18th Industrial Conference on Advances in Data Mining (ICDM 2018)

Poster Proceedings

New York, New York, USA
11-12 July 2018

Editors:

Petra Perner

ISBN: 978-1-5108-9513-3

Printed from e-media with permission by:

Curran Associates, Inc.
57 Morehouse Lane
Red Hook, NY 12571

Some format issues inherent in the e-media version may also appear in this print version.

ibai-publishing
Arno-Nitzsche-Str. 45
04277 Leipzig, Germany

info@ibai-publishing.org

Additional copies of this publication are available from:

Curran Associates, Inc.
57 Morehouse Lane
Red Hook, NY 12571 USA
Phone: 845-758-0400
Fax: 845-758-2633
Email: curran@proceedings.com
Web: www.proceedings.com

Table of Content

Petra Perner (Ed.)

Advances in Data Mining

18th Industrial Conference, ICDM 2018
New York, USA, July 2018

Poster Proceedings

ibai Publishing
www.ibai-publishing.org

Petra Perner (Ed.)

Advances in Data Mining

16th Industrial Conference, ICDM 2018
New York, USA, July 2018

Poster Proceedings

ibai - publishing

Preface

The 18th event of the Industrial Conference on Data Mining ICDM was held in New York again (www.data-mining-forum.de) under the umbrella of the World Congress on Frontiers in Intelligent Data and Signal Analysis, DSA 2018 (www.worldcongressdsa.com).

After the peer-review process, we accepted 25 high-quality papers for oral presentation. The topics range from theoretical aspects of data mining to applications of data mining, such as in multimedia data, in marketing, in medicine and agriculture, and in process control, industry, and society. Extended versions of selected papers will appear in the international journal *Transactions on Machine Learning and Data Mining* (www.ibai-publishing.org/journal/mldm).

In all, 20 papers were selected for poster presentations and six for industry paper presentations, which are published in the ICDM Poster and Industry Proceedings by ibai-publishing (www.ibai-publishing.org).

The tutorial days rounded up the high quality of the conference. Researchers and practitioners got an excellent insight in the research and technology of the respective fields, the new trends, and the open research problems that we would like to study further.

A tutorial on Data Mining, a tutorial on Case-Based Reasoning, a tutorial on Intelligent Image Interpretation and Computer Vision in Medicine, Biotechnology, Chemistry and Food Industry, and a tutorial on Standardization in Immunofluorescence were held before and in between the conferences of DSA 2018.

We would like to thank all reviewers for their highly professional work and their effort in reviewing the papers.

We also thank the members of the Institute of Applied Computer Sciences, Leipzig, Germany (www.ibai-institut.de), who handled the conference as secretariat. We appreciate the help and understanding of the editorial staff at Springer, and in particular Alfred Hofmann, who supported the publication of these proceedings in the LNAI series.

Last, but not least, we wish to thank all the speakers and participants who contributed to the success of the conference. We hope to see you in 2019 in New York at the next World Congress on Frontiers in Intelligent Data and Signal Analysis, DSA 2019 (www.worldcongressdsa.com), which combines under its roof the following three events: International Conferences Machine Learning and Data Mining, MLDM (www.mldm.de), the Industrial Conference on Data Mining, ICDM (www.data-mining-forum.de), and the International Conference on Mass Data Analysis of Signals and Images in Medicine, Biotechnology, Chemistry, Biometry, Security, Agriculture, Drug Discovery and Food Industry, MDA (www.mda-signals.de), as well as the workshops, and tutorials.

July 2018 Petra Perner

Organization

Chair

Petra Perner	IBaI Leipzig, Germany

Program Committee

Ajith Abraham	Machine Intelligence Research Labs (MIR Labs), USA
Brigitte Bartsch-Spörl	BSR Consulting GmbH, Germany
Orlando Belo	University of Minho, Portugal
Bernard Chen	University of Central Arkansas, USA
Antonio Dourado	University of Coimbra, Portugal
Jeroen de Bruin	Medical University of Vienna, Austria
Stefano Ferilli	University of Bari, Italy
Geert Gins	KU Leuven, Belgium
Warwick Graco	ATO, Australia
Aleksandra Gruca	Silesian University of Technology, Poland
Hartmut Ilgner	Council for Scientific and Industrial Research, South Africa
Pedro Isaias	Universidade Aberta (Portuguese Open University), Portugal
Piotr Jedrzejowicz	Gdynia Maritime University, Poland
Martti Juhola	University of Tampere, Finland
Janusz Kacprzyk	Polish Academy of Sciences, Poland
Mehmed Kantardzic	University of Louisville, USA
Eduardo F. Morales	INAOE, Ciencias Computacionales, Mexico
Samuel Noriega	Universitat de Barcelona Spain
Juliane Perner	Cancer Research, Cambridge Institutes, UK
Armand Prieditris	Newstar Labs, USA
Rainer Schmidt	University of Rostock, Germany
Victor Sheng	University of Central Arkansas, USA
Kaoru Shimada	Section of Medical Statistics, Fukuoka Dental College, Japan
Gero Szepannek	Stralsund University, Germany
Markus Vattulainen	Tampere University, Finland

Additional Reviewers

Dimitrios Karras
Calin Ciufudean
Valentin Brimkov
Michelangelo Ceci
Reneta Barneva
Christoph F. Eick
Thang Pham
Giorgio Giacinto
Kamil Dimililer

Effective Mechanism of Mapping Labels in Financial Tables using Machine Learning

Yan Chen[1], Agrima Srivastava[2], and Dakshina Murthy Malladi[3]

[1] Factset Research Systems Inc. New York, USA
[2] Factset Research Systems Inc. Hyderabad, India
ychen@factset.com, agrima.srivastava@factset.com and dakshinamurthy.malladi@factset.com

Abstract. In order to give a better picture of a company's financial health to the investors we need to map the reported financial labels in the current year with the labels reported in past. The main issue in mapping these labels is that the companies keep changing their reporting patterns and the same labels which are semantically similar across the years may or may not remain the same syntactically. Hence, in this work we have proposed, built and analyzed an effective mechanism for mapping semantically similar and syntactically dissimilar financial labels of a company across the years. We map the problem statement as a classification task, make use of machine learning to build models and use it to predict an appropriate matching label for the newly reported filings.

Keywords: Finance · xbrl · Support Vector Machine · Natural Language Processing

1 Introduction

With the fast moving markets, the investors have to analyze the current market trends and make quick decisions [1][2]. In order to do so they need to apply business intelligence on a holistic view of statements over the period of years [3]. To achieve this task we need to map all the financial labels in the newly reported filing with the financial labels of the filings reported in the past. These financial labels can differ across the years as they may or may not be reported in the same way each time the reports are filed. For e.g. the financial label "Property, plant and equipment, net" could have been reported as "Plant, rental machines and other property net" in the past. Therefore, there is a need for an efficient, scalable and intelligent mapping service which can not only speed up the entire process and reduce the manual effort, but can also learn from the prior experience, thereby providing highly accurate predictions in future.

In summary, the main contributions of the work are as follows : To the best of our knowledge we are the first ones to come up with this problem statement for the financial domain and have proposed, built and analyzed an effective solution for mapping syntactically dissimilar financial labels. We extract financial labels from the highly unstructured and voluminous financial data, build classification models and deploy a scalable and fault tolerant solution for mapping them.

2 Related Work

An extensively used method for the similar kind of problem is the Latent Semantic Analysis (LSA) which comes under the corpus based similarity method [4]. In general LSA is more appropriate for longer texts whereas the shorter sentences would result in sparse representations. Anna et al [5] have experimented with wide varieties of distance functions and similarity measures and have used it for clustering. They have compared and analyzed the effectiveness of these measures in clustering the text documents. On the similar lines, Islam et al have proposed a normalized and modified version of the Longest Common Subsequence (LCS) string matching algorithm in order to measure the text similarity [6]. Financial labels are too scarce as a unit to support effective statistical analysis [7]. Therefore, we apply feature based approach in order to find semantic similarities between the labels and map them with an appropriate label in the previous filings.

3 The Overall Workflow

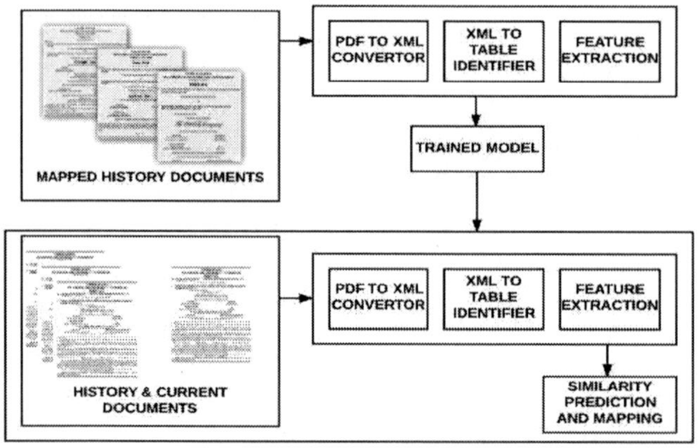

Fig. 1. The overall work flow for the mapping process.

Figure 1 shows the complete work flow of the proposed solution. We fetch all the history or past mapping data for a company over a period of specified years as well as the current filing which has to be mapped. The filings obtained in the form of pdf are converted to XML which is then used to identify the financial tables followed by feature extraction and model building [8]. We load the trained classification model and make row maps of financial labels between the current filing and the history filings. We then perform feature extraction and make predictions for each of them and return the mappings having the highest prediction score.

4 Data Collection, Feature Extraction and Model Training

For data collection we iterate through the list of 500 companies for which we collect the manually mapped financial labels. Some companies also report financial labels in the eXtensible Business Reporting Language (XBRL) format along with the traditional format [9] [10] which is why we come up with three categories of row maps i.e. the xbrl to xbrl, xbrl to html and the html to html. A filing falls under the category of xbrl if it has been reported using XBRL standards, otherwise we categorize it as HTML.

For feature extraction we decided to go with various similarity metrics. Hierarchy of the labels plays an important role while mapping the labels. For e.g. the financial label "Depreciation and Amortization Expense" can come from the parent label "Cash Flow from Operating Activities" and also from the parent "Expenses". Therefore we take a combination of hierarchy based and non-hierachy based features. For feature extraction we mainly calculate the cosine similarity, context similarity, bi-gram and tri-gram similarity between the hierarchy labels, non-hierarchy labels and the xbrl labels. We train three different models for each of the row map category and train the feature vectors using the Support Vector Machine algorithm.

To achieve a higher accuracy we select output thresholds for each model from a fixed set of threshold values. We ran our experiment on a total of 125 combinations of thresholds and recorded the value for precision and recall for each of them. The baseline precision and recall value was recorded as 72.74% and 95.66% which went up to a precision of 83.56% and a good enough recall of 92.28% with the threshold of 0.6,0.6 and 0.4 for xbrl,xbrl-html and html models respectively.

5 Final Label Mapping

For final mapping we extract the financial labels from the the current filing and predict the financial labels in the past filings with which it best matches to. The following algorithm illustrates the same :

Algorithm 5.1: DATA MAPPING($RowMaps, Models$)

Extract features for xbrlRowMap
- Load xbrlmodel
- Using the trained model and extracted features
- xpred = Predict(xbrlRowMap,xbrlModel)

Extract features for xbrlhtmlRowMap
- Load xbrlhtmlmodel
- Using the trained model and extracted features
- xhpred = Pred(xbrlhtmlRowMap,xbrlhtmlModel)

Extract features for htmlRowMap
- Load htmlmodel
- Using the trained model and extracted features
- hpred = Predict(htmlRowMap,htmlModel)

Finalpred = xpred + xhpred + hpred
Sort FinalPred scores in descending order
for each $RowMap_i$ ϵ FinalPred
- If $RowMap_i$ not in the ResultSet
- ResultSet = Insert $RowMap_i$

6 Performance Evaluation

We trained our models with various classification algorithms namely the Logistic Regression, Random Forest, Gradient Boosted Tree Model and Support Vector Machine. We observed that the SVM outperforms the other algorithms used here. Figure 2 below shows the label mapping ratio vs the average collection time taken. Here the X axis represents the mapping rate and the Y axis represents the mapping time. For example, for filings where mapping rate accuracy is 100%, the research analysts only need less than 10 minutes of processing time. Without, such a service in place they will have to manually go through each filing and map the labels which is tedious and is susceptible to incorrect mappings. On an average without such a service in place it would take hours to process the filing whereas the average time taken now is reduced to a few seconds. Figure 3 below shows the graph between the mapping rate and the percentage of filings processed. X axis represents the mapping rate and Y axis represents the percentage of filings. From the graph we can infer that a significant number of filings have a mapping rate of greater than 85% percent. The service makes use

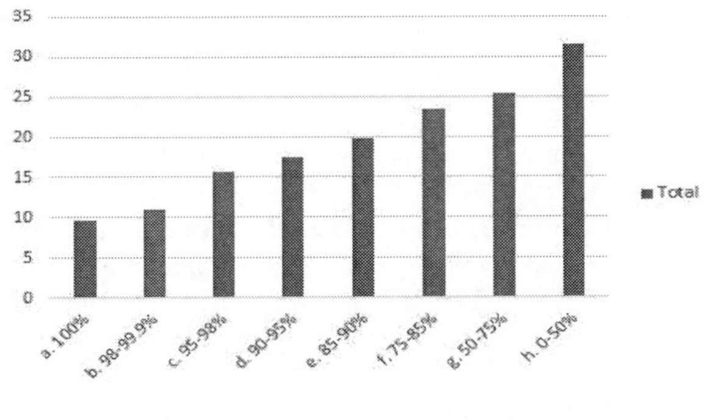

Fig. 2. Mapping vs average.

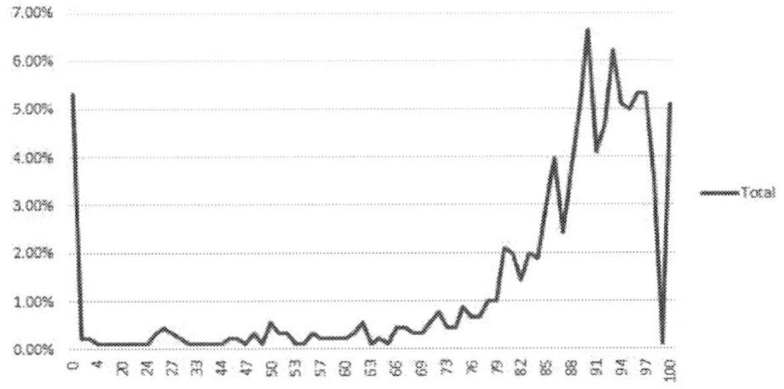

Fig. 3. The mapping rate.

of Apache Spark as the parallel processing framework. During the peak seasons the analyst receives more than thousands of documents and there are over millions of data points that the service has to process in real time. We maintain a work-queue at the back end which is responsible for preventing any sort of thundering herd problem.

7 Conclusion and Future Work

In order to provide one stop data solutions to the investors we devised an effective feature based mechanism to map semantically similar yet syntactically different financial labels by making use of support vector machines. Our algorithm achieves a pretty good accuracy and has reduced the manual efforts greatly. As part of our future work we plan to optimize our code, improve the overall speed of the process and make our service language agnostic.

8 Credits

Special thanks to Sarah Hoffman, Ajaya Mallapaty, Naveen Kudupudi and Geetika Digumarthy who have helped us shape the solution. We would also thank the

Factset Fundamentals Technical Operations (FFTO) team for contributing their time and providing us with relevant feedbacks while testing the service.

References

1. Fox, Merritt B and Glosten, Lawrence R and Rauterberg, Gabriel V ,2015. *The new stock market: sense and nonsense*, Duke LJ, Pages : 65–191
2. Biddle, Gary C and Hilary, Gilles and Verdi, Rodrigo S ,2009. *How does financial reporting quality relate to investment efficiency?*, *Elsevier* Volume : 48, Number : 2, Pages : 112–131
3. Alfaro, Laura and Chanda, Areendam and Kalemli-Ozcan, Sebnem and Sayek, Selin ,2004. *FDI and economic growth: the role of local financial markets*, *Journal of international economics* Volume : 64, Pages : 189–112
4. Landauer, Thomas K and Foltz, Peter W and Laham, Darrell ,1998. *An introduction to latent semantic analysis*, Discourse processes Volume : 25, Pages : 203–212
5. Huang, Anna ,2008. *Similarity measures for text document clustering*, Proceedings of the sixth new zealand computer science research student conference (NZC-SRSC2008), Christchurch, New Zealand, Pages : 49–56.
6. Islam, Aminul and Inkpen, Diana ,2008. *Semantic text similarity using corpus-based word similarity and string similarity*, ACM Transactions on Knowledge Discovery from Data (TKDD) Volume : 2
7. Hatzivassiloglou, Vasileios and Klavans, Judith L and Eskin, Eleazar ,1999. *Detecting text similarity over short passages: Exploring linguistic feature combinations via machine learning*, *Proceedings of the 1999 joint sigdat conference on empirical methods in natural language processing and very large corpora* Pages : 203–212
8. Dejean Herve, Meunier, Jean-Luc ,2006. *A system for converting PDF documents into structured XML format*, Document Analysis Systems VII, Springer, Pages : 129–140
9. Cong, Yu and Hao, Jia and Zou, Lin ,2014. *The impact of XBRL reporting on market efficiency*, Journal of Information Systems, Volume : 28, Number : 11, Pages : 81–207
10. Bonsall, Samuel B and Leone, Andrew J and Miller, Brian P and Rennekamp, Kristina ,2017. *A plain English measure of financial reporting readability*, *Journal of Accounting and Economics* Volume : 63, Number : 2, Pages : 329–357

Evaluation of Community Structure Finding Algorithms on Social Network Data Sets

Abdul Qadar Kara and Harun Pirim

Systems Engineering Department,
King Fahd University of Petroleum and Minerals
PO Box 5067, Dhahran, 31261, Saudi Arabia
{aqkara, harunpirim}@kfupm.edu.sa

Abstract. Community structure finding is investigated since decades. Different class of algorithms exist without a clear winner. We compare three different classes of community structure finding algorithms to comprehend on the performance based on modularity, VI, NMI, and ARI. Three network data sets are employed for the comparison. The results suggest concentrating on optimization based methods to find community structures. Optimization models can be used to guide heuristic methods for larger data sets.

Keywords: Community structure, Clustering, Modularity, Graph partitioning

1 Introduction

Most of the real word systems and data sets can be represented by networks. Networks span diverse fields such as computer science, i.e. Internet [1], computer networks, and social sciences, i.e. social networks [2,10]. Analogous among these networks are two basic components, individual *nodes* or *vertices* represented by web-pages, computers, humans etc. and *edges* or *connections* represented by wired (or wireless) connections, relationships, similarities between entities etc. This network representation has enabled scientists to study various aspects of these systems, allowing them to understand more about them and explaining associated features or underlying behaviors. One of these aspects is to study the sub-grouping of the network or "community structure", that is smaller groups of nodes closely connected to each other compared to other nodes. Connectivity can be due to higher density of edges between these nodes than with the rest of the network. This finding of smaller well-connected communities among larger network is an interesting problem and has been well studied in the literature (see [12,13] and references there in). One of the recent approaches that has gained popularity in recent literature [12,13] is based on benefit function known as *Modularity.*

According to [3], modularity is a measure of the difference between the existing connectivity within separate communities and expected connectivity. The stronger the connectivity within communities, the larger is the difference. Then for a network $G(V, E)$, where V denotes set of vertices, whose cardinality is n and E denotes set of edges, with cardinality of m, mathematically, the modularity can be written as:

$$Q = \frac{1}{2m} \sum_{ij} (A_{ij} - P_{ij}) \delta(C_i, C_j) \tag{1}$$

where and j are vertices belonging to V, the pair ij denotes an edge in E. m denotes the total number of edges in E. A is the adjacency matrix, P_{ij} is the expected number of edges between the vertices in the null model. The $\delta-$function is 1 if both vertices i and j belong to the same community denoted by C_i $(C_i = C_j)$, 0 otherwise. For the null model, we expect (as in [3,6] among others) the degree of each vertex is equal to its actual degree in the network. This entails $P_{ij} = \frac{k_i k_j}{2m}$, where k_i is the number of edges from vertex i to any other vertex in the network. Therefore, equation (1) translates to,

$$Q = \frac{1}{2m} \sum_{ij} (A_{ij} - \frac{k_i k_j}{2m}) \delta(C_i, C_j) \tag{2}$$

The goal is to find communities that increase the modularity function. In practice, a value greater than 0.3 is considered to be evidence for existence of stronger community structure.

In this paper, we have taken three different methods from the literature based on the concept of modularity and compared them on three different data sets. Next section starts with describing briefly our algorithm choices. It then proceeds to explaining the data sets used and the performance measure we use to analyze different algorithms. All methods are implemented in R language with igraph library [4]. The last section describes results of the comparative analysis and conclusion.

2 Methodology

For our comparative analysis, we choose three algorithms.that all use the concept of modularity, but differ in their approach of maximizing it.

Algorithm 1 Our first choice of algorithm is by Clauset et. al [6]. This is an improved version of the earlier algorithm proposed in [5]. This method is an agglomerative hierarchical clustering method, where vertices are iteratively joined together to form larger communities in order to increase modularity. The process starts from n communities (each node is community). At each iteration, we select an edge to be added such that the modularity is maximally increased (minimally decreased) from the current setup resulting in one merging of two communities into one. Change in modularity ΔQ is computed at each merge as $\Delta Q = 2(e_{CD} - a_C a_D)$, where e_{CD} refers to edges between communities C and D and a_C refers to all edges out of community C. This algorithm ends when there is only community left. ΔQ only changes where there is an edge between two communities otherwise it is 0. e_{CD} is updated if the corresponding communities (i.e. C and D) merge. The method we used makes use of efficient data structures, a sparse matrix to store ΔQ_{CD} for each pair of community C, D as a *balanced binary tree*, a *max-heap* containing the largest element of each row of matrix of ΔQ_{CD} and a vector containing values of a_C. The running time is therefore $\mathcal{O}(mdlogn)$, where d is the depth of the *dendrogram* describing the network community structure.

Algorithm 2 Our second choice of algorithm is based on the concepts from graph partitioning and spectral optimization. *Modularity matrix* **B** is introduced where its elements are defined as $B_{ij} = A_{ij} - \frac{k_i k_j}{2m}$. Let **s** be vector representing partition of graph into two clusters C and D, where each element represents node $i \in V$, $s_i = +1$ if the node belongs to community C or $s_i = -1$ if it belongs to D. The modularity function (defined in eq(2)) is then transformed into $Q = \frac{1}{4m}\mathbf{s^T B s}$. Further dividing **s** into linear combination of normalized eigenvectors u_i of the modularity matrix, $\mathbf{s} = \sum_{i=1}^{n} a_i u_i$ with $a_i = u_i^T s$, we get $Q = \frac{1}{4m}\sum_i a_i^2 \beta_i$, where β_i is the eigenvalue of **B** corresponding to the eigenvector u_i. The algorithm then tries to find the eigenvector with highest value of corresponding eigenvalue. We use the signs of the elements in the eigenvector to divide the nodes into two groups. We repeatedly apply this approach to all the subgroups until we cannot find a positive eigenvalue that can further divide the resulting subgroups. The average running time (based on the average length of dendrogram as $d = logn$) is $\mathcal{O}((m+n)nlogn)$.

Algorithm 3 Our third choice of algorithm is based on the framework of mathematical programming, more specifically Integer Linear Programming (ILP)[8]. This is a very simple and intuitive ILP model that maximizes the modularity function (described above) based on the relationship of reflexivity, symmetry and transitivity. For a network of n nodes, they define n^2 binary decision variables $X_{ij} \in 0, 1$, one for each pair of nodes. The idea is, if the two nodes belong to same community then the corresponding variable is 1. The constraints include reflexivity, that $X_{ii} = 1, \forall i \in V$, symmetry $X_{ij} = X_{ji}, \forall i, j \in V$ and transitivity $\forall i, j, l$ if $X_{ij} = 1 \wedge X_{jk} = 1 \rightarrow X_{il} = 1$ (linearized version). The objective function is then to maximize eq(2) where $\delta(C_i, C_j)$ is replaced by X_{ij}. The simplified version of this ILP has only $\binom{n}{2}$ variables and $\binom{n}{3}$ constraints. No polynomial algorithms exist for general ILP problems.

2.1 Performance Measures

In order to compare the aforementioned algorithms, we used three performance measures, apart from modularity, that indicates the performance of each algorithm on each data set.

- **Adjusted Rand Index (ARI)**[14] Adjusted Rand Index is corrected-for-chance version of the Rand index. It is one of the partition similarity measure based on *pair counting*.

- **Normalized Mutual Information (NMI)[15]** Normalized Mutual Information (NMI) is similarity measure based on *information theory* and is widely used to determine correctness of partitioning scheme.
- **Variation of Information (vi)** Variation of Information (vi) is another similarity measure based on *information theory.* It measures locally, i.e. it looks at the difference of the partitions themselves and not on the overall network.

2.2 Data sets

We chose the following three data sets to test the algorithms. These are well-known data sets in the literature and has been used by many approaches to test their effectiveness in identifying the right number of communities as well as correct membership for each of its vertices.

- **Karate club** The first data set we chose is a relatively well-known data set known as Zachary's network of karate club. There are a total of 34 members (represented as nodes) in this network, a total of 78 connections between them (indicating interaction between members) and two sub-groups [9].
- **Dolphin Social Network** Another commonly used data set to benchmark algorithms is a network of dolphins living in New Zealand as analyzed by Lusseau [10]. The nodes in this data set represent dolphins and the edges represent animals that were seen together with higher than expected value.There are total of 62 members in this network with a total of 159 connecting edges and two sub-groups.
- **Schedule of American College Football** This data set refers to the schedule of Division I games for the 2000 season [11]. The vertices represent the teams and the edges between them represent if these teams play against each other according to the schedule.This data set contains a total of 115 nodes, 613 edges and a total of 12 communities (conferences)

3 Results and Conclusions

We compared three community structure finding algorithms based on modularity, vi, NMI, and ARI values (as shown in Table 1). The optimization based method generated the best modularity values. This is expected as the method maximizes the modularity globally. The method generates better NMI values as well compared to other methods. The method finds the best partition for the largest data set, football, with the highest ARI score. The greedy method finds better ARI values while the eigenvector based method generates better vi values. The optimization based method finds 6 best values, the greedy method finds 4 best values, and the eigenvector based method finds 3 best values. More optimization based methods can be compared using more data sets and validation metrics for a future study. Efficient heuristic methods can be guided by optimization models to find community structures for bigger data sets.

Algorithm1	Q	vi	NMI	ARI
Karate	0.3990796	0.2922759	0.8255182	0.8027464
Dolphins	0.4954907	0.7770066	0.5727005	0.4508546
Football	0.5497407	1.269104	0.6977317	0.4740983
Algorithm2	Q	**vi**	**NMI**	**ARI**
Karate	0.4118179	0.7278128	0.6551704	0.504765
Dolphins	0.4911989	1.212381	0.4489142	0.2830055
Football	0.4926058	1.339205	0.6986702	0.4640505
Algorithm3	Q	**vi**	**NMI**	**ARI**
Karate	0.419	0.629	0.687	0.541
Dolphins	0.5285194	0.886768	0.5864663	0.3734515
Football	0.604	0.519	0.890	0.807

Table 1. Results of the comparative analysis

References

1. Faloutsos M. ,Faloutsos P. and Faloutsos C., On power-law relationships of the Internet topology. SIGCOMM Comput. Commun. Rev. 29, 4 , 251-262. DOI: https://doi.org/10.1145/316194.316229 (1999)
2. Kottak C.P., Cultural Anthropology, McGraw-Hill, New York, USA, 2004
3. Newman M. E. J. and Girvan M. , Finding and evaluating community structure in networks. Phys. Rev. E 69, 026113 (2004)
4. Csardi G, Nepusz T: The igraph software package for complex network research, InterJournal, Complex Systems 1695. 2006.
5. Newman M.E.J. , Fast algorithm for detecting community structure in networks, Phys. Rev. E 69 (6) 066133.(2004)
6. Clauset A. , Newman M.E.J. , Moore C. , Finding community structure in very large networks, Phys. Rev. 70 66111(2004)
7. Newman M. E. J. Newman, Finding community structure in networks using the eigenvectors of matrices. Physical Review E, vol. 74, Issue 3, id. 036104, (2006)
8. Brandes U. et al., On Modularity Clustering, In: IEEE Transactions on Knowledge and Data Engineering, vol. 20, no. 2, pp. 172-188, (2008)
9. Zachary W.W. ,An information flow model for conflict and fission in small groups, J. Anthropol. Res. 33 (1977) 452-473.
10. Lusseau D. , The emergent properties of a dolphin social network, Proc. R. Soc. London B 270 (2003) S186-S188
11. Girvan M. ,Newman M.E.J., Community structure in social and biological networks, Proc. Natl. Acad. Sci. USA 99 (2002) 78217826.
12. Fortunato S. , Community detection in graphs, Phys. Rep. 486 (2010) 75174.
13. Fortunato, S. Hric, D., Community detection in networks: A user guide, Physics Reports, Volume 659, p. 1-44. (2016)
14. Hubert L and Arabie P: Comparing partitions. Journal of Classification 2:193-218, 1985.
15. Danon L, Diaz-Guilera A, Duch J, Arenas A: Comparing community structure identification. J Stat Mech P09008, 2005.
16. Meilă M., Comparing clusteringsan information based distance, J. Multivariate Anal. 98 (5) 873895, (2007).

Applying Chromathics to Data Processing and Computations

Tony Nolan[1], Warwick Graco[2], Emily Nolan[1], Stewart Turner[2], Garry Mitchell[3], and Charles Palmer[4]

[1] G3N1U5
[2] Australian Taxation Office, Australia
[3] Analytics Workshed
[4] ACT Electricity, Water and Gas
tony@g3n1u5.com

Abstract. This paper describes a colour approach to doing data processing and computations and it illustrates this with everyday applications. Everything can be represented as light with examples including text, numbers, objects and patterns. They can be each given a unique colour code.
Computers that use light to perform data processing and computations are referred to either as chromatic computers or photonic computers. Light can be decomposed into a colour spectrum and colours can be used to represent data and to do mathematical operations.
Chromathics is a process of doing calculations and transformations with light. Light-based operations can be performed at speeds faster than digital ones and can compress data better than can be done with digital computers.
This paper will explain both chromatic computers and chromathics. It will provide everyday examples to illustrate the use of a colour approach to computing.

Keywords: chromatic · chromathics · photonic

1 Introduction

Colour is an integral part of the universe. Everything has colour. Sometimes it is natural and other times it is artificial. Colour is simply the wavelength of light.

In nature, certain animals have specific colours and patterns which allow them to function, survive, mate and similar. For example a gecko changes the colour of its skin to match the colour of its background. This gives it protection against predators.

2 Analogue versus Digital Computers

There are different views on analogue computers versus digital ones. An analogue computer [1] uses continuous values to represent electrical, mechanical or physical quantities that are employed in the problem being solved. In contrast, digital computers [2] represent quantities in binary form as '0s' and '1s' and perform high speed calculations using binary numbers.

Analogue computers operate on mathematical variables in the form of physical quantities. Examples include temperature, pressure and electrical currents. Any real physical process can be represented by a mathematical model. This is the basis of analogue computing. After the modelling of the physical process has been completed, the computations performed by analogue computers are easy to do and convenient.

The advantage of analogue computers are that they can show the solutions in a graphical manner. In an analogue computer the output can be connected to an oscilloscope and results can be viewed by users. In a digital computer the modelling may require complex programming and the use of graphical applications to represent the results.

The disadvantages of analogue computers are that they are not versatile and they may not be as accurate as digital computers. The accuracy of the analogue computers is limited and dependent on a number for factors such as the circuit parameters and the wiring of the computer and are prone to external influences such as magnetic effects and ambient temperature and pressure.

Examples of analogue computers include slide rules, tide predictors, the Norden bomb sight, electric integrators that solve partial differential equations, electronic machines that solve differential equations, machines that solve algebraic equations and neural networks.

Digital computers deal with mathematical variables in form of numbers that represent discrete values of physical quantities. The advantages of digital computers are that they are versatile, programmable, accurate, and less affected by outside influences in contrast to analogue computers. As pointed out calculations are performed using binary numbers. Most modern computers, laptops, and calculators are digital in their operations.

The disadvantages of digital computers include the way they deal with larger numbers. These are denoted using a sequence of 0s and 1s digits called bits and bytes. They are therefore computationally slower, because they have to pass more data in a data stream to achieve the same results.

3 Chromatic Computers

Chromatic also can be called 'photonic' computers use light to do data processing and numerical operations. Light can be decomposed into a colour spectrum and the different colours can be used to represent data and to do mathematical procedures.

Chromatic computers can work in either analogue or digital mode. They can also be applied in an integrated manner such as with hybrid computers. Specific combinations of these different computers can differ from hardware to hardware, from situation to situation and from problem to problem i.e. they can be used in digital, in analogue or in both modes of operation.

4 Chromathics

This is about doing calculations and transformations using light. It works along the same lines as logarithms, where numbers are transformed into log values, mathematical operations are performed on the numbers such as addition or subtraction, and then the results are converted back to numerical results. Chromathics, as with logarithms, involves transforming numbers into colours, sometimes mathematical operations are performed with the data and the resulting results are converted back into numbers [3].

A similar approach can also be used with text where it is converted to colour and transmitted from one location to another and then converted back to text. This can be used with the encryption of messages. This will be illustrated and discussed later in the paper.

5 Chromathic Operations

These are used to perform operations where data in transformed and transmitted in colour rather than digital form. They include the use of three basic colours of red, green and blue. These three colours can be combined two at a time to form other colours. For example, a combination of red and green gives a yellow tone and a combination of red and blue gives purple tone.

Information is stored as bits and bytes in a digital computer. A bit is the smallest unit for storing information. A bit contains either a '0' or '1'. This is insufficient to represent characters used for conveying information and representing numbers.

A byte consists of 8 bits and is used to signify a character such as 'A', '9' or '#'. This is done using an 8 bit binary code of '0s' and '1s'. Therefore a byte is the standard binary packet that is used by computers to represent characters. A byte of 8 bits can furnish 256 or 2^8 patterns. Therefore a byte can store a number between 0 and 255 for numerical values. It can also represent 256 colours.

Each pulse containing a chromatic representation of data consists of the three basic colours of red, blue and green. Each pulse can also represent a number between 0 and 16,777,216 based on the following calculation:

256 (red tone) * 256 (green tone) * 256 (blue tone) = 16,777,216 or 2^{24} colours.

If a second pulse is sent this enables a number between 0 to 281,474,976,710,656 or 2^{48} to be used. The upper limit increases exponentially as more pulses are added to the signals.

The above description shows what can be achieved with quantity of numbers. It ignores the costs of the conversions from numerical to a colour representation and vice versa. The costs of the conversion process is considered to be a hardware issue. It depends on the hardware available and how it is configured as to how much it costs to do these conversions. For example, if parallel processing is employed the number of conversions and transfers can be increased substantially.

6 Coloured Barcode

The concept of a coloured barcode was selected to represent entities and events using colour. It is based on the QR code system [4]. QR stands for quick response.

6.1 QR Code

The QR code system was invented in 1994 by the Japanese company Denso Wave. Its purpose was to track vehicles during manufacturing. It was designed to allow high-speed component scanning. QR codes are now used in a much broader context, including both commercial tracking applications and convenience-oriented applications aimed at mobile-phone users (termed mobile tagging). They may be used to display text to the user, to open a Uniform Resource Identifier (URI), or to compose an email or text message. There are now many QR code generators available.

A QR code consists of either black squares arranged in a square grid on a white background or it can be any mix of colours provided with contrast high enough to allow differentiation of cells. It can be read by an imaging device such as a camera and is processed using Reed-Solomon error correction [5] until the image can be correctly interpreted. The required data is then extracted from the QR patterns that are present in both horizontal and vertical components of the image as shown below.

Fig. 1. The overall work flow for the mapping process.

The QR code has become one of the most-used types of two-dimensional code. A QR code uses four standardized encoding modes (numeric, alphanumeric, byte/binary, and kanji) to efficiently store data. Extensions may also be used.

6.2 Colour Barcode

A barcode is a machine-readable optical label that contains information about the item or event which it represents. The coloured barcode employed in the applications described in this paper are the equivalent of a pixelated image where each colour bar contains information arranged in a sequence. The colour employed in each bar is the combination of three basic colours highlighted previously of red, green, and blue. Examples are shown later in the paper.

Doing mathematical operations with chromathics are still being explored. However, early results look promising.

Chromathics enables a numerical value between 0 and 16,777,216 to be represented in a single colour square. In this form, mathematical calculations can be performed in the same way as logarithms.

By placing these coloured squares in a three-part sequence of 'number operator', 'number operator' and 'number operator' computations, a chromatic barcode can be produced. A number of coloured squares can be assembled together to make a barcode to give higher numerical values. As was previously mentioned in this paper, a numerical value of up to 281.5 trillion can be represented by two coloured squares. The squares are a categorical representation of the different mathematical operations in a list. This list is repeated three times for the variable it is applied to.

The key difference doing this computationally is that chromathics can decompose the numerical value into three parts and apply different mathematical operations to any of these parts. By doing chromathics in a barcode, means that each colour represents a mathematical operation of a number. There is no variation required for the mathematical operations because they are standardised.

However, numerical representative colours can represent whole numbers, negative numbers or decimal points. But a barcode is just a number of coloured squares in a sequence. It can be read left to right or all at one time i.e. in sequence or in parallel. So in this case a barcode can be an imprint on a page, an image file or a pulse of light. The pulses (i.e. segments) need to be consistent. If whole positive numbers are employed then each pulse is a value between 0 and 16,777,216. If decimal numbers are used, then the same range can be applied with an adjustment calculation in the computer. If however negative numbers are required, then the range is between -8,421,504 and +8,421,504. This is exactly half way and this needs to be balanced like this to accommodate pulses in either direction.

7 Advantages

There are advantages in using chromatic computers. One is the compression ratios that can be achieved with data, the second is more efficient computer operations and the third is that it can use fuzzy logic.

7.1 Data Compression

Three columns and 2520 rows of data represents 105 kb in a CSV file [6]. A jpg file [7], which is used for web pages, can store the same data using 8.48 kb. It is to be noted that JPG uses lossy compression techniques [8] where as a CSV is a literal compression. This illustrates that the files are smaller in size than using CSV representations.

The compression advantage with chromathics is that the combination of three lights in one pulse and that light has a higher range of values in a single pulse than using a black and white representations.

7.2 Colour versus Binary Operations

Chromathics is more efficient than traditional binary operations. This is illustrated with weather systems where three sensors employed provide real-time measurements of air pressure, humidity, and temperature would be compressed into single pulses which are then transmitted at optical speed. The optical pulses received by a sensor decodes them using optical bypass filters to be processed to provide weather data.

If these operations were done in a binary system, the values from each sensor would have to be converted into binary code and then transmitted as pulses. The binary codes would then have to be converted back to their original values. This would require more computer processing because of the use of binary code than using a colour approach.

7.3 Fuzzy Logic

This is an approach to computing based on degrees of truth in which the truth values of variables can be any real number between '0' and '1' rather than 'true or false' or '0' or '1' with crisp logic on which digital computers are based. The concept of fuzzy logic was first advanced by Lotfi Zadeh [9] from the University of California at Berkeley in the 1960s. It is employed to handle problems and issues involving partial truths where the truth value may range between completely true and completely false.

Chromathics can use fuzzy logic to enable it to manage values that range between a minimum and maximum value. This enables observations to be represented with real values. In contrast binary representations can become exponentially cumbersome to process.

8 Electromagnetic Spectrum

Light is part of the electromagnetic spectrum [10]. This spectrum is divided into separate bands according to frequency and wavelength. They include radio waves, microwaves, infrared radiation, the visible region that is perceived as light, ultraviolet, X-rays and gamma rays.

The question can be raised why not use the whole of the electromagnetic spectrum instead of the narrow band that covers light to perform chromathic operations. Light has two advantages over using the whole of the electromagnetic spectrum. The first is that is easier to use with filters and the second is that it is easy to combine numbers using light.

The main reasons for this are simple logistics and the type of user. From a machine point of view, the main reason is the question of which technology gives the best definition between the pulses, to run the processes and to achieve an end result. For humans it is different. They, except the visually impaired, are used to dealing with light and most of the technology used in the world rely on the use of light. In addition users often want to examine the process that the technology is designed to deliver as it is happening such as seeing a sequence of events to detect any emerging patterns. It is a truism that people want to be able to examine the results and they do this normally using visual perception. Another possible futuristic reason is that human beings may want to communicate with nonhuman living beings such as monkeys, dolphins, dogs and even possibly plants. This may seem farfetched at this point in time. But at some future point scientists may focus on enhancing the cognitive ability of these non-human lifeforms to provide a functional labour force. Chromathics may provide a solution to facilitate this human to other animal and plant communications.

9 Examples

These are a number of the ways chromathics can be applied to real-world applications. Examples include tracking horse leg movements, sending encoded messages, picking colours for house decorations, measuring vibrations, finding the loudest sound source and mapping changes in cloud cover for adverse weather developments. Examples of these uses are illustrated below.

9.1 Control of Movements

Colour can be used to transmit commands to robots. An example is a robot receiving its instructions from colour transmitted from devices in the floor of a room where colour conveys information about the distance and height of the next movement taken by a robot. The robot would be able to adjust its behaviour based on the information conveyed by the colour transmitters. In hospitals, the same systems can be employed to control service delivery and cleaning activities. This would allow robotic units to be simplified in their design and therefore be made less prone to failure because control is exercised by the transmitters delivering colour instructions rather than code stored in the robots memory. It is acknowledged that this solution does not necessarily reduce failure rates.

9.2 Capturing Movements

When movements are being mapped, a chromathic process gives 16,777,216 different three dimensional (3D) positional data points. This creates a mosaic pattern where the movements are represented as single colours. When multiple observations are taken and are visually examined, rhythmic patterns and positional variations within those rhythmic patterns can be identified. For example, if a 3D sensor was mounted on a horse and then the horse was ridden around a set course for a specified time, it would be possible to identify specific way points and any variations in the horses movements. This data could be used to identify any anomalies in the horses gait which could indicate possible lameness and the degree of lameness. If a regular starting point could be established, then the data set could be turned into a time series data set with comparison of performances possible over repeated occurrences.

This mosaic is an example of horse movement. The first column ranges from standing still to walking. The second column ranges from walking to trotting. The third column is trotting to cantering and easing back to at rest. The last column is coming to rest and the removal of the sensor equipment

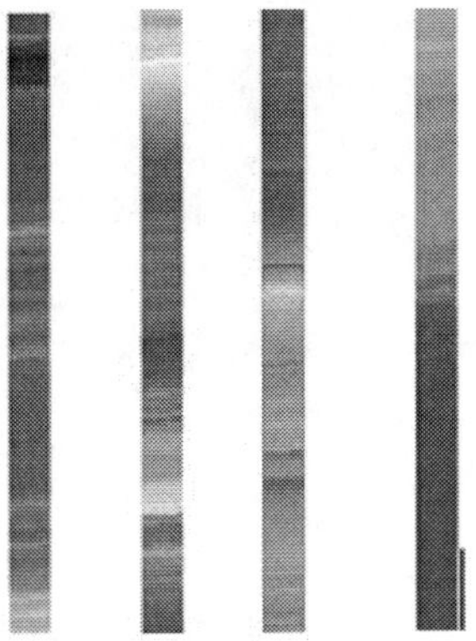

Fig. 2. Capturing Movements

Another practical example is Chinese calligraphy where a human uses brush strokes to produce Chinese characters. This is a highly skilled art. Once a starting point is established the person painting can progress through a number of 3D way points using sound to provide feedback on the precision of the strokes. A musical chord across three octaves informs the person printing of the deviation and distance from the desired way point position. To establish the persons position compared to the way point would be a difference measure between both positions in 3D, and if the person is greater than the desired position, then a combination of high octave notes sound. If the person is below the position, then a combination of low octave notes are heard. Then when the person is within + or 2.5% of the desired way point, then a combination of middle octave notes are heard. The greater the loudness of the chord, the greater the distance from the persons position to the way point position. It is expected that this use of light and sound would speed up the development of precision with the brush strokes. The same solution can be applied learn yoga and to improve stroke play in sports such as golf, tennis, cricket and baseball.

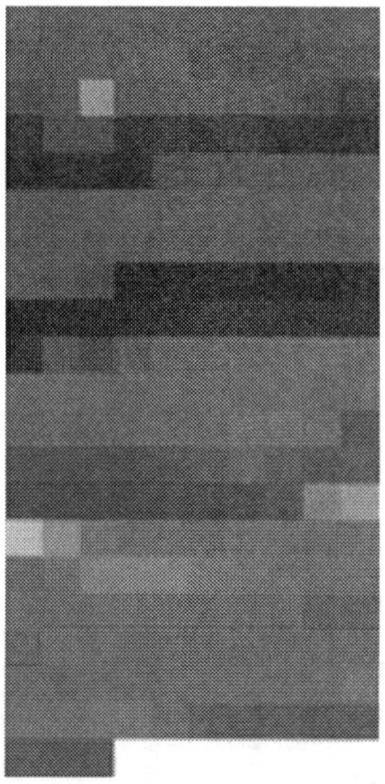

Fig. 3. Series of Yoga exercises

9.3 Traffic Flows

The mosaic below (Traffic Flows) is of motor vehicles going through an intersection with a sample rate of 300 milliseconds. This is an example of how to sample quickly car colours. The black colour is the other side of the road. The other colours in the squares represent different coloured vehicles. These entries allow traffic flows to be assessed.

9.4 Audio Events

The mosaic below (Audio Events) shows the sounds of outside noise and birds singing as well as music playing on a radio. The audio spectrum is broken up into three equal segments. With each colour representing a 1/3rd, the computer can detect the different tones better than the human eye. While this image appears to have maybe 20 different tones there are over 50 different colours.

9.5 Weather Events

The mosaic below (Weather Events) is of a series of 10 minutes observations of weather sensors. The three sensors are air pressure, humidity, and temperature.

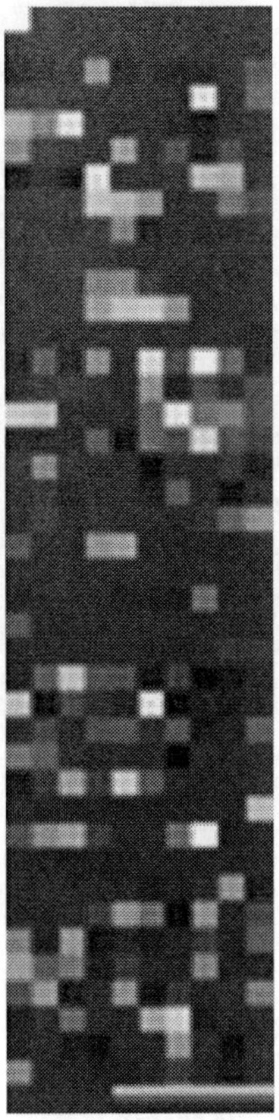

Fig. 4. Traffic Flows

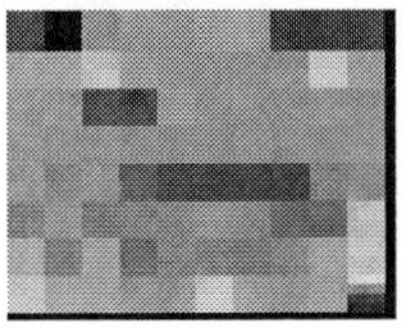

Fig. 5. Audio Events

Each square represents the combination of the three sensors and transmitted to a receiving sensor that is programed to adjust the environmental controls when it detects a specific colour.

The next mosaic (time lapse example of rain and storm) is a time lapse example of rain and storm clouds with lightning going past. The change in the grey tones gives an indication of the severity of the storm.

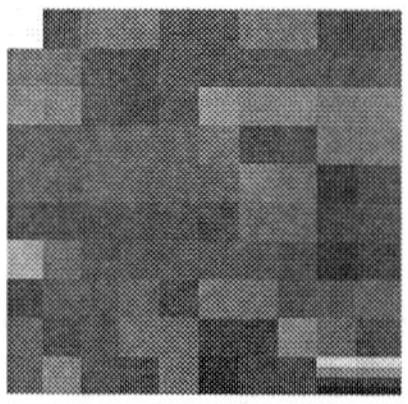

Fig. 6. Weather Events

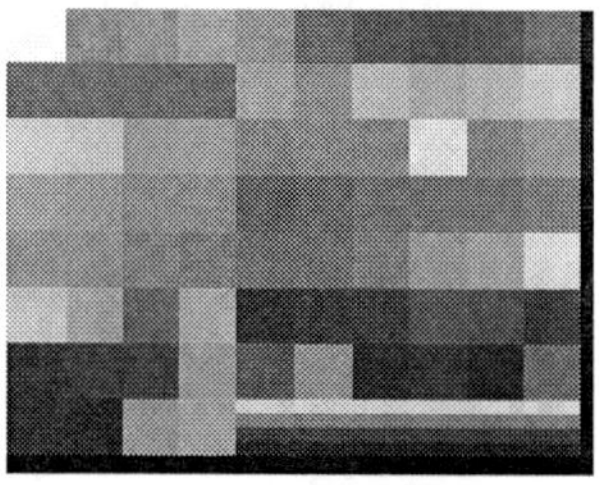

Fig. 7. Time lapse example of rain and storm

9.6 Chemical Assays

This mosaic (Chemical Assays) contains observations taken of bricks, plants, and metal. However an astronomical spectrometer optical filter was used in a similar manner to organic chemistry spectroscopy. This process uses reflected light from the sun to give a chemical assay of objects.

Fig. 8. Chemical Assays

9.7 Encryption of Messages

With a chromatic approach able to compress and store data in an optical format, this allows it to be transferred and accessed from an image file rather than an ASCII based file. In the following example, the image is of the Lords Prayer which has been transformed and compressed from text to a colour mosaic where one tile contains three pieces of data. However, the image can have a number of adjustments made to make it harder to decode and read. By changing the colour combination order, or by adding a weighting factor, the message within the image is encrypted and could not easily be deciphered without the key.

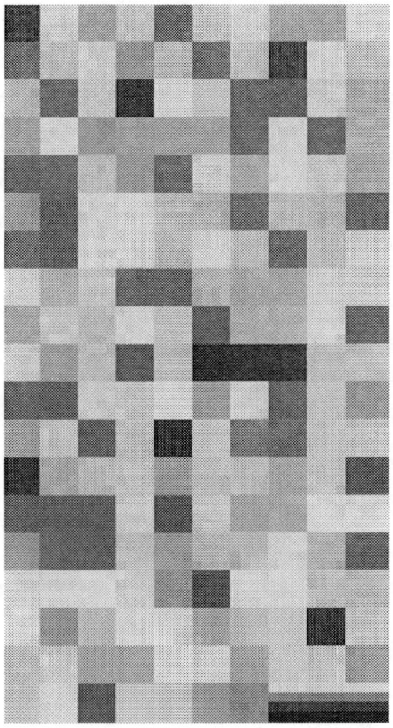

Fig. 9. Encryption of Messages

This mosaic (Encryption of Messages) is of a single piece of text repeated twice. The before the three black squares is the standard text. Following the three black squares is the same text but slightly scrambled. Each square has a possible 16,777,216 possible combinations of characters. This type of data storage can also be used for encryption

10 Discussion

The above examples illustrate that there are potentially many practical uses of a colour approach to computing including it can be used to store and transmit compressed and encrypted data, it can track the movements of people, other animals and mechanical objects and it can identify their colour signatures. This can assist with safeguarding data from unauthorized intrusions, with controlling traffic flows, with teaching intricate and highly skilled movements in sports such as with tennis shots and with detecting criminals, terrorists and similar where chromatic detection is used with facial recognition [11]. It can also assist with measuring the nutrients, moisture and pesticides in agriculture fields and with diagnosing diseases based on their spectral patterns. The potential uses of chromatic computing and chromathics are many. The above suggested uses have to be confirmed by further research. One application where a chromatic computing could confer a significant advantage is with the authentication of users.

Malicious actors now have access to increasingly powerful computer capabilities that threaten governments and private enterprise. An example is to decrypt a 12 character password consisting of upper and lower case numeric and non-alpha characters. This takes less than 500th of a second using a high-end video card from a leading vendor [12]. They offer much more processing power than many desktop personal computers.

Using a chromatic approach to certificate based authentication could provide a chromatic certificate that changes colour every time it is accessed in a similar manner to blockchain [13]. It can authenticate users who have a corresponding chromatic certificate key. The permutations here are huge thus making it difficult for malicious actors to compromise these certificates. The certificates could also decide what access privileges a user is conferred based on the contents of his/her chromatic certificate and the period of time they cover. This too has to be tested to see if these expectations are supported.

It is also considered that a chromatic approach could fill the gap between traditional digital computers and the promise of quantum computers. Quantum computing uses quantum-mechanical principles to perform numerical operations. They would theoretically be able to solve certain problems much more quickly than any classical computers that use even the best currently known algorithms. Quantum computers [14] promise to run calculations far beyond the reach of any conventional supercomputer. They might revolutionize the discovery of new materials by making it possible to simulate the behaviour of matter down to the atomic level. They could upend cryptography and security by cracking otherwise invincible codes. There is even hope they will supercharge artificial intelligence by crunching through data more efficiently.

Chromatic computers will not process numbers at the super speed of quantum computers but they offer the possibility to outperform conventional computers in data processing and scientific calculations. They can do this without the current technical complications of quantum computers that are very sensitive to temperature and other environmental conditions. Quantum computers can become quite unstable if conditions change.

The future may see the progression of digital computers, chromatic computers and quantum computers with each having particular strengths and each having a particular niche where they perform optimally.

11 Conclusion

The potential of chromatic computing and chromathics is considered immense. They could confer many possible advantages with storage, transformation and transmission of data, with doing mathematical operations, with encryption of information and with authentication of people and the provision of privileges. The next steps are to see to what extent these potential uses can be realised. As suggested above chromatic computing could fill the gap between digital computers and the great promise of quantum computers.

References

1. https://en.wikipedia.org/wiki/Analog_computer, J.S. Small (2001) The Analogue Alternative. London/New York: Routledge and C. Bissell (2001) A great disappearing act: the electronic analogue computer. Presented at IEEE Conference on the History of Electronics, Bletchley Park, UK, 28-30 June ,2001. UK, 28-30 June,
2. S. Sangun (2010) Difference between Analog and Digital Computing. www.brighthubengineering.com/diy-electronics-devices/97571-difference-between-analog-and-digital-computing/
3. Al Williams pointed out that there is a video showing how to solve 2D mathematical equations using colour. He stated that colours are a clever way of representing vectors and can be applied to complex numbers. See https://hackaday.com/2018/03/26/solve-2d-math-equations-colorfully/
4. https://en.wikipedia.org/wiki/QR_code
5. https://en.wikipedia.org/wiki/Reed%E2%80%93Solomon_error_correction
6. https://en.wikipedia.org/wiki/Comma-separated_values
7. https://en.wikipedia.org/wiki/JPEG
8. https://en.wikipedia.org/wiki/Lossy_compression
9. D. McNeil and P. Freiberger (1993). Fuzzy Logic: The discovery of a revolutionary computer technology - and how it is changing our world. New York: Simon & Schuster
10. https://en.wikipedia.org/wiki/Electromagnetic_spectrum
11. https://en.wikipedia.org/wiki/Facial_recognition_system
12. https://en.wikipedia.org/wiki/Video_card, https://computer.howstuffworks.com/graphics-card1.htm, https://en.wikipedia.org/wiki/Graphics_processing_unit and https://www.techspot.com/community/topics/cracking-passwords-using-nvidias-latest-gtx-1080-gpu-its-fast.229218/
13. https://en.wikipedia.org/wiki/Blockchain and I. Bashir (2017). Mastering Blockchain. Packt Publishing, Ltd and D. Tapscott and A. Tapscott (2016). Blockchain Revolution: How the Technology Behind Bitcoin Is Changing Money, Business and the World. London: Portfolio Penguin
14. https://en.wikipedia.org/wiki/Quantum_computing and A. Wichert (2014). Principles of Quantum Artificial Intelligence. World Scientific Publishing Co and S. Akama (2014). Elements of Quantum Computing: History, Theories and Engineering Applications. Springer International Publishing

Development of High-Speed Engineering Data Transfer Technique

Zixian Zhang[1], Ichiro Kataoka[2], and Yixiang Feng[3]

Research and Development Group, Hitachi Ltd., Tokyo, Japan
zixian.zhang.kh@hitachi.com

Abstract. With the development of globalization of research and development, technologies are required which will enable us to do quality evaluation from domestic computing environment soon after a change occurs in customized design. In this research, a high-speed engineering data transfer technique to reduce transfer time to 1/100 based on data mining was developed. Thus design simulation platform can be executed from overseas sites, and high-quality customize design became possible.

Keywords: Simulation · Data Transfer · Data Mining · Design Cloud

1 Introduction

With the expansion of overseas business of international companies, localization of product design for each region is also expanding rapidly. With the expansion of overseas business of international companies, localization of product design for each region is also expanding rapidly. In FY12, research project called design cloud, targeting at whole Hitachi Group, was started by Hitachi to fast establishment of overseas design sites and realize high-reliability design same with Japan, the structure of which is shown in Fig.1. Data centers are built in the mother factory in Japan, and overseas design sites, including America and India. In data center of Japan, design environment including analysis tools such as simulation software, super computer, and PC cluster are equipped.

The design cloud is targeting at evaluating automotive parts design in the US and the design of power electronics in India. In this research, US with high-end communication network, and India with 1 order lower communication network than Japan, are selected as evaluation objects. In the future, design cloud will be deployed to global design environment.

For the evaluation of automotive parts design, in March 2013, an environment was established that allows design site in US to access technical computing environment in Japan and do evaluation with vHILS (Virtual Hardware In the Loop Simulation) technology developed by Hitachi. For the collaboration with India, customized design in HHPE which is a joint venture of Hitachi is selected as object, for the development of design cloud with softwares, such as thermo-fluid simulation software called PESDAP developed by Hitachi. However, because of low transfer speed between Japan and India, data transfer

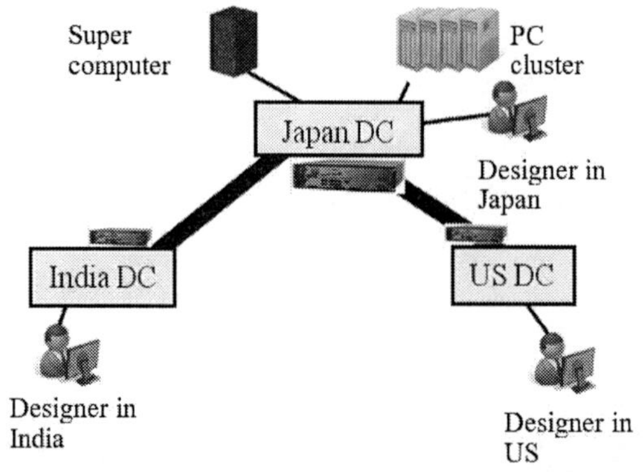

Fig. 1: Concept of the design cloud.

time became the bottle neck for high efficient simulation. High speed data transfer technique for reducing transfer time of engineering data became necessary.

Engineering cloud is being developed in Fujitsu since 2009. By applying super computer inside the company, simulation environment for constructure simulation and electronics simulation can be provided [1]. For urgent simulation task, calculation resources such as super computer bacame necessary, and engineering cloud is developed to provide the service by allocating calculation resources. In Fujitsu Ltd., system for sharing design information is constructed between Japan and overseas design sites [2]. The company of NEC is also developing a computing environment called HPC cloud by connecting to super computer and PC cluster, and the computing service is being provided. Rajendran, A. [3] proposed technique towards obtaining maximum through in large data transfer by optimizing and fine-tuning scientific and applications and mid-dleware at 100 Gbps speeds, achieving 80-90 Gbps in most test cased with a peak transfer rate of 100 Gbps.

Our research is targeting on thermo-fluid simulation, and reducing thermo-fluid simulation time from the current 100 hours to 20 hours is required by design engineers, therefore the design job and simulation job can be applied parallelly and smooth design process can be accomplished. Therefore, it is necessary to reduce transfer time of 4GB data between Japan and overseas design site from the current 16 hours to within 0.16 hours. Our development goal is that, with WAN accelerator technique developed in Hitachi, the time for data transfer will be reduced to 1/100 of that of the previous methods.

2 High-speed Engineering Data Transfer Technique

A high-speed engineering data transfer technique is developed, including both net-work acceleration technique and engineering data compression technique. For net-work acceleration, WAN accelerator technique developed by Hitachi is applied. And for data size reduction, a novel compression technique based on analysis knowledge of simulation result is developed. We focus on the thermo-fluid simulation. The simulation result commonly reaches large data size, and takes quit a long transfer time from the data center in Japan to overseas designs sites. Inside thermo-fluid simulation result, evaluation area which should be evaluated, and non-evaluation area which is not necessary to be evaluated, are focused. Evaluation area extraction tech-nique, and non-evaluation compression technique with higher compression rate than conventional technique, was developed. The work flow of the developed method is introduced below.

Conventionally, designers evaluate simulation results manually. Therefore it costs long time for evaluation area extraction. We interviewed designers, summarized evaluation areas, and completed the software which can extract evaluation area automatically. Thermo-fluid simulation result is taken as research object. And tech-nique that can extract to check thermo-generation area and flow distribution was developed.

In some area of thermo-fluid simulation result, precise simulation result data is required for high precision evaluation, and we call it evaluation area. In some other areas, only the trend is analyzed, and small error is acceptable. Because the error may be generated with compression, in the former case, compression should not be applied. And we call this kind area non-compression area. The other kind of area is called compression area. To maintain high precision of evaluation area, evaluation area should be extracted.

The evaluation area extraction method is developed to correct the error by tensor compression method. For high-quality verification, necessary evaluation areas of power electronics equipment are summarized by interviewing experienced designer in mother factory in Japan. We classified them into 3 kinds as below.

The first kind is high-temperature areas. Temperature of each element is checked. If an element is with higher temperature than input threshold, it is extracted.

The second kind is thermo accumulation areas. Thermo accumulation area means in a relatively large area, all the elements are with higher temperature than an input threshold. Although the temperature threshold here is lower than threshold in the first kind, the parts surrounded by hot air is hard to be cooled, and trend to become higher temperature. Thus the thermo accumulation areas are with danger and focused by design engineers. To extract the thermo accumulation areas, high-temperature location next to the thermo generation parts is searched.

The third kind is locations surrounding thermo generation parts. Fluid velocity of elements surrounding thermo generation parts is evaluated. Thermo exchange be-tween thermos generation parts and air is not efficient in the low velocity area, and thermos generation parts usually trend to become higher temperature. Therefore these areas with low fluid velocity are focused by design engineers. If the velocity of an element is lower than the input threshold, the element is extracted.

The evaluation areas extracted are separated from the whole simulation result, and saved as independent file, so as to maintain high precision.

Areas besides evaluation areas are compressed by tensor decomposition based compression technique. The tensor decomposition based compression technique can obtain a quite high compression ratio, which can reach 1/1000, despite compression error. But the error is acceptable in the non-evaluation area, because only the trend of simulation result is analyzed. By applying the compression technique, compressed data with much smaller size are obtained.

For compression of non-evaluation area, we focus on property that result data from thermo-fluid simulation is orthogonal mesh format, thus can construct a tensor. Because the 3-dimension tensor can be decomposed into three 2-dimension matrices and one 3-dimension matrix, and total size of theses matrixes is much smaller than the compression technique is developed. These matrixes can be recovered to the original format, so as to approximate the tensor.

Compressed data by tensor decomposition is presented by the three 2-dimension matrix and one 3-dimension matrix. Theses matrix are combined together to recovery the original simulation data format, by matrix operation. Thus in the recovered file, error occurs even the evaluation area.

Data combination is used for correcting the error generated in recovery of com-pressed data. Simulation result of the evaluation area without compression is combined with recovered data, so as to correct the error generated by compression.

With this technology, transfer time can be shortened even with very narrow band-width, and simulation result can be evaluated in India with high precision.

3 Data Transfer Experiment Between Japan-India

Model 1 in Table 1 is a converter for 3MW wind power generator, and thermo-fluid simulation result is used to verify the developed technique. Simulation data (Fig.2 (a)) before compression is 130MB, among which non-compress area is extracted by pro-posed method. In this experiment, if temperature difference between a surface element which is higher than 50 and the element which is 8mm away from surface is lower than 5, the area is extracted as non-compress area (Fig.2 (a)). Data size of compressed data (Fig.2 (b)) and non-compress area (Fig.2 (a)) is reduced to 2MB. Thus the compression rate reached to 1/70. Data transfer speed from Japan to HHPE is 44kbps, which can be improved to 110kbps by applying WCC data transfer tech-nique with 2.5 times transfer speed. The total transfer time is reduced to 139s (transfer time 130s and compress-recover time 9s), gaining a reduction rate of 1/173. The recovered data is illustrated in Fig.2 (c). We can see that the compressed data is with error, and recovered data by applying developed technique is without error. Model 2 in Table 1 is a converter for 2MW wind power generator, and data transfer time is reduced to 190s. The research goal of 1/100 is accomplished (Table 1).

Table 1: Result of proposed technique

	Data Size	Transfer time	Compress and recover Time	Total time
Model 1 before	130MB	240×10^2 s	0s	240×10^2 s
after	2MB	130s	9s	139s
Model 2 before	294MB	550×10^2 s	0s	550×10^2 s
after	2MB	180s	10s	190s

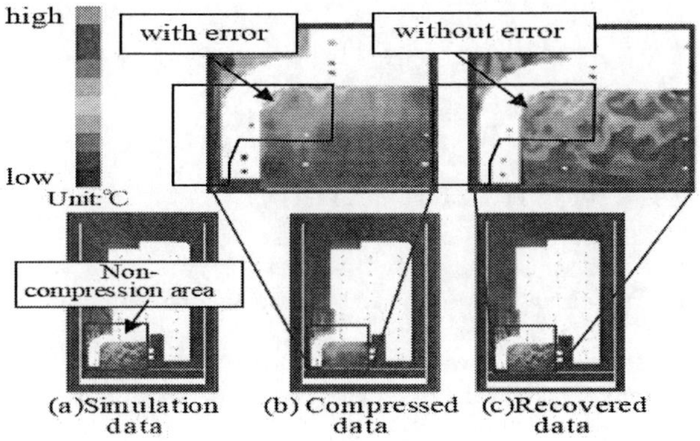

Fig. 2: Data transfer experiment.

4 Conclusion and Future work

A high-speed engineering data transfer technique to reduce transfer time to 1/100 based on data mining was developed in this research. Thus design simulation plat-form can be executed from overseas sites, and high-quality customize design became possible. High-speed engineering data transfer technique is going to be deployed to other business departments, so as to take advantage of design cloud. The understanding of design process would be necessary to contribute to the realization of high-quality customized design for utilizing simulation tools, such as not only vHILS and thermo-fluid simulation but other kinds of software.

References

1. Fujitsu Homepage,http://pr.fujitsu.com/jp/news/2012/05/15-4.html, last accessed 2018/01/04. NEC HPC OnLinehttp://jpn.nec.com/manufacture/machinery/hpc_online/index.html, last accessed 2018/01/04.
2. Rajendran, A., Mhashilkar, P.: Optimizing Large Data Transfers over 100Gbps Wide Area Networks, 13th IEEE/ACM international symposium on cluster, cloud, and grid computing, pp. 26-33, (2013).

Improving Sales Forecasting with Customer Behavior Analysis

Yusuke Yamaura[1], Yiou Wang[2], and Takeshi Onishi[3]

Fuji Xerox Co., Ltd. Japan
{Yusuke.Yamaura,Yiou.Wang,Takeshi.Onishi}@fujixerox.co.jp

Abstract. In this paper, we explore the utility of customer behavior analysis of un-structured video data for improving sales forecasting, which is an important task for supply chain management in retail store. Our work is motivated by the observation that *the needs and interest of customers will influence the sales performance and customers' needs and interest can be reflected in some degree by monitoring and analyzing the customers' behavior in a store.* To the best of our knowledge, this is the first work that introduces the customer behavior analysis of monitoring video data to sales forecasting task. In order to validate our observation, we conducted a series of experiments in a physical retail store and demonstrated that integrating video-based customer behavior analysis into a conventional sale forecasting model results in a performance improvement.

Keywords: Customer behavior analysis, sales forecasting

1 Introduction

Sales Forecasting is an important task for supply chain management, business planning, and customer relationship management in retail industries [1]. In particular, retail stores provide short shelf-life food products and inaccurate forecast tends to cause stock-outs and food waste [2]. Therefore the accurate prediction is required for reliable planning and optimization.

A number of studies on sales forecasting have been conducted in the past decades. Recently machine learning based forecasting methods have achieved high accuracy compared with traditional statistical time series methods, such as moving average model [3,4]. To improve the performance, demand influence factors have been explored[5,6]. Generally, weather conditions, holidays, and public events are considered due to their impact on demand and public availability[5].

On the other hand, behavior intelligence and insight play an important role in data understanding and business problem solving [7,8]. Customer behavior contains valuable information for marketing analysis. Therefore, it is attractive to considering exploiting customer behavior analysis in sales forecasting. The idea of combining customer behavior analysis with sales prediction been previously reported in online sales forecasting, which consider visitor's behavior tracked in their online EC-site [9,10,11]. However, little research has been conducted in this direction for offline cases. Customer behavior inside a physical store, which represents a shopping process until purchasing or non-purchasing but not explicitly included in the point-of-sales (POS) data or other external data, is often neglected.

In this paper, we present an approach to improve the performance of sales forecasting by incorporating the customer behavior analysis into a conventional sales forecasting model. Specifically, we develop video-based customer behavior analysis system for monitoring and analyzing customer's shopping behavior, then extract the information about how the customers interact with the stores and products, and finally design a framework to incorporate the customer behavior analysis into a sales forecasting model. To demonstrate the effectiveness of our approach, we conduct a series of experiments in a physical retail store. We show that our approach yields improvements for all the test collections and achieves better results than the conventional sale forecasting method.

To the best of our knowledge, this is the first work that introduces the customer behavior analysis of monitoring video data to sales forecasting task. Overall, the main contributions of this paper are as follows:

- We present a new approach to encode customer behavior information to sales forecasting.
- The relation between customer behaviors and sales is investigated.
- We make behavioral forecasting to predicts customer behavior and translate it into sales.

2 Proposed Method

In this section, we introduce our approach for incorporating customer behavior analysis into a conventional approach for sales forecasting. We first describe an overview of our video-based customer behavior analysis system, which can monitor the customer's shopping behavior inside a store. Second, we discuss what types of shopping behaviors are relevant to sales. Third, we make behavioral forecasting to predicts customer behavior and translates it into sales. Finally, we explain the way to integrate new customer behavior features to the traditional method effectively. Figure 1 shows an overview of our approach for incorporating customer behavior analysis into a conventional model. This is the framework that we utilize the unstructured video data for financial forecast, which is traditionally based on structured data.

2.1 Customer Behavior Analysis

We developed video-based customer behavior analysis system for capturing and analyzing customer's shopping behavior in real stores. Our system is composed of multiple IP cameras and PCs with image processing modules installed. Specifically, surveillance cameras, which is utilized for monitoring, marketing, or security in a physical store, was installed. We developed several retail-oriented

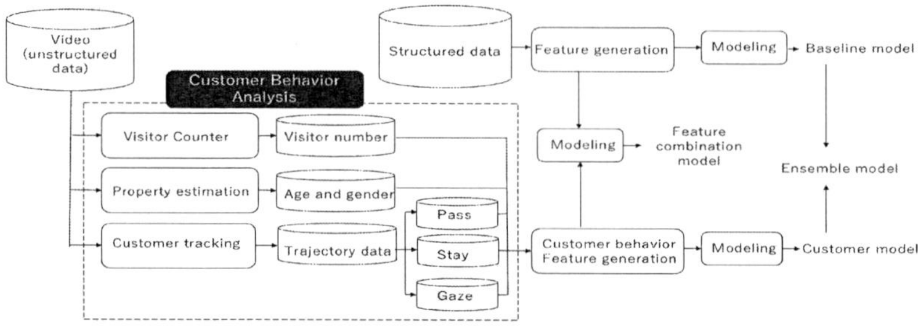

Fig. 1. Overview of the proposed approach

intelligent video analysis modules for analyzing customer's behavior inside a store.

- **Visitor counter module** receives video frames from a surveillance camera just above the store entrance and counts the number of customers who visit or leave the store.
- **Property estimation module** also receives video frames from a surveillance camera just above the store entrance and estimate the age and gender of customers.
- **Customer tracking module** processes video data from multiple cameras mounted on the ceiling inside the store and this module conduct several image recognitions sub-modules,

Specifically, customer tracking module includes people detection sub-module, head orientation estimation sub-module and trajectory reconstruction sub-modules. People detection sub-module first detects the region where a customer is in a video frame based on background subtraction technique, and then detects the head and body part. head orientation estimation sub-module analyzes the head orientation and outputs the category of head orientation (e.g. front, left, back, right). Trajectory reconstruction sub-module reads sequential images, detects locations, estimates head orientation, and reconstructs a trajectory inside the store. All the data is aggregated in real time and transported to our cloud server per 5 minutes. Using this system, we can collect the customer information of the visitor number, customers' age and gender, customer shopping trajectory and shopping actions.

2.2 Customer Behavior Feature Selection

Customer behavior is the center point of behavioral forecasting and sales forecasting. In this section, we will discuss how do customers behave in a store and how does this impact sales.

In the case of physical store, if a customer has no interest to the product, he or she will neither look at the shelf nor turn to the shelf. As an initial interest level, he or she will go to the shelf and stay in front of the shelf. If the customer has more interest, he or she will stay in front of the shelf for a long time. If the customer has further interest, his or her gaze will fall upon the product and gaze the shelf for a long time. If the customer has further interest, he or she probably stretches arm and touches the product. Based on these observations, in sales forecasting task, we assume that the following shopping behaviors are strongly related to customer's demand, reveals the interest of customer to the product and reflected the way in which customers interact with the store and products:

1. Visit the store
2. Pass the shelf
3. Stay in front of the shelf
4. Gaze the shelf
5. Purchase the shelf

Because of some technical limitations (such as low resolution images, lighting conditions, and occlusions) of the customer behavior analysis system described in section 2.1, we can only analyze the previous four behaviors.

To capture the relation between the behaviors and sales, we investigated the relationship between customer behaviors and sales using the history data of shopping video data and POS data, and made the following two observations:

Observation 1: The sales was impacted by customer behaviors.

Figure 2 shows the tendency of sales, the visitor number and behavior number. We can see that the tendency of the visitor number and behavior number is the same as that of sales.

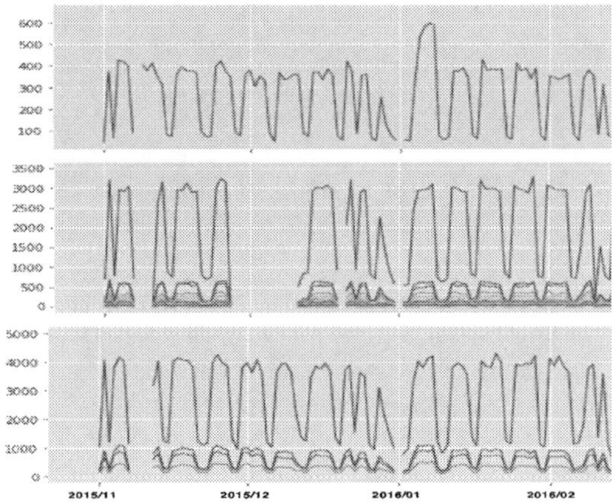

A: Tendency of the sales of rice balls.

B: Tendency of visitor numbers in different groups. The red line is the total number of visitors. Note that there are some data missing in December 2015.

C: Tendency of customer numbers in different behaviors. The red line is the total number of customers passing the shelf of rice balls

Fig. 2. Plot of sales, visitor numbers and behavior numbers

Observation 2: The relations between the behaviors and sales are different for different specific customer segments.

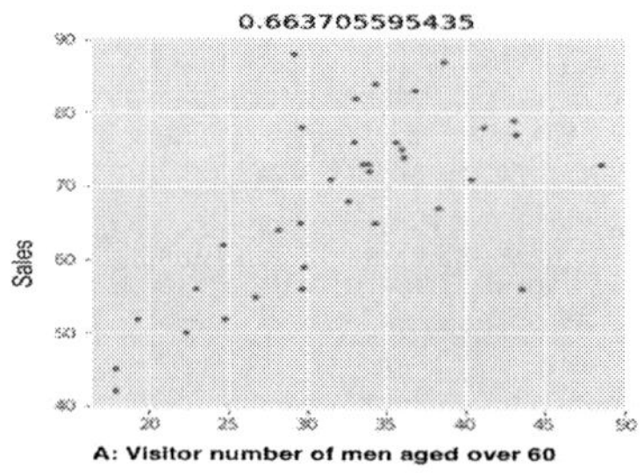

Fig. 3. Correlation of sales and visitor numbers of different gender groups

We investigated the correlation coefficients of customer behavior and sales. Figure 3 is the plot of the correlation coefficients between sales and visitor numbers of different gender groups. The number of male customers is more relevant to sales than that of female customers. Customers in different gender groups impact the sales in a different way.

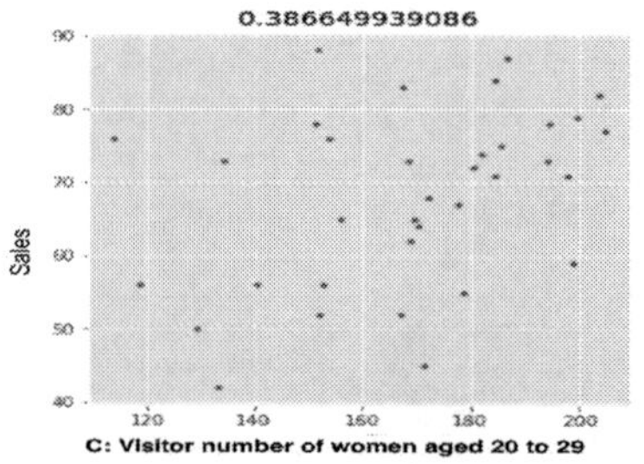

Fig. 4. Correlation of sales and visitor numbers of different age groups

Figure 4 is plot of correlation coefficients between sales and visitor numbers of different age groups. The number of female customers aged 20 to 29 is more relevant to sales than that of female customers above 60. Customers in different age groups also impact the sales in a different way. As the store is located in the business center area in Tokyo, the salarymen and young female staffs are tend to be frequent buyers while the female customer above 60 are tend to be occasional customers. Our findings are consistent with the situation of the physical store.

From this point of view, we propose to encode the customer behavior information separately for different customer segments and different activities. We categorize customers into groups by gender and age, then investigate how different customer groups are relevant of sales and encode the behavior of specific customer groups as distinct new features for sale forecasting. Specifically, visitors' age is categorized into 6 groups, under 19, 20-29, 30-39, 40-49, 50-59, 60 or over. We make the activities (behaviors) features in the same way. Activities include pass by the shelf, stay in front of the shelf over 5/10 seconds, gaze the shelf over 1 second. We calculate the number of people who act these behaviors from trajectory data acquired by the customer behavior analysis system. Consequently, we extract customer behavior features, including the daily number of visitors to the store at each age group and gender, people who pass by the shelf, stay in front of the shelf over 5/10 seconds, gaze the shelf over 1 second.

2.3 Behavioral Forecasting

We must predict the sales in advance. However it is impossible to know the customer behavior information of the prediction target day in advance. Therefore in order to add the customer behavior information into sale forecasting, we must make behavioral forecasting too. We apply time series analysis to model seasonal patterns of customer behaviors and here predict the customer behaviors of a target day using simple moving average (SMA) method. We adopted moving average of same days of week in past 4 weeks because daily sales are strongly related to the day of week. To put it simply, for example, customer behavior of the week day is different from the holidays and the effects of weekends and holidays should be considered. We found that predicted customer behavior information is close to the actual situation except for some special days such as some special holidays, and can capture recent trends of customer behavior. We finally generate customer behavior features by behavioral forecasting result. Table 1 shows generated customer behavior features.

Feature Type	Feature	Description
Visitor features	$N_{visitor}, visitorg$	SMA of number of visitor for each age and gender group.
Activity features	N_{pass}	SMA of number of people who pass by the shelf.
	N_{stay_five}	SMA of number of people who stay in front of the shelf over 5 seconds.
	N_{stay_ten}	SMA of number of people who stay in front of the shelf over 10 seconds.
	N_{gaze}	SMA of number of people who gaze the shelf over 1 seconds.

Table 1. Customer Behavior Features

2.4 Feature Integration

To integrate the customer behavior features into a structured data based traditional model, the following two integration strategies are adopted:

- **Feature combination**

This is a simple concatenation of separate features and requires only single model. There is a possibility that high dimensional features cause overfitting or complexity of interpretation.

– **Ensemble learning**

Ensemble learning is an algorithm to acquire more accurate outcome by combining the predictions of multiple models. Ensemble modeling is most effective when large variance of outcomes or large difference among input data type. We here adopt the simplest way of ensemble averaging described as follows:

$$f_i(X) = \frac{1}{M}\sum_{i=1}^{M} \hat{f}_i(X)$$

Here, $\hat{f}_i(X)$ is the output of model i among all the multiple models and M is the number of models.

3 Experiments

3.1 Experimental Setting

In this paper, we chose rice balls sale forecasting in a physical store as as our prediction task. Specifically, we predict the daily sales number of rice ball in one week before the prediction target day. In our study, we don't consider type difference of rice balls and the target value is total number of all types of rice balls. Our video-based customer behavior analysis system is installed in a physical store, which is composed with two surveillance cameras for visitor analysis, three omnidirectional cameras for acquisition of customer's trajectory inside the store, and two PCs with image processing modules installed.

The experiment is conducted from October 2015 to May 2016. In order to evaluate the generalization performance appropriately, we choose the last week of March, April, and May 2016 as validation period (Test1, Test2, and Test3). As we define forecasting day as one week before the target day, the training period covers from October 2015 to the day when one week before the target day as shown Figure 5.

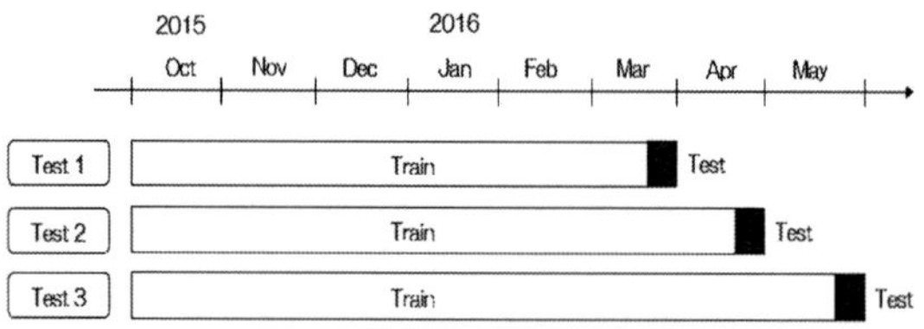

Fig. 5. Experimental data sets

3.2 Baseline Models

The baseline model is a conventional approach based on machine learning generally using the structured information, such as weather, calendar, and event information. We train our baseline model on Gradient Boosting Decision Tree (GBDT) proposed by Friedman [12], which is demonstrated to be one of the most effective algorithms and is becoming a mainstream in forecasting competitions as well as Kaggle challenges. Baseline features are as follows:

- POS information: the same days of the week in past 4 weeks.
- Weather information: lowest/highest temperature, precipitation, humidity, wind speed, and categorized day-time/night weather (sunny, cloudy, rainy, snow).
- Calendar information: year, month, the day of week, seasons, quarters, public holiday, holiday, before/after holiday, between holidays, consecutive holidays, annual events, elapsed years/month/weeks/days, number of weeks in corresponding month.
- Promotion information: discount sales, special lottery, collaboration campaign, etc.

We use XGBoost[13] library for implementation of GBDT, which has become widely popular tool among various competitions. We tune the hyper parameters of XGBoost step by step for acquiring generalization ability as follows: (i) fix a relatively high learning rate (e.g. η=0.1) and find the optimal number of trees under the fixed learning rate by cross-validation. (ii) tune tree-specific parameters such as the maximum number of depth, the minimum weight at child nodes, the ratio of subsamples, etc. (iii) tune regularization parameters which help to reduce model complexity. (iv) lower the learning rate (e.g. η=0.01) and recalibrate the number of trees.

In addition to the conventional machine learning model, we built a moving average model with daily sales of same day of week in past 4 weeks for comparision. This is the widely-used simplest way for sales forecasting and our collaborative retail company also adopt this method for daily sales forecasting.

3.3 Experimental Results

We evaluated the effectiveness of our proposed method in a series of experiments. Specifically, we investigate the effect of incorporating customer behavior features, which is described in Section2.2, into a traditional model.

We used Accuracy as evaluation metrics.

$$Accuracy = (100 - MAPE)\%$$

Here, Mean Absolute Percentage Error(MAPE) is defined as follows:

$$MAPE = \frac{100}{N} \sum_{i=1}^{N} \frac{f_i - y_i}{y_i}$$

Methods	Test1 (%)	Test2 (%)	Test3 (%)	Average (%)
Sales SMA model	87.18	91.28	83.55	87.34
Baseline model	88.78	92.68	87.31	89.59
+ (a) visitor features	**90.37**	93.78	84.46	89.54
+ (b) activity features	88.1	95.8	85.86	89.92
+ (a), (b)	87.44	**95.97**	86.07	89.83
Customer model	89.62	94.21	86.04	89.96
Ensemble model	89.2	93.71	**88.83**	**90.58**

Table 2. The results of prediction models

Here, f_i is the predict value, y_i is the actual value and N is the predict data number.

Table 2 shows the final results for all experiments. Our experiments demonstrate that the customer behavior information contributes to the improvement of prediction performance even though the customer related features are generated by behavioral forecasting. We investigated the cases with great improvement and found the following points contribute to the performance gains:

(i) The latest trends of the customer behavior have impact on the sales of a product and the balance among the kinds of customer behavior can be considered by our method. For example, if the number of visitors is increasing while the number of customers passing the shelf is stable, it perhaps indicates the customers are interested in other products but not in the predict target product, the sales of the targeted product is not increasing.

(ii)The latest trends of some specific customer segment sometimes impact the sales greatly and the trends of the specific customer segment can be encoded by our method. For example, in some cases, the tendency of the female customers over 60 and under 12, who belong to the occasional customer segment, changed greatly and such change can be reflected by our method and lead to a more precise prediction.

In general, structured POS data only include the buyers information, while customer behavior data provides more detailed information, which includes the information of latent buyers and represents the whole shopping process. Such information is effective for the sales prediction.

4 Conclusion

In this paper, we presented an approach to improve the performance of sales forecasting by incorporating customer shopping behavior analysis and investigated the impact of several strategies which can integrate the unstructured customer behavior features into a conventional structure data based model. The experimental results showed that customer behavior information provided improvements for all the test collections. Customer behavior analysis was demonstrated effective in sales prediction task. In future, we will evaluate our method with large data sets and introduce the confidence of the customer behavior information to the behavioral forecasting model.

References

1. Mentzer, J. T. and Bienstock, C. C.: Sales forecasting management: understanding the techniques, systems and management of the sales forecasting process.Thousand Oaks, CA: Sage publications (1998)
2. Mena, C., Terry, L. a, Williams, A. and Ellram, L.: Causes of waste across multi-tier supply networks: cases in the UK food sector, Int. J. Prod. Econ. 152, 144 -158. (2014)
3. Alon, Q.Min and R.J.Sadowski : Forecasting aggregate retail sales: a comparison of artificial neural networks and traditional method, J.Retail.Consum.Serv.8 (3) 147-156.(2001)
4. Dilek Penpece and Orhan Emre Elma.: Predicting Sales Revenue by Using Artificial Neural Network in Grocery Retailing Industry: A Case Study in Turkey, In: International Journal of Trade, Economics and Finance, 5(2) pp. 435-440 (2014)
5. Mykola Pechenizkiy and Patrick Meulsteea: Food Sales Prediction: "If Only It Knew What We Know", In: IEEE International Conference on Data Mining Workshops 128, pp. 128-143 (2008)
6. Chen, C.-Y., Lee, W.-I., Kuo, H.-M., Chen, C.-W., and Chen, K.-H. : The study of a forecasting sales model for fresh food, Expert Systems with Applications, 37(12), 7696-7702. (2010)
7. Zimu Zhou, Longfei Shangguan, Xiaolong Zheng, Lei Yang and Yunhao Liu: Design and Implementation of an RFID-Based Customer Shopping Behavior Mining System, Networking IEEE/ACM Transactions on, vol. 25, pp. 2405-2418, (2017)
8. Jingwen Liu, Yanlei Gu and Shunsuke Kamijo: Customer Behavior Recognition in Retail Store from Surveillance Camera, Multimedia (ISM) 2015 IEEE International Symposium on, pp. 154-159, (2015)
9. Currie, C. S. M., and Rowley, I. T.: Consumer behavior and sales forecast accuracy: What's going on and how should revenue managers respond? Journal of Revenue and Pricing Management, 9(4), 374-376, (2010)
10. Lohse, C. L., Bellman, S., and Johnsone, E. J. (2000). Consumer buying behavior on the Internet: Findings from panel data. journal of lnteractive Marketing, 74, pp.15-29, (2000)
11. Yuan, H., Xu, W and Wang, M. : Can online user behavior improve the performance of sales prediction in E-commerce? IEEE International Conference on Systems, Man, and Cybernetics, pp 2377-2382, (2014)
12. Friedman, J. . Greedy function approximation: A gradient boosting machine. Annals of Statistics, 29, pp. 1189 - 1232, (2001)
13. T. Chen and C. Guestrin: Xgboost: A scalable tree boosting system, In Proceedings of the KDD, San Francisco, California, (2016)

Electricity Short Term Load Forecasting

Gassan Abujumra[1] and Mohamed Bouguessa[2]

University of Quebec at Montreal
Department of Computer Science
Montreal, Quebec, Canada

Abstract. Electricity load forecasting refers to the estimation of future load demand. This is very important for real-time contingency analysis, maintenance scheduling, infrastructure development, etc. In this short paper, we analyze the behavior of supervised learning models such as Multi-Layer Perceptron and Support Vector Regression for the purpose of short-term load forecasting. We highlight the weakness of such learning models and we describe our ongoing work to enhance the prediction of existing approaches.

Keywords: Electricity consumption · Load forecasting · Supervised learning.

1 Context

Forecasting electricity demand and energy, is being used throughout all segments of the electric power industry, including generation, transmission, distribution, and retail. Applications of load forecasts include power supply planning, transmission and distribution systems planning, demand side management, power systems operations and maintenance, financial planning, rate design, and so forth. Due to the fundamental role of load forecasting in the utility business operations, inaccurate load forecasts may result in financial burden to, or even bankruptcy of a utility company. While load forecasting provides a key input to power systems operations and planning, inaccurate load forecasts can lead to equipment failures or even system wide blackout [1].

Electric load forecasting refers to the estimation of future load demand. A typical forecasting process involves modeling the relationship between load and its influential factors, such as temperature, wind speed, and day type (e.g. week day, week end, holiday). Load forecasting can be roughly classified into four categories based on its forecasting horizon: (1) Very Short-Term Load Forecasting (VSTLF) for few minutes to one hour time interval – VSTLF applications may include optimal power flow and real-time contingency analysis; (2) Short-Term Load Forecasting (STLF) for one hour to one week timestamp – STLF applications may include unit commitment and economic dispatch; (3) Medium-Term Load Forecasting (MTLF) for one week or one year – MTLF applications may include reserve requirement decision and maintenance scheduling; and finally, (4) Long-Term Load Forecasting (LTLF) for one year and above – LTLF applications include infrastructure development and financial planning. In the experiments reported in this document, we focus on STLF. Specifically, we define STLF as a 24-hour-ahead load forecast whose results will provide an hourly electric load forecast in megawatts for the next 24 hours (a 24-hour load profile). In the following section, we present some experiments related to the STLF problem. In Section 3, we discuss our ongoing work.

2 Experiments

2.1 Data Preparation

We conducted experiments using hourly data taken from ISO New England (ME station) [2], an independent electricity system operator in the USA. The time period for the collected data is from January 1, 2015 to December 31, 2016. The data contains 17,522 instances and 14 features. Since we want to forecast one day ahead, we aggregate the hourly data to one day. Also, we generate a weekend index to mark weekday and weekend (1 for a weekend and 0 for a weekday.) For the load forecast, the input parameters include the following: (1) Day of the week; (2) Weekend indicator (0 or 1); (3) Previous 24-hr average load; (4) Previous 24-hr average demand; (5) Previous 24-hr average Dry bulb temperature; (6) Previous 24-hr average Dew point temperature.

We used a windowing technique to transform the above time series data into a generic data set; this step will convert the last row of a window within the time series into a label or target variable. Our window size is 8; that will use the previous 7 days data to predict one day ahead. That means we will use the previous 7 days data (weekend indicator, average load, average demand, average Dry-bulb temperature, average Dew point temperature) to predict the 8th day load value. This will generate a new data set with 34 attributes, and the target variable will be the load attribute.

2.2 Comparing Algorithms and Evaluation Metrics

In our experiments, we compared the performance of two load forecasting supervised methods: (1) Multi-Layer Perceptron (MLP) and (2) Support Vector Regression (SVR) [3]. The selected models (MLP and SVR) are trained with data from January 1, 2015 to December 31, 2015 and tested on out-of-sample data from January 1, 2016 to December 31, 2016. The test set is completely separate from the training sets and it is not used for model estimation or variable selection. In order to evaluate the forecast performance, we used a sliding windows validation technique. This technique uses a certain window of examples for training and uses another window (after horizon examples, i.e. time points) for testing. The window is moved across the example set and all performance measurements are averaged afterwards. The performance measure that we have used to evaluate the quality of the forecasting, that is, to compare between the predicted load $p_1,\dots,p_n$ and the actual load $a_1,\dots,a_n$ (over n instance

	MLP	SVR
Mean Absolute Error	**42.326**	49.003
Relative Absolute Error	**3.20%**	3.84%
Correlation Coefficient	**0.863**	0.824

Table 1: Results over the full feature space.

	MLP	SVR
Mean Absolute Error	**42.001**	53.876
Relative Absolute Error	**3.26%**	4.25%
Correlation Coefficient	**0.843**	0.786

Table 2: Results over a subset of selected features.

in the testing set), are : (1) Mean Absolute Error $MAE = \frac{|p_1 - a_1| + \cdots + |p_n - a_n|}{n}$ which look at the average difference between the predicted load p and the actual load a; (2) Relative Absolute Error $RAE = \frac{|p_1 - a_1| + \cdots + |p_n - a_n|}{|a_1 - \overline{a}| + \cdots + |a_n - \overline{a}|}$ which divide the differences between p and a by the variation of a (note that $\overline{a}$ denotes the average load over a) - so RAE has a scale from 0 to 1 such that lowest values (close to 0) suggest good prediction; and (3) Correlation Coefficient $CC = \frac{S_{PA}}{\sqrt{S_P S_A}}$, $S_{PA} = \frac{\sum_i^n (p_i - \overline{p})(a_i - \overline{a})}{n-1}$, $S_P = \frac{\sum_i^n (p_i - \overline{p})^2}{n-1}$, $S_A = \frac{\sum_i^n (a_i - \overline{a})^2}{n-1}$ ($\overline{p}$ denotes the average load over p). The Correlation Coefficient tells us how much p and a are related. It gives values between -1 and 1, where values close to 1 suggest a strong relation between p and a.

2.3 Results

We performed two experiments. In the first experiment, all the 34 attributes of the training data was fed to both MLP and SVR. Then, the learned model was applied to the entire testing data set. In the second experiment, we performed features selection using Correlation weighting scheme. This metric calculates the weight of attributes with respect to the label attribute by using correlation. The higher the weight of an attribute, the more relevant it is considered. We select all the attributes that have a correlation value above 0.5. Specifically, 14 attributes have been selected. We repeated the first experiment with the new data set generated from the feature selection process. Table 1 and Table 2 illustrate the results of MLP and SVR evaluated with the Mean Absolute Error, Relative Absolute Error and Correlation Coefficient. Bold values correspond to the best results. As can be seen, MLP performs better than SVR. MLP has a small (mean and relative) absolute error and a higher correlation coefficient compared to SVR. Features selection leads SVR to score the worst result as compared with the first experiment. A tiny improvement has been observed for MLP after features selection. For the purpose of illustration, in Figure 1 we show the actual and the predicted load plot by MLP and SVR using all the set of features as well as a subset of selected features. These figures corroborate the metrics values in

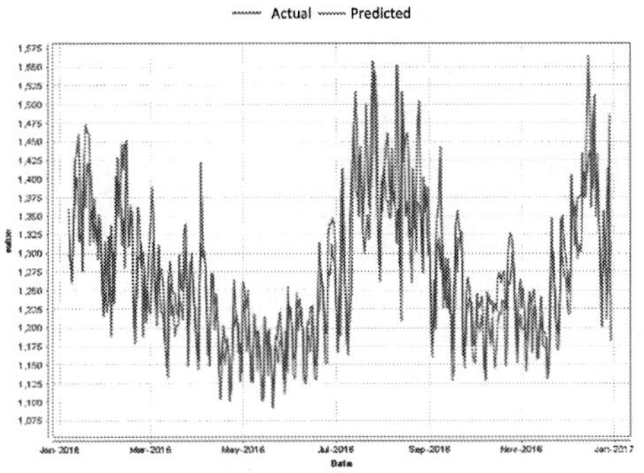

(a) MLP over the full space.

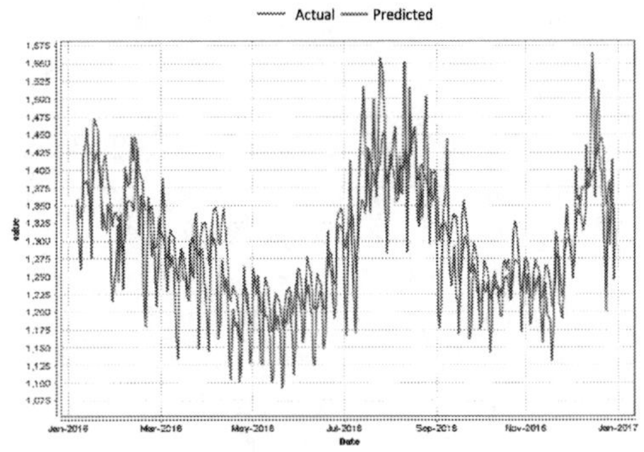

(b) SVR over the full space.

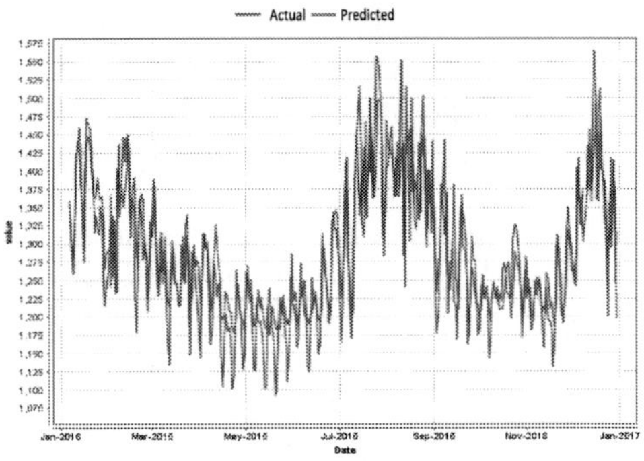

(c) MLP over a subset of selected features.

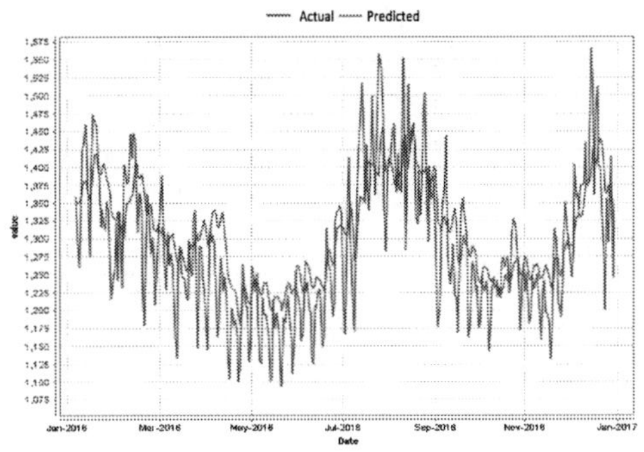

(d) SVR over a subset of selected features.

Fig. 1: The actual and the predicted load plots using: all features ((a) & (b)) and a subset of selected features ((c) & (d)).

Table 1 and Table 2 in the sense that MLP tends to provide accurate prediction compared to SVR.

3 Discussion and Ongoing Work

Most machine learning models used in the field of energy analysis [4], [5], are capable of forecasting electricity load with quite good accuracy. We believe this is simply due to the fact that some customers tend to exhibit repetitive behavior from one period to another, yielding periodic load profiles. On the other hand, however, the repetitively fluctuating nature of customers consumption may pose difficulties for highly accurate forecasting using supervised learning models. For instance, customer electricity consumption forecasts, treated as streaming data, are usually dominated by outdated historic information which tends to hamper existing models. This is essentially due to the fact that individual customers may change their consumption behavior at any moment. In other words, we completely lose the time varying aspect of customer consumptions which might completely change with time. Forecasting electricity load with such non-stable/variable customers' consumption over time requires the use of historical data that, indeed, reflect these variations. However, we observed in our empirical investigation, if the historical load is long and includes variable behaviors, existing learning models encounter difficulties to predict consumption at a further time point (short and medium term forecasting).

To alleviate the aforementioned problems, we are currently implementing a sliding window analysis from which we will develop a time varying model that simultaneously exploits an ensemble of learning approaches. The goal is to simulate load evolution patterns and temporal relations in a single framework to predict future electricity consumption over short and long-time scales. In our work, we will model the data under investigation as a type of sequence data. Different from the classical vector representation, sequence data encompass temporal information related to energy consumption. The data sequence refers to an ordered list of events associated with a single row data object. Each row records the occurrences of events associated to a specific customer at a different time stamp. We will next devise a statistical tracking model to analyse sequence data of phase 1 in order to track the consumption of each customer over time. This tracking process allows us to detect all critical events that may occur during different time periods. Based on the result of the tracking process, we will be able to identify features that reflect a causal relationship between customers energy consumption at different time points. Finally, the identified features will be used in a unified ensemble-learning framework that includes various learning approaches. Our objective is to develop an approach that aggregates the predictions of multiple learning techniques in a single framework. By doing so, we aim to enhance the prediction of various combined learning algorithms and avoid their pitfalls. This work is underway.

References

1. Hong T., Pinson P., and Fan S.: Global Energy Forecasting Competition 2012, International Journal of Forecasting, vol. 30, no. 2, pp. 357–363, 2014.
2. ISO New England: Energy, Load, and Demand Reports, `https://www.iso-ne.com/isoexpress/web/reports/pricing/-/tree/zone-info`
3. Ogcu G., Demirel O. F., and Selim Zaim S.: Forecasting Electricity Consumption with Neural Networks and Support Vector Regression, Procedia - Social and Behavioral Sciences, vol. 58, pp. 1576–1585, 2012.
4. Srivastava A. K, Pandey A. S, and Singh D., Short-Term Load Forecasting Methods: A Review, International Conference on Emerging Trends in Electrical Electronics & Sustainable Energy Systems, pp. 130–138, 2016.
5. Azimi R., Ghayekhloo M., Ghofrani M.: A Hybrid Method Based on a New Clustering Technique and Multilayer Perceptron Neural Networks for Hourly Solar Radiation Forecasting, Energy Conversion and Management, vol. 118. pp. 331–344, 2016.

Echo State Network Optimized by Cross-Entropy for Short-Term Load Forecasting of a Large Power Plant

Gabriel Trierweiler Ribeiro[1], Flavia Bernardo Pinto[2], Viviana Cocco Mariani[1,2], and Leandro dos Santos Coelho[1,3]

[1] Department of Electrical Engineering, Federal University of Parana Zip code 81531-980, Curitiba, PR, Brazil
[2] Mechanical Engineering Graduate Program (PPGEM) Pontifical Catholic University of Parana (PUCPR)
[3] Industrial and Systems Engineering Graduate Program (PPGEPS) Pontifical Catholic University of Parana (PUCPR)
leandro.coelho@pucpr.br

Abstract. Load forecasting means to know beforehand how much load will be demanded in given the following period. It is useful for power plants planning, since they need to guarantee enough power generators and resources available to supply the de-manded load, besides the need to comply with regulatory terms such as reservoir level and economical penalties imposed in case of lack of energy supply. In this study a cross-entropy optimization of Echo States Networks (ESN) hyperpa-rameters for load forecasting of a large power plant in Brazil is presented. The ESN control hyperparameters were set as variables to be optimized, then the cross-entropy optimization algorithm is employed to find the best set of ESN control hyperparameters, that are used for predictions. Results are evaluated in terms of accuracy, optimization convergence and computational effort.

Keywords: Echo State Networks · Load Forecasting · Cross-Entropy Optimization

1 Introduction

Load forecasting means to know beforehand how much load will be demanded in a given period. It is main useful for power plants planning, since they need to guaran-tee enough power generators and resources available to supply the demanded load, besides the need to comply with regulatory terms such as reservoir level and econom-ical penalties imposed in case of lack of energy supply. However, the growing introduction of renewable distributed energy sources together with the changed load pro-files of consumers requires that recent approaches to load forecasting make use of a huge amount of available load time series data to produce machine learning algorithms for load forecasting [1-3]. Recently, ESN, which is a type of reservoir for recur-rent neural networks trained through the learning approach of reservoir computing, has been successfully applied in a variety of engineering problems, including load [4] and time series [5-7] forecasting problems.

ESN requires initially the definition of a set of parameters, and this may be done through optimization techniques. The main contribution of this study is the investigation of Cross-Entropy (CE) for optimize ESN control hyperparameters in load forecasting applied to a large power plant located in Brazil. The remainder of the paper is organized as follows. In Section 2 a theoretical background for ESN and the cross-entropy optimization algorithm is provided. Next, in Section 3, the proposed materials and methods are presented. The results analysis and conclusion are presented in Section 4.

2 Theoretical Background of the ESN

ESN is a Recurrent Neural Networks (RNN) which use least squares learning algorithm to modify the output weights based on the inputs and reservoir weights previously randomly assigned [7-8]. Network weights are input weights W^{in}, reservoir weights W, output weights W^{out} and feedback weights from output W^{back}. The hidden layer state vector is named reservoir and is composed of fully connected nonlinear neurons. The reservoir outputs are named echo states, updated according to (1) where t is the time, x, u and y are vectors of reservoir states, inputs and outputs, respectively, f(.)are the reservoir neurons activation functions.

$$x_{t+1} = f(W^{in}.u_{t+1} + W.x_t + W^{back}.y_t) \tag{1}$$

Output y is calculated according to (2) where f^{out} is the activation function,

$$y_{t+1} = f^{out}(W^{out}.[u_{t+1}, x_{t+1}, y_t]) \tag{2}$$

The training is realized in the sense of least squares minimization as in (3) where d is the desired output vector. The matrix inversion is usually made by means of the Moore-Penrose operator or the pseudoinverse.

$$W^{out} = (x_{t+1}^T.x_{t+1})^{-1}).x_{t+1}^T.d \tag{3}$$

A sufficient condition to the echo state property existence is that the absolute value of highest eigenvalue of W, named spectral radius, must be lower than the unity [9].

2.1 Cross-Entropy Optimization

In the CE first values are randomly generated based on a distribution controlled by dynamic parameters, then are adjusted based on the set of function. Suppose the set of M possible solutions, X(k)=$\{x_1,...,x_M\}$ is defined by the mean μ, and variance σ^2. The objective function S(x), the set $\{s(x_1),...,s(x_M)\}$ is sorted from the lower to the higher value, the lowest values of the set (determined by the rarity parameter ρ) are selected to update the parameters μ, and σ^2. The random generator parameters are,

$$\mu(k+1) = \alpha \cdot mean(X'(k)) + (1-\alpha) \cdot \mu(k) \tag{4}$$

$$\sigma^2(k+1) = \beta \cdot std(X'(k)) + (1-\beta)\sigma^2(k) \tag{5}$$

where X ' is the elite set, fixed values to and βmay sometimes lead to local minima and so a modified version, named dynamic smoothing, is employed keeping fixed and varying βas,

$$\beta(k+1) = \beta(k) - \beta(k)\left(1 - \frac{1}{k}\right)^q \tag{6}$$

3 Materials and Methods

The dataset was composed of hourly loads records in MW from five consecutive weeks, the first three weeks for training, the fourth for validation and the fifth re-served for testing. In terms of optimization, was considered two cost functions to be minimized, the first was the MSE (Mean Squared Error) validation error of ESN with hyperbolic tangent activation function (tanh-ESN) and the validation error of ESN with sigmoid activation function (sig-ESN). The hyperparameters (variables) and UB (upper boundary) and LB (lower boundary) are presented in Table 1.

Hyperparameter	**LB tanh-ESN**	**UB tanh-ESN**	**LB sig-ESN**	**UB sig-ESN**
Spectral radius	0.01	1.5	0.01	6.00
Bias scaling	-3	3	-1	1.5
Input scaling	-10	10	-2	2
Bias shift	-7	7	-40	40
Input shift	-15	15	-20	20
Teacher Scaling	-1	1	0	1
Teacher shift	-2	0	-1	0
Feedback scaling	-1	1	-1	1
Noise level	-1	1	-20	20

Table 1. Optimized hyperparameters with respective bounds

4 The Overall Workflow

Figure 1 shows the complete work flow of the proposed solution. We fetch all the history or past mapping data for a company over a period of specified years as well as the current filing which has to be mapped. The filings obtained in the form of pdf are converted to XML which is then used to identify the financial

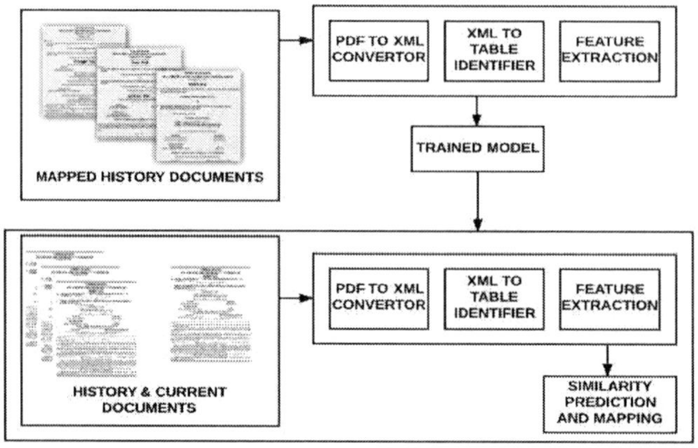

Fig. 1. The overall work flow for the mapping process.

tables followed by feature extraction and model building [8]. We load the trained classification model and make row maps of financial labels between the current filing and the history filings. We then perform feature extraction and make predictions for each of them and return the mappings having the highest prediction score.

5 Data Collection, Feature Extraction and Model Training

For data collection we iterate through the list of 500 companies for which we collect the manually mapped financial labels. Some companies also report financial labels in the eXtensible Business Reporting Language (XBRL) format along with the traditional format [9] [?] which is why we come up with three categories of row maps i.e. the xbrl to xbrl, xbrl to html and the html to html. A filing falls under the category of xbrl if it has been reported using XBRL standards, otherwise we categorize it as HTML.

For feature extraction we decided to go with various similarity metrics. Hierarchy of the labels plays an important role while mapping the labels. For e.g. the financial label "Depreciation and Amortization Expense" can come from the parent label "Cash Flow from Operating Activities" and also from the parent "Expenses". Therefore we take a combination of hierarchy based and non-hierachy based features. For feature extraction we mainly calculate the cosine similarity, context similarity, bi-gram and tri-gram similarity between the hierarchy labels, non-hierarchy labels and the xbrl labels. We train three different models for each of the row map category and train the feature vectors using the Support Vector Machine algorithm.

To achieve a higher accuracy we select output thresholds for each model from a fixed set of threshold values. We ran our experiment on a total of 125 combinations of thresholds and recorded the value for precision and recall for each of them. The baseline precision and recall value was recorded as 72.74% and 95.66% which went up to a precision of 83.56% and a good enough recall of 92.28% with the threshold of 0.6,0.6 and 0.4 for xbrl,xbrl-html and html models respectively.

6 Final Label Mapping

For final mapping we extract the financial labels from the the current filing and predict the financial labels in the past filings with which it best matches to. The following algorithm illustrates the same :

Algorithm 6.1: DATA MAPPING($RowMaps, Models$)

Extract features for xbrlRowMap
$\left\{\begin{array}{l}\text{Load xbrlmodel}\\ \text{Using the trained model and extracted features}\\ \text{xpred} = \text{Predict(xbrlRowMap,xbrlModel)}\end{array}\right.$
Extract features for xbrlhtmlRowMap
$\left\{\begin{array}{l}\text{Load xbrlhtmlmodel}\\ \text{Using the trained model and extracted features}\\ \text{xhpred} = \text{Pred(xbrlhtmlRowMap,xbrlhtmlModel)}\end{array}\right.$
Extract features for htmlRowMap
$\left\{\begin{array}{l}\text{Load htmlmodel}\\ \text{Using the trained model and extracted features}\\ \text{hpred} = \text{Predict(htmlRowMap,htmlModel)}\end{array}\right.$
Finalpred = xpred + xhpred + hpred
Sort FinalPred scores in descending order
for each $RowMap_i \in$ FinalPred
$\left\{\begin{array}{l}\text{If } RowMap_i \text{ not in the ResultSet}\\ \text{ResultSet} = \text{Insert } RowMap_i\end{array}\right.$

7 Performance Evaluation

We trained our models with various classification algorithms namely the Logistic Regression, Random Forest, Gradient Boosted Tree Model and Support Vector Machine. We observed that the SVM outperforms the other algorithms used here. Figure 2 below shows the label mapping ratio vs the average collection time taken. Here the X axis represents the mapping rate and the Y axis represents the mapping time. For example, for filings where mapping rate accuracy is 100%, the research analysts only need less than 10 minutes of processing time. Without, such a service in place they will have to manually go through each filing and map the labels which is tedious and is susceptible to incorrect mappings.

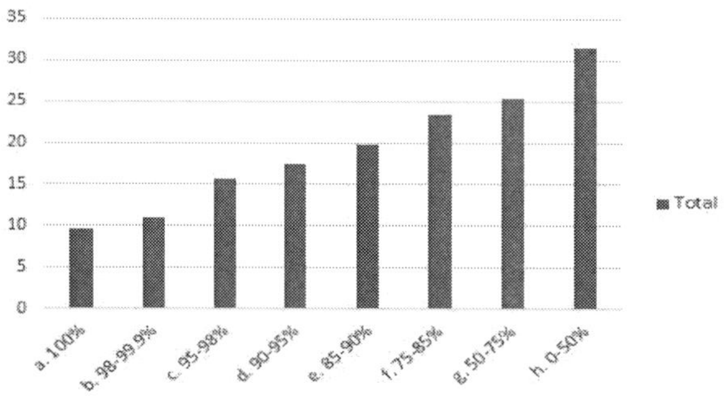

Fig. 2. Mapping vs average.

On an average without such a service in place it would take hours to process the filing whereas the average time taken now is reduced to a few seconds. Figure 3 below shows the graph between the mapping rate and the percentage of filings processed. X axis represents the mapping rate and Y axis represents the

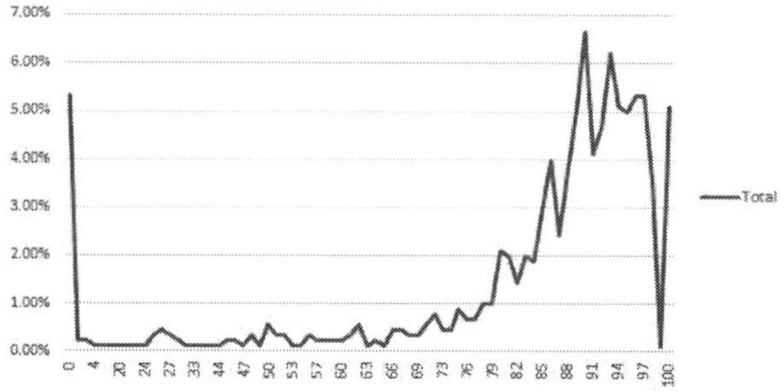

Fig. 3. The mapping rate.

percentage of filings. From the graph we can infer that a significant number of filings have a mapping rate of greater than 85% percent. The service makes use of Apache Spark as the parallel processing framework. During the peak seasons the analyst receives more than thousands of documents and there are over millions of data points that the service has to process in real time. We maintain a work-queue at the back end which is responsible for preventing any sort of thundering herd problem.

8 Conclusion and Future Work

In order to provide one stop data solutions to the investors we devised an effective feature based mechanism to map semantically similar yet syntactically different financial labels by making use of support vector machines. Our algorithm achieves a pretty good accuracy and has reduced the manual efforts greatly. As part of our future work we plan to optimize our code, improve the overall speed of the process and make our service language agnostic.

9 Credits

Special thanks to Sarah Hoffman, Ajaya Mallapaty, Naveen Kudupudi and Geetika Digumarthy who have helped us shape the solution. We would also thank the Factset Fundamentals Technical Operations (FFTO) team for contributing their time and providing us with relevant feedbacks while testing the service.

References

1. Qiu, X., Ren, Y., Nagaratnam, P., Amaratunga, G. A. J.: Empirical Mode Decomposition based ensemble deep learning for load demand time series forecasting. Applied Soft Compu-ting Journal, 54, (2017) 246-255
2. Ribeiro, G. T., Gritti, M. C., Ayala, H. V. H., Mariani, V. C., Coelho, L. S.: Short-term load forecasting using wavenet ensemble approaches. In: International Joint Conference on Neu-ral Networks (IJCNN), IEEE, Vancouver, Canada (2016) 727-734
3. Li, S., Wang, P., Goel, L. A novel wavelet-based ensemble method for short-term load fore-casting with hybrid neural networks and feature selection. IEEE Transactions on Power Sys-tems 3, 31, (2016) 17881798
4. Bianchi, F. M., De Santis, E., Rizzi, A., Sadeghian, A.: Short-Term Electric Load Forecast-ing Using Echo State Networks and PCA Decomposition. Access, 3, (2015) 1931-1943
5. Velasco Rueda, C.: EsnPredictor: Time series forecasting application based on echo state networks optimized by genetics algorithms and particle swarm optimization. Thesis, Pontifcia Universidade Catlica do Rio de Janeiro, Rio de Janeiro, Brazil (2014)
6. Liu, C., Zhang, H., Yao, X., Zhang, K.: Echo state networks with double-reservoir for time-series prediction. In: Seventh International Conference on Intelligent Control and Infor-mation Processing (ICICIP), IEEE, Siem Reap, Cambodia (2016) 196-202
7. Siqueira, H., Boccato, L., Attux, R., Lyra, C.: Unorganized machines for seasonal stream-flow series forecasting. International Journal of Neural Systems 3, (2014) 1-6
8. Jaeger, H.: The echo state approach to analyzing and training recurrent neural networks with an Erratum note 1. Technical Report, Fraunhofer Institute for Autonomous Intelligent Systems (2010)
9. Yaslan, Y., Bican, B.: Empirical mode decomposition based denoising method with support vector regression for time series prediction: A case study for electricity load forecasting. Measurement, 103, (2017) 52-61

Identification of Human Activity Change using Time Series Analysis

Yulei Pang[1] and Xiaozhen Xue[2]

Southern Connecticut State University, New Haven CT 06515, USA
URU Video Inc, New York, USA

Abstract. Human motion analysis is a grand research question and it continues attracting attention in both academia and industry. Its applications include surveillance systems, patient monitor-ing systems and so on. In recent years, most human activity analysis techniques are based on machine learning and deep learning algorithms [2],[3],[4]. Although the empirical study demonstrated the effectiveness of these algorithms, an important factor, the time stamp, was absent from studying. In this paper, we studied the human activity in the per-spective of time series analysis. More specially, we used changepoint analysis (CPA) technique to identify whether, when and where a change has taken place in human activity time series.

Keywords: Human Activity Recognition(HAR) · Changepoint Analysis(CPA) · Time Series Analysis

1 Introduction

Through this paper, we aim at proposing a technique, for segmenting the human activity time series, thus identifying human activity change. The proposed technique can be applied in both industry and academia. The major contribution of this paper is to:

a) Introduce an innovative technique for identification of human activity change based on the application of time series data analysis technique;

b) Evaluate and report the performance of proposed technique based through some experiments;

c) Discuss the implications of findings and the influence of factors involved, including the as-sumed distribution, measuring methods, and penalty function.

2 Datasets

In this paper, we use a dataset publicly available online [1]. To collect the date, previous research-ers have carried out an experiment with a group of 30 volunteers within an age range of 19-48 years. Each observation performed six activities (walling, walking upstairs, walking downstairs, sitting, standing, laying) wearing a smartphone (Samsung Galaxy S II) on the waist. The experi-ments have been video-recorded to label the data manually.

3 Methodology

We have conducted some preliminary study, and has verified the feasibility of the application of time series data analysis into human activity change. There are many perspectives and methods for analyzing time series data, and one of the most useful techniques is changepoint analysis (CPA). The purpose of CPA is to identify whether, when and where a change has taken place in a time series. There are many reasons to do this kind of analysis. A few good ones are:

a) to identify when a change has occurred so that you can respond somehow to that change;

b) to pinpoint when a change has occurred so you can attempt to identify its cause;

c) to predict future change. In this study, we will focus on the application of CPA in human activ-ity change.

3.1 An illustrative example

For instance, a person is sitting somewhere. At some time stamp, he stands up and starts walking.

This use case has a lot of real world applications including healthcare monitoring, security checking, and others. We formalize the data as following:

$$Data = X_1, X_2, ..., X_n \tag{1}$$

Where

$$X_i = (x_i, y_i, z_i, t_i) \tag{2}$$

X_i is one record; x_i, y_i, z_i are the position values; and t_i is the time stamp. Intuitively we can extract more info like velocity of movement and acceleration; and both of them are time series data. Now we take one window of data as an illustrative example. This piece of data contains two sequential activities: 1) a person was sitting between 1 to 190 time stamp; 2) he stands up at 191. We extract the velocity information and plot the data: Now we apply the changepoint

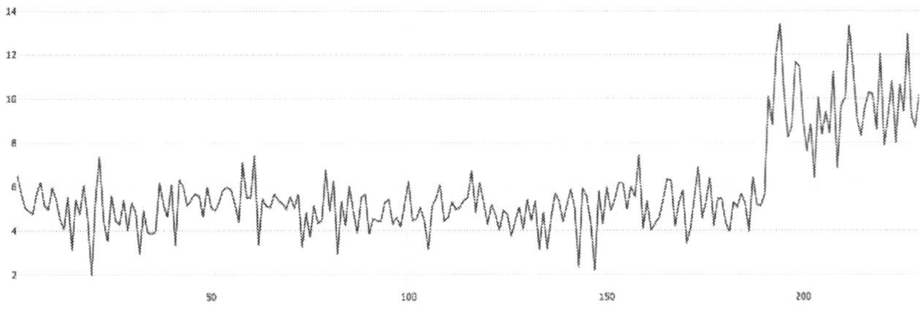

Fig. 1. The time series of a persons arm moving velocity .

identification technique [5] to locate the stand up time stamp by measuring the change in mean. Below is the plot of the results.

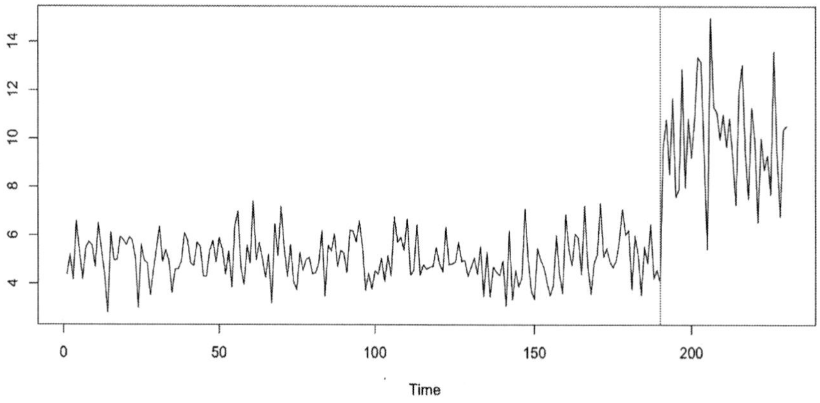

Fig. 2. The change from sitting to standing, in mean .

This picture depicts the two segmentations through redlines and it indicates that the changepoint is at 190, which exactly matches the ground truth. Although the mean function works perfectly in this case (we did more experiment, see Fig. 3) there are scenarios where it doesnt. For another activity change from walking upstairs to walking downstairs, the velocity means are very similar to each other before and after the change, so that we can not find out the changepoint through measuring change in mean. Fortunately there are other options, like measure by variance and so on. We plan to investigate the performance when different distributions are measured, and various methods to select; also all penalty functions are applied.

4 Conclusion

In this paper, we propose changepoint analysis to perform efficient smartphone-based human activity recognition. We will find a scalar to measure the precision for the proposed technique and explore more time series analysis method in this study.

5 Acknowledgments

This work is supported by the Connecticut State University American Association of University Professors Research Grants and Minority Recruitment and Retention Committee (MRRC) in Southern Connecticut State University.

h

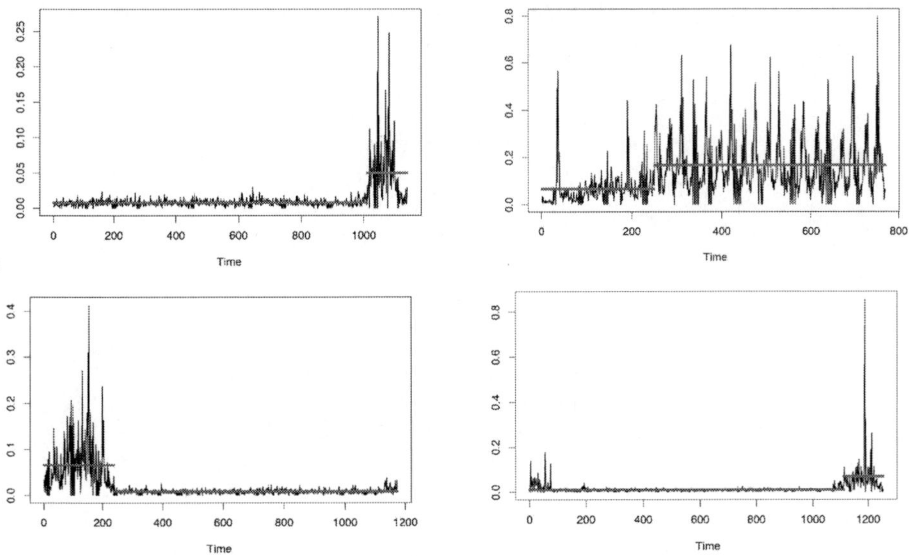

Fig. 3. More examples to show the change from "sitting" to "standing", in mean

References

1. Davide Anguita, Alessandro Ghio, Luca Oneto, Xavier Parra and Jorge L. Reyes-Ortiz. A Pub-lic Domain Dataset for Human Activity Recognition Using Smartphones. 21th European Sympo-sium on Artificial Neural Networks, Computational Intelligence and Machine Learning, ESANN 2013. Bruges, Belgium 24-26 April 2013.
2. Davide Anguita, Alessandro Ghio, Luca Oneto, Xavier Parra and Jorge L. Reyes-Ortiz. Human Activity Recognition on Smartphones using a Multiclass Hardware-Friendly Support Vector Machine. International Workshop of Ambient Assisted Living (IWAAL 2012). Vitoria-Gasteiz, Spain. Dec 2012
3. Jorge Luis Reyes-Ortiz, Alessandro Ghio, Xavier Parra-Llanas, Davide Anguita, Joan Cabesta-ny, Andreu Catal. Human Activity and Motion Disorder Recognition: Towards Smarter Interac-tive Cognitive Environments. 21th European Symposium on Artificial Neural Networks, Compu-tational Intelligence and Machine Learning, ESANN 2013. Bruges, Belgium 24-26 April 2013.
4. Ronao CA, Cho SB (2016) Human activity recognition with smartphone sensors using deep learning neural networks. Expert Syst Appl 59:235244.
5. Killick R, Eckley IA (2014). changepoint: An R Package for Changepoint Analysis. URL http://www.jstatsoft.org/v58/i03/.

Flow Prediction Versus Flow Simulation Using Machine Learning Algorithms

Milan Cisty

Slovak University of Technology in Bratislava, Slovakia
milan.cisty@stuba.sk

Abstract. The paper deals with differences between two types of machine learning river flow modelling, i.e., their simulation and prediction. In this paper, simulation means a determination of river flows from only meteorological data. The second type of modelling, i.e., prediction, additionally includes preceding flows in the input data. Preceding flows are known at the time of making a prediction. For this reason, i.e., because less input data serve for the simulation, it is a more difficult task than the prediction, and its degree of precision is also usually lower. The authors focused on the improvement of flow simulation methodology, i.e., the determination of river flows only from climate data. Several machine learning models were tested for this purpose, and their results are compared in the paper with a conceptual hydrological model. Three options were evaluated in the paper for the improvement of the precision of the machine learning type of flows simulation: 1) the effect of the use of different types of models, 2) the impact from the expansion of input data utilizing feature engineering, and 3) improving the accuracy of the simulation by applying an ensemble paradigm. An increased degree of precision (approximately 12%) of the flow simulation was obtained after the incorporation of the above methodological enhancements to the computations (when compared to standard hydrological methods). The authors believe that the proposed methodology will be a promising alternative to the usual hydrological simulation, and it would be useful to test it in an extended study in which more streams would be evaluated.

Keywords: Flow Simulation, Flow Prediction, Data-driven Methods

1 Introduction

Since the mid-1990s, many papers have been published in the hydrological literature which deals with the application of machine learning methods for the modelling of the rainfall-runoff process (these methods are also called data-driven modelling). Most of these papers only consider flow predictions [1, 2, 3] (we are mentioning only review papers due to the many published works). In the present study, the authors have followed this research and are emphasizing the existence of two types of such machine learning modelling, i.e., simulation and prediction. The difference between simulation and prediction is characterized below.

Flow *prediction* using machine learning models is usually based on input data consisting of a time series of climatic variables and on the known flow at the time the prediction is being made. The values of such variables are typically used in input data from several time steps before the prediction date. A flow predicted is one or more time steps (e.g., hours, days) ahead. This type of prediction has several advantages compared to a determination by other hydrology models, such as physical GIS-based models or conceptual models. The benefits of machine learning models include their simplicity, reduced amount of input data, and the higher degree of precision of the results, which in the scientific literature has been mainly demonstrated for short-term predictions [4].

In the terminology used in this paper flow *simulation* is the second type of modelling and is defined as the modelling of river flows only from data which is describing the factors directly causing it, i.e., rain, evaporation, melting of snow, and similar climate variables. In such a way understood simulation is applicable, e.g., for the generation of flows in the context of climate change impact studies. Its purpose could be to provide a long time series of a flow, which together with other data (usually simulated as well), e.g., temperatures and precipitation, can serve for statistical analyses of an expected drought, an investigation of irrigation demands, verifications of the future functioning of a water supply reservoir, etc. When comparing to the prediction a positive difference, with regard to its impact on the degree of precision, is that in a simulation (or flow generation), climate data can also be used from the same time step as is the time step for which the flow is simulated and not only from previous days (which is not possible in river flow prediction).

However, what is more important, in the context of a simulation, flows from previous days cannot be used as input data, since previous flows are not available (the entire flow time series is unknown and is going to be simulated). This difference in the amount of data that can be used as an input for prediction and simulation is substantial. This disadvantage is further underlined by the fact that flows have a strongly autocorrelative nature. From this property of river flows, it follows that the modelled flow mostly depends on its previous value. So, if the preceding flow is included in the input data, the accuracy of the calculations is much better. In contrast, the absence of data for previous flows makes a flow simulation substantially more difficult than its prediction. The result of this difference between the input data for simulation and prediction is that the precision of the simulation is more demanding to achieve.

The primary goal of this paper is an analysis of options for the improvement of flow simulation based on climate variables. In a search for the improvement of the precision of such calculations, the effects of three factors were investigated. The first is the selection of the algorithm, where a typical conceptual hydrological model and machine learning methods were compared. An analysis of the possibilities of feature engineering was the second possibility analyzed for the improvement of the calculation results. Feature engineering is constructing new input variables which are derived in various ways from primary climate data. The third option investigated was an experiment with the application of an ensemble paradigm and an analysis of its contribution to the precision of the simulated flows.

2 Material and Methods

In the real application of the proposed method for streamflow generation, climate inputs obtained by a weather generator, specifically a daily time series of temperatures and precipitation, will be used. However, the proposed method must be verified using actual data to ensure the climatic and hydrological compatibility of all the time series. For this purpose a daily time series of the temperatures, precipitation and stream flows of the Parna Creek in the Carpathian region of Slovakia were used (Figure 1).

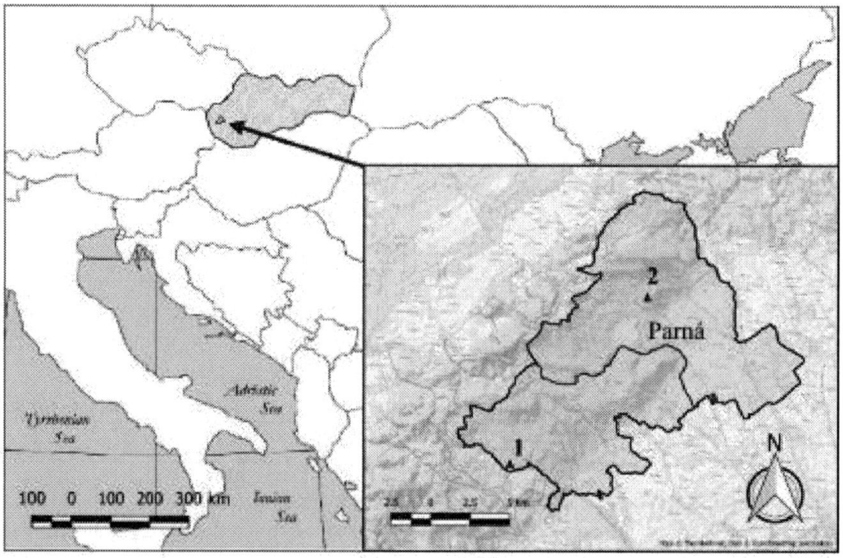

Fig. 1. Location of the test site and indication of the CarpatClim points (1, 2) from which climate data were acquired

The temperature and precipitation data were obtained from the CarpatClim [5], a publicly available geodatabase (http://www.carpatclim-eu.org). The authors therefore also verified in this article the applicability of climate data from this database to simulate water discharges in small streams, such as the Parna Creek. The CarpatClim database provides climate data in a square grid of points located in the Central Carpathian region. Figure 1 shows two of these points (labeled 1 and 2), which are located near the Parna, and from which precipitation and minimum and maximum temperatures have been obtained for the years 1961-2010. An overview of the flow regime of this creek and the regime of the climatic characteristics in its watershed is provided in Figure 2.

In this paper one hydrological and three data driven methods for generation of flows were used. Basic principle of this methods is described in following paragraphs.

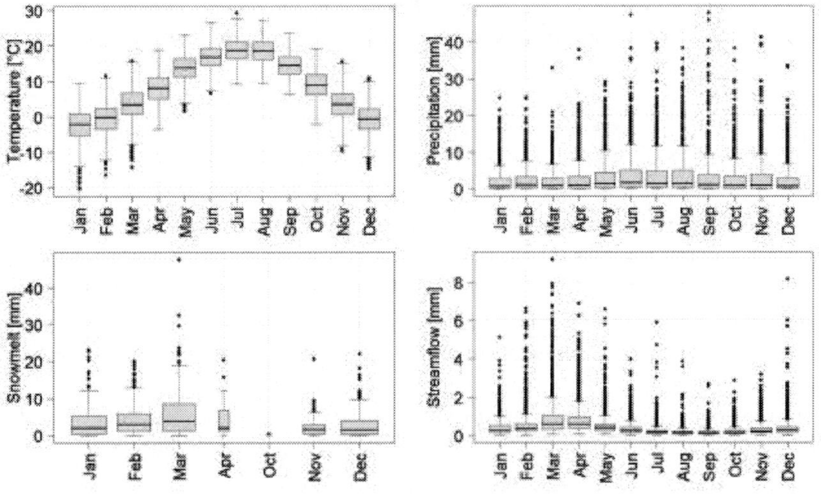

Fig. 2. Overview of the flow regime of Parna creek and the regime of the climatic characteristics in its watershed

The hydrological model used in this paper was developed at the Vienna University of Technology and is freely available as a package (add-in) for R software [6]. It is a semi-distributed conceptual rainfall-runoff model, following the structure of the well-known HBV model [7]. The model runs on a daily time step and consists of a snow routine, a soil moisture routine, and a flow routing routine. The snow routine represents snow accumulation and melting by a simple degree-day concept; it uses a degree-day factor and a melt temperature as parameters. The soil moisture routine represents runoff generation and changes in the soil moisture state of a catchment. Runoff routing on the hillslopes is represented by an upper and lower soil reservoir. Excess rainfall enters the upper reservoir and leaves by three paths, i.e., outflow from the reservoir based on a rapid storage coefficient; percolation to the lower zone with a constant percolation rate; and, if a threshold of the storage state is exceeded, by an additional outlet based on a very fast storage coefficient. Water leaves the lower zone based on a slow storage coefficient. The outflow from both reservoirs is then routed by a triangular transfer function that represents runoff routing in the streams [8]. A genetic algorithm [9] was used to calibrate this conceptual rainfall-runoff model with fifteen parameters.

In this work, three machine learning algorithms were applied, namely Random Forest, XGBoost and Deep Learning Neural Network. They are used for supervised learning problems in this study, where we use the training data (with multiple features) to predict a target variable. The Random Forest (RF) algorithm, which was initially proposed by Breiman (2001), is an ensemble method that generates a set of individually trained decision trees and combines their results. The regression trees are a series of decision rules that dictate how a target variable is computed from the input (predictor) variables. A forest is a collection of trees, and an RF consists of a group or ensemble of simple tree predictors, each one of which can evaluate a target variable by using a set of predictor values. The variability in solving a given regression problem by individual members of the ensemble is realized such that RF is random in two ways. Firstly, each tree is based on a random subset of the observations (bootstrap sample), and secondly, each split in each tree is created on a random subset of all the available variables [20]. The benefit of the RF 's randomness is robustness against over-fitting and good generalization abilities. Given the number of trees created, the degree of accuracy increases up to a certain point. When used as a regression method, decision trees can describe complex relationships fairly accurately among multiple variables; by aggregating the results of these regression trees into a forest, an even more accurate solution is generated. In addition to these characteristics, RF parameterization is not particularly complicated nor is RF model tuning too difficult. This study used an RF add-on package [11] with R statistical software [12]. Although it has several parameters, only two parameters specified by the user are necessary to tune to run RF: the number of trees in the forest, ntree, and the number of variables randomly sampled at each split, mtry. This study operated RF with a default value of ntree 500 and of mtry, which was found by a cross-validation procedure.

XGBoost is an abbreviation of Extreme Gradient Boosting, where the term Gradient Boosting was proposed in the [13]. As stated by the XGBoost algorithm author in [4], his algorithm is based on this original model. Gradient Boosting is a forwardly learning ensemble method, e.g., it builds a model in a stage-wise fashion (not in a parallel fashion, as in the case of RF). The guiding idea is that a good predictive model can be obtained through increasingly refined approximations. Gradient boosting evaluates the precision of a model in a previous stage and then develops the next model, which computes the differences between the current results computed and the known target values (i.e., not the original target values). The next models are thus mainly concentrating on the previously incorrectly computed samples. Such "boosting" continues until the desired level of accuracy is reached. In this way, gradient boosting produces a prediction model as an ensemble of weak prediction models (usually shallow decision trees). The algorithm used in this work, XGBoost, follows the principle of gradient boosting. However, there are some differences in the modelling details. XGBoost uses a more regularized model formalization to control over-fitting, which gives it a better performance in comparison with previously evolved boosting algorithms. The XGBoost developers have also made other significant performance enhancements to different features of the XGBoost implementation. These result in significant differences in speed and memory utilization due to 1) the use of sparse matrices with sparsity aware algorithms, 2) improved data structures for better utilization of the processor cache, thereby making it faster, and 3) better support for multicore processing, which reduces overall training time [14]. From the point of view of the users of boosting algorithms, when they use GBM and XGBoost for training large datasets (e.g., 5 million or more records), they can experience significantly reduced memory usage for the same dataset; it is also easier to use multiple cores to reduce training time. The cost of the advantages of using XGBoost (compared, e.g., with an RF algorithm) is that XGBoost has several parameters to tune, while RF is almost tuning-free, which is why we included both algorithms in this study. In this work, the *xgboost* R package was used. Seven parameters were tuned, so genetic algorithms were applied in the tuning process.

The optimized parameters were the maximum number of iterations, learning rate, minimum loss reduction gamma, maximum tree depth, minimum child weight, subsample ratio of the training instance, and subsample ratio of the columns when constructing each tree. A description of the parameters and various recommendations for setting them can be found at XGBoost WWW [15].

A Deep Learning Neural Network (DLNN) is a tool that has significantly expanded the boundaries the real-world applicability of machine learning in recent years in computer vision, speech recognition, various recommendation systems, and predictions of some types of sequential data, such as time series. It is a new generation of artificial neural networks characterized by a "deeper" architecture compared to a multilayer perceptron, which was in use at the end of the previous century. Deep learning has been enhanced by a number of recently developed improvements. These enhancements have been published and put into practice in the last five years and cover new types of activation functions, new network architectures, improved network initialization before training, and an improvement of the training process. Deep learning is a subfield of machine learning that emphasizes learning successive layers to increasingly meaningful representations of searched patterns in the data. Even though the superiority of DLNN could probably be better shown for more complex projects than our task in this work, we wanted to test its performance in the hydrological field; to our knowledge, DLNN has rarely been tested in this area. The more complex tasks mentioned in the previous sentence means that they have a larger and more complex data structure, such as computer vision. We have used the TensorFlow software tool developed by researchers and engineers working as part of the Google brain team. Construction of the neural network, its settings for training, and training was accomplished using the keras R package [16].

Calibration of all the models was performed on data from the above case study from Slovakia using data from the years 1961-1995. The basic inputs in all the models consisted of a time series of the average daily precipitation, evapotranspiration, air temperatures and river flows. The verification of the precision of all the models was accomplished on test data from 1996 - 2010. To illustrate the difference between prediction and simulation when using machine learning models, the calculation of the flow prediction for one day in advance was also performed. It includes the flow from the predication day and other previous flows among the input data. To illustrate the usefulness of using advanced machine learning models, the simulation was also accomplished with multiple linear regression.

The evaluation of the precision of the simulation included a comparison of the simulated flows with monitored data, which in our case was flows measured on the River Parna in Slovakia. The quality of the simulation was assessed using several criteria for statistical precision. For an assessment of the model's precision, the Nash-Sutcliffe coefficient was prioritized due to its frequent use in hydrological calculations, which allows for a better comparison of our results with the results of other authors.

3 Results and Discussion

In this chapter, three options for the improvement of the precision of flow simulation methods are assessed. In the first part, the effect of the selected method on the accuracy of the results of the flow simulation is evaluated. In the second subchapter, methods for the application of feature engineering and an evaluation of its impact on the precision of the calculations are quantified. In the third part, the models created in the context of a simple ensemble are described and evaluated.

The expected or required range of the precision of the simulation was identified using two calculations. The simulation using a hydrological model defined its lower limit, as the use of machine learning models has no meaning when the degree of precision is lower. By using a Deep Learning Neural Network (the most efficient among the models tested), the prediction of the flows was performed which determined the upper limit for the precision of a simulation. Such an identification of the upper limit results from the fact that the precision of prediction using machine learning models is higher than the precision of simulation, due to the integration of flows from the previous time steps into the input data. The results of these calculations, as characterized by selected statistical indicators, are given in Table 1.

3.1 Effect of the Selection of the Model

In this part, we have evaluated the simulation of flows using several models, by using their standard application. Feature engineering was not applied in these computations. This group of calculations includes calculations using the TUW hydrological model mentioned above. The calculation of the river flows was also performed using multiple linear regression (MLR) and the Random Forest (RF), Extreme Gradient Boosting (XGBoost) and Deep Learning Neural Network (DLNN) machine learning models. The optimization of the internal parameters of the machine learning models was accomplished by tenfold cross-validation. A description of the parameters necessary to tune each of the algorithms is given in the Methods section. The river flows, precipitation, temperatures and potential evapotranspiration data from the years 1961 - 1995 were used for all the models. The climate data for the linear regression and machine learning models were used in models from 20 days before the date for which the flow was simulated. The number of days affecting the calculation of the flows was acquired empirically. Usually, data from fewer days are applied in, e.g., the prediction of flows. A larger volume of the previous climate data was used in the inputs because it is the simulation that is solved in this case. Because of this the previous data on the flows are not available in this type of modelling. Additional data on the climate variables from more days should partially eliminate the lack of this information. These models are evaluated in Table 1 using standard RMSE and R2 statistics (we are not giving their description here). KGE and NSE statistics, which are frequently used in hydrology and PBIAS (percentual bias between simulated and observed values), were also used for the evaluation of the model's performances. The Nash-Sutcliffe Efficiency (NSE) is a normalized statistic that determines the relative magnitude of the residual variance compared to the measured data variance [17]. KGE is Kling-Gupta efficiency, which was developed by Gupta [18] and later refined by Kling [19]. Both statistics can take values between minus infinity and 1; the ideal model has a value of 1. The percent bias (PBIAS) measures the average tendency of the simulated values to be larger or smaller than corresponding observed ones. The optimal value of the PBIAS is 0.0. Positive values indicate an overestimation bias, whereas negative values indicate the models underestimation bias. From these statistical indicators, NSE is considered herein as primary, as it is the most frequently used statistic in hydrology.

Table 1. Evaluation of models that did not use feature engineering

Model	RMSE	R2	NSE	KGE	PBIAS
TUW	0.31	0.67	0.67	0.76	-6.2
DLNN prediction	0.17	0.92	0.90	0.79	-14.8
XGBoost	0.43	0.37	0.35	0.43	21.2
RF	0.44	0.35	0.32	0.38	23.2
DLNN	0.41	0.41	0.39	0.39	5.3
MLR	0.46	0.25	0.24	0.34	11.1

RMSE root mean square error, R^2 coefficient of determination, NSE - Nash-Sutcliffe efficiency, KGE Kling-Gupta efficiency, PBIAS percent of bias

The first two lines of Table 1 contain an evaluation of two reference models that identify the theoretical minimum and maximum precision of the simulations using machine learning models. The TUW hydrological model has better values of the statistical indicators than the machine learning models. This means that the machine learning models in their basic use, are for simulation of flows (not prediction), less precise than the conceptual hydrological model. Linear regression has the worst precision indicators. Besides the hydrological model, DLNN has the best results but is also below the required minimum precision limit.

3.2 Feature engineering and its influence on the precision of a model

Additional models evaluated in this study included feature engineering, while their input data were prepared. Constructed variables were added to the basic climate inputs for modelling the flows, which is described in this subchapter. Their construction was motivated by applying knowledge gained from the domain of hydrology. A typical example of this approach was the creation of the variable that quantifies the melting of snow, as snow (i.e., a type of precipitation which is a basic climate input) is not the direct initiator of an outflow because an outflow only comes only after the melting of snow. The potential evapotranspiration was also calculated because it is a more direct detector of water leaking from a watershed to the atmosphere than is the temperature. As the resulting flow from a basin is influenced not only by the current values of climate variables but also by their values from previous days, we also included climate data from four days before the date of the simulated flow in the model inputs. On the smaller streams with which this study deals, the outflow from the watershed is influenced by precipitation maximally from 1 or 2 preceding days. Precipitation from earlier days creates water reserves in a basin, which are a source of so-called base flow. Data from days three to four were included due to the possibility of subsequent precipitation, which makes a watershed saturated with water. Including more climate variables from previous days to the inputs did not seem to be a very useful option, which can be evaluated from the calculations in the previous subchapter (Tab. 1). However, as the history of the hydro-climate developments in the basin must in some way be included in the model and quantified in the input data, a variable summarizing the previous precipitation (cumRAIN) and a variable summarizing the previous evapotranspiration (cumPET) were constructed for the 60 days before the day on which the flow was simulated. The last experiment with the tuning of the input data involved a modification of the target variable, i.e., the flow. Figure 3a shows the probability distribution of the measured flow from our case study using a histogram. We can see that this variable has a right-skewed distribution, which may be unsuitable for some models.

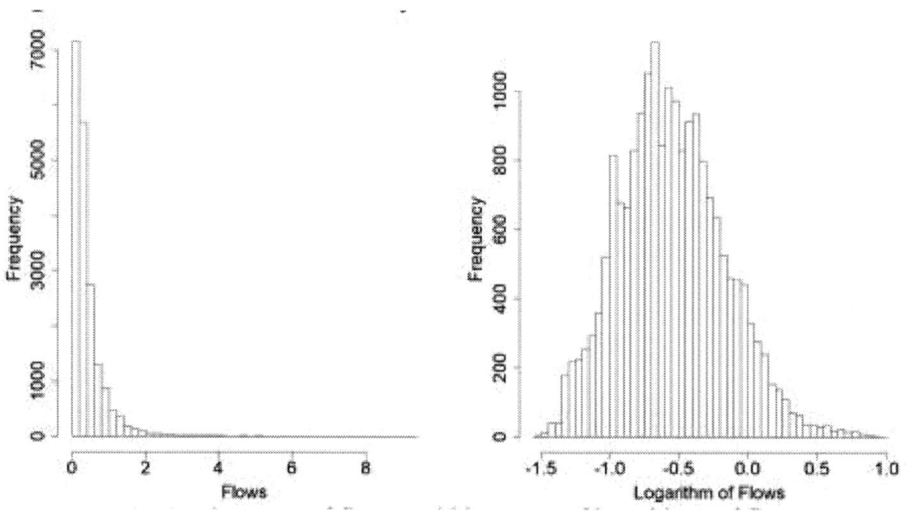

Fig. 3. Histogram of flows and histogram of logarithms of flows

For this reason, in all the models, the flow (the target variable) was replaced by its logarithm. The evaluation provided, which is in Table 2, only shows the models where such a step leads to the improved precision of a model. A histogram of the logarithms of the flows is shown in Fig. 3b, which is apparently more normally distributed.

A total of 22 explanatory variables were acquired; three of them are basic, and the remaining 19 are the result of the feature engineering.

The results of the individual calculations were evaluated using NSE and other statistical indicators and are shown in Tab. 2. Without using feature engineering, the precision of the models according to NSE is in a range of 0.24 - 0.39 (Table 1). When feature engineering was applied, the degree of precision was significantly improved and, as shown in Table 2, it is now in a range of 0.42 - 0.69.

Table 2. Evaluation of models in which feature engineering was used

Model	RMSE	R2	NSE	KGE	PBIAS
MLR	0.41	0.48	0.42	0.46	34
MLR with log of target	0.31	0.67	0.67	0.76	-6.2
RF	0.34	0.64	0.59	0.64	27.4
XGBoost	0.33	0.66	0.61	0.62	30.6
XGBoost with log of target	0.29	0.71	0.69	0.76	14.1
DLNN	0.31	0.67	0.66	0.77	0.6

RMSE root mean square error, R^2 coefficient of determination, NSE - Nash-Sutcliffe efficiency, KGE Kling-Gupta efficiency, PBIAS percent of bias

An interesting point is the notable influence of the logarithm applied to the target variable (the predicted flow). This alteration significantly influenced the precision of the linear model and the precision of the XGBoost model. Although the reasons and conditions for the transformation of the target variable using a logarithm of the target were not further investigated, we consider this result, particularly regarding the XGBoost model, to be quite interesting and worth analyzing in future research.

Because we did experiment with the input data, we also evaluated the impact of individual variables on the resulting modelling. For an illustration and confirmation of the importance of feature engineering, Figure 4 shows the relative importance of the individual variables in the XGBoost model.

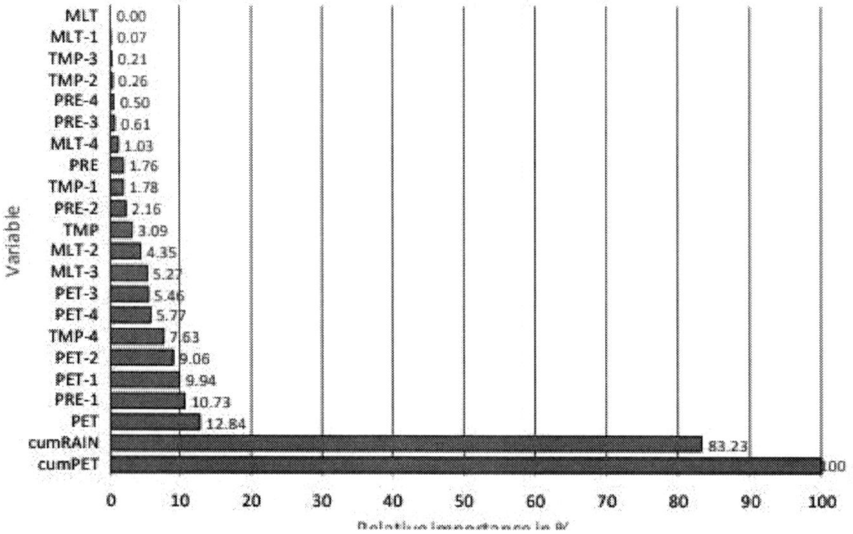

Fig. 4. Variable importance (PET potencial evapotranspiration, PRE precipitation, TMP temperatures, MLT snow melting; number indicate day before prediction)

The most significant influences on the model have both summation variables, i.e., the variables summing the previous precipitation and evapotranspiration. At this point, all the models coincided. This finding shows that entering precipitation and evapotranspiration data on a day-by-day basis for many previous days as done in the preceding subchapter is less favorable than the use of cumulative values. For further research on this phenomenon, it would be useful to optimize the number of backward days in the summation and review the effect of using a weighted sum instead of the standard sum of such data, where the older data would receive a lower weight. Such calculation experiments were not done in this study; we are mentioning them only as possible options for improving the effect of feature engineering on the precision of a model.

3.3 Ensemble method

Ensemble regression models calculate the target variable by a combination of its multiple specifications for several models. Ensembles can be classified as those which contain many individual models (e.g., Random Forest) and ensembles composed of a smaller number of models, which are also a subject of interest of this paper. In this second type of ensemble, the precision of the participating models is the first precondition for the selection of the model into an ensemble and its success in improving an overall prediction. This degree of precision for models selected for an ensemble should be similar and as high as possible. The second precondition is that the prediction should be more precise for different domains of hydrological inputs, i.e., the correlation between the individual models in the ensemble should be as low as possible.

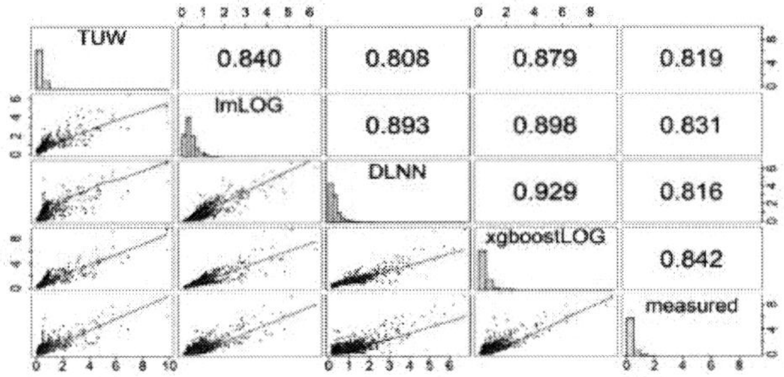

Fig. 5. Correlation between TUW model, linear regression and XGBoost with logarithm of target variable (lmLOG and xgboostLOG), DLNN, and observed flows

Based on such conditions, a conceptual hydrological model (Table 1) and three of the data-driven models tested (Table 2) were selected as members of the ensemble, i.e., the linear and the XGBoost model with a logarithm of the target variable and the DLNN model. The flows calculated through these four models have a comparable degree of accuracy but are not identical. This follows from the fact that the models are evaluated differently by various statistical indicators. The different results of the individual models are also demonstrated by Figure 5, which summarizes the correlation of the four best models with the measured flows and the mutual correlation between these models. The correlation coefficients are in the part above the diagonal. The diagonal identifies the models and indicates the probability distribution of their results (in the form of a histogram), and the part below the diagonal expresses always the dependence of the two models (identified by horizontal and vertical projections on the diagonal) graphically.

The figure shows that the models have different histograms and therefore a different probability distribution function and different mutual relations expressed by the small charts below the diagonal. The correlation coefficients between the flows calculated by these models are in a range of 0.81 - 0.93.

Such a level of correlation means that each model can better simulate flows on different days, which is a precondition for the cooperation of models in an ensemble. The resulting value of the simulation can be obtained, for example, by algebraic combination of the results of the individual models or using a suitably selected meta-model with the inputs being the flows calculated by different models. Such a methodology is typical in a stacking regression [20]. The specific form and parametrization of such a metamodel must be optimized based on the results of a flow simulation from the test folds of the cross-validation by which the individual models were tuned. However, this is not possible if the hydrological model is intended to be kept in an ensemble (as it is a wellestablished model). This is because the hydrological model does not use cross-validation during its calibration (so we do not have test folds for it). It cannot use it because the flows are simulated in a continuous sequence of days when using a hydrological model. As a metamodel cannot be optimized, it was decided to use an average of the results of the individual models (which could be considered as a simple meta-model). The flows obtained as an average of the simulations using a hydrological model and the three selected machine learning models have an NSE of 0.75, i.e., a degree of precision which is better by almost 12 % compared to the original hydrological model. If the ensemble considers the hydrological model and only two of the machine learning models, the average NSE value of such acquired simulated flows is 0.74 (there are three such possible combinations). For the three possible combinations of the hydrological model with only one selected machine learning model, the average value of NSE is 0.73.

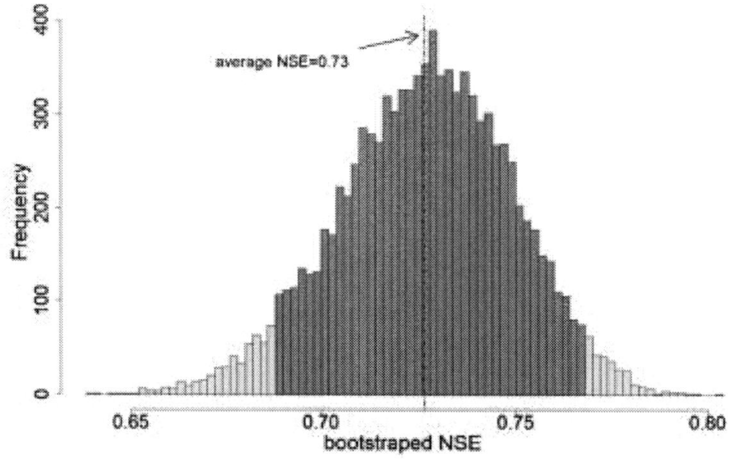

Fig. 6. NSE values of the ensemble created from bootstrap replications

Figure 6 shows a histogram of NSE values of the ensemble created in this way from 10,000 bootstrap replications selected from the four specified models. As shown in this figure, most of the NSE values have a higher degree of precision than the original hydrological model. The average NSE value from this calculation experiment is 0.73, and the 95% level of the confidence interval for this value is 0.69 0.77 (highlighted in Figure 4 by darker color), which is quite a promising result from this approximate testing.

4 Conclusion

The authors dealt in this paper with specific features of two types of machine learning river flow modelling, i.e., with prediction and simulation. The simulation represents tasks such as the generation of flow from precipitation and temperatures in the context of climate change impact and adaptation studies or in the calculation of unknown flows in unmeasured streams using an analogy method. Data on previous flows cannot be used as inputs for such simulation tasks. In comparison with prediction, simulation usually is less precise by 10-20%; in the case study addressed in this paper, it was 17%, according to the NSE statistic. In this paper, the authors have focused on improving the precision of simulation by using constructed variables which were included in the inputs, by using the most recent machine learning models, and by the application of simple ensemble simulations. Although the precision of the individual machine learning models did not significantly exceed the precision of the hydrological model, the connection of the individual models into an ensemble showed better results by 12% than the original hydrological model. These results show the potential of the above methodology as an alternative to traditional calculation methods.

The case study which verifies the proposed procedures is focused on a specific stream located in southwest Slovakia (Central Europe). For further application of this methodology, it would be useful to accomplish some refinements, which are mentioned in the paper and verification through case studies in different locations in the future.

ACKNOWLEDGEMENTS

This work was supported by the Slovak Research and Development Agency under Contract No. APVV-15-0489 and by the Scientific Grant Agency of the Ministry of Education of the Slovak Republic and the Slovak Academy of Sciences, Grant No. 1/0665/15.

References

1. ASCE Task Committee on Application of Artificial Neural Networks in Hydrology. Artificial neural networks in hydrology. I: Preliminary concepts. Journal of Hydrologic Engineering 5(2), 115-123 (2000).
2. Papacharalampous, G. A., Tyralis H., Koutsoyiannis, D.: Comparison of stochastic and machine learning methods for multi-step ahead forecasting of hydrological processes. Journal of Hydrology (2017).

3. Maier, H. R., Dandy, G. C.: Neural networks for the prediction and forecasting of water resources variables: a review of modelling issues and applications. Environmental modelling & software 15(1), 101-124 (2000).
4. Yaseen, Z. M., El-Shafie, A., Jaafar, O., Afan, H. A., & Sayl, K. N.: Artificial intelligence based models for stream-flow forecasting: 20002015. Journal of Hydrology, 530, 829-844. (2015).
5. Szalai S., Spinoni J., Galos B., Bessenyei M., Molar P., Szentimrey T.: Use of regional database for climate change and drought. 5th IDRC Davos 2014: Global Risk Forum GRF Davos, Switzerland (2014).
6. Viglione, A., Parajka, J.: TUWmodel: Lumped Hydrological Model for Education Purposes. R package version 0.1-8. Homepage, https://CRAN.R-project.org/package=TUW model (2016).
7. Lindstrm, G., et al.: Development and test of the distributed HBV-96 hydrological model. Journal of hydrology 201(1-4), 272-288 (1997).
8. Parajka, J., Merz, R., Blschl, G.: Uncertainty and multiple objective calibration in regional water balance modelling: case study in 320 Austrian catchments. Hydrological processes 21(4), 435-446 (2007).
9. Boisvert, J., El-Jabi, N., St-Hilaire, A., El Adlouni, S. E.: Parameter Estimation of a Distributed Hydrological Model Using a Genetic Algorithm. Open Journal of Modern Hydrology 6(3), 151-167 (2016).
10. Breiman, L.: Random forests. Machine learning 45(1), 5-32, (2001).
11. Liaw, A. Wiener, M.: Classification and Regression by randomForest. R News 2(3), 18-22 (2002).
12. R Core Team. R: A language and environment for statistical computing. R Foundation for Statistical Computing, Vienna, Austria. Homepage, https://www.R-project.org/ (2017).
13. Friedman, J. H.: Greedy function approximation: a gradient boosting machine. Annals of statistics, 1189-1232 (2001).
14. Chen, T., Guestrin, C.: Xgboost: A scalable tree boosting system. In: Proceedings of the 22nd acm sigkdd international conference on knowledge discovery and data mining. ACM. 785-794 (2016).
15. Xgboost Homepage, https://xgboost.readthedocs.io/en/latest/, last accessed 2018/03/16.
16. Allaire, J.J., Chollet, F.: keras: R Interface to 'Keras'. R package version 2.1.4. https://CRAN.R-project.org/package=keras (2018).
17. Nash, J. E., Sutcliffe, J. V.: River flow forecasting through conceptual models part I-A discussion of principles. Journal of hydrology 10(3), 282-290 (1970).
18. Gupta, H. V., et al.: Decomposition of the mean squared error and NSE performance criteria: Implications for improving hydrological modelling. Journal of Hydrology 377(1-2) 80-91 (2009).
19. Kling, H., Fuchs M., Paulin M.: Runoff conditions in the upper Danube basin under an ensemble of climate change scenarios. Journal of Hydrology 424, 264-277 (2012).
20. Breiman, L.: Stacked regressions. Machine learning 24(1), 49-64 (1996).

Gap in pagination due to formatting issues.

Pages 73-75

Improving Sales Forecasting with Customer Behavior Analysis

Yusuke Yamaura[1], Yiou Wang[2], and Takeshi Onishi[3]

Fuji Xerox Co., Ltd. Japan
{Yusuke.Yamaura,Yiou.Wang,Takeshi.Onishi}@fujixerox.co.jp

Abstract. In this paper, we explore the utility of customer behavior analysis of un-structured video data for improving sales forecasting, which is an important task for supply chain management in retail store. Our work is motivated by the observation that *the needs and interest of customers will influence the sales performance and customers' needs and interest can be reflected in some degree by monitoring and analyzing the customers' behavior in a store.* To the best of our knowledge, this is the first work that introduces the customer behavior analysis of monitoring video data to sales forecasting task. In order to validate our observation, we conducted a series of experiments in a physical retail store and demonstrated that integrating video-based customer behavior analysis into a conventional sale forecasting model results in a performance improvement.

Keywords: Customer behavior analysis, sales forecasting

1 Introduction

Sales Forecasting is an important task for supply chain management, business planning, and customer relationship management in retail industries [1]. In particular, retail stores provide short shelf-life food products and inaccurate forecast tends to cause stock-outs and food waste [2]. Therefore the accurate prediction is required for reliable planning and optimization.

A number of studies on sales forecasting have been conducted in the past decades. Recently machine learning based forecasting methods have achieved high accuracy compared with traditional statistical time series methods, such as moving average model [3, 4]. To improve the performance, demand influence factors have been explored[5, 6]. Generally, weather conditions, holidays, and public events are considered due to their impact on demand and public availability[5].

On the other hand, behavior intelligence and insight play an important role in data understanding and business problem solving [7, 8]. Customer behavior contains valuable information for marketing analysis. Therefore, it is attractive to considering exploiting customer behavior analysis in sales forecasting. The idea of combining customer behavior analysis with sales prediction been previously reported in online sales forecasting, which consider visitor's behavior tracked in their online EC-site [9–11]. However, little research has been conducted in this direction for offline cases. Customer behavior inside a physical store, which represents a shopping process until purchasing or non-purchasing but not explicitly included in the point-of-sales (POS) data or other external data, is often neglected.

In this paper, we present an approach to improve the performance of sales forecasting by incorporating the customer behavior analysis into a conventional sales forecasting model. Specifically, we develop video-based customer behavior analysis system for monitoring and analyzing customer's shopping behavior, then extract the information about how the customers interact with the stores and products, and finally design a framework to incorporate the customer behavior analysis into a sales forecasting model. To demonstrate the effectiveness of our approach, we conduct a series of experiments in a physical retail store. We show that our approach yields improvements for all the test collections and achieves better results than the conventional sale forecasting method.

To the best of our knowledge, this is the first work that introduces the customer behavior analysis of monitoring video data to sales forecasting task. Overall, the main contributions of this paper are as follows:

- We present a new approach to encode customer behavior information to sales forecasting.
- The relation between customer behaviors and sales is investigated.
- We make behavioral forecasting to predicts customer behavior and translate it into sales.

2 Proposed Method

In this section, we introduce our approach for incorporating customer behavior analysis into a conventional approach for sales forecasting. We first describe an overview of our video-based customer behavior analysis system, which can monitor the customer's shopping behavior inside a store. Second, we discuss what types of shopping behaviors are relevant to sales. Third, we make behavioral forecasting to predicts customer behavior and translates it into sales. Finally, we explain the way to integrate new customer behavior features to the traditional method effectively. Figure 1 shows an overview of our approach for incorporating customer behavior analysis into a conventional model. This is the framework that we utilize the unstructured video data for financial forecast, which is traditionally based on structured data.

2.1 Customer Behavior Analysis

We developed video-based customer behavior analysis system for capturing and analyzing customer's shopping behavior in real stores. Our system is composed of multiple IP cameras and PCs with image processing modules installed. Specifically, surveillance cameras, which is utilized for monitoring, marketing, or security in a physical store, was installed. We developed several retail-oriented

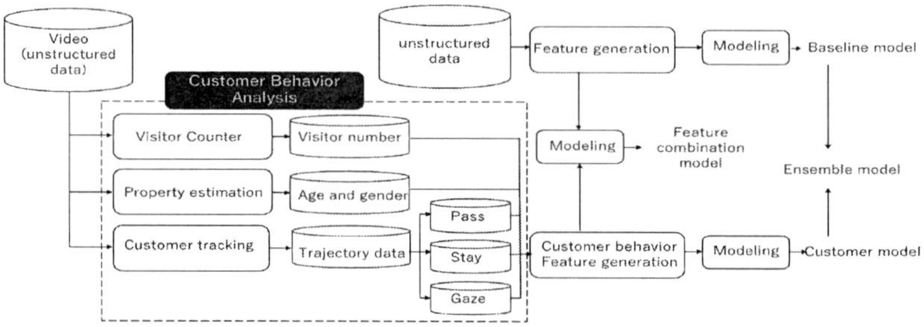

Fig. 1. Overview of the proposed approach

intelligent video analysis modules for analyzing customer's behavior inside a store.

- **Visitor counter module** receives video frames from a surveillance camera just above the store entrance and counts the number of customers who visit or leave the store.
- **Property estimation module** also receives video frames from a surveillance camera just above the store entrance and estimate the age and gender of customers.
- **Customer tracking module** processes video data from multiple cameras mounted on the ceiling inside the store and this module conduct several image recognitions sub-modules,

Specifically, customer tracking module includes people detection sub-module, head orientation estimation sub-module and trajectory reconstruction sub-modules. People detection sub-module first detects the region where a customer is in a video frame based on background subtraction technique, and then detects the head and body part. head orientation estimation sub-module analyzes the head orientation and outputs the category of head orientation (e.g. front, left, back, right). Trajectory reconstruction sub-module reads sequential images, detects locations, estimates head orientation, and reconstructs a trajectory inside the store. All the data is aggregated in real time and transported to our cloud server per 5 minutes. Using this system, we can collect the customer information of the visitor number, customers' age and gender, customer shopping trajectory and shopping actions.

2.2 Customer Behavior Feature Selection

Customer behavior is the center point of behavioral forecasting and sales forecasting. In this section, we will discuss how do customers behave in a store and how does this impact sales.

In the case of physical store, if a customer has no interest to the product, he or she will neither look at the shelf nor turn to the shelf. As an initial interest level, he or she will go to the shelf and stay in front of the shelf. If the customer has more interest, he or she will stay in front of the shelf for a long time. If the customer has further interest, his or her gaze will fall upon the product and gaze the shelf for a long time. If the customer has further interest, he or she probably stretches arm and touches the product. Based on these observations, in sales forecasting task, we assume that the following shopping behaviors are strongly related to customer's demand, reveals the interest of customer to the product and reflected the way in which customers interact with the store and products:

1. Visit the store
2. Pass the shelf
3. Stay in front of the shelf
4. Gaze the shelf
5. Purchase the shelf

Because of some technical limitations (such as low resolution images, lighting conditions, and occlusions) of the customer behavior analysis system described in section 2.1, we can only analyze the previous four behaviors.

To capture the relation between the behaviors and sales, we investigated the relationship between customer behaviors and sales using the history data of shopping video data and POS data, and made the following two observations:

Observation 1: The sales was impacted by customer behaviors.

Figure 2 shows the tendency of sales, the visitor number and behavior number. We can see that the tendency of the visitor number and behavior number is the same as that of sales.

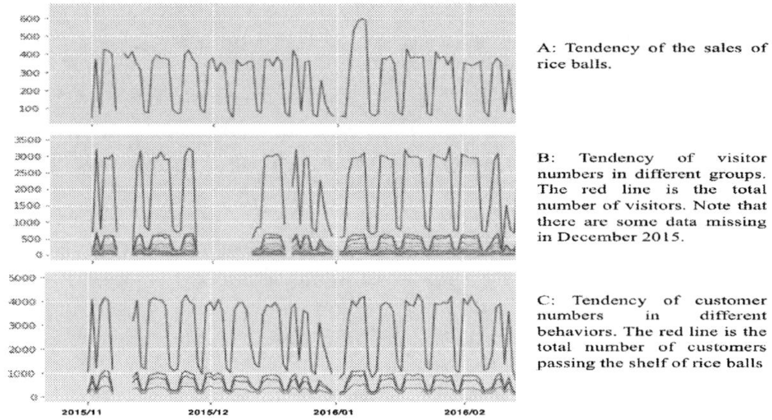

Fig. 2. Plot of sales, visitor numbers and behavior numbers

Observation 2: The relations between the behaviors and sales are different for different specific customer segments.

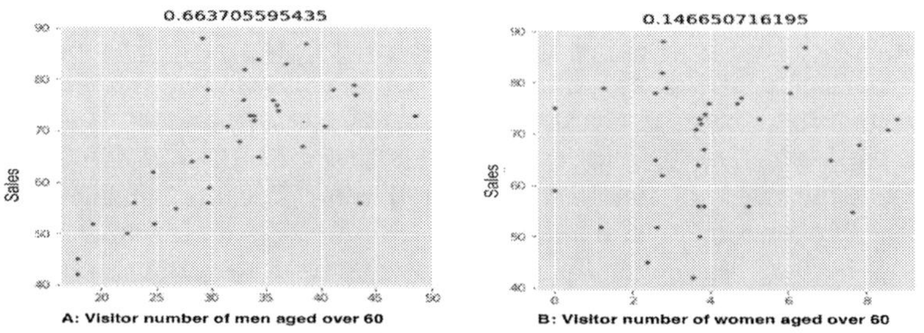

Fig. 3. Correlation of sales and visitor numbers of different gender groups

We investigated the correlation coefficients of customer behavior and sales. Figure 3 is the plot of the correlation coefficients between sales and visitor numbers of different gender groups. The number of male customers is more relevant to sales than that of female customers. Customers in different gender groups impact the sales in a different way.

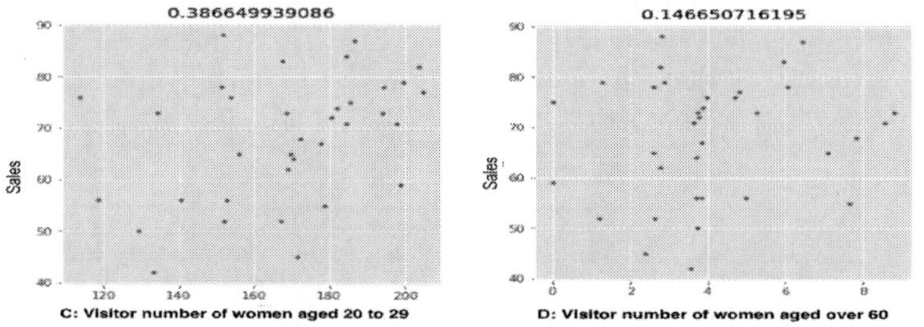

Fig. 4. Correlation of sales and visitor numbers of different age groups

Figure 4 is plot of correlation coefficients between sales and visitor numbers of different age groups. The number of female customers aged 20 to 29 is more relevant to sales than that of female customers above 60. Customers in different age groups also impact the sales in a different way. As the store is located in the business center area in Tokyo, the salarymen and young female staffs are tend to be frequent buyers while the female customer above 60 are tend to be occasional customers. Our findings are consistent with the situation of the physical store.

From this point of view, we propose to encode the customer behavior information separately for different customer segments and different activities. We categorize customers into groups by gender and age, then investigate how different customer groups are relevant of sales and encode the behavior of specific customer groups as distinct new features for sale forecasting. Specifically, visitors' age is categorized into 6 groups, under 19, 20-29, 30-39, 40-49, 50-59, 60 or over. We make the activities (behaviors) features in the same way. Activities include pass by the shelf, stay in front of the shelf over 5/10 seconds, gaze the shelf over 1 second. We calculate the number of people who act these behaviors from trajectory data acquired by the customer behavior analysis system. Consequently, we extract customer behavior features, including the daily number of visitors to the store at each age group and gender, people who pass by the shelf, stay in front of the shelf over 5/10 seconds, gaze the shelf over 1 second.

2.3 Behavioral Forecasting

We must predict the sales in advance. However it is impossible to know the customer behavior information of the prediction target day in advance. Therefore in order to add the customer behavior information into sale forecasting, we must make behavioral forecasting too. We apply time series analysis to model seasonal patterns of customer behaviors and here predict the customer behaviors of a target day using simple moving average (SMA) method. We adopted moving average of same days of week in past 4 weeks because daily sales are strongly related to the day of week. To put it simply, for example, customer behavior of the week day is different from the holidays and the effects of weekends and holidays should be considered. We found that predicted customer behavior information is close to the actual situation except for some special days such as some special holidays, and can capture recent trends of customer behavior. We finally generate customer behavior features by behavioral forecasting result. Table 1 shows generated customer behavior features.

Feature Type	Feature	Description
Visitor features	$N_{visitor}, visitorg$	SMA of number of visitor for each age and gender group.
Activity features	N_{pass}	SMA of number of people who pass by the shelf.
	N_{stay_five}	SMA of number of people who stay in front of the shelf over 5 seconds.
	N_{stay_ten}	SMA of number of people who stay in front of the shelf over 10 seconds.
	N_{gaze}	SMA of number of people who gaze the shelf over 1 seconds.

Table 1. Customer Behavior Features

2.4 Feature Integration

To integrate the customer behavior features into a structured data based traditional model, the following two integration strategies are adopted:

- **Feature combination**

  This is a simple concatenation of separate features and requires only single model. There is a possibility that high dimensional features cause overfitting or complexity of interpretation.

– **Ensemble learning**

Ensemble learning is an algorithm to acquire more accurate outcome by combining the predictions of multiple models. Ensemble modeling is most effective when large variance of outcomes or large difference among input data type. We here adopt the simplest way of ensemble averaging described as follows:

$$f_i(X) = \frac{1}{M}\sum_{i=1}^{M} \hat{f}_i(X)$$

Here, $\hat{f}_i(X)$ is the output of model i among all the multiple models and M is the number of models.

3 Experiments

3.1 Experimental Setting

In this paper, we chose rice balls sale forecasting in a physical store as as our prediction task. Specifically, we predict the daily sales number of rice ball in one week before the prediction target day. In our study, we don't consider type difference of rice balls and the target value is total number of all types of rice balls. Our video-based customer behavior analysis system is installed in a physical store, which is composed with two surveillance cameras for visitor analysis, three omnidirectional cameras for acquisition of customer's trajectory inside the store, and two PCs with image processing modules installed.

The experiment is conducted from October 2015 to May 2016. In order to evaluate the generalization performance appropriately, we choose the last week of March, April, and May 2016 as validation period (Test1, Test2, and Test3). As we define forecasting day as one week before the target day, the training period covers from October 2015 to the day when one week before the target day as shown Figure 5.

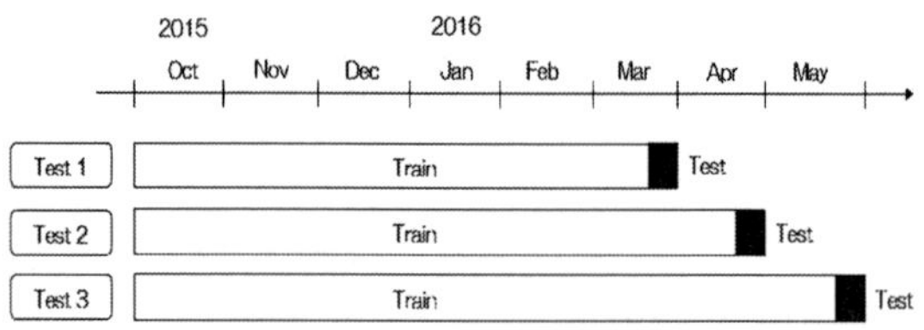

Fig. 5. Experimental data sets

3.2 Baseline Models

The baseline model is a conventional approach based on machine learning generally using the structured information, such as weather, calendar, and event information. We train our baseline model on Gradient Boosting Decision Tree (GBDT) proposed by Friedman [12], which is demonstrated to be one of the most effective algorithms and is becoming a mainstream in forecasting competitions as well as Kaggle challenges. Baseline features are as follows:

- POS information: the same days of the week in past 4 weeks.
- Weather information: lowest/highest temperature, precipitation, humidity, wind speed, and categorized day-time/night weather (sunny, cloudy, rainy, snow).
- Calendar information: year, month, the day of week, seasons, quarters, public holiday, holiday, before/after holiday, between holidays, consecutive holidays, annual events, elapsed years/month/weeks/days, number of weeks in corresponding month.
- Promotion information: discount sales, special lottery, collaboration campaign, etc.

We use XGBoost[13] library for implementation of GBDT, which has become widely popular tool among various competitions. We tune the hyper parameters of XGBoost step by step for acquiring generalization ability as follows: (i) fix a relatively high learning rate (e.g. η=0.1) and find the optimal number of trees under the fixed learning rate by cross-validation. (ii) tune tree-specific parameters such as the maximum number of depth, the minimum weight at child nodes, the ratio of subsamples, etc. (iii) tune regularization parameters which help to reduce model complexity. (iv) lower the learning rate (e.g. η=0.01) and recalibrate the number of trees.

In addition to the conventional machine learning model, we built a moving average model with daily sales of same day of week in past 4 weeks for comparision. This is the widely-used simplest way for sales forecasting and our collaborative retail company also adopt this method for daily sales forecasting.

3.3 Experimental Results

We evaluated the effectiveness of our proposed method in a series of experiments. Specifically, we investigate the effect of incorporating customer behavior features, which is described in Section2.2, into a traditional model.

We used Accuracy as evaluation metrics.

$$Accuracy = (100 - MAPE)\%$$

Here, Mean Absolute Percentage Error(MAPE) is defined as follows:

$$MAPE = \frac{100}{N} \sum_{i=1}^{N} \frac{f_i - y_i}{y_i}$$

Methods	Test1 (%)	Test2 (%)	Test3 (%)	Average (%)
Sales SMA model	87.18	91.28	83.55	87.34
Baseline model	88.78	92.68	87.31	89.59
+ (a) visitor features	**90.37**	93.78	84.46	89.54
+ (b) activity features	88.1	95.8	85.86	89.92
+ (a), (b)	87.44	**95.97**	86.07	89.83
Customer model	89.62	94.21	86.04	89.96
Ensemble model	89.2	93.71	**88.83**	**90.58**

Table 2. The results of prediction models

Here, f_i is the predict value, y_i is the actual value and N is the predict data number.

Table 2 shows the final results for all experiments. Our experiments demonstrate that the customer behavior information contributes to the improvement of prediction performance even though the customer related features are generated by behavioral forecasting. We investigated the cases with great improvement and found the following points contribute to the performance gains:

(i) The latest trends of the customer behavior have impact on the sales of a product and the balance among the kinds of customer behavior can be considered by our method. For example, if the number of visitors is increasing while the number of customers passing the shelf is stable, it perhaps indicates the customers are interested in other products but not in the predict target product, the sales of the targeted product is not increasing.

(ii)The latest trends of some specific customer segment sometimes impact the sales greatly and the trends of the specific customer segment can be encoded by our method. For example, in some cases, the tendency of the female customers over 60 and under 12, who belong to the occasional customer segment, changed greatly and such change can be reflected by our method and lead to a more precise prediction.

In general, structured POS data only include the buyers information, while customer behavior data provides more detailed information, which includes the information of latent buyers and represents the whole shopping process. Such information is effective for the sales prediction.

4 Conclusion

In this paper, we presented an approach to improve the performance of sales forecasting by incorporating customer shopping behavior analysis and investigated the impact of several strategies which can integrate the unstructured customer behavior features into a conventional structure data based model. The experimental results showed that customer behavior information provided improvements for all the test collections. Customer behavior analysis was demonstrated effective in sales prediction task. In future, we will evaluate our method with large data sets and introduce the confidence of the customer behavior information to the behavioral forecasting model.

References

[1] Mentzer, J. T. and Bienstock, C. C.: Sales forecasting management: understanding the techniques, systems and management of the sales forecasting process.Thousand Oaks, CA: Sage publications (1998)

[2] Mena, C., Terry, L. a, Williams, A. and Ellram, L.: Causes of waste across multi-tier supply networks: cases in the UK food sector, Int. J. Prod. Econ. 152, 144 -158. (2014)

[3] Alon, Q.Min and R.J.Sadowski : Forecasting aggregate retail sales: a comparison of artificial neural networks and traditional method, J.Retail.Consum.Serv.8 (3) 147-156.(2001)

[4] Dilek Penpece and Orhan Emre Elma.: Predicting Sales Revenue by Using Artificial Neural Network in Grocery Retailing Industry: A Case Study in Turkey, In: International Journal of Trade, Economics and Finance, 5(2) pp. 435-440 (2014)

[5] Mykola Pechenizkiy and Patrick Meulsteea: Food Sales Prediction: "If Only It Knew What We Know", In: IEEE International Conference on Data Mining Workshops 128, pp. 128-143 (2008)

[6] Chen, C.-Y., Lee, W.-I., Kuo, H.-M., Chen, C.-W., and Chen, K.-H. : The study of a forecasting sales model for fresh food, Expert Systems with Applications, 37(12), 7696-7702. (2010)

[7] Zimu Zhou, Longfei Shangguan, Xiaolong Zheng, Lei Yang and Yunhao Liu: Design and Implementation of an RFID-Based Customer Shopping Behavior Mining System, Networking IEEE/ACM Transactions on, vol. 25, pp. 2405-2418, (2017)

[8] Jingwen Liu, Yanlei Gu and Shunsuke Kamijo: Customer Behavior Recognition in Retail Store from Surveillance Camera, Multimedia (ISM) 2015 IEEE International Symposium on, pp. 154-159, (2015)

[9] Currie, C. S. M., and Rowley, I. T.: Consumer behavior and sales forecast accuracy: What's going on and how should revenue managers respond? Journal of Revenue and Pricing Management, 9(4), 374-376, (2010)

[10] Lohse, C. L., Bellman, S., and Johnsone, E. J. (2000). Consumer buying behavior on the Internet: Findings from panel data. journal of lnteractive Marketing, 74, pp.15-29, (2000)

[11] Yuan, H., Xu, W and Wang, M. : Can online user behavior improve the performance of sales prediction in E-commerce? IEEE International Conference on Systems, Man, and Cybernetics, pp 2377-2382, (2014)

[12] Friedman, J. . Greedy function approximation: A gradient boosting machine. Annals of Statistics, 29, pp. 1189 - 1232, (2001)

[13] T. Chen and C. Guestrin: Xgboost: A scalable tree boosting system, In Proceedings of the KDD, San Francisco, California, (2016)

Deep Learning in Large-Scaled Time Series Forecasting

Chuanyun Zang

AT&T Services, Inc., Alpharetta GA, USA
cz692t@att.com

Abstract. The project aims to discuss the technique of combining deep learning especially Long-Short Memory (LSTM) Networks, decision trees and basic statistics in multiple multistep time series prediction. Other features are available besides time series, so decision trees are built first. At each leaf level, LSTMs study patterns of variation in all the sequences of time series from a large scope and another LSTMs decode the learned trends as well as other features information into future sequence, meanwhile the well selected medians for each sequence can keep the special seasonality of different time series so that the future trend will not fluctuate too much from the reality.

Keywords: Time Series · LSTM · Deep Learning

Suppose the problem is to forecast the monthly values of certain job for each requested level. Given approximately 38K levels with their historical monthly values, starting from 2016-01 to 2017-12, the goal is to forecast future monthly value, from 2018-01 up until 2018-06 for each level.For example, we can simply use value of this month to predict the value of next month. The challenge here is that there are approximately 38K time series instead of only one, and the available historical data points are limited to 24 months.It is not feasible to get different model for each time series, and traditional art of state models like ARIMA cannot efficiently handling such huge different time series. We combine deep learning, decision trees and statistics on this problem which showed power in tackling it. A decision tree is built first, and then two techniques are used at each leaf. One is Neural Network with LSTMs, the other is the simply selected medians.

Decision Trees are built according to the descriptive statistics of levels and their time series.(Fig. 1).

LSTM Implementation. We partition the preprocessed features into two parts according to if it belongs to time series,i.e time series of values are into one part called X_ts and all remaining into X_cat.X_ts is first trained by LSTM and then concatenated to X_cat. The resulted inputs are then trained by several fully connected layers, and finally trained by another LSTM layer. (Fig. 2). For loss function, we define SMAPE in Keras. For optimization algorithm, RMSProp performs well for Recurrent Neural Networks as also documented in Keras.

Chuanyun Zang.

Medians. Due to the outliers (i.e. high spikes), medians are used to get a relevantly stable statistic for each time series. Further because of the variation of different time series along 24 months, median of different shorter periods are used to capture different patterns or information about the time series.

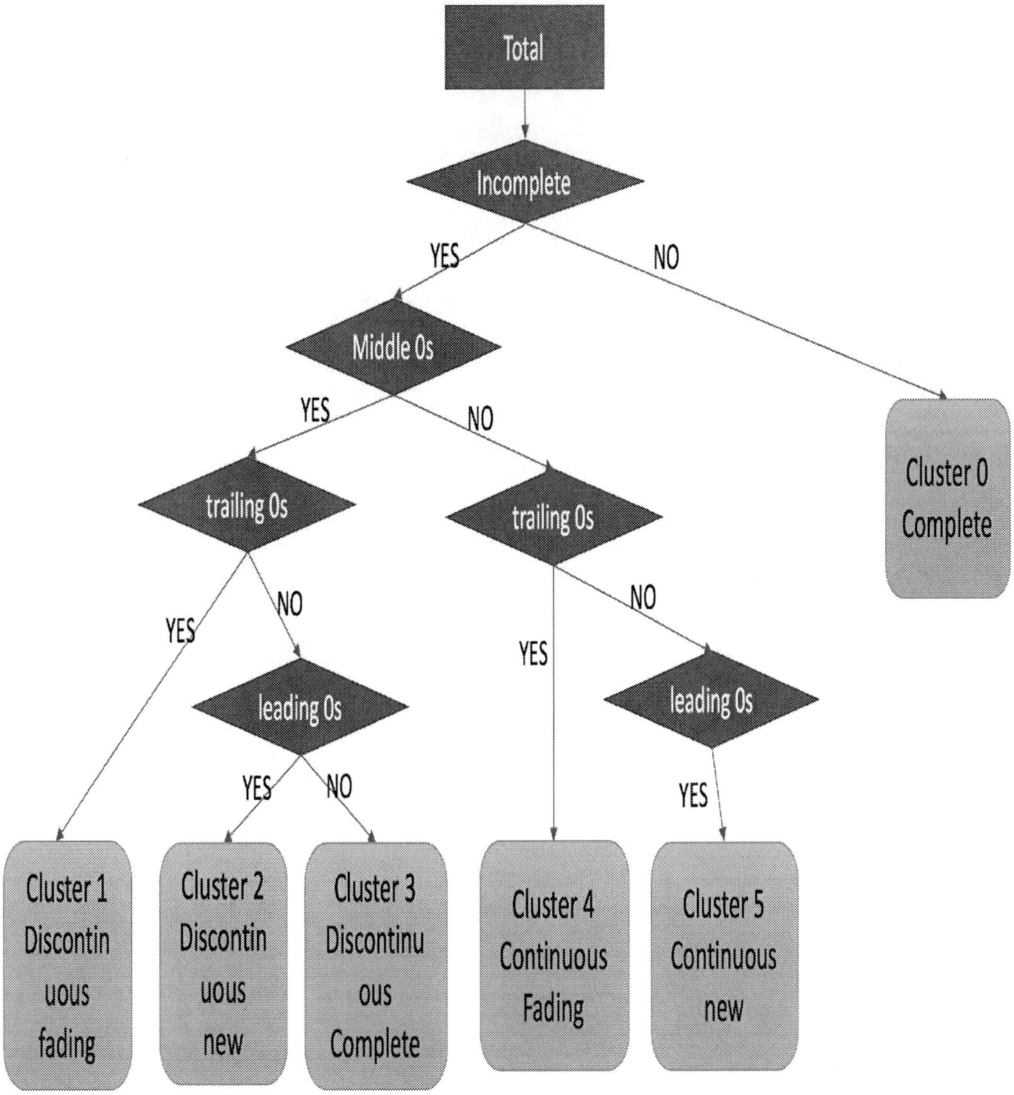

Fig. 1. Decision Trees.

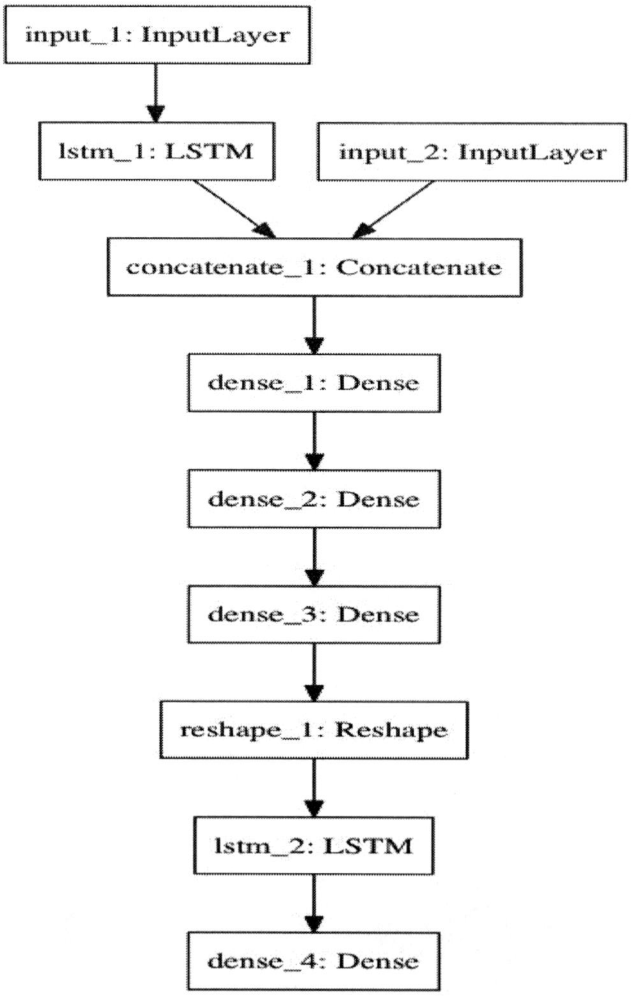

Fig. 2. Deep Neural Network Architecture.

References

1. Hochreiter, S., Jrgen S. Long short-term memory.Neural computation9.8 (1997): 1735-1780.
2. Keras Documentation. https://keras.io/

Research on evaluation indicators weigh computing method of scientific research institutions based on Linked Open Data

Shiyin Jiang

National Science Library, Chinese Academy of Sciences
jiangsy@mail.las.ac.cn

Abstract. Evaluation indicators weigh compute method of scientific research institutions will directly affect the accuracy and objectivity of the evaluation re-sults of scientific research institution.Linked Open Data, offers a large number of semantically described and linked concepts in various domains. In this paper, we propose a novel approach to take advantage of this structured data in the domain of scientific research institutions to compute the indicators weigh.Derived from information theory, our approach of computing the Infor-mation Content for semantic relations and ranking universities based on these indicators weigh achieved results comparable to the Shanghai Jiao Tong Uni-versity.The score correlation and rank correlation of the above two ranking re-sults are very strong, which proves the validity of the weight computing method based on the Linked Open Data in this study.

Keywords: Linked Open Data, evaluation indicators, evaluation of scientific research institutions, weigh compute.

1 Introduction

The multi indicators comprehensive evaluation method is widely used in the quantita-tive evaluation of scientific research institutions, and the weight design of indicators has always been a key and difficult point of technology. The semantic relations between scientific research institutions and their achieve-ments, personnel, education, awards and other information have been established in the Linked Open Data, and the specific semantics under these semantic relations are highly correlated with the evaluation indicators of scientific research institu-tions.Besides these semantic relationships are relatively authoritative and accurate, providing a guarantee for the use of semantic relations to compute the weight of the indicators .

2 Methodology

Base on the concept of entropy in Information Theory,after giving a set of evaluation indicators, the relative intensity of each indicator in the competition sense is considered from the perspective of information. It represents the degree of the effective infor-mation quantity provided by the evaluation indicator in the problem. Details available semantics relations regarding scientific research institutions include its awards and prizes, doctoral students, publication, notable work, and other key contributions (see Figure 1) [1].The semantic relations extracted from Linked Open Data can be em-ployed as indicators.We propose a novel metric to compute the Information Content of semantics relations that signify the indicator weigh in the Linked Open Data. We pro-ceed to experiment with indicator weigh computing which based on the aggregated Information Content of each indicator.

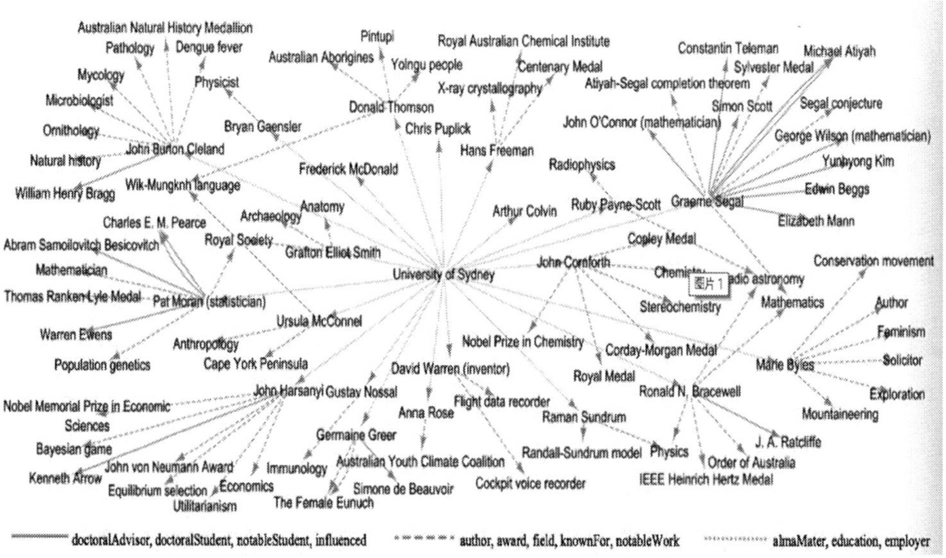

Fig. 1. Part of Linked Open Data graph regarding scientific research institutions.

2.1 Information Content Measurement

In information theory, Information Content (IC), is the amount of bits required to re-construct the transmitted information source[2].Based on probability theory, Infor-mation Content is computed as a measure of generated amount of surprise:

$$IC(a) = -log(\pi(a)) \tag{1}$$

such that π(a) is the probability of appearance of the term or concept a in its context.In this paper, a represents a semantic relationship.

2.2 Indicator Information Content

In Linked Open Data, a single evaluation indicator may correspond to multiple semantic relationships.

$$L = \{l1, l2, , l|L|\}$$

is the set of semantics relations, in which li is the relation, defined as

$$< a, li, b >$$

, connecting resource a to resource b.

$$I = \{I1, I2, , I|I|\}$$

is the set of research evaluation indicators, semantic relations

$$(L_i \in L)$$

,is a subset of L corresponding to each indicator Ii.Based on information theory, The weight of a single evaluation indicator is the sum of all semantic relations information content corresponding to the indicator[3]

$$(IW_{\forall I_i I}(I_i) = \Sigma_{l_i \in L_i} IC(l_i)) \tag{2}$$

3 Experiment

3.1 Experimental Context

The main Linked Dataset employed in our experiments was DBpedia (structured con-tent from the information created in the Wikipedia).Using the proposed indicator com-pute method to compute the weight of indicators (Ns&Pub,Hici,Alumni,Award) Shanghai Jiaotong University World University RankingsSJTUuses, a rank experiment for the top 100 universities, according to the two ranking results to compare and analyze.

- DownLoad DBPedia 3.8 and load the data into OpenLink Virtuoso.
- Find out all the semantic relationships corresponding to each indicator.
- Compute the information content for each indicator.
- Rankings for the top 100 universities of Shanghai Jiaotong University rankings based on the computing weight values of the indicators.
- Comparing our results with existing Shanghai Jiaotong University rankings.

3.2 Results

The indicators and corresponding semantic relations in DBpedia used in the experi-ment,See table 1. Part of lod-based top 100 universities ranking,see table 2.The score results using the proposed weight computing method and the SJTU existing weight score results,Pearson correlation was 0.980,Spearman correlation was 0.939.Its rank-ing order and ranking order of SJTU, Pearson correlation and Spearman correlation was 0.939,see table 3. The score correlation and rank correlation of the above two ranking results are very strong, which proves the validity of the weight computing method based on Linked Open Data.

Indicators	Semantic relations	Weight value
Research Output(Ns&Pub)	bo:author,dbo:publisher	10.044929211724337
Research Team(Hici)	dbo:employer,dbo:occupation, dbo:training,dbo:team	9.009842851681144
Talent cultivation(Alumni)	dbo:almaMater,dbo:education	10.294329936963663
Prizes(Award)	dbo:award	10.460661878821565

Table 1: The indicators and corresponding semantic relations in DBpedia.

rank	university	score	SJTU score
1	Harvard University	4985.469309	1
2	University of Cambridge	3514.994267	5
3	University of California, Berkeley	3468.672932	3
4	Massachusetts Institute of Technology	3451.373995	4
5	Stanford University	3441.811203	2
6	Columbia University	3071.002103	6
7	University of Chicago	2912.113239	10
8	Princeton University	2884.626794	11
9	University of Oxford	2834.65499	7
10	Yale University	2738.671839	8
...	...	...	...
100	cole Polytechnique Fdrale de Lausanne	966.427745	89

Table 2: Part of lod-based top 100 universities.

Pearson		Spearman	
score	rank	score	rank
0.980	0.939	0.939	0.939

Table 3: The correlation between lod-based and SJTU.

4 Conclusion

Linked Open Data,as a structured and reliable source of semantic data, it can offer significant benefits for a low-cost and accurate performance computing of evaluation indicators weigh of scientific research institutions.

We will focus more on the accuracy of the compute by capturing more semantic re-lations from Linked Open Data cloud and by eliminating any trace of redundancy.

References

1. Meymandpour R, Davis J G. Ranking Universities Using Linked Open Data[C]// Linked Data on the Web. 2013.Author, F., Author, S.: Title of a proceedings paper. In: Editor, F., Editor, S. (eds.) CONFERENCE 2016, LNCS, vol. 9999, pp. 113. Springer, Heidelberg (2016).
2. Edwards, S.: Elements of information theory, 2nd edition[J].Information Processing & Management,44(1), 400401 (2008).
3. Meymandpour, R. and Davis, J. G. 2013. Linked Data Informativeness. Web Technologies and Applications, 7808, 629-637. Springer Berlin Heidelberg.

Extracting Rate-changes in Transcriptional Regulation by Word Embedding with Sentence Structure and Domain Knowledge in Deep Neural Networks

Wenting Liu[1] and Yilei Zhang[2]

School of Public Health and Management, Hubei University of Medicine, China
Nanyang Technological University, Singapore
YLZhang@ntu.edu.sg

Abstract. As the rapid increase of bio-literature, its very necessary to develop document analysis tools to automatically and accurately extract biological knowledge and events from bio-literatures. The vast majority of biological data-bases do not record temporal information of gene regulations, which are very important to understand the underlying mechanism of many diseases and biolog-ical processes. We previously constructed a corpus of time-delays related to the transcriptional regulation (bio-events) of yeast from the PubMed abstracts, sum-marized the knowledge rules of the bio-events as rate-changes in transcriptional regulation ontology, and obtained 86% accuracy by using the decision tree clas-sifier with the ontology rule features. Deep neural networks (DNN) achieve great success in many machine learning applications including document analysis. The word2vec model learned the word embedding features from documents can achieve 50-70% accuracy on most of text classification tasks. However, the sen-tence structure and domain knowledge are rarely considered in DNNs of docu-ment classification. We proposed to combine word2vec features, sentence struc-ture, and our ontology rule features to improve the DNNs for bio-events detection in document analysis. Experimental results show that on predicting transcription regulation events, the word2vec in DNN model achieves 73% accuracy, while our combined features in DNN with same parameters achieves 96% accuracy; on predicting the rate-changes in transcription regulation events, word2vec in DNN achieves only 59% accuracy, and our combined features in DNN achieves 90% accuracy. This shows the power of domain knowledge and sentence structure features with DNN in document analysis.

Keywords: Deep neural networks, biomedical events mining, rate-changes in transcriptional regulation.

1 Introduction

1.1 Background

Due to the increasing publications, literature mining is becoming useful for both hy-pothesis generation and biological discovery[1]. Its important but still challenge to 2 automatically and accurately extract biological knowledge and events from biomedical literature [2][3][4]. The current state-of-the-art performance clearly shows that close to 80% in F1-score have been achieved in extracting simple bio-events, but the complex events such as binding and regulation events is still limited, the best performance achieved remains 30%40% lower than that for simple events [2].

Inspired by the big success of deep learning in natural language processing, we applied it on our previous established corpus of bio-events of the rate changes in transcriptional regulation[5]. The vast majority of biological databases do not record temporal infor-mation of gene regulations, which are very important to understand the underlying mechanism of many diseases and biological processes. We previously constructed a corpus of time-delays related to the transcriptional regulation (complex bio-events) of yeast from the PubMed abstracts. By summarizing the textual patterns of the biological knowledge rules of the transcriptional regulation events, we established the rate-changed transcriptional regulation ontology. And it achieved 86% accuracy to predict transcriptional regulation by using the ontology rule features in the decision tree clas-sifier[5].

In this paper, we applied the state-of-the-art word embedding and deep neural network model, combined with the domain knowledge from our ontology features and sentence structure features to improve the performance to infer the complex rate-changed tran-scriptional regulation events from our corpus.

1.2 Related Works

Deep neural networks (DNN) achieve great success in many machine learning applica-tions including document analysis[6]. Word embedding methods represent words as continuous vectors in a low dimensional space which capture lexical and semantic prop-erties of words. They can be obtained from the internal representations from neural network models of text[7]. The word2vec model learned the word embedding features from documents can achieve 50-70The convolutional and recurrent neural networks have been shown to capture effective hidden structures within sentences via continuous representations, thereby significantly advancing the performance of relation extraction[8][9].

However, the sentence structure and domain knowledge [10] are rarely considered in DNNs of document classification[6]. Nguyen and Grishman [5] combine the traditional feature-based method, the convolutional and recurrent neural networks to simultane-ously benefit from their advantages. The approach is demonstrated to achieve the state-of-the-art performance on the ACE 2005 and SemEval datasets.

2 Methods

2.1 Corpus for rate changes in transcriptional regulation

The manually labeled corpus of events relating to rate changes in transcriptional regu-lation for yeast is available in https://sites.google.com/site/wentingntu/data. The cre-ated ontologies summarized both biological causes of rate changes in transcriptional regulation and corresponding positive and negative textual patterns from the corpus. We annotated the corpus by manually labeling sentences containing transcriptional reg-ulation rate changing events as positive instances and others as negative instances. For positive instances, we identified trigger words that indicate mentions of transcriptional regulation processes or rate changes of the processes. These words were annotated to facilitate the creation of our time-delay (transcriptional regulation rate change) ontol-ogy. In the negative class, the sentence may only include information about gene regu-lation without rate changes or about a biological process other than transcriptional reg-ulation. Both direct and indirect evidences exist in the positive instances. We thus fur-ther annotate the positive class with two types of events: (i) events with specific infor-mation about regulator, regulatee and rate changes in transcription regulation, and (ii) indirect evidences for transcription regulation rate changing events.

2.2 Representation learning

We employ the natural language toolkit, (NLTK)[11] to tokenize a sentence into the sequence of tokens. For each feature of interest, retrieve the corresponding vector by word2vec[12] [13], a feed-forward neural network (NN) that takes input sparse vector and produces a output dense vector [14]. The input vector encodes features such as words, part-of-speech tags or other linguistic information. The sparse-input linear mod-els to neural-network based models is to stop representing each feature as a unique dimension (the so called one-hot representation) and representing them instead as dense vectors. The embeddings (the vector representation of each core feature) can then be trained like the other parameter of the function NN. The feature embeddings (the values of the vector entries for each feature) are treated as model parameters that need to be trained together with the other components of the network[15].

2.3 Sentence into vector

A sentence vector model [16] [17] is comprised of an unsupervised learning algorithm that learns fixed- size vector representations for variable-length pieces of texts such as sentences and documents[18]. The vector representations are learned to predict the sur-rounding words in contexts sampled from the paragraph. We adopted the Doc2Vec [19] from Gensim, a python package, to get sentence embeddings using the word vectors.

2.4 Domain Knowledge Integration for Feature Combinations

The Transcriptional Regulation Rate Change Ontology [5] include the textual pat-terns of biological processes that may result in transcriptional regulation rate change. We previously propose a feature-based method that incorporates diverse lexical, syn-tactic and semantic features to automatically extract transcriptional regulation relations as follows.

Keyword-tag: a combination of the keywords defined in our ontologies, and their POS tags, which indicate their grammatical roles in sentences. The keywords in the features are normalized to reduce the diversity of words with the same tags.

Word-relation-word: two words concatenated by the name of their dependency relation type. The relation is extracted from the shortest relation path between genes and key-words in the dependency tree derived from the Stanford NLP parser [23].

Gene-keyword-distance: a triplet of gene, keyword, and length of the shortest relation path between them in the dependency tree. The contextual features provide general characteristics of the sentence or neighborhood where the target token is present.

2.5 Deep Neural Networks, multi-layer feed-forward networks

Feed-forward networks include networks with fully connected layers, such as the multi-layer perceptron, as well as networks with convolutional and pooling layers[20]. All of the networks act as classifiers, but each with different strengths. The non-linearity of the network, as well as the ability to easily integrate pre-trained word embeddings, often lead to superior classification accuracy. We adopted multi-layer feed-forward net-works, which can provide competitive results on sentiment classification[1].

3 Results

From the corpus, the 1000-dimension word vectors were produced with deep learning via word2vec of gensim, a python package. Each sentence is then transformed a vec-tor by adding the word vectors of the sentence. For each classification task, we perform 10-fold cross-validation to evaluate the classification performance. The positive sen-tences and negative ones are by randomly partitioned into 10 equal groups. For each round, one group is used as testing set, the other 9 groups are training set, a three layer deep neural networks (DNN) with 10, 20, 10 units, respectively, is built from the train-ing set in 2000 steps by tensorflow; then the testing sentences are predicted by the DNN as positive or negative, and the accuracy is reported.

3.1 Predicting transcription regulation events

The following Table shows the performance of different feature set in DNN model and previous decision tree model on predicting the transcription regulation events in the 1309 sentences with 10-fold cross-validation. Experimental results show that on pre- 5 dicting transcription regulation events, the word2vec in DNN model achieves 73% ac-curacy, while our combined features in DNN with same parameters achieves 96% ac-curacy, which is significantly better than the 86% accuracy of previous ontology rules features in decision tree classifier.

Features	Dimensions	Classifier	Accuracy (%)
Ontology Rules	115	Decision Tree	86
Word2vec	1000	Deep Neural Network	73
Word2vec +Ontology	1115	Deep Neural Network	96

Table 1. Performance on predicting transcription regulation events..

4 Predicting the rate-changes in transcription regulation events

The following Table shows the performance of different feature set in DNN model and previous decision tree model on predicting the rate-changes in transcription regulation events from the 359 sentences of transcription regulation events with 10-fold cross-validation. It shows that on predicting the rate-changes in transcription regulation events, word2vec in DNN achieves only 59% accuracy, same performance as previous combined features by decision tree classifier. By combing our domain knowledge and sentence structure combined features into word embedding, the DNN classifier achieves 90% accuracy.

Features	Dimensions	Classifier	Accuracy (%)
Ontology Rules	115	Decision Tree	54
Domain +Sentence Structure Feature	669	Decision Tree	59
Word2vec	1000	Deep Neural Network	59
Word2vec + Domain +Sentence Struc-ture Feature	1669	Deep Neural Network	90

Table 2. Performance on predicting the rate-changes in transcription regulation events.

5 Discussion and Future Work

In this paper, we proposed to combine the domain knowledge summarized in rate-changed transcriptional regulation ontology and sentence structure features into word embedding, to predict the complex transcriptional regulation events and the rate changes in them by DNN classifier. The experimental results show that both classifica-tion tasks achieve above 90% accuracy. Note that the domain knowledge and sentence structure features are directly combined into the word embedding features learned by word2vec model. 6 Recently, the dependency-based word embedding tool, word2vecf [21], is used for bi-omedical event trigger detection[22]. Specifically, all available PubMed abstracts are parsed with Gdep parser [10], a dependency parse tool specialized for biomedical texts, and train the dependency-based word embedding based on the contexts in dependency relations. Well learn the ontology rules and sentence structure features embedding from our corpus based on supervised training. We also employ the dependency-based word embedding, which contains more functional semantic information, to better cap-ture semantics of the events. In the future, well use tree-based deep learning model such as tree Long Short-Term Memory (LSTM) convolutional and recurrent neural net-works which can automatically learn features from dependency tree for the trigger words and phrases.

References

1. L. J. Jensen, J. Saric, and P. Bork, Literature mining for the biologist : from information retrieval to biological discovery, vol. 7, no. February, pp. 119129, 2006.
2. Biddle, Gary C and Hilary, Gilles and Verdi, Rodrigo S J. A. Vanegas, S. Matos, F. Gonzlez, and J. L. Oliveira, An Overview of Biomolecular Event Extraction from Scientific Documents, vol. 2015, 2015.
3. S. T. Ahmed, R. Nair, C. Patel, and H. Davulcu, BioEve : Bio-Molecular Event Extraction from Text Using Semantic Classification and Dependency Parsing, no. June, pp. 99102, 2009.
4. H. Kilicoglu, G. Rosemblat, M. Fiszman, and T. C. Rindflesch, Sortal anaphora resolution to enhance relation extraction from biomedical literature, BMC Bioinformatics, pp. 116, 2016.
5. Huang, Anna W. Liu, K. Miao, G. Li, K. Chang, J. Zheng, and J. C. Rajapakse, Extracting rate changes in transcriptional regulation from MEDLINE abstracts, BMC Bioinformatics, vol. 15, no. Suppl 2, pp. 112, 2014.
6. Islam, Aminul and Inkpen, Diana M. Allahyari et al., A Brief Survey of Text Mining: Classification, Clustering and Extraction Techniques, 2017.
7. T. Mikolov, K. Chen, G. Corrado, and J. Dean, Distributed Representations of Words and Phrases and their Compositionality, pp. 19.
8. Dejean Herve, Meunier, Jean-Luc T. H. Nguyen and R. Grishman, Relation Extraction: Perspective from Convolutional Neural Networks, Work. Vector Model. NLP, pp. 3948, 2015.
9. Cong, Yu and Hao, Jia and Zou, Lin T. H. Nguyen and R. Grishman, Combining Neural Networks and Log-linear Models to Improve Relation Extraction, no. i, 2015.
10. D. Erhan, A. Courville, and P. Vincent, Why Does Unsupervised Pre-training Help Deep Learning ?, J. Mach. Learn. Res., vol. 11, pp. 625660, 2010.
11. S. Bird and E. Loper, NLTK : The Natural Language Toolkit.
12. J. Lilleberg, Support Vector Machines and Word2vec for Text Classification with Semantic Features, pp. 136140, 2015.

13. S. Arora, Y. Li, Y. Liang, T. Ma, and A. Risteski, Linear Algebraic Structure of Word Senses, with Applications to Polysemy, pp. 122, 2016.
14. Y. Bengio, A. Courville, and P. Vincent, Representation Learning: A Review and New Perspectives, no. 1993, pp. 130, 2012.
15. M. Amit and S. Adi, Word Embeddings and Their Use In Sentence Classification Tasks, Empir. Methods NLP, 2015.
16. S. Arora, Y. Liang, and T. Ma, A simple but tough to beat baseline for sentence embeddings, Iclr, pp. 114, 2017.
17. C. Features, M. Pagliardini, P. Gupta, and M. Jaggi, Unsupervised Learning of Sentence Embeddings.
18. P. Bojanowski, E. Grave, A. Joulin, and T. Mikolov, Enriching Word Vectors with Subword Information, 1996.
19. J. H. Lau and T. Baldwin, Practical Insights into Document Embedding Generation, 2014.
20. Y. Goldberg, A primer on neural network models for natural language processing, arXiv Prepr. arXiv1510.00726, pp. 176, 2015.
21. O. Levy and Y. Goldberg, Dependency-Based Word Embeddings, pp. 302308, 2014.
22. J. Wang et al., Biomedical event trigger detection by dependency-based word embedding, BMC Med. Genomics, vol. 9, no. Suppl 2, 2016.
23. The Stanford Parser. http://nlp.stanford.edu/software/lex-parser.shtml.

Applications of Data Mining in Insurance Sector: Ex-plorations into Techniques of Leveraging Big Data

Dr. Darshan Desai[1] and Om Desai[2]

Berkeley College, New York, NY 10017, USA Academy of Information Technology, NJ 07076, USA

Abstract. This paper addresses the issues and techniques for insurance companies using data mining techniques and leveraging big data. Data mining includes various methods of discovering hidden predictive information from large data sets, and is a process of analyzing data from different perspectives and summarizing it into useful information - information that insurers can use to increase revenue, cut costs, or both. Many scholars have researched useful applications of datamining in the context of the insurance industry. However, the issues and techniques of leveraging big data while applying data-mining techniques in the insurance sector are largely unex-plored. This research aims to uncover the most common insurance industry applica-tion areas where leveraging big data can add significant value. It also explores dif-ferent techniques of leveraging big data across multiple sectors of the insurance in-dustry. With cross-case analysis the intra-industry differences in these techniques and applications are also highlighted.

Keywords: Datamining, Insurance Sector, Big Data.

1 Introduction

Insurance is a mechanism people use to limit their exposure to risk. It is a sector that extends its scope to almost everyone. Companies in the insurance industry charge premium to cover certain risks. When these covered risks happen, they pay claims. A range of activities is important for insurance operations, and risk management is one of these central activities. These activities include identifying the risks that can be covered, deciding the premium to be charged, preparing agreements, executing these agreements, maintaining relationships with customers, claims handling, etc. (Pathak and Jha, 2017). Historically, the industry has been a data and information intensive industry. However, it is accustomed to comparatively slow evolution, and is not very comfortable with fast-paced change

With a shifting data and technology landscape, a storm is being predicted in the insur-ance industry, and it will rain information. According to the results of a recent survey (2018) of insurance CEOs conducted by PWC, more insurance

CEOs are concerned about the pace of technological change (85%) than leaders in almost any other indus-try. Technological advances are changing the business and operating models of an industry thats accustomed to slow evolution rather than rapid transformation. And, in this kind of industry climate, to remain competitive, insurance companies are increas- ingly relying on data mining and big data to reduce claims, create value for their cus-tomers, and help proactively monitor risks to minimize customer losses.

Many scholars (for example, Pathak and Jha, 2017, Yan and Li, 2015, Abtab et al, 2013) researched useful applications of datamining in the context of the insurance industry. However, the issues and techniques of leveraging big data while applying data-mining techniques in the insurance sector are largely unexplored and need fur-ther attention. This paper aims to uncover the relevance, issues, and techniques for insurance companies to leverage big data while applying data-mining techniques.

This research discusses the role of big data in the insurance industry. Through a re-view of literature and case study research, the paper uncovers the most common in-surance industry application areas where leveraging big data can add significant val-ue. In addition, the research further explores different techniques of leveraging big data across multiple sectors of the insurance industry and concludes by highlighting intra-industry differences with cross-case analysis, and areas of future research.

2 Role of Big Data in Insurance

The operational activities of this industry usually generate a huge volume of internal data. Data and information are required not only as a part of the claim management process but also as input for future insurance activities. However, some insurance activities also use data from other sources.

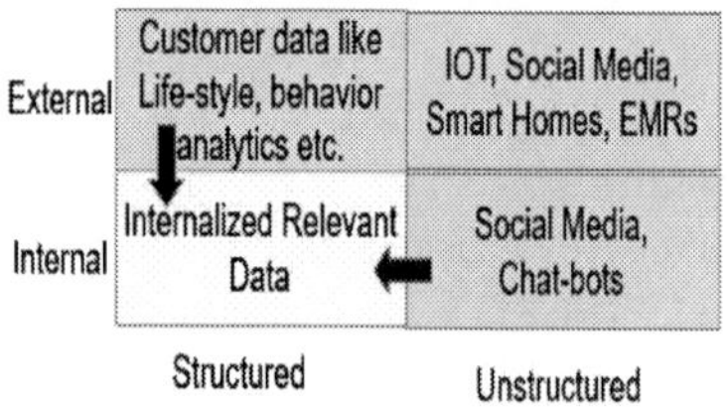

Fig. 1. Different types of data sources used in mining insurance data.

As shown in Fig.1, external data is rapidly growing in volume and relevance, which is causing a gradual shift in companies from relying on internal data to using both inter-nal and external data. In addition, brand new sources of data are appearing. Wearable devices, smart homes, mobile phone apps, chat bots, social media, electronic medical records, and other things will all make it possible to continue to collect more and more data.

For example, in the past, an insurance company might have used historical data to predict the cost of future property damage claims. But now, real-time weather data can alert the company to an impending storm, and within hours it can combine that information with geographical data to determine the probability of snow, ice, or flooding in low-lying areas. The company can identify customers who live in low-lying elevations or blizzard-prone areas, and use digital channels to warn them about property protection. Advancements in processing power and data exploitation are enabling companies to fully exploit external and unstructured data. These are all op-portunities for insurance companies. The challenge lies in digesting the rising tide of data and making sense of it. To get these real time insights, insurance companies must expand their analytics practices beyond traditional ad hoc reporting. In the past, they would run business intelligence reports on a batch basisweeks or months apartand use this data to make predictions about future trends. These practices are still valuable, but insurance companies must evolve their analytics processes to remain competitive: they must monitor information on an ongoing basis, analyzing it proac-tively to search for insights. In this journey towards higher analytics maturity and shift from descriptive analytics toward predictive and prescriptive analytics, big data is playing an increasingly important role.

3 Big Data Application Areas and Techniques

With the increasingly important role of big data, insurers want to get insights about common and valuable big data applications areas. At this time, techniques of leveraging big data in insurance data mining applications need more scholarly attention. Therefore, based on multi-case research and a review of literature, this research has identified the most common big data application areas and techniques in the section below.

3.1 Product Management and Marketing

Data-mining and predictive analytics are widely accepted in marketing and product management to help target the right cus-tomers and to predict those who may churn. In many cases, insurers use classification algorithms such as logistic regression and support vector machine (SVM) to classify various entities like customers, agents, etc. based on some pre-formulated classifica-tion rules. External structured and unstructured data like behavioral analytics, compet-itor and social media data enable insurers to proactively manage their customer port-folio with better prediction of customer value and risk.

Through real-time behavioral analytics and data ingestion from multiple sources, insurers can use analytics interventions for customer engagement. These classes are then used in forming strategies and interventions related to differentiated relationship management, product offerings, various promotional activities, etc. (Pathak and Jha, 2017). Sometimes decision tree techniques are also used to find out the rules of classi-fication (Xiahou, et al. 2016). In using traditional classification methods, fragmented insurance business data and uncertainty about customers' purchasing characteristics lead to a serious imbalance in the category of product data, which brings difficulties in user classification and recommendation of insurance products. Hence, Lin et al, (2017) proposed a heuristic bootstrap sampling approach combined with the ensemble learning algorithm for leveraging bid data in insurance data mining. They proposed an ensemble random forest algorithm that uses the parallel computing capability and memory cache mechanism optimized by Spark. This proposed algorithm outper-formed SVM and other classification algorithms in both performance and accuracy within the imbalanced data. This technique is useful for leveraging big data to im-prove the performance of product management and marketing-related datamining applications.

3.2 Risk-based Pricing and Underwriting.

In underwriting, big data can enable better risk assessment and classification of customers, which leads to better pricing. They also lead to dynamic pricing and better customer profitability and value man-agement. In the case of auto insurance companies, one such big data application is known as telematics. Telematics directly monitors a drivers behavior to provide a more accurate risk assessment score for the customer that can help insurers to create tailor-made policy that a client can ask for. Another life and health reinsurance com-panyleveraged big data to predict mortality risks among cancer patients in remission. A robust mortality model simplified underwriting since low-risk applicants can avoid manual medical verification, and it also reduced claims costs by identifying high-risk patients.

In academic literature, both supervised and unsupervised learning applications have been used for leveraging big data in this context, though supervised learning is more common. Baecke and Bocca (2017) leveraged big data from sensors to improve the risk selection process in an insurance company. More specifically, several risk as-sessment models based on three different supervised data mining techniques (a lo-gistic regression, random forests, and artificial neural networks model) were aug-mented with driving behavior data collected from in-vehicle data recorders. Standard telematics variables significantly improved the risk assessment of customers. As a result, insurers were better able to tailor their products to customers' risk profiles. In another study, Brambilla, Mascetti and Mauri (2017) researched different driving behaviors, using unsupervised learning methods, to cluster drivers with similar behav-ior. They studied driver behavioral characteristics by collecting information from GPS sensors on the cars and by applying three different analysis approaches (DP-means, Hidden Markov Models, and Behavioral Topic Extraction). In both of these studies, the approaches/techniques identified were useful in leveraging big data to improve data-mining model performance.

3.3 Medical/Clinical Risk and Cost Prediction.

Huge cost pressures have created enormous demand for better data across a range of players in the healthcare industry. Non-healthcare consumer data, IoT health device data, and clinical data related to EMRs are creating a supply of relevant data at an unprecedented scale. Significant advances in the ability to combine claims and clinical data are catalysing the trans-formative changes in the sector of medical/clinical cost and risk prediction. In the case of one health insurer, harnessing clinical analytics enabled them to gain actiona-ble insights that can be the key to improving population healthcare management.

On academic side, more recently, for leveraging big data, Hashi, Zaman and Hasan (2017) proposed a system that assists doctors with predicting diseases correctly and helps patients and insurers. Their research used the Decision Tree and K-Nearest Neighbor (KNN) Algorithms to diagnose diabetes, as it is a great threat to human life worldwide. However, many of the existing risk models typically draw on claims data and focus on one specific disease or event, and do not predict multiple outcomes. Lin et al. (2017) proposed a technique to leverage big data relating to patients electronic health records to attain enhanced risk profiling. Patients with chronic diseases often face risks of not just one, but an array of adverse health events, and they adopted a principled approach called Bayesian multitask learning (BMTL) to coordinate a set of baseline modelsone for each eventand communicate training information across the models. These type of innovative approaches and techniques for leveraging big data can potentially create significant impacts on clinical practice in reducing failures and delays in preventive interventions.

3.4 Insurance Fraud Detection and Frictionless Claims.

Risk prediction is also an important defense against insurance claims fraud. Insurance fraud is one of Americas largest crimes, and predictive analytics can better detect and flag potential fraudu-lent claims. In the case of a short-term insurance provider, they were facing difficul-ties in settling claims where the length of the process was hurting the companys reputation. Due to a very high risk of fraud, the insurer had to conduct a detailed as-sessment of every claim. Big data separated potential fraud into different categories with given risks. This helped them save money and significantly reduce the length of the process.

Additionally, this data is also mined to identify various valuable patterns and make use of them in fraud detection or prevention (Pathak and Jha, 2017). Unsupervised machine learning is more closely aligned with the idea that a computer can learn to identify complex processes and patterns without a human providing guidance along the way. Some examples of unsupervised machine learning algorithms include k-means clustering, principal and independent component analysis, and pattern match-ing and association rules. Predicting insurance fraud often requires unsupervised learning approaches as insurance companies often dont collect information as to whether a claim is suspected of fraud or abuse.

4 Conclusion

Big data applications related to insurance fraud prevention, fraud detection, predictive claims, customer relationship and product management, risk-profiling and underwriting, and management decision-making are becoming increasingly common across all types of insurers. Data ingestion from multiple sources for real-time behavioral analytics is more relevant in cases of health and life insurance. This is because, more specifically in these cases, certain behaviors and life-styles are more closely linked to having a higher risk, and such analytics interventions are very valuable for the well-being of the member. Though use of telematics is prevalent only in the cases of the auto-insurance industry, the applications and techniques related to integrating unstructured sensor data and data coming from IOT devices into datamining is affecting everyone in the industry, and is an important area for future research.

This level of maturity involves digesting new kinds of data. In the past, rigid, rela-tional databases held the lions share of information. These data structures are no longer adequate in an age of real-time, unstructured information from a growing vari-ety of sources. Insurance companies must pull these data elements together so they can analyze it all seamlessly. This means breaking down information silos. The insur-ance sector is known for its conservative nature. In this sector, data-mining and ana-lytics were mostly used for descriptive purposes on historical data. The amount of confidence insurers wanted in their predictive models was not feasible to have with the companys internal historical data. Now, with advancement in technology, big-data enabled analytics is shifting the insurers more towards predictive analytics. Big data analytics based prediction of customer value or risk can improve management decisions and light up many opportunities for different insurance business processes across the value chain

References

1. Aftab, S., Abbas, W., Bilal, M. M., Hussain, T., Shoaib, M., & Mehmood, S. H. (2013, September). Data mining in insurance claims (DMICS) two-way mining for extreme values. In Digital Information Management (ICDIM), 2013 Eighth International Conference on (pp. 1-6). IEEE.
2. Hashi, E. K., Zaman, M. S. U., & Hasan, M. R. (2017, February). An expert clinical decision support system to predict disease using classification tech-niques. In Electrical, Computer and Communication Engineering (ECCE), International Conference on (pp. 396-400). IEEE.
3. Lin, W., Wu, Z., Lin, L., Wen, A., & Li, J. (2017). An Ensemble Random Forest Algorithm for Insurance Big Data Analysis. IEEE Access, 5, 16568-16575.
4. Lin, Y. K., Chen, H., Brown, R. A., Li, S. H., & Yang, H. J. (2017). Healthcare Predictive Analytics For Risk Profiling In Chronic Care: A Bayesian Multitask Learning Approach. MIS Quarterly, 41(2)
5. Pathak, G., & Jha, A. N. (2017). Critical Review of Data Mining Techniques for Insurance Service Operations. In International Conference on Technolo-gy and Business Management April(Vol. 10, p. 12).

6. Xiahou, J., Xu, Y., Zhang, S., & Liao, W. (2016, August). Customer profita-bility analysis of automobile insurance market based on data mining. In Computer Science & Education (ICCSE), 2016 11th International Con-ference on (pp. 603-609). IEEE.
7. Yan, C., & Li, Y. (2015, September). The Identification Algorithm and Model Construction of Automobile Insurance Fraud Based on Data Mining. In Instrumentation and Measurement, Computer, Communication and Con-trol (IMCCC), 2015 Fifth International Conference on (pp. 1922-1928). IEEE.

Clustering Professional Baseball Players with SOM and Deciding Team Reinforcement Strategy with AHP

Kazuhiro Kohara[1] and Shota Enomoto[2]

Chiba Institute of Technology
2-17-1 Tsudanuma, Narashino, Chiba 275-0016, Japan
kohara.kazuhiro@it-chiba.ac.jp

Abstract. In this paper, we propose an integration method that uses self-organizing maps (SOM) and the analytic hierarchy process (AHP) to cluster professional baseball players and to make decision on team reinforcement strategy. We used data of pitchers in the Japanese professional baseball teams. First, we collected data of 223 pitchers and clustered these pitchers using the following fourteen features: number of games pitched, number of wins, number of loses, number of save, number of hold, number of innings pitched, rate of strikeout, ERA (earned run average), percentage of hits a pitcher allows, WHIP (walks plus hits per inning pitched), K/BB (strikeout to walk ratio), FIP (fielding independent pitching), LOB% (left on base percentage), RSAA (runs saved above average). Second, we created pitcher maps of all teams and each team with SOM. Third, we examined main features of each cluster. Fourth, we considered team reinforcement strategies by using the pitcher maps. Finally, we used AHP to determine the team reinforcement strategy.

Keywords: clustering, visualization, data mining, business intelligence, sport industry, baseball, decision making, self-organizing maps, AHP

1 Introduction

Machine learning and data mining techniques have been extensively investigated, and various attempts have been made to apply them to baseball [e.g., 1-5]. Tolbert et al. applied SVM (Support Vector Machine) to predicting MLB (Major League Baseball) championship winners [1]. Ishii applied K-means clustering to identifying undervalued baseball players [2]. Pane applied K-means clustering and Fisher-wise criterion to identifying clusters of MLB pitchers [3]. Tung applied PCA (Principal Component Analysis) and K-means clustering to analyzing a multivariate data set of career batting performances in MLB [4]. Vazquez applied time series and clustering algorithms to predicting baseball results [5]. In this paper, we propose an integration method that uses Self-Organizing Maps (SOM) [6] and the analytic hierarchy process (AHP) [7] to cluster professional baseball players and to make decision on team reinforcement strategy. We used data of pitchers in Japanese baseball teams. First, we collected data of 223 pitchers and clustered these pitchers using fourteen features. Second, we created pitcher maps of all teams and each team with SOM. Third, we examined main features of each cluster. Fourth, we considered team reinforcement strategies by using pitcher maps. Finally, we used AHP to determine the team reinforcement strategy.

2 Clustering Professional Baseball Players with SOM

The SOM algorithm is based on unsupervised, competitive learning [6]. It provides a topology preserving mapping from the high dimensional space to map units. Map units, or neurons, usually form a two-dimensional lattice and thus the mapping is a mapping from high dimensional space onto a plane.

Previously, we proposed a way of purchase decision support using SOM and AHP. First, we provided two class boundaries, which divide the range between the maximum and minimum of an input feature value into three equal parts. Second, we created self-organizing product maps using the classified inputs. We applied our way to five kinds of products and confirmed its effectiveness [8]. When we previously compared SOM with the other clustering algorithms (hierarchical clustering and Kmeans clustering) for product clustering, SOM were superior to the other clustering algorithms for both visibility and clustering ability [9]. Therefore, we used SOM for baseball players clustering.

We used data of pitchers of NPB (Nippon Professional Baseball Organization) [10]. We collected data of 235 pitchers in 2015 from Japanese professional baseball database [10, 11]. We clustered these pitchers using the following fourteen features: number of games pitched, number of wins, number of loses, number of save, number of hold, number of innings pitched, rate of strikeouts, ERA (earned run average), percentage of hits a pitcher allows, WHIP (walks plus hits per inning pitched), K/BB (strikeout to walk ratio), FIP (fielding independent pitching), LOB% (left on base percentage), RSAA (runs saved above average).

In each feature, we provide two class boundaries, which divide the range between the maximum and minimum of an input feature value into three equal parts. For classifying the data of the number of games pitched, we divided the number into three classes: under 27, over 28 to 50, and over 51. For classifying the data of the number of wins, we divided the number into three classes: under 5, over 6 to 10, and over 11. For classifying the data of the number of loses, we divided the number into three classes: under 4, over 5 to 8, and over 9. For classifying the data of the number of save, we divided the number into three classes: under 13, over 14 to 27, and over 28. For classifying the data of the number of hold, we divided the number into three classes: under 13, over 14 to 26, and over 27. For classifying the data of the number of innings pitched, we divided the number into three classes: under 74, over 75 to 140, and over 141. For classifying the data of the rate of strikeouts, we divided the rate into three classes: under 6.09, over 6.10 to 10.15, and over 10.16. For classifying the data of ERA, we divided ERA into three classes: under 3.52, over 3.53 to 6.64, and over 6.65. For classifying the data of the percentage of hits a pitcher allows, we divided the percentage into three classes: under 8.35, over 8.36 to 13.08, and over 13.09. For classifying the data of WHIP, we divided WHIP into three classes: under 1.36, over 1.37 to 2.08, and over 2.09. For classifying the data of K/BB, we divided K/BB into three classes: under 4.70, over 4.71 to 8.85, and over 8.86. For classifying the data of FIP, we divided FIP into three classes: under 3.20, over 3.21 to 5.27, and over 5.28. For classifying the data of LOB%, we divided LOB% into three classes: under 0.661, over 0.662 to 0.814, and over 0.815. For classifying the data of RSAA, we divided RSAA into three classes: under -2.1083, over -2.1082 to 16.65, and over 16.66. Table 1 shows a part of the feature matrix for pitchers.

Table 1: A part of the feature matrix for pitchers.

Name	Number of games pitched			Number of wins		
	under 27	over 28 to 50	over 51	under 5	over 6 to 10	over 11
Makita	0	1	0	0	1	0
Hamada	1	0	0	1	0	0
Sawamura	0	0	1	0	1	0
Settu	1	0	0	0	0	1
Wakui	0	1	0	0	0	1
Arihara	1	0	0	0	1	0
Masui	0	0	1	1	0	0
Fujinami	0	1	0	0	0	1
Yamaguchi	0	0	1	1	0	0

We inputted the data of all pitchers into SOM and created pitcher maps of all teams. Figure 1 shows self-organizing map of pitchers of all teams. Figures 2, 3 and 4 show examples of component maps of pitchers.

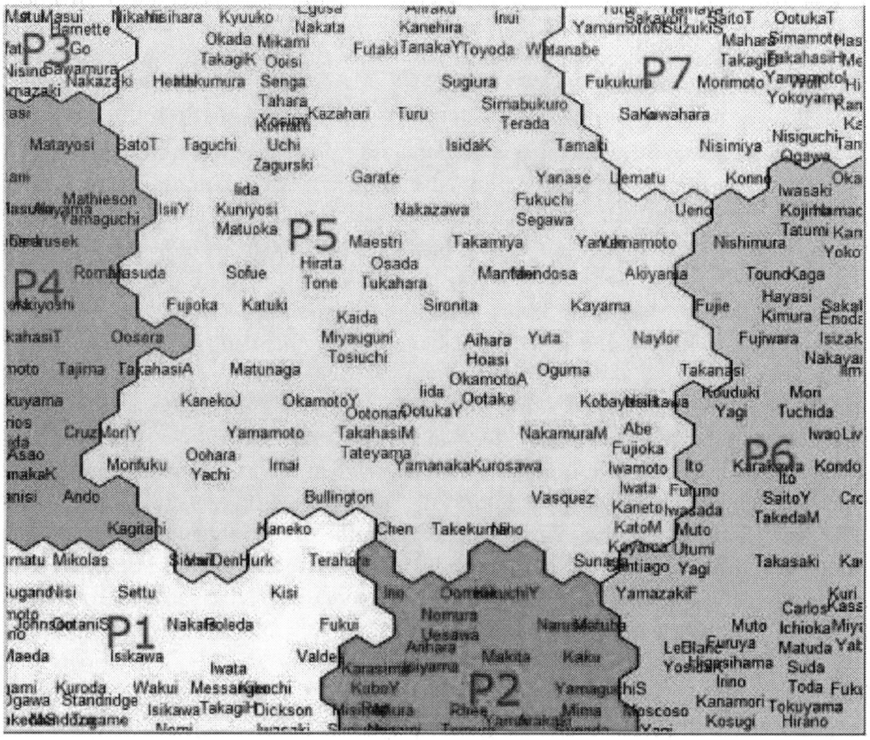

Fig. 1. Self-organizing cluster map of pitchers of all teams.

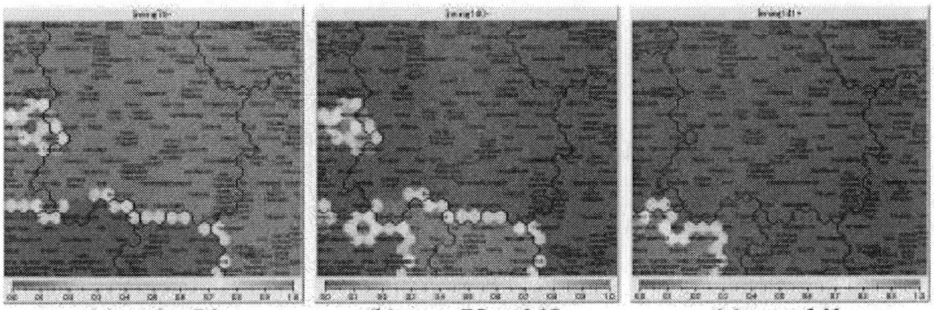

Fig. 2. Component map of pitchers of all teams: number of innings pitched.

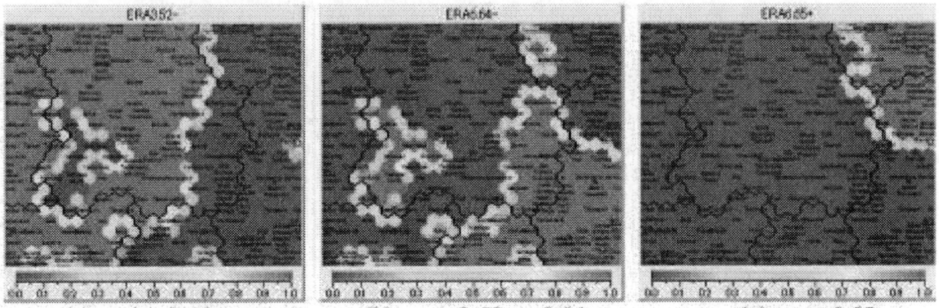

Fig. 3. Component map of pitchers of all teams: ERA (Earned Run Average).

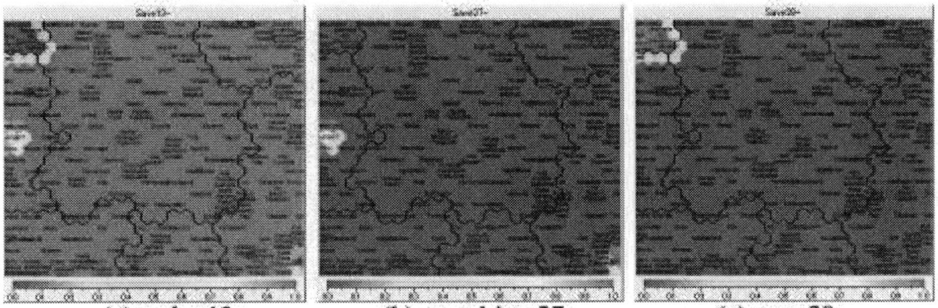

Fig. 4. Component map of pitchers of all teams: number of save.

There were seven clusters in Figure 1. When inspecting component maps, the feature of each cluster is clear. For example, red neurons correspond to over 141 innings pitched in Figure 2 (c) and red neurons correspond to over 75 to 140 innings pitched in Figure 2 (b). Red neurons correspond to under 3.52 ERA in Figure 3 (a) and red neurons correspond to over 3.53 to 6.64 ERA in Figure 3 (b). Red neurons correspond to over 28 save in Figure 4 (c).
As the number of innings pitched is large (over 141) and ERA is small (under 3.52) in cluster P1, a pitcher belonging to P1 is one of the best starting pitcher. As the number of innings pitched is medium (over 75 to 140) and ERA is medium (over 3.53 to 6.64) in cluster P2, a pitcher belonging to P2 is one of the second

best starting pitcher. As the number of save is large (over 28) and ERA is small (under 3.52) in cluster P3, a pitcher belonging to P3 is a *closer*. We inspected every component maps and understand that features of Clusters P1 to P7 are as shown in Table 2.

Table 2: Main features of all NPB pitchers in 2015 in each cluster.

Cluster	Features	Main feature
P1	Number of innings pitched is large. Both ERA and WHIP are small.	Best starting pitchers
P2	Number of innings pitched is medium. Both ERA and WHIP are medium.	Second best starting pitchers
P3	Number of save is large.	Closer
P4	Number of hold is large.	Best setup pitchers
P5	Number of wins and loses is small.	Third best starting pitchers or second best setup pitchers
P6	Number of wins and loses is small. Both ERA and WHIP are large.	Fourth best starting pitchers or third best setup pitchers
P7	Number of innings pitched is small. Both ERA and WHIP are large.	Bad pitchers

3 Considering Team Reinforcement Strategies

Next, we inputted the data of pitchers belonging to Chiba Lotte Marines into SOM and created pitcher maps. Figure 5 shows self-organizing pitcher maps of Lotte.

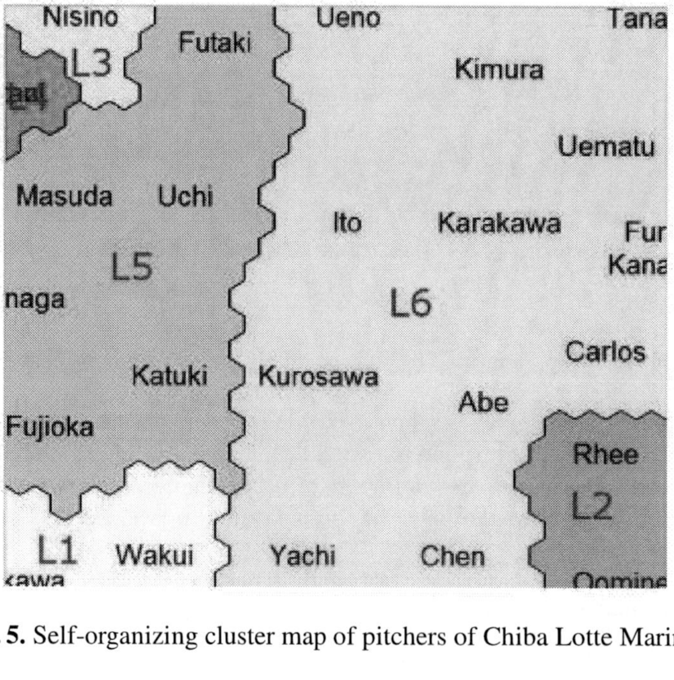

Fig. 5. Self-organizing cluster map of pitchers of Chiba Lotte Marines.

We inspected every component maps and understand that main feature of Clusters L1 to L6 are as shown in Table 3.

Table 3: Main features of pitchers of Chiba Lotte Marines in 2015 in each cluster.

Cluster	Main feature (# of pitchers)	Name (Cluster in all NPB pitchers)
L1	Best starting pitchers (2)	Wakui, Isikawa (P1)
L2	Second best starting pitchers (2)	Rhee, Oomine (P2)
L3	Closer (1)	Nisino (P3)
L4	Best setup pitchers (1)	Ootani (P4)
L5	Second best setup pitchers (6)	Masuda, Fujioka, Matunaga, Uchi, Niki (P5), katuki (P6)
L6	Substitutes (13)	Kurosawa, Yachi, Abe, Chen (P5), Kanamori, Furuya, Carlos (P6)

Here, we assumed that organization of pitchers in a strong team is as follows: the number of starting pitchers is five to six, the number of setup pitchers is one to two, the number of closer is one to two, and the number of relief pitchers is three to five. When comparing Lottes organization of pitchers with a strong teams organization, we understand that the number of starting pitchers is not enough.
Here, we chose alternatives for reinforcement strategies of starting pitchers as follows.

Step 1: We choose pitchers (1) who belong to Clusters P1, P2, P5 or P6, (2) whose contract have been expired or who declared *free agent,* and (3) whose number of innings pitched was large or whose percentage of hits he allows was small. We chose Stanridge and Bullington.

Step 2: We choose pitchers (1) who belong to Clusters P1, P2, P5 or P6, (2) who are young and whose salary is low, (3) whose number of innings pitched was medium or whose FIP was small or whose RSAA was not small. We chose Iida and Mima.

Table 4 shows the data of four alternatives for a reinforced starting pitcher.

Table 4: Data of alternatives for a reinforced starting pitcher.

Name	Innings pitched	Hit ratio	RSAA	FIP (million yen)	Salary	Age	Right/ left
Standridge	144.3	9.4	-0.52	3.79	200	37	right
Bullington	73.6	7.3	2.378	3.18	150	35	right
Mima	86.3	10.6	-7.035	3.53	40	29	right
Iida	41.3	6.5	2.169	3.19	4	24	left

Hit ratio: percentage of hits a pitcher allows,
Right/left: right throw or left throw.

4 Decision Making on Team Reinforcement Strategy with AHP

AHP is a multi-criteria decision method that uses hierarchical structures to represent a problem [7]. Pairwise comparisons are based on forming a judgment between two particular elements rather than attempting to prioritize an entire list of elements. The AHP scales of pairwise comparisons are shown in Table 5.

Table 5: The AHP scales for pairwise comparisons.

Intensity of importance	Definition and explanation
1	Equal importance
3	Moderate importance
5	Essential or strong importance
7	Demonstrated importance
9	Extreme importance
2, 4, 6, 8	Intermediate values between the two adjacent
	judgments when compromise is needed.

Figure 6 shows an example of the relative measurement AHP model created for the task of deciding a high capable pitcher. Here, we used the following four criteria: innings pitched, hit ratio (percentage of hits a pitcher allows), RSAA and FIP.

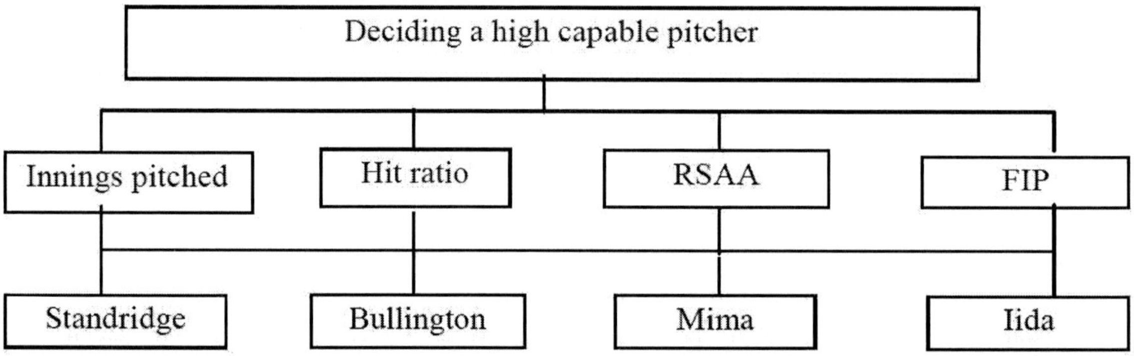

Fig. 6. AHP model for deciding a high capable pitcher.

We assumed the pairwise comparison matrix for Ciba Lotte Marines. The pairwise comparison matrix for the four criteria is shown in Table 6. Here, we assumed that large innings pitched is most important, small hit ratio is second most important, and small FIP is third most important. As a result, innings pitched is most important and its weight is 0.565.

Table 6: Pairwise comparisons of four criteria.

	Innings pitched	Hit ratio	RSAA	FIP	Weight
Innings pitched	1	3	7	5	0.565
Hit ratio	1/3	1	5	3	0.262
RSAA	1/7	1/5	1	1/3	0.055
FIP	1/5	1/3	3	1	0.118

Consistency index = 0.039

Consistency index shows whether the pairwise comparison is appropriate or not. When the index is lower than 0.1, the pairwise comparison is appropriate. When the index is over 0.1, the comparison is not appropriate and should be corrected. In this case, consistency index was 0.01 and the pairwise comparison was appropriate.

The pairwise comparisons of four alternatives with respect to innings pitched are shown in Table 7. The weight of Standridge was highest, because the number of innings pitched of Standridge was largest.

Table 7: Pairwise comparisons of alternatives with respect to innings pitched

	Standridge	Bullington	Mima	Iida	Weight
Standridge	1	6	5	8	0.636
Bullington	1/6	1	1/2	5	0.127
Mima	1/5	2	1	6	0.195
Iida	1/8	1/5	1/6	1	0.042

Consistency index = 0.086

The pairwise comparisons of four alternatives with respect to hit ratio are shown in Table 8. The weight of Iida was highest, because the hit ratio of Iida was smallest.

Table 8: Pairwise comparisons of alternatives with respect to hit ratio.

	Standridge	Bullington	Mima	Iida	Weight
Standridge	1	1/2	2	1/3	0.154
Bullington	2	1	4	1/2	0.288
Mima	1/2	1/4	1	1/5	0.081
Iida	3	2	5	1	0.477

Consistency index = 0.007

The pairwise comparisons of four alternatives with respect to RSAA are shown in Table 9. The weight of Bullington was highest, because the RSAA of Bullington was largest.

Table 9: Pairwise comparisons of alternatives with respect to RSAA

	Standridge	Bullington	Mima	Iida	Weight
Standridge	1	1/5	2	1/2	0.125
Bullington	5	1	6	3	0.577
Mima	1/2	1/6	1	1/3	0.077
Iida	2	1/3	3	1	0.222

Consistency index = 0.011

The pairwise comparisons of four alternatives with respect to FIP are shown in Table 10. The weight of Bullington was highest, because the FIP of Bullington was smallest.

Table 10: Pairwise comparisons of alternatives with respect to FIP.

Model	RMSE	R2	NSE	KGE	PBIAS
	Standridge	Bullington	Mima	Iida	Weight
Standridge	1	1/6	1/2	1/3	0.079
Bullington	6	1	5	2	0.533
Mima	2	1/5	1	1/2	0.130
Iida	3	1/2	2	1	0.253

Consistency index = 0.008

Table 11 shows final results of AHP. Standridge was the most capable pitcher, because we assumed that large innings pitched is most important and small hit ratio is second most important. The number innings pitched of Standridge is largest.

Table 11: Final results of deciding a high capable pitcher

Criteria	Innings pitched	Hit ratio	RSAA	FIP	Result
Weight of criteria	0.565	0.262	0.055	0.118	
Standridge	0.636	0.154	0.125	0.079	0.416
Bullington	0.127	0.288	0.577	0.533	0.242
Mima	0.195	0.081	0.077	0.130	0.151
Iida	0.042	0.477	0.222	0.253	0.191

Figure 7 shows an example of the relative measurement AHP model created for the task of deciding a reinforced starting pitcher. Here, we used the following five criteria: capability, salary, age, right/left throw and feasibility.

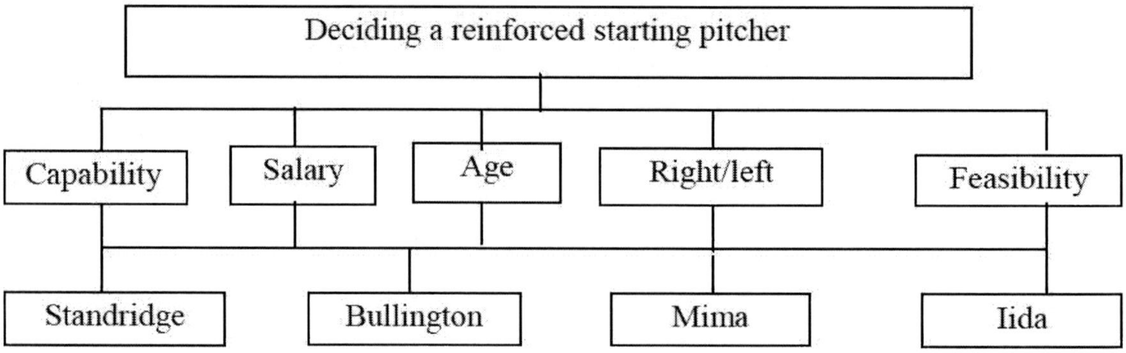

Fig. 7. AHP model for deciding a reinforced starting pitcher.

We assumed the pairwise comparison matrix for Chiba Lotte Marines. The pairwise comparison matrix for the five criteria is shown in Table 12. Here, we assumed that capability and feasibility are most important, and right/left throw is third most important. As a result, capability and feasibility are most important and their weights are 0.362.

Table 12: Pairwise comparisons of five criteria

	Capability	Salary	Age	Right/left	Feasibility	Weight
Capability	1	7	5	3	1	0.362
Salary	1/7	1	1/3	1/5	1/7	0.039
Age	1/5	3	1	1/3	1/5	0.076
Right/left	1/3	5	3	1	1/3	0.161
Feasibility	1	7	5	3	1	0.362

Consistency index = 0.034

The weights of four alternatives with respect to capability are shown in Table 11.

The pairwise comparisons of four alternatives with respect to salary are shown in Table 13. The weight of Iida was highest, because the salary of Iida was cheapest.

Table 13: Pairwise comparisons of alternatives with respect to salary.

	Standridge	Bullington	Mima	Iida	Weight
Standridge	1	1/2	1/4	1/6	0.074
Bullington	2	1	1/2	1/4	0.138
Mima	4	2	1	1/2	0.275
Iida	6	4	2	1	0.513

Consistency index = 0.004

The pairwise comparisons of four alternatives with respect to age are shown in Table 14. The weight of Iida was highest, because Iida is youngest.

Table 14: Pairwise comparisons of alternatives with respect to age

	Standridge	Bullington	Mima	Iida	Weight
Standridge	1	1/2	1/4	1/6	0.074
Bullington	2	1	1/2	1/4	0.138
Mima	4	2	1	1/2	0.275
Iida	6	4	2	1	0.513

Consistency index = 0.004

The pairwise comparisons of four alternatives with respect to right/left throw are shown in Table 15. The weight of Iida was highest, because left throw is a few and important for Chiba Lotte Marines.

Table 15: Pairwise comparisons of alternatives with respect to right/left.

	Standridge	Bullington	Mima	Iida	Weight
Standridge	1	1	1	1/2	0.2
Bullington	1	1	1	1/2	0.2
Mima	1	1	1	1/2	0.2
Iida	2	2	2	1	0.4

Consistency index = 0

The pairwise comparisons of four alternatives with respect to feasibilty are shown in Table 16. The weights of Standrige and Bullington were highest, because they declared *free agent.*

Table 16: Pairwise comparisons of alternatives with respect to feasibility

	Standridge	Bullington	Mima	Iida	Weight
Standridge	1	1	3	3	0.375
Bullington	1	1	3	3	0.375
Mima	1/3	1/3	1	1	0.125
Iida	1/3	1/3	1	1	0.125

Consistency index = 0

Table 17 shows final results of AHP. Standridge was the best. Because we assumed that capability and feasibility are most important. Capability and feasibilty of Standridge are highest. Standridge is selected as the final choice. Actually, Chiba Lotte Marines acquired Standridge as a reinforced starting pitcher.

Table 17: Final results of AHP

Criteria	Capability	Salary	Age	Right/left	Feasibility	Result
Weight of criteria	0.362	0.039	0.076	0.161	0.362	
Standridge	0.416	0.074	0.074	0.2	0.375	0.327
Bullington	0.242	0.138	0.138	0.2	0.375	0.271
Mima	0.151	0.275	0.275	0.2	0.125	0.164
Iida	0.191	0.513	0.513	0.4	0.125	0.238

5 Conclusion

We proposed a way of clustering professional baseball players with SOMs, considering several team reinforcement strategies using player maps, and deciding team reinforcement strategy with AHP. We used data of pitchers of Japanese professional baseball teams. We used data of pitchers in Japanese baseball teams. First, we collected data of 223 pitchers and clustered these pitchers using fourteen features. Second, we created pitcher maps of all teams and each team with SOM. Third, we examined main features of each cluster. Fourth, we considered team reinforcement strategies by using pitcher maps. Finally, we used AHP to determine the team reinforcement strategy. In future work, we will apply our way to the other sports such as football and basketball. We will use other types of AHP [7] and ANP [12] for decision making.

References

1. Tolbert, B., Trafalis, T.: Predicting Major League Baseball Championship Winners through Data Mining. Athens Journal of Sports. Retrieved from: https://www.athensjournals.gr/sports/2016-3-4-1-Tolbert.pdf (2016)
2. Ishii, T.: Using Machine Learning Algorithms to Identify Undervalued Baseball Players. Retrieved from: http://cs229.stanford.edu/proj2016/report/Ishii-UsingMachineLearningAlgorithmsToIdentifyUndervaluedBaseballPlayersreport.pdf (2016)
3. Pane, M.: Trouble with the Curve: Identifying Clusters of MLB Pitchers using Improved Pitch Classification Techniques. Retrieved from: http://repository.cmu.edu/cgi/viewcontent.cgi?article=1184&context=hsshonors (2013)
4. Tung, D.: Data Mining Career Batting Performances in Baseball. Retrieved from: http://vixra.org/pdf/1205.0104v1.pdf (2012)

5. Vazquez Fernandez de Lezeta, M.: Combining Clustering and Time Series for Baseball Forecasting. Retrieved from:
https://repositorio.uam.es/bitstream/handle/10486/661046/vazquez_fernandez_de_lezeta_miguel_tfg.pdf (2014)
6. Kohonen, T.: Self-Organizing Maps. Springer, New York (1995)
7. Saaty, T.: The Analytic Hierarchy Process. McGraw-Hill, New York (1980)
8. Kohara, K., Tsuda, T.: Creating Product Maps with Self-Organizing Maps for Purchase Decision Making. Transactions on Machine Learning and Data Mining, Vol.3, No. 2, 51-66 (2010)
9. Doizoe, J., Kohara, K.: Clustering and Visualization of Goods with SelfOrganizing Maps, Proc. of 70th Annual Convention of Information Processing Society of Japan, Vol.4, 911-912 (2008) (in Japanese)
10. NPB (Nippon Professional Baseball Organization). http://npb.jp/
11. Professional Baseball Data. http://baseballdata.jp/
12. Saaty, T.: The Analytic Network Process. Expert Choice, Arlington (1996)

A Novel Parallel Algorithm for Frequent Itemsets Mining in Large Transactional Databases

Huan Phan and Bac Le

University of Social Sciences and Humanities Vietnam
huanphan@hcmussh.edu.vn

Abstract. Since the era of data explosion, data mining in large transactional databases has become more and more important. There are many data mining techniques like association rule mining, the most important and well-researched one. Furthermore, frequent itemset mining is one of the fundamental but time consuming steps in association rule mining. Most of the algorithms used in literature find frequent itemsets on search space items having at least a minsup and are not reused for subsequent mining. Therefore, in order to decrease the execution time, some parallel algorithms have been proposed for mining frequent itemsets. Nonetheless, these algorithms merely implement the parallelization of Apriori and FP-Growth algorithms. To deal with this problem, several parallel NPA-FI algorithms are proposed as a new approach in order to quickly detect frequent itemsets from large transactional databases using an array of co-occurrences and occurrences of kernel item in at least one transaction. Parallel NPA-FI algorithms are easily used in many distributed file system, namely Hadoop and Spark. Finally, the experimental results show that the proposed algorithms perform better than other existing algorithms.

Keywords: Association rules, Co-occurrence items, Frequent itemsets, Parallel algorithm

1 Introduction

Mining frequent itemsets is a fundamental and essential problem in many data mining applications such as the discovery of association rules, strong rules, correlations, multi-dimensional patterns, and many other important discovery tasks. The problem is formulated as follows: Given a large database of set of items transactions, find all frequent itemsets, where a frequent itemset is one that occurs in at least a userspecified percentage of transaction database [4].

In the last three decades, most of the mining algorithms for frequent itemsets, proposed by various authors around the world, are based on Apriori [5] and FP-Tree [6,9]. Simultaneously to speed up the implementation of the mining frequent itemsets, authors worldwide propose the parallelization of algorithms based on the Apriori [1,7] and FP-Tree [8]. In this paper, we propose a novel sequential algorithm that mines frequent itemsets, and then, parallelizing the sequential algorithm to demonstrate the multi-core processors in an effective way as follows.

- **Algorithm 1:** Computing Kernel_COOC array of co-occurrences and occurrences of kernel item in at least one transaction;
- **Algorithm 2:** Generating all frequent itemsets based on Kernel_COOC array;
- Parallel **NPA-FI** algorithm quickly mining frequent itemsets from large transactional databases implemented on the multi-core processors.

This paper is organized as follows: in section 2, we describe the basic concepts for mining frequent itemsets, benchmark datasets description and data structure for transaction databases. Some theoretical aspects of our approach relies, are given in section 3. Besides, we describe our sequential algorithm to compute frequent itemsets on large transactional databases. After that we parallelize the proposed sequential algorithm. Details on implementation and experimental tests are discussed in section 4. Finally, we conclude with a summary of our approach, perspectives and extensions of this future work.

2 Background

2.1 Frequent Itemset Mining

Let $I = \{i_1, i_2, \cdots, i_m\}$ be a set of m distinct items. A set of items $X = \{i_1, i_2, \cdots, i_k\}, \forall i_j \epsilon I (1 \leq j \leq k)$ is called an itemset, an itemset with k items is called a $k - itemset$. **D** be a dataset containing n transaction, a set of transaction $T = \{t_1, t_2, \cdots, t_n\}$, and each transaction $t_j = \{i_{k1}, i_{k2}, \cdots, i_{kl}\}, \forall i_{kl} \epsilon I (1 \leq k_l \leq m)$.

Definition 1. The support of an itemset X is the number of transaction in which occurs as a subset, denoted as $sup(X)$.

Definition 2. Let $minsup$ be the threshold minimum support value specified by user. If $sup(X) \geq minsup$, itemset X is called a frequent itemset, denoted FI is the set of all the frequent itemset.

Property 1. $\forall X \subseteq Y$, if $sup(Y) \geq minsup$ then $sup(X) \geq minsup$.

Property 2. $\forall X \subset Y$, if $sup(X) < minsup$ then $sup(Y) < minsup$.

Table 1. The Transaction database D used as our running example.

TID	Items	TID	Items
t1	A C E F	t6	E
t2	A C G	t7	A B C E
t3	E H	t8	A C D
t4	A C D F G	t9	A B C E G
t5	A C E G	t10	A C E F G

Table 2. Mining frequent itemsets.

k-itemset	FI (minsup = 2)	FI (minsup = 3)	FI (minsup = 5)
1	D, B, F, G, E, A, C	F, G, E, A, C	G, E, A, C
2	BE, BA, BC, DA, DC, FE, FG, FA, FC, GE, GA, GC, EA, EC, AC	FA, FC, GE, GA, GC, EA, EC, AC	GA, GC, EA, EC, AC
3	BAC, BEA, DAC, FEA, BEC, FEC, FGA, CFG, FAC, GEA, GEC, EAC, GAC	FAC, GEA, GEC, GAC EAC	GAC, EAC
4	BEAC, FGAC, FEAC, GEAC	GEAC	

Example 1. See Table 1. There are eight different items $I = \{A, B, C, D, E, F, G, H\}$ and ten transactions $T = \{t1, t2, t3, t4, t5, t6, t7, t8, t9, 10\}$. Table 2 shows the frequent itemsets at three different minsup values - 2 (20%), 3 (30%) and 5 (50%) respectively.

2.2 Benchmark Description

Djenouri et al categorized the datasets: Three types of well-known instance details the characteristic of these benchmarks [10].

2.3 Data Structure for Transaction Database

The binary matrix is an efficient data structure for mining frequent itemsets [2,3]. The process begins with the transaction database transformed into a binary matrix BiM, in which each row corresponds to a transaction and each column corresponds to an item. Each element in the binary matrix BiM contains 1 if the item is presented in the current transaction; otherwise it contains 0.

Table 3. Datasets description.

Instance type	#Trans	#Items	#Avg. Length
Medium	6,000 *to* 9,000	500 *to* 16,000	2 *to* 500
Large	100,000 *to* 500,000	1,000 *to* 1,600	2 *to* 10
Big	*up* 1,600,000	*up* 500,000	

TID	A	B	C	D	E	F	G	H
t1	1	0	1	0	1	1	0	0
t2	1	0	1	0	0	0	1	0
t3	0	0	0	0	1	0	0	1
t4	1	0	1	1	0	1	1	0
t5	1	0	1	0	1	0	1	0
t6	0	0	0	0	1	0	0	0
t7	1	1	1	0	1	0	0	0
t8	1	0	1	1	0	0	0	0
t9	1	1	1	0	1	0	1	0
t10	1	0	1	0	1	1	1	0

Fig. 1. A binary matrix BiM representation of example transaction database.

3 The Proposed Algorithms

3.1 Generating Array of Co-occurrence Items of Kernel Item

In this part, we illustrate the framework of the algorithm generating co-occurrence items of items in transaction database.

Definition 3. Project set of item i_k on database $D : \pi(i_k) = \{t_j \epsilon D | i_k \subset t_j\}$ is is set of transaction contain item $i_k(\pi - decreasingmonotonic)$. According to Definition 1:

$$sup(i_k) = \mid \pi(i_k) \mid \quad (1)$$

Definition 4. Project set of itemset $X = \{i_1, i_2, \cdots, i_k\}, \forall i_{j=\overline{1,k}} \epsilon I : \pi(X) = \pi(i_1) \cup \pi(i_2) \cdots \pi(i_k)$.

$$sup(X) = \pi(X) \tag{2}$$

Definition 5. Let $i_k \epsilon I$ is called a kernel item. Itemset $X_{cooc} \subseteq I$ is called co-occurrence items with kernel item i_k, so that satisfy $\pi i_k \equiv \pi(i_k \cup X_{cooc})$. Denoted as $cooc(i_k) = X_{cooc}$.

Example 2. See Table 1. Consider item B as kernel item, we detect co-occurrence items with item B as $cooc(B) = \{A, C, E\}$ and $sup(B) = sup(BACE) = 2$.

Definition 6. Let $i_k \epsilon I$ is called a kernel item. Itemset $Y_{looc} \subseteq I$ is called occurrence items with kernel item i_k in as least one transaction,but not co-occurrence items, so that satisfy $1 \leq |\pi(i_k \cup i_{looc})| < |\pi(i_k)|, \forall i_{looc} \ \epsilon \ Y_{looc}$. Denoted as $looc(i_k) = Y_{looc}$.

Example 3: See Table 1. Consider item B as kernel item, we detect occurrence items with item B in as least one transaction $looc(B) = G$ and $\pi(BG) = \{t9\} \subset \pi(B) = \{t7, t9\}$.

Algorithm Generating Array of Co-occurrence Items

This algorithm is generating co-occurrence items of items in transaction database and archive into the *Kernel_COOC* array. Each element within the *Kernel_COOC*, 4 fields:

- Kernel_COOC[k].item : kernel item k;
- Kernel_COOC[k].sup : support of kernel item k;
- Kernel_COOC[k].cooc : co-occurrence items with kernel item k;
- Kernel_COOC[k].looc : occurrence items k kernel item in least one transaction.

The framework of **Algorithm 1** is as follows:

Algorithm 1. Generating Array of Co-occurrence Items

Input : Dataset D
Output: Kernel_COOC array, matrix BiM

foreach Kernel_COOC[k] **do**
Kernel_COOC[k].item = i_k
Kernel_COOC[k].sup = 0
Kernel_COOC[k].cooc = 2^m - 1
Kernel_COOC[k].looc = 0
foreach $t_j \epsilon T$ **do**
foreach $i_k \epsilon t_j$ **do**
Kernel_COOC[k].sup ++
Kernel_COOC[k].cooc = Kernel_COOC[k].cooc **AND** vectorbit(t_j)
Kernel_COOC[k].looc = Kernel_COOC[k].looc **OR** vectorbit(t_j)
sort Kernel_COOC array in ascending by support

We illustrate **Algorithm 1** on example database in Table 1.
Initialization of the Kernel_COOC array, number items in database m = 8;

Item	**A**	**B**	**C**	**D**	**E**	**F**	**G**	**H**
sup	0	0	0	0	0	0	0	0
cooc	11111111	11111111	11111111	11111111	11111111	11111111	11111111	11111111
looc	00000000	00000000	00000000	00000000	00000000	00000000	00000000	00000000

Read once of each transaction from $t1$ to $t10$

Transaction $t1 = \{A, C, E, F\}$ has vector bit representation **10101100**;

Item	**A**	**B**	**C**	**D**	**E**	**F**	**G**	**H**
sup	1	0	1	0	1	1	0	0
cooc	10101100	11111111	10101100	11111111	10101100	10101100	11111111	11111111
looc	10101100	00000000	10101100	00000000	10101100	10101100	00000000	00000000

Transaction $t2 = \{A, C, G\}$ has vector bit representation **10100010**;

Item	**A**	**B**	**C**	**D**	**E**	**F**	**G**	**H**
sup	2	0	2	0	1	1	1	0
cooc	10100000	11111111	10100000	11111111	10101100	10101100	10100010	11111111
looc	10101110	00000000	10101110	00000000	10101100	10101100	10100010	00000000

Transaction $t3 = \{E, H\}$ has vector bit representation **00001001**;

Item	**A**	**B**	**C**	**D**	**E**	**F**	**G**	**H**
sup	2	0	2	0	2	1	1	1
cooc	10100000	11111111	10100000	11111111	00001000	10101100	10100010	00001001

looc	10101110	00000000	10101110	00000000	10101101	10101100	10100010	00001001

Transaction $t4 = \{A, C, D, F, G\}$ has vector bit representation **10110110**;

Item	**A**	**B**	**C**	**D**	**E**	**F**	**G**	**H**
sup	3	0	3	1	2	2	2	1
cooc	10100000	11111111	10100000	10110110	00001000	10100100	10100010	00001001
looc	10111110	00000000	10111110	10110110	10101101	10111110	10110110	00001001

Transaction $t5 = \{A, C, E, G\}$ has vector bit representation **10101010**;

Item	**A**	**B**	**C**	**D**	**E**	**F**	**G**	**H**
sup	4	0	4	1	3	2	3	1
cooc	10100000	11111111	10100000	10110110	00001000	10100100	10100010	00001001
looc	10111110	00000000	10111110	10110110	10101111	10111110	10111110	00001001

Transaction $t6 = \{E\}$ has vector bit representation **00001000**;

Item	**A**	**B**	**C**	**D**	**E**	**F**	**G**	**H**
sup	4	0	4	1	4	2	3	1
cooc	10100000	11111111	10100000	10110110	00001000	10100100	10100010	00001001
looc	10111110	00000000	10111110	10110110	10101111	10111110	10111110	00001001

Transaction $t7 = \{A, B, C, E\}$ has vector bit representation **11101000**;

Item	**A**	**B**	**C**	**D**	**E**	**F**	**G**	**H**
sup	5	1	5	1	5	2	3	1
cooc	10100000	11101000	10100000	10110110	00001000	10100100	10100010	00001001
looc	11111110	11101000	11111110	10110110	11101111	10111110	10111110	00001001

Transaction $t8 = \{A, C, D\}$ has vector bit representation **10110000**;

Item	**A**	**B**	**C**	**D**	**E**	**F**	**G**	**H**
sup	6	1	6	2	5	2	3	1
cooc	10100000	11101000	10100000	10110000	00001000	10100100	10100010	00001001
looc	11111110	11101000	11111110	10110110	11101111	10111110	10111110	00001001

Transaction $t9 = \{A, B, C, E, G\}$ has vector bit representation **11101010**;

Item	**A**	**B**	**C**	**D**	**E**	**F**	**G**	**H**
sup	7	2	7	2	6	2	4	1
cooc	10100000	11101000	10100000	10110000	00001000	10100100	10100010	00001001

looc	11111110	11101010	11111110	10110110	11101111	10111110	11111110	00001001

The last, transaction $t10 = \{A, C, F, G, H\}$ has vector bit representation **10101110**;

Item	**A**	**B**	**C**	**D**	**E**	**F**	**G**	**H**
sup	8	2	8	2	7	3	5	1
cooc	10100000	11101000	10100000	10110000	00001000	10100100	10100010	00001001
looc	11111110	11101010	11111110	10110110	11101111	10111110	11111110	00001001

After the processing of **Algorithm 1**, the Kernel_COOC array as follows:

Table 5. Kernel_COOC array are ordered in support ascending order.

Item	**A**	**B**	**D**	**F**	**G**	**E**	**A**	**C**
sup	1	2	2	3	5	7	8	8
cooc	E	A,C,E	A,C	A,C	A,C		C	A
looc	G	F,G	D,E,G	B,D,E,F	A,B,C,F,G,H	B,D,E,F,G	B,D,E,F,G	

See Table 3, we have cooc(A) = $\{C\}$ and cooc(C) = $\{A\}$. In this case, the frequent itemset generated from A and C items will be duplicated. We provide a Definition 7, 8 to eliminate the duplication when generating frequent itemsets.

Definition 7.Let $i_k \epsilon I(i_1 \prec i_2 ... \prec i_m)$ items are ordered in support ascending order,i_k is called a kernel item. Itemset $X_{lexcooc} \subseteq I$ is called co-occurrence items with the kernel item i_k, so that satisfy $\pi(i_k) \equiv \pi(i_k \cup i_j)$,$i_k \epsilon i_j$, $\forall i_j \epsilon X_{lexcooc}$ Denoted as $lexcooc(i_k) = X_{lexcooc}$.

Definition 8.Let $i_k \epsilon I(i_1 \prec i_2 ... \prec i_m)$ items are ordered in support ascending order,i_k is called a kernel item Itemset $Y_{lexlooc} \subseteq I$ is called occurrence items with kernel item i_k in as least one transaction,but not co-occurrence items, so that satisfy $1 \leq \mid \pi(i_k \cup i_{lexlooc}) \mid < \mid \pi(i_k) \mid, \forall_i lexlooc \epsilon Y_{lexlooc}$. Denoted as $lexcooc(i_k) = Y_{lexcooc}$.

Additional command line 12, 13 and 14 into **Algorithm 1**:

12: **foreach** $i_k \epsilon t_j$ **do**
13: Kernel_COOC[k].cooc = lexcooc(i_k)
14: Kernel_COOC[k].looc = lexlooc(i_k)

We have looc(G) = {B, D, E, F}, where B,D $\prec$ F $\prec$ G $\prec$ {E}, so $lexlooc(G) = E$. Execute command line 12, 13 and 14 has result on Table 4.

Table 7. the Kernel_COOC array are co-occurrence items ordered in support ascending order.

Item	A	B	D	F	G	E	A	C
sup	1	2	2	3	5	7	8	8
cooc	E	A,C,E	A,C	A,C	A,C	ϕ	C	ϕ
looc	ϕ	G	F,G	G,E	E	A,C	ϕ	ϕ

3.2 Algorithm Generating All Frequent Itemsets

In this part, we illustrate the framework of the algorithm generating all frequent item-sets bases on the $Kernel_COOC$ array.

Lemma 1. $\forall\, i_k \epsilon$ I, if $sup(i_k) \geq minsup$ and $X_{lexcooc}$is powerset of $lexcooc(i_k)$ then $sup(i_k \cup x_{lexcooc}) \geq minsup$, $\forall x_{lexcooc} \epsilon X_{lexcooc}$.

Proof. According to Definition 8, (1) and (2): then $\pi(i_k) \equiv \pi(i_k \cup x_{lexcooc})$ and $sup(i_k) \geq minsup$.Therefore, we have $sup(i_k \cup x_{lexcooc}) \geq minsup$.

Example 4. See Table 4. Consider the item F as kernel item (minsup = 2), we detect co-occurrence items with the item F as $lexcooc(F)$ = {A,C} and $X_{lexcooc} = \{A, C, AC\}$ then $sup(FA) = sup(FC) = sup(FAC) = 3 \geq minsup$.

Lemma 2. $\forall\ i_k\ \epsilon$, $Y_{lexlooc}$ is powerset of $lexcooc(i_k), \forall y_{lexlooc} \epsilon Y_{lexlooc}$, if $sup(i_k \cup y_{lexlooc}) \geq minsup$ and $X_{lexcooc}$ is powerset of $lexcooc(i_k)$ then sup(i_k $\cup$ $y_{lexlooc} \cup x_{lexcooc}$) $\geq$ minsup, $\forall$ $x_{lexcooc}\ \epsilon\ X_{lexcooc}$.

Proof. According to Definition 8, 9: then $\mid \pi\ (i_k \cup y_{lexlooc}) \mid$ ¡ $\mid \pi(i_k) \mid = \mid \pi(i_k \cup x_lexcooc) \mid$ and sup($i_k \cup y_lexlooc$) $\geq$ minsup.Therefore we have sup($i_k \cup y_lexlooc \cup x_lexcooc$) $\geq$ minsup,$\forall$ $x_lexcooc\ \epsilon\ X_lexcooc$, $\forall$ $y_lexlooc\ \epsilon\ Y_lexlooc$.

Example 5. See Table 4. Consider the item G as kernel item (minsup = 2), we detect co-occurrence items with item G as $lexcooc(G) = \{A, C\}, X_lexcooc = \{A, C, AC\}; lexcooc(G) = E$ and $sup(GE) = 3 \geq minsup$ then $sup(GEA) = sup(GEC) = sup(GEAC) = 3 \geq minsup$.

The framework of Algorithm 2 is presented as follows:

Algorithm 2. Generating all frequent itemsets satisfy minsup

Input : minsup, Kernel_COOC array, Dataset D
Output: FI
1: **foreach** $Kernel\_COOC[k].sup \geq minsup$ **do**
2: FI[k] = i_k
3: **if**(Kernel_COOK[k].sup=minsup) **then**
4: Co ← GenSub(Kernel_COOC[k].cooc)//generating noempty subsets of cooc
5: **foreach** is_j ϵ CO **do**
6: $FI[k] = FI[k] \cup i_k \cup is_j$
7: **else**
8: **if**(Kernel_COOC[k].cooc =ϕ)**then**
9: Lo ← GenSub(Kernel_COOC[k].looc)//generating noempty subsets of looc
10: **foreach** $is_j \epsilon Lo$ **do**
11: $FI[k] = FI[k] \cup i_k \cup is_j$
12: **else**
13: Co ← GenSub(Kernel_COOC[k].cooc)
14: **foreach** is_j ϵ CO **do**
15: $F_t = F_t \cup i_k \cup is_j$
16: Lo ← GenSub(Kernel_COOC[k].looc)
17: **foreach** is_j ϵ LO **do**
18: $F_k = F_k \cup i_k \cup is_j$
19: **foreach** $f_i \epsilon f_t$ **do**
20: **foreach** is_j ϵ LO **do**
21: $FI[k] = FI[k] \cup f_i \cup is_j$
22: FI[k] = FI[k] $\cup F_t$
23: sort **FI** in descending by support

We illustrate **Algorithm 2** on example database in Table 1, and minsup = 3. After the processing **Algorithm 1**, the Kernel_COOC array in Table 5 is showed.

Line 3, consider items satisfying minsup as kernel items {F, G, E, A, C}; Consider kernel item F, sup(F) = 3 = minsup (Lemma 1- form line 5 to 6) generating all frequent with kernel item F as $FI_{[F]}$ = {(F, 3), (FA, 3), (FC, 3), (FAC, 3)}. Consider the kernel item G (from line 12 to 21): the powerset of co-occurrence items of kernel item G as set Co ={A, C, AC}, generating frequent itemsets F_t = {(GA, 5), (GA, 5), (GAC, 5)}; line 16 generating noempty subsets of looc field Lo = {E}, F_k = {GE} generating frequent itemsets $FI_{[G]}$ = {(G, 5), (GA, 5), (GC, 5), (GAC, 5), (GE, 3), (GEA, 3), (GEC, 3), (GEAC, 3)}.

Consider the kernel item E (from line 8 to 11) – generating noempty subsets of looc field Lo = {A, C, AC}, line 10 and 11 generating frequent itemsets $FI_{[E]}$ = {(E, 7), (EA, 5), (EC, 5), (EAC, 5)}.

Consider the kernel item A (similary kernel item G): Co = {C}, F_t ={(AC, 8)}, Lo = {ϕ}, F_k = {ϕ} generating frequent itemsets $FI_{[A]}$ = {(A, 8), (AC, 8)}. Consider the kernel item C (similary kernel item E): Lo = {ϕ} generating fre-quent itemsets $FI_{[C]}$ = {(C, 8)}.

Table 9. All frequent itemsets satisfy minsup = 3 (example database in Table 1).

Kernel item	Frequent itemsets - **FI**	
F	(F,3)	(FA,3) (FC,3) (FAC,3)
G	(GE,3)	(GEA,3) (GEC,3) (GEAC,3) (GA,5) (GC,5) (GAC,5) (G,5)
E	(EC,5)	(EA,5) (EAC,5) (E,7)
A	(A,8)	(AC,8)
C	(C,8)	F,G

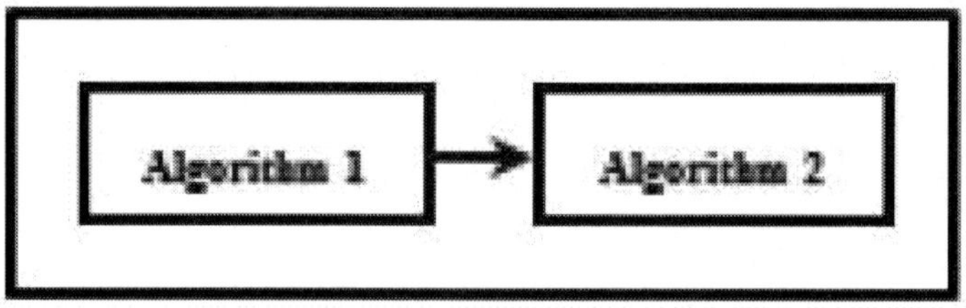

Fig. 2. The diagram sequential algorithm for frequent itemsets mining (SEQ-FI).

3.3 Parallel NPA-FI Algorithm Generating All Frequent Itemsets

In this section, we illustrate parallel algorithms and experimental setup on the multicore processors (MCP). We proposed a parallel **NPA-FI** algorithm for because it quickly detects frequent itemsets on MCP using **Algorithm 1** and **Algorithm 2**.

The parallel **NPA-FI** algorithm for generating all frequent itemsets, including 2 phases:

- Phase 1: Computing Kernel_COOC array by parallelization **Algorithm 1**;
- Phase 2: Generating all frequent itemsets by parallelization **Algorithm 2**;

Phase 1 - Parallelization **Algorithm 1** is shown in the diagram:

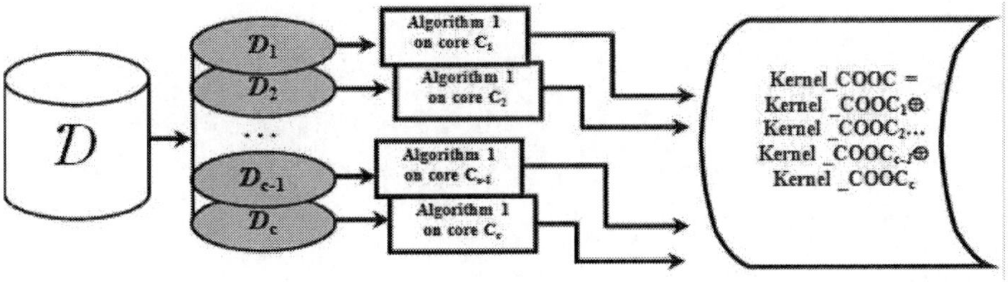

Fig. 3. The diagram parallelization Phase 1.

In Figure 3, we split the transaction database D into c (number of core on CPU) parts $D_1, D_2, ..., D_c$.After that, the core j^{th} executes **Algorithm 1** with input transaction database D_j, output the $Kernel\_COOC_{D}j$ array.The $Kernel\_COOC_D$ array for the transaction database D, we compute the following equation:

$$Kernel\_COOC_{Dj} = Kernel\_COOC_{D1} \oplus Kernel\_COOC_{D2} \oplus ... \oplus Kernel\_COOC_{Dc} \tag{3}$$

$\oplus$ denoted as **sum** for *sup*, **AND** for *cooc*, **OR** for *looc* field of each element array.
The next step, we sort the Kernel_COOC array in ascending order by supporting, executing commands line 12, 13 and 14 of the **Algorithm 1**.

Example 6. See Table 1. We split the transaction database D into 2 parts: the data-base D_1 consists 5 transaction $\{t1, t2, t3, t4, t5\}$ and database D_2 consists 5 transaction $\{t6, t7, t8, t9, t10\}$.

The processing of **Algorithm 1** on database D_1

Item	A	B	C	D	E	F	G	H
sup	4	0	4	1	3	2	3	1
cooc	10100000	11111111	10100000	10110110	00001000	10100100	10100010	00001001
looc	10111110	00000000	10111110	10110110	10101111	10111110	10111110	00001001

The processing of **Algorithm 1** on database D_2

Item	A	B	C	D	E	F	G	H
sup	4	2	4	1	4	1	2	0
cooc	10100000	11101000	10100000	10110000	00001000	10101110	10101010	11111111
looc	11111110	11101010	11111110	10110000	11101110	10101110	11101110	00000000

Results of equation (3), we have the Kernel_COOC array as presented in Table 5. Phase 2 Parallelization of **Algorithm 2** is shown in the diagram:

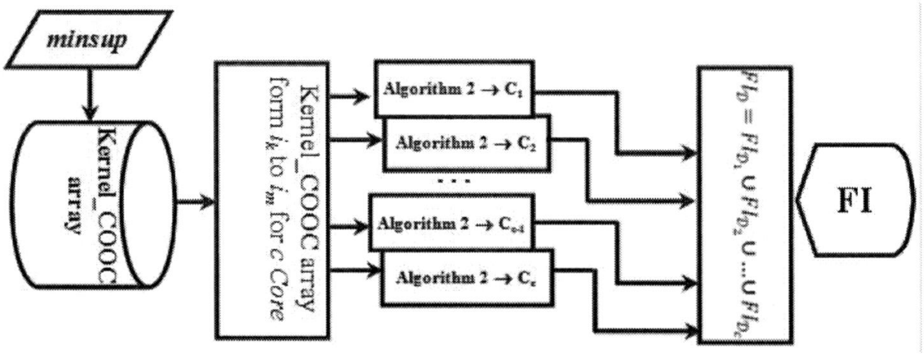

Fig. 4. The diagram parallelization Phase 2.

In Figure 4, we split the $Kernel\_COOC_D$ array from element i_k to $i_m(sup(i_k) \geq minsup)$ into c parts. After that, the core j th execute **Algorithm 2** with input $Kernel\_COOC_D$ array from $k+(j-1)*((m-k+1)divc)$ to $k+j*((m-k+1)divc)$ element returns results frequent itemsets FI_{Dj}. The frequent itemsets FI_D for the transaction database D, we compute the following equation:

$$FI_D = FI_{D1} \cup FI_{D2} \cup ... \cup FI_{Dc} \quad (4)$$

Example 7. See Table 1. Generating all frequent itemsets satisfy minsup= 3, the transaction database D split into 2 parts as Example 6. Results of phase 1 paralleliza-tion, we have the $Kernal\_COOC_D$ array as Table 5.

The processing of **Algorithm 2** on the Kernel_COOC array form item F to E:

Kernel item	Frequent itemsets - FI_{D1}	
F	(F,3)	(FA,3) (FC,3) (FAC,3)
G	(GE,3)	(GEA,3) (GEC,3) (GEAC,3) (GA,5) (GC,5) (GAC,5) (G,5
E	(EC,5)	(EA,5) (EAC,5) (E,7)

The processing of **Algorithm 2** on the Kernel_COOC array form item A to C:

Kernel item	Frequent itemsets - FI_D1

A	(A,8)	(AC,8)
C	(C,8)	

Results of equation (4), we have all frequent itemsets as presented in Table 6.

4 Experiments

All experiments were conducted on a PC with a Core Duo CPU T2500 2.0 GHz *(2 Cores, 2 Threads)*, 4Gb main memory, running Microsoft Windows 7 Ultimate. All codes were compiled using C#, Microsoft Visual Studio 2010, .Net Framework 4.
We experimented on two instance types of datasets:

- Two real datasets that belong to medium instance are form of UCI Machine Learning Repository [http://archive.ics.uci.edu/ml] as **Pumsb** and **Retail** datasets.
- Two synthetic datasets that belong to large instance using the software are generated by IBM Almaden Research Center [http://www.almaden.ibm.com] as **T40I1KD100K** and **T40I1KD200K** datasets.

Table 13. Datasets description in experiments.

Instance type	Name	#Trans	#Items	#Avg.Length	Type
Medium	Pumsb	49,046	2,113	74	Dense
	Retail	88,162	16,470	10	Sparse
Large	T40I1KD100K	100,000	1,000	40	Sparse
	T40I1KD200K	200,000	1,000	40	Sparse

Deng et al, proposed the **PrePost** [9] algorithm for constructing a FP-tree-like and mining frequent itemsets from a database. In recent years, **PrePost** algorithm shows the better performance result. We have compared the parallel **NPA-FI** algorithm with sequential algorithms (SEQ-FI) and **PrePost** algorithm.

Performance implementation parallel NPA-FI algorithm on multi-core processors:

$$P = 1 - \left(T_M - \frac{T_S}{c}\right) \Big/ \left(\frac{T_S}{c}\right) \tag{5}$$

Where:

1. T_S : executing time of the sequential algorithm;

2. T_M executing time of the parallel algorithm;
3. c number of the core on CPU.

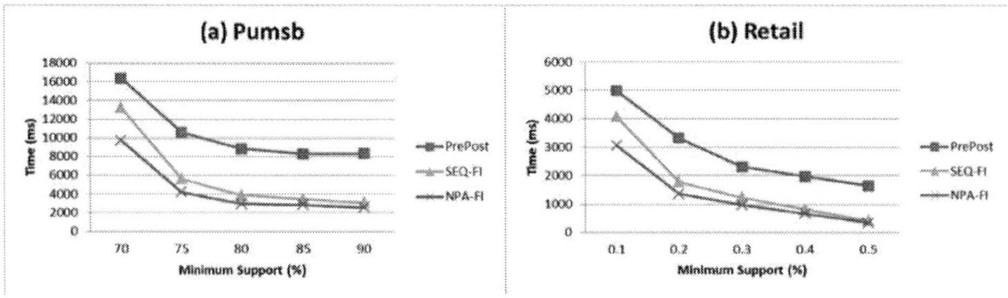

Fig. 5. Running time of the three algorithms on Medium datasets.

Figure 5 (a) and (b) show the running time of the compared algorithms on medium datasets **Pumsb** and **Retail**. **SEQ-FI** runs faster **PrePost** algorithm under all minimum supports; **NPA-FI** runs faster **SEQ-FI** algorithm. Average performance of the parallel **NPA-FI** algorithm in turn: **Pumsb** as $\bar{P} = 0.78$; $\sigma = 0.048$ and Retail as $\bar{P}= 0.79$; $\sigma = 0.032$. Fig.

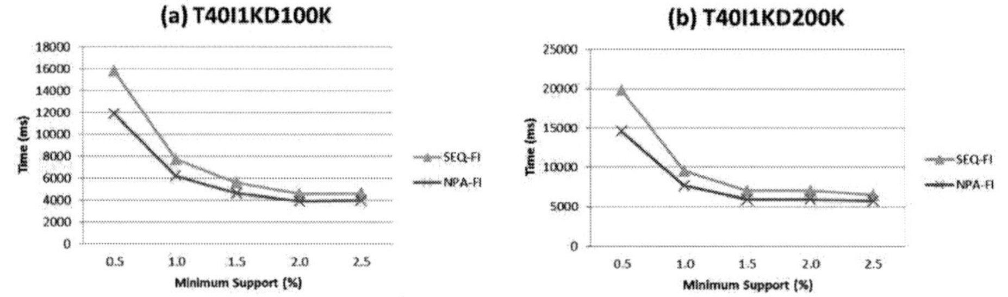

Fig. 6. Running time of the two algorithms on Large datasets

Figure 6 (a) and (b) show the running time of the compared algorithms on large datasets **T40I1KD100K** and **T40I1KD200K**. **PrePost** algorithm fails to frequent itemsets mining on large datasets; **NPA-FI** runs faster **SEQ-FI** algorithm. Average performance of the parallel **NPA-FI** algorithm in turn: **T40I1KD100K** as $\bar{P}= 0.81$; $\sigma = 0.045$ and **T40I1KD200K** as $\bar{P} = 0.81$; $\sigma = 0.052$.

In summary, experimental results suggest the following ordering of these algorithms as running time is concerned: **SEQ-FI** runs faster **PrePost** algorithm;

NPA-FI runs faster **SEQ-FI** algorithm. Average performance of the parallel **NPA-FI** algorithm on datasets experimental is $\bar{P}= 0.80$; $\sigma= 0.042$.

5 Conclusion

In this paper, we have proposed a sequential architecture mining frequent itemsets on large transaction databases, consisting of two phases: the first phase, quickly detect a the Kernel_COOC array of co-occurrences and occurrences of kernel item in at least one transaction; the second phase, the algorithm is proposed for fast mining all frequent itemset based on Kernel_COOC array. Besides, when using mining frequent itemsets with other minsup value then the proposed algorithm only performs mining frequent itemsets based on the Kernel_COOC array that is calculated previously, reducing the significant processing time. The next step, we develop a sequential algorithm for mining frequent itemsets and thus parallelize the sequential algorithm to effectively demonstrate the multi-core processors. The experimental results show that the proposed algorithms perform better than other existing algorithms.

The results from the algorithm proposed: In the future, we will expand the algorithm to be able to mining frequent itemsets on weighted transaction databases, as well as to expand the parallel NPA-FI algorithm on distributed computing systems such as Hadoop, Spark.

References

1. Agrawal R., Shafer J.: Parallel mining of association rules. IEEE Transactions on Knowledge and Data Engineering 8, 962?969 (1996).
2. Dong J., Han M.: BitTableFI: An efficient mining frequent itemsets algorithm. Knowledge-Based Systems 20(4), 329?335 (2007).
3. Song W., Yang B.: Index-BitTableFI: An improved algorithm for mining frequent itemsets. Knowledge-Based Systems 21, 507?513 (2008).
4. Philippe F. V., Jerry C. W. L., Bay V., Tin C. T., Ji Z., Bac L.: A survey of itemset mining.Wiley Interdisc. Rew - Data Mining and Knowledge Discovery, 7(4) (2017).
5. Agrawal R., Imilienski T., Swami A.: Mining association rules between sets of large databases. Proceedings of the ACM SIGMOD International Conference on Management of Data, Washington, DC, pp. 207?216 (1993).
6. Han J., Pei J., and Yin Y.: Mining frequent patterns without candidate generation. In Proc. 2000 ACM-SIGMOD Int. Conf. Management of Data (SIGMOD?00), Dallas, TX, pp. 1? 12 (2000).
7. Lin M. Y., Lee P. Y., Hsueh S. C.: Apriori-based frequent itemset mining algorithms on MapReduce, Proc of the 6th International Conference on Ubiquitous Information Management and Communication, New York, NY, USA, pp. 76?76 (2012).

8. Moonesinghe H. D. K., Chung M. J., and Tan P. N.: Fast parallel mining of frequent itemsets. Technical Report No. 2, Department of Computer Science and Engineering, Michigan State University, (2006).
9. Deng Z. H., Wang Z. H. and Jiang J. J.: A new algorithm for fast mining frequent itemsets using N-lists. Science China Information Sciences, 55(9), 2008-2030 (2012).
10. Djenouri Y., Bendjoudi A., Djenouri D., Habbas Z.: Parallel Processing and Applied Mathematics, ISBN 978-3-319-32148-6, pp.258-268, (2016).

Using Clusters in network threat detection

Tsigkritis Theocharis[1], Groumas Georgios[2], and Schneider Moti[3]

MSDS R&D, PCCW Global, Athens, Greece
{ttsigkritis, gggroumas, mschneider }@pccwglobal.com

Abstract. We describe a process to identify suspicious behaviors of network entities. We utilize the dynamical clustering approach to create clusters to classify behaviors from collected data and fuzzy matching to identify threatful activities. We will de-scribe the process of creating the clusters, present the different algorithms related to the process and discuss the results.

Keywords: network security; clusters; fuzzy logic, similarity measures

1 Introduction

1.1 General

Network threats are proliferating globally and at an unprecedented rate. To improve overall security posture, prevent intrusion [9,20] by detecting anomaly behavior [13] and outliers [19], organizations require a real-time analysis of network & network security events to determine quickly and accurately insights regarding network security status [4]. This objective, however, is getting more difficult in cases where networks of different entities have different level & quality of information is available.

In network infrastructures there are many distributed or centralized entity types (e.g., network nodes, network elements, network components or devices, subnets, IPs, spe-cific service an IP uses), The challenge of network and security monitoring is to detect or determine unusual or suspicious activity corresponding to a network entity on a stream of network and security events of extreme volume and velocity. Events can be distinguished from each other by attributes, which can be either categorical (e.g. location, Autonomous Systems Numbers (ASN) [17] or numerical (e.g. packet count, payload size of a session).

1.2 Related work

Many classification techniques are used to determine fraud behavior. But those approaches can only predict already well known attacks [21,22] and are easily out-dated due to the evolution of the methods used by the attackers. Many different algorithms were introduced to fight intrusion and detect anomaly in the network or cloud. Examples are: k-nearest neighbor [3][7][16], local outlier factor [6], outlier detection for high-dimensional data [19] support vector machines [12], neural net-works [15], Cluster analysis-based outlier detection [14], association rules and fre-quent itemsets, and fuzzy logic based outlier detection [23].

We used the clustering approach. Clustering is an unsupervised method to group data points into groups such that the data points within a group are similar to each other and very dissimilar to data points in different groups. There are several different clustering algorithms. Probably the most popular clustering algorithm is the K-means algorithm [1,8] that has two different approaches. In the first one, the user predefines the number of clusters (K) and places the data points based on the dis-tance between the data points and the centers of the clusters [10]. In the second ap-proach, the dynamic approach, where the user defines the inner distance between the data points within the clusters, and assigns the data accordingly [2]. Another method to generate clusters is via the hierarchical method [1].

Another interesting approach is the fuzzy approach and let an element to belong to multi clusters. Each sample can be assigned to multiple clusters with [23]. Bezdek [5] used fuzzy logic to create clusters. We use the dynamic approach to K-means clustering method, by using fuzzy logic for the matching process. This will be dis-cussed further below.

1.3 The Data Set

The features we used for our approach are aggregated metrics and could be split into four categories, namely traffic related (e.g number of connections, emails, num-ber of unique external IPs, number of unique countries, number of unique services), security related (e.g threat logs, failed logins, spam emails), policy violations (e.g fire-wall blocks, access control blocks) and list of categorical at-tributes set (e.g services used, location, ASN).

2 Fuzzification as a similarity measure

The most fundamental concept of the fuzzy set theory is the membership func-tion. This function computes the distance of an element to the center of the fuzzy set. It can be assumed that the center of the fuzzy set is a place where the membership grade is 1. We also can assume that it is possible to convert any number to a fuzzy term by defining the terms borders.

This means that any value can transformed from being a singleton to being a fuzzy term. The membership grade of 1 represents the original center point of the cluster, and the two end points represent the borders of the membership function (as displayed below).

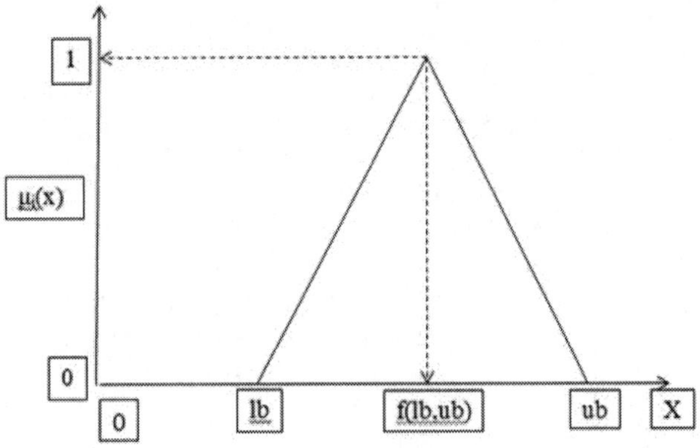

Fig. 1. Logical structure of the fuzzy term.

To match between a new data D and C, we only need to perform the fuzzification process. The fuzzification process filters the domain data D through the membership function to get the membership grade as shown below. The fuzzification process has two major advantages; it avoids the need to normalize the data base and it is the matching process itself. In the following section, we present the process of cluster creation.

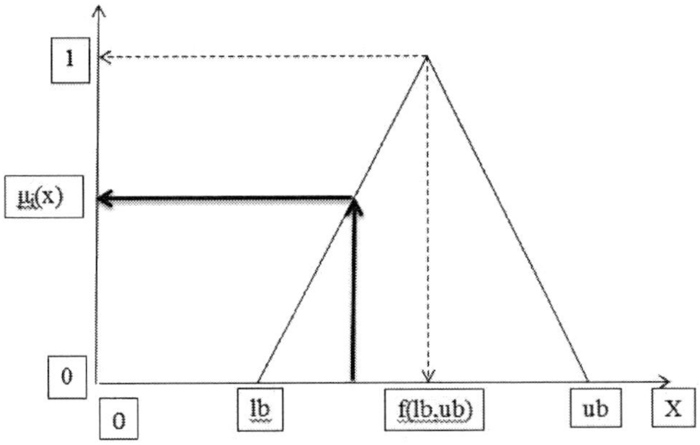

Fig. 2. Example of a fuzzy variable.

3 The clustering system

3.1 Overview

Clusters are defined as groups of data points that are closely similar to each other. On the other hand, the clusters themselves have to be as far as possible from each other to be easily distinguishable.

In the clustering environment, we test how well the clusters recognize a set of given data points. When simulating the performance, we create the clusters with one set of data and test it with another. The most important concern we have is to make sure that the learning data set and the testing data set will be different. To avoid bias, we require that the learning data set will be created randomly.

There are two major procedures to create the clusters:

- Fixed cluster construction – In this approach we define a priory the number of clusters we want to create
- Variable cluster construction – Here we let the system to determine the optimal number of clusters, based on a set of parameters that will be described later.

In our approach, we chose the dynamic approach to create clusters. That is, we let the system to determine the optimal number of clusters. When the process of constructing clusters is completed, the center of each cluster is transformed into a fuzzy term associated with some fuzzy membership function.

Fig. 3 illustrates the overview of our clustering system, based on the above remarks. Please note that from a given data set, a learning data set is created by randomly selected data points and is used for the cluster creation process (right leaf in Fig. 3), while the remaining data points are used for the testing process (left leaf in Fig. 3). Both cluster creation and testing processes will be discussed in the following sections.

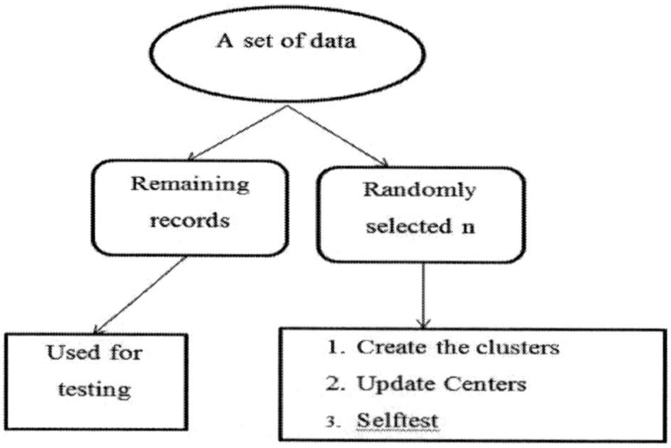

Fig. 3. Clustering system overview.

3.2 Creating the Learning Data Set

As mentioned above, the most important concern we have is to make sure that the learning data set and the testing data set will be different. To avoid bias, we require that the learning data set will be created randomly. In the following, we present our learning data set creation process.

1. Let n be the size of the complete data set. Choose a random number r such that
   $0.4 * n < r < 0.6 * n$
   In other words, we want the learning data set be about half of the size of the en-tire data set.
2. From the entire data set choose r different data points:
   For i=1 to r do
   Generate a random number m between 1 and n
   If m − th data point in the initial data set is not in the learning data set, add it to the learning data set

At the end of this process we have created a data set containing r different and randomly chosen data points from the initial data set.

3.3 The Matching Process

The matching process is a fundamental sub-process in cluster creation process. The matching process compares two data points to find out their similarity. These two data points are the center of the cluster and a new incoming data. A data point is defined as a collection of variables, each with a different type and each has a differ-ent weight. In other words, the data that is collected and analyzed contain many attributes. Some of these attribute may be more important (or influential) than oth-ers. This importance can be expressed as the weight of the attribute (or variable). In our final decision making we will take the weight into account. If the variables are numeric then the result is numeric within [0,1]. Otherwise, it is Boolean, i.e. 1 if the two attributes are identical and 0 otherwise.

This can be summarized graphically in Fig.4:

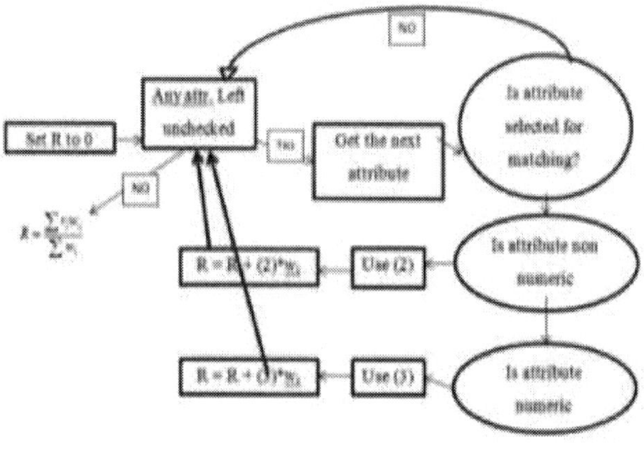

Fig. 4. The matching process.

So, the matching process can be summarized as follows, assuming that ac be the attribute of the cluster center and ad is the attribute of the testing data point.

- In case that a_c and a_d are Boolean or linguistic data then:

$$r_i = \begin{cases} 1, & \text{if } a_c, a_d \quad are \quad identical \\ 0, & \text{otherwise} \end{cases} \tag{1}$$

- In case that a_c and a_d are numeric then matching r_i is the fuzzification process of ad in a_c:

$$r_i = \mu_{a_c}(a_d) \tag{2}$$

To take into account each attributes weight, we add the results from all the matches performed on the attributes of the two data points, such that the final result R is defined as:

$$R = \frac{\sum r_i w_i}{\sum w_i} \tag{3}$$

where r_i is the matching result and w_i is the attribute weight. It is important to note that all the posterior information is not included in the matching process. This includes the IP number, IP group number, and the information whether or not this record represents a false activity.

3.4 The process of creating clusters

As mentioned above, we test how well the clusters recognize a set of given data points. When simulating the performance, we create the clusters with one set of data and test it with another. To avoid bias, we require that the learning data set will be created randomly. The process of creating clusters is divided into three steps:

1. **Creating the clusters**. We choose a data point and assign it to the first cluster. This data point becomes the center of the cluster. Then we pick the next point match it against the first cluster. If R (3) is above some threshold T, then we add the new data point to the cluster. If not, we create the second cluster and assign the new data point as the center of the second cluster. We repeat the process until every da-ta point belongs to some cluster.
2. **Updating the centers of the clusters**. For each attribute, if the attribute is numeric we compute the average value of the attribute, and if not we do not alter the value of the center.
3. **Self-testing**. After changing the centers of the clusters, we have to repeat the pro-cess of matching (as described in step 1) to ensure that data points did not move to other clusters. That will ensure stability of the learning process. If there was a change, go back to step 1, and repeat the process.

By the end of the clusters creation process we have several clusters that have data points that are very similar, and each cluster is distinctively far from other clusters. This fact will ensure a better recognition and classification during testing.

4 The Testing Procedure

In this stage, as illustrated below, we match a new incoming data point that represents an IP behavior with the set of clusters defined above. We define two classes, threat and normal. A data point that belongs to threat class is associated with at least one threat event. On the other hand, a data point, and therefore its related IP behavior, which belongs to normal class, is not associated with any threat and security events. If the data point is correctly assigned to its class, we have a true identification else we have a false identification. Briefly, we take a data point from the test file and compare it with the clusters. If the similarity between the cluster set and the data point is above a certain threshold, then we have a match. Also, if we do have a match, the procedure supplies the index of the specific cluster that was matched against the data.

The above process can be specified as follows:

1. Match the new incoming data point against the clusters center.
2. If the matching result (R) is above a given threshold, then go to step 5, else go to 3.
3. If the matching result is less than the threshold, move the index to the next cluster
4. Go to 1.
5. Extract the cluster that recognized the new data point. Lets call it C.
6. From C, create a set of data points that have the same IP as the data point in question. Denote this list as L.
7. Count the number of threats/normal data records in L. Let L_t and L_n be the threat/normal subsists, respectively, then we define the threat ratio and the normal ratio as:

$$Tratio = \frac{\mid L_t \mid}{\mid L_t \mid + \mid L_n \mid} \tag{4}$$

and

$$Nratio = \frac{| L_n |}{| L_t | + | L_n |} \tag{5}$$

8. If the threat ratio (Tratio) is above a threshold, and the data point is a threat, then we mark a success.
9. If the normal ratio (Nratio) is above a threshold and the data point is normal, then we mark a success.
10. Otherwise we mark a failure.
11. Get the next data point to be tested (if there is one and go back to step 1). If not exit the loop.

So, the idea is to assign the data point in question with one of the following categories:

1. The incoming data records IP indicates threat behavior.
2. The incoming data records IP does not indicates threat behavior.
3. The incoming data records IP group is a threat group. A threat group is defined as a group of IPs most of its IPs have a threatful behavior.
4. The incoming data records IP group is not a threat group.

We check one option at the time until we find a similarity. If nothing found, we place the result in the outlier bin. This may indicate a new type of data point or a corrupted one. With respect to threat class, our clustering system can check whether:

The above procedure is illustrated in Fig. 5.

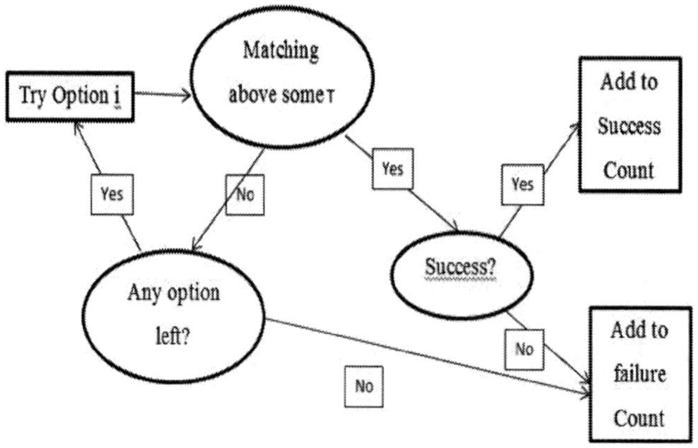

Fig. 5. Testing the system using clusters

5 Parameters Configuration

In this section we describe how to choose the best attributes from the data base. The learning system determines which variables will be used in identifying a threat, and the best values for the chosen variables.

5.1 Choosing Variables and Possible Values

In our system we chose all the variables that can contribute to the identification of a threat. Different variables have different values. Due to the fact that some of the variables are Boolean, we can assign them the values 0 or 1. Some variables are linguistic (i.e. have a finite non numeric values), so we need to check all possible values. Other variables are numeric. In this case we have to choose some representative values. For example, the variable threshold is numeric. It represents how well a certain record matches the set of clusters. It is logical to assume that the matching should be between 0.7 and 1. In other words, if the matching between the record and the cluster center is below 0.7 then it should not be accepted as a member of that cluster. We divided the range of accepted matches to low (above 0.7), medium (above 0.85) and high (above or equal to 0.99). The more options we provide, the more complex will be the computation (this will be described below).

After examining all the variables, we create a multivariable loop. Let x_i be a variable of type integer. Also, x_i corresponds to a real variable (such as threshold, etc.), y_i. Also let a_i be the lowest value in the domain of x_i and b_i the highest value in this domain. So a simple loop will be:
For $x_i = a_i$ to b_i do S,
where S is an executable statement.
In the example above the loop will execute from 0 to 2, such that the value 0 in x_i corresponds to 0.7 in the real variable threshold. It should be noted that the number of permutations can be large. In particular, for a set of n variables, let P be the number of permutations, so, we have:
P=$X_1 \times X_2 \times ... \times X_{n-1}$

Generally, the algorithm for variable selection is O(t*2n). t: the number of threshold's levels (e.g. 3, levels:[0.7 , 0.85 ,0.99]) n: the number of features (e.g 7,[firewall_block_count, failed_login_count, email_count, spam_count, msg_bytesize, orgid, value])

Each Boolean variable shows if some numerical variable participates in the computation. For example, If the 6th Boolean is set to false, this means that the numerical variable orgid does not participate in the simulation. So, in this case P=27*3*3 1 =1151 cases. So, in the first stage we simulate the system with all possible values. This means that we run the simulation 1151 times (we omit the case where all Boolean variables are false) and place the simulation results on some file. The result file contains all the results computed above. It also contains the information regarding the variables participated in the simulation. After this first stage is completed we proceed to the tune up stage.

5.2 Tuning up and testing

The tuning up process deals with finding the best values for the variables chosen to be part of the system. The learning system determines which variables will be used in identifying a threat, and the best values for the chosen variables.

As was stated, first we choose all the variables that can contribute to the identifica-tion of a threat. Basically, these are all the variables in the database containing numeric or Boolean information. Different variables have different values. After running the system once, we get P different results (in our case p=1151). From this set we choose the cases that their Success rate is the highest. In other words, we choose the permutations that generated the best results in the matching of the new data point with the clustering system to find out if the new data point is a threat or not.

If we select more than one case, we observe the number of outliers (# of cases the system rejects). In our system we allow less than 10% of outliers (from the given test files). The reason for having a threshold for checking the number of outliers in the system is only for reducing the amount of valid results. If the number of the outliers is more than 10%, then the possibility of rejecting non threat data increases. Note that the idea here is to reduce the number of possible permutations. The goal is to generate one set of values that will stand the tests we will describe later.

If we still have more than one option we will select the case that the integer values are the highest. We have 2 numbers in the variable pool, each having the values 0.7, 0.85, 0.99. One of the two variables is the threshold. It determines if the new record belongs to a cluster or not. We test the data with low threshold (0.7), medium threshold (0.85) and a high threshold (0.99). We obviously look for the high threshold. The problem is that high threshold will not guarantee stability. Therefore, we need to test several thresholds. The second numeric variable is responsible for the shape of the centre of each attribute in the centre vector of the cluster (we denote it as the shape variable). Let x be the value representing the centre of an attribute of the cluster and S be the shape value. Then we want to expend x to a fuzzy term with a trapezoid shape as described in Fig. 6:

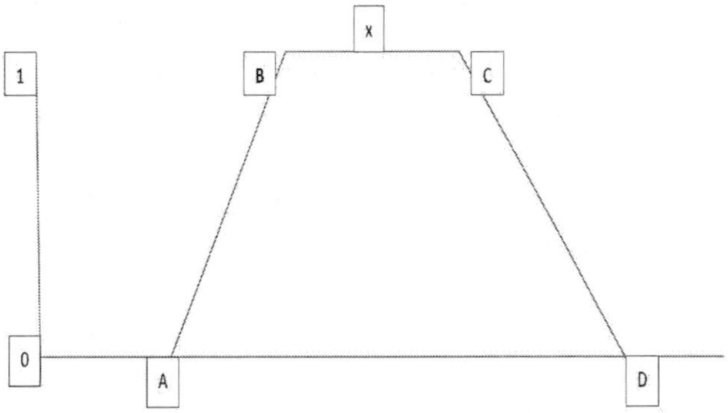

Fig. 6. Fuzzy term described as a trapezoid

The values of the points A, B, C, and D in Fig. 7 are computed as:

$$\begin{aligned} B &= xS \\ A &= BS \\ C &= x + (1 - S)x = x(2 - S) \\ D &= C + (1 - S)C = C(2 - S) \end{aligned} \tag{6}$$

For example, if $x = 100$, then $B = 70$, $A = 49$, $C = 130$, $D = 169$. The trapezoid created is not symmetric. If we want to make the trapezoid symmetric, we define y such that

$$y = xS \tag{7}$$

And

$$\begin{aligned} A &= x - 2y \\ B &= x - y \\ C &= x + y \\ D &= x + 2y \end{aligned} \tag{8}$$

If we still have more than one option we will select the case that has the most Boolean variables having the value true. This means that we chose the case where as many as possible variables from the variable list described above are participating in the simulation. This guarantee that the system will choose only one case and this case has the best characteristics.

After selecting the best variables and the best values for those variables we move to the final stage, or the final test.

After choosing the best set of values for the variables to determine if some IP is a threat or not, we use these values to simulate the system 200 times to ensure con-sistency. The reason for choosing this large number is because of the rule of large numbers. If we show consistency in this simulation we can ensure that statistically the consistency will hold. Consistency is defined as having the same results (or very close to it). The results are stored on a file for further analysis. The analysis showed that in almost all cases we simulated (98%), we got very high success. Success is defined as a case where the prediction (threat/normal) is the same as the actual values.

We have repeated the entire process described above 500 times and got consistent and very good results.

5.3 Example

As was stated above, in the first run we simulate results with all permutated values (1151). This is shown in Fig. 7.

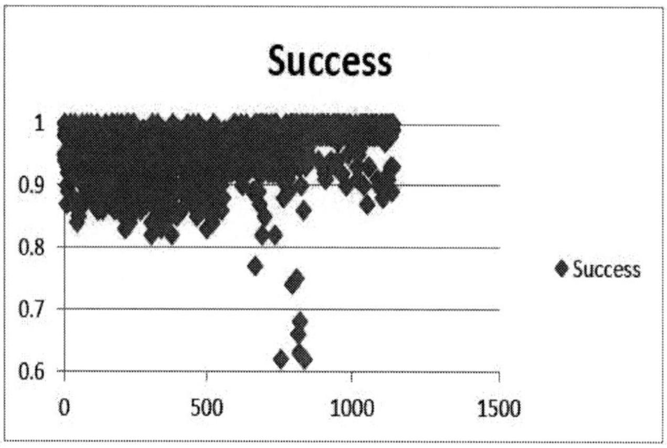

Fig. 7. Initial results

The system sorts the results and selects only the results that their success rate is above 98%. After cutting the results with less than 98% success we are left with 51 cases. This is shown in Fig. 8:

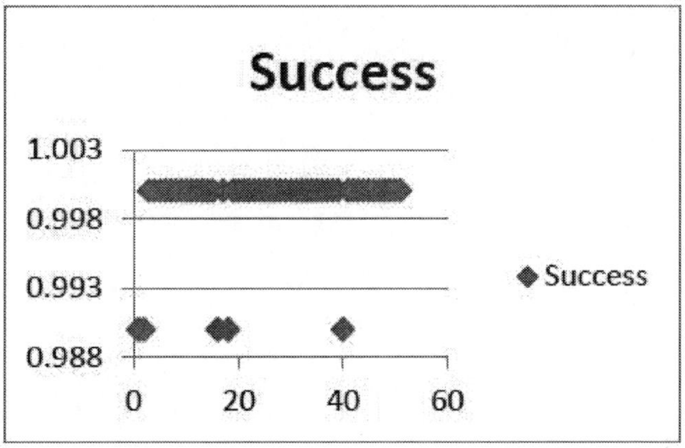

Fig. 8. Results after first cut

From the 51 cases remained, the system selected 16 cases in which the number of outliers is less than 10%. Out of these 16 cases we found one case in which T was 0.99 and S was 0.85. This permutation was chosen.

Then we run the system 100 times to check consistency. The results are depicted in Fig. 9.

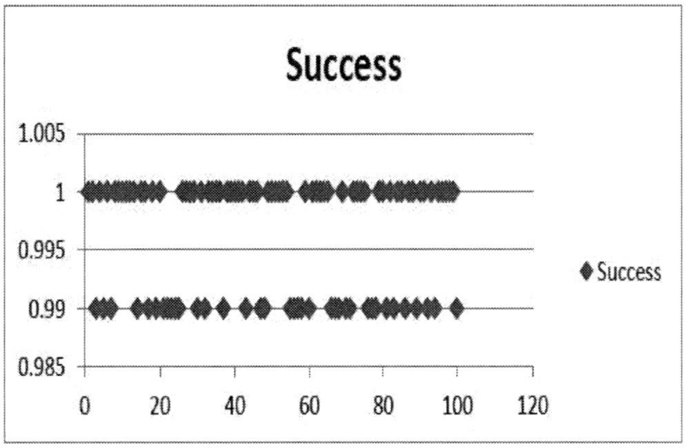

Fig. 9. Simulating the system 100 times

The success rate was 99%. Success is measured by counting the number of cases we predicted correctly divided by the number of cases tested. The outlier rate was less than 10%, that is, the number of records that were rejected due to the fact that their matching result was below the given threshold, was 7%.

The matching threshold T was set to 0.99 (almost a binary case) and the shape value S was set to 0.84. That concluded that the system was very consistent.

We repeated the process 500 times and the results were consistent with the selected permutations.

6 Conclusions

The approach described above was implemented and tested using actual network traffic from PCCW Global backbone network. It is used to generate early notifica-tions regarding suspicious IPs that although no security information was available, were observed with similar traffic behavior with IPs that have been involved in net-work security incidents in given time context. We used random numbers to generate the learning and testing data, by running the simulations 200 times to optimize pa-rameters. The presented approach is related to intellectual property protected by the US patent (provisional) with US Application No.: 62/439,332.

Approach enhancements that are planned as future work are to apply a historical threat severity score model to each entity type, extract temporal patterns and apply a set of techniques considering other unsupervised learning techniques to reason about the final decision. An automated framework for applying appropriate weights to features and feature selection using dimensionality reduction techniques in conjunc-tion with PCCW Global security analysis feedback is under research.

References

1. Agrawal, R.; Gehrke, J.; Gunopulos, D.; Raghavan, P. (2005). "Automatic Subspace Clustering of High Dimensional Data". Data Mining and Knowledge Discovery. 11: 533.
2. Amorim, R.C.; Hennig, C. (2015). "Recovering the number of clusters in data sets with noise features using feature rescaling factors". Information Sciences. 324: 126145.
3. Angiulli, F.; Pizzuti, C. (2002). Fast Outlier Detection in High Dimensional Spaces. Principles of Data Mining and Knowledge Discovery. Lecture Notes in Computer Science. 2431. p. 15.
4. Bailey, M.; Oberheide, J.; Andersen, J.; Mao, M.; Jahanian, F. and Nazario, J. (2007). Automated classification and analysis of internet malware, In Proceedings of International Symposium on Recent Advances in Intrusion Detection (RAID'07).
5. Bezdek, James C. (1981). Pattern Recognition with Fuzzy Objective Function Algorithms. ISBN 0-306-40671-3.
6. Breunig, M. M.; Kriegel, H.-P.; Ng, R. T.; Sander, J. (2000). LOF: Identifying Densitybased Local Outliers (PDF). Proceedings of the 2000 ACM SIGMOD International Conference on Management of Data. SIGMOD. pp. 93104
7. Campello, R. J. G. B.; Moulavi, D.; Zimek, A.; Sander, J. (2015). "Hierarchical Density Estimates for Data Clustering, Visualization, and Outlier Detection". ACM Transactions on Knowledge Discovery from Data. 10 (1): 5:151.

8. Celebi, M. E., Kingravi, H. A., and Vela, P. A. (2013). "A comparative study of efficient initialization methods for the k-means clustering algorithm". Expert Systems with Applications. 40 (1): 200210.
9. Chou, Hui-Hao , Wang,; Sheng-De. (2015). An adaptive network intrusion detection approach for the cloud environment. International Carnahan Conference on Security Technology
10. Cornish, (2007). Cluster Analysis, Mathematics Learning Support Chapter 3.1.
11. Figueiredo, M.A.T.; Jain, A.K. (March 2002). "Unsupervised Learning of Finite Mixture Models". IEEE Transactions on Pattern Analysis and Machine Intelligence. 24 (3): 381 396.
12. Fox, K.; Henning, R.; Reed, J. (1990). "A neural network approach toward intrusion detection", Proc. 13th Nat. Computer Security Conf.
13. Garca-Teodoroa, P; Daz-Verdejoa, J.; Macia-Fernandeza, G.; Vazquezb, E. (2009). Anomaly-based network intrusion detection: Techniques, systems and challenges. computers & security 28 (2009) 1828. Elsevier Publishing.
14. Hawkins, Simon; He, Hongxing; Williams, Graham; Baxter, Rohan (2002). "Outlier Detection Using Replicator Neural Networks". Data Warehousing and Knowledge Discovery. Lecture Notes in Computer Science. 2454. pp. 170180.
15. He, Z.; Xu, X.; Deng, S. (2003). "Discovering cluster-based local outliers". Pattern Recognition Letters. 24 (910): 16411650
16. Knorr, E. M.; Ng, R. T.; Tucakov, V. (2000). "Distance-based outliers: Algorithms and applications". The VLDB Journal the International Journal on Very Large Data Bases. 8 (34): 237253.
17. IANA, Autonomous System (AS) Numbers, last updated on 2016-09-08
18. Rokach, L., and Oded, M., "Clustering methods." Data mining and knowledge discovery handbook. Springer US, 2005. 321-352.
19. Ramaswamy, S.; Rastogi, R.; Shim, K. (2000). Efficient algorithms for mining outliers from large data sets. Proceedings of the 2000 ACM
20. Sandhya G, Anitha Julian. (2014). Intrusion detection in wireless sensor network using genetic K-means algorithm. IEEE International Conference on Advanced Communications, Control and Computing Technologies.
21. Sommer, R., Paxson, V., Outside the closed world: On using machine learning for network intrusion detection, in Proceedings of the 2010 IEEE Symposium on Security and Privacy, ser. SP 10, 2010.
22. Timm, K., "Strategies to reduce false positives and false negatives in nids", Tech. Rep., [online] Available:
23. Zadeh, L.A. (1965). "Fuzzy sets". Information and Control. 8 (3): 338353

Promoting Connectivity: Social Network Analysis to Support Entrepreneurs

Cristina Feniser[1], Ken Brown[2[0000-0001-8863-1410]], Arik Sadeh[3], and Javier Bilbao[4]and Gabriel Plesa[5]

Technical University of Cluj-Napoca, Faculty of Machine Building, Romania
Letterkenny Institute of Technology, Port Road, Letterkenny, Co. Donegal, Ireland
Holon Institute of Technology, Israel
University of the Basque Country,Applied Mathematics Department, Engineering School,Spain
Technical University of Cluj-Napoca, Faculty of Machine Building, Romania
cristina.feniser@mis.utcluj.ro,ken.brown@lyit.ie,sadeh@hit.ac.il,javier.bilbao@ehu.es,gabiplesa_viva@yahoo.com

Abstract. The capabilities of deep data extraction and consideration of relationships and in-fluences of data have been explored in theoretical and empirical studies within the domain of entrepreneurial development. The ability to model and develop an envi-ronment conducive to the, promotion of growth, stimulation of activity, support of knowledge transfer and maintenance of a commercially acceptable level of in-tegrity, is central to the framework necessary for engagement with entrepreneurs. This study considers a case study demonstrating potential for increased commer-cial awareness based on the relationships of data present on the web but which may not be in an easily recognised or useful format. Analysis of the relationships of the data, the perceived levels of influence the data may have, and its relevance to the enquirer, whilst presenting the outputs in a standard form which is readily accessible offers scope for future intervention and support. The framework anal-yses and subsequently reports obscure data in a meaningful and easily digested manner and this article considers how this improved flow of information and knowledge is beneficial to entrepreneurial activity.

Keywords: entrepreneur, social network analysis, data extraction, connectivity.

1 Introduction

Contemporary economic competitiveness is highly dependent on access to high qual-ity, market focused, information. This paper considers the potential offered by social network analysis (SNA) for the enhancement and promotion of start-ups.

Social networking employs relationship knowledge based on a modelled structure of the strengths of connections between information agents. Many interactions are not immediately visible (Freeman, 1979) particularly where human interactions are concerned as may be found in clustered environments. Social structures, infrastruc-ture, communications and human capital resources are potential relational infor-mation agents which may be considered appropriate within the decision process (Scott, 2012). The structures of the data, and nuances determined by them, form the core of the linkages between entities on which the decisions may be made. The map-pings and interconnected relationships, both intra-agent and extra-agent, between entrepreneurs, government departments, support groups, Universities (Pinheiro, Lucas and Pinho, 2015), Internet and other sources of agency generate patterns (Maharani and Gozali, 2015). Analysis of the socially interacting patterns and the resultant nodes produced in the graphing produces information relevant to activities within the network. Of greatest importance within the network is the social capital which is intrinsic to the entrepreneurial network; this social capital is considered critical for the performance of start-ups (Stam, Arzlanian and Elfring, 2014).

Selection of entrepreneurial partners and clusters is not always a straightforward process and may lead to unprofitable dead-ends if the available information is not suitably relevant and high level of quality (Dvir et. al., 2010). Successful transactional activities such as technology transfer, development and management of intellectual property, engagement within regional and cultural norms, and deep social interaction (Landry et al, 2002) are requirements of a successful start-up. The diversity of actors within the cluster and associated with it varies according to region, availability of human capital, industrial scale and government policies (national and local). These diverse agents create a level of complexity which may be difficult to decipher in the decision-making process. The strengths of relationship between actors and by actors are not all equal, hence their effects within any alliance of, small to medium sized enterprises, start-ups, or clusters of complimentary organisations do not have equal weightings. The quantity and type of agent with a role in the start-up decision making process is not always easy to determine and each context will demonstrate different respective weightings.

The methodology employed within the study produces an influence on the infor-mation output from the analysis. The degree of subjectivity of the extracted infor-mation (Frasquet et al, 2011) depends on the relational agent of trust within the mod-el, hence it is advisable to explore any pre-existing relationships to determine how this may be weighted. The SNA may not interpret all agents which may affect the start-up, hence any limitations must be clearly signposted.

The relationships within the social network depend on the influential behaviour of the nodes. Nodes with the highest degrees of centrality describe agents of high levels of connectivity with other nodes. These nodes are given the greatest weightings to represent high levels of connectivity and high levels of interactions. Centrality is the means by which these high levels is described. The degrees of centrality are an im-portant element in the analysis of the human interaction process; the variety of inter-actions, types of interaction and communication means, all affect the relationship model.

Small to medium sized company clusters naturally contain old and new firms op-erating within a range of high and low technologies and may be situated in emerging or more established economic zones. Start-ups wishing to engage with these activities will be affected by network diversity. Stam et al (2014) determined that performance is closely connected to network diversity especially for new firms. The performance levels of older, established firms are better in larger social networks with strongly es-tablished ties. Evolution of start-up status within the requires adaptability of the model as the social capital varies. Therefore, the way the entrepreneur relates and interacts with the social network is not constant and is dependent on the levels of awareness of the entrepreneur and supporting organisations to changing conditions. The methodology employed within the SNA is determined by the status and maturity of the cluster.

Better connected entrepreneurs (Hoang and Antonic, 2003) are viewed as having large nodes demonstrating high levels of interaction with supporting and collaborative actors. The identification of opportunities and subsequent mobilisation of resources social capital, finances and personal networks is a constructive process, however, extraction of data to determine model effect is not without difficulty. Data may be sparse but highly central to the model leading to concern regarding the objectivity and accuracy of the model. Data is contextually dependent and where empirical data is not accessible there may be a need to construct a simulated node which may be updated on receipt of error information.

The entrepreneurial context reveals a generalisation of network effects is not easily obtained when esoteric terms such as social capital are considered. The definitions of social capital vary (McEvily and Zaheer, 1999; Batjargal, 2010) as does the degree of homogeneity of the network under consideration.

Lee (2015) considered the use of SNA to foster entrepreneurs within Korean crea-tive industries. The expectation that successful activities may be created simply through provision of bricks and mortar has been debunked. The activities of the start-up should be integrated into the social and industrial fabric of the region to attract entrepreneurial attention. Effective marketing of the newly developed assets and strategic allocation of support structures to aid the creation and involvement of net-worked activities. Unpredictability and rapidly changing trends are characteristics of many new industries leading to uniqueness of circumstance. Access to a broad, available, qualified workforce, potential partners and financial support are just some of the agents affecting the networked cluster. The innovative elements may not be state based requiring close interaction between individuals. Internet enabled technol-ogies may support new and established firms, however, geographical and relational issues are considered important to extant activities and subsequent growth.

2 Data Extraction Networks: Supporting knowledge transfer and social capital growth

The primary function of social network analysis is the process of identification of the primary agents or central nodes in the network. The central node is that which is most popular in terms of connectivity and perceived importance to the function of the network. The degree of centrality describes the flow of information to and around each node to determine its central function. This technique may be used across many domains such as epidemiology, town planning, building design, transportation. In this study, the degree of centrality is explored to ascertain the optimal sources of infor-mation and support for entrepreneurs in local clusters to aid growth and development of small to medium sized enterprises.

Influence is a measure or perception of quality of interaction, and influential in-teractions are fundamental to the relationships between, and in collaboration with, entrepreneurs. The influences of agents within the network play a large role and may be tacit depending on context. Rachman et al (2013) implemented social network design based on Kretschmer (2007) methods to determine those agents with greatest influence. The actions of influence are paramount however, the analysis must remain cognizant of content within the influencing agents and how this content is distributed across the web. Adapting to the needs of entrepreneurs, in a world where accurate keywords act as agents to enable a targeted analysis in a time sensitive framework, is key to the following case study. The keywords entered in the system form the lens of analysis for the dominant nodes, and the model adapts to changes requested where an output is considered to not be relevant to the search.

The objective of this paper is to propose a model based on case studies of small to medium sized organisations using the extraction of non-transparent Internet based data to support entrepreneurial activity. The proposed model, or selection of adaptive models, will consider relationships applicable to a case study within the context of web distributed start-up support.

3 Case Study

RandomStartup, as its name suggests, is a free start-up discovery engine that allows users to find startups from all around the world which was developed by a team of students from the USA, Romania and Honduras. The website and the apps are user friendly and simple to use: You just need to press refresh and another startup will pop up.

Fig. 1. Start Page.

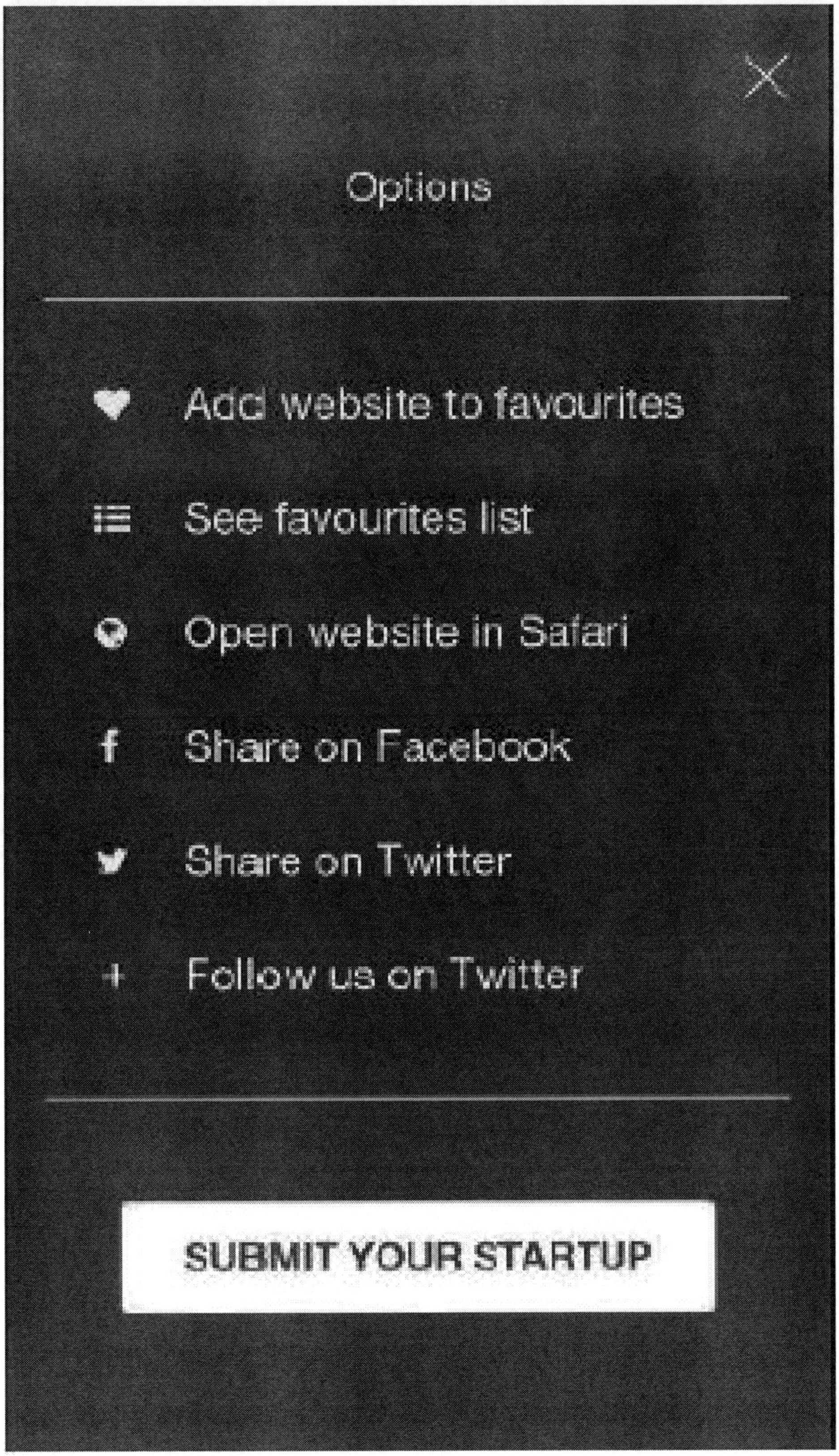

Fig. 2. Menu Page.

The website www.randomstartup.org is operational and gathers data from more than 2500 worldwide start-ups. The iOS and Android apps are under construction with a design emphasis on interactive features: Search button using keywords (music, travel, promote, marketing, education, en-trepreneur, etc) so user can discover start-ups in their area of interest and determine influencing information. Save button allows users to save start-ups they like or use.

Fig. 3. With every refresh a new start-up popsup

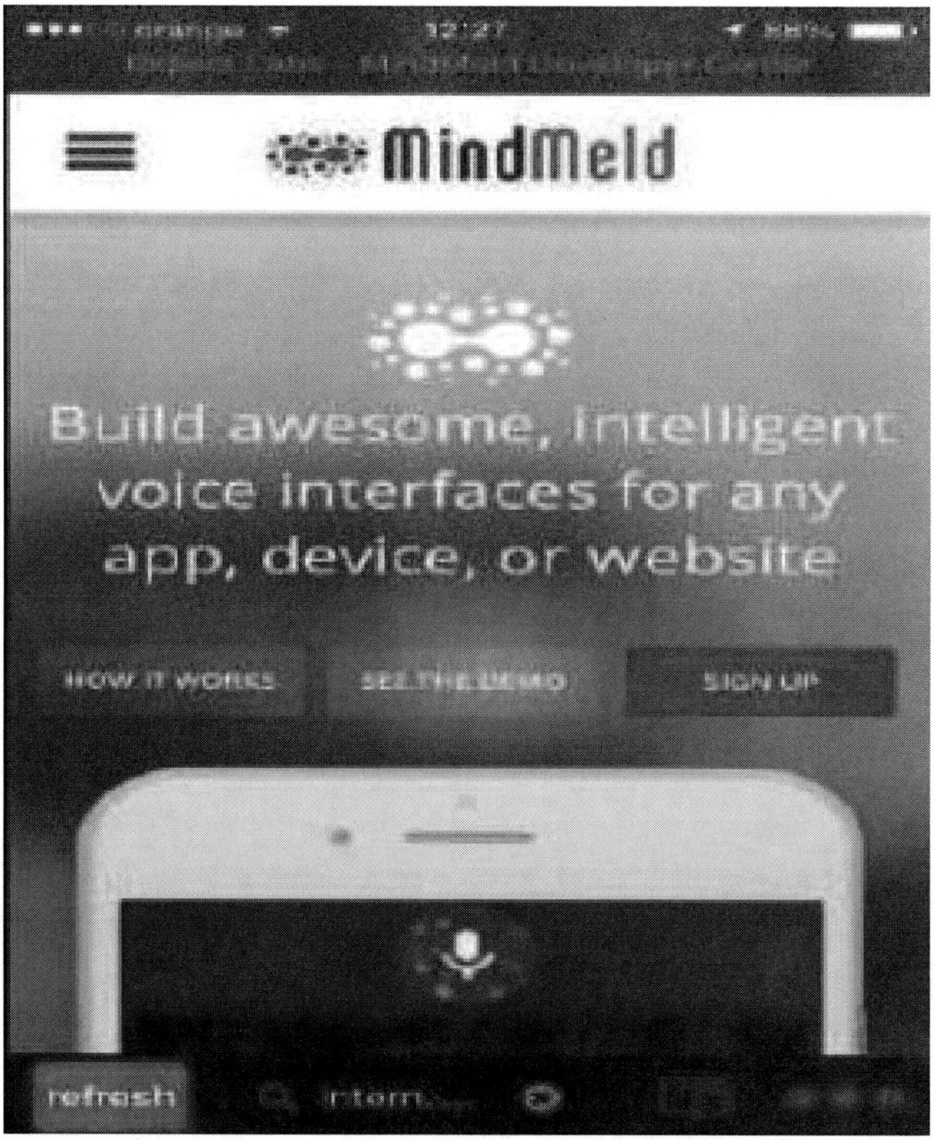

Fig. 4. For every refresh a new start-up will appear

While loading the value proposition of the start-up pops-up

The main purpose of this online platform is to connect start-ups with potential us-ers or buyers and generate social capital. At the same time, it can serve as inspiration for people seeking ideas with a desire to start a new venture. It also works for those that already have started a new business and want to see what their competitors are doing or for those that are simply looking for partnership. Some users who have al-ready tried the product describe it is a healthy alternative to scrolling Facebook feeds.

Products must have a minimum level of viability and may be promoted through the website URL or app; submissions of ideas on RandomStartup are free. After submission, the websites are carefully analyzed for viability and integrity before ap-proval by the RandomStartup team.

Each start-up has equal chances to be known to the world (the logo a yellow equal) and the order of appearance of the start-ups is completely randomized. So, the chronological time doesn‘t matter when a person introduces a start-up, but rather the knowledge that the company is in the start-up phase. Hence, each start-up has an equal chance of appearance to the public searches. Randomstartup is all about entrepreneurship and about connecting the world of entrepreneurs on a single platform.

With RandomStarup mobile app they will be able to customize their search by intro-ducing keywords to determine levels of influence. For example, if the user writes IoT the app will determine those businesses and ideas where this keyword is central to the analysis. This works as well for tourism, travel, music, innovation, etc. RandomStartup also has a save button to revisit outputs at a later stage for further consideration.

Nowadays, many people have ideas but few of them succeed in making those ideas become reality. When they finally succeed in building a prototype or a mini-mum viable product they struggle to become known to the world. Now, things are starting to change because with Internet connection you may access information no matter where your location is. So, even if you are based in Asia, if you have a good product or service you can have users or clients from other parts of the world. In this regard RandomStartup wants to play the connector role.

RandomStartup is a pool where start-ups are swimming. The purpose is to help them become known to the world and strive in this competitive world. Practically, start-ups connect with potential users or buyers and in this way they grow their busi-ness. Also, it is a good source of inspiration for people that are coming from emerging economies to increase the wealth of their co-citizens by applying ideas from devel-oped countries. The reverse is also available, people from emerging countries can also build useful products or services that can be used by people all around the world and at competitive prices.

By using the Randomstartup platform (website or apps) entrepreneurs can im-prove their business or come up with new innovative solution. From, intelligent soft-ware services and smart devices to cloud services, hidden data can be discovered and used.

RandomStartup‘s aim is to conquer complexity with simple user rules. Playing the role of a connector that has impact both on start-up owners and users. The novelty of RandomStartups comes mainly from its simplicity. Think about a photo frame where instead of photos you may find accurate real ideas from all around the world. Be-cause the user doesn‘t know what may come next, the sentiment of serendipitously finding something interesting and useful makes you hit the refresh button again and again.

There are also other start-up generators, but most of them took the approach of building a website where they put links and stories about the startup. At Random-Startup it is all about the ability of a start-up owner to present his/her product in a way that resonates with entrepreneurial activity because its content is employed di-rectly. In time, only some start-ups survive, so the system is very careful to promote only websites that work.

Since the first day the website was launched (September 2014) the number of people submitting their start-ups has been continuously growing. Entrepreneurs are searching for different ways to promote their products and services mainly because most of them have international applicability. When building a start-up resources may be limited at the beginning, so the best thing you can do is to try to invest them efficiently. RandomStartup started from zero startups in September 2014 and now has more than 2500 start-ups. Some start-ups ceased to function along the way but this industry is tremendously growing with the goal of becoming the biggest start-up discovery engine around the world.

The company quickly realized that next to promoting start-ups there is also a need for recognition and support along the way. The path of building the dream may be-come very difficult and some may give up easily if they don't see immediate results. The importance of feedback, services, and skills exchanges, between complementary start-ups can enhance the chances for a start-up to survive. At RandomStartup meaningful partnership are built with start-ups that were previously featured with the program with the mantra that growing start-ups through start-ups could represent a big step forward for entrepreneurship.

RandomStartup began as an initiative which is now in practice. It started with the website (www.randomstartup.org) and the next phase is about to begin via the launch of the iOS app and the android app.

Internal developments include: Improvingthe database over time by introducing more details about the start-ups and gather more information about the users. External developments include: increasing in terms of scalability) the on-line presence to create RandomStartup Ambassadors in more than 190 countries. At the beginning of our journey more start-ups were located in the USA, but as time passed by the website received requests from Europe, Asia and Australia. In the future, the intention is that visitors will be able to discover start-ups from Latin America and from Africa. Introducing new features and data analysis, and building more partnerships with startups and help other startups connect

When running a start-up, you need to expect the unexpected, so to sum up it is planned to adapt the system Every amazing journey starts with a first step. And RandomStartup did it and up to this point they are on the right path. Still, there are so many challenges that must be overcome along the way.

Adapt the product to clients needs while still preserving its authenticity and integri-ty. Usually people give feedback and expect that their idea will be applied immedi-ately. In the real world this is impossible because there simply isnt sufficient time to test all the suggested ideas. It is necessary to decide what goes best for the global picture on the long run.

Monetize the product. Currently the services are free and the company is investing resources to build a viable product. Future plans include a freemium version of the apps.

4 Conclusion

The findings of this study demonstrate the contingent value of social capital for en-trepreneurs and displays how supportive, user design, and authentic information pro-duction aids this process. For entrepreneurs, the results clearly indicate the importance of cultivating rich personal networks and contextually relevant networking strategies according to the status of the business. Social network analysis is an additional tool for successful entrepreneurship, but difficulties may arise over vague boundaries and expectations. The rapid growth development of Internet enabled media, is producing value added capabilities in marketing strategies, networking and decision making. Through appropriate selection of influential data, start-up companies can access and disseminate information, products, and marketing, more effectively and efficiently. This case study although limited to a single organization is an indicator of success supporting success through diligent design. Future research to design and implement more in-depth analysis, using socially networked influential user data, may produce more focused and relevant outputs rapidly and effectively.

The authors thank Silvia Dusa - the owner of Randomstartup - for the courtesy of providing us with information about this site.

References

1. Batjargal, B. (2010) The effects of network's structural holes: polycentric institutions, prod-uct portfolio, and new venture growth in China and Russia. Strategic Entrepreneurship Jour-nal, 4 (2), 146163.
2. Dvir D. A. Malach-Pines and A. Sadeh (2010) The Fit between Entrepreneurs' Personalities and the Profile of the Ventures they Manage and Business Success: An Exploratory Study, J. of High Technology Management Research, 21,(43-51)
3. Frasquet, M, H Caldern and A Cervera (2011). Universityindustry collaboration from a relationship marketing perspective: An empirical analysis in a Spanish University. Higher Education, 64(1), 8598, doi: 10.1007/s10734-011-9482-3.
4. Freeman LC. (1979) Centrality in social networks conceptual clarification. Social networks. Elsevier; 1:215239.
5. Hoang, H., Antoncic, B. (2003) Network-based research in entrepreneurship: a critical re-view. Journal of Business Venturing, 18, 165187.
6. Kretschmer H, Kretschmer T. (2007) A new centrality measure for social network analysis applicable to bibliometric and webometric data. Collnet Journal of Scientometrics and In-formation Management. Taylor & Francis, 1:17.
7. Landry, R, N Amara and M Lamari (2002). Does social capital determine innovation? To what extent? Technological Forecasting and Social Change, 69(7), 681701, doi: 10.1016/S0040-1625(01)00170-6.
8. Lee M. (2015) Fostering connectivity: a social network analysis of entrepreneurs in creative industries, International Journal of Cultural Policy, 21:2, 139-152.
9. Maharani W, Gozali AA. (2015) Collaborative Social Network Analysis and content-based approach to improve the marketing strategy of SMEs in Indonesia, Procedia Computer Sci-ence, 59:373-381.
10. McEvily, B., Zaheer, A. (1999) Bridging ties a source of firm heterogeneity in competitive capabilities. Strategic Management Journal, 20, 11331156.
11. Pinheiro ML, Lucas C and Pinho JC. (2015) Social Network Analysis as a new methodo-logical tool to understand university-industry cooperation, International Journal of Innova-tion Management, 19:1:1-22
12. Rachman ZA, Maharani W, others. (2013) The analysis and implementation of degree cen-trality in weighted graph in Social Network Analysis. Information and Communication Technology (ICoICT), International Conference of. IEEE; 2013. p. 7276.
13. Scott, J (2000). Social Network Analysis A Handbook, 2nd edn., p. 110. London: Sage Publications.
14. Stam W, Arzlanian S and Elfring T. (2014) Social capital of entrepreneurs and small firm performance: A meta-analysis of contextual and methodological operators, Journal of Busi-ness Venturing 29: 152-173

Ensemble of Heterogeneous Regressors Applied to Forecasting in Cosmetics Industry

Leandro dos Santos Coelho[1,2], Viviana Cocco Mariani[1,3],
Frederico Gonzalez Colombo Arnoldi[4] and Donald Neumann[5]

[1] Department of Electrical Engineering, Federal University of Parana (UFPR)
[2] Industrial and Systems Engineering Graduate Program (PPGEPS)
[3] Mechanical Engineering Graduate Program (PPGEM),
Pontifical Catholic University of Parana (PUCPR)
[4] O Boticário, São José dos Pinhais, Curitiba, PR, Brazil
[5] Department of General and Applied Management, Federal University of Parana (UFPR)
leandro.coelho@pucpr.br

Abstract. Cosmetic products serve the beautifying purposes and cover a wide range of products. Despite the recent advances in production, planning and management processes in the cosmetic industry, few studies have explored machine learning (ML) methods to predict the derived demand from point-of-sales (sell-in) based on end consumer demand (sell-out). In terms of regression, ML can be useful to identify and discover patterns in complex datasets related to products and predict point-of-sales behavior affecting the sell-in demand. The contribution of this paper is the comparison of the predictive performance of ten regressors and its heterogeneous ensemble generating estimates of the sell-in demand using datasets from a Brazilian cosmetics company that operates in a franchising business model. The results show that ensemble learning method can be a convenient and accurate approach to predict monthly cosmetic sales up to 200 SKUs (Stock Keeping Units) with 15 steps ahead, reducing the Bullwhip Effect, improving stock and service levels along the supply chain.

Keywords: Ensemble learning, Forecasting, Regression, Cosmetics Industry, Supply chain management, Bullwhip effect.

1 Introduction

During the last years, the cosmetic industry has dramatically diversified its managerial and marketing orientation towards customer requirements due to the growth in response to the customer trends towards a healthier lifestyle and requirements for natural cosmetics [1]. In 2015 the industry generated $56.2 billion in the United States. Hair care is the largest segment with 86,000 locations. Skin care is a close second and growing fast, expected to have revenue of almost $11 billion by 2018. This growth is being driven in part by a generally increasing awareness of the importance of skin care, but also specifically due to an increase in the market for men [2]. Since the turn of the century the cosmetic markets of the BRIC countries (Brasil, Russia, India and China) have been growing fast. In 2011 all those countries generated 81% of the global cosmetics sales growth, according to *Euromonitor International's* data, more than half of which (54%) was attributed to BRIC [3]. According to Euromonitor, the Brazilian market for Beauty and Personal Care (BPC) products was about 102 billion of real in 2016 and should reach 120 billion of real in 2020. Although it is a health market, the compound annual growth rate (CAGR) is expected to decrease from 8.3% (2011-2016) to 4.8% (2016-2021) with a weak period in 2016 and 2017 with a CAGR of 2.6% [4]. This scenario motivates many companies to review internal processes in order to eliminate inefficiencies.

The Brazil BPC market has many different product categories, with hundreds and even thousands of products within each group. As consequence, a large company can have thousands of SKUs in its portfolio and complex demand plans along the whole supply chain, from consumer (independent, sell-out demand) to OME (derived, sell-in demand) are necessary to keep the global efficiency of system. Increase in the BPC complexity and the massive data production have caused an exponential growth in databases and repositories. In addition, forecasting is crucial for the cosmetic industry, but an effective sales forecasting model is challenging due to the sizeable amount of purchasing information obtained from diverse sources in a BPC industry. Machine learning (ML) and big data methods are emerging technologies actively being adopted across many knowledge fields. In last years, several ML applications for regression approaches have been studied and proposed using ensemble-based frameworks [5-7].

The main contribution of this paper is a validation of ten regressors (multilayer perceptron, Elman partially recurrent network, support vector regressor, extreme learning machine, Cubist, *k*-nearest neighbor, multivariable adaptive regressor splines, ordinary random forest, regularized random forest, and extreme gradient boosting) and the combination of the mentioned methods in the ensemble approaches for regression. The regressors were evaluated with a dataset including 200 SKUs from a Brazilian cosmetics company that operates in a franchising business model with thousands of stores. The remainder of the paper is organized as follows. In Section 2, we briefly introduce the regression case study of the Brazilian cosmetics company. In Sections 3, comments about the adopted ensemble form are mentioned. Section 4 presents a results analysis. Finally, this short paper is concluded in Section 5.

2 Brief Description of Case Study in Cosmetics Industry

This complexity of the BPC is leveraged by the fact that sales usually happen in two distinct stages, from industry to stores (sell-in) and from stores to end consumers (sell-out). In the long term, the sell-in volume is similar to the sell-out one. However, in the short-term they are significantly different as the sell-in demand is deeply affected by the behavior of the independent, fully autonomous buying agent at the point-of-sale. This phenomenon is well known in the supply chain literature as the Bullwhip Effect, caused by sub-optimal decision policies, time delays, uncertainties and speculative behavior of the buying agent [10]. In case these differences are not forecasted, over stocking or out-of-stocks can happen in both stages, leading to inefficiencies in the management of the company's financial resources. Different approaches were tested to identify which methodology would help companies to convert sell-out forecasts to sell-in volumes, i.e. predict the behavior of the autonomous buying agent. Sell-out and sell-in volumes were made equivalent in time by adding the lead-time of the delivering products, differences in volume were the subject of our study. A schematic of the case study related to a regression problem is illustrated in Fig. 1.

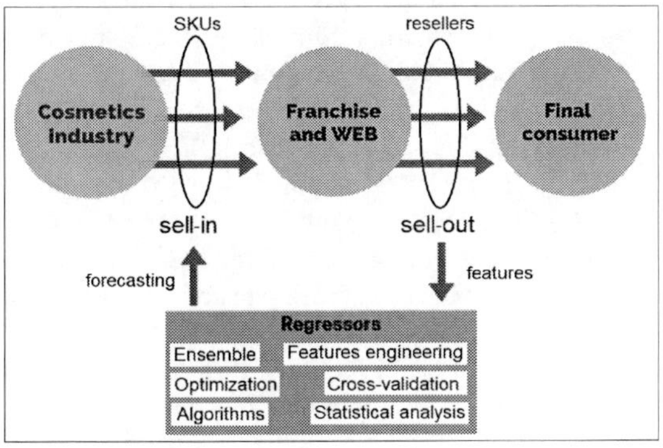

Fig. 1. Schematic linking the cosmetics industry and regressors.

3 Ensemble Learning

The process of ensemble learning for regression can be divided into three phases: the generation phase, in which a set of candidate models is induced, the pruning phase, to select of a subset of those models and the integration phase, in which the output of the models is combined to generate a prediction [4]. In this paper the proposed ensemble learning for regression is composed of simple and heterogeneous base models (base learners) linked with cross-validation procedure, including the following procedures:

Dataset setup: The dataset has 56 features for 200 SKUs as inputs and one output variable of the regressors. Among these features are holidays and marketing variables that affect the buying behavior of the downstream members of the chain. The time unit is the selling cycle of the company and forecasting horizon of the sell-in (output variable) was 15 steps ahead. More details about the contents of the dataset were not authorized by Brazilian cosmetics industry.

Features selection: The adopted design of ensemble learning of this research was based in the combination of three procedures: (i) correlation analysis of inputs to the output; (ii) ranking of the information gain obtained by a gradient boosting machine for regression called xgboost [8] in regression task; and (iii) features clustering linked with correlation analysis. General result of features selection was a decreasing of 43 initial to 36 to forecasting horizon with 15 steps ahead to 200 SKUs.

Model validation: Cross-validation (CV) is a resampling technique often used in ML for model selection and estimation of the prediction error in regression problems. In this paper, CV was equal to 10 folds repeated 100 times.

4 Results Analysis

Ten ML approaches were designed and tested alone in R Studio computational environment. In the tests phase, different combinations using a weighted sum of regressors outputs linked with a factorial experimental design [9] approach to the alone design was validated to obtain a best ensemble regressor in terms of generalization to prevent from having overfitting in a forecasting for 200 SKUs. The performance criterion adopted was the MAPE (Mean Absolute Percentage Error) to be minimized with 15 steps ahead of forecasting. The validated ten regressors were the following: multilayer perceptron (MLP), Elman partially recurrent network (EPRN), support vector regressor (SVR), extreme learning machine (ELM), Cubist, *k*-nearest neighbor (*k*NN), multivariable adaptive regressor splines (MARS), ordinary random forest (ORF), regularized random forest (RRF), and extreme gradient boosting (XGB). The best results with alone approaches were RRF, ORF and XGB, and for all tested approaches, in terms of MAPE performance (k=10 folds repeated 100 times) was the ensemble (BestEns) obtained by weighted sum of *k*NN, SVR, Cubist and XGB as illustrated in Table 1.

The SO, sale of franchisees to the final consumer, utilized as forecaster was more efficient than the regressors in SKUs. This result confirms the hypothesis that in many cases the behavior of the downstream agent is not rational could be identified over the sell-out demand. According to the supply chain literature, this might be due to uncertainties, sub-optimal decision policies and time delays for the agent to react to the consumer demand [10]. Even though this might appear to be a not very good result, for the company knowing which types of products are not subject to rational buying behavior helps to mitigate the amplification of the demand signal (bullwhip effect) upward in the chain. For another set of products, significant variables were identified, which drive buying behavior downstream on the chain. Business understanding of these variables helps preparing stocks assuring adequate service level.

Table 1. Mean quartile results of MAPE criterion. First best results in bold, second and third best results are underlined.

Regressors	Quartile (25%)	Quartile (50%)	Quartile (75%)
SO (Sell-Out)	0.130	0.273	0.464
MLP[1]	0.131	0.331	0.562
EPRN[1]	0.292	0.575	0.913
SVR[2]	0.231	0.440	0.654
ELM[3]	0.305	0.596	0.932
Cubist[4]	0.136	0.304	0.654
*k*NN[5]	0.153	0.315	0.573
MARS[6]	0.136	0.289	0.571
ORF[7]	0.122	*0.271*	0.510
RRF[7]	0.125	0.263	0.517
XGB[8]	*0.126*	0.278	*0.481*
BestEns	**0.104**	**0.239**	**0.430**

* Comprehensive R Archive Network (*https://cran.r-project.org/*)

5 Conclusion and Future Research

Ensemble methods has been proved be a promising alternative in many applications (see details in [5,6]). The combination of many regressors in an ensemble is a well-known method of increasing the quality of recognition and forecasting tasks. In this paper, the performance of ten ML approaches was applied alone and also in an ensemble form based in weighted sum. The solution obtained by this research was further extended for the whole product portfolio and implemented in a solution that combines R and SPSS and was fully deployed into the Integrated Sales and Operations process of the company. As a future research to do, the systematic way to improve the ensemble design based on bagging, boosting, and stacking approaches.

Acknowledgments

The authors would like to thank CNPq (Grants: 150501/2017-0-PDJ, 303906/2015-4-PQ, 303908/2015-7-PQ, 405101/2016-3-Univ, 404659/2016-0-Univ, 204910/2017-0-PDE and 204893/2017-8-PDE) for its financial support of this work.

References

1. Dimitrova, V., Kaneva, M., Gallucci, T. (2009), "Customer knowledge management in the natural cosmetics industry", Industrial Management & Data Systems, 109 (9), 1155-1165.
2. Beauty Industry Analysis 2018 - Cost & Trends, Available at: Beauty Industry Analysis 2015 - Cost & Trends, *https://www.franchisehelp.com/industry-reports/beauty-industry-analysis-2018-cost-trends/* (Accessed on: March 15, 2018).
3. A. Łopaciuk and M. Łoboda, Global beauty industry trends in the 21st century, Management, Knowledge, and Learning International Conference, 2013.
4. Euromonitor, Beauty and personal care in Brazil, May, 2017. *http://www.euromonitor.com/beauty-and-personal-care-in-brazil/report*
5. Moreira, J. M., Soares, C., Jorge, A. M., De Sousa, J. F.: Emsemble approaches for regression: a survey. ACM Computing Surveys, 45 (1), Article No. 10, 2012.
6. Ren, Y., Zhang, L., and Suganthan, P.N.: Ensemble classification and regression — recent developments, applications and future directions. IEEE Computational Intelligence Magazine, 11 (1), 41-53, 2016.
7. Ribeiro, G. T., Gritti, M. C., Ayala, H. V. H., Mariani, V. C., Coelho, L. S.: Short-term load forecasting using wavenet ensemble approaches. In: International Joint Conference on Neural Networks (IJCNN), pp. 727-734. IEEE, Vancouver, Canada (2016).
8. Chen, T., Guestrin, C.: XGBoost : Reliable large-scale tree boosting system. In: Proceedings of the 22nd ACM SIGKDD International Conference on Knowledge Discovery and Data Mining (KDD'16), San Francisco, CA, USA, pp. 785-794 (2016).
9. Onyaih, L. C.: Design and analysis of experiments: classical and regression approaches with SAS, Chapman and Hall/CRC, 2008.
10. Neumann, D.: Collaborative Systems: a systems theoretical approach to interorganizational collaborative relationships. Peter Lang Verlag. Frankfurt am Main, 2012.

Segmenting Biosignals using Hierarchical Clustering

David Yuan[1] and Vangelis Metsis[2]

[1] University of Texas, Austin TX 78712, USA
[2] Texas State University, San Marcos TX 78666, USA

Abstract. Biosignals are measurable signals produced by living beings. Information obtained by measuring and analyzing human biosignals provide vital insights into diagnosing and treating many medical conditions. However, raw biosignals must first be preprocessed before sophisticated tools such as machine-learning can be applied to extract useful information. One of the most critical steps of preprocessing is signal segmentation, where long, heterogeneous signals are segmented into smaller, homogeneous windows. The traditional approach is to segment the signal into short, fixed-length windows. However, doing so often leads to sub-optimal results. In this paper, we address these challenges by developing a novel segmentation algorithm based on an unsupervised hierarchical clustering approach to identify the boundaries of homogeneous segments. We also develop a metric for evaluating segmentation quality and use it to test the performance of our algorithm.

1 Introduction

Biosignals provide vital information for the medical field. Sleep disorder diagnosis [1], mobile activity detection [2], and emotion recognition [3] are some of the most well-known applications. The advancement of computing technology has allowed sophisticated learning algorithms to automatically extract meaningful information from large datasets and facilitate decision support for domain experts [4].

The accuracy of machine learning classification methods is largely determined by the quality of the data. As a result, data preprocessing is critical for learning algorithms to work efficiently. Specifically, in signal analysis, long, heterogeneous signals that represent multiple events in chronological order must first be separated into shorter, homogeneous segments that represent singular events. This is because most classification algorithms will only be able to identify segments as a single event, and if the signal segments are too long and contain multiple events, they are likely to be misclassified. On the other hand, if signal segments are too short, classification algorithms have less data to analyze, thus decreasing classification accuracy. Traditionally, signals are segmented into short, fixed-window segments before classification [5]. The advantage of fixed-window segmentation is that it requires relatively little computation power, and a sufficiently small window size can prevent heterogeneity. However, a small window size can also lead to over-segmentation, where certain events of interest exceed the size of the window.

Following, we elaborate on previous solutions proposed to this problem. In [6], the authors use Simulated Annealing on MRI segmentation, and demonstrate the improved results if used with an expensive wavelet optimization. [7] uses the equipartition principle segmentation and gives signal segments that have equal errors in reconstruction, selecting the most suitable model amongst wavelet, Fourier and polynomial modeling to find each segment. [8] segments audio signals by extracting a sequence of short-term and mid-term feature vectors, then computing a dissimilarity measure for each pair of successive feature vectors to detect the local maxima. The authors in [9] performed multichannel EEG signal segmentation by using two sliding overlapping windows for detecting signal property changes for signal segmentation. In [10], an adaptive segmentation was performed using a wavelet transform by combining the amplitude and frequency contents of the wavelet-decomposed signals to detect boundaries. In [11], the authors combine QRS detection with an adaptive threshold to segment EEG signals. [12] performs segmentation on cyclic biosignals by measuring the temporal alignment distance between a template cycle and the testing signal, and extracting at local minima. In [1], (2015) the authors used the modified Varri method for segmenting data. In this method, two sliding windows are used, one for measuring amplitude values, and the second for estimating frequency values in the windows.

The Modified Varri method has the advantage of requiring relatively low computing power to calculate the frequency and amplitude windows. However, it also has two weaknesses. The first is that the algorithm requires the size of the sliding windows to be very small in order to set precise boundaries. With relatively little data to work with, each individual window becomes susceptible to random noise, leading to inaccurately large differences between consecutive windows, and resulting in over-segmentation. The second weakness is that the Modified Varri method can only measure amplitude and frequency-estimates within the windows. If the user wanted to classify post-segmentation signals based on more complex and accurate features, for example, power spectral density, segmentations based on amplitude and amplitude differences may be inaccurate.

In this paper, we propose a new segmentation algorithm to address the weakness of previous approaches. Using an adaptation of the unsupervised learning algorithm, known as Agglomerative Hierarchical Clustering [4], we will first divide the signal into very small segments, and then repeatedly merge the most similar consecutive segments based on a proximity function. The proximity function allows the user to compare consecutive segments based on complex features, while the merging algorithm allows similar sub-segments to be merged into larger homogeneous segments for more accurate classification. We compare our algorithm against the Varri method. Although our algorithm requires more computational power than the Modified Varri method, we expect the resulting segments to be more accurate in representing different events within the signal, as the proximity function can incorporate any number of signal features and is not limited only to amplitude and frequency.

Our segmentation algorithm is based off the Agglomerative Hierarchical Clustering algorithm, which takes a set of data points as input, and repeatedly merges the most similar data points together. Since a merged "group" of data points can be combined with another similar "group," each individual data point will belong to nested set of groups, called hierarchies.

2 Hierarchical Segmentation

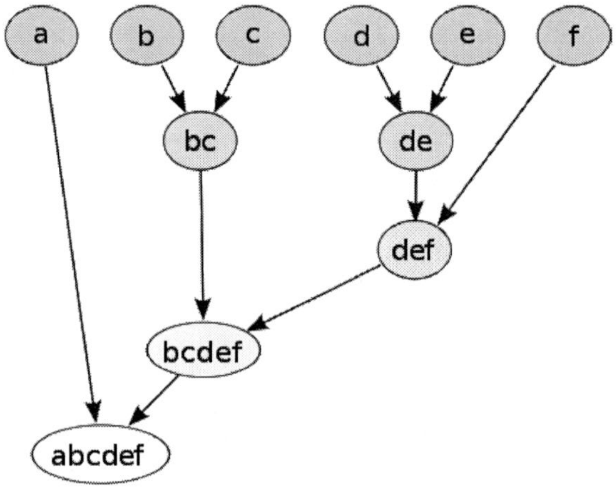

Fig. 1. A visual depiction of the Agglomerative Hierarchical Clustering [4] algorithm process of merging neighboring data points.

As with most clustering algorithms, each step of the merging process is only locally optimal. Two groups that are the most similar in a particular iteration of the algorithm may actually be better off in different groups after the algorithm finishes. However, there are exponentially many ways to partition a set of data points into groups, making it infeasible to compute the globally optimal set of groups. As a result, the weakness of the Agglomerative Hierarchical Clustering algorithm is one which is currently unsolvable, and shared by all clustering algorithms [4].

Algorithm 1 is demonstrates our segmentation algorithm, which we will call the Hierarchical Segmentation algorithm.

For our purposes, the Hierarchical Segmentation Algorithm differs from the clustering algorithm in three ways. First, rather than initializing the starting groups as individual data points, our algorithm will initialize starting groups as small segments. This is because for biosignals, individual points are more susceptible to random noise than segments of points. Furthermore, many important

Algorithm 1 Hierarchical Segmentation

function HIERARCHYCLUSTER(*signal, initialSegmentSize, tolerance*)
    Create initial segments of length *initialSegmentSize* from *signal.*
    Calculate proximity matrix between consecutive segments.
    repeat
        Find minimum proximity value.
        Merge closest two consecutive segments.
        Update proximity matrix to reflect the proximity between the new segment and the original segments.
    until minimum proximity value $<$*tolerance*, or only one segment remains.
end function

biosignal features such as frequency and entropy are meaningless for individual points, but become more important for larger segments. Second, since signals are chronological, and a single event will span a continuous range of the signal, our algorithm will only compare chronologically consecutive segments for potential mergings. This is important because comparing all N(N-1) different pairs of segments is often computationally infeasible. By only comparing consecutive segments, we just need to check (N-1) pairs. Third, we will not be keeping track of nested hierarchies, only the final set of segments when the algorithm ends. As a result, we want the algorithm to end as soon as the closest consecutive segments are sufficiently different from each other.

Calculating the Proximity Matrix is the most complex step of the algorithm. To calculate how similar two consecutive segments are, we first need to describe each segment in terms of quantifiable features. This process, called feature extraction, allows users to incorporate existing knowledge of a signal's properties into the segmentation process. For example, EEG signals are known to have important frequency properties, so users analyzing EEG signals can choose Power Spectral Density Estimate as a defining feature of segments. Other commonly used features include energy, power, zero-crossing rate, and energy entropy [1].

After extracting a list of feature values from the segments, which we will call the feature vector, the algorithm needs to calculate the relative similarity between consecutive segments using a distance function. Some common distance metrics include Euclidean distance, correlation distance, and cosine distance [4]. After every merging, the distance between the new segment and its adjacent neighbors must be calculated. If the list is stored in an array, the array must be re-indexed as well.

The loop runs until the most similar consecutive segments that remain have a greater distance than some user defined tolerance, with at most N-1 iterations. During each iteration, the algorithm 1) finds the closest consecutive segments, 2) merges the consecutive segments, 3) calculates the feature vector of the new segment, and 4) calculates the proximity of the new segment to its adjacent neighbors. Steps 1 and 2 can run in O(N) time, while step 4 can run in constant time. However, the complexity of step 3 depends on the feature extraction function. If the extraction function has only homomorphic features, then step 3 can be run in constant time, where the algorithm simply calculates the new feature values based on the old one. An example of such a feature would be average amplitude. On the other hand, features such as power spectral density must be recalculated for every new segment, and since the size of segments increases after each iteration, the extraction step would run at $\mathcal{O}(g)$ time, where g is the complexity of the extraction function. As a result, the overall runtime of the Hierarchical Segmentation Algorithm is $max(\mathcal{O}(N * g), \mathcal{O}(N^2))$.

3 Segmentation Evaluation

In order to test our segmentation algorithm, we need an evaluation method for testing segmentations. Several types of evaluations exist, but the most direct way is to use an empirical discrepancy evaluation method [13]. Empirical discrepancy methods evaluate a generated segmentation by comparing it to a segmentation accepted as the "correct" segmentation, known as the ground truth. In signal analysis, the ground truth is either a manual segmentation by experts or an automated segmentation by machines that experts accept to be perfectly accurate.

However, as far as we know there does not exist an empirical discrepancy evaluation for signal segmentation. Such an evaluation method must take into account how well the generated segmentation represents the ground-truth, as well as measuring oversegmentation. As a result, we developed such a signal evaluation method based on an existing image segmentation evaluation method [13].

Let us first define the distance between a segmentation and a boundary. Since a segmentation is simply a set of boundaries which create segments, we can define the distance *dist* to be

$$\begin{aligned} dist(boundary segments) = \\ min(|boundary - segments_j|) \end{aligned}$$

for all $j = 1, 2, ..., N$, where N is the number of boundaries in *segments* (Fig. 2).

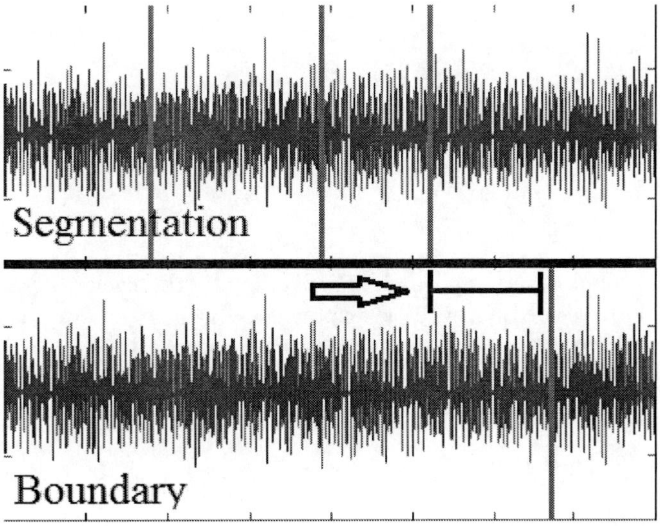

Fig. 2. Distance between a boundary and a segmentation [14].

In other words, the distance between a boundary and a set of boundaries should be the distance between the boundary and the nearest boundary in the set. A boundary that is near a segmentation's boundary is considered "close" to the segmentation as a whole, while a boundary that is far from all boundaries in a segmentation is considered "far."

Now, let us define *genSegs* to be the computer generated segmentation of the signal, while *truthSegs* is the ground-truth segmentation.

The value $\sum_i dist(truthSegs_i, genSegs)$ is how well the generated segments represent the ground-truth segments (representative distance). Each iteration of the summation measures how far a specific ground-truth boundary is from the generated segmentation, and a large representative distance means there are certain ground-truth boundaries that are far from the generated segmentation. Similarly, $\sum_i dist(genSegs_i, truthSegs)$ measures how well the generated segments fit the ground-truth segments (fit distance). Each iteration of the summation measures how far a specific generated boundary is from the ground-truth segmentation, and if over-segmentation occurs, the summation will be very large.

We now define the distance between the generated segmentation and the ground truth to be a weighted sum of the representative distance and the fit distance

$$\begin{aligned} & dist(genSegs, truthSegs) = \\ a & \sum_i dist(truthSegs_i, genSegs) + \\ b & \sum_i dist(genSegs_i, truthSegs) \end{aligned} \tag{1}$$

where a and b are weight coefficients specified by the user. Overall, this evaluation formula gives the difference, or disparity, between a generated segmentation and the ground-truth segmentation, taking into account both representation and over segmentation.

4 Testing Results

Using the signal evaluation method, we evaluated how well our hierarchical segmentation algorithm works on real polysomnographic data.

The data was collected in sleep study sessions at the Texas State Sleep center, using Compumedics Profusion PSG 3, and converted to anonymous format for research use. Profusion PSG allows the recording of 28 different biosignal channels with different sampling rates, including 8 electroencephalogram (EEG) channels and 2 EMG signals from the legs. In addition to signal recording, Profusion also provides annotations of events such as sleep stage, limb movement, and respiratory events by using software built and optimized for its sensors to analyze the collected signals. Theses annotations provided by Profusion are trusted by sleep experts to assess sleep disorders [1], and therefore we consider them accurate enough to be our ground truth segmentations. In our tests, we used data from a full night sleep study, approximately 7.5 hours long, of one patient. At a sampling rate of 128Hz, each data channel consists of 3,456,128 data points.

In the first test, we ran our algorithm on EMG signals used to detect leg movement. Because EMG signals are mainly characterized by amplitude features [1], we used power, mean, and standard deviation as our features in the extract function. In the second test, we ran our algorithm on EEG signals used to detect arousal, or periods of wakefulness. Because EEG signals are characterized by frequency and amplitude features [1], we used power spectral density estimate, amplitude, and standard deviation as our features in the extract function. In both tests, we set initial segment size to 0.5 seconds, because all movement/arousal events were longer than 0.5 seconds. We also used Euclidean distance to measure the distance between feature vectors.

After each test, we evaluated the generated segmentation using the evaluation method described in the previous section. We then compared the results to existing segmentation algorithms. In the EMG test, we compared our algorithm with the fixed window algorithm, while in the EEG test, we compared our algorithm with the Modified Varri algorithm [1]. For the fixed window approach, a 30-second window size was used, which is considered as the standard "epoch" size in sleep studies. Based on the ground-truth labels, there were 291 left leg movement events, 318 right leg movement events, and 67 sleep arousal events. Each event marked two boundaries (beginning and end of movement).

Figures 3 - 5 show the results of the comparisons. As it can be noted the vertical axis in Fig. 3 is in exponential scale. The sum of all the differences, as calculated by Equation 1, ends up being a large number as it multiplies the number of event occurrences with the number of data points of difference between the correct (ground truth boundaries) and the predicted ones for each event.

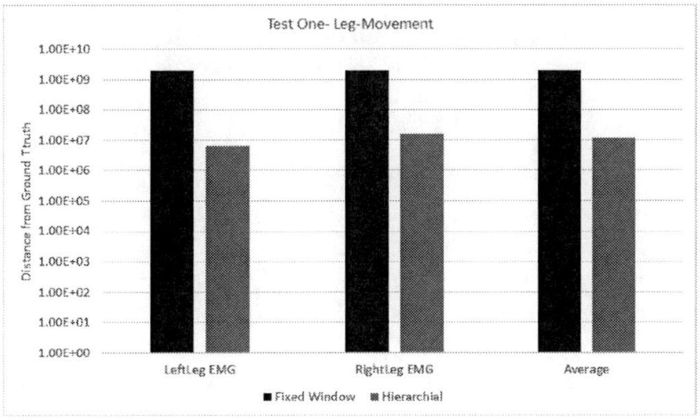

Fig. 3. Sum of distances (in exponential scale) of predicted segmentation boundaries from ground truth for leg movement events in EMG Signals Left Leg, Right Leg and Average between the two.

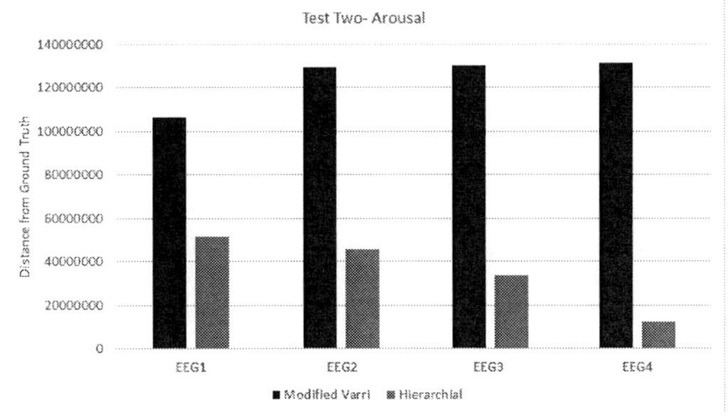

Fig. 4. Sum of distances of predicted segmentation boundaries from ground truth for Arousal events in EEG signal channels 1-4.

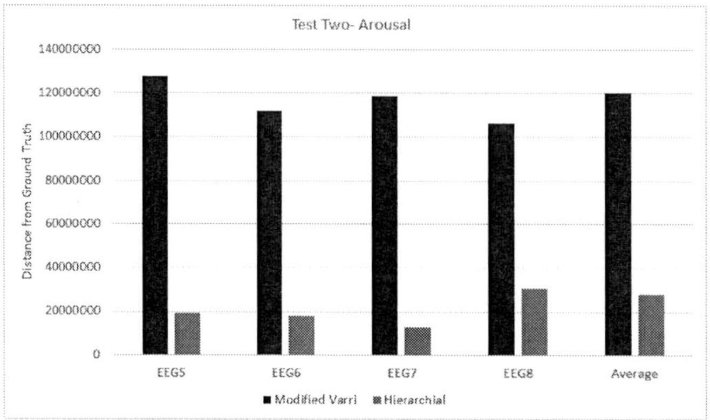

Fig. 5. Sum of distances of predicted segmentation boundaries from ground truth for Arousal events in EEG signal channels 5-8 and Average over all 8 channels.

As it can be seen, the hierarchical segmentation algorithm performs significantly better than the fixed window algorithm and the Modified Varri algorithm. In both cases, hierarchical segmentation had a significantly smaller fit distance than its counterparts, while having similar representative distances. In other words, while Fixed window and Modified Varri suffered from over-segmentation, hierarchical segmentation was able to identify ground-truth boundaries while minimizing extraneous boundaries.

As with every clustering approach, the proximity function (or distance metric) used to measure the distance between neighboring points can significantly affect the outcome. However, our method allows the user to choose the proximity function that is deemed appropriate for each application, contrary to other existing segmentation methods which use predetermined metrics to recognize signal variability.

5 Conclusion

Fixed window segmentation, the traditional method of preprocessing signals for machine learning, often results in heterogeneous segments or over segmentation. In this paper, we proposed a new segmentation method, the Hierarchical Segmentation Algorithm, which uses machine learning algorithms to identify boundaries between homogeneous segments. By segmenting signals based on complex features, our algorithm allows users to increase segmentation accuracy using pre-existing knowledge of the signal itself. Experimental testing on real life data confirms that our algorithm significantly outperforms existing solutions in terms of segmentation accuracy. For future study, we hope to perform tests on different types of signals, and to investigate segmentation algorithms of lower complexity.

References

1. Espiritu, H., Metsis, V.: Automated detection of sleep disorder-related events from polysomnographic data. In: Healthcare Informatics (ICHI), 2015 International Conference on, IEEE (2015) 562–569
2. Florentino-Liano, B., O'Mahony, N., Artés-Rodríguez, A.: Hierarchical dynamic model for human daily activity recognition. In: BIOSIGNALS. (2012) 61–68
3. Katsis, C.D., Katertsidis, N., Ganiatsas, G., Fotiadis, D.I.: Toward emotion recognition in car-racing drivers: A biosignal processing approach. IEEE Transactions on Systems, Man, and Cybernetics-Part A: Systems and Humans **38**(3) (2008) 502–512
4. Tan, P.N., et al.: Introduction to data mining. Pearson Education India (2006)
5. Reyes-Ortiz, J.L., Oneto, L., Samà, A., Parra, X., Anguita, D.: Transition-aware human activity recognition using smartphones. Neurocomput. **171**(C) (January 2016) 754–767
6. Cigale, B., Divjak, M., Zazula, D.: Application of simulated annealing to biosignal classification and segmentation. In: Computer-Based Medical Systems, 2002.(CBMS 2002). Proceedings of the 15th IEEE Symposium on, IEEE (2002) 165–170
7. Panagiotakis, C., Tziritas, G.: Signal segmentation and modelling based on equipartition principle. In: Digital Signal Processing, 2009 16th International Conference on, IEEE (2009) 1–6
8. Giannakopoulos, T., Pikrakis, A.: Introduction to Audio Analysis: A MATLAB® Approach. Academic Press (2014)
9. Procházka, A., Mudrová, M., Vyšata, O., Háva, R., Araujo, C.P.S.: Multi-channel eeg signal segmentation and feature extraction. In: Intelligent Engineering Systems (INES), 2010 14th International Conference on, IEEE (2010) 317–320
10. Hassanpour, H., Shahiri, M.: Adaptive segmentation using wavelet transform. In: Electrical Engineering, 2007. ICEE'07. International Conference on, IEEE (2007) 1–5
11. Lourenço, A., Silva, H., Leite, P., Lourenço, R., Fred, A.L.: Real time electrocardiogram segmentation for finger based ecg biometrics. In: Biosignals. (2012) 49–54
12. Kurtek, S., Wu, W., Christensen, G.E., Srivastava, A.: Segmentation, alignment and statistical analysis of biosignals with application to disease classification. Journal of Applied Statistics **40**(6) (2013) 1270–1288
13. Zhang, H., Fritts, J.E., Goldman, S.A.: Image segmentation evaluation: A survey of unsupervised methods. computer vision and image understanding **110**(2) (2008) 260–280
14. Bhoi, A.K., Phurailatpam, D., Tamang, J.S.: Evaluation of frequency domain features for myopathic emg signals in mat lab. Int. Journal of Engineering Research and Application **3** 622–627

Research on evaluation indicators weigh computing method of scientific research institutions based on Linked Open Data

JiangShiyin[1]

[1] National Science Library, Chinese Academy of Sciences
jiangsy@mail.las.ac.cn

Abstract. Evaluation indicators weigh compute method of scientific research institutions will directly affect the accuracy and objectivity of the evaluation results of scientific research institution.Linked Open Data, offers a large number of semantically described and linked concepts in various domains. In this paper, we propose a novel approach to take advantage of this structured data in the domain of scientific research institutions to compute the indicators weigh.Derived from information theory, our approach of computing the Information Content for semantic relations and ranking universities based on these indicators weigh achieved results comparable to the Shanghai Jiao Tong University.The score correlation and rank correlation of the above two ranking results are very strong, which proves the validity of the weight computing method based on the Linked Open Data in this study.

Keywords: Linked Open Data, evaluation indicators, evaluation of scientific research institutions, weigh compute.

1 Introduction

The multi indicators comprehensive evaluation method is widely used in the quantitative evaluation of scientific research institutions, and the weight design of indicators has always been a key and difficult point of technology.

The semantic relations between scientific research institutions and their achievements, personnel, education, awards and other information have been established in the Linked Open Data, and the specific semantics under these semantic relations are highly correlated with the evaluation indicators of scientific research institutions.Besides these semantic relationships are relatively authoritative and accurate, providing a guarantee for the use of semantic relations to compute the weight of the indicators .

2 Methodology

Base on the concept of entropy in Information Theory,after giving a set of evaluation indicators, the relative intensity of each indicator in the competition sense is considered from the perspective of information. It represents the degree of the effective information quantity provided by the evaluation indicator in the problem. Details available semantics relations regarding scientific research institutions include its awards and prizes, doctoral students, publication, notable work, and other key contributions (see Figure 1) [1].The semantic relations extracted from Linked Open Data can be employed as indicators.We propose a novel metric to compute the Information Content of semantics relations that signify the indicator weigh in the Linked Open Data. We proceed to experiment with indicator weigh computing which based on the aggregated Information Content of each indicator.

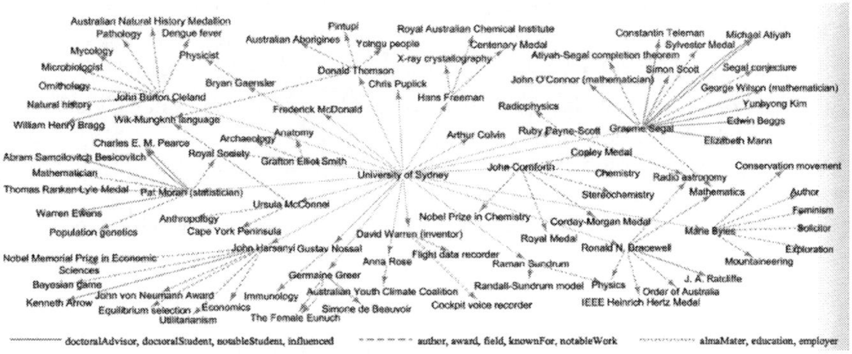

Fig. 1. Part of Linked Open Data graph regarding scientific research institutions.

2.1 Information Content Measurement

In information theory, Information Content (IC), is the amount of bits required to reconstruct the transmitted information source[2].Based on probability theory, Information Content is computed as a measure of generated amount of surprise:

$$\mathrm{IC(a)} = \qquad a)) \tag{1}$$

such that $a)$ is the probability of appearance of the term or concept a in its context.In this paper, a represents a semantic relationship.

2.2 Indicator Information Content

In Linked Open Data, a single evaluation indicator may correspond to multiple semantic relationships.L=$\{l_1,l_2,\ldots,l_{|L|}\}$ is the set of semantics relations, in which l_i is the relation, defined as <a,l_i,b>, connecting resource a to resource b. I=$\{I_1,I_2,\ldots,I_{|I|}\}$ is the set of research evaluation indicators, semantic relations $L_i \in$ L ,is a subset of L , corresponding to each indicator I_i.Based on information theory, The weight of a single evaluation indicator is the sum of all semantic relation's information content corresponding to the indicator[3]:

$$) = \sum \qquad) \tag{2}$$

3 Experiment

3.1 Experimental Context

The main Linked Dataset employed in our experiments was DBpedia[4]（structured content from the information created in the Wikipedia）.Using the proposed indicator compute method to compute the weight of indicators (Ns&Pub,Hici,Alumni,Award) Shanghai Jiaotong University World University Rankings（SJTU）uses, a rank experiment for the top 100 universities, according to the two ranking results to compare and analyze.

1. DownLoad DBPedia 3.8 and load the data into OpenLink Virtuoso.
2. Find out all the semantic relationships corresponding to each indicator.
3. Compute the information content for each indicator.
4. Rankings for the top 100 universities of Shanghai Jiaotong University rankings based on the computing weight values of the indicators.
5. Comparing our results with existing Shanghai Jiaotong University rankings

3.2 Results

The indicators and corresponding semantic relations in DBpedia used in the experiment,See table 1. Part of lod-based top 100 universities ranking,see table 2.The score results using the proposed weight computing method and the SJTU existing weight score results,Pearson correlation was 0.980,Spearman correlation was 0.939.Its ranking order and ranking order of SJTU, Pearson correlation and Spearman correlation was 0.939,see table 3. The score correlation and rank correlation of the above two ranking results are very strong, which proves the validity of the weight computing method based on Linked Open Data.

Table 1. The indicators and corresponding semantic relations in DBpedia.

Indicators	Semantic relations	Weight value
Research Output (Ns&Pub)	dbo:author,dbo:publisher	10.044929211724337
Research Team (Hici)	dbo:employer,dbo:occupation, dbo:training,dbo:team	9.009842851681144
Talent cultivation (Alumni)	dbo:almaMater,dbo:education	10.294329936963663
Prizes (Award)	dbo:award	10.460661878821565

Table 2. Part of lod-based top 100 universities.

rank	university	score	SJTU score	SJTU rank
1	Harvard University	4985.469309	130	1

2	University of Cambridge	3514.994267	86.47	5
3	University of California, Berkeley	3468.672932	89.86	3
4	Massachusetts Institute of Technology	3451.373995	89.14	4
5	Stanford University	3441.811203	93.5	2
6	Columbia University	3071.002103	79.65	6
7	University of Chicago	2912.113239	70.56	10
8	Princeton University	2884.626794	70.49	11
9	University of Oxford	2834.65499	76.8	7
10	Yale University	2738.671839	74.92	8
...	...	...	...	...
100	École Polytechnique Fédérale de Lausanne	966.427745	34.34	89

Table3. The correlation between lod-based and SJTU.

Pearson		Spearman	
score	rank	score	rank
0.980	0.939	0.939	0.939

4 Conclusion

Linked Open Data,as a structured and reliable source of semantic data, it can offer significant benefits for a low-cost and accurate performance computing of evaluation indicators weigh of scientific research institutions.

We will focus more on the accuracy of the compute by capturing more semantic relations from Linked Open Data cloud and by eliminating any trace of redundancy.

References

1. Meymandpour R, Davis J G. Ranking Universities Using Linked Open Data[C]// Linked Data on the Web. 2013.Author, F., Author, S.: Title of a proceedings paper. In: Editor, F., Editor, S. (eds.) CONFERENCE 2016, LNCS, vol. 9999, pp. 1–13. Springer, Heidelberg (2016).
2. Edwards, S.: Elements of information theory, 2nd edition[J].Information Processing & Management,44(1), 400–401 (2008).
3. Meymandpour, R. and Davis, J. G. 2013. Linked Data Informativeness. Web Technologies and Applications, 7808, 629-637. Springer Berlin Heidelberg.
4. DBpedia[EB/OL].[2016-03-11].http://dbpedia.org/ontology/.

A New Approach for Mining Representative Patterns

Abeda Sultana, Hosneara Ahmed, and Chowdhury Farhan Ahmed

Dept. of Computer Science and Engineering, University of Dhaka, Bangladesh
{abida1616@gmail.com,hosneara_17@yahoo.com,farhan@du.ac.bd}

Abstract. With the revolution of science and technology, we step into the age of information, particularly age of data. As the amount of data is expanding, scarcity of knowledge is also increasing. Hence analysis for more useful and interesting knowledge is on demand. Representative patterns can be a solution to it to represent data in the more concise way. Different efficient methods for mining frequent and erasable patterns exist in representative pattern mining field that are regarded as significant. We have proposed a new type of pattern called decaying pattern. These patterns are characterized as those patterns that were frequent for a time being and then decayed with time. These patterns of declining nature as to frequency can give us the opportunity to analyze reasons behind items' decrease such as extinct animals, finding unsolved accidental news, analysis of buying behavior of customers that require further inspection.

Keywords: Frequent Pattern, Erasable Pattern, Representative Pattern, Data Mining, Pattern Tree, Decaying Pattern

1 Introduction

Data mining is the process of analyzing large amount data to discover knowledge and finding patterns and relationship among them. By means of data mining we can renovate huge amount of information into useful information and knowledge. This knowledge are immensely important on various applications and research field. Frequent pattern mining is one of the most significant field of data mining. Pattern of any itemset having frequency of more than a given threshold is called frequent in a given dataset.Another important domain of data mining is mining representative patterns. Different kind of frequent patterns can be formed in itemsets, sequences, episodes and substructures and so on. Representative frequent pattern mining is finding precise, distinctive and explicable set of patterns of each class that represent their key characteristics among other classes. Representative patterns represent a dataset and extract the significant knowledge from huge amount of data. This representation can be done in many criteria. Many efficient and noble works are already done on these e.g. some patterns are most significant in the database, that are mined as representative frequent patterns, some patterns are so insignificant that it is better to prune them, this patterns are mined as representative erasable patterns[10,11,12]. Again maximal, closed, top rank-k, top-k frequent regular [7,8,9] are also developed for representative pattern mining.

There are some patterns which are frequent in a database for some time being, then they are lost. These patterns could be in representative frequent pattern set but due to their decaying nature, they fail to get a place here. This type of patterns are ignored but have importance in various research fields. We focus on this decaying representative patterns which can be a means of mining important knowledge from huge amount of data.

1.1 Motivation

With the existing algorithms we can only find the patterns which are most frequent or too scarce. Patterns having both characteristics that are once frequent but have become infrequent with time are not mined yet. This type of patterns are not observed but have importance in various research fields.

Motivating Example

Suppose a large electronics company sells various types of products like laptops, smartphones, smartwatches, tablets etc. Laptops and smartphones are very popular among the buyers of that company. These two products were sold throughout the year. On the other hand, smart watches are not greatly welcomed by the customers, so the sale of smartwatches remained below the expectation. However for tablet the case was slightly different. When company released it first, it was a very demandable product. After there second release, the sale suddenly decreased.

After two or three years when a data analyst of that company mined for the most remunerative products, he got laptop and smart phone as the number of sale was higher and so the profit. Again as least profitable product he got smart watch. Company will take action for better development of smartwatch. As tablets do not fit in any of the two categories, company will never know the problem why the sale of tablets decreased and it will not take any necessary step. If analyst would observe decaying nature in the trade, this tablet will come to light for finding the reason behind consumers' sudden disinterest toward this product.

There are more important applications of decaying patterns. Everyday accidental or unusual occurrences are happening which appear in newspaper and social media so frequently for some days and then perish of unnotice. In most cases they remain unsolved. Mining those patterns can help correspondents write follow-ups. Again we can find this pattern in species data of animals and plants which have become extinct such as Sea Mink, Tasmanian Tiger, West African Black Rhinoceros and so on. In many cases this decaying nature is prevailing but do not come to light. This gradual going off detection is our main purpose of proposing new type of pattern.

1.2 Contributions

- We have proposed a concept of new type of representative patterns named "Decaying patterns" which represents those which were once in frequent pattern set but decayed with time. This could be put into representive pattern set but due to degradation, they fail to stay there.
- We have developed an algorithm to mine this type of patterns from real life large datasets which are collected from famous data mining repositories FIMI and SPMF.
- Data that we have used to test are considered as stream of data so we have divided it into set of windows and for any current window we have observed whether it is frequent or erasable which assures getting recent result always.
- We have run our algorithm on six real life datasets, two synthetic datasets. Further our own web service to collect news from prominent online newspapers provided us with floods of daily news. We have pre-processed that huge data and applied our algorithm. From all of these real life large dataset, significant number of decaying patterns have been obtained.

The rest of the paper is organized as follows. In section 2 some overview of related works on representative pattern has been given. Section 3 consists of our proposed approach, algorithm and a small example simulation based on the algorithm. Section 4 contains the experimental analysis based on different performance metrics by running the algorithm on many real life and synthetic datasets. Finally in section 5 we concluded with discussion on the future scope of contribution on our proposed algorithm.

2 Related Work

Maximal Frequent Itemsets[1]: Low min_sup generates large number of patterns. Bayardo[1] proposed for storing long patterns(maximal frequent itemsets) in roughly linear scale. If a pattern is X is frequent, all Y where $Y \subset X$ is frequent.

FPclose[2] implements another distinction of FP-tree known as CFI-tree (Closed Frequent Itemset Tree). Four fields are necessary for this tree structure - item name, count, node link and level. Subset test of maximality is done with level. Count works for checking if the support count is equal to it's superset and if it is not, both superset and subset are stored in memory. FP-close is the fastest among the algorithms of that time when minimum support is low but when minimum support is high it becomes slow than Apriori.

TFP[3]: For mining top-k frequent closed items, TFP is an efficient algorithm. The common factor among all approaches of frequent pattern mining is the usage of *min_sup* threshold which ensures generation of accurate and entire set of frequent item sets which leads to two problems stated below -

First, an appropriate *min_sup* is taken as input but this requires detailed knowledge on mining query. Again setting min support is quite problematic in the sense that a too small threshold may produce thousands of itemsets on the other hand a too big threshold may generate no answers.
Second, Due to the downward closure property, when a long itemset is mined, it may generate an exponential number of itemsets.
To solve these problems they proposed a new approach of mining top-k frequent closed itemsets of minimum length *min_l*, where k is user given number of frequent closed itemset that they want to be mined. k is easy to specify and top-k means k most frequent closed itemsets. *min_l* helps to mine long itemset without mining the short ones first.

ECP(Erasable Closed Pattern)[4]: In factories, for the optimization of production plans erasable pattern(EP) mining plays an important role. For efficient mining of these patterns various algorithms have been proposed. Nevertheless, number of EPs becomes numerous because of large threshold values which cause memory usage overhead. Hence it becomes requisite to mine compressed EPs representation. This paper first came up with the concept of erasable closed patterns (ECPs). These ECPs can be represented without losing information. They at first gave a theory to detect ECPs based on a structure name dPidset and proved it. Then two efficient algorithms, ECPat and dNC-ECPM are proposed. Their result of experiment on these two algorithm shows that for sparse datasets ECPat performs the best but ECPM algorithm is more efficient in the case of memory usage and runtime for rest of the datasets.

DSTree(Data Stream Tree)[5]: In this paper, Leung et. al. proposed the concept of data stream tree. Transactions are sorted in any canonical order chosen by user. Each node keeps a list for frequency count. With the appearance of a new batch of transaction, it is appended to the list to each of the node and frequency count of that node in the current batch. The last entry of a certain node N is the frequency count of that node in the current batch. When the next batch of transactions arrives after fulfilling the batches in a window, the list is shifted to left to place the newest batch to be added as the most recent one. In DSTree costly deletion is not required, only shifting and updating the frequency list will suffice to update tree.

3 Our Proposed Approach

Decaying patterns are important and useful for analysis and many other purposes in many data repository. To the best of our knowledge, it is the first approach for mining decaying pattern. By observing the enormous application in many sectors, we hope these patterns will be effective and useful for gaining knowledge. We are using a tree similar to data stream tree with sliding window approach. The sliding window is for observing the frequency variation effectively and the tree formation is for mining frequent sub patterns. Again a pattern tree will be constructed with the frequent sub patterns from where decaying patterns can be mined efficiently.

3.1 Preliminaries

A window is comprised of a set of batch and a batch consists of a set of transactions.

- *win_F* (Frequent window length in decaying pattern) The number of consecutive windows where a the pattern has to be frequent.
- *win_IF* The number of consecutive windows where a pattern need to be infrequent (Difference between total window size & *win_F*).
- *min_WT* (Minimum window support threshold) The minimum support threshold that is to be crossed by a pattern by occurrence for being frequent in a window.
- *ET* (Error threshold in *win_F*) The maximum number of batches in *win_F* where pattern can be infrequent.
- *ET'* (Error threshold in *win_IF*) The maximum number of batches in *win_IF* where pattern can be frequent.

Definition 1 (Decaying pattern) Consider a set of batches of transactions $B=\{b_1, b_2, b_3,...,b_n\}$ where each batch consists of a number of transactions $T=\{t_1, t_2, t_3,...,t_m\}$. If a pattern is frequent(meets *min_WT*) in frequent windows (each window of *win_F*) and then becomes infrequent in decay windows (each window of *win_IF*), it is called decaying pattern.
e.g. a pattern with a window length 9 and the frequency list of the pattern in these windows is [9,5,10,4,3,3,2,0,0]. Let the *min_WT* is 4, frequent window length *win_F* is 4. Here the for first four window[9,5,10,4] the pattern meets *min_WT*(4). The pattern remains infrequent for last five windows *win_IF* [3,3,2,0,0]. So this pattern is our desired decaying pattern.

- Batch size and window size generation

  The size of batch and windows will be based on the number of transaction in a database. In a database with small transaction this value should be kept as small as possible. If user wants to observe the decaying characteristics intensely then he should keep batch size small because the window will move slowly in that case. In general case with increment of batch size the number of decaying patterns increase. For sparse dataset batch size should be as large as possible for this reason.
- *win_F* and *win_IF* generation

  For dense dataset

$$win\_F = \frac{Total\ window\ size}{2}$$

  or

$$win\_F = \frac{2 \times Total\ window\ size}{3}$$

For sparse dataset

$$win\_F = \frac{Total\ window\ size}{3}$$

$$win\_IF = Total\ window\ size - win\_F$$

But this can be tuned by user according to his demand.

- Minimum window support min_WT

  We represent the minimum window support as a percentage value. A minimum window support threshold of 60% would mean a pattern would have to be appear in at least 60% of all the transactions in current window of the data stream. The min_WT value is calculated as follows:

  $min\_WT = minimum\ support\ percentage \times\ number\ of\ transactions\ in\ WS$

- ET and ET' generation

  The error threshold in win_F and win_IF should be 1% for dense dataset which refers that a pattern which remains frequent in at least 99% windows of win_F and remains infrequent in at least 99% windows of win_IF, patterns will be excepted as decaying pattern. For sparse dataset ET and ET' can vary from 10% to 20%

3.2 Tree Construction and Mining

Our tree construction will follow the mechanism of DSTree[5] construction but we have changed it according to our our purpose.
The transactions in the tree will be sorted in frequency descending order for static database. In case of data stream any canonical order can be maintained like alphabetic order or order based on any specific property. With every node in the tree a frequency list is added which contain the frequency of current batches of that item. A batch of transactions is inserted at a time and frequency of each item is appended in the frequency list of each item node. When new batch is added, the list is shifted to left and the oldest batch frequency is removed. This has the same effect as deleting the transactions in the oldest batch from the window.

In each window, the frequent patterns are mined with any frequent pattern mining algorithm. We used FP-growth[6] algorithm for mining frequent patterns in a window. These patterns from each window is added to a new pattern tree. Each node in a pattern tree is also consists of a frequency list. Frequent patterns generated from each window of data stream tree considered as a batch of transactions for the pattern tree. The frequency list of each node contained the frequency of that node in a particular batch. Each batch of frequent patterns are inserted at a time in tree. When a complete pattern tree is generated, we will extract the patterns of our interest by checking only the leaf node. If a leaf node meets the condition of a decaying pattern the whole branch and the sub-branch of a path including the leaf node will be considered as decaying pattern

Example Workout

- In table.1 a small transaction dataset is shown. There are seven items a,b,c,d,e,f,g and fifteen transactions. We have divided the transactions into five batches. Each batch consists of three transactions, batch length BS is 3. Each window consists of 2 batches, window size WS is 2.
  We consider our minimum window support threshold min_WT as 3 which means that a pattern can be frequent in a window if the total frequency of a pattern is at least 3 in that window.
  Frequent window length in decaying pattern, win_F is 2.

- Now we have to construct a DSTree with these batches. In figure.1a the tree is constructed with batch-1 and batch-2. The frequency of each batch is inserted in the frequency list with each node e.g. 'a' has value 3 and 2 in its list which refers to the frequency of 'a' in first batch is 3 and in second batch is 2. In each window we mine frequent pattern from the tree with FP-growth algorithm. The total frequency of 'a' in window 1 is 5 which is greater than min_WT, so 'a' is a frequent pattern for window 1.
  In this window, we have found {a}, {b}, {d}, {a,b}, {b,d}, {a,d}, {a,b,d} as frequent patterns.

Batch	Transactions	Contents
First	t1 t2 t3	{a,b,d,e} {a,b,f,d} {a,b}
Second	t4 t5 t6	{a,b,d,f} {b,f} {a,b,d}
Third	t7 t8 t9	{a,b,d,e,f} {d,e} {a,f}
Fourth	t10 t11 t12	{a,d,f} {d,e,g} {a,e,f,g}
Fifth	t13 t14 t15	{a,d} {a,d,f} {d,e,g}

Table 1: Transactions are arranged in frequency descending order

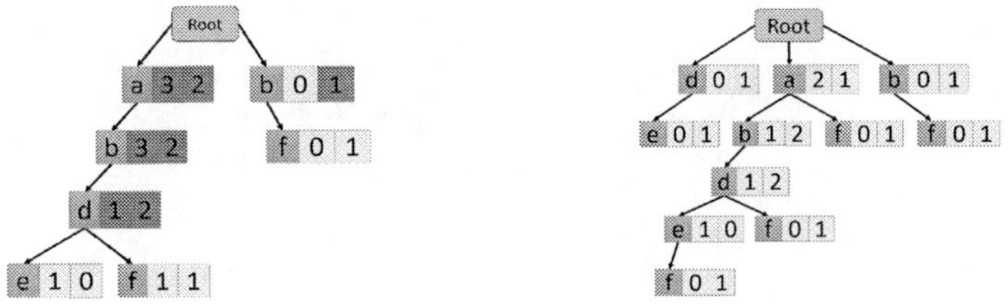

(a) Tree after including first two batch (b) Tree after inserting 3rd batch

Fig. 1: Window 1 & 2

- For second window, we have to insert third batch by removing the oldest batch from the tree. We shifted the frequency list of each node to left direction and added the frequency of new batch to the rightmost. Again by mining frequent pattern we got {a}, {b}, {d}, {f}, {a,b}, {a,d}, {b,d}, {a,b,d}. [Figure.1b]

(a) Tree after inserting 4th batch (b) Tree after inserting 5th batch

Fig. 2: Window 3 & 4

- For third window [Figure.2a], after inserting fourth batch we got {a}, {e} as frequent patterns.

- On fourth window[Figure.2b] we got {a} and {g} as frequent patterns.

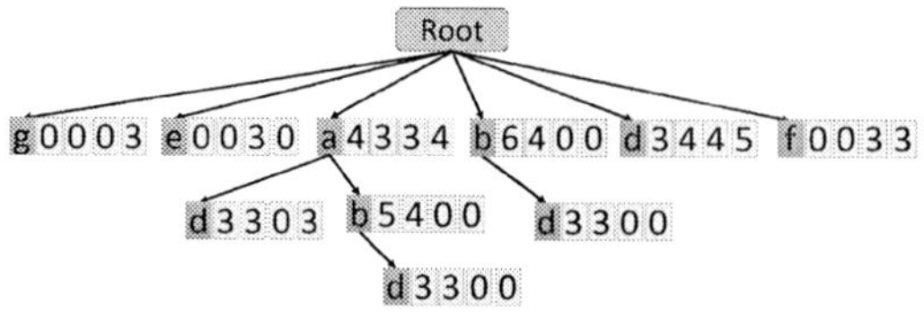

Fig. 3: Pattern tree with the frequent patterns from all windows

- We have built a pattern tree with all the patterns found above, considering the patterns from each window as a batch of transactions to insert in the tree. Each node also consists of a frequency list. [Figure 3]
- Now from this pattern tree, we can easily find out desired pattern only by checking the leaf nodes. The decaying patters are - {a, b, d}, {b, d}, {a, d}. [Figure.3]

Algorithm 1: Algorithm for Mining Decaying Patterns

Input : transactions[] where each transaction consists of items, *min_sup*, *win_F* and *win_IF*, *ET* and *ET'*
Output: List of decaying patterns in structure named *Decay_Patterns*

Sort transactions[] in lexicographic order
root← ***Add_Batch_to_Tree***(Batch$_0$,...,Batch$_m$)
PatternSet ←***FPgrowth***(tree)
foreach *Remaining batch Batch$_i$* **do**
  Add_batch_to_tree(*Batch_i,root*)
  Pattern_set[window++] ← ***FP_growth***(tree)
  Pattern_tree(*pattern_set, root*)
end
Decay_Patterns ← ***Extract_Pattern***(root)
Function ***Extract_Pattern(root)***
  foreach *leaf node in tree* **do**
    if *ItemFreq in win_F* $\geq$ *min_WT and ItemFreq in each batch of win_IF == 0* **then**
      keep the node in *tree*
      Decay_Patterns[count++] = $\beta \cup$ leaf node
      Prune the leaf node upto root;
    else
  end
  return *Decay_Patterns*

Algorithm 2: Algorithm for Mining Decaying Patterns

```
Function Add_Batch_to_Tree(batch[], root)
    if root is NULL then
        foreach batch_i in batch[] and transaction t in batch_i do
            add t to tree and nodeFrequency to list
        end
    else
        Shift left each node in tree
        foreach batch_i in batch[] and each transaction t in batch_0 do
            add t to tree
            add frequency of node to list
        end
    end
    if frequency of each window is 0 of any node in tree then
        delete node and its successors
    end
    return root
Function Pattern_Tree(patterns[])
    foreach pattern_i in patterns[] do
        Add pattern_i to tree
        insert frequency of node to freq_list
    end
```

4 Experimental Results

We tested our algorithm on six real life and two synthetic datasets- chess, mushroom, pumsb, accidents, connect, c73d10k, c20d10k. Also we have a web service where we fetch data from some prominent online news portal of Bangladesh. We collected around 59,033 news in 4 months (August to November). We processed the data and applying our algorithm, got our desired result. The algorithm is implemented in JAVA and experiments are performed in Linux environment (Ubuntu 16.04), on a PC with Intel(R) Core-i3-4005U 1.70 GHz processor 4GB main memory. As there is no literature on finding decaying pattern, we could not compare our result with any other algorithm. For this reason we have shown our result on five metrics.

- **Number of patterns with varying minimum window support**
- **Number of patterns with varying window size**
- **Number of patterns with varying batch size**
- **Runtime with varying minimum support**
- **Maximum memory usage with varying minimum support**

4.1 Pattern Count W.R.T. Minimum Window Support

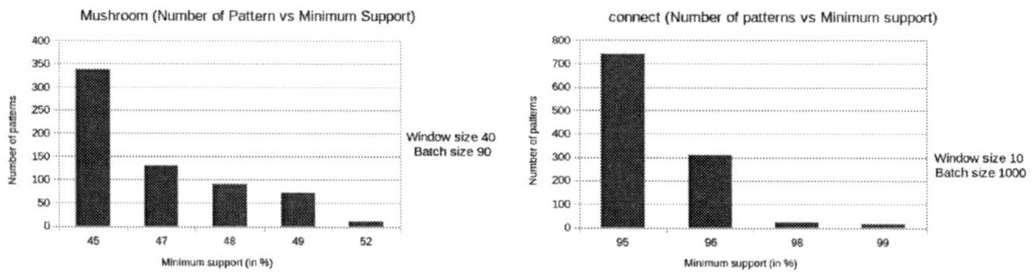

(a) Mushroom dataset (b) Connect dataset

Fig. 4: Pattern number vs Minimum window support (min_WT)

With varying minimum support value number of decaying patterns also varies. For frequent patterns, number of patterns increases when minimum support decreases but in case of decaying pattern this trend does not hold always. It is possible because when minimum support is low, the patterns tend to be frequent in the decaying window(win_IF) and those patterns will be rejected as per the definition of decaying pattern. When minimum support is higher those rejected pattern will be added in decaying pattern list. From figure.4 and result of two dense dataset (fig.4b and 4a) connect and mushroom are showed where pattern number decreases with increasing min_WT but for sparse dataset accident and c20d10k (fig.5b and 5a) the results are different. Number of patterns tends to increase with increasing min_WT for accidents. Nearly reverse nature is noticed for c20d10k. This property actually depends on dataset.

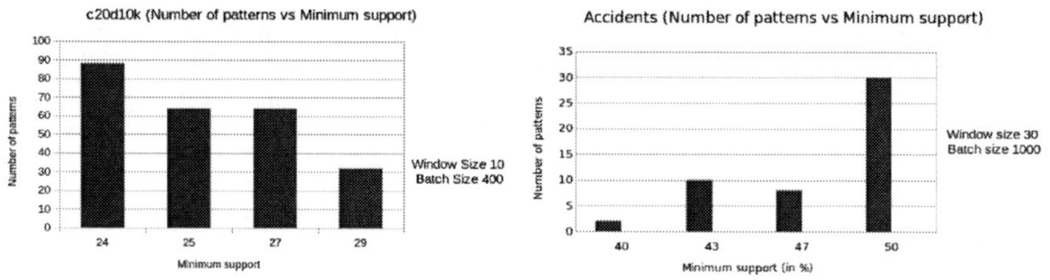

(a) c20d10k dataset (b) Accident dataset

Fig. 5: Pattern number vs Minimum window support (min_WT)

Our news dataset was highly sparse as we got news of four month only. For better output we splitted the dataset by taking two months' news in a group. From the dataset of news August and September we observed several decaying patterns (fig.6a). Most of them are murder incidents including 16th amendments of Bangladesh constitution, floods in northern part of Bangladesh. From the dataset, consists of news of four month August to November(fig.6b) the important decaying news mostly are rape and murder case including some international matters like Rohinga issue, issue of mosque Al-Aqsa in Palestine etc.

4.2 Pattern Count W.R.T. Window Size

In case of dense dataset generally pattern number tends to increase with increasing window size (figure.7a) because in larger window, longer decaying pattern can be generated and in that case there would be a lot of sub patterns. Thus number of patterns increases. But in case of sparse dataset the opposite tendency is noticed(figure.7b) because sparse dataset contains small number of decaying pattern when window size increases possibility of being frequent of a pattern in a large set of transaction decreases. Thus many patterns are rejected for being infrequent in the frequent windows. This characteristic varies with dataset.

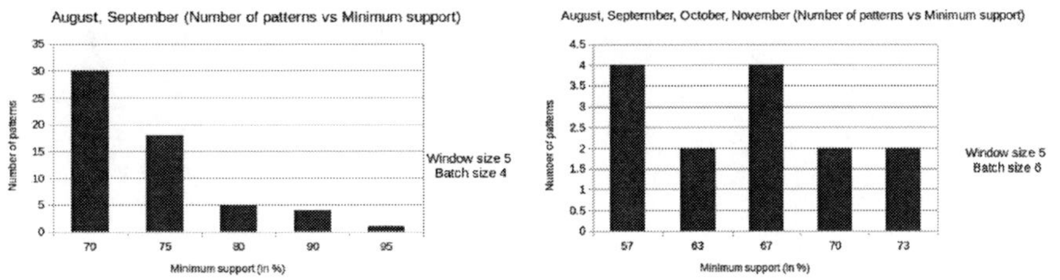

(a) News dataset (August and Semptember)

(b) News dataset (August to November)

Fig. 6: Pattern number vs Minimum window support (min_WT)

4.3 Pattern Count W.R.T. Batch Size

The next metric is number of pattern w.r.t batch size. Similar characteristic maintains with previous metric. In case of dense dataset (figure.8a) number of patterns increase with increasing batch size because of longer pattern generation and when batch size increases total number of window decreases so a pattern has to be frequent and infrequent in small number of windows thus probability of getting decaying pattern increased with increasing batch size. Again for sparse dataset (figure.8b) number of pattern tends to decrease because with batch size is larger window slides faster. Patterns in a sparse dataset which once frequent in

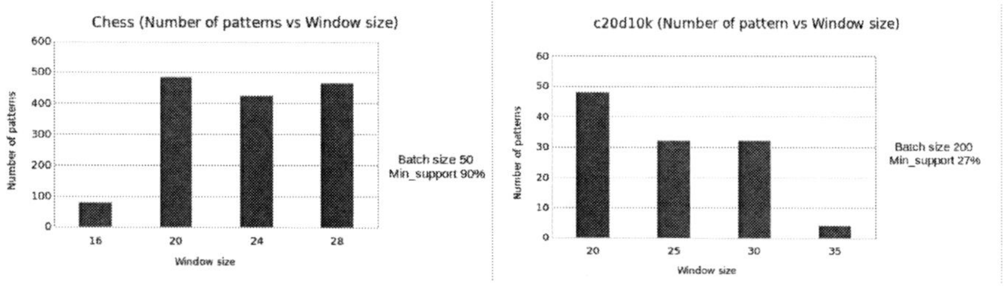

(a) Chess dataset (b) C20d10k dataset

Fig. 7: Pattern number vs Window size

one window tends to become infrequent in subsequent windows thus the number of patterns decrease. This characteristic also varies with dataset.

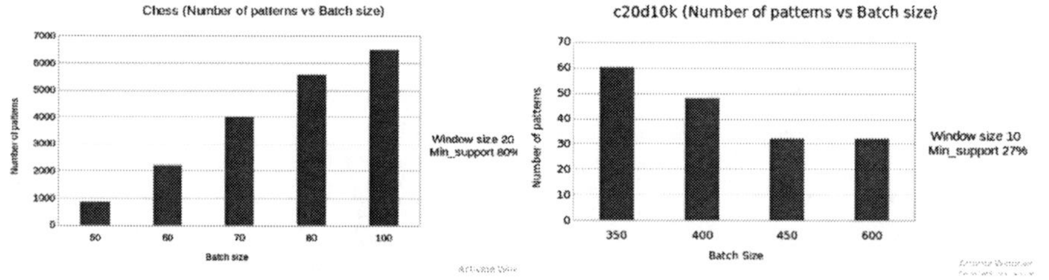

(a) Chess dataset (b) C20d10k dataset

Fig. 8: Pattern number vs Batch size

4.4 Runtime Evaluation

Runtime graphs are showed with varying min_WT on three batches for a dense (figure.9a) and a sparse dataset (figure.9b). Run time depends on number of patterns generated and total number of windows to calculate. From the graph it is clear that run time increases with decreasing minimum support and batch size. For sparse dataset result is bit different. With increasing batch size number of patterns decreases as we showed earlier thus runtime becomes higher. In case of sparse dataset pattern number varies differently with varying win_WT so as the runtime.

4.5 Maximum Memory Usage Evaluation

Memory usage also depends on the number of patterns generated. With varying minimum support the variation of maximum memory usage during run time is

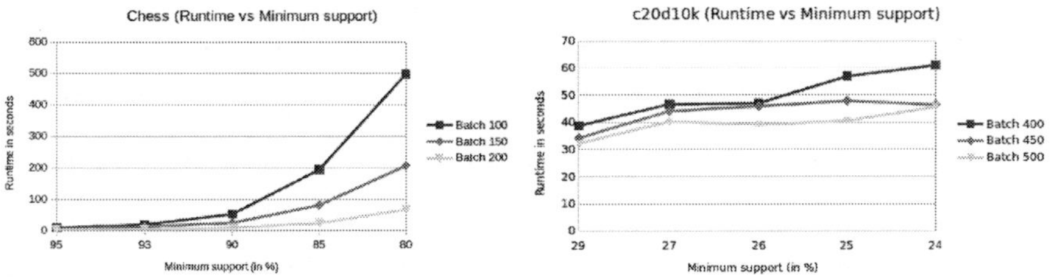

(a) Chess dataset (b) C20d10k dataset

Fig. 9: Runtime (in second) vs *win_WT*

shown. We determined maximum memory usage for any instance. During the execution of the code, we have kept the maximum value of memory usage. If at any instance more memory is used than the value, we have updated it. Here we have shown memory consumption of two dataset- chess (figure.10a) , the dense one and c23d10k (figure.10b), the sparse one.

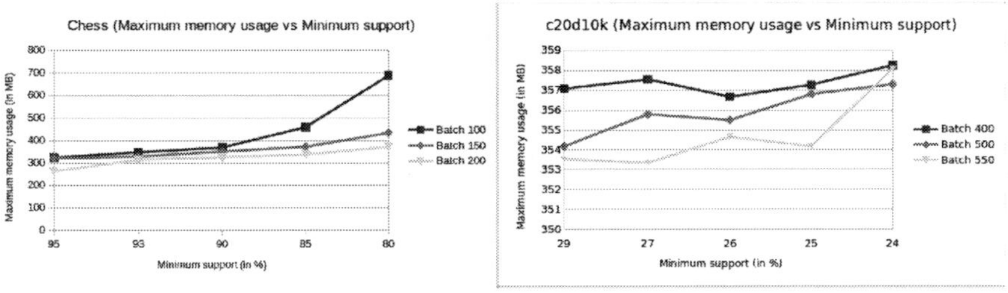

(a) Chess dataset (b) C20d10k dataset

Fig. 10: Maximum memory usage (in MB) vs *win_WT*

5 Conclusions

Many significant patterns are worn out with time which should be in representative pattern and need proper attention. This type of patterns are important because if we only focus on those which are always in representative set, some promising patterns that suddenly started decaying will remain neglected. For this, mining this type of patterns are important for different contexts. We have developed an algorithm for mining decaying patterns and applied it by merging the concept of data stream. We have constructed pattern tree structure which speeds up the mining process. As we are dealing with data stream, more interesting knowledge can be found at any instance of time from the patterns.

The application field of this algorithm is huge beginning from market basket data to find new characteristics in dataset. We applied the work on many real life dataset and have got expected results. Our work is highly applicable for mining decaying news and we also showed significant result from our own processed news data. As a future work we are planning to develop more compressed structure of tree, applying more efficient mining methodology. We will also carry out more research for generalizing the algorithm so that it can be performed with dynamic window adjusting feature to get the best result without user's input.

References

1. Bayardo,R.J. : Efficiently Mining Long Patterns from Databases. In: Proc. ACM-SIGMOD Int'l Conf. Management of Data, pp. 85-93 (1998)
2. Grahne,G., Zhu, J.: Fast Algorithms for Frequent Itemset Mining Using FP-Trees. In: IEEE Transaction on knowledge and data engineering,vol. 17,No 10, pp. 1347-1362 (2005)
3. Wang, J., Han, J., Lu, Y., Tzvetkov, P. : TFP: An Efficient Algorithm for Mining Top-K Frequent Closed Itemsets. In: IEEE Trans. on Knowledge and Data Engineering, Vol 17, No 5, pp. 652-664 (2005)
4. Vo, B., Le, T., Nguyen, G., Hong, T.: Efficient algorithms for mining erasable closed patterns from product datasets. In: IEEE Access ,PP. 1-1 (2017)
5. Leung,C. K. S., Khan, Q. I.: DSTree: A Tree Structure for the Mining of Frequent Sets from Data Streams. In: Proc Sixth International Conference on Data Mining (ICDM '06). IEEE Computer Society, Washington, DC, USA, pp. 928-932 (2006)
6. Han, J., Pei, J., Yin, J.: Frequent Patterns without Candidate Generation A Frequent-Pattern Tree Approach. In: Data Mining and Knowledge Discovery, v.8 n.1, pp.53-87 (2004)
7. Amphawan, K., Lenca, P., Surarerks, A.: Efficient mining top-k regular- frequent itemset using compressed tidsets. In: proc. international workshops on new frontiers in applied data mining, May 24-27, 2011, Shenzhen,China. Lecture notes in computer science, vol. 7104, pp. 124-135 (2012)
8. Amphawan, K., Lenca, P., Surarerks, A.: Mining top-k regular-frequent itemsets using database partitioning and support estimation. In: Expert Systems with Applications, 39(2), 1924-1936 (2012)
9. Han, J., Wang, J., Lu, Y., Tzvetkov, P.: Mining top-k frequent closed pat- terns without minimum support. In: proc. 2002 IEEE international conference on data mining (ICDM 2002), Maebashi City, Japan (pp. 211-218), 9-12 (2002)
10. Nguyen, G., Le, T., Vo, B., Le, B.: Discovering erasable closed patterns. In: Proc. ACIIDS, Bali, Indonesia, pp. 368-376 (2015)
11. Lee, G.,Yun, U., Ryang, H.: Mining weighted erasable patterns by using underestimated constraint-based pruning technique. In: J. Intell. Fuzzy Syst., vol.28, no. 3, pp. 1145-1157 (2014)
12. Nguyen, G., Le, T., Vo, B., Le, B.: EIFDD:An efficient approach for erasable itemset mining of very dense datasets. In: Appl. Intell., vol. 43, no. 1, pp. 85-94 (2015)

Extracting Rate-changes in Transcriptional Regulation by Word Embedding with Sentence Structure and Domain Knowledge in Deep Neural Networks

Wenting Liu[1] and Yilei Zhang[2]

[1] Human Genetics, Genome Institute of Singapore, 138672
[2] Nanyang Technological University, Singapore
YLZhang@ntu.edu.sg

Abstract. As the rapid increase of bio-literature, it's very necessary to develop document analysis tools to automatically and accurately extract biological knowledge and events from bio-literatures. The vast majority of biological databases do not record temporal information of gene regulations, which are very important to understand the underlying mechanism of many diseases and biological processes. We previously constructed a corpus of time-delays related to the transcriptional regulation (bio-events) of yeast from the PubMed abstracts, summarized the knowledge rules of the bio-events as rate-changes in transcriptional regulation ontology, and obtained 86% accuracy by using the decision tree classifier with the ontology rule features. Deep neural networks (DNN) achieve great success in many machine learning applications including document analysis. The word2vec model learned the word embedding features from documents can achieve 50-70% accuracy on most of text classification tasks. However, the sentence structure and domain knowledge are rarely considered in DNNs of document classification. We proposed to combine word2vec features, sentence structure, and our ontology rule features to improve the DNNs for bio-events detection in document analysis. Experimental results show that on predicting transcription regulation events, the word2vec in DNN model achieves 73% accuracy, while our combined features in DNN with same parameters achieves 96% accuracy; on predicting the rate-changes in transcription regulation events, word2vec in DNN achieves only 59% accuracy, and our combined features in DNN achieves 90% accuracy. This shows the power of domain knowledge and sentence structure features with DNN in document analysis.

Keywords: Deep neural networks, biomedical events mining, rate-changes in transcriptional regulation.

1 Introduction

1.1 Background

Due to the increasing publications, literature mining is becoming useful for both hypothesis generation and biological discovery[1]. It's important but still challenge to automatically and accurately extract biological knowledge and events from biomedical literature [2][3][4]. The current state-of-the-art performance clearly shows that close to 80% in F1-score have been achieved in extracting simple bio-events, but the complex events such as binding and regulation events is still limited, the best performance achieved remains 30%–40% lower than that for simple events [2].

Inspired by the big success of deep learning in natural language processing, we applied it on our previous established corpus of bio-events of the rate changes in transcriptional regulation[5]. The vast majority of biological databases do not record temporal information of gene regulations, which are very important to understand the underlying mechanism of many diseases and biological processes. We previously constructed a corpus of time-delays related to the transcriptional regulation (complex bio-events) of yeast from the PubMed abstracts. By summarizing the textual patterns of the biological knowledge rules of the transcriptional regulation events, we established the rate-changed transcriptional regulation ontology. And it achieved 86% accuracy to predict transcriptional regulation by using the ontology rule features in the decision tree classifier[5].

In this paper, we applied the state-of-the-art word embedding and deep neural network model, combined with the domain knowledge from our ontology features and sentence structure features to improve the performance to infer the complex rate-changed transcriptional regulation events from our corpus.

1.2 Related Works

Deep neural networks (DNN) achieve great success in many machine learning applications including document analysis[6]. Word embedding methods represent words as continuous vectors in a low dimensional space which capture lexical and semantic properties of words. They can be obtained from the internal representations from neural network models of text[7]. The word2vec model learned the word embedding features from documents can achieve 50-70% accuracy on most of text classification tasks.
The convolutional and recurrent neural networks have been shown to capture effective hidden structures within sentences via continuous representations, thereby significantly advancing the performance of relation extraction[8][9].

However, the sentence structure and domain knowledge [10] are rarely considered in DNNs of document classification[6]. Nguyen and Grishman [5] combine the traditional feature-based method, the convolutional and recurrent neural networks to simultaneously benefit from their advantages. The approach is demonstrated to achieve the state-of-the-art performance on the ACE 2005 and SemEval datasets.

2 Methods

2.1 Corpus for rate changes in transcriptional regulation

The manually labeled corpus of events relating to rate changes in transcriptional regulation for yeast is available in https://sites.google.com/site/wentingntu/data. The created ontologies summarized both biological causes of rate changes in transcriptional regulation and corresponding positive and negative textual patterns from the corpus. We annotated the corpus by manually labeling sentences containing transcriptional regulation rate changing events as positive instances and others as negative instances. For positive instances, we identified trigger words that indicate mentions of transcriptional regulation processes or rate changes of the processes. These words were annotated to facilitate the creation of our time-delay (transcriptional regulation rate change) ontology. In the negative class, the sentence may only include information about gene regulation without rate changes or about a biological process other than transcriptional regulation. Both direct and indirect evidences exist in the positive instances. We thus further annotate the positive class with two types of events: (i) events with specific information about regulator, regulatee and rate changes in transcription regulation, and (ii) indirect evidences for transcription regulation rate changing events.

2.2 Representation learning

We employ the natural language toolkit, (NLTK)[11] to tokenize a sentence into the sequence of tokens. For each feature of interest, retrieve the corresponding vector by word2vec[12] [13], a feed-forward neural network (NN) that takes input sparse vector and produces a output dense vector [14]. The input vector encodes features such as words, part-of-speech tags or other linguistic information. The sparse-input linear models to neural-network based models is to stop representing each feature as a unique dimension (the so called one-hot representation) and representing them instead as dense vectors. The embeddings (the vector representation of each core feature) can then be trained like the other parameter of the function NN. The feature embeddings (the values of the vector entries for each feature) are treated as model parameters that need to be trained together with the other components of the network[15].

2.3 Sentence into vector

A sentence vector model [16] [17] is comprised of an unsupervised learning algorithm that learns fixed- size vector representations for variable-length pieces of texts such as sentences and documents[18]. The vector representations are learned to predict the surrounding words in contexts sampled from the paragraph. We adopted the Doc2Vec [19] from "Gensim", a python package, to get sentence embeddings using the word vectors.

2.4 Domain Knowledge Integration for Feature Combinations

The "Transcriptional Regulation Rate Change Ontology" [5] include the textual patterns of biological processes that may result in transcriptional regulation rate change. We previously propose a feature-based method that incorporates diverse lexical, syntactic and semantic features to automatically extract transcriptional regulation relations as follows.

Keyword-tag: a combination of the keywords defined in our ontologies, and their POS tags, which indicate their grammatical roles in sentences. The keywords in the features are normalized to reduce the diversity of words with the same tags.

Word-relation-word: two words concatenated by the name of their dependency relation type. The relation is extracted from the shortest relation path between genes and keywords in the dependency tree derived from the Stanford NLP parser [23].

Gene-keyword-distance: a triplet of gene, keyword, and length of the shortest relation path between them in the dependency tree. The contextual features provide general characteristics of the sentence or neighborhood where the target token is present.

2.5 Deep Neural Networks, multi-layer feed-forward networks

Feed-forward networks include networks with fully connected layers, such as the multilayer perceptron, as well as networks with convolutional and pooling layers[20]. All of the networks act as classifiers, but each with different strengths. The non-linearity of the network, as well as the ability to easily integrate pre-trained word embeddings, often lead to superior classification accuracy. We adopted multi-layer feed-forward networks, which can provide competitive results on sentiment classification[1].

3 Results

From the corpus, the 1000-dimension word vectors were produced with deep learning via word2vec of "gensim", a python package. Each sentence is then transformed a vector by adding the word vectors of the sentence. For each classification task, we perform 10-fold cross-validation to evaluate the classification performance. The positive sentences and negative ones are by randomly partitioned into 10 equal groups. For each round, one group is used as testing set, the other 9 groups are training set, a three layer deep neural networks (DNN) with 10, 20, 10 units, respectively, is built from the training set in 2000 steps by "tensorflow"; then the testing sentences are predicted by the DNN as positive or negative, and the accuracy is reported.

3.1 Predicting transcription regulation events

The following Table shows the performance of different feature set in DNN model and previous decision tree model on predicting the transcription regulation events in the 1309 sentences with 10-fold cross-validation. Experimental results show that on predicting transcription regulation events, the word2vec in DNN model achieves 73% accuracy, while our combined features in DNN with same parameters achieves 96% accuracy, which is significantly better than the 86% accuracy of previous ontology rules features in decision tree classifier.

Table 1. Performance on predicting transcription regulation events.

Features	Dimensions	Classifier	Accuracy (%)
Ontology Rules	115	Decision Tree	86
Word2vec	1000	Deep Neural Network	73
Word2vec +Ontology	1115	Deep Neural Network	96

3.2 Predicting the rate-changes in transcription regulation events

The following Table shows the performance of different feature set in DNN model and previous decision tree model on predicting the rate-changes in transcription regulation events from the 359 sentences of transcription regulation events with 10-fold cross-validation. It shows that on predicting the rate-changes in transcription regulation events, word2vec in DNN achieves only 59% accuracy, same performance as previous combined features by decision tree classifier. By combing our domain knowledge and sentence structure combined features into word embedding, the DNN classifier achieves 90% accuracy.

Table 2. Performance on predicting the rate-changes in transcription regulation events.

Features	Dimensions	Classifier	Accuracy (%)
Ontology Rules	115	Decision Tree	54
Domain +Sentence Structure Feature	669	Decision Tree	59
Word2vec	1000	Deep Neural Network	59
Word2vec + Domain +Sentence Structure Feature	1669	Deep Neural Network	90

4 Discussion and Future Work

In this paper, we proposed to combine the domain knowledge summarized in rate-changed transcriptional regulation ontology and sentence structure features into word embedding, to predict the complex transcriptional regulation events and the rate changes in them by DNN classifier. The experimental results show that both classification tasks achieve above 90% accuracy.

Note that the domain knowledge and sentence structure features are directly combined into the word embedding features learned by word2vec model.

Recently, the dependency-based word embedding tool, word2vecf [21], is used for biomedical event trigger detection[22]. Specifically, all available PubMed abstracts are parsed with Gdep parser [10], a dependency parse tool specialized for biomedical texts, and train the dependency-based word embedding based on the contexts in dependency relations. We'll learn the ontology rules and sentence structure features embedding from our corpus based on supervised training. We also employ the dependency-based word embedding, which contains more functional semantic information, to better capture semantics of the events. In the future, we'll use tree-based deep learning model such as tree Long Short-Term Memory (LSTM) convolutional and recurrent neural networks which can automatically learn features from dependency tree for the trigger words and phrases.

References

[1] L. J. Jensen, J. Saric, and P. Bork, "Literature mining for the biologist : from information retrieval to biological discovery," vol. 7, no. February, pp. 119–129, 2006.

[2] J. A. Vanegas, S. Matos, F. González, and J. L. Oliveira, "An Overview of Biomolecular Event Extraction from Scientific Documents," vol. 2015, 2015.

[3] S. T. Ahmed, R. Nair, C. Patel, and H. Davulcu, "BioEve : Bio-Molecular Event Extraction from Text Using Semantic Classification and Dependency Parsing," no. June, pp. 99–102, 2009.

[4] H. Kilicoglu, G. Rosemblat, M. Fiszman, and T. C. Rindflesch, "Sortal anaphora resolution to enhance relation extraction from biomedical literature," *BMC Bioinformatics*, pp. 1–16, 2016.

[5] W. Liu, K. Miao, G. Li, K. Chang, J. Zheng, and J. C. Rajapakse, "Extracting rate changes in transcriptional regulation from MEDLINE abstracts," *BMC Bioinformatics*, vol. 15, no. Suppl 2, pp. 1–12, 2014.

[6] M. Allahyari *et al.*, "A Brief Survey of Text Mining: Classification, Clustering and Extraction Techniques," 2017.

[7] T. Mikolov, K. Chen, G. Corrado, and J. Dean, "Distributed Representations of Words and Phrases and their Compositionality," pp. 1–9.

[8] T. H. Nguyen and R. Grishman, "Relation Extraction: Perspective from Convolutional Neural Networks," *Work. Vector Model. NLP*, pp. 39–48, 2015.

[9] T. H. Nguyen and R. Grishman, "Combining Neural Networks and Log-linear Models to Improve Relation Extraction," no. i, 2015.

[10] D. Erhan, A. Courville, and P. Vincent, "Why Does Unsupervised Pre-training Help Deep Learning ?," *J. Mach. Learn. Res.*, vol. 11, pp. 625–660, 2010.

[11] S. Bird and E. Loper, "NLTK : The Natural Language Toolkit."

[12] J. Lilleberg, "Support Vector Machines and Word2vec for Text Classification with Semantic Features," pp. 136–140, 2015.

[13] S. Arora, Y. Li, Y. Liang, T. Ma, and A. Risteski, "Linear Algebraic Structure of Word Senses, with Applications to Polysemy," pp. 1–22, 2016.

[14] Y. Bengio, A. Courville, and P. Vincent, "Representation Learning: A Review and New

Perspectives," no. 1993, pp. 1–30, 2012.
[15] M. Amit and S. Adi, "Word Embeddings and Their Use In Sentence Classification Tasks," *Empir. Methods NLP*, 2015.
[16] S. Arora, Y. Liang, and T. Ma, "A simple but tough to beat baseline for sentence embeddings," *Iclr*, pp. 1–14, 2017.
[17] C. Features, M. Pagliardini, P. Gupta, and M. Jaggi, "Unsupervised Learning of Sentence Embeddings."
[18] P. Bojanowski, E. Grave, A. Joulin, and T. Mikolov, "Enriching Word Vectors with Subword Information," 1996.
[19] J. H. Lau and T. Baldwin, "Practical Insights into Document Embedding Generation," 2014.
[20] Y. Goldberg, "A primer on neural network models for natural language processing," *arXiv Prepr. arXiv1510.00726*, pp. 1–76, 2015.
[21] O. Levy and Y. Goldberg, "Dependency-Based Word Embeddings," pp. 302–308, 2014.
[22] J. Wang *et al.*, "Biomedical event trigger detection by dependency-based word embedding," *BMC Med. Genomics*, vol. 9, no. Suppl 2, 2016.
[23] The Stanford Parser. http://nlp.stanford.edu/software/lex-parser.shtml.

Rise, Fall, and Implications of the New York City Medallion Market

Sherraina Song[1[0000-1111-2222-3333]]

[1] Shrewsbury High School, Shrewsbury, MA 01545, USA
sherraina.s@gmail.com

Abstract. Capping the number of licenses and granting exclusive right to street hailing passengers, the New York City (NYC) medallion system manipulated the demand and supply of taxicab services and created a medallion market. The lasting system turned the right to operate taxis in NYC into a private property of scarcity and an investment vehicle with disguised risks. Integrating data published by the NYC Taxi and Limousine Commission (TLC), this research identified four phases of the medallion market and argued that 1) the market collapsed because technology and ride-sharing economy have materially weakened the assumptions underlying the market; 2) Yellow Cab is fighting a lost battle against players of ride-sharing economy; and 3) the deregulation of the NYC taxicab industry will adapt and continue despite its adverse impact on the medallion interest groups.

Keywords: App-Based, Boro Taxis, For-Hire Vehicle, FHV, Green Cab, Haas Act, Medallion, New York City, NYC, Street Hail Livery, SHL, Ride-Sharing, Taxicab, Taxi & Limousine Commission, TLC, Uber, Yellow Cab

1 Introduction

1.1 NYC Taxicab Market

The NYC taxicab market is one of the largest in the world, with about one million passengers per day and annual revenue of two billion US dollars. By the local government regulations, summarized in Table 1. Classification of NYC Taxicab Services and Providers, the market consists of two sectors of service demand (street hailing and pre-arranged pick-up) and three major classes of service suppliers: Yellow Taxi Cab (Yellow Cab), For-Hire Vehicles (FHVs), and Street Hail Livery (SHL).

Street hailing services are provided by taxicabs in response to hails by passengers on the streets. Pre-arranged pick-up services are provided by taxicabs in response to requests made to a taxicab's affiliated service dispatching base.

Identifiable by the color of canary yellow, Yellow Cab taxis are providers of street hailing services. They are permitted to pick up passengers anywhere in all the five NYC boroughs. More, they are granted exclusive right to street hailers in Manhattan, LaGuardia Airport, and John F. Kennedy International Airport [1], where most of the traditional NYC taxi traffic is originated or destined. Customers access this mode of transportation by standing in the street and hailing with hands. A medallion, the metal plate attached to a car's hood, is the proof of legal license, i.e., the right for a car to provide street hailing services. There is a cap on the number of available licenses.

Table 1. Classification of NYC Taxicab Services and Providers

	Right to Street Hailing Passengers	**Right to Pre-Arranged Pick-ups**
Yellow Cab	All NYC	Not Permitted
FHVs	Not Permitted	All NYC
Green Cab	Northern Manhattan (north of West 110th street and East 96th street) and outer-boroughs (Bronx and Queens excluding the airports)	All NYC

FHVs include Community Cars (aka Liveries), Black Cars, and Luxury Limousines. Those taxicabs can pick up passengers throughout the five NYC boroughs, but only by appointments [2]. Customers access this mode of transportation by submitting a request, via phone, mobile apps, website, or other methods, to a TLC-licensed base or a TLC-licensed dispatch service provider who then direct FHV taxicabs to the customers. Important to note, app-based service providers such as Uber and Lyft are classified as FHVs. They were not permitted to enter the NYC taxicab market until the middle 2011. However, once permitted, they became disruptive against street hailing service providers as smart phones made FHVs as convenient (if not more so) as traditional taxicabs.

SHL, painted apple green and known as "Boro Taxis" or "Green Cabs", is a hybrid between Yellow Cab taxis and FHVs. They are permitted to accept pre-arranged rides in all the five NYC boroughs, and, beginning in June 2013, are permitted to pick up hailing passengers from the street in northern Manhattan (north of West 110th street and East 96th street) and the outer-boroughs: the Bronx and Queens (excluding the airports), areas historically underserved by Yellow Cab [3].

1.2 Medallion System

Licenses for both drivers and vehicles are required to operate taxicabs in NYC. However, regulations vary on Yellow Cabs, Green Cabs, and FHVs. Yellow Cabs have the strictest licensing. The right to serve street hailers had been exclusively assigned to Yellow Cabs until 2013 – the year Green Cab was created. The number of Yellow Cab Taxis permitted on streets is controlled via medallion licensing, by which the New York state's legislative body approves additional medallions and the NYC TLC holds auctions to sell them to public.

Introduced in 1937, the medallion system added only limited number of Yellow Cabs with only three legislative approvals in year 1996, 2004, and 2013. Today, only 13,587 Yellow Cab taxis are permitted on the NYC streets, corresponding to the same number of medallions.

2 Evolution of NYC Medallion Market

Based on the data integrated from the TLC websites, annual transfer volumes and average prices for Yellow Cab medallion transactions are graphed in Fig. 1. NYC Yellow Cab Medallion Annual Transfers and Average Sales Prices. According to the price and volume movements, the market can be described in four different phases,

- Born but no value (1937 – 1946)
- Formed and established (1947 – 1986)
- Investment tool and booming (1987 – 2013)
- Collapsed and falling (2014 – Present)

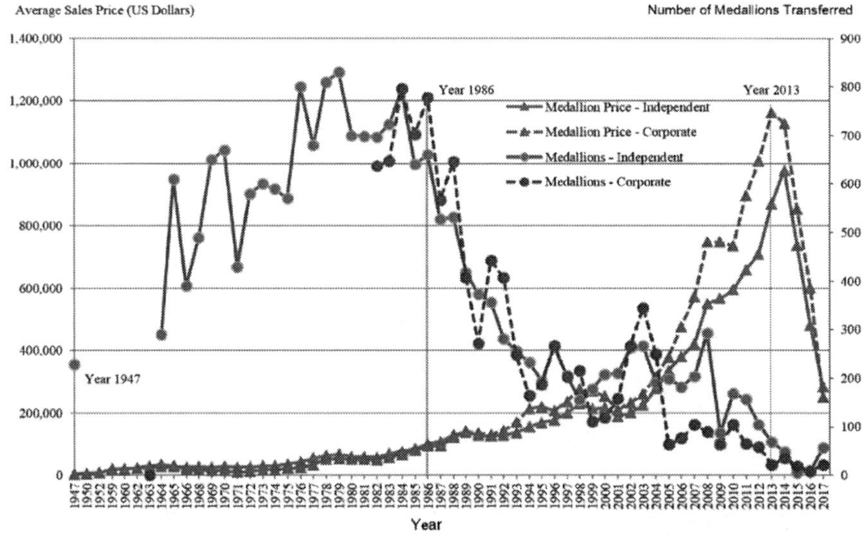

Fig. 1. NYC Yellow Cab Medallion Annual Transfers and Average Sales Prices

Data details are in Table 2. NYC Yellow Cab Medallion Annual Issuance and Sales Transfer.

2.1 Born but No Value (1937 – 1946)

The first phase of nine years from 1937 through 1946 carried no market values for the medallions. After the great depressions in early 1930s, NYC was flooded with 30,000 drivers. Sometimes there were more taxi cabs than passengers on the streets. Out of concerns about congestion, pollution, and crimes, the Haas Act was legislated in 1937 and official taxis were introduced with medallions attached. The law limited the number of cab licenses to the existing 16,900, but only 13,595 were in active use due to registration lapses [4]. The active licenses dwindled to 11,787 in 1947 due to reduced renewals and stood the same for 50 years until 1996 when 266 more were issued.

Table 2. NYC Yellow Cab Medallion Annual Issuance and Sales Transfer

Medallion Market	Year	Total Medallions				Independent Medallions		Corporate Medallions	
		Approved	Issued	Active	Sales Transfer	Average Price ($)	Numbers Traded	Average Price ($)	Numbers Traded
Phase I	1937-1946	16,900	13,595	13,595	0	0	0	0	0
	1947					2,500		2,500	
	1950					5,000		5,000	
	1952					7,500		7,500	
	1959					19,500		20,000	
	1960					20,825		19,450	
	1962					22,000		23,400	
	1963					25,000		28,773	
	1964			11,787	290	26,000	290	34,145	
	1965			11,787	610	26,000	610	30,000	
	1966			11,787	390	25,000	390	19,000	
	1968			11,787	490	27,000	490	16,000	
	1969			11,787	650	24,500	650	15,000	
	1970			11,787	670	28,000	670	14,000	
	1971			11,787	430	25,000	430	10,000	
	1972			11,787	580	26,000	580	12,000	
	1973			11,787	600	30,000	600	17,000	
	1974			11,787	590	30,000	590	17,000	
	1975			11,787	570	35,000	570	22,000	
	1976			11,787	800	42,000	800	24,000	
	1977			11,787	680	55,000	680	33,000	
	1978			11,787	810	63,000	810	52,000	
	1979			11,787	830	67,000	830	53,000	
	1980			11,787	700	60,000	700	50,000	
	1981			11,787	699	60,000	699	50,000	
	1982			11,787	1,334	57,500	697	49,300	637
	1983			11,787	1,371	68,600	723	57,900	648
	1984			11,787	1,591	75,900	795	66,200	796
Phase II	1985			11,787	1,344	84,900	641	79,000	703
(1947-1986)	1986			11,787	1,438	101,600	660	92,900	778
	1987			11,787	1,094	108,700	527	94,600	567
	1988			11,787	1,178	129,700	532	121,500	646
	1989			11,787	826	139,100	418	141,400	408
	1990			11,787	646	128,400	374	135,700	272
	1991			11,787	800	126,067	357	130,360	443
	1992			11,787	688	128,577	281	143,199	407
	1993			11,787	504	137,196	256	170,200	248
	1994			11,787	396	155,633	232	214,221	164
	1995			11,787	381	169,750	194	219,958	187
	1996	400	266	12,053	531	176,333	264	207,292	267
	1997		134	12,187	408	199,875	205	236,500	203
	1998			12,187	370	229,000	155	277,318	215
	1999			12,187	289	212,917	178	269,500	111
	2000			12,187	327	217,125	208	253,864	119
	2001			12,187	368	188,958	210	209,458	158
	2002			12,187	529	200,333	262	232,250	267
	2003			12,187	611	224,958	266	260,917	345
	2004	1,050	554	12,741	440	277,583	191	315,636	249
	2005		38	12,779	263	335,583	199	378,556	64
	2006		249	13,028	259	379,000	182	476,000	77
	2007		120	13,148	308	420,964	204	573,489	104
	2008		89	13,237	383	550,000	293	747,000	90
	2009			13,237	150	566,732	87	746,746	63
	2010			13,237	274	595,118	169	736,200	105
	2011			13,237	222	657,665	157	895,462	65
Phase III	2012			13,237	164	709,643	105	1,007,203	59
(1987-2013)	2013	2,000	200	13,437	90	870,059	69	1,162,381	21
	2014		150	13,587	84	977,729	49	1,127,371	35
	2015			13,587	24	736,667	6	852,500	18
Phase IV	2016			13,587	17	479,191	9	600,266	8
(2014 -)	2017			13,587	78	285,168	57	249,891	21

The number-capped medallion system had little impact on the NYC taxi industry during this initial phase. Due to the World War II and lack of demand for taxi services, many medallion owners valued a medallion not worth the annual $10 renewal fee and chose not to renew. No evidences suggest that, in capping the number of taxis, the law makers of Haas Act intended to turn the right to operate taxicabs on the NYC streets into a property with tradable market value. The establishment of medallion was not much different from other Depression-era legislative efforts: to stabilize and revive the taxicab industry diagnosed suffering from excessive competition [5].

However, the Haas Act did have an ordinance allowing transfer of licenses between owners, conditionally upon the NYC's approval of new owners' qualifications. This transferability was critical to establish medallion values and trade in future when economic conditions improved and demand for taxicabs rose.

2.2 Formed and Established

A medallion market was formed and stabilized during the second phase of almost four decades from 1947 through 1986. Until 1947 had there been no demand adequate to utilize the existing medallions from individuals seeking to drive a taxi. Rationing of fuel and car parts during World War II turned more people to taxis for transportation and the post-World War II prosperity created more business, which led to more drivers than the medallions available [6]. Medallions started to assume value and a medallion market formed in response to the need of medallion trading.

In 1947, the New York Times reported that taxicab owners received bonuses averaging $1,500 or $2,500 from selling their medallions with used cabs [7]. In 1950, the "bonus" rose to $5,000. The "bonus", on the top of the sales price for a cab, effectively put a price tag on a medallion and indicated the birth of a standalone market. In early 1960s, a medallion was traded around $25,000.

In 1971, the NYC TLC was created pursuant to Local Law 12 of 1971 to license taxicab vehicles and drivers by establishing and enforcing standards and criteria [8]. The creation and functioning of the TLC brought regulation transparency and consistency, which contributed to the health and stability of the NYC taxicab industry. It also led to legitimatization of "gypsy cabs" into what known today as livery cars, community cars, car services or for-hire vehicles [9]. In its annual reports, the TLC stated "taxicab licenses are transferable, and may be pledged as security for loans. ..., the license has a considerable value" [10]. Explicitly, the TLC pointed to the tradable value of the medallion and existence of a medallion market.

In addition to purchasing that requires a large amount of payment up front, drivers can pay medallion owners for the right of use by operation shift or certain hours, i.e., leasing. The Haas Act mandated that 60 percent of the medallions go to fleets who hold two or more licenses and can rent them to drivers. In 1979, TLC legalized leasing. Through waves of conversion to lessee-driving from owner-driving - fleet leasing in 1980s and independent owner leasing in 1990s, nearly all fleet drivers and most independent drivers were lessees [11]. Medallion ownerships were effectively separated from their right of use, which made it easy to price and trade medallions. Independent agencies were founded to broker and manage leasing on behalf of medallion owners.

During the second phase, demand for taxicabs rose due to a growing NYC population – residents and tourists, most of whom did not drive, while the number of medallions was capped the same for the whole period. Sales transfer of medallions increased at steadily higher prices. In 1984, the trading volumes went as high as 1,591, or 13.5% of the medallions in circulation. In 1986, 1,438 medallions or 12.2% of existing medallions changed hands. Thereafter both the number of medallions traded and its percentage in the total continued to decrease. As such, year 1986 was deemed the end of this forming phase. In the same year the average sales price for a medallion crossed $100,000 for the first time, forty times the price at the beginning of this phase (inflation was not adjusted). Without new supply, this phase of the NYC medallion market was characteristic of more transactions, rising prices, and establishment of a regulation agency, the NYC TLC.

2.3 Investment Tool and Booming

During the third phase of 1987 through 2013 (or quarter 2 of 2014 concisely), the medallion price continuously rose, but trading volumes were thin, and thinner. This trend continued despite additional 1,650 or 14% more licenses were issued between 1996 and 2013. Both private sales transfers and official auctions kept recording prices historically high. Medallions were bought and held in anticipation for value appreciation. The license became an investment vehicle, no longer limited to the way gaining the right to drive to make a living in the city. Medallion-owner drivers populously counted on selling their medallions later to make comfortable retirements.

The annually averaged prices peaked at $1.16 million for a corporate medallion in 2013 and $0.98 million for an independent one in 2014. Only 90 medallions were transacted in 2013, 21 corporate and 69 independent, less than 0.67% of the total in use. The price was so high that fractions of a medallion were recorded in sales transfer. Except temporary setbacks from the economic recessions in early 1990s and following the terrorist attack on September 11 of 2001, the price trend line was straight up, projecting the medallion as a safe investment risking nothing; the volume trend line was straight down, telling few owners would like to sell. The two lines crossed and formed the shape like a pair of scissors in Fig. 1.

Rising price and known entry control made the NYC medallion a safe bet and gave it many attributes of the bundle of right as a private property [12]. It has been routinely bought and sold, leased, and used as collateral for loans and counted as assets in estate, bankruptcy, divorce, and inheritance settlements. Purchases were financed through credit unions, banks, and other financial institutes. In 1995, Medallion Financial was founded as a firm specialized in originating, acquiring, and servicing loans that finance taxicab medallions and various derivatives. It was listed and actively traded one year later in NASDAQ stock exchange [13]. Taking the Schaller Consulting's estimate that 15% of a medallion's total revenues went to its owners [14], the annual return was computed between 3% and 9% during this period, better than investment in gold and oil in the comparable years. Calculated according to the rate rules in the TLC Promulgation of Rules issued in 2012 [15], a medallion owner can earn $30,000 to $80,000 annually by leasing out one medallion. It was commonly believed that buying, holding, and leasing out medallions was a wise business decision. The environment of low interest rate following 2008 financial crisis provided widely accessible, low-cost loans and contributed to the medallion hype as well.

Medallion auctions administrated by the TLC also enforced the perception that investing in the medallion was safe. "Strong medallion sale prices have historically been used to judge the overall health and viability of the industry" [16] was frequently presented in the TLC annual reports. It was no coincidence that TLC auctions always set price records.

2.4 Collapsed and Falling

The good time peaked and started to end in the second half of 2014. Viewed quarterly, the average sales price for a corporate medallion peaked at $1.26 million in quarter 2 of 2014 and then fell straight to $208,411 in quarter 4 of 2017, a drop of 83.5%; the average sales price for an independent medallion peaked at $1.0 million in quarter 3 of 2014 and then fell straight to $191,749 in Quarter 3 of 2017, a drop of 80.8% (Fig. 2. NYC Yellow Cab Medallion Quarterly Sales Prices). The fall was steep and fast. It took almost twenty years to rise to $1 million for a medallion in 2013, but less than three years to fall back where it was: around $200,000. Quarterly data details for individual years are in Table 3. NYC Yellow Cab Medallion Quarterly Sales and Prices.

Not only were the prices low, but also the transaction volumes were light. Unlike the third phase with few sellers due to appreciation expectations, the fourth phase had fewer sellers because of no buyers when no retainable floor prices were in sight. Corporate and independent medallions combined, only 24 changed hands in 2015 and 17 in 2016, out of the total 13,587. Together, those transactions made a sale of only $20 million in 2015 and less than $9 million in 2016. The market, valued over $14 billion prior to quarter 4 of 2014, collapsed.

Without buyers, many owners were unable to pay back their loans and filed for bankruptcy. Between quarter 3 of 2014 and quarter 4 of 2017, 15 corporate medallions were foreclosed, defaulting loans valued over $16.3 million, averaged $1.09 million per piece; 72 independent medallions were foreclosed, defaulting $35.8 million, averaged about $0.5 million each. In contrast, there was only one foreclosure recorded (in 2011) prior to quarter 3 of 2014 (Table 4. NYC Yellow Cab Medallion Foreclosures). Not a surprise, impact on independent medallions owned by drivers is far more severe than that on those medallions owned by corporates.

Many medallions are now in possession of credit unions and banks who financed the purchases. In the middle September of 2017, for a total of $8.56 million, or $186,000 per medallion, a hedge fund company won the auction sale of 45 medallions foreclosed from an owner who once owned 800 medallions [17]. More foreclosures are likely to follow. Aware of the market distress, the TLC had to hold off auctioning the remaining 1,650 of the 2,000 Yellow Cab medallions authorized in 2013.

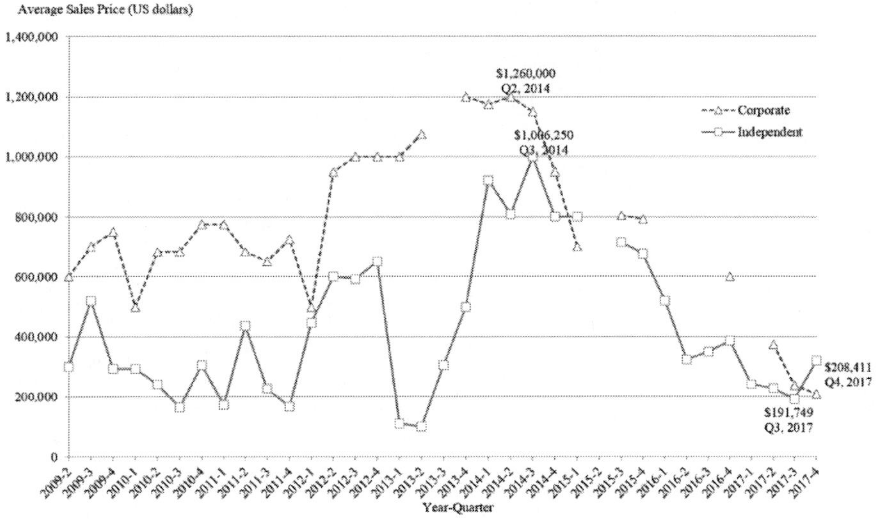

Fig. 2. NYC Yellow Cab Medallion Quarterly Sales Prices

Table 3. NYC Yellow Cab Medallion Quarterly Sales and Prices

Year	Quarter	Corporate						Independent					
		Transactions	Medallions		Price ('000 US dollars)			Transactions	Medallions		Price ('000 US dollars)		
			Transacted	Transferred	High	Low	Average		Transacted	Transferred	High	Low	Average
2009	2	13	27	27	763	600	735	28	28	27	578	300	561
2009	3	16	32	32	775	700	755	52	52	49	594	520	572
2009	4	2	4	4	775	750	763	11	11	11	600	293	557
2010	1	14	29	29	800	500	721	45	45	39	620	293	577
2010	2	18	36	36	800	685	741	43	43	39	610	242	589
2010	3	13	27	27	825	685	713	51	51	44	615	165	596
2010	4	6	13	13	850	775	807	53	53	48	700	305	614
2011	1	5	10	10	950	775	915	37	37	31	660	173	608
2011	2	9	18	18	975	685	878	74	74	58	695	438	661
2011	3	9	19	19	950	650	862	43	43	35	705	227	675
2011	4	8	18	18	1,000	725	938	37	37	35	710	167	679
2012	1	5	10	10	1,000	500	890	25	25	24	715	447	683
2012	2	6	12	12	1,050	950	996	38	38	35	712	600	703
2012	3	11	22	22	1,125	1,000	1,039	35	35	31	750	592	708
2012	4	7	15	15	1,125	1,000	1,048	16	16	16	850	650	769
2013	1	3	6	6	1,210	1,000	1,103	19	19	16	950	112	822
2013	2	3	6	6	1,320	1,075	1,165	26	26	26	1,100	100	914
2013	3				0	0	0	13	13	13	1,050	305	833
2013	4	4	9	9	1,200	1,200	1,200	14	14	14	1,000	499	878
2014	1	6	12	12	1,254	1,175	1,205	25	25	25	1,050	920	985
2014	2	2	5	5	1,300	1,200	1,260	17	17	15	1,050	808	1,002
2014	3	3	6	6	1,200	1,150	1,183	4	4	4	1,025	1,000	1,006
2014	4	6	12	12	1,000	950	967	5	5	4	866	800	827
2015	1	4	8	8	950	700	863	2	2	2	800	800	800
2015	3	2	4	4	875	805	840	3	3	3	715	715	715
2015	4	3	6	6	875	793	848	1	1	1	675	675	675
2016	1				0	0	0	2	2	2	580	520	550
2016	2				0	0	0	4	4	4	600	325	476
2016	3				0	0	0	2	2	2	570	350	460
2016	4	4	8	8	675	475	600	1	1	1	388	388	388
2017	1				0	0	0	1	1	1	241	241	241
2017	2	1	2	2	375	375	375	8	8	8	300	150	228
2017	3	10	19	19	140	236	236	9	9	9	256	130	192
2017	4	1	1	1	208	208	208	39	39	39	628	150	320

Table 4. NYC Yellow Cab Medallion Foreclosures

Year	Quarter	Corporate					Independent				
		Foreclosures	Medallions	Recorded Unit Value ('000 US dollars)			Foreclosures	Medallions	Recorded Unit Value ('000 US doallars)		
			Floreclosed	Highest	Lowest	Average		Foreclosed	Highest	Lowest	Average
2011	3						1	1	635	635	635
2014	3						1	1	900	900	900
2014	4	1	1	1,925	1,925	1,925	3	3	905	840	873
2015	1						1	1	800	800	800
2015	2						3	3	777	700	745
2015	3						3	3	725	603	681
2015	4						3	3	725	326	585
2016	1										
2016	2						7	7	615	540	574
2016	3	10	10	1,500	1,250	1,325	5	5	620	550	602
2016	4						3	3	600	550	583
2017	1						1	1	550	550	550
2017	2	1	2	738	738	369	7	9	500	220	348
2017	3	1	2	202	202	202	17	20	581	185	420
2017	4						8	13	450	200	354

3 The Uber Disruption

Blames have been quickly played against Uber for the meltdown of the NYC medallion market – less regulated than Yellow Cab and thus gained an edge in competition.

Table 5. NYC Taxicab Ridership and Market Share by Provider

Year-Quarter	Total Market Trips (million)	Share of Total Market Trips (%)				
		Yellow Cab	Green Cab	FHVs		
				Uber	Lyft	Other FHVs
2015-1	52.8	73.01	9.10	12.51	0.02	5.37
2015-2	55.1	69.99	9.24	12.69	0.54	7.54
2015-3	55.3	61.39	8.27	18.65	1.75	9.95
2015-4	64.7	54.26	7.38	19.16	2.09	17.11
Year Total	227.8	64.14	8.44	15.93	1.15	10.34
2016-1	67.1	50.85	6.68	21.57	2.96	17.94
2016-2	71.2	49.04	6.30	22.23	4.05	18.37
2016-3	67.9	44.71	5.51	26.77	4.55	18.46
2016-4	73.7	42.65	4.92	29.33	4.69	18.41
Year Total	279.8	46.74	5.84	25.04	4.08	18.30
2017-1	75.6	38.59	4.30	31.62	6.48	19.01
2017-2	53.5	37.64	4.00	32.94	7.18	18.24
Year to Date	129.1	38.19	4.17	32.17	6.77	18.69

Uber and Lyft have been winning both market shares and revenues. Beginning for year 2015, the TLC published trip data for all the providers - Yellow Cab, Green Cab, and FHVs, which made it possible to view individual providers' market shares (Table 5. NYC Taxicab Ridership and Market Share by Provider). By quarter 2 of 2016 Yellow Cab had retreated to take less than 50% of the NYC taxicab service market. While the quarterly market size increased to 75.6 million trips in the first quarter of 2017 with a growth of 43% over the same period two years ago, Yellow Cab's trips dropped to 29.2 million, a loss of 9.4 million or 24%; and its market share dropped to 38.6% from 73%. Not only failed Yellow Cab in grabbing a share from the market growth but also it failed in customer retention – many riders who used to hail a Yellow Cab taxi now turned to Uber, Lyft, or other small FHVs. In the first quarter of 2017, FHVs as one group served 57.1% of the NYC taxicab trips and became NYC riders' first choice. Uber alone captured 31.6%, up from 12.5% two years ago. Fig. 3. Market Share of NYC Taxicab Ridership by Provider illustrated the wining stride of Uber and Lyft, in contrast with Yellow Cab's drastic retreat, quarter after quarter.

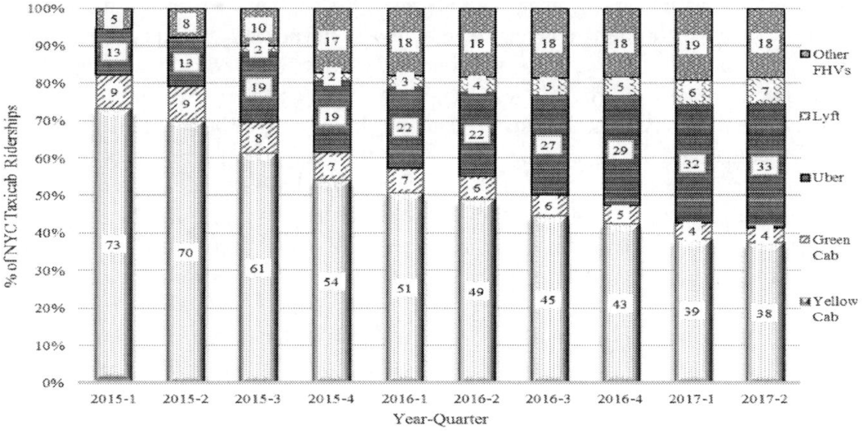

Fig. 3. Market Share of NYC Taxicab Ridership by Provider

Table 6. NYC Yellow Cab Annual Trips and Revenues

Year	Medallions	Trips			Revenues		
		Total	Per Medallion	Year over Year Change %	Total ($)	Per Medallion ($)	Year over Year Change %
2010	13,237	168,983,489	12,766		1,789,049,841	135,155	
2011	13,237	176,866,900	13,362	4.67	1,992,549,043	150,529	11.37
2012	13,237	177,996,949	13,447	0.64	2,134,910,742	161,284	7.14
2013	13,437	173,136,240	12,885	-4.18	2,322,802,868	172,866	7.18
2014	13,587	165,104,282	12,152	-5.69	2,268,307,017	166,947	-3.42
2015	13,587	146,107,068	10,753	-11.51	2,097,292,315	154,360	-7.54
2016	13,587	130,789,390	9,626	-10.48	1,906,905,626	140,348	-9.08

Trips and revenues per medallion also dropped. Between 2013 and 2016, Yellow Cab's annual trips per medallion dropped 25%, to less than 10 thousand from around 13 thousand, and annual revenues per medallion dropped 19%, to $140 thousand from over $170 thousand (Table 6. NYC Yellow Cab Trips and Revenues). Taking 15% as medallion owner's share, an average Yellow Cab medallion earned a return of only

$21,000 in 2016, compared to $25,900 just three years earlier, and $30,000 to $80,000 during its booming period.

4 Economic and Regulation Implications

4.1 Breakdown of Market Assumptions

Market functioning and values of the NYC medallions have been relying on one supply policy - restricting issuance of medallions and thus controlling the number of taxicabs on streets and one demand assumption - street hailing and pre-arrangement are two different demand for taxicab services and can be met with two different service products. Thus, it goes that government can segment the market and designate different service providers accordingly and exclusively. It was further assumed there be growing number of street hailers out of growing economy, visitors, and residents who prefer not to drive or conscious of traffic congestion, air pollution, and inconvenience in driving, which has been mostly true. As such, the supply holds flat while the demand grows, medallion values and driver revenues are assured to rise – law of economics 101.

However, those assumptions, even if used to be true, have been disrupted by emergence and advance in technology-enabled ride-sharing economy. By 2015, 96% of NYC residents had owned mobile phones and 79% of those were smart phones [18]. Almost all taxicab riders can tap mobile apps or dial up from handset devices to pre-arrange a cab, anywhere and anytime, on streets or off streets. The lagging time between hailing and pre-arranging became no longer significant and meaningful. When there are enough taxicabs nearby waiting for the calls, callers can get the benefit of immediacy and convenience, almost no different (if not better off) from that of hailing Yellow Cab taxis. Even more, people would prefer to call their cabs prior to getting off flights, leaving restaurants and coffee shops, and from places of comfort instead of hailing in cold weather or in the rains. App-based on-demand pre-arrangement offers the benefits of instant planning and predictability. The demand for street hailing or pre-arranged taxicabs has become hardly differentiable from street hailing, or at least the attributes used to enable riders to differentiate the two have diminished or blurred in riders' eyes. The two have become two units of one product that transports people, substitutable to each other, and should be regulated as one product [19]. The primary assumptions, upon which the NYC medallion market and government regulations have been based and functioning, have been fundamentally uprooted.

4.2 Ride-Sharing Economy

When demand for app-based riding rose and the number of Yellow Cab taxis on the NYC streets were restricted, FHVs responded by adding more vehicles and drivers. There were no FHVs legally permitted on NYC streets when the medallion system was born. But the number of FHVs was more than doubled to 80,881 and the FHV drivers increased by 120% to 122,997 between 2011 (the year Uber entered NYC) and 2016. For the same period, only 300 Yellow Cab taxis were added (Table 7. NYC Taxicabs and Drivers). More, 19,463 Yellow Cab drivers quit and most of them switched to

FHVs. The net result is that FHVs outnumbered Yellow Cab taxis by 6:1; FHV drivers outnumbered Yellow Cab drivers by 4:1; and up to four drivers had to share driving one Yellow Cab vehicle by shift due to the medallion restriction. Uncapped licensing seemingly did give FHVs advantages over Yellow Cabs under the existing regulations.

Table 7. NYC Active Taxicabs and Drivers

Year	Drivers		Vehicles		Vehicle Driver Ratio	
	Yellowcab Divers	FHV Drivers	Yellowcab Medallions	FHVs	Yellocab	FHVs
1937			13,595	0		
1964			11,787	2,513		
1992			11,787	27,613		
2000	35,160	48,271	12,187	41,813	2.9	1.2
2005	42,512	51,060	12,779	40,449	3.3	1.3
2010	49,129	53,755	13,237	37,782	3.7	1.4
2015	55,390	90,284	13,587	66,604	4.1	1.4
2016	30,488	122,997	13,587	80,881	2.2	1.5

Successes in business models like Uber's are not uncommon in the era of digital economy– eBay, Amazon, Facebook, Google, etc. Leveraging Internet and smart phones, they built platforms to connect and assemble buyers and sellers directly to create a market ecosystem, economy of scale, and even monopolies via "Size begets size" [20]. Different for Uber, a pioneer in sharing economy, it explores and exploits resources idle prior to the Internet economy – private cars at the times not being driven and personnel at the times outside regular jobs, which makes it theoretically possible for almost everyone to become an Uber driver and thus provides options and flexibilities in offering, scheduling, and pricing to compete. As it evolves and adapts to market demand and regulations, new features can be expected to address public concerns the medallion system initially intended to address – traffic congestion, air pollution, and safety. For example, dynamic pricing with surcharges can be explored to contain traffic through crowded areas; access to driver and passenger information and their mutual rating can be explored to improve safety. There are advantages over Yellow taxicab drivers who must earn or lease a medallion up front and adhere to stricter licensing criteria and regulated pricing.

Globalization and market size matters too. An estimated online advertising market of $1 trillion has created the legendary Google and Facebook. The global market for personal mobility is as much as 10 times that [21]. Appealing to investors with the ambition to be another Google or Facebook, Uber has attracted $18 billion in funding since its setup in 2010 and now carries a valuation closed to $70 billion, the largest startup in history that raised the most money even before going public. The large capital enabled Uber to extend its platform and business model to more than 450 cities in 78 countries [22] and to build its fleets of autonomous driving for future. In contrast, the medallion system in NYC or the similar ones in other cities confine their taxicab service providers to a geographic locale, potentially blocking their riders from not only the benefits of sharing economy but also the prospects for Uber or any of its existing or potential competitors to replicate those legendary successes in an era of digital age.

4.3 Deregulation Trend

Consumers are standing to benefit from the ride-sharing economy. In the era of mass intelligence and digital economy, the new service mode of ride-sharing has made taxi riding more accessible and affordable, which helps grow the market. In 2016, total NYC taxicab ridership has got bigger, to 280 million, up 23% from one year ago. Meanwhile Uber and Lyft gained not only from the market incremental but also from what Yellow Cab lost: 5.3 million trips and 17.4% market share during the same period. If not lost to Uber, it would have lost to someone else who can materialize the benefit. Technology is there, demand is there, and consumers are ready to make moves in their riding and opinions on taxicab regulations. Uber and the likes are in right places at right times. But nothing is assured who will be the eventual winner, facing evolving technology, increasing market competition, and regulations that certainly will adapt.

Though the perpetuation of the medallion system was the result of political process subject to more influence from interested supplier groups – owners, drivers, agencies, and creditors than from consumers, political winds seem to shift toward deregulations favoring Uber and the likes who run their business on national and global scale beyond localized monopolies. The advantage of financial power, easily identified common interest, and ease of organizing the medallion interest groups over insufficiency in funding and difficulty in organizing consumers (whose individual interests in taxicab market are scattered and ambiguous), is among the main reasons why the medallion system was perpetuated and lasting [23]. Now Uber, with sufficient funding, concentrated investor interest, and organization power in influencing law makers and public opinion, is up to the task to challenge the traditional order and medallion interest groups. It mobilized public support and launched political campaigns to change regulations. It started "principled confrontation" program in 2015, searching for compromises with local municipalities for entry into their markets. In the summer of 2015, Uber won against NYC and foiled the city's efforts to cap the number of Uber vehicles on the grounds of traffic congestion [24]; in September of 2015, the New York City won a legal victory against three lawsuits brought by Melrose Credit Union, the largest lender who made almost $2.5 billion in loans for 5,331 city-issued medallions and claimed it was illegal for Uber and other app companies to operate in New York City [25]; In May of 2016, the New York state senate passed bill to legalize Uber statewide [26]. Similar efforts and successes in other places have produced ordinances favorable to app-based services in more than 23 states in the United States.

The deregulation process of the taxicab industry has started and hardly can that be turned back by any foreseeable political winds. After all, the New York medallion is a "problematic private property" - created in the past, controversial in the present, and potentially burdensome in the future [27]. Instead of patching and reviving the medallion system, local and federal regulations should adapt and, progressively but decisively, catch up with technological innovations and changes in consumer demand. The essence is to let the free market play freely and let the once protected medallion monopoly adapts or dies. Instead of holding Uber and the likes back, regulations will foster their growth, monitor their expansions, and intervene timely to prevent them from propelling into monopoly powers like Google, Facebook, and Amazon.

Source Data

1. **TLC Annual Reports (2002-2016)** http://www.nyc.gov/html/tlc/html/archive/annual.shtml. Summarized the TLC work, including licensing and regulation updates.
2. **Medallion Transfer Reports (2009 – 2017)** http://www.nyc.gov/html/tlc/html/archive/archive.shtml. Click on a link for a year, then the link of Medallion Transfers.

   Trip and Revenue Data (2010-2017) http://www.nyc.gov/html/tlc/html/technology/aggregated_data.shtml. Data for Yellow Cab and Green Cab at monthly level and data for FHVs at weekly level were integrated to derive metrics of taxicab trips and revenues.

Acknowledgements

The author would like to thank the three anonymous reviewers for their encouragement and comments that helped me greatly improve the manuscript. I am immensely grateful to Kaitlin Andryauskad for her mentorship, inspirations, and insights that motivated and helped me to develop the project and finalize this paper.

References

1. Yellow Taxi, http://www.nyc.gov/html/tlc/html/industry/yellow_taxi.shtml, last accessed 2018/04/16.
2. For-Hire Vehicles, http://www.nyc.gov/html/tlc/html/industry/for_hire.shtml, last accessed 2018/04/16.
3. Taxi Info for Boro Taxis, http://www.nyc.gov/html/tlc/downloads/pdf/shl_boro_taxi_info_content_final_070313.pdf, last accessed 2018/04/16.
4. Gelder, V. Lawrence: Medallion Limits Stem From the 30's. The New York Times, May 11, 1996, https://www.nytimes.com/1996/05/11/nyregion/medallion-limits-stem-from-the-30-s.html, last accessed 2018/04/16.
5. Wyman, Katrina: Problematic Private Property: The Case of New York Taxicab Medallions. Yale Journal on Regulation, Volume 30, 169 (2013), pp. 169.
6. Regulation and Prosperity: 1935-1960, http://www.nyc.gov/html/media/totweb/taxioftomorrow_history_regulationandprosperity.html, last accessed 2018/04/16.
7. Wyman, Katrina: Problematic Private Property: The Case of New York Taxicab Medallions. Yale Journal on Regulation, Volume 30, 169 (2013), pp. 170.
8. The NYC TLC 2002 Annual Report, http://www.nyc.gov/html/tlc/downloads/pdf/annual_report03.pdf, pp. 1, last accessed 2018/04/16.
9. The Modern Taxi: 1960-2010, http://www.nyc.gov/html/media/totweb/taxioftomorrow_history_themoderntaxi.html, last accessed 2018/04/16.

10. The NYC TLC 2002 Annual Report, http://www.nyc.gov/html/tlc/downloads/pdf/annual_report03.pdf, pp. 7, last accessed 2018/04/16.
11. Gilbert, Schaller and Gorman: Villain or Bogeyman? New York's Taxi Medallion System, http://www.schallerconsult.com/taxi/taxi2.htm#first, last accessed 2018/04/16.
12. Wyman, Katrina: Problematic Private Property: The Case of New York Taxicab Medallions. Yale Journal on Regulation, Volume 30, 169 (2013), pp. 135-139.
13. Reuters: Medallion Financial Corp, https://www.reuters.com/finance/stocks/companyProfile/MFIN.O, last accessed 2018/04/18.
14. Schaller Consulting: The New York City Taxicab Factbook, http://www.schallerconsult.com/taxi/taxifb.pdf, pp. 35, last accessed 2018/04/16.
15. Notice of Promulgation of Rules, http://www.nyc.gov/html/tlc/downloads/pdf/lease_cap_rules_passed.pdf, pp. 3, last accessed 2018/04/16.
16. The NYC TLC 2005 Annual Report, http://www.nyc.gov/html/tlc/downloads/pdf/2005_annual_report.pdf, pp. 5, last accessed 2018/04/16.
17. Hernandez, Raul: A Mysterious Hedge Fund Just Scooped Up the Foreclosed Medallions from New York City's 'Taxi King', http://www.businessinsider.com/nyc-taxi-king-foreclosed-medallions-scooped-up-by-hedge-fund-2017-9, last accessed 2018/04/18.
18. New York City Mobile Services Study, https://www1.nyc.gov/assets/dca/MobileServicesStudy/Research-Brief.pdf, las accessed 2018/04/18.
19. Wyman, Katrina: Taxi Regulation in the Age of Uber. http://www.nyujlpp.org/wp-content/uploads/2017/04/Wyman-Taxi-Regulation-in-the-Age-of-Uber-20nyujlpp1.pdf, pp. 4, last accessed 2018/04/18.
20. Parkins, David: Taming the Titans. The Economist, January 18th, 2018.
21. The Economist: "From zero to seventy (billion)". The Economist, September 3rd, 2016.
22. DMR: 90 Amazing Uber Statistics, Demographics, and Facts, March 2018, https://expandedramblings.com/index.php/uber-statistics/, last accessed 2018/04/18.
23. Wyman, Katrina: Problematic Private Property: The Case of New York Taxicab Medallions. Yale Journal on Regulation, Volume 30, 169 (2013), pp. 156-164.
24. Grisworld, Alison: Uber Won New York, http://www.slate.com/articles/business/moneybox/2015/11/uber_won_new_york_city_it_only_took_five_years.html, last accessed 2018/04/18.
25. Harshbarger, Rebecca: Yellow Cab Industry Dealt Legal Blow as It Loses Court Battle against Taxi App Companies, https://www.amny.com/transit/nyc-yellow-cabs-lose-legal-battle-to-uber-taxi-apps-1.10825964, last accessed 2018/04/18.
26. Campbell, Jon: NY Senate Passes Bill to Fast Track Uber, Lyft, https://www.democratandchronicle.com/story/news/politics/albany/2017/05/17/ny-senate-passes-bill-fast-track-uber-lyft/101800922/, last accessed 2018/04/18.
27. Wyman, Katrina: Problematic Private Property: The Case of New York Taxicab Medallions. Yale Journal on Regulation, Volume 30, 169 (2013), pp. 187.

Parsimonious Modeling for Binary Classification of Quality in a High Conformance Manufacturing Environment

Carlos A. Escobar Diaz[1,2], Ruben Morales-Menendez[2]

[1] General Motors, Research and Development, Warren MI 48092, USA,
carlos.1.escobar@gm.com
[2] Tecnológico de Monterrey, Monterrey, NL. 64849, México,
rmm@itesm.mx

Abstract The world of *big data* is changing dramatically; in the domain of data mining, machine learning and pattern recognition, the feature access has grown from tens to hundreds or even thousands. This trend presents enormous challenges, specially for classification problems. In manufacturing, classification of quality is one of the most important applications; however, feature explosion, combined with high conformance production rates are two of the most important challenges for *big data* initiatives. Empirical evidence shows that discarding irrelevant or redundant features improves prediction, helps in understanding the system, reduces running time requirements, and reduces the effect of dimensionality. In this paper, the *Hybrid Correlation- and Ranking-based (HCR)* and *ReliefF* filter feature elimination algorithms are presented as a wrapper method, which uses the *Naive Bayes* as the learning algorithm. To boost parsimony, the algorithms are combined with the *Penalized Maximum Probability of Correct Decision* – a model selection criterion – to develop a *Hybrid Feature Selection and Pattern Recognition* framework aimed at rare quality event detection. A flexible approach that can be widely applied to various machine learning algorithms.

Keywords Quality control · Manufacturing systems · Feature elimination algorithm · Model selection criterion · Unbalanced binary data · Defect detection

1 Introduction

We are living in a world that is highly influenced by the rise of *big data*. The information explosion that companies are facing with ever-increasing amounts of data highlights the importance of information extraction techniques. When analyzing large volumes of data, data mining, machine learning and pattern recognition techniques are used for data-driven knowledge discovery (e.g., model discovery), pattern recognition (e.g., classification) and/or to display hidden patterns in the data. In these *big data*-driven techniques, a feature (e.g., variable) is an individual measurable property of a phenomenon being observed [1]; the prediction ability of a learning algorithm is mainly determined by the inherent class information available in the features included in the analysis [2]. And generalization refers to the prediction ability of a learning algorithm-based model on unseen data.

Theoretical analysis and empirical evidence show that irrelevant and redundant features are not helpful in solving pattern recognition problems: (1) they may have negative effect on the classification performance because of the mutual effect between the features; (2) they may significantly increase computational time; and (3) it is more difficult to extract high-level knowledge from the analysis [3–5].

Dependence can be described as any statistical relationship between two random variables. Correlation refers to a broad class of statistical relationships involving dependence. The most common measure of linear dependence is the Pearson product-moment correlation coefficient[6].

In this context, a feature may be considered good if its inherent class information is relevant to one of the class labels, but is not redundant to other good features. If the correlation of two variables is used as a goodness measure, a good feature should be highly correlated to one of the class labels, but not highly correlated to any other features – redundant [5, 7]. On the other hand, a feature may be considered irrelevant if the information that it contains is independent from the class label. In the *Feature Selection (FS)* domain, the selection of relevant features and elimination of irrelevant and redundant ones is one of the main challenges [8].

1.1 *Big Data* in Manufacturing

Manufacturing companies are intense users of *big data*, this industry generates and stores more data than any other [9]. Learning algorithms e.g, support vector machine, logistic regression, decision trees to name a few, are applied for quality monitoring and process control [10]. Classification of quality is one of the most important applications, where relevant quality characteristics of the process or product are observed and related to an ordinal or binary output aimed at detecting defects [11]. *Big data* initiatives have the potential to solve a whole range of hitherto intractable manufacturing problems [12].

When a new manufacturing process is initially deployed, it often occurs that engineers do not fully understand the physics of the process and the huge amount of information is used to create tens, hundreds or even thousands of features, which frequently include relevant, irrelevant and redundant ones. This may cause serious problems to many learning algorithms with respect to the scalability and learning performance [5]. Because most mature manufacturing organizations generate only a few defects per million of opportunities, another common challenge when analyzing manufacturing-derived data sets is their highly unbalanced data structure. The feature explosion combined with high conformance production rates are two of the most important challenges of *big data* initiatives in manufacturing.

Table 1: Acronyms Table

Acronym	Definition
FN	False Negatives
FP	False Positives
FS	Feature Selection
HCR	Hybrid Correlation- and Ranking-based
HFSPR	Hybrid Feature Selection and Pattern Recognition
MPCD	Maximum Probability of Correct Decision
MS	Model Selection
NB	Naive Bayes
PMPCD	Penalized Maximum Probability of Correct Decision
SUFL	Sorted and Uncorrelated Feature List
TN	True Negatives
TP	True Positives

In contrast with other industries, where prediction is the main goal, in manufacturing, model interpretation – from a physics perspective – is very important. Since the extracted information of the cases yielding high quality can be used by engineers to plan and to design randomized experiments to find optimal levels of process/product parameters. This problem representation highlights the importance of finding a few good empirical-data-derived features to approximate the patterns of manufacturing systems (parsimony [13]).

Parsimonious modeling aimed at detecting rare quality events is the main driver of this research. Parsimony is induced through *FS* and *Model Selection (MS)*.

The *Hybrid Correlation- and Ranking-based* [14], is a filter *FS* algorithm aimed at eliminating redundant features, where the *Pearson*'s correlation coefficient is used as a measure of redundancy. The basic idea of the algorithm is to keep the *best* feature – highest ranked – from a set of two or more highly correlated variables and eliminate the rest. It uses the *ReliefF* algorithm to rank the features according to their discriminative capacity.

In this paper, *HCR* and *ReliefF* algorithms are presented as a wrapper method. Due to the strong assumption of independence of variables, the *Naive Bayes (NB)* is used as the learning algorithm. To boost parsimony, the algorithms are combined with the *Penalized Maximum Probability of Correct Decision (PMPCD)* – a model selection criterion [15] – to develop a *Hybrid Feature Selection and Pattern Recognition (HFSPR)* framework; aimed at analyzing highly unbalanced data structures.

This paper is organized as follows: it starts with a review of the theoretical background in section 2. Section 3 describes the *HFSPR* framework, followed by a binary classification empirical study in section 4. Finally, conclusions and opportunities for future research are included in section 5.

Table 2: Variables Table

Variable	Description
α	type I error
β	type II error
δ	high-correlation threshold
F	list of features in descending order
FC	feature correlation matrix
k	number of nearest neighbors
K	number of features in the candidate model
m	number of sampled instances
n	number of features
r_{xy}	Pearson correlation coefficient
τ	feature relevance threshold
$\bar{x}$	mean of variable x
x_i	data point i of variable x
x, y	correlated variables
$\bar{y}$	mean of variable y
y_i	data point i of variable y

2 Theoretical Background

2.1 Feature Selection Methods

Feature selection can be defined as the process of choosing a subset of good features, and eliminating irrelevant and redundant ones from the original feature set. From a given data set, evaluating all possible combinations (2^n) becomes an NP-hard problem as the number of features grows [16]. The FS methods broadly fall into two classes: filters and wrappers [17].

Filter methods select variables independently of the classification algorithm or its error criteria, they assign weights to features individually and rank them based on their relevance to the class labels. A feature is considered good and thus selected if its associated weight is greater than the user-specified threshold [5]. The advantages of feature ranking algorithms are that they do not over-fit the data and are computationally faster than wrappers, and hence they can be efficiently applied to big data sets containing many features [7].

Wrappers, use the learning algorithm as a black-box to evaluate the relative performance of a feature subset [18, 19]. In this procedure, a set of candidate features are input to the learning algorithm, and the prediction performance is used as the objective function to evaluate the feature subset. Although the wrapper methods can become computationally intensive, they perform better than filters due to the bias induction by the algorithm [17]. However, the classifier may learn the training data too well (i.e., become over-fitted), but exhibit poor generalization ability. To avoid this situation, a holdout set can be used to track the classifier's accuracy on unseen data.

Recently, hybrid approaches have been proposed by [3] to take advantage of the particular characteristics of each method. These approaches mainly focus on combining filter algorithms with either wrappers or regularization to solve the scalability problem and to achieve the best possible learning performance with a particular algorithm. The basic idea is to break down the *FS* problem into several stages, namely feature ranking, correlation-based feature elimination, and prediction optimization.

2.2 *Relief* and *ReliefF*

The basic idea of *Relief* is to estimate the quality of features according to how well their values distinguish between instances that are near to each other [20]. Its advantages are that it is not dependent on heuristics, it runs in low-order polynomial time, and it can be applied to nominal or numerical features. However, *Relief* does not eliminate redundant features, cannot deal with incomplete data and is limited to two-class problems.

ReliefF is an extension of the *Relief* algorithm, it was improved by Kononenko to generalize to multiclass problems. In addition, the improved algorithm (*ReliefF*) is more robust to incomplete and noisy data sets [21]. *ReliefF* searches for a k of its nearest neighbors from the same class, called nearest *hits*, and also a k nearest neighbors from each of the different classes, called nearest *misses*, this procedure is repeated m times, which is the number of randomly selected instances. Thus, features are weighted and ranked by the average of the distances (*Manhattan* distance) of all *hits* and all *misses* [22] to select the most important features [20], developing a significance threshold τ. Features with an estimated weight below τ are considered irrelevant and therefore eliminated. The proposed limits for τ are $0 < \tau \leq 1/\sqrt{\alpha m}$ [22]; where α is the probability of accepting an irrelevant feature as relevant.

2.3 Correlation-Based Redundancy Measure

The *Pearson* product-moment correlation coefficient (or *Pearson* correlation coefficient) is used as a measure of redundancy between two random variables [6]. The *Pearson* correlation coefficient (r_{xy}), is a measure of strength of linear relationship between two variables (x, y), and it can take a range of values from +1 to -1, eq. (1). A value of 0 indicates that there is no linear relationship between the two variables, while an absolute value of 1 (or close to 1) indicates strong linear relationship, and therefore considered highly redundant.

$$r_{xy} = \frac{\sum_i (x_i - \bar{x})(y_i - \bar{y})}{\sqrt{\sum_i (x_i - \bar{x})^2}\sqrt{\sum_i (y_i - \bar{y})^2}} \tag{1}$$

2.4 Naive Bayes

Naive Bayes is a probabilistic algorithm based on *Bayes* theorem of conditional probabilities. The basic classification process consists on determining a score based on the training data values. In a simple binary classification problem, a high score is associated with one class and a small score is related to the other class. The result is compared with a threshold to determine the final class [23]. *NB* is fast calculating the needed probabilities as it only performs one scan to the data [24]. *NB* has a strong independence of variables assumption [25]. Another assumption of *NB* is that numerical values have always a normal distribution. *NB* is easy to develop [23] and its classification process is easy to understand as well. It also offers computational time savings for training as it only needs a small amount of data; it is also fast classifying and requires minor storage space in both previous tasks . Besides, it is not affected by missing values as it omits them. In this sense, *NB* is suitable for working with high amount of data [23]. *NB* cannot remove irrelevant features and its performance is highly dependent on the feature selection procedure used. Finally, this algorithm is very affected by irrelevant features [24].

2.5 Maximum Probability of Correct Decision

In predictive analytics, a confusion matrix [26] is a table with two rows and two columns that reports the number of *False Positives (FP)*, *False Negatives (FN)*, *True Positives (TP)*, and *True Negatives (TN)*. This allows more detailed analysis than just the proportion of correct guesses since it is sensitive to the recognition rate by class. A type-I error (α) may be compared with a *FP* prediction; a type-II (β) error may be compared with a false *FN* [6]. They are defined as:

$$\alpha = \frac{\mathrm{FP}}{\mathrm{FP} + \mathrm{TN}}, \quad \beta = \frac{\mathrm{FN}}{\mathrm{FN} + \mathrm{TP}}. \tag{2}$$

The *MPCD* is a probabilistic-based measure of classification performance. It is more sensitive to the recognition rate by class than just the proportion of correct guesses. The α, and beta β errors are combined to estimate *MPCD*:

$$\mathrm{MPCD} = (1 - \alpha)(1 - \beta) \tag{3}$$

where higher score ($0 \leq MPCD \leq 1$) indicates better classification performance.

2.6 Penalized Maximum Probability of Correct Decision

It is a *MS* criterion for binary classifiers in highly unbalanced data structures (i.e., 0.1-3% of defects) [15]. This criterion solves the posed tradeoff between model complexity (e.g., number of features) and prediction ability.

$$PMPCD = (1 - \alpha)(1 - \beta) - ln(K)/34.55 \tag{4}$$

where K is the number of features, and the model with the highest estimated value on the validation set [27–29] is the preferred one.

The term $(1 - \alpha)(1 - \beta)$ rewards the prediction capacity, while the penalty function $ln(K)/34.55$ induces parsimony by decreasing the *PMPCD* value based on the extra features. Since the natural logarithm is a monotonically increasing function, the penalty values follow the same pattern, with no penalty imposed for a single-feature model.

2.7 Hybrid Correlation and Ranking-based Algorithm

The *HCR* algorithm [14] eliminates redundant features based on *Pearson*'s correlation coefficients and the *ReliefF* algorithm ranking. The basic idea is to keep the *best* feature – highest rank – from a set of two or more highly correlated variables and eliminate the rest in that group.

3 Hybrid Feature Selection and Pattern Recognition

Parsimonious modeling is induced through feature selection and model selection, Fig. 1. Since most manufacturing systems are time-dependent, cross-validation methods are not encouraged. Instead, time-ordered hold-out method seems to be more appropriate. The data set should be splitted into training, validation and testing sets (e.g., 50%, 25%, 25% respectively) [28]. And the search space defined by many candidate pairwise combinations – based on different values of k for *ReliefF* and δ for *HCR*. The values of k can be determined by generating a logarithmically spaced vector [30] – p logarithmically spaced points between decades 10^a and 10^b, where $X = sum(bad)$ in the training set, $a = 0$ and $b = log10(X)$.

1. Feature selection
   The primary purpose of this stage, is to find a small subset of features with high prediction capacity. Since the optimal combination – with respect to prediction – of k and δ is not known in advance, a hyperparameter [31] optimization is performed through a grid search [32, 33]. Using the training set, irrelevant and redundant features are eliminated by applying *ReliefF* and *HCR* algorithms. First, features are ranked based on *ReliefF* and irrelevant features are eliminated based on τ – feature relevance (significance) threshold. From the selected features, high correlations are eliminated based on δ. These two steps are performed in a filter-type approach, where the learning algorithm is not considered. The outcome of this step, is a subset of relevant features with no high correlations.
   A *candidate* model is developed with the subset of features at each pairwise combination, and the predictive fitness of each model is evaluated to find the *incumbent* (best so far) model – highest validation *MPCD*. The features in the *incumbent* model are selected and their associated *ReliefF* ranking recorded.
2. Model selection
   Although a good feature subset has been obtained in the previous step, their individual relevance in the model is not known in advance. To evaluate their prediction-contribution, a set of n *candidate* models are developed – where n is the number of selected features – using the top 1 feature in the first *candidate* model, and the top 2 features in the second one, and so on. Finally, the *PMPCD* of each *candidate* model is estimated and used as a *MS* criterion to induce parsimony – solve the tradeoff between model complexity and prediction ability. The *final* model is the one with the highest *PMPCD* score.

3. Generalization evaluation
   To obtain an unbiased estimation (or closest to) of the generalization ability of the *final* model, the prediction on testing set (unseen data) should be reported in a confusion matrix [26] .

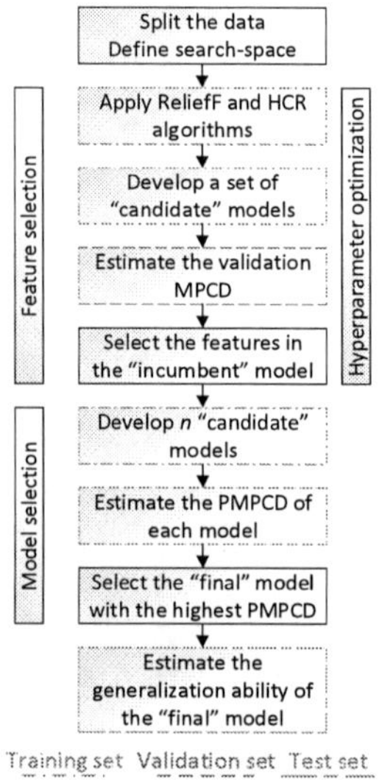

Fig. 1: *HFSPR* framework.

4 Case Study – Ultrasonic Metal Welding

To validate the practical and theoretical advantages of the *HFSPR* approach a manufacturing-derived data set is analyzed. Due to the strong independence of variables assumption, the *NB* learning algorithm is used in this analysis, however, the proposal can be virtually applied to any binary classifier. The data used for this analysis is derived from the *Ultrasonic Metal Welding* of battery tabs for the *Chevrolet Volt* [11], an extended range electric vehicle. A very stable process, that only generates a few defective welds per million of opportunities.

4.1 Hybrid Feature Selection and Pattern Recognition

The collected data set contains a binary outcome (*good/bad*) with 54 features. The data set is highly unbalanced since it contains only 35 *bad* batteries out of 30,731 examples. To run the analysis, the data set is partitioned following a time-ordered hold-out validation scheme: training set (18,495, including 20 *bad*), validation set (12,236 - 8 *bad*), testing set (9,500 - 7 *bad*).

1. Feature selection
   The search space contains 35 pairwise combinations; for *ReliefF*, 7 logarithmically spaced points are defined – $k = \{1, 2, 3, 4, 7, 12, 20\}$ – and for δ, 10 even spaced points – $\delta = \{0.50, 0.55, ..., 0.95\}$. At each iteration, feature relevance is determined by comparing their weights with $\tau = 0.0329$ – calculated with an α of 0.05, and m of 18,495. Prediction results and number of features of each *candidate* model are shown in Fig. 2.

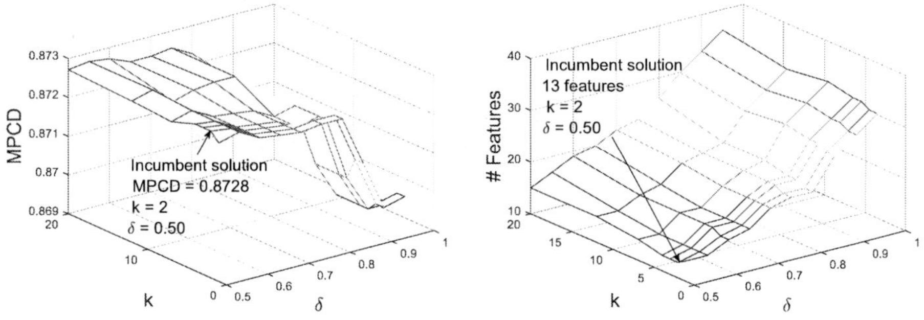

(a) Validation *MPCD*. (b) Number of features.

Fig. 2: Candidate model information (denoted by line intersections).

   According to the grid search results, the *incumbent* model has an estimated validation $MPCD = 0.8728$, Fig. 2(a), and 13 features, Fig. 2(b). This model was developed with the following relevant hyperparameters – $k = 2, \tau = 0.0329, \delta = 0.50$. All *candidate* models failed to detect one of the defective items, therefore, the $\beta = 0.125$ in all models. And they are basically competing over the α error. As displayed by the plots, as the number of low quality features included in the model increases, the α error increases too. The proposed hyperparameter optimization allowed to find a good subset of features.
2. Model selection
   To induce parsimony, 13 *candidate* models are create, and *PMPCD* is used as a model selection criterion to find the *final* model. The basic idea is to evaluate the individual prediction-contribution of each of the 13 selected features, Fig. 3 shows the selected features and their associated ranking. *Candidate* model 1 contains top 1 feature (25), *candidate* model 2 contains the top 2 features (25,5) and so on.
   According to the model selection criterion, *Candidate* model 2 should be selected, with an estimated $PMPCD = 0.8501$, Fig. 4. This analysis, discloses that only two features are needed to approximate the pattern in the manufacturing system, since the prediction improvement is not significant if more features are added to the *final* model.

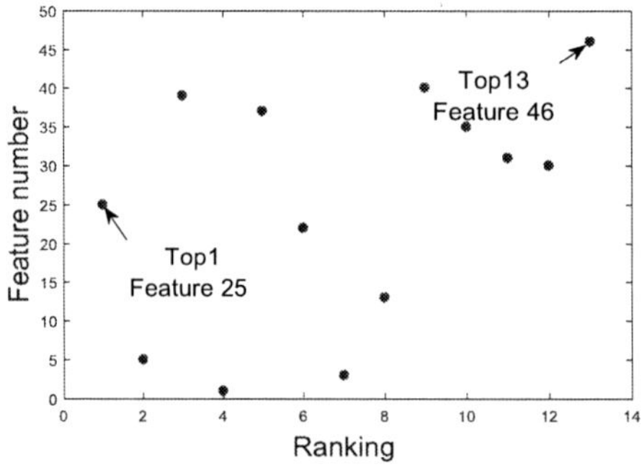

Fig. 3: Features in the *incumbent* model.

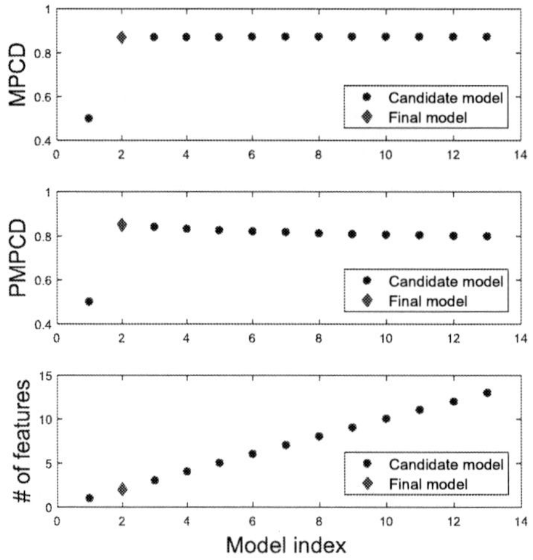

Fig. 4: *Candidate* models using the top 13 features.

3. Generalization evaluation
The testing set is used to estimate the generalization ability of the *final* model, recognition rates are summarized in the confusion matrix, Table 3. This model includes only two features (25,5), and it correctly detected the seven defective items with only five *FP*s – $MPCD = 0.9995$. It is clear that the system can be explained by only these two features.

Table 3: Confusion Matrix

	Declare good	Declare bad
good	9488	5
bad	0	7

4.2 Solution Evaluation and Discussion

Although the feature combination is subject to combinatorial explosion, 1.80144E+16 number of combinations in this case study, the *HFSPR* approach only required 48 models to find a solution. To evaluate its relative quality, an exhaustive search (due to computational feasibility) is performed with all the possible combinations – up to two features – and compared with the *final* model. Since no model selection is performed, the training set is used to develop the models and the testing set to evaluate their generalization ability: (1) 54 ($_{54}C_1$) one-feature models, Fig. 5(a); and (2) 1431 ($_{54}C_2$) two-feature models, Fig. 5(b).

Based on exhaustive search, no single-feature model has better generalization ability. Whereas six two-feature models outperformed the *final* model, Table 4 summarize their relevant information. However, evaluating all possible combinations to find an optimal solution rapidly becomes unfeasible as the feature space grows.

The optimal solution could be defined as the model with the least number of features and the highest prediction ability. For example, in this case study, if there is no other model with an estimated $MPCD > 0.9998$, the optimal solutions would be model indexes 1032 and 1035, Table 4. However, since the number of combinations is huge, a model with more features may have greater *MPCD*. In this context, oftentimes due to the tradeoff between model complexity and prediction ability, there is no straight forward optimal solution. Instead, this tradeoff should be solved.

Although the *HFSPR* did not find the optimal solution, it did promptly find a good quality solution – a model that efficiently addresses the posed tradeoff. Fig. 5 show the relative location of the solution – *final* model.

5 Conclusions and Future Work

In manufacturing domain, traditional quality initiatives have merged to create a more coherent approach, therefore most mature organizations generate only

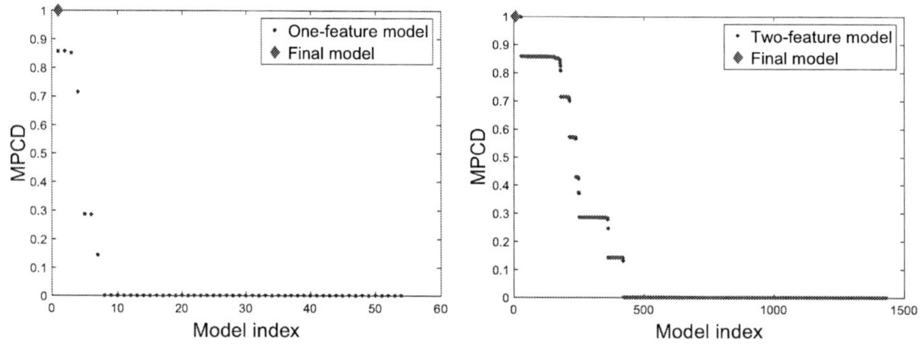

(a) One-feature models. (b) Two-feature models.

Fig. 5: *MPCD* exhaustive search in the one-feature and two-feature spaces.

Table 4: Top models (**HFSPR* solution)

Model index	Features	MPCD	FN
1032	26,33	0.9998	2
1035	26,36	0.9998	2
413	9,26	0.9997	3
1042	26,43	0.9997	3
1044	26,45	0.9997	3
1045	26,46	0.9996	4
Final	5,25	0.9995	5*

a few defects per million of opportunities. As shown in this paper, machine learning, pattern recognition and data mining techniques have the potential to detect these very few defects, and therefore move quality standards forward. However, several intellectual challenges have to be addressed to explode the full potential of *big data* initiatives.

A *Hybrid Feature Selection and Pattern Recognition* approach aimed at detecting rare quality events was developed. Although it does not guarantee to find the optimal solution (if exists), it does promptly find a good quality solution.

Although the proposed approach was inspired by the challenges that manufacturing companies are facing in detecting rare quality events – (1) feature explosion; and (2) high conformance production rates – it can be generalized to other domains, where the main challenge is to detect rare events through a parsimonious model.

In this paper, hyperparameter optimization was performed through a grid search. Future research along this path, can focus on developing an algorithm to improve the hyperparameter optimization process.

Bibliography

[1] C. Bishop, *Pattern Recognition and Machine Learning.* springer, 2006.

[2] P. Bradley and O. Mangasarian, "Feature Selection via Concave Minimization and Support Vector Machines," in *ICML*, vol. 98, 1998, pp. 82–90.

[3] F. Wang, Y. Yang, X. Lv, J. Xu, and L. Li, "Feature Selection using Feature Ranking, Correlation Analysis and Chaotic Binary Particle Swarm Optimization," in 5th *Int Conf on Software Eng and Service Science*, 2014, pp. 305–309.

[4] C. Shao, K. Paynabar, T. Kim, J. Jin, S. Hu, J. Spicer, H. Wang, and J. Abell, "Feature Selection for Manufacturing Process Monitoring using Cross-Validation," *J. of Manufacturing Systems*, vol. 10, 2013.

[5] L. Yu and H. Liu, "Feature Selection for High-Dimensional Data: A Fast Correlation-based Filter Solution," in *ICML*, vol. 3, 2003, pp. 856–863.

[6] J. Devore, *Probability and Statistics for Engineering and the Sciences.* Cengage Learning, 2015.

[7] M. Hall, "Correlation-based Feature Selection of Discrete and Numeric Class Machine Learning," in *Proc of the* 17th *Int Conf on Machine Learning.* University of Waikato, 2000, pp. 359–366.

[8] S. Wu, Y. Hu, W. Wang, X. Feng, and W. Shu, "Application of Global Optimization Methods for Feature Selection and Machine learning," *Mathematical Problems in Eng*, 2013.

[9] M. Baily and J. Manyka, "Is Manufacturing'Cool'Again," *McKinsey Global Institute*, 2013.

[10] G. Köksal, İ. Batmaz, and M. C. Testik, "A Review of Data Mining Applications for Quality Improvement in Manufacturing Industry," *Expert systems with Applications*, vol. 38, no. 10, pp. 13 448–13 467, 2011.

[11] J. A. Abell, D. Chakraborty, C. A. Escobar, K. H. Im, D. M. Wegner, and M. A. Wincek, "Big Data Driven Manufacturing — Process-Monitoring-for-Quality Philosophy," *ASME J of Manufacturing Science and Eng on Data Science-Enhanced Manufacturing*, vol. 139, no. 10, 2017.

[12] C. A. Escobar, M. Wincek, D. Chakraborty, and R. Morales-Menendez, "Process-Monitoring-for-Quality — Applications," *to appear in SME Manufacturing Letters*, 2018.

[13] K. P. Burnham and D. R. Anderson, *Model Selection and Multimodel Inference: a Practical Information-Theoretic Approach.* Springer Science & Business Media, 2003.

[14] C. A. Escobar and R. Morales-Menendez, "Machine Learning Techniques for Quality Control in High Conformance Manufacturing Environment," *DOI:10.1177/1687814018755519, Advances in Mechanical Eng*, 2018.

[15] Carlos A. Escobar and Ruben Morales-Menendez, "Process-Monitoring-for-Quality — A Model Selection Criterion," *DOI:10.1016/j.mfglet.2018.01.001, SME Manufacturing Letters*, 2018.

[16] G. Chandrashekar and F. Sahin, "A Survey on Feature Selection Methods," *Computers & Electrical Eng*, vol. 40, no. 1, pp. 16–28, 2014.

[17] A. Ng, "On Feature Selection: Learning with Exponentially Many Irrevelant Features as Training Examples," in *Proc of the* 15th *Int Conf on Machine Learning*. MIT, Dept. of Electrical Eng and Computer Science, 1998, pp. 404–412.

[18] H. Deng and G. Runger, "Feature Selection via Regularized Trees," in *Int Joint Conf on Neural Networks*, 2012, pp. 1–8.

[19] J. Weston, S. Mukherjee, O. Chapelle, M. Pontil, T. Poggio, and V. Vapnik, "Feature Selection for SVMs," in *NIPS*, vol. 12, 2000, pp. 668–674.

[20] K. Kira and L. Rendell, "The Feature Selection Problem: Traditional Methods and a New Algorithm," in *AAAI*, vol. 2, 1992, pp. 129–134.

[21] I. Kononenko, "Estimating Attributes: Analysis and Extensions of RELIEF," in *European Conf on Machine Learning*. Springer, 1994, pp. 171–182.

[22] M. Robnik-Šikonja and I. Kononenko, "Theoretical and Empirical Analysis of ReliefF and RReliefF," *Machine Learning*, vol. 53, no. 1-2, pp. 23–69, 2003.

[23] X. Wu, V. Kumar, Q. Ross, J. Ghosh, Q. Yang, H. Motoda, and D. Steinberg, "Top 10 Algorithms in Data Mining," *Knowledge and Information Systems*, vol. 14, pp. 1–37, 2008.

[24] K. Al-Aidaroos, A. A. Bakar, and Z. Othman, "Naive Bayes Variants in Classification Learning," in *Int Conf on Information Retrieval and Knowledge Management: Exploring the Invisible World*, 2010, pp. 276–281.

[25] P. Valente Klaine, M. Ali Imran, O. Onireti, and R. Demo Souza, "A Survey of Machine Learning Techniques Applied to Self Organizing Cellular Networks," *IEEE Comm Surveys & Tutorials*, p. 1, 2017.

[26] T. Fawcett, "An Introduction to ROC Analysis," *Pattern Recognition Letters*, vol. 27, no. 8, pp. 861–874, 2006.

[27] S. Arlot and A. Celisse, "A Survey of Cross-Validation Procedures for Model Selection," *Statistics Surveys*, vol. 4, pp. 40–79, 2010.

[28] J. Friedman, T. Hastie, and R. Tibshirani, *The Elements of Statistical Learning*. Statistics Springer, Berlin, 2001, vol. 1.

[29] C. A. Escobar and R. Morales-Menendez, "Machine Learning and Pattern Recognition Techniques for Information Extraction to Improve Production Control and Design Decisions," in *P. Perner Advances in Data Mining, ICDM*. Springer Verlag, 2017, pp. 285–295, lncs 10357.

[30] T. M. Inc. (2017) Logspace. [Online]. Available: https://www.mathworks.com/help/matlab/ref/logspace.html

[31] M. Kuhn and K. Johnson, *Applied Predictive Modeling*. Springer, 2013, vol. 810.

[32] J. Bergstra and Y. Bengio, "Random Search for Hyper-parameter Optimization," *Journal of Machine Learning Research*, vol. 13, no. Feb, pp. 281–305, 2012.

[33] M. Claesen and B. De Moor, "Hyperparameter search in machine learning," *arXiv preprint arXiv:1502.02127*, 2015.

Dynamic Classifier and Sensor Using Small Memory Buffers

Gelbard R.[1[0000-0003-0923-5706]] and Khalemsky A.[1[0000-0002-0817-6575]]

[1] Information Systems, Bar-Ilan University, Ramat-Gan 5290002, Israel
gelbardr@mail.biu.ac.il, anna.khalemsky@gmail.com

Abstract. The model presented in current paper designed for dynamic classifying of real time cases received in a stream of big sensing data. The model comprises multiple remote autonomous sensing systems; each generates a classification scheme comprising a plurality of parameters. The classification engine of each sensing system is based on small data buffers, which include a limited set of "representative" cases for each class (case-buffers). Upon receiving a new case, the sensing system determines whether it may be classified into an existing class or it should evoke a change in the classification scheme. Based on a threshold of segmentation error parameter, one or more case-buffers are dynamically regrouped into a new composition of buffers, according to a criterion of segmentation quality.

Keywords: Dynamic Classifier, Dynamic Rules, Big Data, Sensing Data, Memory Buffers, Clustering; Classification.

1 Introduction

Sensors are located in environments that change dynamically and are required not only to detect the values of all parameters measured, but also to assess the situation and alert accordingly, based on predefined rules managed by a "Classifier-engine". Since the environments are dynamically changed and there may be new situations that were not known in advance, which are reflected in new combinations of parameter values, there is a need for a dynamic updating of the sensor's classifier.

One exemplary application for such dynamic classification unit (DCU) is a screening gate including biometric sensors that screen travelers entering a high security area such as an airport. The sensors may be configured to test multiple parameters of a traveler, such as heart rate, heart pressure, perspiration, etc. The classification system may be set to measure two classes of travelers, the bulk of travelers who have "normal" parameters and should pass the biometric screening without interference, and those who should be checked by security personnel. Upon receiving a new case, the sensing system determines whether it may be classified into one of the existing classes, or it should evoke a change in the classification scheme. Thus, over the course of a day, environmental conditions may change; ranges of values that haven't been observed before may appear causing dynamic changes-updates in sensor's classifier.

Changes in the sensor's classifier (i.e. classification scheme) are triggered based on a threshold of segmentation error parameter. The sensor's classifier is based on small data buffers and collects remembers a limited set of "representative" cases for each class (case-buffers). As a result of the trigger's appeal, one or more case-buffers are dynamically regrouped into a new composition of buffers, according to segmentation quality criteria.

The novelty of this real-time mechanism lies in the fact that the entire process is based on the use of limited memory buffers. In addition, each DCU, which is a remote autonomous sensing system, can communicate with multiple additional remote autonomous sensing systems. In such situations, the case buffers, as well as the case history, can be synchronized and managed via a central controller. Furthermore, in a distributed environment, regardless the existence of a central controller, the contents of the case buffers and the classifier scheme of each DCU can be synchronized between the multiple remote autonomous agents (sensing-systems). Synchronization may be performed after each regrouping process. That is to say that each incremental updating at any local DCU may initiate synchronization among all connected autonomous agents.

2 Related work

In the reality of the dynamic data environment, when a huge amount of raw data and information flows ceaselessly, the main purpose of individuals and organizations is discovering the optimal way to find a hidden potential in it, through the constant cooperation of human intelligence and machine capabilities. The techniques and models that successfully functioned in stable data environment are outdated and need to be corrected to deal with dynamic data environment. "Databases are growing in size to a stage where traditional techniques for analysis and visualization of the data are breaking down" [1], [2]. Because of the constant increase in data volume, interpreting of similarities of different sub-populations becomes the new dimension of data mining goal. The data usually flows from different sources and has to be handled and processed simultaneously [3].The development of new and advanced techniques in data mining in dynamic data environment covers more and more fields, for instance, computer sciences, medicine [4], security systems [5] and social networks [6], [7]. And it is not just an application of existing algorithmic tools in these fields, but the inclusion of elements and logic and even tools, that were created purposefully for them.

As a result of the constant need to get real-time solutions, the research is naturally directed into a new field – incremental data processing. The motivation is to maximize the quality of solutions through minimizing the process cost [8], [9], [10]. The algorithmic tools have to be adjusted to dynamic data environment and be capable to absorb significant amounts of data, possibly to handle with the Big Data environment. The main idea of incremental techniques is to use small segments of data and not the whole historical data [11], [12], [13].

One of the commonly used directions in data mining is classification process, in which the objects are classified into homogeneous groups, with a maximal diversity between groups and minimal within groups. The proximity of an object to group centroid is usually measured by similarity measures, such as RMSE (root mean square error), used in the current paper [14]. The classification tasks are usually divided into two main types: if the target attribute is previously known, the process is called "classification", and if the target attribute is not known, it is called "clustering" [15], [2], [16], [10]. In the case of clustering problems, the interpretation of achieved clusters is one of the main challenges. For example, if a higher education consultant has to recommend the future student what is the best faculty for him, he will probably pick the faculty name from the existing list in the university. On the other hand, if the security system bank controller needs to identify the type of a new financial fraud trend, he needs to be very open-minded and be able to classify the action undertaken by a fraudster to an absolutely different type and give it an appropriate description. In some cases, there is a need to create a set of groups/classes based on items/customers/actions that are needed to be classified without any information about the target attribute. Different kinds of classification/clustering tasks in dynamic data environment in combination of existing and new techniques became the basis for extensive research [17], [18], [19].

The current research presents a dynamic classifier based on incremental dynamic clustering process. It permits the use of small data buffers that represent existing groups. This approach is significantly different from other approaches and methods, considered in the literature.

The dynamic classifier, proposed in the current paper, functions as a sensor. It works as a screening gate that distinguishes between "regular" items that are close enough to at least on of existing groups and alerts when the relatively "different" item occurs. The model permits not just an alert in such situation, but the action required to classify the item. Lots of studies combine different sensors in decision making processes [20], [21], [22], [23].

3 Model architecture

Figure 1 presents a schematic architecture of the proposed system, showing one DCU connected to a central controller as well as to other remote autonomous sensors-agents.

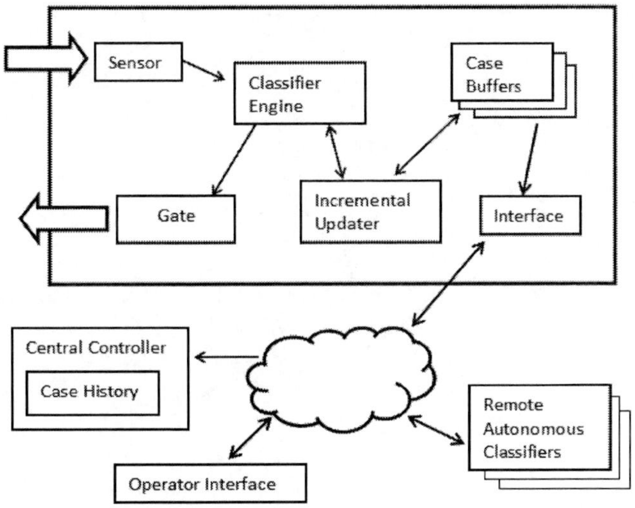

Fig. 1. Schematic architecture of the system.

The real-time data flows through the "Sensor" (Fig.1, first component) to the "Classifier-engine". The "Classier-engine" performs a decision process based on a classification scheme, as described in the flow diagram in Figure 2. The "Gate" component represents the output, or, in other words, the decision regarding the classification of object. Based on a threshold of segmentation error parameter and segmentation quality criteria, the DCU incrementally updates the population of the relevant "Case-buffers". The mechanism that manages the population (i.e. cases) stored in each buffer can use diverse policies, such as FIFO policy (First-In First-Out), or a selection policy that may store extreme-farthest cases of each group ("outliers" that are still classified to that group).

The term "Sensor" represents the "funnel" through which the data stream flows. Thus, a sensor can be a physical object, as well as a logical handshake through which the data flows into the system. The flow chart, illustrated in Figure 2, presents the real-time decision-making process for each new sensing data element (i.e. each new case). Table 1 presents the notations used in the flowchart, illustrated in Figure 2.

The mechanism presented in Figure 2 works as follows: The new item X_i passes through the sensor, the distance measure between the new item and the centroids of existing groups are calculated and the minimal value e is registered. The threshold level δ, the maximal buffer size Zmax and the rest of parameters have to be determined at this point of time. If the minimal distance e is less than a threshold, no rearrangement needed and a new case X_i joins the closest group (completion). If e exceeds the threshold level, the number of items in the buffer is checked. If there are not enough cases (the number of cases is less than Zmin), the new case creates an absolutely new group. If there are enough cases in the buffer, the new case removes the oldest case and a new distribution is created (by splitting or merging of the existing groups).

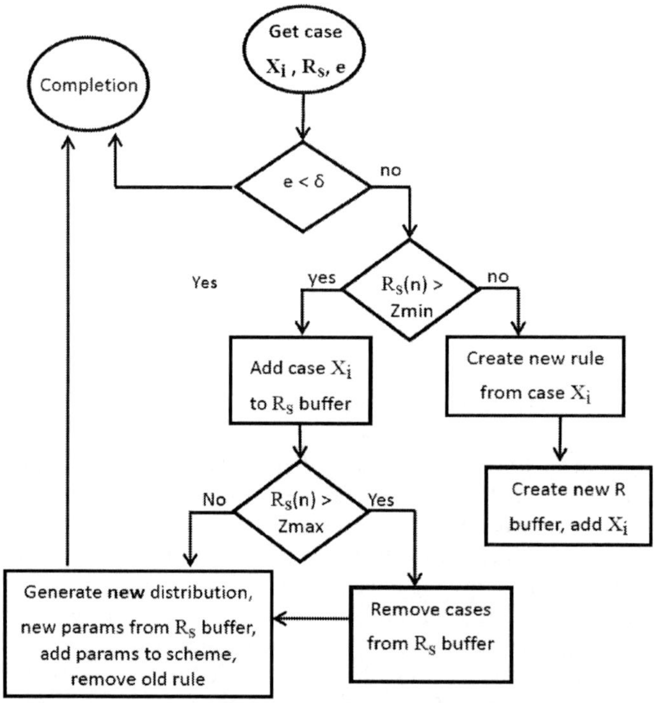

Fig. 2. A flow diagram of a process for real-time data classification based on dynamic updating of sensor's classifiers.

X_i	New case
R_s	The closest group
e	Minimal distance measure RMSE between a new case and existing groups centroids
δ	Threshold that determines the decision of update
R	New group
$R_s(n)$	Number of cases in the buffer
Z_{min}	Minimal number of cases in buffer that justifies the update of the buffer
Z_{max}	The buffer size – maximal number of cases stored in the buffer

Table 1. Notations

The version control is managed by sequential numbering approach, such as used in WBS notation.

4 Model validation

Since the model deals with a stream of real-time data, which is a continuous flow of new cases, the validation was based on datasets of classification problems. The model is implemented by the code developed in Python and combines the k-means algorithm package [24]. The following datasets were used: (1) "ERA" dataset, donated by Prof. Ben-David [25]. This data set was originally gathered during the academic decision-making experiment. Input attributes are candidates' characteristics (such as past experience, verbal skills etc.), output attribute is a subjective judgement of a decision-maker to which degree he/she tends to accept the applicant to the job or to reject him. All the input and output attributes have ordinal values. The data set contains 1000 instances, four input attributes and one output attribute. (2) "Car Evaluation" dataset that was retrieved from the UCI Machine Learning Repository [26], [27], [28]. Input attributes are cars properties and an output attribute is a class value (unacceptable, acceptable, good and very good). The data set contains 1728 instances.

4.1 Optimal situation as a baseline

The theoretical optima in such case is the situation in which the algorithm runs across the entire dataset. Thus, based on the results obtained by the clustering k-means algorithm, while analyzing all the records in the dataset, we can find the best set of rules, and the required total number of rules, that achieve the best classification accuracy.

4.2 The initial stage

According to widely used methodology in machine learning, each dataset was divided into training set (with about two thirds of data) and test set (with about one third of data). The training set provides the initial groups and the test set simulates a new data stream. Worth mention that the initial stage is mainly used to shorten the "reset-cycle" of the decision-making process. In cases where there is no urgency, the system can stat with no decision rule at all, and with totally empty "Case-buffers".

4.3 The "Dynamic-Flow" stage

The test set was used in an unsupervised mode (while hiding the target-labeled field). The records flowed through the "Sensor" to the "Classifier-engine" without any information regarding the right classification-filtering.

- The "Classifier-engine" and the "Incremental-updater" used the flow diagram mechanism described in Fig. 2.
- The delta symbol (δ), in Fig.2, represents Root-mean-square error (RMSE) that was used as a threshold.
- The parameters in each experiment were set as follows:
  ERA data-set: three threshold levels: 2, 2.25, 2.5; initial number of groups:10; buffer size: 25; training set = 600, test set=400.
  Car evaluation data-set: three threshold levels: 0.8, 0.9, 1; initial number of groups: 15; buffer size: 25; training set=1400, test set=328.

In accordance with the schematic architecture of the system (illustrated in Fig.1), a case is either directly classified, or initiates an incremental reevaluation (supported by the "Incremental-updater" component) till the threshold is satisfied, then the "Case-buffers" and the "Classifier-engine" are dynamically updated.

5 Results and discussion

As shown in Figures 3,4 and in Table 2, we can see that although the learning mechanism uses only small data increments, it succeeds to perform good and consistent results. Figures 3,4 represent the dynamics of group set updating for different threshold levels. The process converges in both data sets for all sensitivity levels.

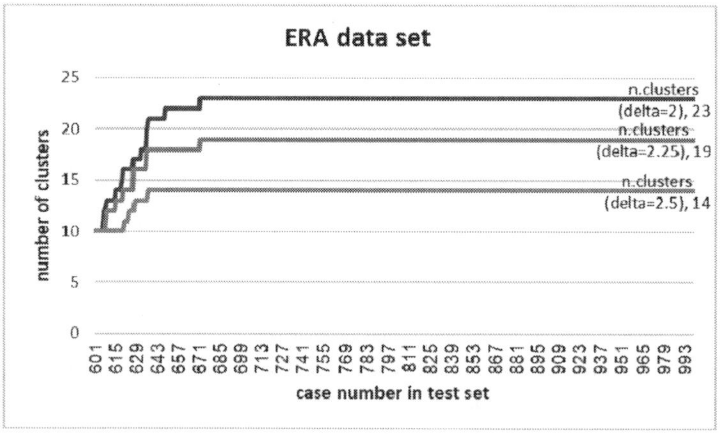

Fig. 3. Rules Convergence using k-means with "ERA" Dataset.

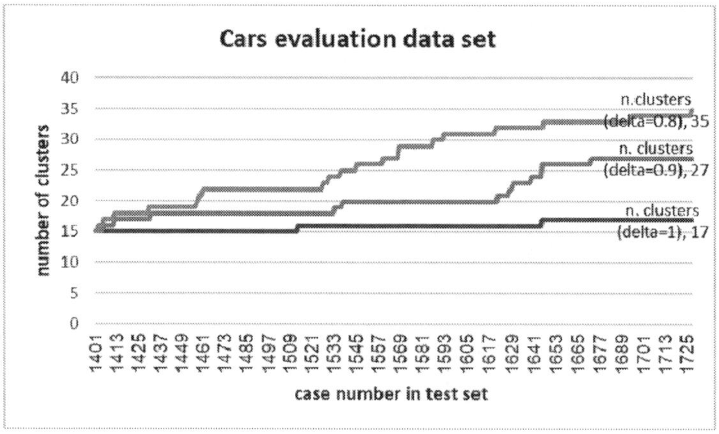

Fig. 4. Rules Convergence using k-means with "Car evaluation" Dataset.

We can see that in all three threshold values a reach a convergence of the classification process. In order to trace the dependence of aggregate rate of total number of groups on the sensitivity level, we chose three threshold levels for each data set. We can see that the convergence is faster as the threshold refers to lower accuracy value, but even at a high accuracy threshold, a relatively rapid convergence was achieved. The application of this result is very practical: on one hand, the dynamic data environment dictates us to act in real time, that is why we use small increments of data to be able to classify objects immediately; on the other hand, we need to provide good classification results and identify new trends or significant changes in data distribution. The convergence of classification process shows the ability of the proposed model to catch the critical moments when an update is needed, without too much computational effort. The updated groups set becomes more and more representative, that is why the periods of time between every two updates lengthens.

Table 2 presents the numerical results of all experiments in two data sets. The distance measure RMSE was calculated for each classified item (in most cases the distance between the item and at least one of the existing groups is less than a threshold level, so the item is joins the existing group; sometimes the threshold is achieved and the update is needed). The average and standard deviation of all minimal RMSE values are calculated for each experiment. The total number of groups in the end of each experiment is presented in addition. As sensitivity of a threshold level decreases (higher values of δ), the average distance measure grows. This result is expected: if a threshold level is relatively high, less items are defined as "far" or "non-similar" and more items succeed to join existing groups. Their minimal RMSE value is weighted into the calculation of average RMSE and we get bigger result. The same effect usually happens in standard deviation.

Data set	$\boldsymbol{\delta}$	**Average RMSE for classified instances**	**Std.dev.**	**Number of Clusters**
ERA	2	0.9048	0.6349	23
Initial number of	2.25	1.1967	0.6677	19
Clusters = 10	2.5	1.4455	0.5842	14
Cars evaluation	0.8	0.6	0.1133	35
Initial number of	0.9	0.6871	0.1184	27
Clusters = 15	1	0.7433	0.1199	17

Table 2. The dynamic incremental updating of group set, according to threshold level.

In the conclusion of the above facts, we can see that the proposed incremental dynamic mechanism succeeds to achieve good results, that can be adopted in industry or in academical research as well.

6 Conclusions

Dynamic incremental classifier presented in this paper is designed to improve the classification process in state of dynamic data environment. The constant changes in data characteristics and preferences require from the mechanism immediate solutions. In addition to this obligatory condition, the process has to be economic. There is no dispute that the most qualitative solution will be obtained through the update of whole relevant data, but it is not possible in dynamic data environment. We assume that it is not possible to revise all previous data, so we choose to demonstrate the incremental mechanism that functions using small data buffers.

Experiments with different data sets showed that the loss of quality in classification results is not significant and the mechanism succeeds to identify the important changes in data stream and converges during the process.

The further research is planned in different possible directions: dealing with a big data sets that simulate big data environment; new trend and outlier detection; text data processing etc.

Acknowledgment: This work was supported in part by a grant from the MAGNET program of the Israeli Innovation Authority; who also submitted this work as a patent application.

References

1. Fayyad U, Stolorz P (1997) Data mining and KDD: Promise and challenges. Future Gener Comput Syst 13:99–115 . doi: 10.1016/S0167-739X(97)00015-0
2. Gelbard R, Goldman O, Spieger I (2007) Investigating diversity of clustering methods: An empirical comparison. Data Knowl Engeneering 155–166
3. Fan J, Han F, Han L (2014) Challenges of Big Data analysis. Natl Sci Rev 293–314
4. Darema F (2004) Dynamic Data Driven Applications Systems: A New Paradigm for Application Simulations and Measurements. In: Computational Science - ICCS 2004. Springer, Berlin, Heidelberg, pp 662–669
5. Ren K, Wang C, Wang Q (2012) Security Challenges for the Public Cloud. IEEE Internet Comput 16:69–73 . doi: 10.1109/MIC.2012.14
6. Li J, Xu H (2016) Suggest what to tag: Recommending more precise hashtags based on users' dynamic interests and streaming tweet content. Knowl-Based Syst 106:196–205 . doi: 10.1016/j.knosys.2016.05.047
7. Miller Z, Dickinson B, Deitrick W, et al (2014) Twitter spammer detection using data stream clustering. Inf Sci 260:64–73 . doi: 10.1016/j.ins.2013.11.016
8. Shah Siddharth, Chauhan N.C., Bhandery S.D. (2012) Incremental Mining of Association Rules: A Survey. Int J Comput Sci Inf Technol 3:4041–4074
9. Cheung DW, Han J, Ng VT, Wong C. (1996) Maintenance of Discovered Association Rules in Large Databases: An Incremental Updating Technique. pp 106–114
10. Grira N, Crucianu M, Boujemaa N (2005) Unsupervised and Semi-supervised Clustering: a Brief Survey. Rev Michine Learn Tech Process Multimed Content
11. G S (2016) Web Data Mining and the Development of Knowledge-Based Decision Support Systems. IGI Global
12. Song YC, Meng HD, Wang SL, et al (2009) Dynamic and Incremental Clustering Based on Density Reachable. In: Fifth International Joint Conference on INC, IMS and IDC, 2009. NCM '09. pp 1307–1310
13. Mishra N, Hsu M, Dayal U (2002) Computer implemented scalable, incremental and parallel clustering based on divide and conquer
14. Deza M.M., Deza E. (2014) Encyclopedia of Distances, 3rd ed. Springer
15. Jain A.K., Murty M.N., Flynn P.L. (1999) Data Clustering: a Survey. ACM Comput Surv 31:
16. Vempala S, Wang G, Kannan R, Cheng D (2010) Techniques for Clustering a Set of Objects
17. Thomas S, Bodagala S, Alsabti K, Ranka S (1997) An Efficient Algorithm for the Incremental Updation of Association Rules in Large Databases.
18. Zhang C-Q, Ou Y (2009) Method for Data Clustering and Classification by a Graph Theory Model - Network Partition into High Density Subgraphs
19. Lughofer E (2012) A dynamic split-and-merge approach for evolving cluster models. Evol Syst 3:135–151 . doi: 10.1007/s12530-012-9046-5
20. Toth CK, Grejner-Brzezinska D (2006) Extracting dynamic spatial data from airborne imaging sensors to support traffic flow estimation. ISPRS J Photogramm Remote Sens 61:137–148 . doi: 10.1016/j.isprsjprs.2006.09.010
21. Zhang Y, He S, Chen J (2016) Data Gathering Optimization by Dynamic Sensing and Routing in Rechargeable Sensor Networks. IEEEACM Trans Netw 24:1632–1646 . doi: 10.1109/TNET.2015.2425146

22. Okeyo G, Chen L, Wang H, Sterritt R (2014) Dynamic sensor data segmentation for real-time knowledge-driven activity recognition. Pervasive Mob Comput 10:155–172 . doi: 10.1016/j.pmcj.2012.11.004
23. Ni Q, Patterson T, Cleland I, Nugent C (2016) Dynamic detection of window starting positions and its implementation within an activity recognition framework. J Biomed Inform 62:171–180 . doi: 10.1016/j.jbi.2016.07.005
24. Download Python. In: Python.org. https://www.python.org/downloads/. Accessed 20 Apr 2018
25. Ben-David A (1992) Automatic Generation of Symbolic Multiattribute Ordinal Knowledge - Based DSS's: Methodology and Applications. Decis Sci 1357–1372
26. UCI Machine Learning Repository: Data Sets. https://archive.ics.uci.edu/ml/datasets.html. Accessed 10 Dec 2016
27. Bohanec M, Rajkovic V (1988) Knowledge Acquision and Explanation for Multi-Attribute Decision Making. pp 1–19
28. Bittmann RM, Gelbard R (2009) Visualization of multi-algorithm clustering for better economic decisions — The case of car pricing. Decis Support Syst 47:42–50 . doi: 10.1016/j.dss.2008.12.012

An Efficient Approach for Mining Weighted Sequential Patterns in Dynamic Databases

Sabrina Zaman Ishita, Faria Noor, and Chowdhury Farhan Ahmed

Department of Computer Science and Engineering, University of Dhaka
sz.ishita@gmail.com,faria.noor93@gmail.com,farhan@du.ac.bd

Abstract. In modern time of flowing data where more data accumulate every minute than we can store or make sense of, a fast approach for analyzing incremental or dynamic database has a lot of significance. In a lot of instance, the data are sequential and the ordering of events has interesting meaning itself. Algorithms have been developed to mine sequential patterns efficiently from dynamic databases. However, in real life not all events bear the same urgency or importance, and by treating them as equally important the algorithms will be prone to leaving out rare but high impact events. Our proposed algorithm solves this problem by taking both the weight and frequency of patterns and the dynamic nature of the databases into account. It mines weighted sequential patterns from dynamic databases in efficient manner. Extensive experimental analysis is conducted to evaluate the performance of the proposed algorithm using large datasets. This algorithm is found to outperform previous method for mining weighted sequential patterns when the database is dynamic.

Keywords: Dynamic databases, Weighted sequential pattern, weighted support, Incremental mining

1 Introduction

Data Mining is the analysis of data, usually in large volumes, for uncovering useful relationships between events or items that make up the data. Frequent pattern mining is an important data mining problem with extensive application; here patterns are mined which occur frequently in a database. Another important domain of data mining is sequential pattern mining where the ordering of items in a sequence is important. Unless weights (value or cost) are assigned to individual items, they are usually treated as equally valuable. However, that is not the case in most real life scenarios. When the weight of items is taken into account in a sequential database, it is known as weighted sequential pattern mining.

As technology and memory devices improve at an exponential rate, their usage grows along too, allowing for the storage of databases to occur at an even higher rate. This calls for the need of incremental mining for dynamic databases whose data are being continuously added. Most organizations that generate and collect data on a daily basis have unlimited growth. When a database update occurs, mining patterns from scratch is costly with respect to time and memory. It is clearly unfeasible. Several approaches have been adopted to mine sequential patterns in incremental database that avoids mining from scratch. This way, considering the dynamic nature of the database, patterns are mined efficiently. However, the weights of the items are not considered in those approaches.

Consider the scenario of a supermarket that sells a range of products. Each item is assigned a weight value according to the profit it generates per unit. In the classic style of market basket analysis, if we have 5 items { "milk", "perfume", "gold", "detergent", "pen" } from the data of the store, the sale of each unit of gold is likely to generate a much higher profit than the sales of other items. Gold will therefore bear a high weight. In a practical scenario, the frequency of sale of gold is also going to be much less than other lower weight everyday items such as milk or detergent. If a frequent pattern mining approach only considers the frequency without taking into account the weight, it will miss out on important events which will not be realistic or useful. By taking weight into account we are also able to prune out many low weight items that may appear a few times but are not significant, thus decreasing the overall mining time and memory requirement.

Existing algorithms for mining weighted sequential patterns or mining sequential patterns in incremental database give compelling results in their own domain, but have the following drawbacks: existing sequential pattern mining algorithms in incremental database do not consider weights of patterns, though low-occurrence patterns with high-weight are often interesting, hence they are missed out if uniform weight is assigned. Weighted sequential patterns are mined from scratch every time the database is appended, which is not feasible for any repository that grows incrementally. These motivated us to overcome these problems and provide a solution that gives better result compared to state-of-the-art approaches. In our approach we have developed an algorithm to mine weighted sequential patterns in an incremental database that will benefit a wide range of applications, from Market Transaction and Web Log Analysis to Bioinformatics, Clinical and Network applications.

With this work we have addressed an important sub-domain of frequent pattern mining where several categories such as sequential, weighted and incremental mining collide. Our contributions are: 1) the construction of an algorithm, *WIncSpan*, that is capable of mining weighted sequential patterns in a dynamic databases continuously over time. 2) Thorough testing on real life datasets to prove the competence of the algorithm for practical use. 3) Marked improvement in results of the proposed method when compared to existing algorithm.

The paper is organized as follows: section 2 talks about the preliminary concepts and discusses some of the state-of-the-art mining techniques which directly influence this study. In section 3, the proposed algorithm is developed and an example is worked out. Comparison of results of the proposed algorithm with existing algorithm is given in section 4. And finally, the summary is provided as conclusions in section 5.

2 Preliminary Concepts and Related Work

Let us expand our discussion to better understand the concepts that lie at the heart of mining frequent patterns of different types. Let I be the set of all items $I_1, I_2, \ldots, I_n$. A set of transactions is considered as a transaction database where each transaction is a subset of I. Sequence database is a set of sequences where every sequence is a set of events $< e_1\ e_2\ e_3\ \ldots\ e_l >$. The order in which events or elements occur is important. Here, event e_1 occurs before event e_2, which occurs before e_3 and so on. Each event $e_i \subseteq I$. In table 1, a sequence database is given along with one increment, where in first sequence, there are 2 events: (ab) and (e). For brevity, the brackets are omitted if an event has only one item. Here, (ab) occurs before (e). Given a set of sequences and a user-specified *min_sup* threshold, sequential pattern mining is regarded as finding all frequent subsequences whose support count is no less than *min_sup*. If $\alpha = <$ (ab)b $>$ and $\beta = <$ (abc)(be)(de)c $>$, where a,b,c,d, and e are items, then α is a subsequence of β.

Many algorithms, such as GSP[1] and SPADE[2], mine frequent sequential patterns. GSP uses Apriori based approach of candidate generate and test. SPADE uses the same approach as GSP but it maps a sequence database into vertical data format unlike GSP. They also obey the antimonotone or downward-closure property that if a sequence does not fulfill the minimum support requirement then none of its super-sequences will be able to fulfill it as well. FreeSpan[3] takes motivation from FP-Growth Tree and mines sequential patterns. SPAM[12] mines sequential patterns using a bitmap representation. PrefixSpan[4] maintains the antimonotone property and uses a prefix-projected pattern growth method to recursively project corresponding postfix subsequences into projected databases.

As technology and memory devices improve at an exponential rate, their usage grows along too, allowing for the storage of databases to occur at an even higher rate. This calls for the need of incremental mining for dynamic databases whose data is being continuously added, such as in shopping transactions, weather sequences and medical records. The naive solution for mining patterns in dynamic database is to mine the updated database from scratch, but this will be inefficient since the newly appended portion of the database is often much smaller than the whole database. To produce frequent sequential patterns from dynamic database in an efficient way, several algorithms [14,15,16] were proposed. One of the algorithms for mining sequential patterns from dynamic databases is IncSpan[5]. Here, along with frequent sequences, semi-frequent sequences are also saved to be worked on when new increment is added. For buffering semi-frequent sequences along with frequent sequences, a buffer ratio is used. In our approach, we will use this concept for buffering weighted semi-frequent sequences for further use.

Considering the importance or weights of items, several approaches such as WSpan[6], WIP[7], WSM[8] etc have been proposed for mining weighted frequent patterns. WSpan mines weighted frequent sequential patterns. Using the weight constraint for mining weighted sequential patterns WSpan[6] uses the prefix projected sequential pattern growth approach. According to WSpan, the weight of a sequence is defined as the average weight of all its items from all the events. For example, using the weight table provided in Table 2, we can calculate the weight of the sequential pattern $P = < abc >$ as W(P)=(0.41+0.48+0.94)/3=0.61.

There exists many work in the field of weighted sequential pattern mining and in the field of incremental mining separately. But there has been no complete work in the field of mining weighted sequential patterns in incremental database. A work[9] has attempted to mine weighted sequential patterns in incremental database, but no complete details and comparative performance analysis were provided there. We are proposing a new algorithm *WIncSpan* which provides a complete work of how weighted sequential patterns can be generated from dynamic database and providing detailed experimental results of its performance.

3 The Proposed Approach

In previous section we discussed the preliminary concepts and existing methods of mining frequent sequential patterns separately in weighted and incremental domains. In this chapter we merge those concepts to propose a new method for weighted sequential pattern mining in incremental databases. A sequence database is given in Table 1. Here, from sequences 10 through 50 represent the initial database D and sequences 60 through 80 represent Δdb which is the new appended part of the whole database D'. The corresponding weights of the items of D' is given in Table 2.

Table 1. Appended Database D'

	Sequence ID	Sequences
D	10	$< (ab)e >$
	20	$< ab >$
	30	$< a(dc)e >$
	40	$< (ab)d >$
	50	$< b(dc)e >$
Δdb	60	$< (ab)d >$
	70	$< a(dc)(ab) >$
	80	$< a(ab)e >$

Table 2. Weight Table for Items in D

Item	Weight
a	0.41
b	0.48
c	0.94
d	0.31
e	0.10

Definition 1 (Minimum Weighted Support: *minw_sup*). As we know, for a given minimum support percentage, the *min_sup* value is calculated as: *min_sup = number of transactions in database * minimum support percentage.* We are considering the weight of the items as well, we derive a minimum weighted support threshold *minw_sup:*

$$minw\_sup = min\_sup * avgW$$

Here, $avgW$ is the average weight value. This is the average of the total weight or profit that has contributed to the database upto that point. In initial database of D', item a occurs 4 times in total, similarly b occurs 4, c occurs 2, d occurs 3 and e occurs 3 times in total. The $avgW$ is calculated as: $avgW$ = (4 * 0.41)+(4 * 0.48)+(2 * 0.94)+(3 * 0.31)+(3 * 0.10)/16=0.4169. In initial database D, the $minw\_sup$ for minimum support 60% is therefore calculated as: $minw\_sup$ = 3 * 0.4169 = 1.25 (as min_sup=5 * 60%=3).

Definition 2 (Possible Frequent Sequences). The possible set of frequent sequences is generated to list sequences or patterns in a database that have a chance to grow into patterns that could be frequent later. For a sequence to be possibly frequent, the following condition must be fulfilled:

$$support * maxW \geqslant minw\_sup$$

The notation $maxW$ denotes the weight of the item in the database that has maximum weight. In our example, it would be 0.94 for the item $< c >$. This value is multiplied with the support of the pattern instead of taking the actual weight of the pattern. This is to make sure the anti-monotone property is maintained, since in an incremental database a heavy weighted item may appear later on in the same sequence with less weighted items, thereby lifting the overall support of the pattern. By taking the maximum weight, an early consideration is made to allow growth of patterns later on during prefix projection. The set thus contains all the frequent items, as well as some infrequent items that may grow into frequent patterns later, or be pruned out.

Complete Set of Possible Frequent Sequences First, the possible length-1 items are mined. For item $< a >$ in D, $support_a * maxW = 4 * 0.94 = 3.76 \geqslant minw\_sup$. The item $< a >$ satisfies the possible frequent sequence condition. Items $< b >$, $< c >$, $< d >$ and $< e >$ are found to satisfy the condition as well and therefore are added to the set of possible frequent length-1 sequences.

Possible Frequent length-1 Sequences: $\{< a >, < b >, < c >, < d >, < e >\}$

Next, the projected database for each frequent length-1 sequence is produced using the frequent length-1 sequence as prefix. The projected databases are mined recursively by identifying the local weighted frequent items at each layer, till there are no more projections. In this way the set of possible frequent sequences is grown, which now includes the sequential patterns grown from the length-1 sequences. At each step of the projection, the items picked will have to satisfy the minimum weighted support condition. For example, for item $< a >$, the projected database contains these sequences: $< (\_b)e >$, $< b >$, $< (dc)e >$, $< (\_b)d >$. And the possible sequential patterns mined from these sequences are: $< a >, < ab >, < (ab) >, < ac >, < ad >, < ae >$. In the similar way, possible sequential patterns are also mined from the projected databases with prefixes $< b >, < c >, < d >$ and $< e >$.

Definition 3 (Weighted Frequent and Semi-Frequent Sequences). For static database, at this moment, only the weighted frequent sequences will be saved and others will be pruned out. Considering the dynamic nature of the database, along with weighted frequent sequences, we will keep the weighted semi-frequent sequences too. From the set of possible frequent sequences, set of Frequent Sequences(FS) and Semi-Frequent Sequences(SFS) can be constructed as follows:

$$\text{Condition for FS:} \quad support(P) * weight(P) \geqslant minw\_sup$$
$$\text{Condition for SFS:} \quad support(P) * weight(P) \geqslant minw\_sup * \mu$$

Here, P is a possible frequent sequence and μ is a buffer ratio. If the support of P multiplied by its actual weight satisfies the minimum weighted support $minw\_sup$ then it goes to the FS list. If not, the support of P times its actual weight is compared with a fraction of $minw\_sup$ which is derived from multiplying $minw\_sup$ by a buffer ratio μ. If satisfied, the sequence is listed in SFS as a semi-frequent sequence. Otherwise, it is pruned out.

For example, the single length sequence $< a >$ has weighted support 4 * 0.41 = 1.64. Since 1.64 is greater than the $minw\_sup$ value 1.25, $< a >$ is added to FS. Considering the value of μ as 60%, $minw\_sup * \mu$=1.25*60%=0.75. Here, $< bd >$ has support count of 2 and weight of (0.48+0.31)/2 = 0.395. Its weighted support 2 * 0.395 = 0.79 is greater than 0.75, so it goes to SFS list. For initial sequence database D, mined frequent sequences are: $< a >, < b >, < c >, < (dc) >$ and semi-frequent sequences are: $< (ab) >, < bd >, < d >$. Other sequences from possible set of frequent sequences are pruned out as infrequent. Interestingly, we see that $< d >$ is a semi-frequent pattern but when we consider it in an event with highly weighted item $< c >$, $< (dc) >$ becomes a frequent pattern. This is possible in our approach as a result of considering the weight of sequential patterns.

Dynamic Trie Maintenance An extended trie is constructed from FS and SFS patterns from D which is illustrated in Figure 1. The concept of the extended trie is taken from the work [5]. Each node in the trie will be extended from its parent node as either s-extension or i-extension. If the node is added as different event, then it is s-extension, if it is added in the same event as its parent then it is i-extension. For example, while adding the pattern $< (ab) >$ to the trie, we first go to the branch labeled with $< a >$, increment its support count by the support count of $< (ab) >$, then add a new branch to it labeled with $< b >$ as i-extension. The solid lines represent the FS patterns and the dashed lines represent the SFS patterns. Each path from root to non-root node represents a pattern along with its support.

When new increments are added, rather than scanning the whole database to check the new support count of a pattern, the dynamic trie becomes handy. This trie will be used dynamically to update the support count of patterns when new increments will be added to the database. Traversing the trie to get the new support count of a pattern is performed a lot faster than scanning the whole database.

Increment to Database At this point, if an update to the database is made, which is a common nature of most real-life datasets, it is not convenient to run the procedure from scratch. How the appended part of the database will be handled, how new frequent sequences will be generated using the *FS* and *SFS* lists, how the dynamic trie will be helpful -all are explained below.

The Proposed Algorithm Here, the basic steps of the proposed *WIncSpan* algorithm is illustrated to mine weighted sequential patterns in an incremental database. Further, an incremental scenario is provided to better comprehend the process.

Snapshot of the Proposed Algorithm The necessary steps for mining weighted sequential frequent patterns in an incremental database are:

1. In the beginning, the initial database is scanned to form the set of possible frequent patterns.
2. The weighted support of each pattern is compared with the minimum weighted support threshold *minw_sup* to pick out the actual frequent patterns, which are stored in a frequent sequential set *FS*.
3. If not satisfied, the weighted support of the pattern is checked against a percentage(buffer ratio) of the *minw_sup* to form the set of semi-frequent set *SFS*. Other patterns are pruned out as infrequent.
4. An extended dynamic trie is constructed using the patterns from *FS* and *SFS* along with their support count.
5. For each increment in the database, the support counts of patterns from the trie are updated.
6. Then the new weighted support of each pattern in *FS* and *SFS* is again compared with the new *minw_sup* and then compared with the percentage of *minw_sup* to check whether it goes to new frequent set FS' or to new semi-frequent set SFS', or it may also become infrequent.
7. FS' and SFS' will serve as *FS* and *SFS* for next increment.
8. At any instance, to get the weighted frequent sequential patterns till that point, the procedure will output the set *FS*.

An Incremental Example Scenario When an increment to database D occurs, it creates a larger database D' as shown in Table 1. Here, three new transactions have been added which is denoted as Δdb.

The *minw_sup* will get changed due to the changed value of *min_sup* and *avgW*. Taking 60% as the minimum supprt threshold as before, new absolute value of *min_sup*=8 * 60%=5 and the new avgW is calculated as 0.422. So, the new *minw_sup* value is now: $5 * 0.422 = 2.11$. The sequences in Δdb are scanned to check for occurrence of the patterns from *FS* and *SFS*, and the support count is updated in the trie. When the support count of patterns in the trie is updated, their weighted support are compared with the new *minw_sup* and *minw_sup* $* \mu$ to check if they become frequent or semi-frequent or even infrequent.

After the database update, the newly mined frequent sequences and semi-frequent sequences are listed in 3. Patterns not shown in the table are pruned out as infrequent. Although $< (ab) >$ was a semi-frequent pattern in D, it became frequent in D'. On the other hand, the frequent pattern $< (dc) >$ only appears once in Δdb, but it became semi-frequent now. Another pattern, $< bd >$, which was semi-frequent in D only increases one time in support in D'. So, $< bd >$ falls under the category of infrequent patterns.

Table 3. Weighted Frequent and Semi-Frequent Sequences in D'

Frequent Sequences	Semi-Frequent Sequences
$< a >, < b >, < c >, < (ab) >$	$< (dc) >, < d >$

After taking the patterns from Δdb into account, the updated FS' and SFS' trie that emerges is illustrated in Figure 2.

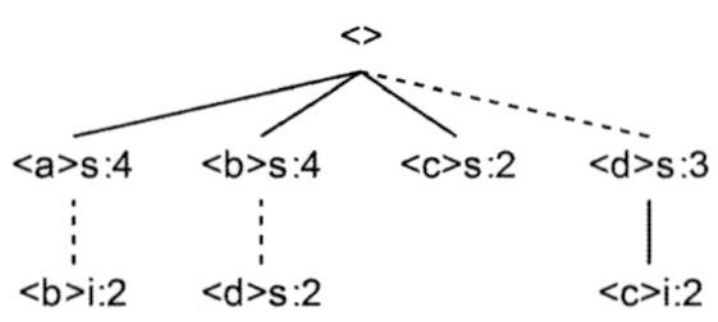

Fig. 1. The Sequential Pattern Trie of *FS* and *SFS* in *D*

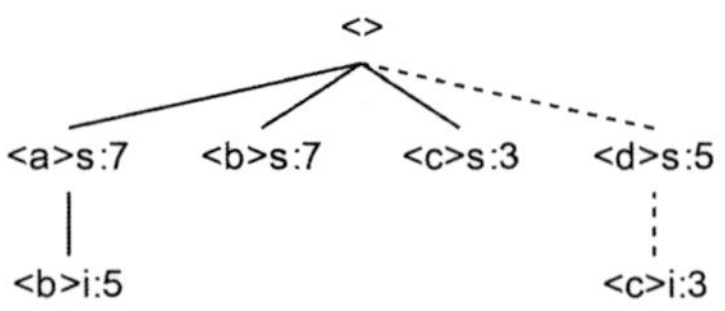

Fig. 2. The Updated Sequential Pattern Trie of FS' and SFS' in D'

3.1 The Pseudo-code

To get the weighted sequential patterns from the given database which are dynamic in nature, we will use the proposed *WIncSpan* algorithm. A sequence database *D*, the minimum weighted support threshold *minw_sup* and the buffer ratio μ are given as input to the algorithm. Algorithm *WIncSpan* will generate the set of weighted frequent sequential patterns at any instance. The pseudo-code is given in Algorithm 1.

Algorithm 1 WIncSpan: Weighted Sequential Pattern Mining in Dynamic Database

Input: A sequence database D, the minimum weighted support threshold *minw_sup*, and the buffer ratio μ
Output: The set of weighted frequent sequential patterns FS.

Method:
Begin

1. Let *WSP* be the set of Possible Weighted Frequent Sequential Patterns, *FS* be the set of Frequent Patterns and *SFS* be the set of Semi-Frequent Patterns.
   Now,
   $WSP \longleftarrow \{\}$, $FS \longleftarrow \{\}$, $SFS \longleftarrow \{\}$
2. *WSP* = Call the modified WSpan(*WSP*, *D*, *minw_sup*)
3. **for** each pattern *P* in *WSP* **do**
4.   **if** *sup(P)) * weight(P)* $\geqslant$ *minw_sup* **then**
5.   insert (FS, *P*)
6.   **else if** *sup(P) * weight(P)* $\geqslant$ *minw_sup* * μ **then**
7.   insert (SFS, *P*)
8.   **end if**
9. **end for**
10. **for** each new increment Δdb in D **do**
11.   *FS*, *SFS* = Call WIncSpan(*FS*, *SFS*, Δdb, *minw_sup*, μ)
12.   output *FS*
13. **end for**

End

Procedure: WIncSpan(*FS*, *SFS*, Δdb, *minw_sup*, μ)
Parameters: *FS*: Frequent Sequences upto now; *SFS*: Semi-Frequent Sequences upto now; Δdb: incremented portion of D; *minw_sup*: minimum weighted support threshold; μ: buffer ratio.

1. Let FS' and SFS' be the set of new frequent and semi-frequent patterns respectively.
2. Initialize $FS' \longleftarrow \{\}$, $SFS' \longleftarrow \{\}$
3. **for** each pattern *P* in *FS* or *SFS* **do**
4.   check $\Delta sup(P)$
5. $sup(P) = sup_D(P) + \Delta sup(P)$
6.   **if** *sup(P) * weight(P)* $\geqslant$ *minw_sup* **then**
7.   insert(FS', P)
8.   **else if** *sup(P) * weight(P)* $\geqslant$ *minw_sup* * μ **then**
9.   insert (SFS', P)
10.   **end if**
11. **end for**
12. return FS', SFS'

At any instance, we can check the *FS* list to get the weighted frequent sequential patterns till that point.

4 Performance Evaluation

In this section, we present the overall performance of our proposed algorithm *WIncSpan* over several datasets. The performance of our algorithm *WIncSpan* is compared with WSpan[6]. Various real-life datasets such as SIGN, BIBLE, Kosarak etc were used in our experiment. These datasets were in spmf[10] format. Some datasets were collected directly from their site, some were collected from the site Frequent Itemset Mining Dataset repository[11] and then converted to spmf format. Both of the implementations of *WIncSpan* and WSpan were performed in Windows environment (Windows 10), on a core-i5 intel processor which operates at 3.2GHz with 8 GB of memory.

Using real values of weights of items might be cumbersome in calculations. We used normalized values instead. To produce normalized weights, normal distribution is used with a suitable mean deviation and standard deviation. Thus the actual weights are adjusted to fit the common scale. In real life, items with high weights or costs appear less in number. So do the items with very low weights. On the other hand items with medium range of weights appear the most in number. To keep this realistic nature of items, we are using normal distribution for weight generation.

Here, we are providing the experimental results of the *WIncSpan* algorithm under various performance metrics. Except for the scalability test, for other performance metrics, we have taken an initial dataset to apply *WIncSpan* and WSpan, then we have added increments in the dataset in two consecutive phases. To calculate the overall performance of both of the algorithms, we measured their performances in three phases.

Performance Analysis w.r.t Runtime We measured the runtime of *WIncSpan* and WSpan in three phases. The graphical representations of runtime with varying min_sup threshold for BMS2, BIBLE and Kosarak datasets are shown in Figure 3, 4 and 5 respectively. Like sparse dataset as Kosarak, the runtime performance was also observed on dense dataset as SIGN. Figure 6 shows the graphical representation.

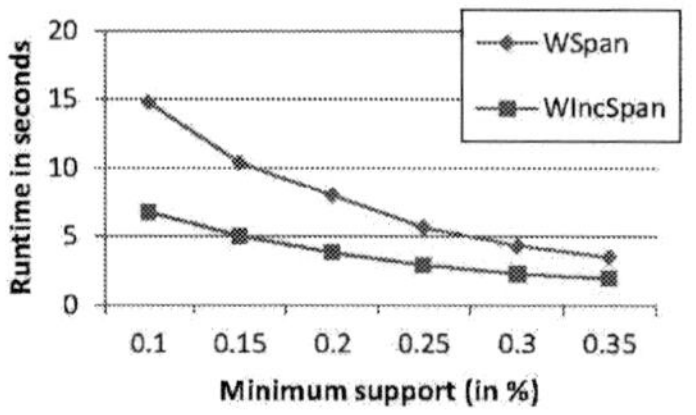

Fig. 3. Runtime for Varying min_sup in BMS2 Dataset.

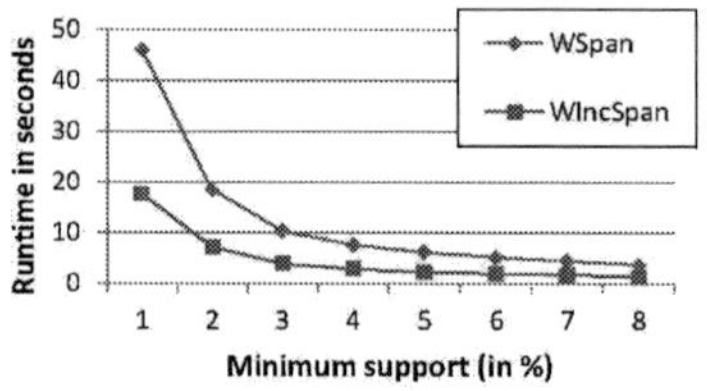

Fig. 4. Runtime for Varying min_sup in BIBLE Dataset.

Table 4. Runtime Performance of WSpan and WIncSpan with Varying min_sup in Kosarak Dataset

min_sup (in %)	Runtime in initial database		Runtime after 1st increment		Runtime after 2nd increment		Runtime Total (in seconds)	
	WSpan	WIncSpan	WSpan	WIncSpan	WSpan	WIncSpan	WSpan	WIncSpan
0.22%	81.3	81.3	66.8	1.66	65.5	1.53	213.6	84.49
0.26%	22.8	22.8	38.4	1.56	51.1	0.82	108.3	25.18
0.3%	14.5	14.5	20.3	0.75	26.8	0.63	61.6	15.88
0.34%	4.63	4.63	8.12	0.56	15.1	0.48	27.85	5.67
0.38%	2.11	2.11	3.11	0.48	5.11	0.54	10.33	3.13

In the figures, we can see that time required to run *WIncSpan* is less than the time required to run WSpan. And their differences in time becomes larger when the minimum support threshold is lowered. To understand how the runtime calculation is done more clearly, Table 4 shows the runtime in each phase for both *WIncSpan* and WSpan in Kosarak dataset. The total runtime is calculated which is used in the graph. It is clear that *WIncSpan* outperforms WSpan with respect to runtime. With the dynamic increment to the dataset, it is desirable that we generate patterns as fast as we can. *WIncSpan* fulfills this desire, and it runs a magnitude faster than WSpan.

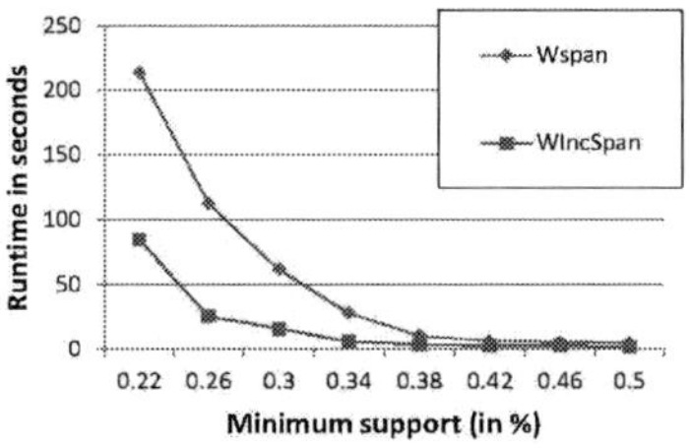

Fig. 5. Runtime for Varying min_sup in Kosarak Dataset.

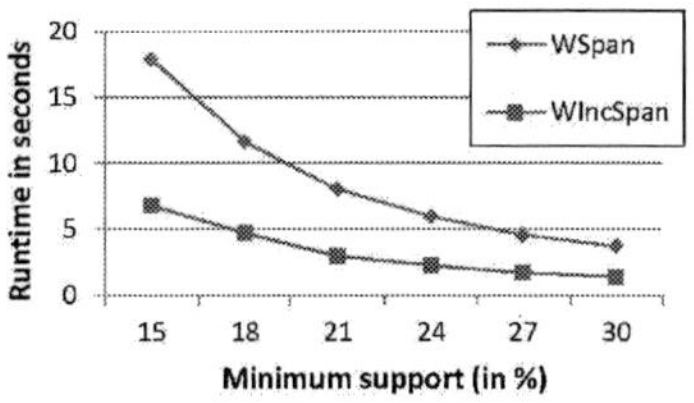

Fig. 6. Runtime for Varying min_sup in SIGN Dataset.

Performance Analysis w.r.t Number of Patterns The comparative performance analysis of *WIncSpan* and WSpan with respect to number of patterns for Kosarak and SIGN datasets are given in Figure 7 and Figure 8 respectively. In these graphs, we can see that the number of patterns generated by WSpan is more than the number of patterns generated by *WIncSpan*. As the minimum threshold is lowered, this difference gets bigger. However, the advantage of *WIncSpan* over WSpan is that it can generate these patterns way faster than WSpan as we saw in the previous section.

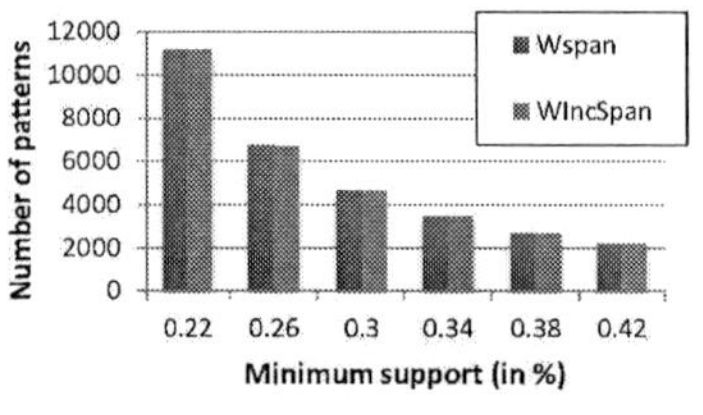

Fig. 7. Number of Patterns for Varying min_sup in Kosarak Dataset.

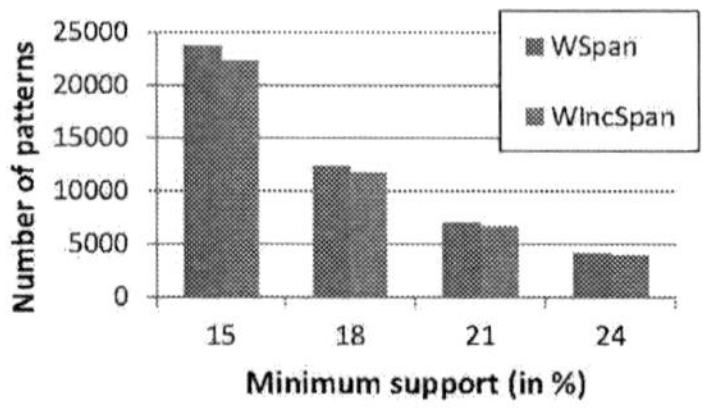

Fig. 8. Number of Patterns for Varying min_sup in SIGN Dataset.

Performance Analysis with Varying Buffer Ratio The lower the buffer ratio is, the higher the buffer size, which can accommodate more semi-frequent patterns. We have measured the number of patterns by varying the buffer ratio. The graphical representation of the results in BIBLE dataset is shown in Figure 9. Here, we can see that by increasing the buffer ratio the number of patterns tend to decrease. Because smaller number of semi-frequent patterns are generated and they can contribute less to frequent patterns in the next phase. We can also see that the number of patterns generated by WSpan is constant for several buffer ratio because WSpan does not buffer semi-frequent patterns, it generates patterns from scratch in every step.

Performance Analysis w.r.t Memory Figure 10 shows memory consumption by both *WIncSpan* and WSpan with varying min_sup in Kosarak dataset. For every dataset, it showed that memory consumed by *WIncSpan* is lower than memory consumed by WSpan. This is because *WIncSpan* scans the new appended part of the database and works on the dynamic trie. Whereas WSpan creates projected database for each pattern and generates new patterns from it. This requires a lot more memory compared with *WIncSpan*.

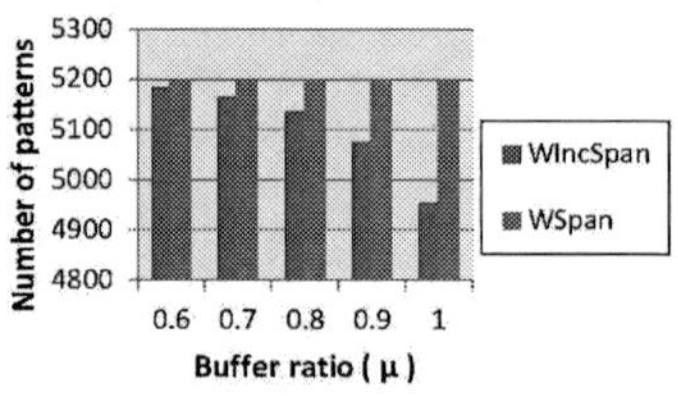

Fig. 9. Number of Patterns for Varying Buffer Ratio (μ) in BIBLE Dataset.

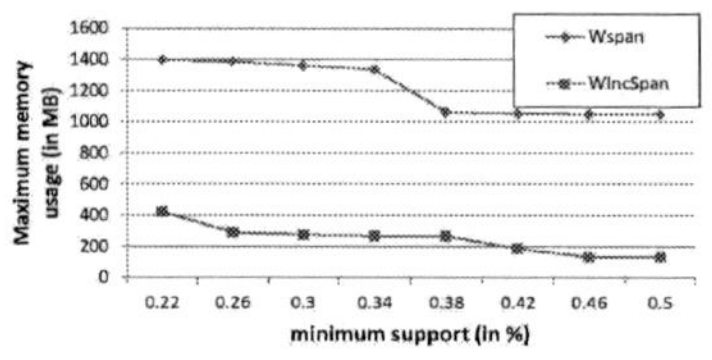

Fig. 10. Memory Usage for Varying min_sup in Kosarak Dataset.

Performance Analysis with Varying Standard Deviation To generate weights for items, we have used normal distribution with a fixed mean deviation of 0.5 and varying standard deviation(0.15 in most of the cases). For varying standard deviation the number of items versus weight ranges curves are shown in figure 11. The range (mean deviation ± standard deviation) holds the most amount of items which is the characteristic of real-life items. In real life, items with medium values occur frequently whereas items with higher or too lower values occur infrequently.

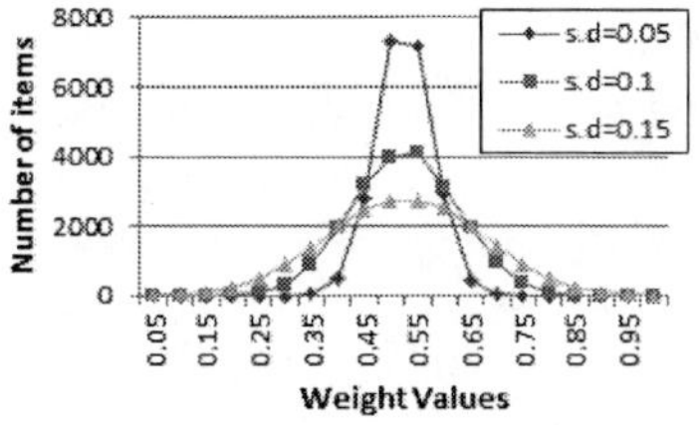

Fig. 11. Weight Values by Normal Distribution with Different Standard Deviations in Kosarak dataset.

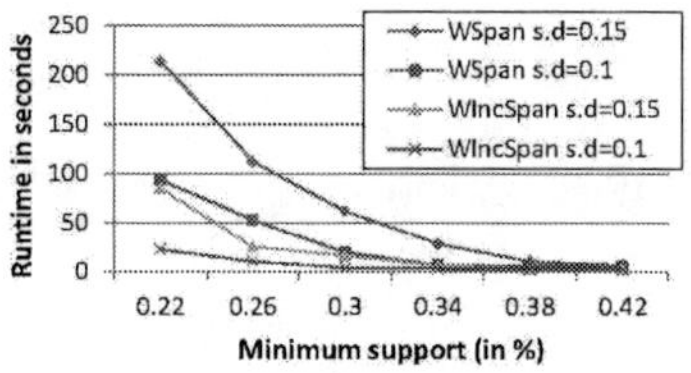

Fig. 12. Runtime Evaluation with Different Standard Deviations in Kosarak Dataset.

Figure 12 and 13 show performance of *WIncSpan* and WSpan with respect to runtime and number of patterns respectively with different standard deviations. *WIncSpan* outperforms WSpan in case of runtime. The number of patterns in each case does not differ a lot from each other. So, it is clear that *WIncSpan* can work better than WSpan with varying weight ranges too.

Scalability Test To test whether *WIncSpan* is scalable or not, we have run it on different datasets with several increments. Figure 14 shows the scalability performance analysis of *WIncSpan* and WSpan in Kosarak dataset when the minimum support threshold is 0.3%. After running on an initial set of the database, five consecutive increments were added and the runtime performance was measured in each step.

Here, we can see that both WSpan and *WIncSpan* take same amount of time in initial set of database. As the database grows dynamically, WSpan takes more time than *WIncSpan*. *WIncSpan* tends to consume less time from second increment as it uses the dynamic trie and new appended part of the database only. From second increment to the last increment, consumed time by *WIncSpan* does not vary that much form each other. So, we can see that *WIncSpan* is scalable along with its runtime and memory efficiency.

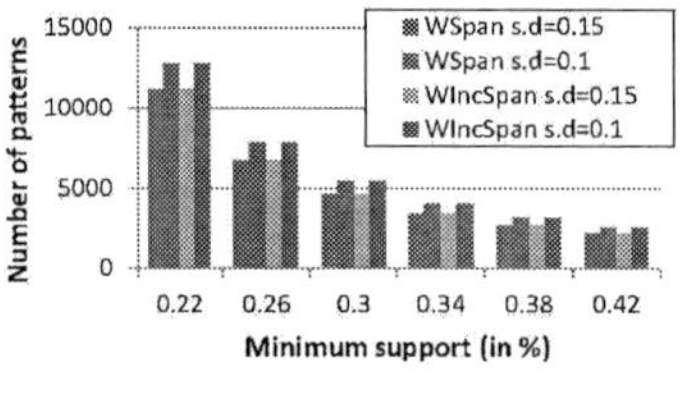

Fig. 13. Number of Patterns for varying Standard Deviations in Kosarak Dataset.

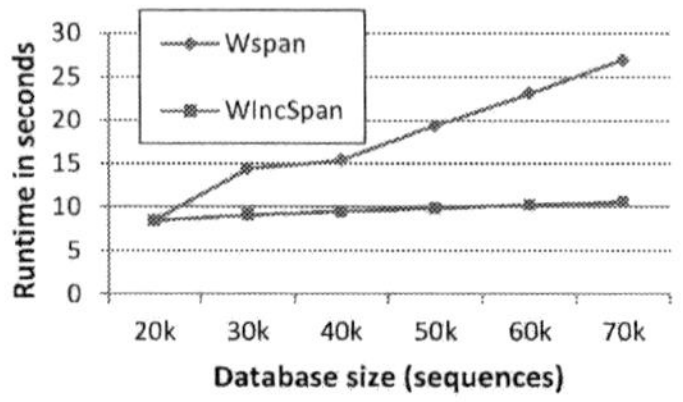

Fig. 14. Scalability Test in Kosarak Dataset (min_sup=0.3%)

The above discussion implies that *WIncSpan* can be applied in real life application where the database tends to grow dynamically and the values(weights) of the items are important. *WIncSpan* outperforms WSpan in all the cases. In case of number of patterns, *WIncSpan* may provide less amount of patterns than WSpan, but this behaviour can be acceptable considering the remarkable less amount of time it consumes. In real life, items with lower and higher values are not equally important. So, *WIncSpan* can be applied in place of IncSpan also where the value of the item is important.

5 Conclusions

A new algorithm *WIncSpan*, for mining weighted sequential patterns in large incremental databases, is proposed in this study. It overcomes the limitations of previously existing algorithms. By buffering semi-frequent sequences and maintaining dynamic trie, our approach works efficiently in mining when the database grows dynamically. The actual benefits of the proposed approach is found in its experimental results, where the *WIncSpan* algorithm has been found to outperform WSpan. It is found to be more time and memory efficient.

This work will be highly applicable in mining weighted sequential patterns in databases where constantly new updates are available, and where the individual items can be attributed with weight values to distinguish between them. Areas of application therefore includes mining Market Transactions, Weather Forecast, improving Health-Care and Health Insurance and many others. It can also be used in Fraud Detection by assigning high weight values to previously found fraud patterns.

The work presented here can be extended to include more research problems to be solved for efficient solutions. Incremental mining can be done on closed sequential patterns with weights. It can also be extended for mining sliding window based weighted sequential patterns over datastreams[13].

References

1. Srikant, R., & Agrawal, R. (1996). Mining Sequential Patterns: Generalizations and Performance Improvements. *EDBT '96 Lecture Notes in Computer Science*, 1-17.
2. Zaki, M. J. (2001). SPADE: An Efficient Algorithm for Mining Frequent Sequences. *Machine Learning, 42*(1-2), 31-60.
3. Han, J., Pei, J., Mortazavi-Asl, B., Chen, Q., Dayal, U., & Hsu, M. (2000). FreeSpan. *Proceedings of the Sixth - KDD '00.*
4. Pei, J., Han, J., Mortazavi-Asl, B., & Pinto, H. (2001). PrefixSpan: Mining Sequential Patterns Efficiently by Prefix-Projected Pattern Growth. *Proceedings of the 17th ICDE '01*, 215.
5. Cheng, H., Yan, X., & Han, J. (2004). IncSpan. *Proceedings of the 2004 ACM SIGKDD - KDD '04.*
6. Yun, U. (2008). A New Framework for Detecting Weighted Sequential Patterns in Large Sequence Databases. *Knowledge-Based Systems, 21*(2), 110-122.
7. Yun, U. (2007). Efficient Mining of Weighted Interesting Patterns with a Strong Weight and/or Support Affinity. *Information Sciences, 177*(17), 3477-3499.
8. Cui, W., & An, H. (2009). Discovering Interesting Sequential Pattern in Large Sequence Database. *2009 PACIIA.*
9. Kollu, A. (2013). Incremental Mining of Sequential Patterns Using Weights. *IOSR Journal of Computer Engineering, 14*(5), 70-73.
10. Fournier-Viger, P., Lin, C.W., Gomariz, A., Gueniche, T., Soltani, A., Deng, Z., & Lam, H. T. (2016). The SPMF Open-Source Data Mining Library Version 2. Proc. *19th PKDD 2016 Part III*, Springer LNCS 9853, pp. 36-40.
11. Goethals, B., & Zaki, M. J. (2003). Frequent Itemset Mining Implementations Repository. Retrieved from http://fimi.ua.ac.be/
12. Ayres, J., Flannick, J., Gehrke, J., & Yiu, T. (2002). Sequential Pattern Mining Using a Bitmap Representation. *Proceedings of the eighth ACM SIGKDD - KDD '02.*
13. Ahmed, C. F., Tanbeer, S. K., Jeong, B., & Lee, Y. (2009). An Efficient Algorithm for Sliding Window-Based Weighted Frequent Pattern Mining over Data Streams. *IEICE Transactions on Information and Systems, E92-D*(7), 1369-1381. doi:10.1587/transinf.e92.d.1369
14. Lin, Chun-Wei & Hong, Tzung-Pei & Gan, Vincent W. & Chen, Hsin-Yi & Li, Sheng-Tun. (2015). Incrementally updating the discovered sequential patterns based on pre-large concept. *Intelligent Data Analysis. 19*, 1071-1089.
15. F. Masseglia, P. Poncelet, and M. Teisseire. (2003). Incremental mining of sequential patterns in large databases. *Data Knowl. Eng., 46*(1):97121.
16. N. Nguyen, Son & Sun, Xingzhi & Orlowska, Maria. (2005). Improvements of IncSpan: Incremental Mining of Sequential Patterns in Large Database. 442-451.

Detection of IP Gangs: Strategically Organized Bots

Tianyue Zhao Xiaofeng Qiu

Abstract. Botnets, groups of malware-infected computers (bots) that perform cybersecurity attacks on the Internet, pose one of the most serious cybersecurity threats to many industries, including smart infrastructure [10,11], Internet based companies, [12] and Internet of Things (IoT) [9]. There are many unconventional methods of organizing bots that are potentially advantageous to attackers. "Botnet", as a technical term, cannot effectively describe these methods. With vast amounts of Internet traffic data collected by security appliances, it is possible to reveal novel behavior of bots using data analysis algorithms. In this paper, we propose a concept called IP Gang to describe groups of bots from the perspective of the attacker's business – we define IP Gangs to be groups of bots that often perform attacks together during a period of time. Crucially, we developed a fast, high-compatibility detection algorithm that can be deployed in wide-scale, industrial applications to effectively defend against IP Gangs. The detection algorithm is inspired by single-linkage clustering, and is optimized for large amounts of data. A test on a month (1.5GB) of real life DDoS log data detected 21 IP Gangs, with 13916 bots in total. To analyze the behavior of the Gangs, we visualized the activity of each Gang with diagrams named "attack fingerprints", and confirmed that 15 of the detected Gangs displayed behavior that the concept of "botnet" alone cannot explain.

Keywords: IP Gang, botnet, cybersecurity, big data

1 Introduction

Botnets, groups of malware-infected computers (bots) that perform cybersecurity attacks on the Internet, pose one of the most serious cybersecurity threats to many industries. Smart infrastructure such as power grids have been hacked to deny hundreds of thousands of people basic services [10,11]. Internet-based industries have been hit with massive Distributed Denial of Service (DDoS) attacks that can render large websites inoperative for entire hours [12]. Internet of Things (IoT) devices such as webcams are regularly hijacked to form bots [9], disabling them in their original purpose and severely disrupting IoT industry operations. With vast amounts of Internet traffic data collected by security appliances, it is possible to reveal novel behavior of bots using data analysis algorithms. Many aspects of botnets have been researched quite thoroughly [1,2,3], such as detection of botnets and communication patterns between bots and command/control (C&C) servers, but these are all technical studies, while few researches consider the perspective of the thriving botnet industry, which conducts cybersecurity attacks as a service.

The botnet industry seeks a high volume of DDoS attacks botnets can perform at any given time, low cost, and resistance to detection algorithms. These goals can be better achieved by organizing his bots with unconventional methods, such as flexible organization.

Here are several scenarios that demonstrate the advantages of flexibly organizing bots from the point of view of the botnet industry: 1) Bots can be controlled as multiple small botnets with distinct technical properties – such as separate C&C servers and different C&C protocols – to evade detection. Many detection algorithms classify large groups of confirmed bots with identical technical properties as a botnet, so these small botnets with distinct properties are much harder to completely detect, and therefore have much better survivability. One way of implementing this is through the "super-botnet" structure proposed and analyzed by Vogt, et al [3]. 2) An attacker can utilize deceitful, advanced attack strategies, which are much more costly and time-consuming to defend against. Botnets could take separate roles in a composite attack strategy. A known composite strategy is the usage of DDoS attacks as smokescreens [5][6] to draw defenders' attention and cover up other attacks. 3) Bots in places where it is night may be turned off. Making bots in places where it is day attack together allows for maximum guaranteed attack volume.

We recognize that the term botnet is not enough to describe the organization of bots. The definition of botnets is from a technical perspective, yet these advantageous scenarios of organizing bots can be achieved in many ways: by creating a network of small botnets each with its own C&C server, by dividing a large botnet into separately managed portions, and more. Therefore, the concept "botnet" is ill-suited at describing these new methods.

This necessitates a new, broad, industry-oriented concept that describes these ways of organizing bots. We propose the concept of IP Gang to meet this demand.

Analyzing IP Gangs allows for smarter, strategic defences. Analysis from the perspective of the cyber-crime industry allows defenders to study, truly understand, and most importantly strategically defend against the behaviors of the attackers. For example, attackers have threatened to launch attacks unless a bribe is paid [8], and the defender can better decide to pay or not thanks to the additional knowledge on the IP Gang. In another situation, if some bots belonging to an IP Gang starts attacking, it would save precious time to immediately quarantine other bots of the IP Gang.

In this paper, we proved the existence of IP Gangs in real life Internet traffic, and developed a fast, high-compatibility detection algorithm that can be deployed in wide-scale, industrial applications to effectively defend against IP Gangs.

For compatibility, we only use the start time, source IP address, and target IP address describing events in easily-obtainable Internet event log data, which widely deployed network security appliances generally output. Other parameters describing the events (such as bytes per packet) are optional, and may help with accuracy if present.

The algorithm is based on the principle of single-linkage clustering [7], but with an additional "packaging" step that reduces the number of nodes to be clustered to increase speed. The detection algorithm outputs each detected IP Gang as a list of IP addresses. The complexity of the algorithm is $O(n^2)$ with a small constant, where n is the number of events in the data. Our test on one month's events from a DDoS attack log detected

21 IP gangs, and showed that our algorithm is fast enough to be used to detect and help defend against IP Gangs on a large scale.

The rest of this paper is structured as follows. Section 2 presents previous works on botnet structure and botnet detection with Internet traffic. In section 3, the formal definition of IP Gang is introduced and its relationship to botnets is analyzed. The principle and algorithm used to detect IP Gangs are detailed in section IV. Next, the test results on real data are presented. We conclude by discussing future work.

2 Related work

Botnet structures that may provide advantages similar to those of IP Gang's have been studied. Most notably, Vogt, et al.[3] proposed the "super-botnet", a network of small, centralized botnets that can perform coordinated attacks, and provided detailed technical analysis of super-botnets. Individual botnets in a super-botnet can be detected, but it is very hard to detect the entire super-botnet. This additional resilience allows attackers to accumulate enough bots to perform very large-scale attacks. However, Vogt, et al. did not provide experimentation on real life data. The concept of super-botnet is possibly related to the concept of IP Gang, but is still fundamentally different - it is still a technical definition, while the definition of IP Gang is business-oriented.

There had been a lot of researches on the detection of botnets based on Internet traffic. Gu, et al.[1] was one of the first to propose and test on real life traffic data a clustering-based botnet detection model, which provides a variety of advantages over previous models that detect botnets by scanning for Command and Control (C&C) traffic between bots and the attacker. Gu, et al. provided experimentation on real life data and analysis of the results.

3 Definition of IP Gang

As discussed in Section I, the concept of IP Gangs and botnets are not comparable. IP Gangs and botnets consider the business and technical perspectives of groups of bots respectively. The former is concerned with how the attacker organizes his bots to his advantage, while the latter is instead mainly concerned with how the bots communicate with each other and with the controller.

Definition:

An IP Gang is a group of malware-infected computers(bots) that are controlled by the same attacker and often perform attacks together - launch attacks directed at the same target within a short period of time t.

A botnet is a group of bots that are organized by a certain network architecture and controlled by the same C&C (Command and Control) protocol by a logically centralized C&C server. Usually, the bots in a botnet have the same behavior from a technical point of view.

There is, however, a significant difference in property between the two: by definition, all the bots in a botnet always receive the same command, while bots in an IP Gang are not subject to such constraint.

IP Gang reveals business level spatial and temporal features of organized bots, which could be in a same botnet or belongs to different botnets (Fig 1). IP Gangs can be intentionally formed by attackers, or unintentionally formed due to logistic conditions, such as when bots of a botnet in the same time zone often attack together.

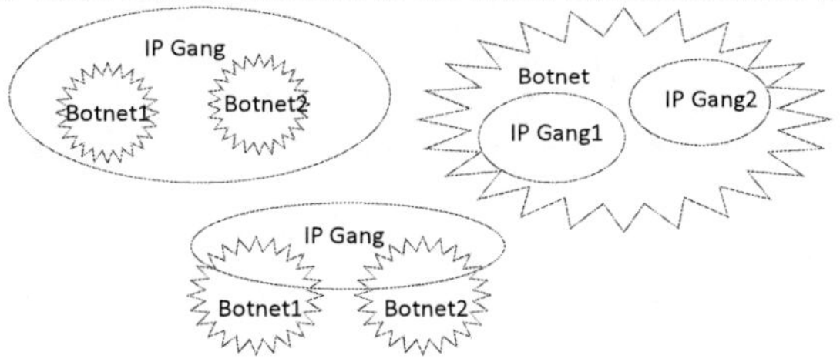

Fig. 1. IP Gang and Botnet

4 IP Gang Detection Algorithm

4.1 Overview

The target of the algorithm is to cluster the IP addresses of bots based on security event log data to detect IP Gangs - groups of bots that often launch attacks together. We designed the detecting method to meet the following challenges:

1) Speed: the method must be fast enough to be deployed on networks which produce large volumes of log data.

2) Use as little information as possible: to ensure compatibility, the method must use only the most basic attack event information found in virtually all event logs: start time, source IP address, and destination IP address.

At the core of the detecting algorithm is a clustering algorithm inspired by single-linkage clustering. Clustering algorithms are inherently time-intensive, and ours yields a complexity of O(N2), where N is the number of nodes to be clustered. Subsequently, reducing the number of nodes is crucial to the speed of the detection algorithm, and we add a packaging step before the clustering step to accomplish this. The algorithm consists of three steps, as illustrated in Fig 2.

1) Packaging: Events reported by security devices are grouped into Organized Attack Events (OAEs).

2) Clustering: OAEs are clustered using a method inspired by single-linkage clustering with each finished cluster, named OAE cluster, representing a Gang.

3) Analyzing: OAE clusters are analyzed to find Gangs of IP addresses. This can also be seen as a "de-packaging" step, extracting IP addresses from OAE clusters.

Each step of our procedure is analyzed in greater detail in the rest of this section, and the performance of the procedure when ran on real life data is discussed in the experimentation section.

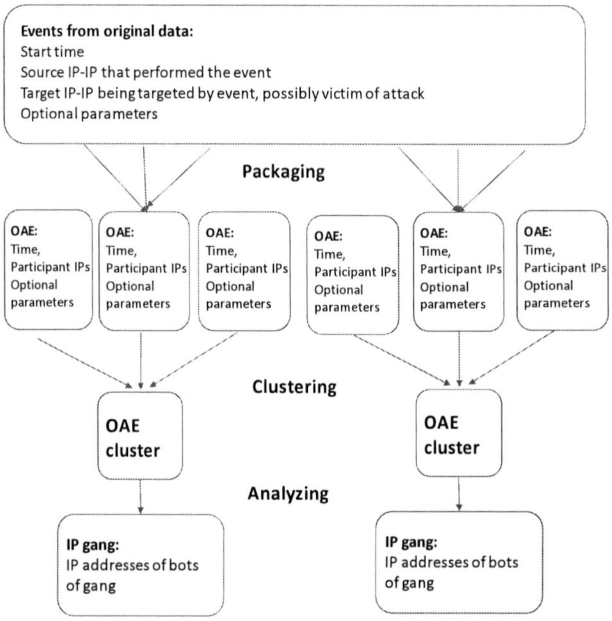

Fig. 2. Procedure of IP Gang detection algorithm

4.2 Packaging: Constructing Organized Attack Events (OAEs) from original data

To decrease the number of nodes that need to be clustered in the clustering stage, we designed a way of packaging individual events with the same target IP address and starting in a time interval *t* into entities called Organized Attack Events(OAEs), which will be nodes in the clustering step.

The definition of an OAE is:

Given A as a subset of attack event, a.IP as the set of all of the source IP address in A. A is an OAE, iff

$$\begin{aligned} &\forall a_1, a_2 \in A, \\ &|a_{1.starttime} - a_{2.starttime}| \leq t \\ &\& \quad a_{1.targetIP} == a_{2.targetIP} \\ &\& \quad |A_{.IP}| \geq min\_size \end{aligned} \tag{1}$$

The set $A_{.IP}$ contains the IP addresses of all the bots that launched this set of Organized Attack Events(OAE).

The optimal value of time *t* varies between log data types.

Generally, attackers will utilize a large number of bots in each organized attack for maximum effectiveness. P2P Zeus, for example, has information of 50 peers in its hard code[4]. Here we use this property to keep organized attacks – which are of use to us –

and discard unorganized, individual attacks by filtering out OAEs with less than *min_size* events in them.

The pseudocode for the packaging process is:

```
id=0, and cur_OAE is initialized to empty
for event in D: #D denotes the input data
    if(|event.start_time-cur_OAE.start_time|<=1 minute)...
        and (event.target_IP==cur_OAE.target_IP):
        cur_OAE.size+=1
        cur_OAE.IP.append(event.source_IP)
        optional_params_tmp.append(event.optional_params)
    else:
        if(cur_OAE.size>=minimum_size): #OAE is disposed if not big enough
            cur_OAE.optional_params=take_most_common_values(optional_params_tmp)
                #if the most common set of values for the
            #optional params do not account for at least
            #50% of the entries in the optional_params_tmp
            #list, cur_OAE.optional_params is set to None

            A.append(cur_OAE)
        cur_OAE.id=id
        id+=1
        cur_OAE.size=1 #initialization with only current event
        cur_OAE.IP=[event.source_IP]
        cur_OAE.optional_params=None
        cur_OAE.start_time=event.start_time
        cur_OAE.target_IP=event.target_IP
```

At the start, the set of current OAE, *cur_OAE*, is initialized to contain only the first event. Afterwards, if the event being processed starts within *t* of *cur_OAE*, and has the same target IP address, it is added to *cur_OAE*. *cur_OAE* is added to the list of OAEs if the number of events it contains exceeds *min_size*. Otherwise, it is discarded and re-initialized.

This step has linear time complexity, and therefore is insignificant in terms of runtime. However, by using OAEs, instead of individual events in the clustering step, we decreased the number of nodes to be clustered by a very large factor, without sacrificing accuracy.

4.3 Clustering: clustering OAEs to form OAE clusters

The OAEs formed in the packaging step are then clustered to form OAE clusters. Given A_1,A_2 are two OAEs, $A_{1.IP}$ as the set of all of the source IP address in A_1, A_1 and A_2 must be put in the same cluster if:

$$s = \frac{|A_{1.IP} \cap A_{2.IP}|}{|A_{1.IP}|} \geq combining\_threshold, \quad (2)$$
$$assuming\ |A_{1.IP}| \leq |A_{2.IP}|$$

In (2), *s* measures the normalized similarity of bots in two OAEs. Two OAEs with similarity larger than combining.threshold should be put in the same OAE cluster.

The clustering algorithm is inspired by single-linkage clustering, but is different in a key way. Single linkage clustering merges the two most similar clusters in each merge step, and stops performing merge steps when a reasonable total number of clusters have been reached. In contrast, we perform all possible merges of OAE clusters satisfying equation (2). In words, the clustering algorithm merges pairs of clusters that contain

OAEs with a similarity score higher than the combining threshold but not yet in the same cluster. We proceed until no such pair exists.

The clustering algorithm is performed with a disjoint set data structure. For each OAE, the clustering algorithm computes the similarity scores between this OAE and all other OAEs. If the similarity score of two OAEs is higher than the combining threshold and the two OAEs are not yet in the same OAE cluster, the OAE clusters of the two OAEs are merged with a *union* operation.

The pseudo code is as follows:

```
1 for OAE A1 in set of all p OAEs:
2      count={} #counts the number of IP addresses
3               #each OAE has with the current OAE
3      for each IP address ip1 in A1.IP:
4          relevant=find(every OAE that contains ip1)
5          #The time this operation takes is near
6          #constant when a key-value database is used
7
8          #Each entry in "relevant" is an OAE that has
9          #at least 1 IP address in common with A1
10
11         #The number of entries in "relevant" is
12         #proportional to q, the average number
13         #of OAEs an IP address contributes to
14         for OAE A2 in relevant:
15             if(A1 and A2 are already in same cluster):
16                 skip iteration
17             if(A2.id is in count):
18                 count[A2.id]+=1
19             else:
20                 count[A2.id]=1
21         for A2 in count:
22             if(A1 and A2 are already in same cluster):
23                 continue
24             if(|A1.IP|<=|A2.IP|):
25                 s=count[A2]/|A1.IP|
26             else:
27                 s=count[A2]/|A2.IP|
28             if(s>=combining threshold):
29                 merge the OAE clusters A1 and A2 are in
30                        with "union" operation
```

In short, the clustering step puts OAEs that are performed by bots of the same gang into the same OAE cluster. This is achieved through computing the percentage of participating IP addresses two OAEs have in common, and merging the clusters the two OAEs are in if the percentage is higher than a threshold.

A NOSQL database is integral to our clustering method, as it greatly speeds up our method. With a relational database, the query at line 4 is very time-consuming, but NOSQL databases can perform this in a near constant time.

The complexity of this implementation is $O(n^2)$, where n is dataset size – the number of individual events in the log data. The number of iterations in the *for* loop in line 1 is p, the total amount of OAEs. The *for* loop in line 3 is independent from data size. The number of iterations in the *for* loops of lines 14 and 21 are both q, the average number of OAEs an IP address contributes to. Therefore, the overall complexity is $O(pq)$. It is apparent that $p \propto n$, as the average number of events in each OAE does not change. We expect $q \propto n$, though the correlation between the two is less strong. Therefore, $pq \propto n^2$, and the complexity is $O(n^2)$.

4.4 Analyzing: identifying gangs by analyzing OAE clusters

After OAE clusters are formed in the previous step, we analyze the OAE clusters to identify gangs of bots, with each bot represented by an IP address. We collect all the IP addresses that have participated in an OAE of an OAE cluster, and only retain IP addresses that have participated in enough OAEs of that cluster.

In words, for each OAE cluster, we calculate the percentage of OAEs in the cluster each IP address contributed to. IP addresses that only contribute to a very small percentage of OAEs may be treated as noise, as they are generally not worthy of studying. A threshold named *validation.threshold* is set in section V of this paper and only the IP address with a contribution percentage larger than the threshold is retained into a gang.

5 Experimentation on Real Life Data

5.1 Overview

The data we used for experimentation is a DDoS log consisting of individual DDoS attack events collected from January 1st, 2016 to January 31st, 2016. The reports of DDoS attacks are collected from several dozens of NSFOCUS Network Traffic Analyzers (NTAs) and Anti-DDoS Systems (ADSs). NTAs and ADSs are deployed at the sites of the customers of NSFOCUS, and construct the DDoS log by analyzing netflow, an industry standard type of metadata.

Our algorithm was written in Python, used the Neo4j graph database, and was ran on a 2012 Thinkpad X230i laptop with hyper-threading disabled. The clustering step took 48 hours with the full 1.5GB of data, and the other steps were insignificant in terms of runtime.

With a *validation.threshold* of 0.05 and a *combining.threshold* of 0.6, our algorithm detected 17350 OAEs and 21 IP Gangs that has at least 10 OAEs. In total, there are 13916 valid bots in all these gangs.

On average, each OAE contained 183 individual events. This means that the packaging step decreased the runtime of the clustering step by a factor of 183^2.

5.2 Discussion of the Parameters

In the “Packaging” step, the optimal time t in equation (1) for our data is found to be 1 minute. We observed in our log data that large groups of events that have the same target IP address typically have start times within 1 minute of each other. Running the packaging step on our data with several different t values confirm *t=1 minute* as the optimal value. We determined the optimal value of *min_size* in equation (1) to be 50 with a similar procedure. In fact, we conducted tests with *t=1,3,5 minutes* and *min_size=20,30,50*, achieving very similar results in each test. We therefore chose *t=1 minute* and *min_size=50* to maximize accuracy.

In the “Analyzing” step, the value of *validation.threshold* greatly influences the final output of IP addresses in an IP gang. As shown in Fig.3, different values of *validation.threshold* resulted in large variations in the total number of IP addresses in these

21 gangs. *Validation.threshold* provides a mechanism to look into an IP gang in different levels of granularity. For example, a larger *validation.threshold* will only output core members of an IP gang so that the defender could monitor the IP gang more efficiently. On the other hand, a smaller threshold will help the defender to get more detailed statistic of an IP gang.

5.3 Visualization and Discussion

We developed a type of diagram that visualizes the attack patterns of IP Gangs, which we denote the "attack fingerprint". Each attack fingerprint represents a Gang, and each red dot on attack fingerprint represents an individual attack event by a bot of the Gang. The *ID* numbers of OAEs are assigned in time order, so the Y-axis is practically a relative measure of time. The X-axis is the *ID* of the bot, so each column of the figure represents the temporal behavior of a bot. The fingerprints in Fig 4 (a),(b), and (c) have *validation.threshold=0.05*, while the one in Fig 4 (d) has *validation.threshold=0.1*.

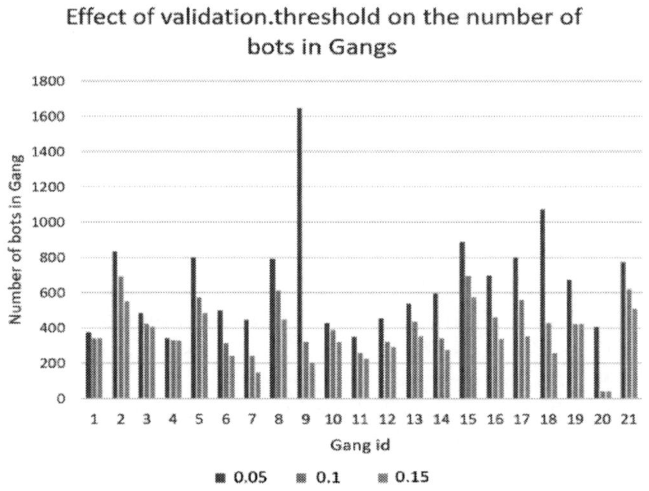

Fig. 3. Influence of *validation.threshold*

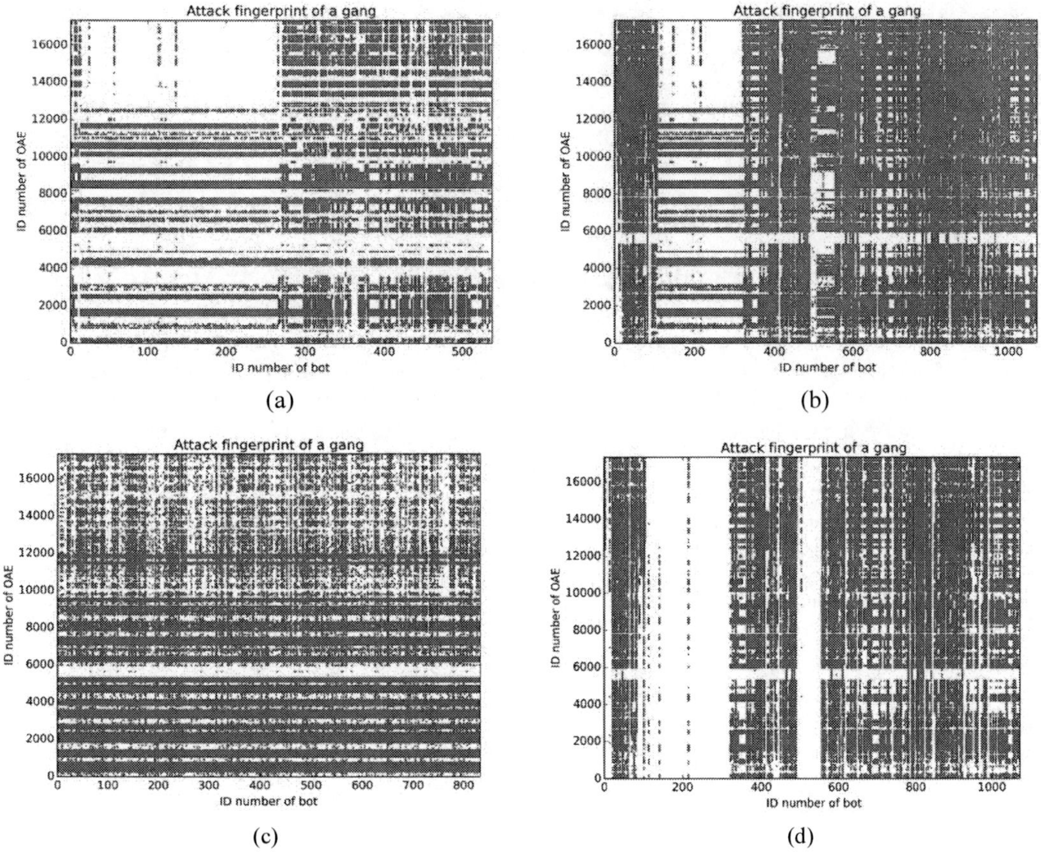

Fig. 4. Fingerprints of gangs

In 6 of the 21 fingerprints, we see that all the columns have nearly the exact same appearance. This tells us that each bot in the gang participated in almost the same OAEs. The attack fingerprints in Fig 4 (c) is an example. This kind of fingerprints can be explained with the conventional concept of botnets, because all the bots are behaving in the same way.

The other 15 fingerprints are difficult to explain with only the concept of botnets, because the behavior of bots often differ from each other. As shown in Fig 4 (a) and (b), the columns take a small number of distinct but still similar appearances. In certain rows, all columns have red dots, but the columns take several distinct patterns in other rows. This shows that the bots are not always behaving in the same way. Notably, different values of *validation.threshold* allows for different parts of the Gang to be analyzed in detail. Fig 4 (d) demonstrates this, as it describes the same Gang as Fig 4 (b), but is drawn with *validation.threshold=0.1*. Clearly, the bots with *id* between 100 and 300 are omitted from the graph, while the other parts are preserved. There are several plausible explanations for this phenomenon. For example, in Fig 3(a), there may be two botnets, one with bots *ID <280*, and another with bot *ID >280*. Sometimes they attack together as shown by the dense horizontal lines, and sometimes they attack separately as shown by the upper part of the fingerprint with OAE *ID >12000*. Another explanation is that these bots belong to one botnet, but sometimes only part of the botnet are able to successfully carry out the attack.

6 Conclusions and Future Work

We demonstrate that IP gangs exist on the internet, and are actively being used by attacker to perform DDoS attacks. They are detectable using clustering-based algorithms, and can clearly be distinguished from conventional botnets.

Analyzing the behavior of IP gangs will be highly beneficial. Doing so can make for a better understanding of the operation, structure, and performance of IP gangs. A more thorough understanding of these is necessary to accurately assess the threat IP gangs pose to cybersecurity, and to defend against IP gangs. For defenders, knowing more about the behavior of Gangs can allow for smarter, strategic defences against Internet attacks.

References

1. Guofei, G., Perdisci, R., Zhang, J., Lee, W.: BotMiner: Clustering Analysis of Network Traffic for Protocol-and Structure-Independent botnet Detection. In: USENIX security symposium. vol. 5, no. 2, pp. 139-154. (2008).
2. Khattak, S., Ramay, N. R., Khan, K. R., Syed, A. A., Khayam, S. A.: A taxonomy of botnet behavior, detection, and defense. IEEE communications surveys & tutorials 16(2), 898-924 (2014).
3. Vogt, R., Aycock, J., Jacobson, M.: Army of botnets. In: Proceedings of NDSS'07 (2007).
4. Soltani, S., Seno, S. A. H., Nezhadkamali, M., Budiarto, R.: A survey on real world botnets and detection mechanisms. International Journal of Information and Network Security, 3(2), 116 (2014).
5. Arbor Networks. (2016, February 3). DDoS as a smokescreen for fraud and theft. https://www.arbornetworks.com/blog/insight/ddos-as-a-smokescreen-for-fraud-and-theft/
6. Kaspersky Lab. (2016, November 22). Research reveals hacker tactics: Cybercriminals use DDoS as smokescreen for other attacks on business. https://www.kaspersky.com/about/press-releases/2016_research-reveals-hacker-tactics-cybercriminals-use-ddos-as-smokescreen-for-other-attacks-on-business
7. Stanford Natural Language Processing Group. (n.d.). Single-link and complete-link clustering. https://nlp.stanford.edu/IR-book/html/htmledition/single-link-and-complete-link-clustering-1.html

8. WeLiveSecurity. (2017, September 25). Spammed-out emails threaten websites with DDoS attack on September 30th. https://www.welivesecurity.com/2017/09/25/email-ddos-threat/
9. Kolias, C., Kambourakis, G., Stavrou, A., Voas, J.: DDoS in the IoT: Mirai and Other Botnets. Computer 50(7), 80-84 (2017).
10. Pultarova, T.: Cyber security - Ukraine grid hack is wake-up call for network operators. Engineering & Technology 11(1), 12-13 (2016).
11. Khan, R., Maynard, P., McLaughlin, K., Laverty, D., Sezer, S.: Threat Analysis of BlackEnergy Malware for Synchrophasor based Real-time Control and Monitoring in Smart Grid. In: Janicke, H., Jones, K., Brandstetter, T. (eds.) 4th International Symposium for ICS & SCADA Cyber Security Research 2016, (pp. 53-63).
12. Kaspersky Lab, Attack on Dyn explained, https://www.kaspersky.com/blog/attack-on-dyn-explained/13325/

Identification of Human Activity Change using Time Series Analysis

Yulei Pang[1] and Xiaozhen Xue[2]

[1] Southern Connecticut State University, New Haven CT 06515, USA

[2] URU Video Inc, New York, USA

Abstract. Human motion analysis is a grand research question and it continues attracting attention in both academia and industry. Its applications include surveillance systems, patient monitoring systems and so on. In recent years, most human activity analysis techniques are based on machine learning and deep learning algorithms [2],[3],[4]. Although the empirical study demonstrated the effectiveness of these algorithms, an important factor, the time stamp, was absent from studying. In this paper, we studied the human activity in the perspective of time series analysis. More specially, we used changepoint analysis (CPA) technique to identify whether, when and where a change has taken place in human activity time series.

Keywords: Human Activity Recognition(HAR), Changepoint Analysis(CPA), Time Series Analysis

1 Introduction

Through this paper, we aim at proposing a technique, for segmenting the human activity time series, thus identifying human activity change. The proposed technique can be applied in both industry and academia. The major contribution of this paper is to:
a) Introduce an innovative technique for identification of human activity change based on the application of time series data analysis technique;
b) Evaluate and report the performance of proposed technique based through some experiments;
c) Discuss the implications of findings and the influence of factors involved, including the assumed distribution, measuring methods, and penalty function.

2 Datasets

In this paper, we use a dataset publicly available online [1]. To collect the date, previous researchers have carried out an experiment with a group of 30 volunteers within an age range of 19-48 years. Each observation performed six activities (walling, walking upstairs, walking downstairs, sitting, standing, laying) wearing a smartphone (Samsung Galaxy S II) on the waist. The experiments have been video-recorded to label the data manually.

3 Methodology

We have conducted some preliminary study, and has verified the feasibility of the application of time series data analysis into human activity change. There are many perspectives and methods for analyzing time series data, and one of the most useful techniques is changepoint analysis (CPA). The purpose of CPA is to identify whether, when and where a change has taken place in a time series. There are many reasons to do this kind of analysis. A few good ones are:
a) to identify when a change has occurred so that you can respond somehow to that change;
b) to pinpoint when a change has occurred so you can attempt to identify its cause;
c) to predict future change. In this study, we will focus on the application of CPA in human activity change.

3.1 Illustrative example

For instance, a person is sitting somewhere. At some time stamp, he stands up and starts walking.
This use case has a lot of real world applications including healthcare monitoring, security checking, and others. We formalize the data as following:

$$\text{Data} = \{X_1\ X_2\ , \ldots , X_n\}$$

Where

$$X_i = (x_i, y_i, z_i, t_i)$$

X_i is one record; x_i, y_i, z_i are the position values; and t_i is the time stamp. Intuitively we can extract more info like velocity of movement and acceleration; and both of them are time series data. Now we take one window of data as an illustrative example. This piece of data contains two sequential activities: 1) a person was sitting between 1 to 190 time stamp; 2) he stands up at 191. We extract the velocity information and plot the data:

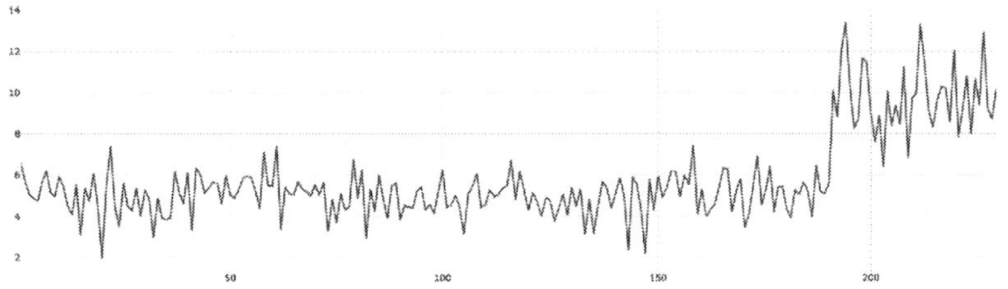

Fig. 1. The time series of a person's arm moving velocity

Now we apply the changepoint identification technique [5] to locate the "stand up time stamp" by measuring the change in mean. Below is the plot of the results.

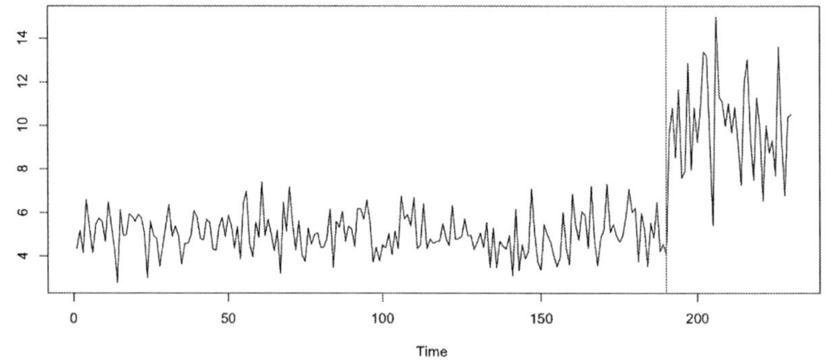

Fig. 2. The change from "sitting" to "standing", in mean

This picture depicts the two segmentations through redlines and it indicates that the changepoint is at 190, which exactly matches the ground truth. Although the "mean" function works perfectly in this case (we did more experiment, see Fig. 3) there are scenarios where it doesn't. For another activity change from "walking upstairs" to "walking downstairs", the velocity means are very similar to each other before and after the change, so that we can not find out the changepoint through measuring change in mean. Fortunately there are other options, like measure by variance and so on. We plan to investigate the performance when different distributions are measured, and various methods to select; also all penalty functions are applied.

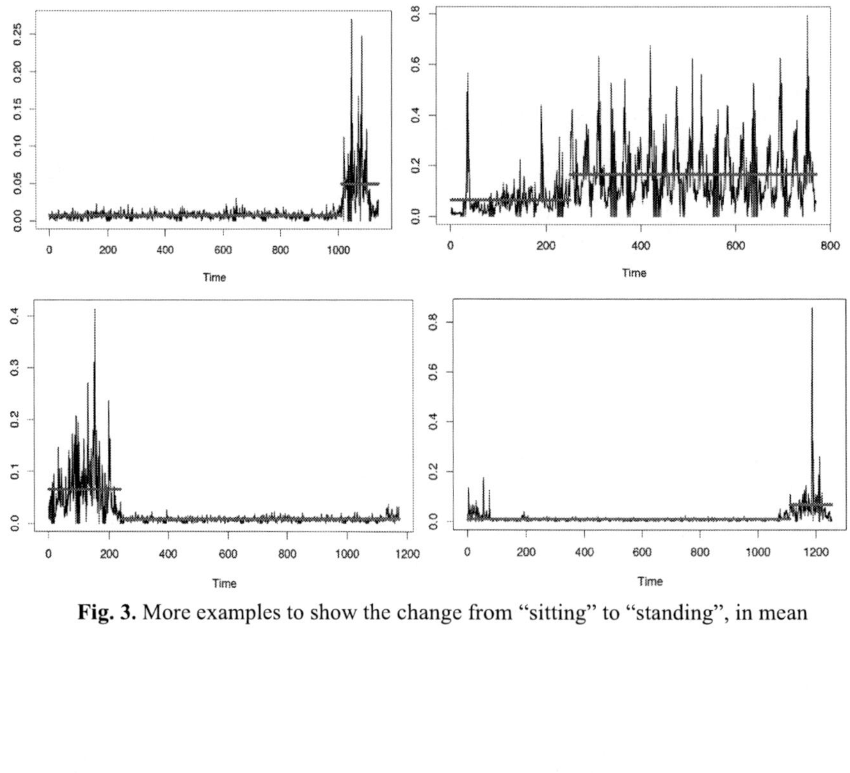

Fig. 3. More examples to show the change from "sitting" to "standing", in mean

4 Conclusion

In this paper, we propose changepoint analysis to perform efficient smartphone-based human activity recognition. We will find a scalar to measure the precision for the proposed technique and explore more time series analysis method in this study.

Acknowledgments

This work is supported by the Connecticut State University American Association of University Professors (CSU-AAUP) Research Grants and Minority Recruitment & Retention Committee (MRRC) Grants in Southern Connecticut State University.

Reference

1. Davide Anguita, Alessandro Ghio, Luca Oneto, Xavier Parra and Jorge L. Reyes-Ortiz. A Public Domain Dataset for Human Activity Recognition Using Smartphones. 21th European Symposium on Artificial Neural Networks, Computational Intelligence and Machine Learning, ESANN 2013. Bruges, Belgium 24-26 April 2013.

2. Davide Anguita, Alessandro Ghio, Luca Oneto, Xavier Parra and Jorge L. Reyes-Ortiz. Human Activity Recognition on Smartphones using a Multiclass Hardware-Friendly Support Vector Machine. International Workshop of Ambient Assisted Living (IWAAL 2012). Vitoria-Gasteiz, Spain. Dec 2012

3. Jorge Luis Reyes-Ortiz, Alessandro Ghio, Xavier Parra-Llanas, Davide Anguita, Joan Cabestany, Andreu Català. Human Activity and Motion Disorder Recognition: Towards Smarter Interactive Cognitive Environments. 21th European Symposium on Artificial Neural Networks, Computational Intelligence and Machine Learning, ESANN 2013. Bruges, Belgium 24-26 April 2013.

4. Ronao CA, Cho SB (2016) Human activity recognition with smartphone sensors using deep learning neural networks. Expert Syst Appl 59:235–244.

5. Killick R, Eckley IA (2014). changepoint: An R Package for Changepoint Analysis. URL http://www.jstatsoft.org/v58/i03/.

A Dynamic Ensemble Learning Approach for Online Anomaly Detection in Alibaba Datacenters

Wanyi Zhu[1] and Xia Ming[1] and Huafeng Wang[1] and Junda Chen[2] and Lu Liu[2] and Zhengong Cai[2]

[1]Alibaba Group, Hangzhou 311121, China
[2]Zhejiang University, Hangzhou, China
wanyi.wyz@alibaba-inc.com, caizhengong@zju.edu.cn

Abstract. Anomaly detection is a first and imperative step needed to respond to unexpected problems and to assure high performance and security in large data center management. This paper presents an online anomaly detection system through an innovative approach of ensemble machine learning and adaptive differentiation algorithms, and applies them to performance data collected from a continuous monitoring system for multi-tier web applications running in Alibaba data centers. We evaluate its effectiveness and efficiency with production traffic data and compare with the traditional anomaly detection approaches such as a static threshold and other deviation-based detection techniques. The experiment results show that our algorithm correctly identifies the unexpected performance variances of any running application, with an acceptable false positive rate. This proposed approach has already been deployed in real-time production environments to enhance the efficiency and stability in daily data center operations.

Keywords: Alibaba Data Centers, Anomaly Detection, Big data computation, Dynamic Ensemble learning.

1 Introduction

In recent years, cloud data center environments are increasingly characterized by extremely large scale and complexity. Thousands of servers have been deployed in cloud datacenters to support large-scale cloud computing services and multi-tiered online applications with various characteristics. Therefore, data center management is a daunting task and failing to quickly respond to anomalies, failures, malfunctions or load may lead to extensive losses in profits and productivity. To ensure high availability, reliability and performance, real-time cloud infrastructure monitoring and analytics become a critical component of today's cloud datacenters' operations and management. At Alibaba, the challenge of scalable data center monitoring calls for: 1) monitoring efficient and lightweight performance metrics that can be a good approximation of application health (application metrics such as throughput and system metrics such as CPU utilization); 2) automatically detect the anomalies and identify the root cause in real-time. Although there exists a large body of prior research in anomaly detection field [1], we found that existing techniques including user-defined thresholds or statistical confidence levels are not effective on production data for detecting performance anomalies owing to a predominant dynamic pattern in the time series data.

To this end, we developed an online anomaly detection system through an innovative analytic approach of ensemble machine learning and modified differentiation algorithm, which can (i) automatically identify the static and dynamic properties of any running application based on its corresponding performance metrics, (ii) calculate dynamic baselines that can be considered normal for the key metrics, and (iii) correctly detect problems in real-time, thereby triggering further investigation of problems.

The first key component of our anomaly detection system is the selection of light-weight performance metrics. Many of the existing metrics are either expensive or non-actionable. For instance, collecting the incoming or outgoing packet statistics of each server in each time interval requires a significant amount of commutating resources as well as memory/storage resource, and are often difficult for the site reliability engineers to act upon without comprehensive interpretation [2]. With the business domain knowledge, a combination of hardware and software system configurations, log files, performance data at the levels of CPU, operating systems and software applications are chosen for further performance monitoring and analytics. To ensure high data integrity, we also develop a novel data schema approach that enable an automated process to convert the raw performance data into the standardized data structure. These data are preprocessed and merged for further analysis.

Another key element of our system is real-time and continuous anomaly detection for large-scale data center systems, which is to determine whether any application is significantly deviating from its normal usage patterns and deserves further investigation. It does so by automatically estimating a dynamic baseline for each performance metric of each running application using an ensemble learning approach (including Time Series mining, regression model and statistical learning approach); then applying an adaptive smoother and differentiator to both actual and predicted baseline to remove the noise from normal patterns and compare the difference in their rate and direction of changes. This approach enables us to identify the anomalies using a fixed baseline and its corresponding confidence levels. Here, we propose to use Savitzky-Golay (SG) filters, with a finite memory, which have been used for decades as data-smoothers for signals [3]. They are extended and modified here by adopting the low-order differentiation function and deriving their inflection point via numerical computation in the time domain. This is the first paper that proposes to use the ensemble learning approach, combined with the smoothing and differentiation methods to evaluate if the difference between the prediction and the actual value is truly anomalous.

Through testing on the real production system in Alibaba datacenters, our system could look beyond the obvious and find the subtle anomalies that could be causing production problems, which can save the reliability engineers from countless hours of late-night hectic, thus improving the efficiency and stability of data center operations.

The rest of this paper is organized as follows. Section II introduces the related work and background of our research. Section III details the proposed system for detecting anomalies in real-time cloud data. Section IV presents an evaluation of our approaches with existing detection approaches in a real-time production system in Alibaba datacenters. Lastly, conclusions and future work are presented in Section V.

2 Background

2.1 Threshold-based Anomaly Detection Approaches

The threshold-based alerting system has been widely deployed in most data centers, which means that if any performance metric (which are being continuously monitored in the data center) goes beyond a certain fixed threshold or statistical boundary of thresholds, an alert is triggered. However, this system still requires enormous manual efforts and prone to false alarms, for instance, an on-call engineer still needs to manually scan through graphs to spot any outliers or anomalies [3].

The major drawbacks of this approach include:

1) These static thresholds for each application are generally set by a domain expert or determined through statistical analysis of historical data and patterns. They tend to remain constant during the entire monitoring process, and sensitive to intermittent bursts and varying workloads, resulting in high false positive rates. In a production system with many distributed applications running, a small false alarm rate can still make the further investigation overwhelming for an application owner.
2) To account for spikes in the data which may occur over time, the upper and lower bounds for the fixed threshold are generally constructed with a wide tolerance based on the assumption of statistical distribution. Moreover, this step requires periodic tuning to account for the varying workloads.

The reasons listed above reduce the accuracy of alerting system and tend to cause false alarms. Here, we developed an online automated alerting system that can improve the precision and sensitivity of performance anomaly detection in cloud data centers.

2.2 Univariate Statistical Learning Approach

Statistical learning has a wide application in anomaly detection [4]. One simple classical approach to screen outlier is to use the deviation-based methods such as standard deviation (SD) and Z-Score method. Any observations which fall outside $\pm$ 2 standard deviation of the mean, or have a absolute Z-score exceeding 3 are considered as anomalies in general. Even though those two methods are quite powerful under well-behaving normal distribution assumtpion, most data in production environments may be stochastic or unknown, or may not conform to specific distributions. Additionaly, both of these two methods are susceptible to masking or swamping problems caused by extreme values with different magnitudes. Moreover, these methods are fundamentally problematic because the statitical indicator mean value can be altered by the presence of outlying values. To avoid these problems, the median and the median of the absolute deviation of the median (MAD) can be used as an alternative to the arithmetic mean and SD in the calculation of modified Z-Score M_i, when handling data that are not evenly distributed or contain extremes values. The decision criterion for outliers can be set and justified depending on the stringency of each detection. Here, we choose a relatively conservative threshold through the simulation of pseudo-normal observations for sample size larger than 10. Any observations with a absolute modified Z-Score greater than 3.5 are suggested to be labeled as potential outliers. Even though the MAD is the most robust dispersion measurement in the presence of outliers in univariate statistics, the observations are required to follow an approximately normal distribution for this detection method.

In parallel with robust statistics, another practical method for outlier detection is Tukey's schematic ("full") boxplot. It does not requires a normality distribution of the data and therefore is flexible and effective in practical settings. Instead of using sample mean and standard variance, this test utililzes quartiles to characterize the statistical distribution and is less sensitive to extreme values of the data. A value beyond the outer fences with a distance of 3 inter quartile range (IQR) below the 25% quartile (Q1) and above 75% quartile (Q3) are considered to be outliers.

2.3 Machine Learning Approaches

With the increasing complexity, volume and velocity of performance data, the machine-learning driven anomaly detection methods have also been proposed as opposed to traditional methods that rely on static profiling or limited sets of historical data [4, 5]. Recently some sophisticated machine-learning techinques are employed to discover the complex features within the large-scale streaming data. The advanced statistical learning techinques have been adopted to analyze the time series streaming data with various distribution properties. For instance, the multivariate adaptive statistical filtering (MASF) is used to determine a specific threshold for data segmented and aggregated by temporal context (time of day, day of week, time of month) [6]. This is the most common and effective statistical technique since the business generally follows specific rhythms of activity. However, MASF relies on the assumption that the time series conform to Gaussian behaviors. Alternatively, other non-parametric statistical testing such as Tukey method is used to set control limits. Although the advantages of both techniques are considerable and field-tested in a variety of process monitoring and control contexts from factories to data centers, they are not effective when the temporal structure or underlying regularity in the streaming data deviate from historical patterns [4]. For this reason, one alternative is to use the multinomial goodness-of-fit test based on the relative entropy statistic, which can detect the extreme variations in temporal pattern structure. Information entropy is used to measure the uncertainty and consistency of a collection of data observations. These have demonstrated adequate accuracy for identifying the anomalies in the performance data from production environment to data captured from multi-tier web applications running on server class machines [1]. However, the statistical learning techniques are usually based on the entire history of individual data points to determine statistical profiles, therefore becoming computationally expensive as the amount of data increases.

Time-series mining is another popular detection method for the performance data collected sequentially in time. The method will first determine the temporal patterns of each metric, build a forecasting model with the history data and ARMA/ARIMA/Holt-Winters exponential smoothing algorithms, and use it to predict future values. The abnormal observations will be considered as anomalies if they fall outside a specific prediction confidence [7, 8]. However, it is difficult to achieve the prediction accuracy with an acceptable level since the time series in cloud datacenters has complex and nonlinear behaviors. Additionally, they are only backward looking and difficult to capture the new patterns/behaviors, thus resulting in false positives [8].

Since unsupervised algorithm-based anomaly detection does not rely on the labeled data, some distance/density-based clustering algorithms, such as k-means, hierarchical clustering algorithm, local outlier factor (LOF) and DBSCAN (Density-Based Spatial Clustering of Applications with Noise), have been utilized in cloud datacenters. They rely on the assumption that outliers can be detected using distance/density measures where data with a substantial distance from any other clusters will be considered as outliers [9,10,11].

However, they have limitations of accuracy and sensitivity due to their assumed data distributions, or limited adaptability to changing workloads, or some of them have poor scalability and lack of correlation analysis (e.g. clustering analysis). Also, few of them can operate at the scale of future data center or cloud computing systems and/or have the "lightweight" characteristic desired for online operation. In contrast, we propose an online anomaly detection through a combination of statistical learning approach, time series mining and regression techniques to estimate the dynamic threshold based on the characteristics of the performance metrics of any running application. Rather than simply using the absolute distance measurement between prediction and actual values or the statistics-based confidence levels to flag the outliers, we choose to utilize the smoothing and differentiation methods to compare the actual rate of change difference between predictive and actual values.

3 The Anomaly Detection System

In this section, we introduce the operation mechanism used for the anomaly detection system, including the performance data collection module, data preprocessing module, anomaly detection module and model implementation module. This suggested real time anomaly detection application collects the resource utilization statistics of datacenter servers and application-specific performance metrics, sends alerts to the datacenter administrators if there are any deviations in the resource usage patterns in the data.

3.1 Performance Data Collection

Alibaba has fitted its servers all over the world with performance monitoring technology, which makes it possible to track every task that is running on these servers and provides insights for its daily operation and management. We collect the data center performance metrics from four main aspects: the hardware (e.g., temperature), the operating system (e.g., number of threads), the runtime system (e.g., garbage collected), and application layers (e.g., transactions completed). Hundreds of counters are collected at each machine per time interval.

For this research, we focus on application-level performance data. This data can be divided into three categories: system-level resource utilization (such as CPU, memory, IO utilization rate); middleware-specific metrics- for instance, number of middleware related incidents (error counts of RPCs, cache hit ratios, etc); and lastly performance measurements from an end user's perspective such as network throughput and latency (response time). More data can be specified by the system administrators, the application developers, or the business owners as necessary. With these performance indicators, we can check the health of the application and detect most anomalies in datacenters.

We developed a real-time ETL system to collect and store these performance metrics [12]. This system is divided into three sub-modules: a log agent, a stream computing system and a datacenter.

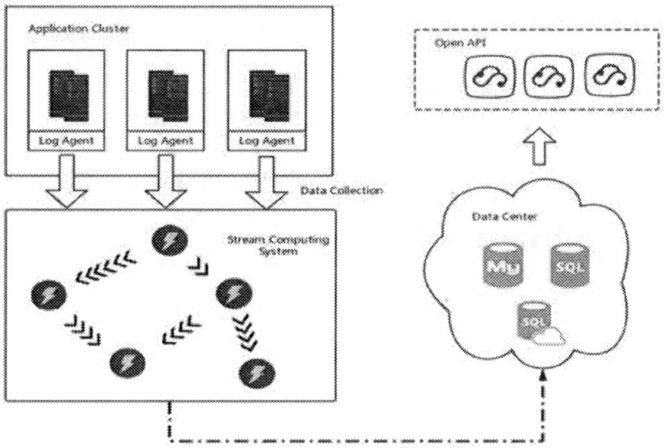

Fig. 1. Architecture of data collection system

First is the log agent, which is a data collection agent installed on each machine. It records fine grained performance data to local disk. Recording, processing and storing data at as fine a grain as the log agent collects can put extraneous pressure on our infrastructure for large applications. The log agent is capable of aggregating the data it collects on each machine level to reduce strain. Second is the stream computing system. Its main task is to collect the aggregated performance data on each machine. It then converts the data into a standardized data model and stores it into the target databases. In order to give a quick overview of application-level performance by allowing engineers to have fast running queries across the metrics they are interested in, the stream computing system applies a second level of aggregation. It does this across several major performance indicators (e.g. service, application, group). Then all the data will be converted into the unified query interface and the standardized data structure before passing into the datacenter module. Last is the datacenter module. The datacenter stores, manages and normalizes all the performance data collected, and provides the standard open API for developers or other data consumers with programmatic access to the real-time performance data, which facilities further data analysis. Normalization is especially important for data analysis. All the time series data from different applications or different metrics are provided in a uniform format to make sure it can be easily analyzed by any different systems.

With negligible overhead, these three modules collect continuous, real-time, and accurate performance data at the datacenter scale, thereby providing performance insights for cloud applications.

3.2 Data Preprocessing

Data preprocessing is an important step in analyzing the real-time performance data because the data issues that might affect the data integrity should be removed first to prevent incorrect analysis results. We propose the preprocessing algorithm 2.1 to eliminate artifacts, normalizes the data, and automatically discards counters that significantly violate assumptions or business rules thereby hinder comparisons.

Algorithm 2.1 The preprocessing algorithm. Receives the raw counters, climinates problematic counters and normalizes the data. $p_{90}(S)$ denotes the 90th - percentile of *S*.

Let $\theta^1 = 0.01, \theta^2 = 2, \theta^n = 6$
Let $z_c(m,t)$ = the last value of counter c on machine *m* before time *t*
Let $n_c(m)$ = number of reports for counter *c* on *m*
for all counter $c \in C`$ **do**
$\quad v_c \leftarrow mean_{m\in M, t\in T}(z_c(m,t))$
$\quad \sigma_c \leftarrow STD_{m\in M, t\in T}(z_c(m,t))$
$\quad$ **for all machine** $m \in M$ and time $t \in T$ **do**
$$y_c(m,t) \leftarrow \frac{z_c(m,t) - v_c}{\sigma_c}$$
$\quad\quad$ **end for**
$\quad$ **for all** machine $m \in M$ **do**
$\quad\quad \mu_c(m) \leftarrow median_{t\in T}(y_c(m,t))$
$\quad\quad mad_c(m) \leftarrow MAD_{t\in T}(y_c(m,t))$
$\quad$ **end for**
$\quad n_c \leftarrow median_{m\in M}(n_c(m))$
$$\psi_c^1 \leftarrow p_{90}\left(\left|\frac{n_c(m) - n_c}{n_c}\right|\right)$$
$\quad u_c \leftarrow median_{m\in M}(u_c(m))$
$$\psi_c^2 \leftarrow p_{90}\left(\left|\frac{u_c(m) - u_c}{mad_c(m)}\right|\right)$$
$\quad$ **If** $(\psi_c^1 \le \theta^1)$ **and** $(n_c \ge \theta^n)$ **and** $(\psi_c^2 \le \theta^2)$ **then**
$\quad\quad$ Add counter *c* to set of selected counters *C*
$\quad\quad$ **for all** machine $m \in M$ and time $t \in T$ **do**
$\quad\quad\quad x_c(m,t) \leftarrow y_c(m,t)$
$\quad\quad$ **end for**
$\quad$ **else**
$\quad\quad$ Discard counter *c*
$\quad$ **end if**
end for

First, not all performance counters are reported or collected at a fixed rate, and even periodic counters may have different periodicities. Non-periodic, infrequent, event-driven counters, or inconsistent values can be automatically detected by looking at the variability of the historical patterns, domain-specific knowledge and are removed by the preprocessing steps. For each counter and machine under the same application group, we expect all machines to have similar number of reports for a periodic counter. We use Median Absolute Deviation (MAD) to robustly detect the typical number of reports for each counter. Any counters for which the 90% percentile of the corresponding normalized MAD is too large will be eliminated from further analysis. We also exclude the infrequent counters. In our experiment, any counters that are being reported less than 6 times a day are excluded from further analysis. Additionally, the performance counters with extreme cases caused by business events (promotion) are removed. After removing the non-periodic or infrequent counters through preprocessing steps, performance counters at equal time intervals (1 minute in our implementation) will be used for further comparison at the same time scale. For the performance counters where the missing values occur less frequently, the median value at the same timestamp is used to replace the missing values.

Secondly, since we are analyzing various performance counters collectively, the raw data have to be normalized to bring them to a common range. The normalization operation, which has been trained using the initial samples, is used to transform the input time series data into a consistent mean and unit-variance data.

Lastly, the identification of pronounced peaks and valleys in performance metrics are also important for setting sensible and adaptive thresholds for alerting or further investigation. A local maximum method is applied as a brute force searching algorithm to find the local maximum in a moving window. The window size is determined by a predefined number of local points. The baseline estimated in the subsequent step will be corrected for the peak-to-valley ratios of the corresponding time period.

3.3 Model Formulation

The processed performance counters are used for the further baseline estimation, including the model selection, model training and anomaly determination module.

First, the biweekly historical data are collected for determining the temporal pattern. Based on the frequency identified from historical data and correlation analysis with other performance metrics, different modeling approaches will be selected for further baseline estimation. The model selection is decided by the temporal pattern of performance metrics (detailed in Algorithm 2.2): 1) if no seasonal or temporal pattern is detected, the time series mining will not be utilized: If there is significant correlation between the metric and other performance counters, the regression module will be recommended; otherwise, the statistical-based model (a modified Z-score MAD-|Mi|) will be used. The observations with the absolute modified Z-score greater than 3.5 will be labeled as outliers; 2) If there are seasonal or other temporal patterns, the time series mining will be utilized. Here, we choose the ensemble learning approach, which is a collection of individual learning algorithms such as ARIMA, STL LOESS decomposition, exponential smoothing algorithms to produce a consensus. The hope is that although one or two learners/algorithms may be off base, the majority will be able to produce the correct decision. The mean absolute percentage error (MAPE), a measure of prediction accuracy of a forecasting method in statistics, will be used to determine which model/models fit best for the estimation of dynamic baseline.

We can thus construct a confidence interval by taking the 99-th percentile of the distances, as the upper limit. The lower limit is not less than 0 since a distance is strictly positive. These intervals provide us with a "normality" interval of healthy data, which we can then use in the test phase to determine if a data sample is normal or not. The performance metrics are often unpredictable due to spiky peak usage in the production environment. Therefore, in addition to the statistical confidence limits for anomaly determination, we have elected to evaluate the performance change by comparing its performance metrics with the Savitzky-Golay filter (SGF). SGF is known to be a good choice for signal cleaning compared to other adjacent averaging filters (moving averages, Local Regression Smoothing), because it tends to preserve the height, width, amplitude and pertinent high frequency components of the signal.

Algorithm 2.2 Ensemble Anomaly Detection Algorithm: Receives the pre-processed counters, estimates the baselines based on the historical pattern and identifies anomalous counter.

---

function ENSEMBLEANOMALYDETECTION (X) $>$ where X - array containing at least 2 weeks performance counters

Phase 1 – Model Determination And Baseline Estimation

1. Use periodogram to determine periodicity/seasonality
2. Split X into training data and validation data

Input:(1) X;(2) SG.
Output:(1) Anomaly
if periodogram(X) is not seasonal but stochastic **then**
modified :

$$Z-score = \frac{0.6745*(X_i - median(X))}{mad(X)}$$

else if periodogram(X) is seasonal and is not correlated with other counters **then**

$F_1 = arima(X)$ $>$ Where F-include both the predictive values and the 0.99 confidence levels
$F_2 = stl(X)$
$F_3 = ewa(X)$
Use bootstrap sampling and choose the best prediction F to minimize

$$MAPE = \frac{100}{n}\sum_{t=1}^{n}\left|\frac{X_t - F_t}{X_t}\right|$$

else if *periodogram is highly correlated with other counters* **then**
$F = lm(X)$
end if

Phase 2 – Anomaly Determination

F = *predicted values*
CI = *c(lowerBound, UpperBound)*
SG = the Savitzky-Golay filter (the 2nd order smoothing and differentiation)
M = *the model determined in Phase 1*
if *M is Time Series Module* $\vee$ *M is Regression Module* **then**
F` = SG(F)
X` = SG(X)
if *[F` - X`]* $> \gamma \wedge$ *X exceed CI* **then**
Anomaly = True
Anomaly = False
else if *M is MAD Module* **then**
if X *exceed CI* **then**
Anomaly = True
Anomaly = False
end if
end if

We firstly use a local least-squares (LS) to regress a small sliding window (m) of the time series data onto a low-order (p) polynomial, then use the polynomial to estimate the point in the center of the window. This continues until every time point has been optimally adjusted relative to its neighbors. This low-pass filter is introduced to smooth the burstiness in performance metrics, so as to exclude the noise from further analysis of the true pattern(s). We then evaluate the resulting smoothed polynomial at a single point within the approximation interval, which is equivalent to discrete convolution with a fixed impulse response. We apply the nth differentiation (n) on the fitted polynomial of predicted baseline and actual observations rather than on original data. This step can filter out the noise (e.g., unreasonable burst) in the data, while preserving its high statistic moments, thus keeping its statistical properties unchanged for more reliable comparison between the prediction and actual values. With the fixed sliding window (m) and smoothing order (p), a curvature threshold (Tr) can be estimated by solving the polynomial equation numerically. The absolute difference (Diff_sg) between baseline and actual values adjusted by SGF were compared against optimal inflection point (Tr), which is time-tiered threshold scaled by different day and night factors. Any Diff_sg values beyond the inflection point (Tr) will be flagged as "anomaly".

Once all the "anomalies" have been flagged for each performance metric based on each detector module, we always convert them to a probability in the [0,1] range. This probability can be interpreted as the detector's belief that a point is an anomaly. Once this score is obtained, we can use it as prior knowledge in a model feedback scheme. It is necessary to have scores on the same scale as to not inadvertently weight some metric as a priori more important than others.

Using the ensemble modeling module, for each application specific metric, we generate a dynamic baseline and comparison between prediction and actual values to help determining anomalous data. the model will be implemented in the production system and connect to the incident management platform for further alerting actions.

3.4 Model Implementation in Production Environment

In order to validate the work described in the previous section in a real, large production system, we implement the anomaly detection system in Alibaba production environment. It includes three functional modules: the effective metric selection, the real-time detection and the incident management module.

Computer systems hosted in datacenters usually involve multiple layers and provide a large set of metrics for tracking their operation. The analysis of all available metrics collected from the performance monitoring system generates drawbacks associated with communication, storage and processing. In order to support anomaly detection and minimize the cost of monitoring, we select metrics that can effectively reflect the system health based on the following aspects:

1) Scope: we choose to limit the scope of performance metrics at five main levels including application, product group, datacenter unit, server room, and instances.
2) Category: we use stable statistical correlations among metrics combined with the domain knowledge to select the performance categories that can represent the system health. The categories of metrics selected include various service calls (e.g.

HTTP, RPC, database, cache and message), system load, or JVM status.

3) Metric: To measure and evaluate the system performance, we select the specific counters such as throughput, response time, hit rate and resource utilization rates.

The real-time anomaly detection is performed once every minute. The entire detection process is divided into four steps as follows:

1) Firstly, the prediction values, including the dynamic baseline, statistical confidence limits and the numerical difference after applying the SG filters, are requested from the data layer based on the corresponding time period.
2) Secondly, we compare the difference between the prediction and actual values, and identify the abnormal point based on the criteria defined in anomaly detection module. The data which exceeds the dynamic upper bound is flagged as an anomaly.
3) Thirdly, all abnormal points are standardized as event models to facilitate subsequent analysis and decision making.
4) Finally, all the anomalous events of the same application will be summarized and quantified as an overall anomaly score for each application

The overall running time of the detection module is less than 50 milliseconds, which is acceptable for the requirement of the real-time production system. Incident management module involves writing the anomaly event to the data layer and sending an alarm notification to the stakeholders including developers and business owners.

1) Each anomaly event will be written back to the data layer so that the front-end monitoring dashboard and other performance-related platforms can get anomaly information in real time through the event interface.
2) Each application's anomaly score triggers an alert when it is higher than the specific alarm threshold. This strategy effectively reduces the false alarm rate at each application level, thus improving the quality of anomaly detection services and avoiding redundant or invalid alerts.

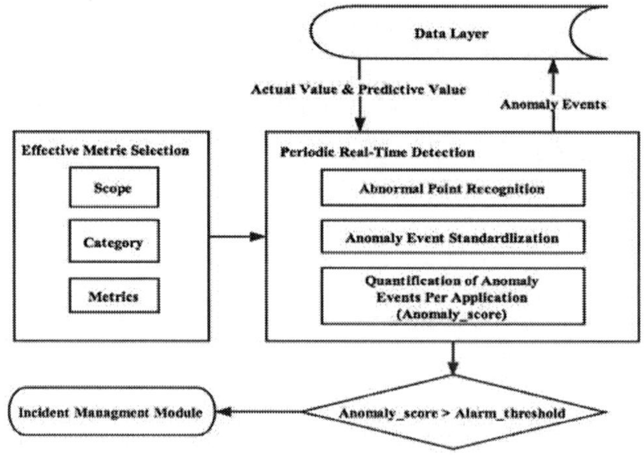

Fig. 2. Model implementation in production environment

In summary, this system can continuously diagnose the abnormal behaviors from normal ones or unexpected performance changes of any running application, with a low false alarm rate. This online anomaly detection system has been implemented in Alibaba datacenters on a daily basis, demonstrating its capability and effectiveness in ensuring the reliability of daily operations and management in cloud datacenters.

4 Evaluation

In this research study, we evaluated the following anomaly detection techniques on the data collected from Alibaba production data centers:

1) our ensemble learning model
2) the static threshold model defined by domain experts
3) the fixed threshold segmented by hour of day
4) 3-sigma outlier
5) multivariate adaptive statistical filtering (MASF)
6) relative percent difference minute-on-minute

Model 2 and 3 are based on the static or multi-level threshold defined by domain experts. The Gaussian distribution is the assumed underlying probability model for both model 4 and 5. MASF is a popular method for anomaly detection in data centers, which first segments the performance data by hour of day and day of week, subsequently, threshold limits are computed based on the standard deviation (σ) of this segregated data. A data point falling outside the $\mu \pm 3\sigma$ range is deemed as a rare event and thus is flagged as an anomaly. 3-sigma model is similar to MASF but no data segmentation needs to be done. In general, a 3-sigma detection is taken as being the minimum to be believed. Model 6 is calculating the relative percent difference per minute and if the relative ratio exceeding the user-defined threshold is flagged as an anomaly. Each model is trained separately on each time-series; i.e., learned parameters do not carry over. Since this is data from production data centers, we had no control of the anomalies that manifested, nor do we have knowledge about them. So, in our evaluations, we will compare the number of anomalies detected by the various techniques.

Figure 3 provides a representative plot of the performance of each model tested on one typical performance measurements (network throughput) collected from a running application in Alibaba production environment. The metrics are sampled every minute. The actual throughput is in red; the blue and green band show the predicted confidence range based on each model. The results are shown for both the actual measurement per minute and the predicted confidence levels.

The alarms (highlighted as red points) raised by different techniques are shown. This metric exhibits a typical pattern of network traffic: throughput peaks during business hours each weekday, when application usage is highest and drops to a local minimum at night. Because that pattern repeats week after week, the anomaly detection algorithm is able to accurately forecast the metric's value, peaks and variation pattern based on time series learning. Our prediction and the relative percent change module match the actual data more closely compared to the other four techniques. The anomalies captured by the relative percent change model has higher false alarm rate, in contrast to our model, due to the fact that it couldn't be easily customized with each peak signal-to-noise ratio or the level of background noise. These pattern/threshold-based anomaly detection techniques make them interpretable and amenable for post-analysis by domain experts to reveal the root cause. However, this generality comes at a cost of high false positive rates, as not all rare occurrences can be attributed to anomalous cases. Also, we observed that our methods detect the first unusual change in network throughput faster than other techniques.

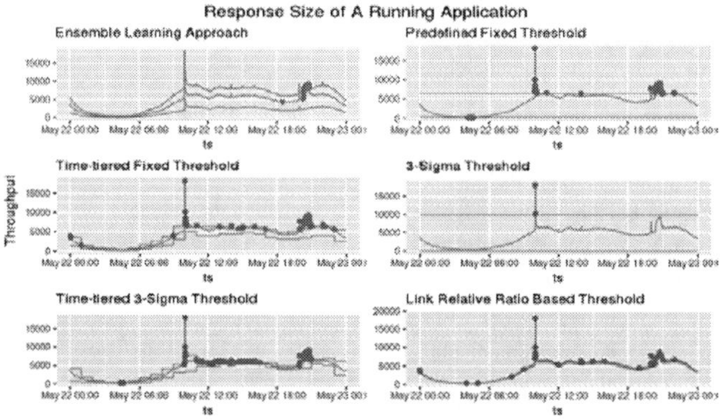

Fig. 3. Model Comparisons tested on the network throughput measurement of a running application in the production environment.

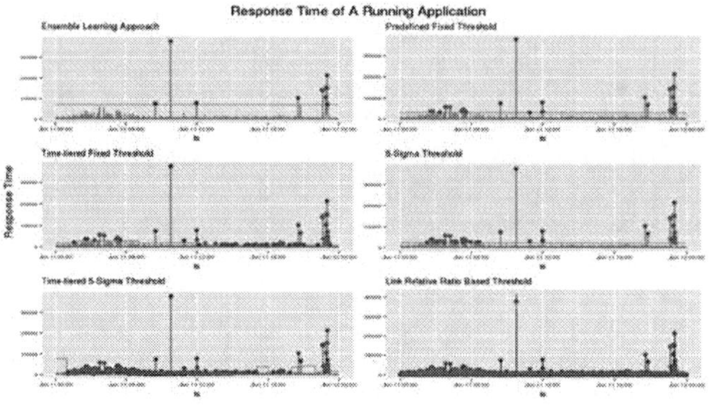

Fig. 4. Model Comparisons tested on the network latency measurement of a running application in the production environment

To assess the efficacy of these six detection models, we computed three standard metrics: Recall, Precision, and F-measure (or the balanced F-score). Precision (also called positive predictive value) is a measure of how many instances are correctly classified among all positive predictions including true and false positives. Recall (also known as sensitivity, true positive rate) is a measure of a proportion of all real positive observations that are correct. F-measure is the weighted harmonic mean of precision and recall.

Recall and precision are two widely used performance metrics in classification. Precision permits to measure the fidelity of the classification model regarding each particular class, whereas recall measures the per-class accuracy.

Table 1. Anomlay detection result.

Metrics	Anomaly Detection Result			
	Type	Prec	Rec	F1
Throughput	Ensemble learning approach	0.9333	0.8235	0.8750
	Predefined fixed threshold	0.5322	0. 9705	0. 6875
	Time-tiered fixed threshold	0. 3626	0. 9705	0. 5280
	3-Sigma threshold	0.0000	0.0000	0.0000
	Time-tiered 3-Sigma threshold	0.0973	0.9705	0.1769
	Link relative ratio	0.1785	0.1470	0.1613
Response time	Ensemble learning approach	1.0000	0.7333	0.8462
	Predefined fixed threshold	0.5357	1. 0000	0. 6977
	Time-tiered fixed threshold	0. 2083	1. 0000	0. 3448
	3-Sigma threshold	0. 3261	1. 0000	0. 4918
	Time-tiered 3-Sigma threshold	0. 0456	1. 0000	0. 0872
	Link relative ratio	0. 0124	0.3333	0. 0244

Table 1 shows the outcome analysis of recall, precision and F-measure relating to the anomaly detection schema and other five different detectors. For the network throughput counter, which exhibits a prominent temporal pattern, our ensemble learning has a highest F-score 86%, with the highest recall rate of 82 and a 93% precision. This approach outperforms the other five techniques.

For the network latency measurement with no significant seasonality or cyclic behavior, our proposed approach achieved the highest 85% F-score. The precision achieved was 100%, meaning that all anomalies detected were true anomalies. Also, the recall rate was very high, achieving about 73% at the 95% confidence level. High F-scores achieved by testing on two typical performance counters, demonstrate that our proposed approach is precise and robust in identifying the anomalous behaviors.

Based on the model comparison, our proposed real-time system for detecting the anomalies in Alibaba data centers is best suited for detecting general anomalies, such as short-term drifts or sudden spikes in the resource utilization of the servers.The proposed system is demonstrated to perform anomaly detection in real time much more efficiently with significantly improving the performance of the anomaly detection in the cloud data centers compared to the other available state of the art solutions.

5 Discussion

The feasibility of our anomaly detection system has been verified with the highly complex, unpredictable and dynamic environment in Alibaba datacenters. This novel solution is capable of detecting the anomalies of the data centers in real time with high accuracy and negligible latency. Our techniques are adaptable and can learn the workload characteristics over time. They also meet the scalability needs of cloud data-centers and can be applied to multiple metrics in data centers.

This suggested system remarkably improves the availability and reliability of the cloud based services running on top of the cloud data centers. However, there are still more work needed to be done. One concern associated with this factor is the process for resolving whether a defect is caused by an error or by actual program performance. As ongoing work, we are performing more evaluations on synthetic as well as real production data. We are also exploring further refinements to the proposed techniques for various metrics and for aggregation across multiple machines at large scale. We also plan to obtain traceability back to the source (individual or authoritative record) that could resolve the nature of the anomaly.

6 Acknowledgement

This work was supported by Alibaba-Zhejiang University Joint Research Institute of Frontier Technologies.

References

1. Wang, Chengwei, F.: Statistical techniques for online anomaly detection in data centers. Integrated Network Management (IM), 2011 IFIP/IEEE International Symposium on. IEEE, 2011.
2. Ren, Gang, F.: Google-wide profiling: A continuous profiling infrastructure for data centers. IEEE micro 30.4 (2010): 65-79.
3. Candan, F., Çağatay, S., Hakan Inan, T.: A unified framework for derivation and implementation of Savitzky–Golay filters. Signal Processing 104 (2014): 203-211.
4. Chandola, F., Varun, S., Arindam Banerjee, T.: Anomaly detection: A survey. ACM computing surveys (CSUR) 41.3 (2009): 15.
5. Chow, F., Kingsum, S., Wanyi Zhu, T.: Software Performance Analytics in the Cloud. Proceedings of the 8th ACM/SPEC on International Conference on Performance Engineering. ACM, 2017.
6. Buzen, F., Jeffrey P., S., Annie W. Shum, T.: Masf-multivariate adaptive statistical filtering. Int. CMG Conference. 1995.
7. Hochenbaum, F., Jordan, S., Owen S. Vallis, T.: Automatic Anomaly Detection in the Cloud Via Statistical Learning. arXiv preprint arXiv:1704.07706 (2017).
8. D. Machiwal, F., M. K. Jha, S.: Hydrologic Time Series Analysis: Theory and Practice, Springer, New York, NY, USA, 2012.
9. Breunig, F., Markus M., S.: LOF: identifying density-based local outliers. *ACM sigmod record*. Vol. 29. No. 2. ACM, 2000.
10. Vallis, F., Owen, S., Jordan Hochenbaum, T.: A Novel Technique for Long-Term Anomaly Detection in the Cloud. HotCloud. 2014.
11. Gander, F., Matthias, S.: Anomaly Detection in the Cloud: Detecting Security Incidents via Machine Learning. EternalS@ ECAI. 2012.
12. Zhao Jun Xia Xiaoling(School of Computer Science and Technology,Donghua University,Shanghai 201620,China); Design and implementation of ETL system in the common data center[J]; Computer Applications and Software; 2011-10.s

A Partial Demand Fulfilling Capacity Constrained Clustering Algorithm to Static Bike Rebalancing Problem

Yi Tang and Bi-Ru Dai

Department of Computer Science and Information Engineering,
National Taiwan University of Science and Technology, Taipei, Taiwan, R.O.C
m10515038@mail.ntust.edu.tw, brdai@csie.ntust.edu.tw

Abstract. Nowadays, bike sharing systems have been widely used in major cities around the world. One of the major challenges of bike sharing systems is to rebalance the number of bikes for each station such that user demands can be satisfied as much as possible. To execute rebalancing operations, operators usually have a fleet of vehicles to be routed through stations. When rebalancing operations are executing at nighttime, user demands usually are small enough to be ignored and this is regarded as the static bike rebalancing problem. In this paper, we propose a Partial Demand Fulfilling Capacity Constrained Clustering (PDF3C) algorithm to reduce the problem scale of the static bike rebalancing problem. The proposed PDF3C algorithm can discover outlier stations and group remaining stations into several clusters where stations having large demands can be included by different clusters. Finally, the clustering result will be applied to multi-vehicle route optimization. Experiment results verified that our PDF3C algorithm outperforms existing methods.

Keywords: Bike rebalancing, clustering, mixed integer linear programming.

1 Introduction

Nowadays, as the first-and-last mile connections, the bike sharing systems have been widely used in major cities around the world, and there are over 1400 systems online [9]. The most convenient feature of bike sharing systems is that a user can borrow a bike in any station and then return it to any other station.

However, user demands for different stations are usually unbalanced such that some stations are short of bikes to be borrowed and some stations do not have enough docks to be hooked. With unbalanced stations, fewer users can be served and the revenue of operators will be reduced. Therefore, operators usually have a fleet of trucks to rebalance the number of bikes between stations. To determine the rebalancing route and rebalancing operations for each truck is the bike rebalancing problem.

Since the traffic congestion and parking locations will not be a problem while the rebalancing fleet travels in the city during the night [11], we focus on the static bike rebalancing problem which assumes the rebalancing operations are executing at nighttime while the user operations at this time are usually small enough to be ignored.

In general, the static bike rebalancing problem can be treated as a One-commodity Capacitated Pickup and Delivery Problem [2] which is an NP-hard problem and will be hard to find the optimal solution in limited time when the problem scale increases. For a 200 station case with 3 trucks, even the advanced optimization model [11] may take several hours to find the optimal solution. While finding out the optimal solution becomes difficult, several works have been tried to find a good enough near-optimal solution during the limited time, where [1] proposed an approximation algorithm, [10, 13, 15] developed different heuristic methods, [2, 4, 6] applied the meta-heuristic techniques and [3, 7, 8, 14] used the clustering techniques to divide the multi-vehicle static bike rebalancing problem into several single-vehicle static bike rebalancing problem to reduce the problem scale.

To further reduce the problem scale, Liu et al. [8] considered outlier stations whose demands are large and hard to be satisfied. However, their method still cannot deal with stations whose demand is larger than the vehicle capacity directly.

In this paper, to deal with stations with large demands and utilize the outlier station discovering to further reduce the problem scale of the static bike rebalancing problem, based on the CCKC algorithm [8], we propose a Partial Demand Fulfilling Capacity Constrained Clustering (PDF3C) algorithm which allows the demands of one station to be partially considered by different clusters and utilizes the average saved shortage to discriminate the considering priority of stations. Experimental results show that for the large-scale static bike rebalancing problem with some stations having large demands, the proposed PDF3C clustering method can get better performance than existing methods.

The rest sections of this paper are organized as follows. We summarize the strategies of existing methods to the static bike rebalancing problem in Section 2. The problem definitions are demonstrated in Section 3. The proposed method is presented in Section 4. Experiment results are presented in Section 5. Finally, the conclusion of this paper is in Section 6.

2 Related Works

In this section, we will briefly summarize the strategies of existing methods and introduce several clustering methods with their reduction to the multi-vehicle static bike rebalancing problem.

When traditional methods cannot get optimal or good enough near-optimal solutions in limited time, some methods were proposed to get better solutions, including heuristic methods [13, 15], meta-heuristic methods [2, 4, 6] and clustering methods [3, 7, 8, 14]. The strategies for these methods are different. The heuristic methods usually give some rules related to the problem to guide the searching or construction of the solution, the meta-heuristic methods apply their own mechanism to utilize the searching experience in solution space to improve the searching process and the clustering methods try to reduce the solution space and keep the solution quality simultaneously. Some of these methods are combined with each other or with other methods to become hybrid methods.

Clustering methods can be used to reduce the problem scale of the multi-vehicle bike rebalancing problem. Schuijbroek et al. [14] proposed a Cluster-First Route-Second approach to divide the multi-vehicle bike rebalancing problem into single-vehicle bike rebalancing problems, where each cluster represents a vehicle, and the travel distance for each cluster is approximated by the Maximum Spanning Star. Forma et al. [3] proposed a 3-step Math Heuristic method. In addition to divide the original problem into several single-vehicle bike rebalancing problems, the travel routes between clusters are determined by Step 2 in their method and the decision variables in the MILP model are reduced according to the travel routes.

To further reduce the problem scale, Liu et al. [8] proposed a Capacity Constrained K-centers Clustering method which use the balance condition to discover outlier stations before solving the bike rebalancing problems. However, this method is not able to deal with outlier stations with the number of rebalancing operations being larger than the vehicle capacity.

3 Problem Formulation

In this section, we will introduce the static bike rebalancing problem and the station clustering problem.

The static bike rebalancing problem is to determine the rebalancing route and rebalancing instructions for each vehicle such that the expected shortage of each station in the next day will be as low as possible. In this paper, the target inventory for each station is determined by the penalty function provided in [12]. Assume the penalty function is given then the static bike rebalancing problem is defined as follows.

Definition 1: Static Bike Rebalancing Problem.

Given one depot and a set of stations with their initial bikes or vacancies, the penalty function for each station, the travel cost between stations and depot, the load and unload time for single rebalancing instruction, the total time budget for rebalancing operations and a weight alpha to tradeoff between travel cost and rebalancing operations, the static bike rebalancing problem is to determine the rebalancing route and rebalancing instructions for each vehicle that minimize the total travel cost and the shortage for each station.

In addition, in order to simplify the original problem and satisfy some stations with large demands, each vehicle is restricted to visit each station at most once but each station can be visited by more than one vehicle.

Usually, after determining the final bike inventory for each station at the end of a day, there are only a few hours remained for solving the static bike rebalancing problem and conducting the rebalancing operations. For the small-scale static bike rebalancing problem, several works [7] have solved it by mixed integer linear programming (MILP) methods. However, for a large-scale static bike rebalancing problem, pure MILP methods are often not able to get the optimal or a good enough near-optimal solution in limited time.

To reduce the problem scale, clustering is a good technique to allocate stations for each vehicle. This is called station clustering problem and is defined as follows.

Definition 2: Station Clustering Problem.

Given a static bike rebalancing problem, the station clustering problem is to allocate stations into clusters, where each cluster represents one vehicle, according to the travel cost and the rebalancing operations to reduce the problem scale of the original problem. Note that some stations are probably not assigned to any cluster and will be regarded as outlier stations.

After problem definitions, the proposed method to solve the identified problems will be introduced in the next section.

4 Proposed Method

In this section, we will first give an overview of our framework and then demonstrate the proposed method in two parts, where the target inventory determination part is in Section 4.2 and the rebalancing route optimization part is in Section 4.3.

4.1 Framework

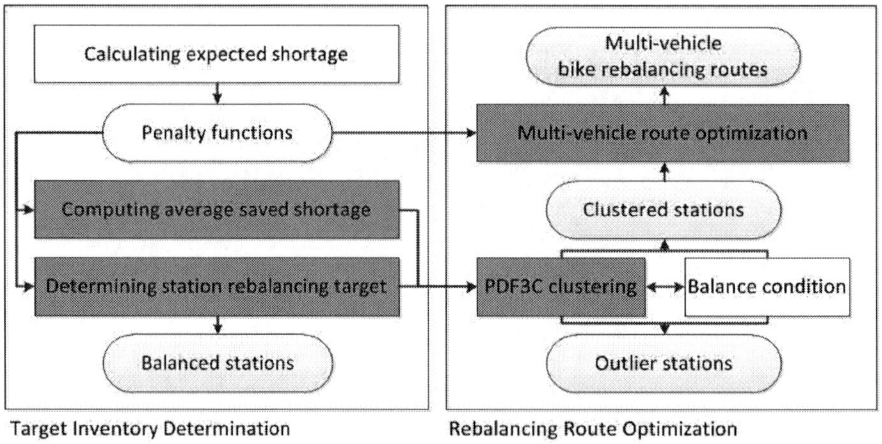

Fig. 1. Proposed framework

The whole framework can be divided into two parts, one is the target inventory determination part and the other is the rebalancing route optimization part. The framework is illustrated in Figure 1, and components filled by gray color are designed or revised by this paper. In the target inventory determination part, we will need to calculate the expected shortage for each station first. This process can be done by different methods, such as some stochastic analysis or demand prediction methods. In this paper, our expected shortage is calculated by the method proposed in [12] and is represented as the penalty function for each station. In order to discriminate the considering priority for each station and discover outlier stations according to the vehicle capacity, the average saved shortage and the station rebalancing target are computed, respectively. During this process, stations with zero rebalancing targets will be regarded as balanced stations and will not be taken into the rebalancing problem. Next, in the rebalancing route optimization part, according to the station rebalancing target and the average saved shortage, we design a clustering algorithm, named PDF3C, to generate clustered stations for each vehicle and discover some outlier stations according to the balance condition. Finally, the penalty function and clustered stations will be taken as inputs of the MILP model to obtain the optimized bike rebalancing routes and rebalancing instructions.

4.2 Target Inventory Determination

In the target inventory determination part, we use the same penalty function as [12] to represent the expected shortage for each station. Then the station rebalancing target can be calculated accordingly. Different from [5], we further define the average saved shortage to determine the priority of stations, as described below.

Penalty function. The penalty function represents the expected shortage number of docks or bikes incurred by users during next day. For each station i having capacity c_i, with a number of bikes s_i after the rebalancing operations, the penalty function $f_i(s_i)$ is defined discretely [12]:

$$shortage = f_i(s_i) \quad s_i = 0,...,c_i \tag{1}$$

Station rebalancing target. The station rebalancing target is the number of bikes required to be load or unload if we want to get the minimum shortage for a bike station. Given the penalty function of station i, since the convexity of penalty function, there exists a number of bikes s_i^* corresponding to the minimum shortage. Assume that the number of bikes before rebalancing operations is s_i^0, the station rebalancing target b_i is defined as:

$$b_i = s_i^* - s_i^0 \tag{2}$$

Average saved shortage. When the rebalancing target of some stations cannot be satisfied, it is necessary to determine which station will have higher priority and need to be satisfied first. Therefore, we define the average saved shortage for each station i as follows:

$$ass_i = \left| \frac{s_i^* - s_i^0}{b_i} \right| \tag{3}$$

Stations with larger average saved shortages will be given higher priority because for such stations, more shortages can be saved by a single rebalancing instruction in average.

In the next part, the station rebalancing target and the average saved shortage for each station will be used to generate station clusters. Then, the multi-vehicle route optimization will be performed based on the penalty function and station clusters.

4.3 Rebalancing Route Optimization

The linear programming model is a common way to solve the static bike rebalancing problem. However, for the large-scale static bike rebalancing problem, even the advanced MILP model [11] will take a very long time to get a good enough solution. In order to reduce the problem scale, we propose a clustering algorithm, named Partial Demand Fulfilling Capacity Constrained Clustering (PDF3C) algorithm, to allow the demands of one station to be partially considered by different clusters. The same balance condition mentioned in [8] will be used in this paper and is stated below.

Balance condition. Given the vehicle capacity of k and a set of stations belonging to cluster I, where $B(I)$ is the absolute value of the sum of rebalancing targets for all stations in cluster I, the balance condition is defined as follows:

$$B(I) \le k \quad where\ B(I) = \left| \sum_{i \in I} b_i \right| \tag{4}$$

If the balance condition is not violated, the rebalancing target for all stations in the same cluster will be fully satisfied in one route using one vehicle. Note that one route represents a vehicle starting from the depot with its initial bikes or vacancies, passing through several stations, and finally going back to the depot.

Partial Demand Fulfilling Capacity Constrained Clustering.
The difficulty of using MILP model to solve the static bike rebalancing problem mainly depends on the number of decision variables and constraints [3]. Although there are several works applying clustering techniques to divide the multi-vehicle static bike rebalancing problem into several single-vehicle bike rebalancing problems to reduce the problem scale [3, 7, 8, 14], only [8] has considered outlier stations, whose rebalancing targets cannot be fulfilled completely, to further reduce the problem scale to get better effectiveness.

Liu et al. [8] proposed a clustering algorithm named Capacity Constrained K-centers Clustering (CCKC) to discovery outlier stations by the capacity balanced condition mentioned above. However, CCKC does not consider the following two points: 1. to deal with stations whose rebalancing targets are larger than the vehicle capacity; 2. to discriminate important stations when the saved shortage for each station by one instruction is heterogeneous.

The importance of considering point 1 is that for those stations whose rebalancing targets are larger than the vehicle capacity, the saved shortage will usually be large and have a serious impact on the revenue of operators. The consideration of point 2 is trying to allow each rebalancing operation and each bike in the system to be utilized to save the bike shortage as much as possible. When the saved shortage for a station by one instruction is heterogeneous, we should satisfy those stations with higher saved shortages first.

In order to overcome these two points, in this paper, we propose the Partial Demand Fulfilling Capacity Constrained Clustering (PDF3C) algorithm which allows the rebalancing target to be partially considered and takes into account the saved shortage for different stations using average saved shortage. The flowchart and the pseudo code of the proposed algorithm are illustrated in Figure 2 and Algorithm 1, respectively.

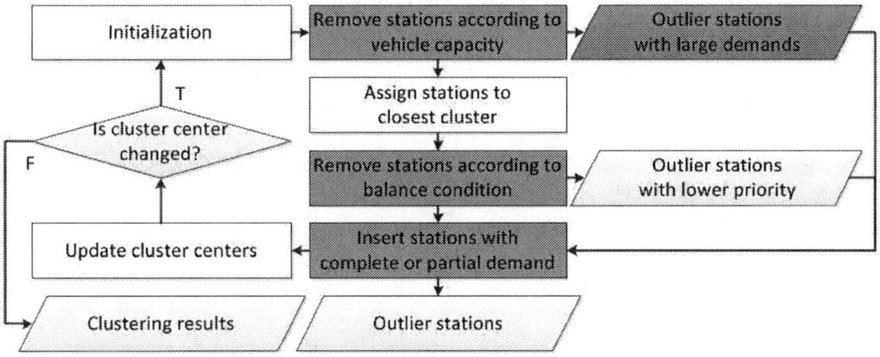

Fig. 2. Partial Demand Fulfilling Capacity Constrained Clustering algorithm flowchart

Before the details of the proposed algorithm, we demonstrate the flowchart first. The initialization step is to clear the cluster assignment for each station and reset the station set. After that, we then markup stations whose rebalancing targets are larger than the vehicle capacity and assign each of the remaining stations to its closest cluster. In the following remove station step, while the balance condition for any one cluster is violated, we keep removing some stations with lower priority until the balance condition is not violated for that cluster. Next, in the insert station step, we try to utilize the remaining capacity for each vehicle to cover outlier stations. After the insert station step, stations still belonging to no cluster are real outlier stations. Finally, cluster centers will be updated and all steps will be repeated until centers are not changed.

Algorithm 1 $PDF3C(\mathbf{TC}, \mathbf{b}, k, C, N_s, N_{ori}, E, \varepsilon)$

Input: $TC_{ij}, b_i, k, C, N_s, N_{ori}, E, \varepsilon$;
Output: C;

1: $N_s \leftarrow N_{ori}$;
2: **for** $i \in N_s$ **do** $c(i) = 0$;
3: **for** $b_i > k,\ i \in N_s$ **do** $c(i) = -2$;
4: **for** $c(i) = 0,\ i \in N_s$ **do** $c(i) = \arg\min_{j \in E}\ (TC_{ij})$;
5: **for** $B(I) > k,\ I \in C$ **do**
6:     **while** $B(I) > k$ **do**
7:         $q = \arg\min_{i \in I^*}\ (\sum_{j \in E} TC_{ij} \cdot ass_i \cdot |b_i|)$, where $I^* = \{i \mid B(I \setminus i) < B(I)\}$
8:         $c(q) = -1,\ I = I \setminus q$;
9: **find** $l = \arg\max_{i, c(i) = -1, -2}\ (\sum_{j \in E} TC_{ij} \cdot ass_i \cdot |b_i|)$
10: create $a = l$;
11: **if** $\exists\ CC = \{I \mid B(I \bigcup a) < k,\ \frac{ass_i \cdot |ab_{Il}|}{\min_{j \in I}(TC_{ij})} > \varepsilon\}$ **then**
12:     **if** $b_l = ab_{Il}$ **then**
13:         delete a, $c(l) = E(I)$, $I = \arg\min_{Q \in CC}(\min_{j \in Q}(TC_{lj}))$
14:     **else**
15:         add a to N_s, $c(a) = E(I)$, $I = \arg\min_{Q \in CC}(\min_{j \in Q}(TC_{lj}))$
16:         $b_l = b_l - ab_{Il},\ b_a = ab_{Il}$;
17:     **for** $c(i) = -3, -4,\ i \in N_s$ **do** $c(i) = c(i) + 2$;
18: **else**
19:     delete a, $c(l) = c(l) - 2$;
20: **go to** step 9 **till** $\nexists\ i$ that $c(i) = -1, -2$;
21: **for** $I \in C$ **do** $E'(I) = \arg\min_{i, c(i) = E(I)}(\sum_{j, c(j) = E(I)} TC_{ij})$;
22: **if** $E' \neq E$ **then** $E = E'$, go to step 1 **else** go to step 23;
23: **return** clustering result C.

We now begin to demonstrate the proposed algorithm. Inputs of Algorithm 1 include the travel cost $\mathbf{TC}$, rebalancing targets $\mathbf{b}$, vehicle capacity k, set of clusters C, set of current station nodes Ns, set of original station nodes $Nori$, set of initial cluster centers E, which can be generated randomly or by some other methods, and the benefit threshold ε. First, in the initialization step, Step 1 resets current station set to the original station set and Step 2 clears the cluster assignments for each station, and then Step 3 markups outlier stations with large rebalancing targets. Step 4 assigns each of the remaining station to its closest cluster. When the balance condition is violated, Step 5~8 keep removing stations with lower priority which is determined by the distance to other clusters and the average saved shortage for that station. Next, in Step 9~20, stations without a cluster assignment are reassigned where the priority of these stations are similar to Step 5~8 but in a contrary way. For each reassigned station, the available candidate cluster set is determined by the benefit which is computed by the average saved shortage and the available rebalancing target where the available rebalancing target is the maximum rebalancing target that can be included into the current considered cluster. If the available rebalancing target is equal to the original rebalancing target, it means that the rebalancing target of the reassigned station can be fully included by the candidate cluster. Therefore, the reassigned station will be assigned to the candidate cluster directly. Otherwise, the reassigned station will be duplicated with the available rebalancing target and the duplicated one will be assigned to the candidate cluster while the rebalancing target of the original reassigned station will be subtracted by the available rebalancing target. In other words, when the available rebalancing target is not equal to the original rebalancing target, we will split the reassigned station into two stations with the available rebalancing target and the remaining rebalancing target respectively. After adjusting the clustering result with considering the balance condition, cluster centers are updated in Step 21. Then, Step 22 determines whether these cluster centers are changed. If not, Step 23 returns the clustering result; otherwise, the algorithm restarts from Step 1 with these updated cluster centers.

In above, we have demonstrated the PDF3C algorithm completely. Since the proposed algorithm is based on the CCKC algorithm, we summarize main differences as follows.

- First, in Step 3, stations with too large rebalancing target are excluded before station assignments. By this way, we avoid the problem occurred in [5] that all stations will be removed from a cluster if the cluster includes a station whose rebalancing target is larger than the vehicle capacity.
- Second, in Step 11~20, to deal with stations with large rebalancing target and fully utilize the capacity of each vehicle, the rebalancing target of a station is allowed to be partially considered by different clusters.
- Third, in Step 11, in addition to the original distance threshold in CCKC algorithm, we also take into account how much shortage can be saved when inserting a station into a cluster to further identify valuable stations to be included.
- Forth, in Step 7 and Step 9, because the penalty function is different for each station, we include the concept of average saved shortage to discriminate which station can save more shortage.

After the PDF3C algorithm, stations whose rebalancing target is not zero will be divided into clusters and some of them will become outlier stations. Next, in the multi-vehicle route optimization step, the MILP model will use the clustering result to reduce the problem scale.

Multi-vehicle Route Optimization.
In this step, we use the Arc Index formulation which is the MILP model proposed by [11] to solve the static bike rebalancing problem. To reduce the problem scale for the MILP model, the creation of decision variables and constraints, which are referenced by vehicles and stations, will be decided according the clustering result. In order to see how many decision variables and constraints can be reduced, we then briefly introduce the Arc Index Formulation where the notations used to describe the MILP model are summarized in Table 1.

Because of the limited space, some details such as the binary and general integrality constraints, non-negativity constraints, sub-tour elimination constraints, penalty function piecewise constraints and the decision variables relative to those constraints, which can be found in [11], will not be introduced here.

Table 1. The summary of notations

Sets and Parameters	Description
V	The vehicle set, indexed by $v = 1, \ldots, \lvert V\rvert$
k_v	Capacity of vehicle $v \in V$
N_s	The station node set, indexed by $i = 1, \ldots, \lvert N_s\rvert$
N_0	The station node set with depot where the depot is indexed by $i = 0$
s_i^0	Number of bikes at station i before the rebalancing operation
c_i	Number of docks at station i
$f_i(s_i)$	The penalty function for station $i \in N_s$
t_{ij}	Travel cost from station i to station j, here is the travel time in seconds
L	Time for remove a bike from a dock and load it onto the vehicle
U	Time for unload a bike from the vehicle and hook it to a dock
T	Total time for the rebalancing operation
α	Trade-off factor of travel cost and bike shortage
Decision variables	**Description**
x_{ijv}	Binary variable equals to 1 if vehicle travels from station i to station j, equals to 0 for otherwise
y_{ijv}	Number of bikes on vehicle when it travels from station i to station j, equals to 0 if vehicle dose not travel from station i to station j
y_{iv}^L	Number of bikes loaded onto vehicle v at station i
y_{iv}^U	Number of bikes unloaded from vehicle v at station i
s_i	Number of bikes at station i after rebalancing operation

The Arc Index (AI) is formulated by following objective function and constraints:

$$\min \sum_{i\in N_s} f_i(s_i) + \alpha \sum_{i\in N_0}\sum_{j\in N_0}\sum_{v\in V} t_{ij}x_{ijv} \tag{5}$$

s.t.

$$s_i = s_i^0 - \sum_{v\in V}\left(y_{iv}^L - y_{iv}^U\right) \quad \forall i \in N_0 \tag{6}$$

$$y_{iv}^L - y_{iv}^U = \sum_{j\in N_0, i\neq j} y_{ijv} - \sum_{j\in N_0, i\neq j} y_{jiv} \quad \forall i \in N_0, \forall v \in V \tag{7}$$

$$y_{ijv} \le k_v x_{ijv} \quad \forall i, j \in \mathrm{N}_0, i \neq j, \forall v \in V \tag{8}$$

$$\sum_{j\in N_0, i\neq j} x_{ijv} = \sum_{j\in N_0, i\neq j} x_{jiv} \quad \forall i \in N_0, \forall v \in V \tag{9}$$

$$\sum_{j\in N_0, i\neq j} x_{ijv} \le 1 \quad \forall i \in N_s, \forall v \in V \tag{10}$$

$$\sum_{j\in N_0, i\neq j} x_{ijv} \le 1 \quad \forall i \in N_0, \forall v \in V \tag{11}$$

$$\sum_{v\in V} y_{iv}^L \le s_i^0 \quad \forall i \in N_0 \tag{12}$$

$$\sum_{v\in V} y_{iv}^U \le c_i - s_i^0 \quad \forall i \in N_0 \tag{13}$$

$$\sum_{i\in N_0} \left(y_{iv}^L - y_{iv}^U \right) = 0 \quad \forall \in \text{V} \tag{14}$$

$$\sum_{i\in N_s} \left(Ly_{iv}^L + Uy_{iv}^U \right) + \sum_{i\in N_s} \left(Ly_{0iv}^L + Uy_{0iv}^U \right) + \sum_{i,j\in N_0 : i\neq j} t_{ij} x_{ijv} \le T \quad \forall v \in V \tag{15}$$

The objective function (5) minimizes the bike shortage and the travel cost with a trade-off parameter α . Constraints (6) are inventory-balance constraints. For each station, the number of bikes after rebalancing operation is the original number of bikes plus the sum of load (positive) and unload (negative) instructions by all vehicles. Constraints (7) represent the conservation of inventory for each vehicle. When a vehicle travels through one station, checking the cross in y_v can determine the past station and the next station, then the difference of two numbers in y_v is the number of bikes loaded or unloaded in that station. Constraints (8) limit the vehicle capacity. If a vehicle does not travel through two stations directly, the corresponding element in x_v will be zero, hence there is no capacity. Constraints (9) ensure the travel frequency from one station is equal to the travel frequency to that station. Constraints (10) restrict each station to be visited at most once by the same vehicle, while the depot can be visited more than one time. To fit our problem definition, we modify constraints (10) to constraints (11) which also restrict that the depot can be visited at most one time. Constraints (12) and constraints (13) limit the pick-up quantity and drop-off quantity for one station by all vehicles respectively. Constraints (14) make sure that the sum of pick-up quantity and the sum of drop-off quantity are equal. Constraints (15) are the time limit constraints for each vehicle which consist of the total instruction time and the total travel time.

In addition, since the execution time allowed for the route optimization is limited, time assignments for each single-vehicle bike rebalancing problem will be difficult because some clusters with more stations will take a longer time. To address the problem of time assignments, we use only one MILP model to solve the multi-vehicle bike rebalancing problem while the decision variables and constraints are still can be reduced according to the clustering result.

After reducing the decision variables and constraints of MILP model, we conduct the optimization to get the final result of the static bike rebalancing problem.

So far, we have already demonstrated the proposed method completely. The proposed method starts from using the penalty function to compute the station rebalancing target and the average saved shortage. The average saved shortage is used to discriminate the importance of each station and the station rebalancing target is used to check the balance condition. Then, before using the MILP model to solve the static bike rebalancing problem, we first utilize the clustering algorithm to divide all stations into several clusters and some outlier stations and then use these assignments to reduce the number of decision variables and constraints in the MILP model. Finally, the MILP model with reduced decision variables and constraints is used to solve the final rebalancing routes and instructions for each vehicle in limited time.

In summary, based on the clustering result generated by the proposed PDF3C algorithm, which allows the station rebalancing target to be partially considered by different vehicles, stations with large rebalancing targets can be satisfied by multiple vehicles. In addition, some outlier stations can be further fulfilled according to the priority provided by the designed average saved shortage.

5 Experiment

In this section, we will introduce the dataset, the baseline method and competitors in Section 5.1, and presents the experiment results in Section 5.2.

5.1 Comparative Environment

We used the dataset provided by [3]. This dataset has 200 stations with different workloads corresponding to different initial inventories according to the light, real and heavy case for each station. There are 3 vehicles with the capacity of 25 in our rebalance planning. The pick-up and drop-off time for each rebalancing instruction is 60s and the time budget for rebalancing operations is 18000s.

To verify the effectiveness of the proposed PDF3C algorithm, denoted as PDF3C, we use the pure MILP model named Arc Index Formulation as the baseline method [11], denoted as Arc Index. In addition to the baseline method, we have two other clustering methods as competitors, one is the original CCKC algorithm [8], denoted as CCKC, and the other is the 3-Step Math Heuristic method [3], denoted as 3-Step MH. All algorithms are adjusted based on the same assumption that the depot can be visited by each vehicle at most once which are similar as the constraint (10) and (11), and outlier station removing is also applied to CCKC to avoid cluster disappearing.

About the parameter setting, for the MILP model, the trade-off factor is 1/900 and the execution time limit is 3600s [3]; for clustering algorithms, according to the trade-off factor, the benefit threshold of PDF3C is also 1/900, the distance threshold of CCKC is 900 and the diameter of 3-Step MH is 800 [3] where this value of diameter is set according to some empirical tuning. We also conducted some experiments to tune the parameter and got a same conclusion of the diameter setting.

5.2 Experiment Results

In our experiments, we compare the objective value and the optimality gap calculated by a commercial solver where the objective value demonstrates the goodness of founded solution and the optimality gap roughly represents how much can the founded solution be improved. In addition, since with different order of the same clustering result to reduce the problem scale of the MILP model will get different results, we observe experiment results both from the average case and the best case for all possible permutations of the clustering result.

All experiments were conducted on an Intel personal computer with Intel(R) Core(TM) i5-3470 CPU, 3.20GHz and 8 GB memory running Microsoft Windows 7 Ultimate system where the MILP models were solved by the Gurobi optimizer [5] with version 7.0 in java code.

Experiment results for the average case and the best case are summarized in Table 2 and the best result for each instance is represented in bold font. In this table, instance names are represented by workload and the number of stations, Obj. represents the objective value of founded solution and Gap. represents the optimality gap of the founded solution in percentage which is calculated by the Gurobi optimizer.

Table 2. Experiment results for the average case and the best case

Instance	PDF3C		CCKC		3-Step MH		Arc Index	
	Avg. Obj.	Avg. Gap.	Avg. Obj.	Avg. Gap.	Avg. Obj.	Avg. Gap.	Obj.	Gap.
light 75	509.555	0.399	**508.463**	0.418	512.222	0.010	520.528	5.194
light 100	**685.204**	0.274	687.854	0.035	688.304	0.010	722.039	8.602
light 125	**855.062**	0.205	855.866	0.250	861.303	0.010	924.101	10.796
light 150	**1039.630**	0.632	1043.454	0.765	1052.244	0.459	1127.402	11.458
light 175	1233.580	1.362	**1233.324**	1.238	1250.976	1.494	1333.669	12.234
light 200	**1444.372**	1.828	1455.367	2.244	1514.556	0.611	1548.963	12.848
real 75	507.252	0.109	**504.384**	0.019	504.724	0.004	516.668	4.733
real 100	668.604	0.146	**667.845**	0.082	668.952	0.010	681.892	4.270
real 125	**834.725**	0.296	837.647	0.420	841.998	0.410	910.069	10.882
real 150	**1018.724**	0.223	1040.734	0.409	1030.525	0.771	1124.391	12.260
real 175	**1206.169**	1.211	1227.719	1.269	1249.441	0.879	1329.185	12.779
real 200	**1428.183**	3.233	1444.278	2.984	1480.173	0.982	1541.856	13.497
heavy 75	561.730	0.911	578.947	0.793	**555.386**	1.249	593.341	12.960
heavy 100	780.531	2.441	804.379	1.333	**767.020**	1.242	951.194	26.050
heavy 125	1023.788	3.577	1035.414	2.286	**1022.520**	2.196	1282.824	28.981
heavy 150	**1302.080**	5.719	1315.156	3.890	1336.187	2.697	1610.413	28.884
heavy 175	1637.992	7.923	**1615.940**	2.596	1632.715	2.370	1921.630	26.361
heavy 200	1991.767	5.803	1995.559	2.573	**1973.379**	2.319	2289.897	22.679
Instance	PDF3C		CCKC		3-Step MH		Arc Index	
	Best Obj.	Gap.	Best Obj.	Gap.	Best Obj.	Gap.	Obj.	Gap.
light 75	509.545	0.397	**508.434**	0.407	512.217	0.010	520.528	5.194
light 100	**684.942**	0.270	687.840	0.021	688.304	0.010	722.039	8.602
light 125	**854.803**	0.179	855.430	0.177	861.303	0.010	924.101	10.796
light 150	**1038.536**	0.527	1041.374	0.558	1051.487	0.347	1127.402	11.458
light 175	**1227.199**	0.854	1228.484	0.839	1248.653	1.298	1333.669	12.234
light 200	**1441.197**	1.686	1446.067	1.549	1513.980	0.573	1548.963	12.848
real 75	507.252	0.088	**504.384**	0.010	504.724	0.000	516.668	4.733
real 100	668.597	0.119	**667.845**	0.076	668.952	0.010	681.892	4.270
real 125	**834.330**	0.245	837.313	0.381	841.496	0.342	910.069	10.882
real 150	**1018.612**	0.209	1039.471	0.287	1030.022	0.737	1124.391	12.260
real 175	**1199.583**	0.639	1219.084	0.556	1249.082	0.852	1329.185	12.779
real 200	**1411.006**	1.776	1424.283	1.687	1477.667	0.834	1541.856	13.497
heavy 75	561.382	0.804	578.746	0.749	**554.514**	1.036	593.341	12.960
heavy 100	777.920	2.140	801.396	0.900	**765.693**	1.123	951.194	26.050
heavy 125	**1014.320**	2.864	1028.533	1.610	1016.794	1.657	1282.824	28.981
heavy 150	**1262.569**	2.719	1304.244	2.971	1333.634	2.499	1610.413	28.884
heavy 175	1607.221	5.917	**1606.779**	1.951	1631.089	2.402	1921.630	26.361
heavy 200	**1939.325**	3.339	1977.846	1.748	1965.346	1.860	2289.897	22.679

As we can see, the proposed PDF3C algorithm outperforms two competitors and the baseline method in most instances, especially in the best case. As for the heavy workload instances in the average case we do not get the best result since the problem scale is still large because too many stations with partial demand are considered. However, the best case can be interpreted as the quality of clustering result. Our PDF3C algorithm utilizes the mechanism of partial demand including and the concept of average saved shortage to cover more valuable stations and generate clusters with higher potential quality.

6 Conclusions and Future Work

In this paper, we proposed a Partial Demand Fulfilling Capacity Constrained Clustering (PDF3C) algorithm to reduce the problem scale of the static bike rebalancing problem. The PDF3C algorithm can discover outlier stations and group remaining stations into several clusters. Furthermore, our PDF3C algorithm allows the demands of one station to be partially considered by different clusters and considers the average saved shortage for each station to increase the potential quality of generated clusters. Experiment results verified that using the clustering results generated by our algorithm to reduce the number of decision variables and constraints in the MILP model can get better results than other clustering algorithms or pure MILP model. In future works, based on current clustering results generated by our PDF3C algorithm, we will try to utilize other reduction manners to further reduce the problem scale to get better results.

References

1. Benchimol, M., Benchimol, P., Chappert, B., De La Taille, A., Laroche, F., Meunier, F., Robinet, L.: Balancing the stations of a self service "bike hire" system. RAIRO-Oper. Res. 45(1), 37-61 (2011).
2. Chemla, D., Meunier, F., and Calvo, R. W.: Bike sharing systems: Solving the static rebalancing problem. Discrete Optim. 10(2), 120-149 (2013).
3. Forma, I.A., Raviv, T., Tzur, M.: A 3-step math heuristic for the static repositioning problem in bike-sharing systems. Transport. Res. B-Meth. 71(Supplement C), 230-247 (2015).
4. Gaspero, L.D., Rendl, A., Urli, T.: Constraint-based approaches for Balancing Bike Sharing Systems. In: Christian, S. (ed.) CP 2013, LNCS, vol. 8124, pp. 758-773. Springer, Heidelberg (2013).
5. Gurobi Optimization, Inc.: Gurobi Optimizer Reference Manual (2016). http://www.gurobi.com
6. Ho, S.C., Szeto, W.Y.: Solving a static repositioning problem in bike-sharing systems using iterated tabu search. Transport. Res. D-Tr.E. 69(Supplement C), 180-198 (2014).
7. Kloimüllner, C., Papazek, P., Hu, B., Raidl, G.R.: A Cluster-First Route-Second Approach for Balancing Bicycle Sharing Systems. In: Roberto, M.D., Franz, P., Alexis, Q.A. (eds.) EUROCAST 2015, LNCS, vol. 9520, pp. 439-446. Springer, Heidelberg (2015).

8. Liu, J., Sun, L., Chen, W., Xiong, H.: Rebalancing Bike Sharing Systems: A Multi-source Data Smart Optimization. In: Proceedings of the 22nd ACM SIGKDD International Conference on Knowledge Discovery and Data Mining, pp. 1005-1014, ACM (2016).
9. Meddin, R., DeMaio, P.: The bike sharing world map (2017). http://www. metrobike.net
10. Papazek, P., Kloimüllner, C., Hu, B., Raidl, G.R.: Balancing Bicycle Sharing Systems: An Analysis of Path Relinking and Recombination within a GRASP Hybrid In: Bartz-Beielstein, T., Branke, J., Filipič, B., Smith, J. (eds.) PPSN 2014, Part XIII, LNCS, vol. 8672, pp. 792-801. Springer, Heidelberg (2014).
11. Raviv, T., Tzur, M., Forma, I.A.: Static repositioning in a bike-sharing system: models and solution approaches. EJTL. 2(3), 187-229 (2013).
12. Raviv, T., Kolka, O.: Optimal inventory management of a bike-sharing station. IIE Transactions 45(10), 1077-1093 (2013).
13. Rainer-Harbach, M., Papazek, P., Raidl, G. R., Hu, B., Kloim¨ullner, C.: PILOT, GRASP, and VNS approaches for the static balancing of bicycle sharing systems. J. Global Optim. 63(3), 597-629 (2015).
14. Schuijbroek, J., Hampshire, R.C., van Hoeve, W.J.: Inventory rebalancing and vehicle routing in bike sharing systems. EJOR. 257(3), 992-1004 (2017).
15. Szeto, W.Y., Liu, Y., Ho, S. C.: Chemical reaction optimization for solving a static bike repositioning problem. Transport. Res. D-Tr.E. 47(Supplement C), 104-135 (2016).

A Novel Parallel Algorithm for Frequent Itemsets Mining in Large Transactional Databases

Huan Phan[1,2[✉]] and Bac Le[3]

[1] Division of IT, University of Social Sciences and Humanities, VNU-HCM, Vietnam
[2] Faculty of Mathematics and Computer Science, University of Science, VNU-HCM, Vietnam
huanphan@hcmussh.edu.vn
[3] Faculty of IT, University of Science, VNU-HCM, Vietnam
lhbac@fithcmus.edu.vn

Abstract. Since the era of data explosion, data mining in large transactional databases has become more and more important. There are many data mining techniques like association rule mining, the most important and well-researched one. Furthermore, frequent itemset mining is one of the fundamental but time-consuming steps in association rule mining. Most of the algorithms used in literature find frequent itemsets on search space items having at least a *minsup* and are not reused for subsequent mining. Therefore, in order to decrease the execution time, some parallel algorithms have been proposed for mining frequent itemsets. Nonetheless, these algorithms merely implement the parallelization of Apriori and FP-Growth algorithms. To deal with this problem, several parallel NPA-FI algorithms are proposed as a new approach in order to quickly detect frequent itemsets from large transactional databases using an array of co-occurrences and occurrences of kernel item in at least one transaction. Parallel NPA-FI algorithms are easily used in many distributed file system, namely Hadoop and Spark. Finally, the experimental results show that the proposed algorithms perform better than other existing algorithms.

Keywords: Association rules, Co-occurrence items, Frequent itemsets, Parallel algorithm.

1 Introduction

Mining frequent itemsets is a fundamental and essential problem in many data mining applications such as the discovery of association rules, strong rules, correlations, multi-dimensional patterns, and many other important discovery tasks. The problem is formulated as follows: Given a large database of set of items transactions, find all frequent itemsets, where a frequent itemset is one that occurs in at least a user-specified percentage of transaction database [4].

In the last three decades, most of the mining algorithms for frequent itemsets, proposed by various authors around the world, are based on Apriori [5] and FP-Tree [6,9]. Simultaneously to speed up the implementation of the mining frequent itemsets, authors worldwide propose the parallelization of algorithms based on the Apriori [1,7] and FP-Tree [8]. In this paper, we propose a novel sequential algorithm that mines frequent itemsets, and then, parallelizing the sequential algorithm to demonstrate the multi-core processors in an effective way as follows.

— **Algorithm 1**: Computing Kernel_COOC array of co-occurrences and occurrences of kernel item in at least one transaction;
— **Algorithm 2**: Generating all frequent itemsets based on Kernel_COOC array;
— Parallel **NPA-FI** algorithm quickly mining frequent itemsets from large transactional databases implemented on the multi-core processors.

This paper is organized as follows: in section 2, we describe the basic concepts for mining frequent itemsets, benchmark datasets description and data structure for transaction databases. Some theoretical aspects of our approach relies, are given in section 3. Besides, we describe our sequential algorithm to compute frequent itemsets on large transactional databases. After that we parallelize the proposed sequential algorithm. Details on implementation and experimental tests are discussed in section 4. Finally, we conclude with a summary of our approach, perspectives and extensions of this future work.

2 Background

2.1 Frequent Itemset Mining

Let $\{i$ $\}$ be a set of distinct items. A set of items $\{i$ $\}$, is called an itemset, an itemset with items is called a set. **D** be a dataset containing transaction, a set of transaction $\{t$ $\}$, and each transaction $t_j = \{i$, $\}$,

Definition 1. The support of an itemset X is the number of transaction in which occurs as a subset, denoted as).

Definition 2. Let be the threshold minimum support value specified by user. If su p, itemset X is called a frequent itemset, denoted FI is the set of all the frequent itemset.

Property 1. $\forall X$

Property 2. $\forall X$

See an example transaction database in Table 1.

Table 1. The Transaction database $\mathcal{D}$ used as our running example.

TID	Items							
t1	A		C		E	F		
t2	A		C				G	
t3					E			H
t4	A		C	D		F	G	
t5	A		C		E		G	
t6					E			
t7	A	B	C		E			
t8	A		C	D				
t9	A	B	C		E		G	
10	A		C		E	F	G	

Table 2. Mining frequent itemsets.

k-itemset	FI (minsup = 2)	FI (minsup = 3)	FI (minsup = 5)
1	D, B, F, G, E, A, C	F, G, E, A, C	G, E, A, C
2	BE, BA, BC, DA, DC, FE, FG, FA, FC, GE, GA, GC, EA, EC, AC	FA, FC, GE, GA, GC, EA, EC, AC	GA, GC, EA, EC, AC
3	BAC, BEA, DAC, FEA, BEC, FEC, FGA, CFG, FAC, GEA, GEC, EAC, GAC	FAC, GEA, GEC, GAC, EAC	GAC, EAC
4	BEAC, FGAC, FEAC, GEAC	GEAC	

Example 1. See Table 1. There are eight different items $\{A, B, C, D, E, F, G, H\}$ and ten transactions $\{t$ $\}$. Table 2 shows the frequent itemsets at three different minsup values–2 (20%), 3 (30%) and 5 (50%) respectively.

2.2 Benchmark Description

Djenouri *et al* categorized the datasets: Three types of well-known instance details the characteristic of these benchmarks [10].

Table 3. Datasets description.

Instance type	#Trans	#Items	#Avg.Length
Medium	6,000 *to* 9,000	500 *to* 16,000	2 *to* 500
Large	100,000 *to* 500,000	1,000 *to* 1,600	2 *to* 10
Big	*up* 1,600,000	*up* 500,000	

2.3 Data Structure for Transaction Database

The binary matrix is an efficient data structure for mining frequent itemsets [2,3]. The process begins with the transaction database transformed into a binary matrix BiM, in which each row corresponds to a transaction and each column corresponds to an item. Each element in the binary matrix BiM contains 1 if the item is presented in the current transaction; otherwise it contains 0.

TID	A	B	C	D	E	F	G	H
t1	1	0	1	0	1	1	0	0
t2	1	0	1	0	0	0	1	0
t3	0	0	0	0	1	0	0	1
t4	1	0	1	1	0	1	1	0
t5	1	0	1	0	1	0	1	0
t6	0	0	0	0	1	0	0	0
t7	1	1	1	0	1	0	0	0
t8	1	0	1	1	0	0	0	0
t9	1	1	1	0	1	0	1	0
t10	1	0	1	0	1	1	1	0

Fig. 1. A binary matrix BiM representation of example transaction database.

3 The Proposed Algorithms

3.1 Generating Array of Co-occurrence Items of Kernel Item

In this part, we illustrate the framework of the algorithm generating co-occurrence items of items in transaction database.

Definition 3. Project set of item i_k on database $\mathcal{D}$: $\pi(i_k) = \{t_j \in \mathcal{D} | i_k \subseteq t_j\}$ is set of transaction contain item i_k ($\pi-decreasing\ monotonic$). According to Definition 1:

(1)

Example 2. See Table 1. Consider item B, we detect project set of item B on database $\mathcal{D}$: $\pi(B) = \{t_7, t_9\}$ then $sup(B) = |\pi(B)| = 2$.

Definition 4. Project set of itemset $X = \{i_1, i_2, \dots i_k\}, \forall i_{j=\overline{1,k}}$
).

(2)

Example 3. See Table 1. Consider item E, we detect project set of item E on database $\{t$ $\}$ then
$|\{t$ $\} \cap \{t$ $\}|$ $|\{t$ $\}|$ 2.

Definition 5. Let is called a kernel item. Itemset is called co-occurrence items with kernel item i_k, so that satisfy). Denoted as .

Example 4. See Table 1. Consider item B as kernel item, we detect co-occurrence items with item as $cooc(B) = \{A$ $E\}$ and $sup(B) = sup(BACE) = 2$.

Definition 6. Let is called a kernel item. Itemset $Y_{looc} \subseteq I$ is called occurrence items with kernel item in as least one transaction, but not co-occurrence items, so that satisfy 1 . Denoted as .

Example 5. See Table 1. Consider item as kernel item, we detect occurrence items with item in as least one transaction $\{G\}$ and $\pi(BG) = \{t_9\}$ $\{t$ $\}$.

Algorithm Generating Array of Co-occurrence Items

This algorithm is generating co-occurrence items of items in transaction database and archive into the *Kernel_COOC* array. Each element within the *Kernel_COOC*, 4 fields:

- Kernel_COOC[k].*item* : kernel item k;
- Kernel_COOC[k].*sup* : support of kernel item k;
- Kernel_COOC[k].*cooc* : co-occurrence items with kernel item k;
- Kernel_COOC[k].*looc* : occurrence items kernel item in least one transaction.

The framework of **Algorithm 1** is as follows:

Algorithm 1. Generating Array of Co-occurrence Items

Input : Dataset D

Output: *Kernel_COOC array, matrix BiM*

foreach Kernel_COOC[k] **do**
  Kernel_COOC[k].item = i_k
  Kernel_COOC[k].sup = 0
  Kernel_COOC[k].cooc = 2
  Kernel_COOC[k].looc = 0
foreach $t_j \in T$ **do**
  foreach $i_k \in t_j$ **do**
    Kernel_COOC[k].sup ++
    Kernel_COOC[k].cooc = Kernel_COOC[k].cooc **AND** vectorbit(t
    Kernel_COOC[k].looc = Kernel_COOC[k].looc **OR** vectorbit(t
sort Kernel_COOC array in ascending by support

We illustrate **Algorithm 1** on example database in Table 1.

Initialization of the Kernel_COOC array, number items in database m= 8;

Item	A	B	C	D	E	F	G	H
sup	0	0	0	0	0	0	0	0
cooc	11111111	11111111	11111111	11111111	11111111	11111111	11111111	11111111
looc	00000000	00000000	00000000	00000000	00000000	00000000	00000000	00000000

Read once of each transaction from *t1* to *t10*

Transaction $t1$ = $\{A \quad F\}$ has vector bit representation **10101100**;

Item	A	B	C	D	E	F	G	H
sup	1	0	1	0	1	1	0	0
cooc	**10101100**	11111111	**10101100**	11111111	**10101100**	**10101100**	11111111	11111111
looc	**10101100**	00000000	**10101100**	00000000	**10101100**	**10101100**	00000000	00000000

Transaction $\{A \quad G\}$ has vector bit representation **10100010**;

Item	A	B	C	D	E	F	G	H
sup	2	0	2	0	1	1	1	0
cooc	**10100000**	11111111	**10100000**	11111111	10101100	10101100	**10100010**	11111111
looc	**10101110**	00000000	**10101110**	00000000	10101100	10101100	**10100010**	00000000

Transaction $\{E \ H\}$ has vector bit representation **00001001**;

Item	A	B	C	D	E	F	G	H
sup	2	0	2	0	2	1	1	1
cooc	10100000	11111111	10100000	11111111	**00001000**	10101100	10100010	**00001001**
looc	10101110	00000000	10101110	00000000	**10101101**	10101100	10100010	**00001001**

Transaction $\{A \quad G\}$ has vector bit representation **10110110**;

Item	A	B	C	D	E	F	G	H
sup	3	0	3	1	2	2	2	1
cooc	**10100000**	11111111	**10100000**	**10110110**	00001000	**10100100**	**10100010**	00001001
looc	**10111110**	00000000	**10111110**	**10110110**	10101101	**10111110**	**10110110**	00001001

Transaction {A G} has vector bit representation **10101010**;

Item	A	B	C	D	E	F	G	H
sup	4	0	4	1	3	2	3	1
cooc	**10100000**	11111111	**10100000**	10110110	**00001000**	10100100	**10100010**	00001001
looc	**10111110**	00000000	**10111110**	10110110	**10101111**	10111110	**10111110**	00001001

Transaction {E} has vector bit representation **00001000**;

Item	A	B	C	D	E	F	G	H
sup	4	0	4	1	4	2	3	1
cooc	10100000	11111111	10100000	10110110	**00001000**	10100100	10100010	00001001
looc	10111110	00000000	10111110	10110110	**10101111**	10111110	10111110	00001001

Transaction {A E} has vector bit representation **11101000**;

Item	A	B	C	D	E	F	G	H
sup	5	1	5	1	5	2	3	1
cooc	**10100000**	**11101000**	**10100000**	10110110	**00001000**	10100100	10100010	00001001
looc	**11111110**	**11101000**	**11111110**	10110110	**11101111**	10111110	10111110	00001001

Transaction {A D} has vector bit representation **10110000**;

Item	A	B	C	D	E	F	G	H
sup	6	1	6	2	5	2	3	1
cooc	**10100000**	11101000	**10100000**	**10110000**	00001000	10100100	10100010	00001001
looc	**11111110**	11101000	**11111110**	**10110110**	11101111	10111110	10111110	00001001

Transaction {A G} has vector bit representation **11101010**;

Item	A	B	C	D	E	F	G	H
sup	7	2	7	2	6	2	4	1
cooc	**10100000**	**11101000**	**10100000**	10110000	**00001000**	10100100	**10100010**	00001001
looc	**11111110**	**11101010**	**11111110**	10110110	**11101111**	10111110	**11111110**	00001001

The last, transaction {A G} has vector bit representation **10101110**;

Item	A	B	C	D	E	F	G	H
sup	8	2	8	2	7	3	5	1
cooc	**10100000**	11101000	**10100000**	10110000	**00001000**	**10100100**	**10100010**	00001001
looc	**11111110**	11101010	**11111110**	10110110	**11101111**	**10111110**	**11111110**	00001001

After the processing of **Algorithm 1**, the Kernel_COOC array as follows:

Table 4. Kernel_COOC array are ordered in support ascending order.

Item	H	B	D	F	G	E	A	C
sup	1	2	2	3	5	7	8	8
cooc	E	A, C, E	A, C	A, C	A, C		C	A
looc		G	F, G	D, E, G	B, D, E, F	A,B,C,F,G,H	B,D,E,F,G	B,D,E,F,G

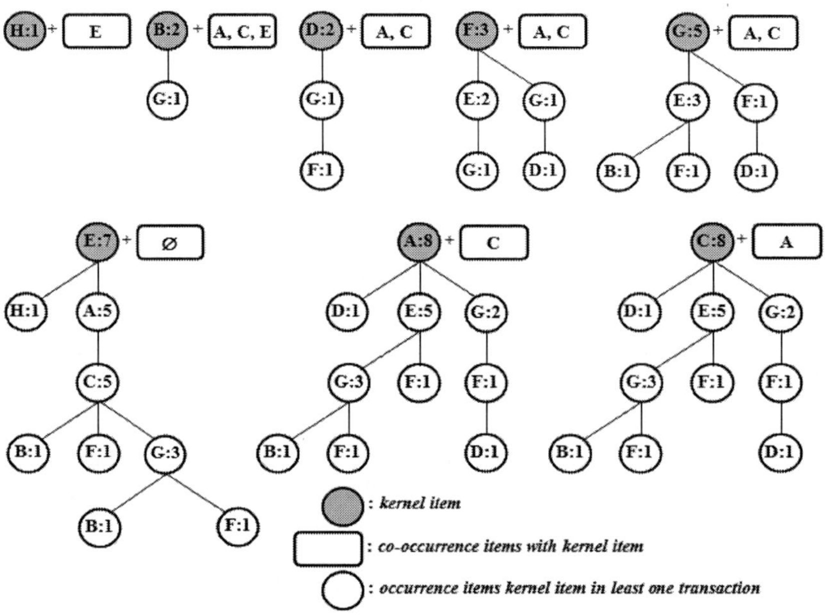

Fig. 2. The pattern-tree of occurrence items with kernel item in as least one transaction.

See Table 3 and Figure 2, we have *cooc*(A) = {C} and *cooc*(C) = {A}. In this case, the frequent itemset generated from A and C items will be duplicated. We provide a Definition 7, 8 to eliminate the duplication when generating frequent itemsets.

Definition 7. Let $i_k \in I(i_1 \prec i_2 \prec \cdots \prec i_m)$ items are ordered in support ascending order, is called a kernel item. Itemset I is called co-occurrence items with the kernel item i_k, so that satisfy $\pi(i_k \cup i_j), i_k \prec i_j, \forall i_j \in X_{lexcooc}$. Denoted as .

Definition 8. Let items are ordered in support ascending order, is called a kernel item. Itemset I is called occurrence items with kernel item in as least one transaction, but not co-occurrence items, so that satisfy . Denoted as

.

Additional command line 12, 13 and 14 into **Algorithm 1**:

```
12:     foreach i_k ∈ t_j do
13:         Kernel_COOC[k].cooc = lexcooc(i_k)
14:         Kernel_COOC[k].looc = lexlooc(i_k)
```

We have *looc*(G) = {B, D, E, F}, where *B*, *E*, so *lexlooc*(G) = {E}. Execute command line 12, 13 and 14 has result on Table 4.

Table 5. the Kernel_COOC array are co-occurrence items ordered in support ascending order.

Item	H	B	D	F	G	E	A	C
sup	1	2	2	3	5	7	8	8
cooc	E	A, C, E	A, C	A,C	A, C	∅	C	∅
looc	∅	G	F, G	G, E	E	A, C	∅	∅

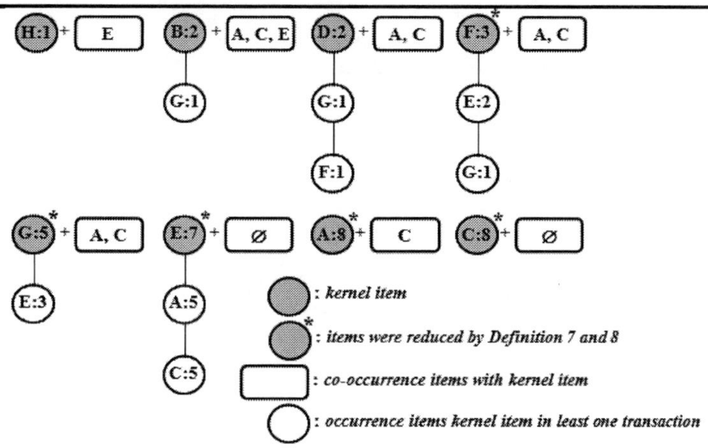

Fig. 3. The pattern-tree was reduced by Definition 7 and 8.

3.2 Algorithm Generating All Frequent Itemsets

In this part, we illustrate the framework of the algorithm generating all frequent itemsets bases on the $Kernel\_COOC$ array.

Lemma 1. $\forall i_k \in I$, if $sup(i_k) \geq minsup$ and) then

Proof. According to Definition 8, (1) and (2): then and ■.

Example 6. See Table 4. Consider the item as kernel item (*minsup* = 2), we detect co-occurrence items with the item F as $\{A\ C\}$ and $\{A \quad AC\}$, then p.

Lemma 2. , if and then p, .

Proof. According to Definition 8, 9: then
and . Therefore, we have
p, ■.

Example 7. See Table 4. Consider the item as kernel item (*minsup* = 2), we detect co-occurrence items with item G as le $= \{A, C\}$, $X_{lexcooc} = \{A, C, AC\}$; *lexlooc*(G) = {E} and *sup*(GE) = 3 ≥ then su
p.

The framework of **Algorithm 2** is presented as follows:

Algorithm 2. Generating all frequent itemsets satisfy *minsup*

```
     Input  : minsup, Kernel_COOC array, Dataset D
     Output: FI
1:   foreach Kernel_COOC[k].sup ≥ minsup do
2:     FI[k] = i_k
3:     if(Kernel_COOC[k].sup = minsup) then
4:       Co ← GenSub(Kernel_COOC[k].cooc)//generating noempty subsets of cooc
5:       foreach is_j ∈ Co do
6:         FI[k] = FI[k] ∪ {i_k ∪ is_j}
7:     else
8:       if(Kernel_COOC[k].cooc = ∅) then
9:         Lo ← GenSub(Kernel_COOC[k].looc)//generating noempty subsets of looc
10:        foreach is_j ∈ Lo do
11:          FI[k] = FI[k] ∪ {i_k ∪ is_j}
12:      else
13:        Co ← GenSub(Kernel_COOC[k].cooc)
14:        foreach is_j ∈ Co do
15:          F_t = F_t  {i        }
16:        Lo ← GenSub(Kernel_COOC[k].looc)
17:        foreach is_j ∈ Lo do
18:          F_k = F_k ∪ {i        }
19:        foreach f_i ∈ F_t do
20:          foreach is_j ∈ Lo do
21:            FI[k] = FI[k] ∪ {f        }
22:        FI[k] = FI[k] ∪
23:  sort FI in descending by support
```

We illustrate **Algorithm 2** on example database in Table 1, and *minsup* = 3. After the processing **Algorithm 1,** the Kernel_COOC array in Table 5 is showed.

Line 3, consider items satisfying *minsup* as kernel items {F, G, E, A, C};

Consider *kernel item F*, *sup*(F) = 3 = *minsup* (*Lemma 1-form line 5 to 6*) generating all frequent with *kernel item F* as $FI_{[F]}$ = {(**F**, 3), (**F**A, 3), (**F**C, 3), (**F**AC, 3)}.

Consider the *kernel item* G (*from line 12 to 21*): the powerset of co-occurrence items of *kernel item* G as set Co ={A, C, AC}, generating frequent itemsets F_t = {(GA, 5), (GA, 5), (GAC, 5)}; line 16 – generating noempty subsets of *looc* field Lo = {E}, F_k = {GE} – generating frequent itemsets $FI_{[G]}$ = {(G, 5), (GA, 5), (GC, 5), (GAC, 5), (GE, 3), (GEA, 3), (GEC, 3), (GEAC, 3)}.

Consider the *kernel item* E (*from line 8 to 11*): generating noempty subsets of *looc* field Lo = {A, C, AC}, line 10 and 11 – generating frequent itemsets $FI_{[E]}$ = {(E, 7), (EA, 5), (EC, 5), (EAC, 5)}.

Consider the *kernel item* A (similary *kernel item G*): Co = {C}, F_t ={(AC, 8)}, Lo = {∅}, F_k = {∅} – generating frequent itemsets $FI_{[A]}$ = {(A, 8), (AC, 8)}.

Consider the *kernel item* C (similary *kernel item* E): Lo = {∅} – generating frequent itemsets $FI_{[C]}$ = {(C, 8)}.

Table 6. All frequent itemsets satisfy *minsup* = 3 (example database in Table 1).

Kernel item	Frequent itemsets - **FI**							
F	(F,3)	(FA,3)	(FC,3)	(FAC,3)				
G	(GE,3)	(GEA,3)	(GEC,3)	(GEAC,3)	(GA,5)	(GC,5)	(GAC,5)	(G,5)
E	(EC,5)	(EA,5)	(EAC,5)	(E,7)				
A	(A,8)	(AC,8)						
C	(C,8)							

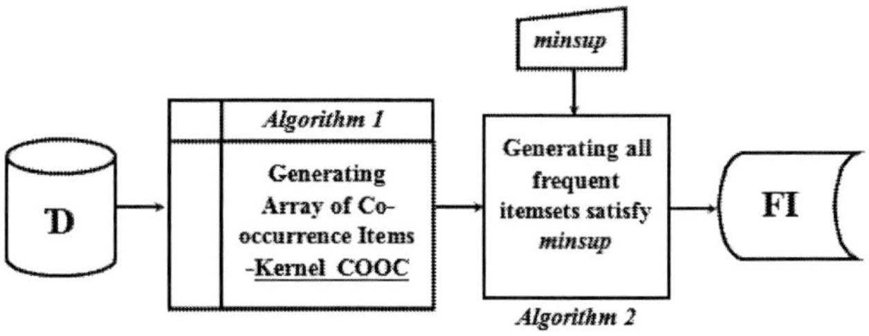

Fig. 4. The diagram sequential algorithm for frequent itemsets mining (SEQ-FI).

3.3 Parallel NPA-FI Algorithm Generating All Frequent Itemsets

In this section, we illustrate parallel algorithms and experimental setup on the multi-core processors (MCP). We proposed a parallel **NPA-FI** algorithm for because it quickly detects frequent itemsets on MCP using **Algorithm 1** and **Algorithm 2**.

The parallel **NPA-FI** algorithm for generating all frequent itemsets, including 2 phases:

- *Phase 1*: Computing Kernel_COOC array by parallelization **Algorithm 1**;
- *Phase 2*: Generating all frequent itemsets by parallelization **Algorithm 2**;

Phase 1 - Parallelization **Algorithm 1** is shown in the diagram:

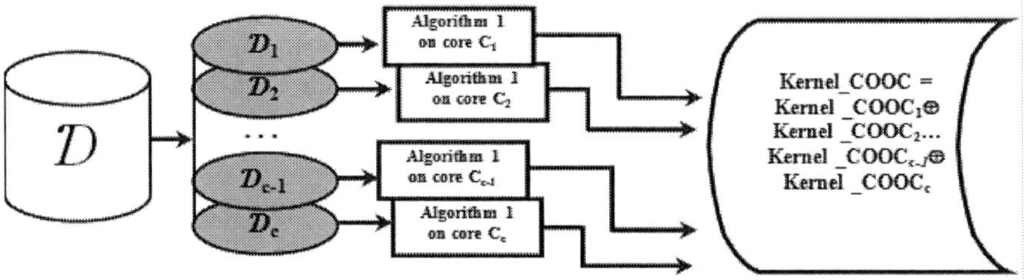

Fig. 5. The diagram parallelization Phase 1.

In Figure 5, we split the transaction database into *c* (*number of core on CPU*) parts $\mathcal{D}$ $\mathcal{D}$. After that, the core executes **Algorithm 1** with input transaction database , output the K array. The $Kernel\_COOC_{\mathcal{D}}$ array for the transaction database $\mathcal{D}$, we compute the following equation:

(3)

denoted as **sum** for *sup*, **AND** for *cooc*, **OR** for *looc* field of each element array.

The next step, we sort the *Kernel_COOC* array in ascending order by supporting, executing commands line 12, 13 and 14 of the **Algorithm 1**.

Example 8. See Table 1. We split the transaction database $\mathcal{D}$ into 2 parts: the database $\mathcal{D}_1$ consists 5 transaction $\{t_1, t_2, t_3, t_4, t_5\}$ and database $\mathcal{D}_2$ consists 5 transaction $\{t$ $t\}$.

The processing of **Algorithm 1** on database

Item	A	B	C	D	E	F	G	H
sup	4	0	4	1	3	2	3	1
cooc	10100000	11111111	10100000	10110110	00001000	10100100	10100010	00001001
looc	10111110	00000000	10111110	10110110	10101111	10111110	10111110	00001001

The processing of **Algorithm 1** on database

Item	A	B	C	D	E	F	G	H
sup	4	2	4	1	4	1	2	0
cooc	10100000	11101000	10100000	10110000	00001000	10101110	10101010	11111111
looc	11111110	11101010	11111110	10110000	11101110	10101110	11101110	00000000

Results of equation (3), we have the Kernel_COOC array as presented in Table 4.

Phase 2 – Parallelization of **Algorithm 2** is shown in the diagram:

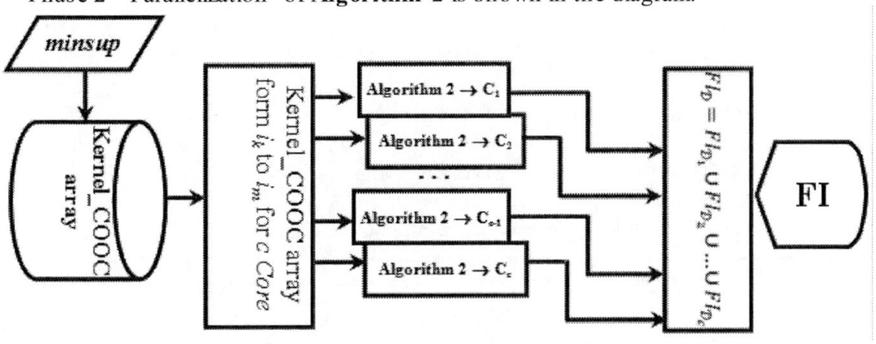

Fig. 6. The diagram parallelization Phase 2.

In Figure 6, we split the $Kernel\_COOC_{\mathcal{D}}$ array from element i_k to i_m (su) into c parts. After that, the core j th execute **Algorithm 2** with input C array from *k+(j-1)*((m-k+1) div c) to k+j*((m-k+1) div c)* element, returns results frequent itemsets $FI_{\mathcal{D}_j}$. The frequent itemsets $FI_{\mathcal{D}}$ for the transaction database $\mathcal{D}$, we compute the following equation:

(4)

Example 9. See Table 1. Generating all frequent itemsets satisfy *minsup= 3*, the transaction database $\mathcal{D}$ split into 2 parts as Example 6. Results of phase 1 parallelization, we have the $Kernel\_COOC_{\mathcal{D}}$ array as Table 5.

The processing of **Algorithm 2** on the Kernel_COOC array form *item* F to E:

Kernel item	Frequent itemsets -							
F	(F,3)	(FA,3)	(FC,3)	(FAC,3)				
G	(GE,3)	(GEA,3)	(GEC,3)	(GEAC,3)	(GA,5)	(GC,5)	(GAC,5)	(G,5)
E	(EC,5)	(EA,5)	(EAC,5)	(E,7)				

The processing of **Algorithm 2** on the Kernel_COOC array form *item* A to C:

Kernel item	Frequent itemsets -	
A	(A,8)	(AC,8)
C	(C,8)	

Results of equation (4), we have all frequent itemsets as presented in Table 6.

4 Experiments

All experiments were conducted on a PC with a Core Duo CPU T2500 2.0 GHz (*2 Cores, 2 Threads*), 4Gb main memory, running Microsoft Windows 7 Ultimate. All codes were compiled using C#, Microsoft Visual Studio 2010, .Net Framework 4.

We experimented on two instance types of datasets:

- Two real datasets that belong to *medium* instance are form of UCI Machine Learning Repository [http://archive.ics.uci.edu/ml] as **Pumsb** and **Retail** datasets.
- Two synthetic datasets that belong to *large* instance using the software are generated by IBM Almaden Research Center [http://www.almaden.ibm.com] as **T40I1KD100K** and **T40I1KD200K** datasets.

Table 7. Datasets description in experiments.

Instance type	Name	#Trans	#Items	#Avg.Length	Type
Medium	Pumsb	49,046	2,113	74	Dense
	Retail	88,162	16,470	10	Sparse
Large	T40I1KD100K	100,000	1,000	40	Sparse
	T40I1KD200K	200,000	1,000	40	Sparse

Deng et al, proposed the **PrePost** [9] algorithm for constructing a *FP-tree-like* and mining frequent itemsets from a database. In recent years, **PrePost** algorithm shows the better performance result. We have compared the parallel **NPA-FI** algorithm with sequential algorithms **(SEQ-FI)** and **PrePost** algorithm.

Performance implementation parallel **NPA-FI** algorithm on multi-core processors:

$$\left(T \quad -\right)/\left(\frac{Ts}{\ }\right) \qquad (5)$$

Where:

- : executing time of the sequential algorithm;
- : executing time of the parallel algorithm;
- : number of the core on CPU.

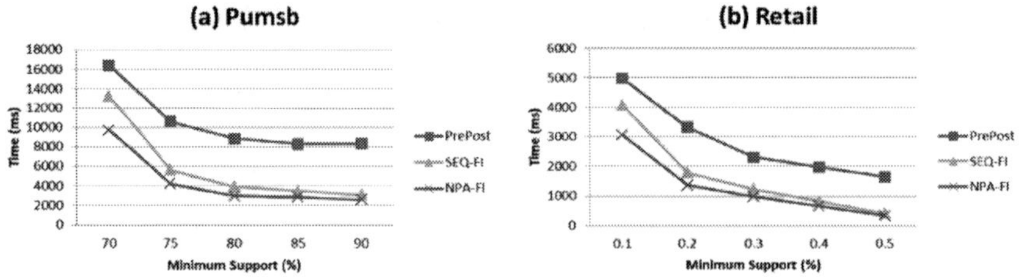

Fig. 7. Running time of the three algorithms on Medium datasets.

Figure 7 (a) and (b) show the running time of the compared algorithms on medium datasets **Pumsb** and **Retail**. **SEQ-FI** runs faster **PrePost** algorithm under all minimum supports; **NPA-FI** runs faster **SEQ-FI** algorithm. Average performance of the parallel **NPA-FI** algorithm in turn: **Pumsb** as $\overline{P}$ = 0.78 (78%); σ = 0.048 and **Retail** as $\overline{P}$ = 0.79 (79%); σ = 0.032.

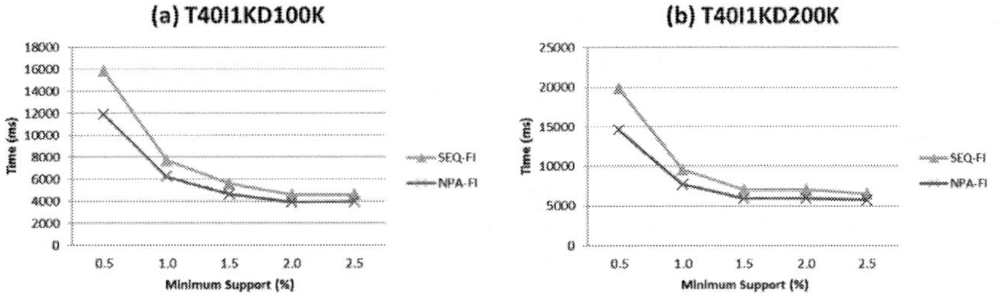

Fig. 8. Running time of the two algorithms on Large datasets.

Figure 8 (a) and (b) show the running time of the compared algorithms on large datasets **T40I1KD100K** and **T40I1KD200K**. **PrePost** algorithm fails to frequent itemsets mining on *large datasets*; **NPA-FI** runs faster **SEQ-FI** algorithm. Average performance of the parallel **NPA-FI** algorithm in turn: **T40I1KD100K** as $\bar{P}$ = 0.81 (81%); σ = 0.045 and **T40I1KD200K** as $\bar{P}$ = 0.81 (81%); σ = 0.052.

In summary, experimental results suggest the following ordering of these algorithms as running time is concerned: **SEQ-FI** runs faster **PrePost** algorithm; **NPA-FI** runs faster **SEQ-FI** algorithm. Average performance of the parallel **NPA-FI** algorithm on datasets experimental is $\bar{P}$ = 0.80 (80%); σ = 0.042.

5 Conclusion

In this paper, we have proposed a sequential architecture mining frequent itemsets on large transaction databases, consisting of two phases: *the first phase*, quickly detect a the Kernel_COOC array of co-occurrences and occurrences of kernel item in at least one transaction; *the second phase*, the algorithm is proposed for fast mining all frequent itemset based on Kernel_COOC array. Besides, when using mining frequent itemsets with *other minsup value* then the proposed algorithm only performs mining frequent itemsets based on the Kernel_COOC array that is calculated previously, reducing the significant processing time. The next step, we develop a sequential algorithm for mining frequent itemsets and thus parallelize the sequential algorithm to effectively demonstrate the multi-core processors. The experimental results show that the proposed algorithms perform better than other existing algorithms.

The results from the algorithm proposed: In the future, we will expand the algorithm to be able to mining frequent itemsets on weighted transaction databases, as well as to expand the parallel NPA-FI algorithm on distributed computing systems such as Hadoop, Spark.

Acknowledgements This work was supported by University of Social Sciences and Humanities; University of Science, VNU-HCM, Vietnam.

References

1. Agrawal R., Shafer J.: Parallel mining of association rules. IEEE Transactions on Knowledge and Data Engineering 8, 962–969 (1996).
2. Dong J., Han M.: BitTableFI: An efficient mining frequent itemsets algorithm. Knowledge-Based Systems 20(4), 329–335 (2007).
3. Song W., Yang B.: Index-BitTableFI: An improved algorithm for mining frequent itemsets. Knowledge-Based Systems 21, 507–513 (2008).
4. Philippe F. V., Jerry C. W. L., Bay V., Tin C. T., Ji Z., Bac L.: A survey of itemset mining.Wiley Interdisc. Rew - Data Mining and Knowledge Discovery, 7(4) (2017).
5. Agrawal R., Imilienski T., Swami A.: Mining association rules between sets of large databases. Proceedings of the ACM SIGMOD International Conference on Management of Data, Washington, DC, pp. 207–216 (1993).
6. Han J., Pei J., and Yin Y.: Mining frequent patterns without candidate generation. In Proc. 2000 ACM-SIGMOD Int. Conf. Management of Data (SIGMOD'00), Dallas, TX, pp. 1–12 (2000).
7. Lin M. Y., Lee P. Y., Hsueh S. C.: Apriori-based frequent itemset mining algorithms on MapReduce, Proc of the 6th International Conference on Ubiquitous Information Management and Communication, New York, NY, USA, pp. 76–76 (2012).
8. Moonesinghe H. D. K., Chung M. J., and Tan P. N.: Fast parallel mining of frequent itemsets. Technical Report No. 2, Department of Computer Science and Engineering, Michigan State University, (2006).
9. Deng Z. H., Wang Z. H. and Jiang J. J.: A new algorithm for fast mining frequent itemsets using N-lists. Science China Information Sciences, 55(9), 2008-2030 (2012).
10. Djenouri Y., Bendjoudi A., Djenouri D., Habbas Z.: Parallel Processing and Applied Mathematics, ISBN 978-3-319-32148-6, pp.258-268, (2016).

Data mining for municipal financial distress prediction

David Alaminos
PhD Student. Department of Finance and Accounting. University of Malaga, Malaga, Spain.
alaminos@uma.es

Sergio M. Fernández
PhD Student. Department of Languages and Computer Sciences. University of Malaga, Malaga, Spain.
sergiofernandezmiguelez@uma.es

Francisca García
Associate Professor. Department of Applied Economics. University of Malaga, Malaga, Spain.
fg_lopera@uma.es

Manuel A. Fernández
Associate Professor. Department of Finance and Accounting. University of Malaga, Malaga, Spain.
mangel@uma.es

Abstract

Data mining techniques are capable of extracting valuable knowledge from large and variable databases. This work proposes a data mining method for municipal financial distress prediction. Using a new proxy of municipal financial situation and a sample of 128 Spanish municipalities, the empirical experiment obtained satisfactory results, which testifies to the viability and validity of the data mining method proposed for municipal financial distress prediction.

Keywords: Financial distress prediction, Data mining, Municipalities, Individual classifiers, Local governments

1. Introduction

Municipal financial distress is a global phenomenon which has captured the attention of researchers and managers of public institutions with the aim of contributing to the continuity and financial sustainability of public services. After the last financial crisis, concerns about the debts incurred by municipalities have increased significantly. Municipal debts are particularly worrying because they affect not only the daily life of citizens but also local private companies, who depend on public decisions [1]. In this context, numerous models have been developed to assess municipal financial distress [2-4]. These models can be divided into two types [5]. On the one hand, the models which analyse the financial situation each year to determine if there exists a state of emergency. On the other hand, the models which analyse fiscal capacity by using tendencies to predict revenues and spending [6].

Although the models for assessing municipal financial distress have achieved significant success, one of the main limitations thereof is related to measurement of financial condition, since it is not directly observed and the researchers have created an index following previous work [7-8]. For this reason, current literature demands new research which will permit a comparison of results using others proxies of the financial situation [9]. With the objective of covering this gap, this work proposes a model for assessing municipal financial distress which incorporates a new proxy of financial situation. This new proxy is the criteria used by Spanish legislation, which refers to the ratio of default to municipal commercial debt. To that end, this work applied a data mining focus to a sample of Spanish municipalities, and this enabled their level of financial distress to be rated convincingly using a set of variables corresponding to 2015.

The work is organised in the following way. After the introduction, the second section offers a review of the literature relating to municipal financial distress prediction. The third section presents the model proposed and the different methodologies used. The fourth section is devoted to data collection and variables. In the fifth section we present the empirical results obtained. And lastly, in the sixth, we present the main conclusions and implications.

2. Literature Review

There is abundant research into municipal financial distress and it is characterised by the differing approaches and methods of analysis used. Initially, statistical techniques of logistic regression and discriminant analysis were used, and more recently, methods based on heuristic approaches, such as multi-criteria methods. For their part, the explanatory variables used have been financial ratios of liquidity, solvency, efficiency and activity and, in other cases, political variables such as fiscal decentralisation or even socio-economic variables such as the level of unemployment, population or quality of infrastructure, varying according to the financial proxy used. The first works to address municipal financial distress were carried out in countries such as the United States of America and Australia, where the availability of information was more advanced than in other developed countries. [10] carried out a study on the prediction and prevention of fiscal crises in local governments in the United States, concluding that less than half the cases attempted to predict municipal financial distress. The analysis determined that the lack of preparation on the part of politicians, business failures, demographic changes and the increase in the cost of public services were the causes of the financial crisis. For their part, [4] applied a model of nine indicators to a sample of municipalities in the state of Michigan, grading their fiscal distress on a scale of 0-10 points, and highlighting the importance of revenue growth and the covering of costs in the budget. Later, [11] developed a statistical model to explain financial distress in Australian municipalities. They concluded that the degree of financial distress is positively associated with the size of their population and the nature of their revenues. [12] analysed municipal financial distress in the United States by addressing four dimensions (cash solvency, budgetary solvency, long-term solvency and services), the socio-economic environment and the size of government, with a binary dependent variable based on payment difficulties. The results led to the conclusion that budgetary surplus, short-term debt and the composition of sources of revenue are essential factors when it comes to determining municipal financial distress.

Ever since European countries started to compile and publish financial details of their municipalities, additional research has also been carried out with reference to the European continent. For example, [13] analysed the unequal implementation of municipal accounting systems in the European Union and the reasons why some countries have resisted carrying out the necessary reforms. [14] constructed a model for predicting financial distress in Greek municipalities using a multi-criteria methodology. They obtained a level of accuracy which varied from 64.7% to 75.9%

in the classification of bankrupt municipalities, and close to 100% for solvent municipalities. For their part, [2] analysed financial performance in Irish municipalities with a benchmarking methodology, concluding that financial autonomy and commercial debt are the most important variables. [15] used logistic regression to study the financial cost of local governments in Spain, calculating the risk premium of the municipalities with a multi-state dependent variable according to the reason for default, which enabled them to predict their possible state of insolvency. With this model, they obtained classifications with a level of accuracy of 76%, showing short-term debt, per capita income and the political ideology of the local government to be significant factors. Furthermore, [16] analysed municipal financial distress in Spain, taking into account three aspects of municipal finances (debt, revenues and services). Their results suggest that municipal revenues are the most significant aspect. [17] developed a multi-criteria model to evaluate the financial performance of French municipalities and reached the same conclusion regarding the importance of own revenues and operating expenses. Recently, [3] studied the municipal financial distress in Italy using a set of financial indicators and the logistic regression methodology. Their work, with a level of accuracy of 75%, reveals that staff costs relative to revenues, the rotation of short-terms debts relative to revenues, and the level of dependency on subsidies are good predictors of municipal financial distress. Finally, [18] examined the factors which influence municipal credit risk, using the case of municipal default as a dependent variable. They found that the size of the population, per capita income and the composition of the debt determine the probability of possible municipal financial distress. Their results achieved a level of accuracy of 69.14% using financial variables and 79.73% when socio-economic variables were also included.

3. Data mining method for municipal financial distress prediction

Data mining is the process of extracting knowledge from databases and other information storage media. It has several functions, such as association, classification and prediction analysis, to name but a few. Each of them can use various alternative data mining algorithms [19]. Data mining for municipal financial distress prediction needs five steps: creating sample, data preprocessing, construction of model, accuracy assessment, and classification and prediction, as shown in Figure 1. Creating sample means obtaining the relevant data from the sources which provide financial information about municipalities. Data preprocessing consists of the discretization of attributes of continuous values, data generalisation, attribute relativity analysis, and the elimination of outlying values. Construction of model refers to learning inductively from the data preprocessed by the algorithms used and choosing the model which best represents the classification of knowledge for municipal financial distress prediction. Accuracy assessment is the task of evaluating the model's predictive accuracy by means of the set of training data and the set of validating data. Finally, classification and prediction consists of using the model developed to predict municipal financial distress.

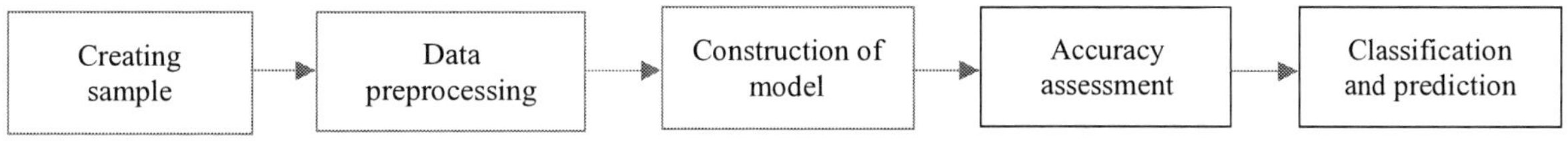

Fig. 1. Data mining steps in municipal financial distress prediction

Data mining which focusses on the prediction of municipal financial distress basically resolves a problem of classification and prediction. For that reason, in this work we use the classifiers which have obtained the best results in previous literature in models of financial distress prediction, specifically, Decision Trees, Naive Bayes, Multi-layer Perceptron, and Deep Belief Network [20].

A Decision Tree (DT) is a graphical, analytical form for classifying data by means of different possible paths [21]. Each of the nodes of the tree represents the different attributes of the data, the branches of the tree represent the possible paths to follow in order to predict the class of a new example, and the end nodes or leaves establish the class to which the test example belongs if the path along the branch in question is followed. The language of description of the DTs corresponds to the formulae in DNF (Disjunctive Normal Form). Thus, and in the event of having 3 attributes available (A, B and C), each of them with two values, x_i and $\neg x_i$, where i = 1, 2, 3, 2n combinations can be constructed in CNF (Conjunctive Normal Form). Each of the combinations in CNF describes a part of the tree, and thus we would have disjunctives of the form expressed in (1).

$$(x_2 \Lambda \neg x_3)\ V\ (x_2 \Lambda x_3)\ V\ (\neg x_2 \Lambda x_1)\ V\ (\neg x_2 \Lambda \neg x_1) \quad (1)$$

These disjunctives are descriptors of the tree constructed, and *22n* possible descriptions could be formed in DNF. As the order of the DT is very large, it is not possible to explore all of the descriptors to see which is the most suitable, and therefore heuristic search techniques are used to find a simple and quick way of doing so. The majority of DT construction algorithms are based on the Hill Climbing strategy, used in Artificial Intelligence to find the maximums or minimums of a function by means of a local search. This is an algorithm which begins with an empty tree and then segments into sets of examples, choosing in each case that attribute which best discriminates between the classes, until the tree is complete. In order to know which attribute is the best, a heuristic function is used, and the choice is irrevocable, and it is therefore essential to ensure that the attribute in question is the closest to the optimum.

For its part, the Naive Bayes (NB) classifier is considered as part of the probabilistic classifiers, which are based on the supposition that quantities of interest are governed by probability distributions, and that the optimum decision can be taken by reasoning about these probabilities together with the data observed. In classification tasks, this algorithm is among the most used [22-23]. [24] presents a basic guide to the different directions taken by research into NB in accordance with the modifications made to the algorithm. In this work we employ the traditional NB. The NB classifier is constructed using a T_r to estimate the probability of each class. In this way, when a new instance is presented, the classifier assigns to it the most probable category, which will be that which fulfils equation (2), i.e. the probability that, once the values which describe this new instance are known, it belongs to class C_i (which is the value of classification function *f(x)* in finite set *C*).

$$c = \arg\max_{c_i \in C} P(c_i \mid i_j) \quad (2)$$

Using the Bayes theorem to estimate probability, we obtain equation (3).

$$c = \arg\max_{c_i \in C} \frac{P(c_i \mid i_j)P(c_i)}{P(i_j)} \quad (3)$$

In equation (3) the denominator does not differ between categories and can therefore be omitted, giving us (4).

$$c = \arg\max_{c_i \in C} P(c_i \mid i_j)P(c_i) \quad (4)$$

If we also resort to the hypothesis of conditional independence, i.e. to the assumption of independence between attributes, it is then possible to assume that the characteristics are conditionally independent given the classes. This simplifies the calculations, resulting in equation (5).

$$c = \arg\max_{c_i \in C} P(c_i) \prod_{k=1}^{n} P(a_{kj} \mid c_i) \tag{5}$$

where $P(C_i)$ is the fraction of examples in T_r which belong to class C_i, and $P(a_{kj}|C_i)$ is calculated in accordance with Bayes' theorem.

The so-called Multi-Layer Perceptron (MLP) is a supervised neural network model, which would be composed of a layer of inputs (sensors), another output layer, and a given number of intermediate layers, called hidden layers in that they have no connections to the exterior. Each input sensor would be connected to the units in the second layer, these in turn to those of the third layer, and so on. The aim of the network is to establish a correspondence between a set of inputs and a set of desired outputs. [25] confirmed that learning in MLP constituted a special case of functional approximation, where no assumption exists regarding the model underlying the data analysed. The learning process means finding a function which correctly represents the learning patterns as well as carrying out a process of generalisation which permits the efficient treatment of individuals not analysed during learning [26]. To do this, weights W are adjusted on the basis of the information deriving from the sample set, considering that both the architecture and the network connections are known, and with the aim of obtaining those weights which will minimize learning error.

Thus, given a set of pairs of learning patterns $\{(x_1, y_1), (x_2, y_2) \ldots (x_p, y_p)\}$ and a function of error ε (W, X, Y), the training process entails the search for the set of weights which minimizes learning error $E(W)$ [26], as expressed by equation (6).

$$\min_{w} E(W) = \min_{w} \sum_{i=1}^{p} \varepsilon(W, x_i, y_i) \tag{6}$$

The majority of the analytical models used to minimize the function of error employ methods which require the evaluation of the local gradient of function $E(W)$, though techniques based on second order derivatives may also be considered [27]. While this is an area in constant development, the learning algorithms for the more common MLP-type networks are the backpropagation algorithm and its different variables, algorithms based on the conjugate gradient and the quasi-Newton models.

Lastly, Deep Belief Network (DBN) is a class of deep neural network where the two upper layers are modelled as an unsupervised bipartite associative memory. For their part, the lower layers of the network constitute a supervised graphical model called a sigmoid belief network. The difference between sigmoid belief networks and DBN lies in the parametrization of the hidden layers [26]. Equation (7) describes a DBN, where v is the vector of visible units, $P(h^{k-1} \mid h^k)$ is the conditional probability of visible units given the hidden ones at level k, and $P(h^{l-1}, h)$ is the joint distribution at the top level for $x(n) = [1, x_1(n), x_2(n), \ldots, x_m(n)]^T$.

$$P(v, h^1, \ldots, h^l) = P(h^{l-1}, h^l)(\prod_{k=0}^{l-2} P(h^{k|} \mid h^{k+1}) \tag{7}$$

When we apply DBN to a set of data, we are looking for a model $Q(h^{l-1}, h)$ for the true posterior $P(h^{l-1}, h)$. The subsequent Qs are all approximations, except for the top level $Q(h^{l-1}, h)$ which is equal to the true posterior $P(h^{l-1}, h)$ and allows us to make an exact inference ([26].

4. Data collection and variables

This work uses a sample of 128 Spanish municipalities. All fulfil the condition of having a population of over 50,000 inhabitants, in line with the criteria proposed by [15]. The information corresponding to the municipalities in the sample refers to 2015 and is provided by the Spanish

Court of Auditors, which publishes data related to the annual accounts of Spanish municipalities. In addition, and in order to validate the models to be estimated and to test predictive ability, test samples were used that were different and unrelated to those used in estimating the model. We then proceeded to divide the data into two different samples, one used to build the model (training data) and another for testing it (testing data).

The majority of the studies which address municipal financial distress have used explanatory variables which refer to the municipalities' financing structure. For this study, we have selected a set of financial variables from among those most used in the previous literature [14-15]. These selected variables comprehensively reflect the financial structure of Spanish municipalities and are related to indebtedness, municipal revenues, the capacity of revenues to pay debts and cover costs, and the volume of subsidies. Moreover, we use variables of political transparency which indicate the quality of information and management of a municipality [18, 28]. Table 1 shows the definition of the variables used in the study.

Table 1. Variables definition

Code	Description
	Financial variables
F1	Financial Debt / Commercial Debt
F2	Own Revenue / Total Revenue
F3	Short-Term Debt / Long-Term Debt
F4	Total Debts / Total Assets
F5	Own Revenue / Total Debts
F6	Short-Term Debt / Own Revenue
F7	Operating Expenses / Own Revenue
F8	Subsidies / Population
F9	Own Revenue / Population
	Transparency variables
T1	Voter turnout
T2	Political competence
T3	Political ideology
T4	Population
T5	Unemployment
T6	Total Debts
T7	Investment
T8	Political party fragmentation
T9	Political fragmentation

Variables F1, F3 and F4 refer to the structure of municipal debt. F1 shows the origin of the debt incurred by the municipality, indicating the proportion deriving from finance by suppliers (commercial debt) and the proportion arising from bank finance (financial debt). For its part, F3 represents the composition and duration of the financial debt. Variable F4 registers the dependency of a municipality on external finance. On the other hand, variables F2 and F9 show the structure of municipal revenues. The first variable measures the degree of autonomy of the municipality compared with possible subsidies received from the central government. The second variable is an indicator of municipal revenue per capita. Variables F5, F6 and F7 refer to the capacity of revenues to pay debts and cover municipal costs. Variable F5 represents the cover provided by municipal revenues in relation to total accumulated debt. Lastly, variable F8 refers to the volume of subsidies which would correspond to each citizen.

With regard to the transparency variables, variable T1 shows the level of citizen involvement in politics and is a proxy of the demand for transparency. Variable T2 is related to the level of approval of the activities of the political parties and the level of pressure for greater transparency. Variables T4 and T5 provide information about the characteristics of the population, while variables T6 and T7 are related to investment and debt, calculated on a per capita basis. Lastly, variables T8 and T9 indicate the composition of the municipal government and the distribution of power. T8 is calculated by dividing the number of councillors belonging to the ruling party by the total number of councillors, and T9 is calculated by dividing the number of parties with representation in the local assembly by the total number of councillors.

Finally, our model incorporates as a dependent variable a new proxy of financial situation and, as mentioned above, makes reference to the ratio of default to municipal commercial debt. This is a point of reference deriving from Spanish Legislation (Organic Law 2/2012, dated 27th April 2012, regarding Budgetary Stability and Financial Solvency and Royal Decree-Law 635/2014, dated 25th July 2014) as an indicator of financial distress. According to this proposal, municipalities are considered to in a good financial situation if the average period for paying debts is less than 30 days. For this purpose, municipalities are classified in two groups according to their average period of payment. In particular, municipalities with an average period of payment of less than 30 days are considered to be in a non-financial distress situation, while those with an average period of payment greater than 30 days are classified as being in a financial distress situation. The above-mentioned Royal Decree-Law 635/2014 stipulates the calculation of the average period of payment as the division of outstanding debts by net acknowledged debts (taking into account in both cases spending on current goods and services and real investments), multiplied by 365 days.

5. Empirical results

The main descriptive statistics of the selected variables for this work are shown in Table 2. Municipalities in a situation of financial distress (FD=1), compared with those that are not (FD=0) are characterized by a higher leverage level (F1, F4), high Short-Term Debt / Own Revenue (F6), and high Operating Expenses / Own Revenue (F7). Also, they present higher average values in Total Debts (T6) and higher Political Fragmentation (T9).

Table 3 and Figure 2 show the results obtained with DT, NB, MLP, and DBN classifiers. The accuracy rates for the training data are 95.45%, 83.97%, 85.52%, and 88.43% respectively. With testing data, the accuracy rates are slightly older, except for DT (79.04%, 84.35%, 93.91%, and 91.27%). Comparing the level of prediction for the model studied, a higher accuracy rate for MLP is seen. With MLP, the significant variables are Short-Term Debt / Own Revenue (F6), Operating Expenses / Own Revenue (F7), Subsidies / Population (F8), Total Debts (T6), and Political Fragmentation (T9), which, taken as a whole, constitute the best set of predictors for municipal financial distress.

Table 2. Descriptive statistics

		F1	F2	F3	F4	F5	F6	F7	F8	F9	T1	T2	T3	T4	T5	T6	T7	T8	T9
FD= 1	Mean	0.892	2.217	1.771	0.464	0.597	0.806	1.131	78.216	1687.146	61.519	16.871	3.357	130679.156	13584.281	1230.222	5495.106	0.265	0.161
	Median	0.324	1.854	1.428	0.281	0.416	0.594	0.843	45.227	1145.26	48.945	9.439	2.158	8851.373	8194.572	1027.358	4087.601	0.149	0.095
	St. Dev.	2.504	3.909	2.324	0.358	2.845	1.258	0.346	33.603	825.373	7.552	13.039	1.749	1317.259	1228.028	874.170	670.118	0.107	0.044
	N	64	64	64	64	64	64	64	64	64	64	64	64	64	64	64	64	64	64
FD= 0	Mean	0.410	2.324	0.613	0.315	0.667	0.450	0.953	89.885	2204.025	62.497	20.799	0.272	217184.328	19969.046	871.569	6721.257	0.096	0.145
	Median	0.294	1.847	0.521	0.254	0.548	0.378	0.683	72.157	1753.548	54.324	15.279	0.168	186536.865	16352.653	594.896	5946.974	0.049	0.114
	St. Dev.	0.411	1.264	0.639	0.238	3.766	0.554	0.285	37.030	120.381	20.799	11.499	0.323	4325.542	3211.803	629.853	191.356	0.089	0.039
	N	64	64	64	64	64	64	64	64	64	64	64	64	64	64	64	64	64	64
P-value (Kruskal-Wallis test)		0.006	0.070	0.057	0.007	0.630	0.000	0.001	0.094	0.208	0.602	0.070	0.931	0.429	0.646	0.007	0.328	0.061	0.027

Table 3. Results of accuracy evaluation

Method	Accuracy classification (%) Training	Accuracy classification (%) Testing	RMSE Training	RMSE Testing	Significant variables
DT	95.45	79.04	1.28	1.35	F2, F5, F6, T2, T8
NB	83.97	84.35	1.69	1.81	F1, F4, T1, T8, T9
MLP	85.52	93.91	0.97	0.92	F6, F7, F8, T6, T9
DBN	88.43	91.27	1.41	1.28	F5, F6, F8, T3, T6, T9

RMSE: Root mean squared error.

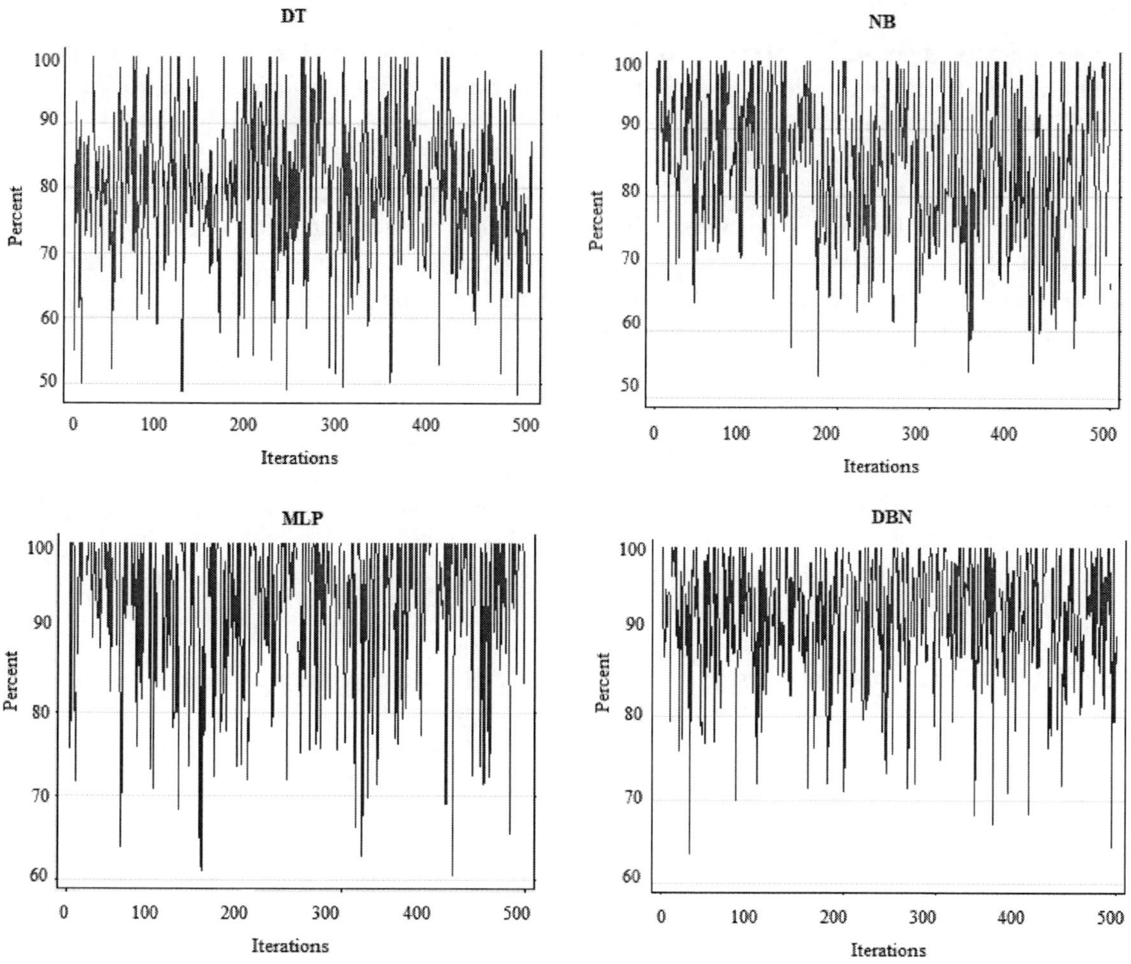

Fig. 2. Accuracy in testing data for 500 iterations

The results of this work show that the model developed increases the ability to predict municipal financial distress, compared with previous studies. Using MLP and the ratio of default to municipal commercial debt as a proxy of financial distress, the prediction accuracy is 93.91%. These results are higher than those contained in previous literature. For example, [15] using logistic regression and a multi-state dependent variable on the basis of the cause of default, obtained a level of accuracy of 76%. [3], also using logistic regression, and with a set of financial indicators, achieved a level of accuracy of 75%. [18] used the case of municipal default as a dependent variable and their results achieved a level of accuracy of 69.14% using financial variables, and 79.73% when also including socio-economic variables.

The accuracy levels obtained exceed those achieved in previous studies, possibly also due to the larger variable set used in this study, which also includes transparency variables such as Voter Turnout and Political Ideology. Transparency is a concept which refers to the availability of information about governmental institutions and which enables citizens and other external agents to verify the performance of public institutions [29-30]. The transparency of municipal governments is related to the financial situation thereof [9], and the use of a set of transparency variables has enhanced the predictive power of the model constructed in this work.

6. Conclusions and implications

Municipal financial distress is a global phenomenon which has captured the attention of researchers and managers of public institutions in recent decades. In this context, numerous models have been developed for evaluating municipal financial distress and one of their main limitations is related to the measurement of financial condition, since it is not directly observed. For this reason, current literature requires new research which will permit a comparison of results using others proxies of financial situation. This work proposes a model for evaluating the financial distress of municipalities which incorporates a new proxy of their financial situation, specifically the ratio of default to municipal commercial debt. To this end, a data mining focus was applied to a sample of Spanish municipalities, and this enabled their level of financial distress to be graded convincingly using a set of variables corresponding to 2015.

Using the MLP method, our model obtained a level of accuracy greater than 93% and has successfully determined the best set variables for predicting municipal financial distress. This set includes financial variables and variables related to the transparency of municipal government. Compared with previous studies, the model developed in this work increases the ability to predict municipal financial distress, and confirms that the use of different proxies of the financial situation of a municipality provides noticeably different results.

Our results contribute to the knowledge of the financial situation of municipalities in various senses. On the one hand, it can help researchers and academics to understand how the use of certain proxies of financial situation can enhance the level of accuracy of municipal financial distress models. On the other hand, our findings could be very helpful to local government financial managers, politicians and tax authorities as we have identified factors whose evolution may influence both the viability of public services and the effectiveness of measures taken to meet the goals of budgetary stability and financial sustainability.

References

[1] Liao, X., Liu, Y.: Local fiscal distress and investment efficiency of local SOEs. China Journal of Accounting Research 7(4), 119-147, (2014). doi: https://doi.org/10.1016/j.cjar.2013.07.002

[2]Turley, G., Robbins, G., McNena, S.: A framework to measure the financial performance of local governments. Local Government Studies, 41(3), 401-420, (2015). doi: 10.1080/03003930.2014.991865

[3] Cohen, S., Costanzo, A., Manes-Rossi, F.: Auditors and early signals of financial distress in local governments. Managerial Auditing Journal, 32(3), 234-250, (2017). doi: https://doi.org/10.1108/maj-05-2016-1371

[4] Kloha, P., Weissert, C.S., Kleine, R.: Developing and testing a composite model to predict local fiscal distress. Public Administration Review, 65(3), 313-323, (2005). doi: https://doi.org/10.1111/j.1540-6210.2005.00456.x

[5] García-Sánchez, I.M., Cuadrado-Ballesteros, B., Frías-Aceituno, J.V., Mordan, N.: A new predictor of local financial distress. International Journal of Public Administration, 35(11), 739-748, (2012). doi: https://doi.org/10.5539/ijbm.v7n1p169

[6] Honadle, B.W., Costa, J.M., Cliger, B.A.: Fiscal health for local governments: An introduction to concepts, practical analysis, and strategies. San Diego: Elsevier Academic Press, (2004). doi: https://doi.org/10.1016/b978-012354751-4.50010-x

[7] Cuadrado-Ballesteros, B., Mordán, N., García-Sánchez, I.M.: Is Local Financial Health Associated with Citizens' Quality of Life? Social Indicators Research, 119, 559-580, (2014). doi: https://doi.org/10.1007/s11205-013-0533-2

[8] Zafra-Gómez, J.L., López-Hernández, A.M., Hernández-Bastida, A.: Developing a model to measure financial condition in local government. The American Review of Public Administration, 39(4), 425-449, (2009). doi: https://doi.org/10.22146/jieb.v29i2.6206

[9] Ferreira, A.C.S., Do Carmo Azevedo, G.M., Da Silva Oliveira, J., Marques, R.P.F.: Global Perspectives on Risk Management and Accounting in the Public Sector. Elsevier B.V. (2016). doi: https://doi.org/10.4018/978-1-4666-9803-1

[10] Honadle, B.W.: The states' role in US local government fiscal crises: A theoretical model and results of a national survey. International Journal of Public Administration, 26(13), 1431-1472, (2003). doi: https://doi.org/10.1081/pad-120024405

[11] Jones, S., Walker, R.: Explanators of local government distress. Abacus, 43(3), 396-418, (2007). doi: https://doi.org/10.1111/j.1467-6281.2007.00238.x

[12] Gorina, E., Maher, C., Joffe, M.: Local Fiscal Distress: Measurement and Prediction. Public Budgeting & Finance. (2017). doi: https://doi.org/10.1111/pbaf.12165

[13] Pina V, Torres L, Yetano A (2009) Accrual accounting in EU local governments: One method, several approaches. European Accounting Review 18(4): 765-807. doi: https://doi.org/10.1080/09638180903118694

[14] Cohen, S., Doumpos, M., Neofytou, E., Zopounidis, C.: Assessing financial distress where bankruptcy is not an option: An alternative approach for local municipalities. European Journal of Operational Research, 218, 270-279, (2012). doi: https://doi.org/10.1016/j.ejor.2011.10.021

[15] Navarro-Galera, A., Rayo-Cantón, S., Lara-Rubio, J., Buendía-Carrillo, D.: Loan price modelling for local governments using risk premium analysis. Applied Economics, 47(58), 6257-6276, (2015). doi: https://doi.org/10.1080/00036846.2015.1068924

[16] Navarro-Galera, A., Rodríguez-Bolívar, M.P., Alcaide-Muñoz, L., López-Subires, M.S.: Measuring the financial sustainability and its influential factors in local governments. Applied Economics, 48(41), 3961-3975, (2016). doi: https://doi.org/10.1080/00036846.2016.1148260

[17] Galariotis, E., Guyot, A., Doumpos, M., Zopounidis, C.: A novel multi-attribute benchmarking approach for assessing the financial performance of local governments: Empirical evidence from France. European Journal of Operational Research, 248, 301-317, (2016). doi: https://doi.org/10.1016/j.ejor.2015.06.042

[18] Lara-Rubio, J., Rayo-Cantón, S., Navarro-Galera, A., Buendía-Carrillo, D.: Analysing credit risk in large local governments: an empirical study in Spain. Local Government Studies, 43(2), 194-217, (2017). doi: https://doi.org/10.1080/03003930.2016.1261700

[19] Sun, J., Li, H.: Data mining method for listed companies' financial distress prediction. Knowledge-Based Systems, 21, 1-5, (2008). doi: https://doi.org/10.1016/j.knosys.2006.11.003

[20] Callejón, A.M., Casado, A.M., Fernández, M.A., Peláez, J.I.: A System of Insolvency Prediction for industrial companies using a financial alternative model with neural networks.

International Journal of Computational Intelligence Systems, 6(1), 29-37, (2013). doi: https://doi.org/10.1080/18756891.2013.754167

[21] Kingsford, C., Salzberg, S.L.: What are decision trees? Nature Biotechnology, 26, 1011-1013, (2008). doi: https://doi.org/10.1038/nbt0908-1011

[22] Escalante, H.J., Morales, E.F., Sucar, L.E.: A naïve Bayes baseline for early gesture recognition. Pattern Recognition Letters, 73, 91-99, (2016). doi: https://doi.org/10.1016/j.patrec.2016.01.013

[23] Feki-Sahnoun, W., Njah, H., Hamza, A., Barraj, N., Mahfoudi, M., Rebai, A., Hassen, M.B.: Using general linear model, Bayesian Networks and Naive Bayes classifier for prediction of Karenia selliformis occurrences and blooms. Ecological Informatics, 43, 12-23, (2018). doi: https://doi.org/10.1016/j.ecoinf.2017.10.017

[24] Lewis, D.D.: Naive (Bayes) at forty: The independence assumption in information retrieval. European Conference on Machine Learning, 4-15, (1998). doi: https://doi.org/10.1007/bfb0026666

[25] De Castro, L.N., Iyoda, E.M., Von Zuben, F.J., Gudwin, R.: Feedforward neural network initialization: an evolutionary approach. Proceedings 5th Brazilian Symposium on Neural Networks. Belo Horizonte, Brazil, 43-48, (1998). doi: https://doi.org/10.1109/sbrn.1998.730992

[26] Bengio, Y.: Learning Deep Architectures For Artificial Intelligence. Foundations and Trends in Machine Learning, 2 (1), 1-127, (2009). doi: https://dx.doi.org/10.1561/2200000006

[27] Flórez, R., Fernández, J.M.: Las Redes Neuronales Artificiales. Fundamentos teóricos y aplicaciones prácticas. Ed. Netbiblo. Coruña, (2008). doi: https://doi.org/10.4272/978-84-9745-246-5.ch1

[28] Araujo, J.F., Tejedo-Romero, F.: Local government transparency index: determinants of municipalities' rankings. International Journal of Public Sector Management, 29 (4), 327-347, (2016). doi: https://doi.org/10.1108/ijpsm-11-2015-0199

[29] Meijer, A.: Understanding the Complex Dynamics of Transparency. Public Administration Review, 73(3), 429-439, (2013). doi: https://doi.org/10.1111/puar.12032

[30] Grimmelikhuijsen, S.: Linking transparency, knowledge and citizen trust in government: An experiment. International Review of Administrative Sciences, 78(1), 50-73, (2012). doi: https://doi.org/10.1177/0020852311429667

Understanding Customers and Their Grouping via WiFi Sensing for Business Revenue Forecasting

Vahid Golderzahi[1,2] and Hsing-Kuo Pao[1,3]

[1] Department of Computer Science and Information Engineering
National Taiwan University of Science and Technology, Taipei 10607, Taiwan
[2] golderzahi@gmail.com
[3] pao@mail.ntust.edu.tw

Abstract. Emerging technologies provide a variety of sensors in smartphones for state monitoring. Among all the sensors, the ubiquitous WiFi sensing is one of the most important components for the use of Internet access and other applications. In this work, we propose a WiFi-based sensing for store revenue forecasting by analyzing the customers' behavior, especially the grouped customers' behavior. Understanding customers' behavior through WiFi-based sensing should be beneficial for selling increment and revenue improvement. In particular, we are interested in analyzing the customers' behavior for customers who may visit stores together with their partners or they visit stores with similarly patterns, called group behavior or group information for store revenue forecasting. The proposed method is realized through a WiFi signal collecting AP which is deployed in a coffee shop continuously for a period of time. Following a procedure of data collection, preprocessing, and feature engineering, we adopt Support Vector Regression to predict the coffee shop's revenue, as well as other useful information such as the number of WiFi-using devices, the number of sold products. Overall, we achieve as good as 7.63%, 11.32% and 14.43% in the prediction on the number of WiFi-using devices, the number of sold products and the total revenue respectively if measured in Mean Absolute Percentage Error (MAPE) from the proposed method in its peak performance. Moreover, we have observed an improvement in MAPE when either the group information or weather information is included.

Keywords: Customer behavior · Group behavior · Received Signal Strength Indicator (RSSI) · Revenue forecasting · WiFi sensing

1 Introduction

Nowadays most stores provide WiFi services for customers who are equipped with WiFi functioning smartphones and interested in accessing Internet. It is well known that WiFi signals, along with other video or non-video-based technology may be helpful in understanding people's behavior for people located in a smart space, or in particular the customers' behavior in stores [12, 3]. In this work, we propose a method based on WiFi sensing given customers' behavioral inputs for store revenue forecasting. In particular, we are interested in the customers' group information where we can observe friends who find each other to go for a drink together or different individuals may share similar visiting behavior even they do not know each other.

Compared to online shopping where all the surfing and purchase behaviors from customers are automatically logged, the marketing in brick-and-mortar business usually face the challenges as they need to deploy the customer analytics framework to the physical realm. In one way or the other, the traditional stores must find solutions to keep track of customers such as when customers may visit the stores, what they prefer to own and what they really purchase in the end based on their judgment between the product quality and price. To understand targeted customers as much as they can to boost the stores' revenue, two major technologies offer the answers: the video and non-video-based approaches. To avoid the privacy leaking issues, the non-video-based approaches are generally favored from the customers' side because they keep the customers' information to its minimum for business analytics. Among the various non-video-based approaches, WiFi-sensing is a major choice due to its popularity. Existing WiFi sensing, which is a cost-effective as well as privacy-preserving technology, can be appropriate for customer behavior analysis [3, 1].

Signal-based indoor sensing for human tracking and business analytics are generally categorized into several categories [14]. A rich set of IoT (Internet of Things) technology with sensors such as passive infrared sensor (PIR), ultrasound, temperature sensors, as well as various vision-based devices can be deployed in the indoor environment for human counting, tracking and activity recognition to name a few. In general, we need to spend efforts on the device deployment physically and the device calibration and threshold setting may not be straightforward for this kind of technology. On the other hand, there are also some devices that we need the humans located in the indoor environment to carry to make the sensing possible. Some wearable devices and smartphones fall into this category. Apparently, we prefer a scenario that is: 1) easy to deploy in the indoor environment, 2) providing high sensing accuracy, and 3) with enough covering rate among people. In another word, we look for a sensing technology where we can: 1) easily implement both in its hardware and software, 2) find convincing tools for analytics and 3) detect as high percentage of people as possible in a given environment where each of the targeted people carries a device that is necessary for sensing. We propose a WiFi-based sensing method [13] where we only assume smartphone carrying from the customers for the indoor customer detection and tracking for business revenue forecasting. By having the technology, we keep the deployment efforts to the minimum and at the same time, we enjoy a decent sensing performance.

The proposed method is realized in a coffee shop where we track and analyze customers' behavior and the associated group information with a WiFi AP. For customers who visit the coffee shop with functioning WiFi, we can collect the

WiFi related information and use it to summarize customers' behavior. One of the reasons why we choose the coffee shop for our study is because drinking coffee and visiting the coffee shop is considered not a mandatory but an optional activity for people where we may choose to have with our friends and when we have certain mood for relaxation or doing business in the environment. This coffee shop is located in Da'an district in Taipei City and close to a university area. Most of its customers are students who may spend their time to have fun with their friends, or work on their homework/projects individually or with a group. From time to time, the coffee shop owner may provide some special discounts to students to encourage them coming to the shop, which could lead to revenue increment.

We use the WiFi related information to track the coffee shop's customers and analyze their behavior using RSSI signals captured via the WiFi AP. We monitor the coming and leaving time for each customer as well as their duration of stay given the RSSI signals. Occasionally, the AP may grab some data from people who pass by the coffee shop or stay in a store nearby. We address these noise data by applying some filters on RSSI signals and the duration of customers' stay. Furthermore, we will extract frequent customers and analyze their behavior to detect the groups of frequent customers. Customers may form a group if they come to the shop together. On the other hand, we also consider a group if customers from the group often come to the coffee shop at some similar time or stay for similar duration. For instance, some people may come the shop before going to work or stay in the shop for almost the whole day long. We believe that they could have similar working patterns or share similar income levels and should behave similarly in their visiting and purchase behavior. In the end, we discuss both of the cases where we may not include or may include the group information as described above in the feature set for prediction. We take turn to predict the total number of customers' devices, the total number of sold products and the total revenue. The prediction model is Support Vector Regression (SVR).

We should emphasize the main contributions and what differentiate the proposed method from the previous solutions for indoor human sensing and business revenue estimation as follows:

- The proposed method is based on an easy-to-deployed scenario where we only assume smartphone carrying from the customers. Moreover, the proposed approach is a *passive* approach where we need customers to open no special software to activate the sensing. On the indoor environment, we need only a tuned AP for WiFi signal collection. By having this property, we can easily convince business stores for its realization.
- We focus on using the customers' group information for revenue forecasting. The group information separates customers from different groups, such as loyal customers, customers with different vocations, customers with different product preferences and customers with different daily or weekly schedule. Knowing the above information may improve the business revenue as the business should have more understanding about its customers.

- The proposed method respects the privacy issue. Unlike many indoor tracking strategies, we collect the information only the part for *signal broadcasting* from customers. Usually, we can assume customers have no objection on releasing the information. It could be hard to hide the broadcasting information in general when a handshaking communication is needed.

The remaining of the paper is organized as follows. An overview of WiFi-based and non-WiFi-based sensing approaches is provided in Section 2. Afterwards, we discuss the proposed method along with all the necessary procedures in Section 3, which is followed by the experiment results and evaluation in Section 4. Finally, we conclude our work in Section 5.

2 The past work

The goal is to adopt indoor sensing on customers for business revenue forecasting. There are a variety of technology that has been developed for this purpose. As we briefly described, the major strategies can be separated into several groups based on whether we need to deploy certain devices or system on the indoor side and whether we assume any devices from the customers to carry to make the sensing possible. In this section, other than the research that we have discussed in Section 1, we mainly discuss the approaches that are directly related to this work. We emphasize that what we plan to detect and track is more than a handful customers where we may not assume any limit for the number of customers. Moreover, identifying the tracked customers is valuable to have in this application. Therefore, the IoT solutions such as PIR, ultrasound and temperature sensing are not precise enough to solve the problem. On the other hand, the vision-based methods may not be the best choice due to the privacy concerns from the general public. We turn our attention to the approaches where we assume customers carrying devices and the devices provide enough information for detection, tracking and analytics.

The user-carrying device approach can be divided into smartphone and non-smartphone categories. The former represents a scenario in which users carry their own smartphones, thereby they are trackable and their identifiable information would be extractable through the smartphones [1]. The latter relies on additional wearable devices that should be carried by users such as bracelets, smart glasses, RFID, etc. For instance, Han et al. [3] implemented a Customer Behavior IDentification (CBID) system based on passive RFID tags. Their system includes three main parts; discovering popular items, revealing explicit correlations, and disclosing implicit correlations to understand customers' purchase behavior. The technology is mainly focused on a small set of people and may have difficulty when we have a large number of unknown people to track and therefore hard to implement in the crowded situation [7, 4].

On the category of smartphones, we have all-in-one devices which have the identifiable information as well as a various set of equipments, sensors and apps for information collection and environmental monitoring. People may prefer to carry smartphones simply because the smartphones play such a role of combining many functionalities in a single device [6, 8]. That implies using smartphones as the assumed carrying device for customer sensing should provide enough covering rate when we use smartphone-related signals to estimate the existence of customers. Among all possibilities, WiFi-equipped smartphones can be considered one of the best solutions to be carried by unknown people or a large number of customers who intend to communicate with public devices due to the built-in identifiable characteristics in the smartphones. By having that, we aim to detect, track and analyze people with their existence and group behavior [6, 11].

Zeng et al. [12] proposed WiWho, which is a method to identify a person using walking gait analysis through the WiFi signals. WiWho consists of two endpoints, a WiFi AP and any WiFi-equipped device for communicating and collecting Channel State Information (CSI). It has some limitations such as assuming the straight walking paths from customers and should have the performance limit while the tracked person turns. Vanderhulst et al. [6, 11] discussed a framework to detect human spontaneous encounters in which spontaneous and short-lived social interactions between a small set of individuals have been detected. It leverages existing WiFi infrastructure and the WiFi signals, so-called "probe" can periodically be radiated by a device to search for available networks. The probes are used to capture radio signals transmitted from users' devices to detect human copresence. The limitations of the proposed method include device variety, a limited number of participants to be allowed for high accuracy detection, and the required application to be installed on users' smartphones.

An extended Gradient RSSI predictor and filter was proposed by Subhan et al. [10]. It is a predictive approach to estimate RSSI values in presence of frequent disconnections. The approach predicts users' positions and movements in terms of their current situations and movements. The distance changes between users' devices and the AP lead to the increase and decrease of the RSSI values and therefore the targeted users as well as their movements can be detected.

As other similar research, Maduskar et al. [6] proposed an approach to trace people's positions and movements using an RSSI measurement of WiFi signals from several APs in predetermined locations. The RSSI-based approaches have the minimum complexity compared to other signal-based indoor localization techniques. In their approach, the larger size of the APs results in more accurate location estimation. The weakness of the approach is that a careful initialization is necessary given a new environment, e.g., customer sensing given an indoor store. Du et al. [2] proposed algorithms for fine-grained mobility classification and structure recognition of social groups using smartphones through their embedded sensors. They have utilized embedded accelerometer to detect group mobility behavior. Afterward, a supervised learning algorithm is applied to recognize different levels of group mobility, such as stationary, walking, strolling, and running. The method can also be used to recognize the relations and structures of a group by monitoring the leader-follower, the left-right relations and distances using smartphones' sensor data. To compare the above two research work, the localization technique is basically not a must to have in our scenario because the main purpose of the proposed method is on understanding when customers visit a store instead of what customers prefer to own. Therefore, it is the visiting behavior not the purchase behavior that interest us. In the next section, we discuss the proposed method in details.

3 Proposed Method

The goal is to predict the number of customers and revenue on each day given the past selling and customers' behavior history. What is different from previous approaches is that we rely on the WiFi signal collection to help us know further about the visiting customers where the WiFi information may tell us the information from the macro scope such as the total number of customers to the micro scope such as the customers' identifiable information. We demonstrate the whole prediction scenario starting from data collection, data preprocessing to prediction model itself in the next few subsections.

3.1 Data Collection

The data for the proposed method includes two parts: the WiFi-based data and others. The WiFi-based data has been collected using a WiFi collecting device, TP-Link TL-WR703N WiFi router in the coffee shop. It is an access point (AP) which operates in IEEE 802.11n mode to collect the data from customers' devices such as smartphone, laptop, tablet, etc. The extracted data from the received WiFi signals per customer includes:

- the physical address (MAC address),
- service set identifier (SSID), and
- received signal strength indicator (RSSI).

Given the MAC address information, we can calculate the number of devices for each day. Usually the number of devices may be close to the number of customers per day if each customer carries only one smart device (further discussed below in the assumption part). The WiFi data has been extracted using the Wireshark packet analyzer[4]. Based on the collected WiFi information, we also derive some information which may be important for the prediction:

- the come-in time of a customer,
- the leaving time of a customer, and
- the way a customer was served, such as "staying in" or "prepared to go".

The come-in time and leaving time are recored based on the first and last signals that we can collect for each specific MAC address (identity). How a customer was served is estimated based on the duration of the WiFi signals that we received per MAC address, such as above or below a predefined threshold (further discussed below). Furthermore, there are customer considered as frequent customers. We add a set of group information features, which are extracted via *frequent customers' behavior analysis*. Note that the above three are individual based, collected for each MAC address. On the other hand, the SSID and RSSI

[4] https://www.wireshark.org

are collected following a predefined sampling rate. In addition to the WiFi related information, we also collect some other information which may have influence on the coffee shop revenue. The information includes:

- temperature, and
- rain probability.

On the side, the analyzed dataset also consists of the number of various sold products and the total revenue for each day. The owner of the analyzed coffee shop is kind to provide the valuable information for us to confirm the performance of the proposed method. Some correlation between the number of sold products, the revenue and the number of devices (MAC address) is further discussed below. The dataset was collected from 2016/09/02 to 2016/12/04 in which the training data is set from 2016/09/02 to 2016/11/20 including 78 days, and the test data is from 2016/11/21 to 2016/12/04 including 14 days. Due to some technical difficulty, we have a few days of missing data. The longest of data missing is a gap of eight days from the 6th to the 7th weeks, shown in Fig. 1. We have consulted the average ratio between the number of devices and the number of sold products to fill the missing values for the study.

Privacy Issues We need to emphasize that we try our best to respect the customers' privacy. The data collection procedure is focused only on the part that the customers broadcast to the environment. We do not attempt to construct a data collection procedure where the customers' browsing history, browsing URLs, etc. may be collected through our AP. That is, we do not trick customers by creating an AP where we may have the above information or even the username or password information from customers.

3.2 Data Preprocessing

The first issue of customer behavior analysis is to identify real customers. In this study, we filter the devices (identified via the MAC address) detected by the WiFi AP by setting thresholds of duration from five minutes to three hours. That is, we assume that each customer stays in the coffee shop no shorter than five minutes and no longer than three hours (5 mins $\leq$ staying time $\leq$ 3 hours). The detected devices with duration shorter than five minutes are assumed to be passing by devices and the devices with duration longer than three hours are likely to be the staff of the coffee shop or neighboring shops. The thresholds are decided based on our visual estimation when we visited the coffee shop. Also, we set a threshold applied to RSSI where we include only the RSSI greater than -70dBm in the data collection (-70dBm $<$ RSSI).

As customers reach the entrance door of the coffee shop, they are in the range of our data collection AP and the RSSI keeps increasing as customers moving into the coffee shop. We record the devices and identify the come-in time when the devices show the above pattern. Recording the customers' leaving time is the opposite. The stay duration for customers can be used for customers' behavior analysis such as the reasons they visit the coffee shop (for study, meeting friends or web surfing, etc.) and whom they go with.

3.3 The Proposed Prediction Method

The complete step-by-step procedure of the proposed method includes: 1) data collection, 2) feature extraction, 3) clustering for group information extraction, 4) model building and 5) prediction. We start by collecting the WiFi data through our modified AP. The WiFi data are compiled into several features and they are combined with the non-WiFi features such as weather information to form a complete feature set for model training. On the side, we have additional information provided by the coffee shop owner such as revenue related information to confirm our evaluation.

Analyzing customers' behavior or more specifically finding customers' group information is a key contribution of the proposed method. We assume customers who are classmates, partners, or colleagues may go to the coffee shop together frequently as a group. On the other hand, some customers, even they may not know each other can behave similarly such as they may visit the shop at similar time or on similar days (all coming in the morning, after lunch, after work or coming during weekdays or weekend), or with similar frequency (once per day or once per week). Given the above group behavioral inputs, we would like to extract a set of features called *group information* to describe different customers. By including those features, we may have a better chance to understand different customers and thus a better chance to predict the revenue of a business.

Given a set of customers' features, we adopt a hierarchical clustering method called Unweighted Pair Group Method with Arithmetic mean (UPGMA) to find customers' group information. Specifically, we have a set of features to describe customer i as:

$$\mathbf{z}_i = (z_{i1}, z_{i2}, \ldots, z_{iK}) \tag{1}$$

where we have K days to consider in our customer analysis and we should use K binary attributes to indicate the presence of customer i in the coffee shop on different days. That is,

$$z_{ik} = \begin{cases} 1 & \text{if customer } i \text{ visits the coffee shop on day } k\,, \\ 0 & \text{otherwise}\,. \end{cases} \tag{2}$$

Given the above inputs, UPGMA builds a rooted tree (dendrogram) that reflects the structure of pairwise similarities between different customers [5]. To describe the similarity between two clusters C_i and C_j, we utilize a proportional averaging formulation written as:

$$\sigma_{ij} = \frac{1}{|C_i| \cdot |C_j|} \sum_{p \in C_i} \sum_{q \in C_j} \sigma_{pq}\,, \tag{3}$$

where $|C_i|$ and $|C_j|$ represent the cardinality of the set (i.e., the size) for C_i and C_j respectively; also, σ_{pq} measures the similarity between two entities p and q from C_i and C_j respectively. We measure the similarity between two customers p and q as:

$$\sigma_{pq} = \sum_k \delta(z_{pk}, z_{qk}) \cdot \delta(z_{pk}, 1)\,, \tag{4}$$

where the function $\delta(x, y)$ outputs 1 if $x = y$ and outputs 0 if $x \neq y$. That is, we count 1 when two show up in the coffee shop on the same day and count 0 otherwise. All pairs of customers are compared through the pairwise computation to form a similarity matrix in the end. Then, a pair of elements with the maximum similarity are recognized and clustered together as a single grouped pair first. Afterwards, the similarity between this pair and all other elements are recalculated to form a new matrix. We go on to find the pair with the maximum similarity for grouping step by step until all are combined into one in the end [4, 5]. The output of UPGMA is a dendrogram and we can find the final grouping result by setting an appropriate number of clusters. In the end, the group information shall be used in building the Support Vector Regression (SVR) model [9] for the prediction on the number of customers' devices, the number of sold products and the total revenue.

3.4 Assumptions and Limitations

The goal is to analyze customers' behaviors that are related to coffee consumption. Due to the WiFi-based data collection nature, we first assume that all customers carry WiFi-based devices and their WiFi signals can be detected easily by the deployed AP. That is, the WiFi function must be on at all times when the customers visit the coffee shop, starting from entering to leaving the coffee shop, for all customers. Based on the assumption, we could capture customers' existence, in particular, we know when customers come to the coffee shop and leave the coffee shop. That is, as soon as we detect RSSI signals for each customer's device, it will be assumed that this is the exact entrance time for the customer. The leaving time of a customer is also assumed to be the time of losing or dropping off of the RSSI signal received from the customer's device. There are also some limitations in this research, such as using just one WiFi AP leads to weak distinguishment of the exact coming and leaving time for each customer. Moreover, we cannot detect the exact location and position of each customer. In the data cleaning phase, removing noisy or irrelevant data is hard especially in a crowded area[5].

4 Experiment Results

We would like to predict the number of customers' devices, the number of sold products and the total revenue given a set of WiFi-based and non-WiFi-based features. There are two scenarios that we discuss:

1. In the first scenario, we take turn to work on three prediction tasks given a sliding window of size L as well as other features such as the day in a week, the weather information, which consists of the temperature and rain forecasting to build the learning model.

[5] There is a convenient store right next to this coffee shop.

Table 1: The statistics of frequent and non-frequent customers.

	The frequent customer (%)	non-frequent customer (%)
The number of customers	11%	89%
The number of visits	27%	73%

2. In the second scenario, we consider additional features, the group information with the same sliding window as described in the first scenario to build the learning model.

We attempt to analyze how the past presence or purchase records can be used to predict the future presence or purchase. In particular, between the first and the second scenarios, we discuss how the group information can help us for better prediction. We utilized Support Vector Regression (SVR) [9] as the predictive model. The size of sliding window L is set as $L = 14$ for this work. The detail result shall be shown below.

4.1 Statistics of frequent and non-frequent customers

Before going on to demonstrate the effectiveness of the proposed method, we first study some basic statistics of the data set. In many retail stores, the transactions from the frequent customers may usually dominate the store revenue. In this case, we also would like to understand the contribution from the frequent and non-frequent customers separately. In Table 1, we show the numbers of frequent and non-frequent customers, which are 11% and 89% out of the whole group of customers who visited the shop during the data collection period. Interestingly, we also observe that this 11% frequent customers contribute 27% of the visiting times in the coffee shop, compared to 73% of the visits from non-frequent customers. It implies a relatively large consumption from the frequent customers compared to the non-frequent ones. When we aim to find a predictive model with good performance, we better to focus more on the prediction of the frequent customers rather than the non-frequent ones. Fortunately, the frequent customers are likely to come to the coffee shop in a regular manner and could be predicted easily if compared to the non-frequent group. Moreover, the prediction on the frequent rather than the non-frequent customers may be easy simply because we usually have a relatively large frequent customers' data in the training set. We discuss more along these two aspects below.

We also analyze the daily visits (in %) from the frequent and non-frequent customers, shown in Fig. 1. From the beginning to the end of data collection period, we observe that the percentage of the frequent customers increases slightly as time moving forward. It may due to that the major group of customers includes a significant percentage of students from a nearby university. The students may know each other better and better starting from September (the beginning of the semester) through November and they may have more chances to go for a coffee when they know each other better. Note that we have a few days of missing values due to data collection difficulty in the period.

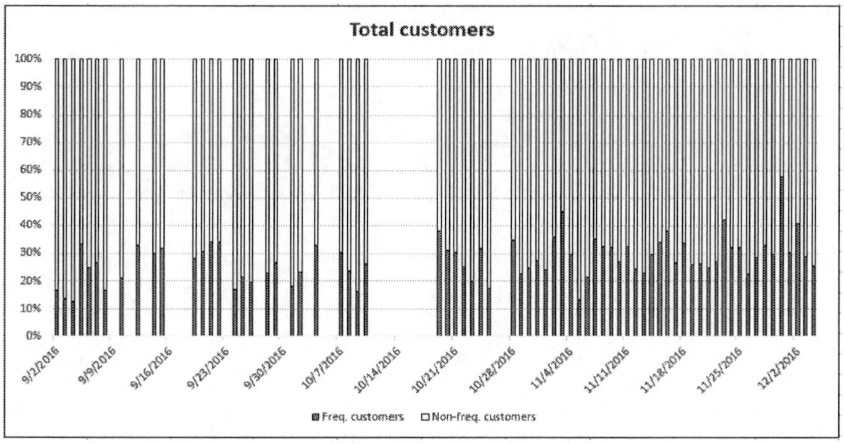

Fig. 1: The percentage of frequent and non-frequent customers per day.

4.2 Features and Results

The Feature Set We first discuss the features that are used in this study. Following the description in the beginning of this section, let us use τ_t, ρ_t and day_t to describe the information such as the temperature forecasting, the probability of raining and the day in a week on the t-th day respectively. The sliding window of size L for the above information (except the day in a week) can be written as:

$$\begin{aligned} \mathbf{temp}_{t,L} &= (\tau_{t-L}, \dots, \tau_{t-1}), \\ \mathbf{rain}_{t,L} &= (\rho_{t-L}, \dots, \rho_{t-1}). \end{aligned} \tag{5}$$

To speak of the group information, we set the number of groups for group information extraction as $K = 4$. Given the assignment, we have the group features written as:

$$\mathbf{g}_t = (g_{t,1}, g_{t,2}, \dots, g_{t,k}, \dots, g_{t,K}), \tag{6}$$

where $g_{t,k}$ records the number of customers from group k who visit the coffee shop on the t-th day. We can describe the group information with the sliding window of size L as:

$$\mathbf{g}_{t,L,k} = (g_{t-L,k}, \dots, g_{t-1,k}), \quad \forall k \in \{1, \dots, K\}. \tag{7}$$

After all, we also write down the sliding window of size L for the target value that we want to predict:

$$\mathbf{y}_{t,L} = (y_{t-L}, \dots, y_{t-2}, y_{t-1}). \tag{8}$$

In the end, the overall feature set in this study can be written as:

$$\begin{aligned} \mathbf{D}^{g}_{t,L} &= (\text{day}_t, \mathbf{temp}_{t,L}, \mathbf{rain}_{t,L}, \mathbf{y}_{t,L}; y_t), \\ \mathbf{D}^{\text{gp}}_{t,L} &= (\text{day}_t, \mathbf{temp}_{t,L}, \mathbf{rain}_{t,L}, \mathbf{y}_{t,L}, \mathbf{g}_{t,L,1}, \dots, \mathbf{g}_{t,L,K}; y_t), \end{aligned} \tag{9}$$

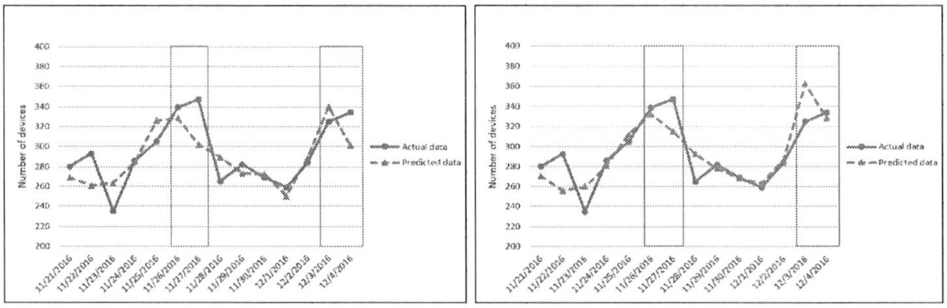

Fig. 2: The prediction on the total number of customers' devices: (a) without and (b) with the group information (weather information not included). The X-axis is the UTC (Epoch time) format and the Y-axis represents the number of customers' devices.

for the case without or with the group information included, respectively. The target value y_t that we want to predict could be the number of customers' devices, the number of sold products or revenue as described before. From time to time, we may have the feature set described in Eq. 9 too large to create the risk of overfitting. To avoid the situation, we reduce the dimensionality by shrinking the feature size of sliding window as follows. For each sliding window, e.g., the sliding window for temperature, we may choose a pre-defined function such as the mean function to compress a long sliding window to a scalar such as:

$$\text{temp}_t = (\tau_{t-L} + \cdots + \tau_{t-1})/L\,. \tag{10}$$

Some other possible functions for shrinkage include minimization, maximization. Now the complete feature set is shrunk to:

$$\begin{aligned} \mathbf{d}^{g}_{t,L} &= (\text{day}_t, \text{temp}_{t,L}, \text{rain}_{t,L}, \mathbf{y}_{t,L}; y_t)\,, \\ \mathbf{d}^{\text{gp}}_{t,L} &= (\text{day}_t, \text{temp}_{t,L}, \text{rain}_{t,L}, \mathbf{y}_{t,L}, \mathbf{g}_{t,L,1}, \ldots, \mathbf{g}_{t,L,K}; y_t)\,, \end{aligned} \tag{11}$$

for the cases of not including the group information or including the group information respectively. Note that we choose the mean function for the shrinkage on all the sliding windows except for the sliding window for the target value.

Result The first experiment is to predict the number of customers' devices given the features described in Eq. 11. In Fig. 2, we demonstrate the effectiveness of the proposed method by showing the difference between the actual and the predicted result on the total number of customers' devices spanning two weeks[6]. First, we notice the ups and downs on the selling between different days where we usually have high selling and revenue during the weekends (Nov. 26, 27, and Dec. 3,

[6] We add random numbers in the Y-axis for Fig. 2, Fig. 3 and Fig. 4 due to a concern from the coffee shop.

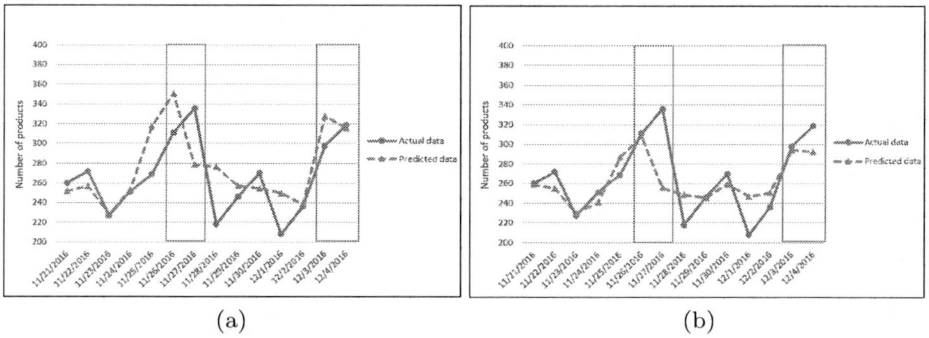

Fig. 3: The prediction on the total number of sold products: (a) without and (b) with the group information (no weather information included). The X-axis is the time and the Y-axis represents the number of products.

4). In fact, those are the days that we have significant gaps between the actual and predicted result. In (a), we have the prediction given the features without the group information and we include the group information for prediction in (b). Overall, we obtain an improvement from 9.11% to 7.63% in MAPE (Mean Absolute Percentage Error) from (a) to (b) if the group information is included and the weather information is not included (also in Table 2).

In the second experiment, we aim to predict the number of sold products. Other than the number of devices which may not be 100% identical to the number of customers, the amount of sold products could be a better quantity to reflect the business profit. In Fig. 3, we can compare between the actual number of sold products and the prediction. Again, we observe more selling during the weekends rather than during the weekdays. The weekend period is also the time that we have worse prediction if compared to the prediction on the weekdays.

To compare between the scenario when we include no group information and the scenario when we do include group information, we found out that including the group information can improve the prediction result from 15.06% to 11.32% in MAPE (without the weather information). It implies that including group information can help us understand more about customers' behavior on visiting the coffee shop. Intuitively speaking, people often visit coffee shops with their partners. The decision about whether people visit a coffee shop or not may be highly influenced by their partners. On the other hand, the group information may also imply a similar behavior on visiting the coffee shop such as the people in the same group may choose to visit the coffee shop on similar days or at similar moments. This kind of group information could reflect the vocations that the customers have or the living style they share. Knowing such information may give us more hints on predicting whether or not certain people visit the coffee shop on a particular day or at a particular moment.

In the end, we discuss the revenue prediction as described in Fig. 4. Again, we have similar result like the prediction on the number of devices and the prediction on the number of sold products. We have the prediction errors improved

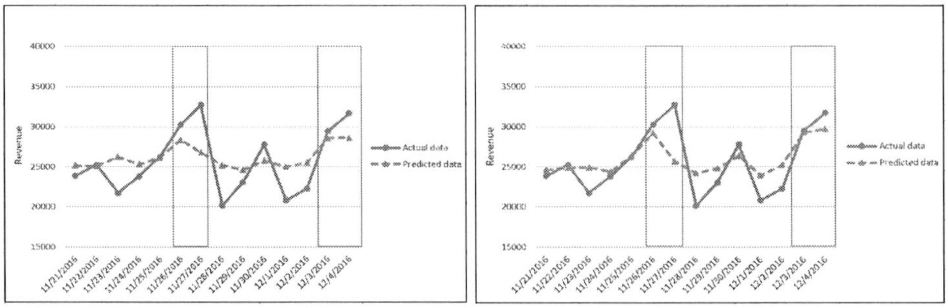

(a) (b)

Fig. 4: The prediction on the total revenue: (a) w/o and (b) w. the group information (no weather information). The X-axis is the time and the Y-axis shows the revenue.

Table 2: The summary of all predictions in MAPE. The boldface numbers show the best performance in each group and the underline, boldface numbers show the best performance across all settings.

	w/o weather		w. weather	
	w/o group info.	w. group info.	w/o group info.	w. group info.
	MAPE (%)	MAPE (%)	MAPE (%)	MAPE (%)
# of devices	9.11	**7.63**	**7.95**	8.43
# of sold products	15.06	**11.32**	**11.60**	12.25
Revenue	18.10	**14.43**	14.58	**14.51**

from 18.10% to 14.43% in MAPE when the weather is not included and from 14.58% to 14.51% in MAPE when the weather is included. Overall, we have the improvement when the group information is included in four out of six different settings, as shown in Table 2 given the settings such as without or with the weather information and for different prediction tasks. In the table, we also noticed the improvement from including the weather information in many of the occasions. Note that including both the weather information and group information may not produce the best result. We believe that too many features may harm the performance due to overfitting and the problem could be eased when more data are collected in the near future.

5 Conclusion

We proposed an easy-to-deployed, low cost and privacy-preserving method for business revenue forecasting based on WiFi sensing. A WiFi collection AP was installed in an indoor environment to collect related WiFi signals for us to understand more about customers who visit the business. The case study was done in a coffee shop where we analyzed the WiFi-based and non-WiFi-based data for 12 weeks for the evaluation. We worked on three prediction tasks such as the prediction on the number of devices, the number of sold products and the total revenue. In the experiment study, we found out the improvement when the weather information is included; more importantly, when the group information is included in most of the prediction tasks even with a limited data collection period. The prediction on the number of devices, the number of sold products and the revenue can reach 7.63%, 11.32%, and 14.43% in MAPE in their peak performance. A large scale data collection and study is on the way for more extensive study in the near future.

References

1. Draghici, A., Steen, M.V.: A survey of techniques for automatically sensing the behavior of a crowd. ACM Comput. Surv. **51**(1), 21:1–21:40 (Feb 2018)
2. Du, H., Yu, Z., Yi, F., Wang, Z., Han, Q., Guo, B.: Recognition of group mobility level and group structure with mobile devices. IEEE Transactions on Mobile Computing **17**(4), 884–897 (April 2018)
3. Han, J., Ding, H., Qian, C., Xi, W., Wang, Z., Jiang, Z., Shangguan, L., Zhao, J.: CBID: A customer behavior identification system using passive tags. IEEE/ACM Transactions on Networking **24**(5), 2885–2898 (October 2016)
4. Lau, E.E.L., Lee, B.G., Lee, S.C., Chung, W.Y.: Enhanced rssi-based high accuracy real-time user location tracking system for indoor and outdoor environments. International Journal on Smart Sensing and Intelligent Systems **1**(2), 534–548 (2008)
5. Loewenstein, Y., Portugaly, E., Fromer, M., Linial, M.: Efficient algorithms for accurate hierarchical clustering of huge datasets: tackling the entire protein space. Bioinformatics **24**(13), i41–i49 (2008)
6. Maduskar, D., Tapaswi, S.: RSSI based adaptive indoor location tracker. Scientific Phone Apps and Mobile Devices **3**(1), 3 (Jun 2017)
7. Nguyen, K.A.: A performance guaranteed indoor positioning system using conformal prediction and the WiFi signal strength. Journal of Information and Telecommunication **1**(1), 41–65 (2017)
8. del Rosario, M.B., Redmond, S.J., Lovell, N.H.: Tracking the evolution of smartphone sensing for monitoring human movement. Sensors **15**(8), 18901–18933 (2015)
9. Smola, A.J., Schölkopf, B.: A tutorial on support vector regression. Statistics and computing **14**(3), 199–222 (2004)
10. Subhan, F., Ahmed, S., Ashraf, K., Imran, M.: Extended gradient RSSI predictor and filter for signal prediction and filtering in communication holes. Wireless Personal Communications **83**(1), 297–314 (Jul 2015)
11. Vanderhulst, G., Mashhadi, A.J., Dashti, M., Kawsar, F.: Detecting human encounters from WiFi radio signals. In: Proceedings of the 14th International Conference on Mobile and Ubiquitous Multimedia, Linz, Austria, November 30 - December 2, 2015. pp. 97–108 (2015)
12. Zeng, Y., Pathak, P.H., Mohapatra, P.: WiWho: WiFi-based person identification in smart spaces. In: 2016 15th ACM/IEEE International Conference on Information Processing in Sensor Networks (IPSN). pp. 1–12 (April 2016)
13. Zeng, Y., Pathak, P.H., Mohapatra, P.: Analyzing shopper's behavior through WiFi signals. In: Proceedings of the 2nd Workshop on Workshop on Physical Analytics. pp. 13–18. WPA '15, ACM, New York, NY, USA (2015)
14. Zhang, D., Xia, F., Yang, Z., Yao, L., Zhao, W.: Localization technologies for indoor human tracking. In: 2010 5th International Conference on Future Information Technology. pp. 1–6 (May 2010)

Social Media Sentiment Analysis Based on Domain Ontology and Semantic Mining

Daoping Wang[1], Liangyue Xu[2] and Amjad Younas[3]

[1] University of Science and Technology Beijing, Beijing 100083, China
[2] University of Science and Technology Beijing, Beijing 100083, China
[3] University of Science and Technology Beijing, Beijing 100083, China

dpwang@ustb.edu.cn
S20171000@xs.ustb.edu.cn.com
Amjad.younas@yahoo.com

Abstract. The rapid development of social media has made numerous users to express their opinions, feelings, and attitudes towards various things through different forums like Twitter, WeChat, and Weibo. However, most existing works just focus on specific product categories to construct the domain ontology, which is a quite narrow use of domain ontology. We propose a new construction of domain ontology based on the semantic features of social media. The topic of posts and opinions also known as topic-opinion pairs, are identified with the domain ontology. The sentiment polarities are determined with the help of the given sentiment polarities. The sentiment polarity of an unknown post is calculated by the weighted average of the sentiment polarities of topics and opinions contained in the post. Preliminary results show that the application of domain ontology can effectively identify the topic-opinion pairs, and according to the known polarity of posts can effectively classify the topic-opinion pairs. The accuracy of sentiment classification is increasing.

Keywords: Domain Ontology, Semantic Mining, Associating Mining, Social Media

1 Introduction

Recent years, with the booming of E-commerce and Social media, numerous netizens express their views, feelings, and attitudes through Twitter, BBS, Weibo, and other different ways. That emotional information of products, topics, and other valuable things not only objectively also were integrated with their own various language emotional colors and text sentiment orientation. It was increasingly being used by governments, companies, and marketers to understand how the crowd thinks.

Semantic analysis is often called viewpoint mining, subjective analysis and evaluation extraction, which is closely related to computer linguistics, natural language processing, and text mining. It usually refers to the data from user's subjective comment and post, using automated or semi-automatic ways to analyze and process. As a result, the opinion and sentiment orientation of individuals and groups on various topics, tasks, and other expressions could be mined. Domain ontology was extracted as a particular domain of the real world into a set of concepts and the relationship between concepts. It systematically describes the basic principles, main entities, and activities of the field, in order to realize the application and sharing of domain knowledge. Although recent years have seen a great progress in sentiment analysis and domain ontology, it still focused on specific category such as mobile phone, cars forum. By analyzing the relationship between the concepts which described in the product comments, the domain ontology for product reviews is constructed. But few papers mentioned the construction of domain ontology in social media (such as Twitter, Weibo, Instagram, etc.). Because of the immediacy of participation, dynamic communication, and the relationship among the posts, it is possible to construct the domain ontology. Therefore, based on the characteristic of the posts, this paper constructs the ontology model with the semantic features in social media. Therefore, the sentiment classification of a post in social media is more accurate and effective.

2 Related work

Sentiment analysis has been extensively studied at different granularity levels. To construct affective dictionary is to use it as a prior knowledge of sentiment analysis and assist the analysis of different granularity. In addition to sentiment dictionary, ontology technology has been widely applied to the research of sentiment analysis. Many researchers try to combine domain ontology with it to improve and optimize the performance and accuracy of sentiment analysis. As a most important feature of ontology, domain ontology aims to standardize concepts and terminology in specific fields and establish a shared conceptual system between different domains. The domain ontology also provides basic support for practical applications in these fields.

Marstawi, A [1] concluded that the sentence-level linguistic rules applied by Ontology-Based Product Sentiment Summarization could provide a more accurate sentiment analysis. Jung, H [2] showed that the applicability of the ontology was validated by examining the representability of 1358 sentiment phrases using the ontology EAV model and conducting sentiment analyses of social media data using ontology class concepts. Sreejith [3] used the `Navarasa' ontology created by the researcher for sentiment analysis in a short story.Hu and Liu [4] used supervised sequential pattern mining method to identify and extract features or viewpoints. Wilson [5] developed an Opinion finder system, which was an automatic recognition of subjective sentences and various subjective components in a sentence (such as opinion source, emotion, direct subjective expression).Kim and Hovy [6] labeled the words that expressed subjectivity in a sentence based on a comment dictionary by manual annotation through defining a fixed-size window which was centered on subjective words. Kobayashi [7] artificially defined evaluation objects and evaluation words and described the modified relation between words and evaluation objects by using eight common modules. Li [8] defined the characteristics and viewpoints film based on WordNet, then aimed to identify features and their opinions through the dependency syntax diagram. Jacob [9] employed the conditional random field algorithm to extract the feature and opinions. Tan [10] tried to apply behavioral relation data on social media to user-level sentiment analysis according to the idea that two users with mutual relationships were likely to hold the same view. Go [11] attempted three machine learning methods, namely Naïve Bayes, support vector machines and maximum Entropy in text sentiment orientation in Twitter, they conclude that the applicability of machine learning model in the sentiment analysis.

On the recognition of the point of view, Alexander Pak [12] considered naive Bayes classifier to identify the point of view based on characteristics extracted by POS tagging and N-gram. Luciano Barbosa [13] used the subjectivity of the words, the polarity of words and negative words as characteristics to classify the subjective and objective nature of Weibo posts. Davidiv [14] extracted tags and emoticons from Twitter as training sets and used an advanced KNN algorithm to classify sentiment on Weibo posts.

Different from most existing studies which concentrate on concrete product, this paper extracts feature entries based on the semantic features of social media and constructs domain ontology. In this study, the emotion value of topic-opinion pairs is weighted by semantic context so that sentiment classification could be more accurate and effective.

3 Construction of Domain Ontology in Social Media

The traditional domain ontology is generally based on collecting characteristics of items. However, many posts in social media are short texts, incorrect writings, and in disorderly sentence structure. The extracted keywords which are really relevant to the central idea may be less than expected, and the word frequency may not be the highest. It means that the accuracy of defining topics and opinions in a post is low, and mining semantic information in the post is an effective way to solve this problem. According to the characteristics of language habits and oral expressions, the content of a post can be generalized not only two main parts topics and comment but also five elements: time, location, object, event, and opinion. It means that to some extent the first four elements can describe the topic. In this paper, we used these four elements as the foundation of the domain ontology in social media.

3.1 Extracting Topic Characteristics of Items

Extracting topic items is the foundation of the constructions of the domain ontology. The existing methods mostly focus on English comment and product comment. Because of the grammatical non-standard, semantic ambiguity and subject missing, the characteristics of Chinese comment increase the difficulty of sentiment classification. Therefore, the representation model of domain ontology is proposed which regards the definition of topic characteristics of items.

Definition 1 *A topic item can be defined as <Time, Location, Object, Event>.*

Due to the colloquial characteristics of social media, there will be a lot of irregular and vague expressions such as "tomorrow", "Yesterday" in a post, and the formulations are various, for example, “3:30 p.m.”, “half past three in the afternoon”, “three thirty”. Those irregular expressions should be standardized. The standard form of time is yyyy-MM-dd-HH-mm-ss. Similarly, the expression of location needs to be standardized as Room, Unit, Building, Road, District, City, Province, and Country.

After standardization, the next step is to mine frequent itemsets with association rules in content. First, all nouns and verbs are extracted from the post to form two itemsets. Then, the frequent 1-itemsets and frequent 2-itemsets are found. By filtering out frequent 2-itemsets which cannot form phrases and that itemsets unrelated to time, location, object, and event, we get the final set of feature words.

After acquiring a set of feature words, by means of the point mutual information (*PMI*) between the feature words, the semantic common frequency of the word is expressed. The higher frequency of the two words in the post shows the higher correlation. Hence, the *PMI* defined as follows:

$$PMI = \log \frac{p(word_1 \,\&\, word_2)}{p(word_1) * p(word_2)} \tag{1}$$

We take $PMI\ (word_1.\ word_2)$ for a frequency of two words’ co-occurrence, $P\ (word_1)$ and $P\ (word_2)$ show frequency of one word appearing respectively. $word_1$, $word_2$ can be taken from the same category of feature words and different category of feature words. After calculating *PMI*, combined those feature words of high *PMI* value to the topic item.

Definition 2 *Domain Ontology uses a 2-tuple representation, O=<C, R>, C represents for the topic item, R represents for the relations between two topic items.*

The topic item is represented by *C=<ID, Topic, List>*. *ID* represents the only number of the topic item, *Topic* represents the descriptive words of this topic item, *List* represents the synonyms of this topic item. The relation between two topic items is represented for $R=< T, R\ (C_1, C_2) >$. We take T for describing three semantic relations: part of, relevant with, and irrelevant with, C_1 and C_2 represent two different topic items.

3.2 Clustering Algorithm of Topic Items

After preprocessing of the post (including syntactic structure, deactivating words and POS tagging), we need to preserve nouns and verbs which are related to time, place, object, and event. In the training sets, we extract four categories which are composed topic items, the *Time* characteristic in *Topic i* items are represented for vector $T_i = \{t_1, t_2, t_3 \ldots t_n\}$, the *Location* for vector $Li= \{l_1, l_2, l_3 \ldots l_n\}$, the *Object* characteristic for vector $O_i= \{o_1, o_2, o_3 \ldots o_n\}$, the *Event* characteristic for vector $E_i= \{e_1, e_2, e_3 \ldots e_n\}$.

The weights of word t_i in *Time* characteristic in the topic item are calculated as follows:

$$\eta_T(t_i, A_i) = \frac{tft(t_i)}{\max tf(A_i)} \log_2 \frac{M}{df(t_i)} \quad (2)$$

We take $tf(t_i)$ for the frequency of t_i appearing in a post A_i; $df(t_i)$ for the number of posts which contained t_i; Function max $tf(A_i)$ for the maximum word frequency in the post A_i; M for the number of posts in the training set. To make the weight between [0, 1], $\eta T\ (t_i, A_i)$ is defined as follows:

$$\eta_t(t_i, A_i) = \frac{\eta_T(t_i,) - \min \eta_T}{\max \eta_T - \min \eta_T} \quad (3)$$

After calculating the average amount of $\eta_T\ (t_i, A_i)$, in the post A_i is calculated as follows:

$$\eta_T(A_i) = \frac{\sum_{i=1}^{M} \eta_t(T_i, A)}{M} \quad (4)$$

Similarly, we get the formulation for the weights of *Location* characteristic $\eta_l\ (A)$, the weights of *Object* characteristic $\eta_o\ (A)$ and the weights of *Event* characteristic $\eta_e\ (A)$.

The similarity between two topic items could be calculated by vector space model, vector A_i, and A_j, $A_i= \{T_i, L_i, O_i, E_i\}$, $A_j= \{T_j, L_j, O_j, E_j\}$, the formulation between A_i and A_j is shown as follows:

$$Sim\ (A_i, A_j) = \eta_T*Sim\ (T_j, T_j)+ \eta_l*Sim\ (L_i, L_j)+ \eta_O*Sim\ (O_i, O_j)+ \eta_e*Sim\ (E_i, E_j) \quad (5)$$

The similarity between the *Time* vector in post A_i and that in post A_j is calculated as follows:

$$Sim(T_i, T_j) = \frac{\sum_{k=1}^{n} \eta_k(T_i) * \eta_k(T_j)}{\sqrt{(\sum_{k=1}^{n} \eta_k^2(T_i)) * (\sum_{k=1}^{n} \eta_k^2(T_j))}} \quad (6)$$

We take $\eta_k(T_i)$ for the kth word in the *Time* vector of post A_i, $\eta_k(T_j)$ for the kth word in the *Time* vector of post A_j.

Similarly, we get the formulation of similarity between the *Location* vector and the *Object* vector.

$$Sim(L_i, L_j) = \frac{\sum_{k=1}^{n} \eta_k(L_i) * \eta_k(L_j)}{\sqrt{(\sum_{k=1}^{n} \eta_k^2(L_i)) * (\sum_{k=1}^{n} \eta_k^2(L_j))}} \quad (7)$$

$$Sim(O_i, O_j) = \frac{\sum_{k=1}^{n} \eta_k(O_i) * \eta_k(O_j)}{\sqrt{(\sum_{k=1}^{n} \eta_k^2(O_i)) * (\sum_{k=1}^{n} \eta_k^2(O_j))}} \quad (8)$$

Based on the Hownet a semantic knowledge resource, calculation of the *Event* vector similarity is the maximum of similarity between their original semantic meanings.

After acquiring the *Topic* items composed of the *Time* vector, the *Location* vector, the *Object* vector, and the *Event* vector, the advanced K-Nearest neighbor algorithm is used to do the cluster analysis. (See Fig 1)

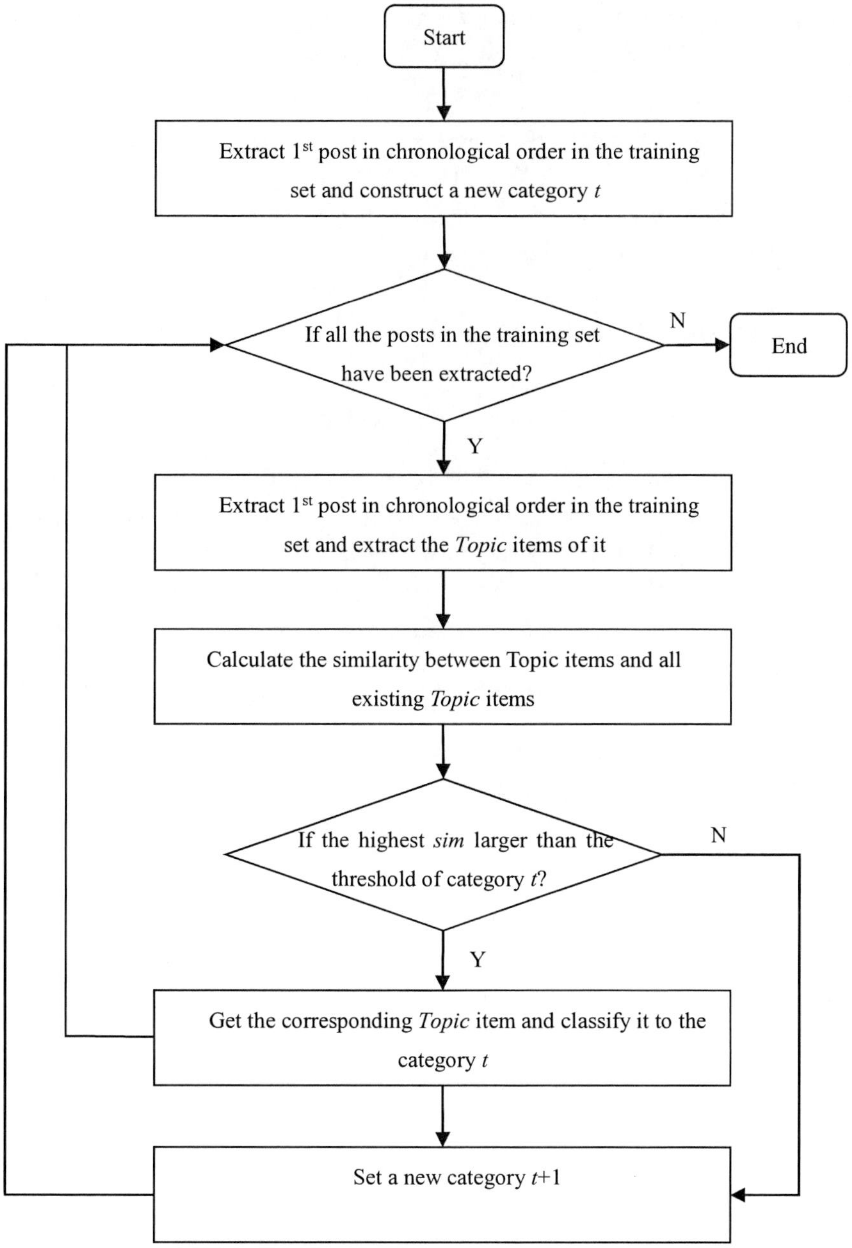

Fig. 1. Clustering algorithm of *Topic* items

4 Identification of Topic-Opinion Pairs Based on Domain Ontology

After the construction of the domain ontology in social media, the next step is to extract the opinion from the post based on semantic mining.

4.1 Identification of Subjective Sentence

The identification of the opinion is the process of classification of sentences building on sentence structure and POS. Using paper [15] and analysis of numerous posts for reference, the three main categories of feature words in the subjective sentence are summarized: sentiment words, asserted words, and modal particle.

Sentiment words. The subjective sentence in a post always contains the standpoint and viewpoints of the author and a strong individual initiative, so the sentiment words could be one of the characteristics of the subjective sentence.

Asserted words. For example, "claim", "blame", "announce", the appearance of these words could be seen as the strong possibility of the subjective sentence.

Modal particle. The emotional punctuations such as "!", "?" and emoticons could express the individual initiative of the author, as well as the Chinese only model particles, such as "吗", "呢", "吧".

4.2 Extraction of Key Subjective Sentence and Relations

The posts in social media are informative but semantic fuzziness. According to the automatic summarization, we extract the keywords for subjective sentence *B*. Based on the topic relevance and three important property, we could decide the key subjective sentence. After weighted summation of the topic relevance, position property, sentiment property, and keyword property, we take the corresponding sentence with the highest value for key subjective sentence. The formulation is shown as follows:

$$key\_Sentence = \lambda_1 * sim(s_i, c_i) + \lambda_2 * keywords(s_i) + \lambda_3 * position(s_i) + \lambda_4 * senti\_words(s_i) \quad (9)$$

We take λ_1, λ_2, λ_3, and λ_4 for the corresponding weight for the four elements.

sim (S_i, C_i) represents the relevance between the subjective sentence and topic. Combining the topic items *C* with the subjective sentence, we get a sequence of topic-opinion which are separated by "," and calculate the similarity in pieces. According to the term frequency-inverse document frequency, we obtain sim $(w_{i,k}, c_{i,k})$ as follows:

$$sim(w_{i,k}, c_{i,k}) = \sum_{c \in C} tf_p(w_{i,k}) * tf(p_{i,k}) * \log_2 \frac{N}{pf(w_{i,k})} \quad (10)$$

Where $w_{i,k}$ denotes the feature words *k* in the subjective sentence *i*, $c_{i,k}$ denotes the feature words *k* contained in the topic items c_i, $p_{i,k}$ denotes the combination of $w_{i,k}$ and $c_{i,k}$, $tfp(w_{i,k})$ denotes the frequency of $w_{i,k}$ in $p_{i,k}$, $f(p)$ denotes the frequency of *p* in the whole post, $pf(w_{i,k})$ denotes the total number of phrases which included $w_{i,k}$, *N* denotes the total number of phrases in the post.

Marked the highest value of sim $(w_{i,k}, c_{i,k})$ as $sim(S_i,C_i)$ in the formulation (11) and the corresponding feature words as the indicator d_{si} of opinion $_i$.

$$sim(S_i, C_i) = \max(sim(w_{i,k}, c_{i,k})) \quad (11)$$

position (s_i) presents for the different part of the speech. People are willing to express their views clearly at the beginning of a speech and summarize at the end, so it attaches great importance the opening phrase and the end of the statement. The formulation (12) presents *position* (s_i).

$$position(s_i) = [i - \frac{num(s_i)}{2}]^2 + 1 \quad (12)$$

Where *num* (s_i) denotes the total number of sentences in a post, the constant 1 is to confirm every sentence in different position has a positive score. From the formulation, it can be seen that the function is a pointing- up parabola which axis of symmetry is at the central position. It confirms that the first and ending sentence has the more location advantages than others.

keywords (s_i) identifies those words which are general and set the tones, such as "anyway", "in a word". If a sentence includes these words, the possibility of being a key-opinion sentence is increasing. The formulation of *keywords* (s_i) is shown as follows.

$$keywords\,(s_i) = \sum_{k=1}^{num(w_{i,k})} keyword\,(w_{i,k}) \tag{13}$$

Where *keyword* ($w_{i,k}$) denotes that whether word $w_{i,k}$ is a summary word or not. If it is, *keyword* ($w_{i,k}$) is 1， otherwise *keyword* ($w_{i,k}$) is 0.

senti_words (s_i) identifies the sentiment orientation of sentences which is shown as follows.

$$senti\_words\,(s_i) = \frac{\sum_{k=1}^{num(w_{i,k})} polarity\,(w_{i,k})}{num\,(w_{i,k})} \tag{14}$$

Where *polarity* ($w_{i,k}$) denotes that whether word $w_{i,k}$ has sentiment orientation or not. If it is, *polarity* ($w_{i,k}$) is 1, otherwise *polarity* ($w_{i,k}$) is 0.

5 Post Sentiment Analysis Based on Domain Ontology

In order to make the sentiment analysis more targeted, we set up rules for matching the post with domain ontology.

Rule 1 The topic items and the opinion indicator are both included in the post and match the post with the domain ontology.

Rule 2 Only topic items are included, not the subjective sentence and opinion indicator, just assume that this post is an objective statement and without any individual initiative. Therefore, filter this post and the extracted topic item does not match any subjective sentences.

Rule 3 Only subjective sentence is included, not the topic items. There is always be ignoring of subject, incidents, and time in speech for example, "We all should engrave what happened on May 5th, 2012 on our mind", we need to identify those implicit topics. Assume that only subjective sentence Bi and topic item *i* without the object *i*, use the extracted topic *i* $<C_i, S, d_{si}>$ as the prior knowledge to calculate the similarity. The missing object *i* is the corresponding *Oi*, *S* of the highest *sim* (C_i, *S*- *Oi*, *S*, (C_i-O_i,), d_{si}, B_i). Similarly, we could get the implicit *Time*, *Location*, and *Event* in the post.

According to the domain ontology and sentiment dictionary, we get the topic item, subjective sentence and sentiment words in the post. In the next step we need to calculate the sentiment orientation of the subjective sentence. The level of affect intensity is $Q= \{q_1, q_2, q_3 \ldots q_i \ldots q_n\}$. When calculate the sentiment value, not only the sentiment polarity and affect intensity should be considered, but also the adverb of degree and negation words appeared closely should also be considered. Therefore, the sentiment value of a sentence is represented as follows.

$$senti\_couple\,(j) = \sum_{k=1}^{num\,(C_k)} sw_k * (-1)^p * d\,(adv) \tag{15}$$

Where *senti_ couple* (*j*) denotes the sentiment value of the topic-opinion pair *j*, sw_k denotes the sentiment value of sentiment words *k*, that is the product of sentiment polarity and affect intensity, *p* denotes the number of negation words appeared closer to the sentiment word *k*, *d* (*adv*) denotes adjustment for adverb of degree appeared closer to the *k*.

The sentiment value of a post *t* is represented as follows.

$$senti\_post(t) = \frac{\sum_{i=1}^{num(senti\_(couple))} senti\_couple(i)}{num(senti\_couple(i))} \quad (16)$$

Where num (*senti_* (*couple*)) denotes the number of topic items included in post *t*.

Due to the strong interactivity of social media, generally every post has comments, likes, and re-posts. To some extent, these behaviors show the affect intensity of posts. According to Paper [16], all users can be divided into five groups by their participation and engagement (see Fig. 2): inactive user R_1, sidelines R_2, participator R_3, criticizer R_4, and key opinion leader R_5.

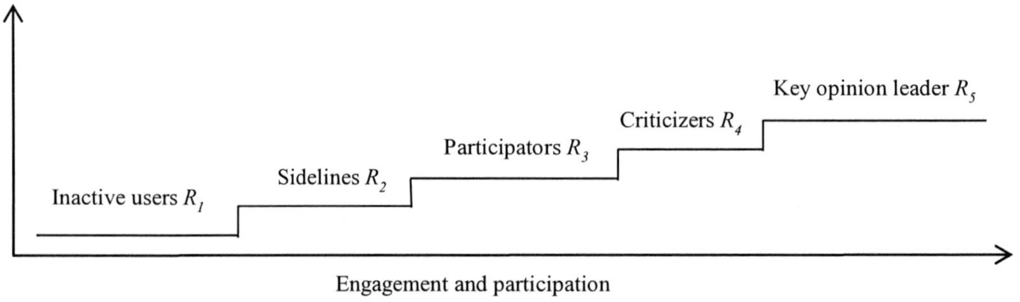

Fig. 2. Five groups of users divided by engagement and participation

Based on the different categories and these interactive behaviors, the sentiment value of a post (t, R_i) can be weighted from *senti_ (post)* as follows.

$$post(t, R_i) = (1 + 0.1 * i) * senti\_post(t) * (1 + 0.05 * num(comment) + 0.02 * num(likes) + 0.05 * num(repost)) \quad (17)$$

Where R_i denotes the group which belongs to, i=1, 2, 3, 4, 5, 6， *num* (*comment*) denotes the number of comments, *num* (*likes*) denotes the number of likes, *num* (*repost*) denotes the number of reposts.

6 Experiments and Conclusion

The experimental steps are designed as follows: first, collect experimental corpus in social media, and remove inactive words and POS tagging with posts. The experimental posts are divided into training sets and test sets. The former is used to construct the domain ontology and compute the polarity of the topic-opinion pairs, while the latter is used to evaluate the validity of the method. Then, the semantic computation of the training sets is carried out and the domain ontology of social media is constructed. Based on it, the topic-opinion pairs of the test set are identified. Then, according to the positive and negative posts in the training sets, the sentiment polarity value of the topic-opinion pairs is calculated and the sentiment classification is obtained. Finally, the experimental results are compared with the manual tagging results in the test set, and the method of this paper is evaluated. Due to limited time, the experiment is still in progress. Preliminary results show that the application of domain ontology can effectively identify the topic-opinion pairs, and according to the known polarity of posts can effectively classify the topic-opinion pairs and has a certain degree of universality.

A post in social media may contain both positive and negative polarity, and sentiment words may change with the context. The existing research used the context-independent sentiment classification method, or only used the simple and empirical method to analyze context and evaluate opinions. These strategies all have some deficiencies, resulting in the lower accuracy of sentiment identification.

Therefore, this research proposes a new sentiment classification method based on social media domain ontology. Compared with the existing methods which mostly focus on the characteristics of the products through the sentiment ontology, this paper employs the semantic features and semantic relation in posts to identify the topic-opinion pairs with the social media domain ontology. Finally, the sentiment classification of each post is obtained according to the user classification and interactive characteristics of social media. This study is not without limitations, for example the neutral posts which are often ignored should be mining out the implied sentiment orientation.

References

1. Marstawi, A., Sharef, N.M., Aris, T.N.M.: Ontology-based Aspect Extraction for an Improved Sentiment Analysis in Summarization of Product Reviews. In: International Conference on Computer Modeling and Simulation. ACM, pp. 100-104, Canberra (2017).
2. Jung, H., Park, H.A, Song, T.M.: Ontology-Based Approach to Social Data Sentiment Analysis: Detection of Adolescent Depression Signals. Journal of Medical Internet Research, pp. 19(7), 259(2017).
3. D, Sreejith., M.P, Devika, N.S, Tadikamalla., S.V, Mathew.: Sentiment Analysis of English Literature using Rasa- Oriented Semantic Ontology. Indian Journal of Science and Technology, Vol 10(24), pp. 1-11(2017).
4. Hu, M., Liu, B.: Mining opinion features in customer reviews. In: National Conference on Artificial Intelligence. AAAI Press, pp. 755-760, San Jose (2004).
5. Wilson, T., Hoffmann, P., Somasundaran, S.: Opinion finder: a system for subjectivity analysis. In Proceedings of Human Language Technology Conference and Conference on Empirical Methods in Natural Language Processing (HLT/EMNLP), pp. 347-354, Canada (2005).
6. Kim, S.M., Hovy, E.: Extracting opinions, opinion holders, and topics expressed in online news media text. In Proceedings of the Workshop on Sentiment and Subjectivity in Text. ACL, pp. 1-8, Sydney (2006).
7. Kobayashi, N., Inui, K., Matsumoto, Y.: Collecting evaluative expressions for opinion extraction. In Proceedings of the International Joint Conference on Natural Language Processing. Springer-Verlag, pp. 596-605, Berlin (2004).
8. Li, Z., Feng, J., Xiao, Z.: Movie review mining and summarization. In Proceedings of the 15th ACM International Conference on Information and Knowledge Management. ACM, pp. 43-50, New York (2006).
9. Jakob, N., Gurevych, I.: Extracting Opinion Targets in a Single and Cross-Domain Setting with Conditional Random Fields. In: Conference on Empirical Methods in Natural Language Processing. Cambridge (2010).
10. Tan, C., Lee, L., Tang, J.: User-level sentiment analysis incorporating social networks. ACM, pp. 1397-1405, San Diego (2011).
11. Go, A., Bhayani, R., Huang, L.: Twitter sentiment classification using distant supervision. Cs224n Project Report, pp. 1-12 (2009).
12. Alexander, P., Patrick, P.: Twitter as a Corpus for Sentiment Analysis and Opinion Mining. In: Proceedings of International Conference on Language Resource and Evaluation, pp. 1320-1326, Lisbon (2010).

13. Barbosa, L., Junlan, F.: Robust Sentiment Detection on Twitter from Biased and Noisy Data. In: Proceedings of the 23rd International Conference on Computational Linguistics, pp. 36-44, Beijing (2010).
14. Davidiv, D., Tsur, O., Rappoport, A.: Enhanced Sentiment Learning Using Twitter Hashtags and Smileys. In: Proceedings of the 23rd International Conference on Computational Linguistics, pp. 241-249. Beijing (2010).
15. Ding, S.C., Ma, M.R., Li, X.: Study of Subjective Sentence Identification Oriented to Chinese Micro blog (in Chinese). Journal of the China Society for Scientific and Technical Information 33(2), pp. 175-182(2014).
16. Ramesh, S., Duerson, D., Ephraims, T.: A managerial perspective on analytics. Chinese Machine Press, Beijing(2015)

Gap in pagination due to formatting issues.

Page 361

Fault Diagnosis of Transformers using Machine Learning Technique: An Application of Support Vector Machine

D. Lam, L. Cuevas, and B. Chattopadhyay

NV Energy, Las Vegas NV 89118, USA
{dlam, lcuevas, bchattopadhyay}@nvenergy.com

Abstract. Power transformers are one of the most important apparatus in an electric transmission and distribution system. As power transformers age over time, the electrical insulating materials and components begin to deteriorate. One of the most useful techniques to get an early identification of incipient faults in power transformers is through monitoring dissolved gas analysis (DGA). There are various methods available to analyze dissolved gases and subsequently detect potential faults. However, many of the conventional methods governed by IEEE and IEC guidelines are based on concentration levels of a single sample of DGA in the transformer rather than a trend over time. In this study, Support Vector Machines (SVM) are employed for transformer DGA. Annual DGA samples were collected from 105 of NV Energy's transformers and used to generate stochastic time series data for the model. Standard feature extraction techniques were then applied for extracting the meaningful characteristics from the time-series data. The dataset is then trained and evaluated on an SVM with 15-fold cross validation. Among the different feature extraction techniques, the piecewise linear representation (PLR) provided over 80% accuracy of the results, whereas discrete wavelet provided consistent outcomes.

Keywords: Dissolved Gas Analysis, Support Vector Machines, Fault Diagnosis, Transformer Oil, Data Mining.

1 Introduction

Power transformers are critical electrical devices within an electric grid. During operation, transformers are subjected to many electrical and thermal stresses which cause insulation deterioration inside the transformer. If not treated, power transformer failures can be disastrous; power flow disruption, operational delays, and safety risk are just some of the few issues that can arise.

Within oil immersed transformers, hydrocarbon gas molecules begin to form in the presence of electrical disturbances, thermal decomposition, or deterioration of electrical insulation. The rate at which these gasses form depend on the temperature and volume of the material and as such, the same quantity of gas will be produced from a transformer with large insulation exposed to medium heat and medium insulation exposed to high heat [1]. These quantities can be measured by performing gas chromatography or photoacoustic spectroscopy on a sample of the oil from the transformer tank and the results can be analyzed using diagnostic methods such as Duval's Triangle or IEC method [2-4]. The entire process is known as Dissolved Gas Analysis (DGA) and is one of the most important methods for evaluating the condition of a transformer's health.

In conventional practice, transformers are typically sampled annually and evaluated using standard diagnostic methods such as Duval's Triangle or IEC method [2-4]. However, these conventional methods are designed to classify faults based on DGA concentration levels provided by one sample instead of a trend over-time. Given that gas levels can vary over-time with changes in temperature and volume, trending DGA levels over-time provide better a significantly better assessment of a transformer's health than individual concentration levels [1]. With the emergence of online DGA monitors, transformers can now be monitored hourly rather than annually and over time, real-time monitoring may be able to provide better insight into fault classification of a transformer's health. Currently, standards for interpreting real-time DGA data do not exist, and as such, using conventional techniques could result in misinterpretation of daily movement in gas levels. This paper focuses on applying a machine learning technique on real time data in order to classify faults within a transformer.

1.1 Conventional Methods

Currently, there are a variety of DGA analysis methods that are used throughout the industry. Methods such as Roger's Ratio, Doernenburg's Ratio, Key Gas Method, IEC Method, and Duval's Triangle are some of the most popular standard methods for diagnosing a transformer's health condition. However, the methods may not be able to correctly predict a fault. For instance, methods such as Duval's Triangle assumes an incipient fault exists at all times which can be problematic if the transformer has no fault present. Other methods propose thresholds for gas concentration levels which are generalized for all transformers and may provide false positive results if misinterpreted. The primary dissolved gases include Hydrogen (H_2), Methane (CH_4), Ethane (C_2H_6), Ethylene (C_2H_4), and Acetylene (C_2H_2). With the quantities of each and using the gas analysis methods above, three general methods of analysis can be discerned: ratio methods, key gas methods, and graphical methods.

Roger's Ratio. Roger's ratio method studies the relationship of ratios between the primary dissolved gases in order conclude a diagnosis. Considering that gases form at different temperatures, Roger's ratio measures the relationship between CH_4/H_2, C_2H_2/C_2H_4, and C_2H_4/C_2H_6. Depending on the ratios between each gas, the method can estimate if thermal decomposition, energy discharges, or normal aging is occurring inside the transformer [1]. If several faults can be classified, the actual classification can be ambiguous and misinterpreted.

Doernenburg's Ratio. Doernenburg's Ratio is similar to Roger's Ratio method but utilizes the following ratios: CH_4/H_2, C_2H_2/C_2H_4, C_2H_6/C_2H_2, and C_2H_2/CH_4. Only three fault classifications are suggested which are thermal decomposition, electrical discharges except corona (low intensity), corona (high intensity), and cellulosic which is concerned with CO and CO_2 values [2]. If the ratios cannot determine a fault, "no interpretation" can be concluded as a result.

Key Gas Method. This method is based on the relative proportions of the primary dissolved gases defined above and CO. There are four fault classifications including overheated oil, partial discharge in oil, arcing in oil, and overheated cellulose [1]. The relative proportions are shown as percentages and show the importance of which dissolved gas dominates the proportion depending on the type of fault. The number of fault classifications are reduced compared to other dissolved gas analysis methods.

IEC Method. IEC 60599 [4] expands on prior ratio-based methods and includes an additional ratio of C_2H_6/CH_4 which helps indicate decomposition levels for another limited temperature range. The IEC method plots each DGA result on a three-dimensional plane to conclude a fault classification [4]. Partial Discharge (PD), Thermal Fault < 300°C (T1), Thermal Fault < 300°C (T2), Thermal Fault 300°C < t < 700°C, Low Energy Discharge (D1), and High Energy Discharge (D2) are the six conditions that are detectable [1-3]. Those cases where a fault classification is not possible can be plotted onto the graph, and its nearest distance to a certain fault region can then be observed.

Duval's Triangle. This method uses values of only three gases CH_4, C_2H_4, and C_2H_2 and their location in a triangular map determines whether partial discharge, electrical fault (high and low energy arcing), or thermal faults (hot spots of various temperature ranges) are present. This is a simple method but false diagnosis may be due to careless implementation of the method because no region of the triangle is designated to normal ageing. Hence before using this method it should be assessed if the amount of dissolved gases is permissible for transformers that have been in service for many years.

1.2 Machine Learning Applications

As data analysis methods are emerging, many machine learning techniques are being applied for fault diagnosis of transformers. An important characteristic of machine learning is its ability to be trained with a dataset and effectively "learn" during the process. Within machine learning, several algorithms have been proposed for fault diagnosis of transformers: Artificial neural networks (ANN), fuzzy logic systems, back propagation neural network (BPNN), and support vector machines (SVM).

Singh et al. [5] shows how taking the incipient fault classifications from IEC 60599 and using them as classifiers can show accurate classification results. The classifiers create a sixth order SVM model which classify individual DGA data. The first classifier determines if the data is experiencing a fault or not. The second classifier divides the fault between a thermal fault or an electrical discharge fault. The other classifiers will determine exactly what type of fault is being used in classification of IEC 60599. Fathima and Venkatasami [6] use a similar hierarchical approach as [5] but also compare results between different basis functions. Fathima and Venkatasami found that radial (or Gaussian) and linear kernels performed best for the classification of DGA. Yan-Cai et al. [7] also uses a hierarchical support vector machine model and found that the addition of fuzzy logic provided high accuracy rates for DGA classification in SVM models. Zhang et al. [8] implemented Pearson's Correlation Coefficient, Principle Component Analysis, and finally used a back propagation neural network which achieved a high percentage of accuracy. Given multiple data sources, their PCA method was able to reduce the dimensionality of the data and only take into account the primary components of the dataset. Another study by Nagpal and Brar [9] utilized neural networks to classify faults and compared the results with IEC 60599.

Many of the research that proposed for DGA classification has been used to compare machine learning based methods against conventional methods for fault classification on a single DGA sample for each transformer. This paper proposes a support vector machine approach in diagnosing faults within a transformer based on real-time data rather than individual oil samples. Support Vector Machine uses classifiers in order to differentiate the outcome. The ability to reveal classifiers in a higher dimensional space allows for the implementation of multiple features that can best fit a dissolved gas dataset.

2 Proposed Methodology

The proposed method involves gathering and generating data, selecting proper features, extracting features from time series, and developing support vector machines (SVM) for the dataset. The conceptual model for the fault diagnosis method of transformers is presented in Fig. **1**.

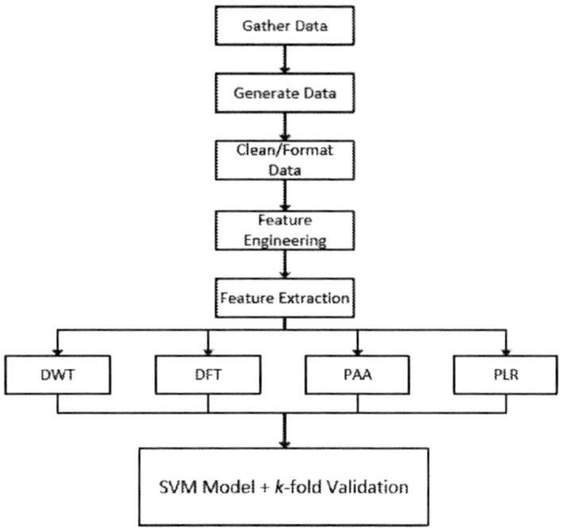

Fig. 1. Proposed method for real-time fault classification of transformer DGA.

2.1 Gathering Data and Additional Data Generation

In this study, DGA samples were collected from approximately 1200 of NV Energy's transformers. The DGA samples were reviewed and classified based on their fault types: Normal condition (N), low thermal fault (T1), medium thermal fault (T2), high thermal fault (T3), partial discharge (PD), low energy discharge (D1), and high energy discharge (D2). Out of the 1200 transformers, a total of 74 samples were utilized for training and testing of the model. Given that machine learning classifiers generally perform poorly on imbalanced datasets, 31 samples needed to be generated to balance the dataset. The generated data was created using a Brownian motion in order to mimic the stochastic nature of real-time dissolved gas in a transformer.

2.2 Geometric Brownian (or Weiner) Motion

Geometric Brownian Motion (GBM) is a common method for generating data for stochastic processes such as stock markets, solar radiation, or wind generation. In this study, Geometric Brownian Motion (GBM) was used to generate the stochastic data between periodic samples of dissolve gas of transformers. As a result, annual dissolve gas samples from transformers can be used to generate hourly data samples in order to mimic data from real-time monitors. Further discussion can be found in [10-11].

2.3 Feature Engineering

Feature engineering is the process of transforming or creating new features from the existing or raw dataset. Rather than supplying the classifier with raw features and expecting the model to determine relationships between the raw data, supplying the classifier with pre-defined relationships between the existing data can improve the machine learning model. In addition, some classical signal processing tools such as Discrete Fourier transform are not suited for analyzing non-stationary signals due to the implicit formulation and assumption that the signal being processed is stationary. As such, calculating the lag or difference between time samples creates a sparse and stationary signal that can be used for the classification. From the raw DGA dataset, normalized gas levels, standard gas ratios, and the rate of change in gas levels were generated.

2.4 Feature Extraction

In order to extract meaningful characteristics from the time-series data, many different feature extraction techniques are used to decompose or transform the multivariate time-series data into a lower dimension. Rather than having the model train on hourly dissolved gas samples, feature extraction techniques provide a sparse representation of the signal by capturing only the most important features of the signal without any loss of information [12]. The following common feature extraction, or data mining, techniques for time-series data are considered for diagnosing transformer faults: Principal Component Analysis (PCA), Discrete Fourier Transformer (DFT), Discrete Haar Wavelet

Transform (DWT), Piecewise Linear Representation (PLR), and Piecewise Linear Approximation (PLA).

Discrete Fourier Transform (DFT). The Discrete Fourier transform decomposes the time-series signal into the spectral components that represent the signal. Rather than having the model train on hourly dissolve gas samples, DFT provide a sparse frequency representation of the time series signal. The reduction in features also enables the machine learning model to better find relationships between features in the dataset. By observing the frequency components of the signal in overlapping sliding windows, DFT can be used to detect events or patterns in the signal [13].

Discrete Wavelet Transform (DWT). Unlike the Fourier Transform, the Discrete Wavelet Transform (DWT) decomposes the time-series signal into fundamental wavelets. While sinusoids are continuous signals with constant frequency, wavelets are finite signals with varying frequencies and zero-mean. In wavelet transform or analysis, small finite wavelets are scaled and modulated throughout each location of time in the signal [14]. As a result, the wavelet transform provides a multiresolution signal characterized by the scale and dilation of wavelet in time. For the DGA time series, a Haar wavelet function is considered as the Haar wavelet function is the simplest wavelet basis function [15]. This observation demonstrates the low order function that is generated from this time series. For this application, Mallat's Pyramid, a recursive algorithm, is employed [16]. The decomposition of the time series is passed through averaging and differencing filters. Once both filters are applied, the resulting vectors are a smoothed version of the original dataset and another vector describing the detail removed due to the smoothing of the other vector [15, 17, 19]. The smoothing of the data is done by convolution which consequently presents boundary problems [18-19]. For the DGA time series, the function is periodic which helps us understand the wavelet coefficients from the averaging and differencing filters.

Piecewise Aggregate Approximation (PAA). Piecewise Aggregate Approximation is another simple dimensionality reduction of time series data. The time series data for this DGA application has a high dimensionality aspect which needs to be reduced to a low space. Like the subspace of a vector, the lower space has properties which fundamentally represent the higher space. In this case, the lower space will underestimate the true distance measure [20]. In order to measure the distance, two methods exist: Euclidean or Dynamic Time Warping [20]. For this application, Euclidean distance shall be used as the true distance measure. Since PAA is a lower bounding function, the time series data can be transformed into another form. This transformation results into the time series data being divided into segments based on w or the lower dimensional space [20]. Visually, the mean value of the data is obtained and shown as a vector in the new space. Each segment is of equal size.

Bottom-Up Segmentation. Bottom-up segmentation aims to create the finest possible approximations of the time series. As discussed in [21], once those approximations are calculated as segments, the adjacent segments are merged until a stopping criterion has been reached. Half of the segments are used to approximate the n-length time series. Next, the cost of merging each pair of adjacent segments is calculated, and the algorithm begins to iteratively merge the lowest cost pair until a stopping criterion is met. When the pair of adjacent segments i and $i+1$ are merged, the algorithm needs to perform some book-keeping. First, the cost of merging the new segment with its right neighbor must be calculated. In addition, the cost of merging the $i-1$ segments with its new larger neighbor must be recalculated. Hence, this process may continue until the stopping criteria is satisfied. The algorithm is further discussed in [21].

Piecewise Linear Representation (PLR). Piecewise Linear Representation is very similar to Piecewise Aggregate Approximation. Segments are developed as a result of the time series analysis and also determines the granularity of the approximation. PLR performs well with time series datasets that trends frequently.

2.5 Support Vector Machines

Support vector machines (SVM) are a set of supervised learning models in machine learning that can be used for outlier detection, regression (ε- or ν- SVM), or classification (C or ν- SVM) [22-23]. Generally, SVM models are binary classifiers that use linear or nonlinear hyperplanes to separate two classes. By maximizing the margins around the hyperplane, the SVM model can make distinctions between the two classes. For multi-class classification, the one-against-one algorithm is used to classify events [24]. The one-against-one algorithm creates SVM classifiers for all possible pairs of classes. Each SVM classifier then "votes" on the class to label the dataset. For this study, a linear multi-class SVM is being utilized for classification of faults in transformers. The *libsvm* library in R is used to develop the SVM models for this study.

2.6 K-Fold Cross Validation

Typically, datasets are split into two disjoint sets in order to train (70%) and test (30%) predictive models for machine learning applications. Rather than using each transformer DGA sample once for either training or testing, k-fold cross validation is used. K-fold cross validation is a technique used to evaluate predictive models by partitioning the dataset into k subsamples of equal size to be used for training and testing the model. For each fold, one subsample is used for testing the model while the other k-1 subsamples are used to train the predictive model. The iterative process is repeated k folds so every subsample can be used for both training and testing the model. The result of each k-fold is then averaged. The advantage of using k-fold cross validation is that all datasets will eventually be used for training and testing of the model. Generally, larger k-fold partitions result in larger variance but minimize the bias [25].

3 Results and Discussion

In this study, DGA samples were collected from approximately 1200 of NV Energy's transformers. The DGA samples were reviewed and classified based on their fault types: Normal condition (N), low thermal fault (T1), medium thermal fault (T2), high thermal fault (T3), partial discharge (PD), low energy discharge (D1), and high energy discharge (D2). Out of the 1200 transformers, a total of 74 samples were utilized for training and testing of the model. Given that machine learning classifiers generally perform poorly on imbalanced datasets, 31 samples needed to be generated or collected from other sources to balance the dataset. The real-time data was then generated using a constrained Brownian motion on existing data in order to mimic the stochastic nature of real-time dissolved gas in a transformer. As a result, a total of 105 transformers (15 per class) were used for the training and testing of the SVM model.

For the study, three different sets of features were created from the raw dataset: rate of change, percent change, and normalized feature sets for gases and ratios. The different feature sets are used in combination with the different feature extraction techniques (DFT, DWT, PLR, and PAA) and evaluated on a 15-fold cross-validation linear SVM model. The partition of 15-fold is selected based on the number of observations for each class and the number of available classes in the dataset. The partitions are stratified such that each subsample contains the same number of observations of each class as the other k-1 subsamples.

Table 1. Feature sets considered for classification of DGA.

	Features				
Normalized Gases & Ratios	H_2	CH_4	C_2H_6	C_2H_4	C_2H_2
	CH_4/H_2	C_2H_2/C_2H_4	C_2H_2/CH_4	C_2H_6/C_2H_2	C_2H_4/C_2H_6
	CO	CO_2	O_2	N_2	CO_2/CO
Percent Change (%)	% H_2	% CH_4	% C_2H_6	% C_2H_4	% C_2H_2
	% CH_4/H_2	% C_2H_2/C_2H_4	% C_2H_2/CH_4	% C_2H_6/C_2H_2	% C_2H_4/C_2H_6
	% CO	% CO_2	% O_2	% N_2	% CO_2/CO
Rate of Change in Gas (Δ)	Δ H_2	Δ CH_4	Δ C_2H_6	Δ C_2H_4	Δ C_2H_2
	Δ CH_4/H_2	Δ C_2H_2/C_2H_4	Δ C_2H_2/CH_4	Δ C_2H_6/C_2H_2	Δ C_2H_4/C_2H_6
	Δ CO	Δ CO_2	Δ O_2	Δ N_2	Δ CO_2/CO

Table 2 shows the model accuracy for different feature extraction techniques used on the rate-of-change in gas and ratio dataset. The best overall performance with the feature set for classification was 72.38% using discrete wavelet transforms. DWT and PLR generally performed well on identifying most types of faults while PAA and DFT generally performed worse overall. However, all methods poorly identified partial discharge in transformers considering the highest accuracy of 13.33%.

In the second experiment, the SVM model was evaluated for feature extraction techniques used on the percent change feature set. Similar to the results completed with the rate-of-change feature set, Table 3 shows that the best performing methods are PLR and DWT where as PAA and DFT general performed worse. However, the model that used PLR performed better than DWT with an accuracy of 86.67%.

The last feature set used was with normalized gas and ratios values. Table 4 shows the model accuracy for each feature extraction technique used on the feature set. The highest performing extraction technique was accomplished using DWT with an accuracy of 79.05%. Unlike the other feature sets, PLR performed significantly worse using the normalized dataset compared to the other sets.

Table 2. Model accuracy for each data mining technique using rate-of-change features.

Class		Fast Fourier Transform (DFT)	Discrete Wavelet Transform (DWT)	Piecewise Linear Representation (PLR)	Piecewise Aggregate Approximation (PAA)
Normal	N	0 (0%)	12 (80%)	14 (93.33%)	13 (86.67%)
Low Energy Discharge	D1	3 (20%)	11 (73.33%)	14 (93.33%)	8 (53.33%)
High Energy Discharge	D2	11 (73.33%)	14 (93.33%)	12 (80%)	10 (66.67%)
Partial Discharge	PD	0 (0%)	2 (13.33%)	1 (6.67%)	1 (6.67%)
Low Thermal Fault	T1	13 (86.67%)	12 (80%)	10 (66.67%)	9 (60%)
Medium Thermal Fault	T2	0 (0%)	13 (86.67%)	12 (80%)	11 (73.33%)
High Thermal Fault	T3	1 (6.67%)	12 (80%)	12 (80%)	1 (6.67%)
Grand Total		28 (26.67%)	76 (72.38%)	75 (71.43%)	53 (50.48%)

Table 3. Model accuracy for each data mining technique using percent difference in features.

Class		Fast Fourier Transform (DFT)	Discrete Wavelet Transform (DWT)	Piecewise Linear Representation (PLR)	Piecewise Aggregate Approximation (PAA)
Normal	N	0 (0%)	15 (100%)	15 (100%)	10 (66.67%)
Low Energy Discharge	D1	5 (33.33%)	14 (93.33%)	15 (100%)	13 (86.67%)
High Energy Discharge	D2	12 (80%)	12 (80%)	14 (93.33%)	12 (80%)
Partial Discharge	PD	1 (6.67%)	5 (33.33%)	5 (33.33%)	1 (6.67%)
Low Thermal Fault	T1	12 (80%)	11 (73.33%)	13 (86.67%)	8 (53.33%)
Medium Thermal Fault	T2	0 (0%)	14 (93.33%)	14 (93.33%)	8 (53.33%)
High Thermal Fault	T3	2 (13.33%)	11 (73.33%)	15 (100%)	5 (33.33%)
Grand Total		32 (30.48%)	82 (78.1%)	91 (86.67%)	57 (54.29%)

Table 4. Model accuracy for each data mining technique using normalized gas and ratio features.

Class		Fast Fourier Transform (DFT)	Discrete Wavelet Transform (DWT)	Piecewise Linear Representation (PLR)	Piecewise Aggregate Approximation (PAA)
Normal	N	0 (0%)	14 (93.33%)	11 (73.33%)	10 (66.67%)
Low Energy Discharge	D1	0 (0%)	13 (86.67%)	9 (60%)	12 (80%)
High Energy Discharge	D2	11 (73.33%)	13 (86.67%)	7 (46.67%)	11 (73.33%)
Partial Discharge	PD	0 (0%)	5 (33.33%)	6 (40%)	1 (6.67%)
Low Thermal Fault	T1	13 (86.67%)	12 (80%)	10 (66.67%)	8 (53.33%)
Medium Thermal Fault	T2	0 (0%)	11 (73.33%)	11 (73.33%)	13 (86.67%)
High Thermal Fault	T3	5 (33.33%)	15 (100%)	5 (33.33%)	1 (6.67%)
Grand Total		29 (27.62%)	83 (79.05%)	59 (56.19%)	56 (53.33%)

A summary of the results of each feature set and feature extraction techniques are shown in Table 5. Although DWT performed consistently well with an average of 76.51% accuracy, PLR performed the best overall with an 86.67% classification rate with the percent-difference feature set. Furthermore, the results suggest that DWT and PLR may be feasible solutions for real-time fault classification in transformers.

Despite the feature set and extraction techniques used, the accuracy for identification of partial discharge was significantly lower than the classification of other faults in the transformer. When observing the results and comparing the prediction against the actual outcome for each dataset, many of the fault mis-classifications occur when the model attempts to distinguish thermal faults from partial discharge. The accuracy of the model could be drastically improved with actual transformer results.

Table 5. Model accuracy results.

	Fast Fourier Transform (FFT)	Discrete Wavelet Transform (DWT)	Piecewise Linear Representation (PLR)	Piecewise Aggregate Approximation (PAA)
Rate of Change	26.67%	72.38%	71.43%	50.48%
% Difference	30.48%	78.10%	86.67%	54.29%
Raw PPM Values	27.62%	79.06%	56.19%	53.33%
Grand Average	28.26%	76.51%	71.43%	52.70%

4 Conclusion

Given that many fault diagnosis methods for transformers only involve studying the dissolved gas concentrations in one sample, this study proposes a method for the classification of real-time DGA. Given that many of the transformers at NV Energy are not equipped with real-time monitors, the real-time dataset was generated from existing data using a constrained Brownian motion. Given different pairs of feature extraction methods and feature sets, the accuracy of each SVM model were then evaluated and compared. Overall, the best result obtained an accuracy of 86.67% by utilizing Piecewise Linear Representation (PLR) with the percent change or difference in the raw time-series dataset. Although PLR performed the best, discrete wavelet transform (DWT) performed consistently well with an average accuracy of 76.51%. The paper also highlighted that Machine Learning application works well when hourly real-time data is available from monitoring devices.

References

1. Hamrick, L.: Dissolved gas analysis for transformers. NETA World Journal. 1-3 (2009).
2. IEEE Std. C57.104-2008.: Guide for the interpretation of gases generated in oil-immersed transformers. (2008).
3. IEEE Std. C57.139-2015.: Guide for dissolved gas analysis in transformer load tap changers. (2015).
4. IEC 60599.: Mineral oil-filled electrical equipment in service – guidance on the interpretation of dissolved and free gases analysis. (2015).
5. Singh, J., Kaur, K., Kumari, P., Swami, A.: Condition assessment of power transformer using SVM based on DGA. Al-Sadiq International Conference on Multidisciplinary in IT and Communication Techniques. , Baghdad (2016).
6. Fathima, J., Venkatasami, A.: Transformer fault classification using support vector machine method. International Journal of Advanced Information and Communication Technology. 1, 168-172 (2014).

7. Yan-cai, X., Gui-qing, N., Qing, Z., Xiao, H.: Transformer fault diagnosis based on hierarchical fuzzy support vector machines. TELKOMNIKA Indonesian Journal of Electrical Engineering. 11, (2013).
8. Zhang, J., Zhu, Y., Shi, W., Sheng, G., Chen, Y.: An improved machine learning scheme for data-driven fault diagnosis of power grid equipment. International Conference on High Performance Computing and Communications (HPCC). IEEE, New York (2015).
9. Nagpal, T., Brar, Y.: Neural network based transformer incipient fault detection. Advances in Electrical Engineering (ICAEE). IEEE, Vellore (2014).
10. Reddy, K., Clinton, V.: Simulating Stock Prices Using Geometric Brownian Motion: Evidence from Australian Companies. Australasian Accounting, Business and Finance Journal. 10, (2016).
11. Sigman, K.: Geometric brownian motion. , http://www.columbia.edu/~ks20/FE-Notes/4700-07-Notes-GBM.pdf (2006).
12. Kordik, P.: Feature extraction for time series. , Czech Technical University (2012).
13. Discrete Fourier Transform. , http://www.robots.ox.ac.uk/~sjrob/Teaching/SP/l7.pdf.
14. Mueen, A.: Data transformation and dimensionality reduction. , University of New Mexico (2014).
15. Essentials in Wavelet Theory. https://www.colorado.edu/engineering/CAS/courses.d/ASEN5519.d/kaist.lecture.11.pdf.
16. Mallat, S.: A theory for multiresolution signal decomposition: the wavelet representation. IEEE Transactions on Pattern Analysis and Machine Intelligence. 11, 674-693 (1989).
17. Lacoste, A.: Wavelet transform for dimensionality reduction. University of Montreal (2005).
18. Graps, A.: An introduction to wavelets. IEEE Computational Sciences and Engineering. 2, 50-61 (1995).
19. Theodoridis, S., Koutroumbas, K.: Pattern recognition. Academic Press, San Diego (2009).
20. Lin, J., Keogh, E., Wei, L., Lonardi, S.: Experiencing SAX: a novel symbolic representation of time series. Data Mining and Knowledge Discovery. pp. 107-108. Springer (2007).
21. Keogh, E., Chu, S., Hart, D., Pazzani, M.: Segmenting Time Series: A Survey and Novel Approach. In: Mark, L., Kandel, A. and Bunke, H. (ed.) Data Mining in Time Series Databases. pp. 1-21. World Scientific, New Jersey (2018).
22. Burges, C.: A tutorial on support vector machines for pattern recognition. Data Mining and Knowledge Discovery. 2, 121-167 (1998).
23. Meyer, D.: Support Vector Machines: the interface to libsvm in package e1071. (2017).
24. Knerr, S., Personnaz, L., Dreyfus, G.: Single-layer learning revisited: a stepwise procedure for building and training a neural network. In: Fogelman, J. (ed.) Neurocomputing: Algorithms, Architectures and Applications. Springer-Verlag (1990).
25. Kohavi, R.: A study of cross-validation and bootstrap for accuracy estimation and model selection. International Joint Conference on Artificial Intelligence (IJCAI). pp. 1137-1143. Morgan Kaufmann, San Francisco (1995).
26. Last, M., Kandel, A., Bunke, H.: Data mining in time series databases. World Scientific, New Jersey (2005).

Learning to Rank and Discover for E-commerce Search

Anjan Goswami[1] and Chengxiang Zhai[2] and Prasant Mohapatra[1]

[1] University of California, Davis agoswami,pmohapatra@ucdavis.edu
[2] University of Illinois Urbana-Champaign cheng@uiuc.edu

Abstract. E-Commerce (E-Com) search is an emerging problem with multiple new challenges. One of the primary challenges constitutes optimizing it for relevance and revenue and simultaneously maintaining a discovery strategy. The problem requires designing novel strategies to systematically "discover" promising items from the inventory, that have not received sufficient exposure in search results while minimizing the loss of relevance and revenue because of that. To this end, we develop a formal framework for optimizing E-Com search and propose a novel epsilon-explore Learning to Rank (eLTR) paradigm that can be integrated with the traditional learning to rank (LTR) framework to explore new or less exposed items. The key idea is to decompose the ranking function into (1) a function of content-based features, (2) a function of behavioral features, and introduce a parameter epsilon to regulate their relative contributions. We further propose novel algorithms based on eLTR to improve the traditional LTR used in the current E-Com search engines by "forcing" exploration of a fixed number of items while limiting the relevance drop. We also show that eLTR can be considered to be monotonic sub-modular and thus we can design a greedy approximation algorithm with a theoretical guarantee. We conduct experiments with synthetic data and compare eLTR with a baseline random selection and an upper confidence bound (UCB) based exploration strategies. We show that eLTR is an efficient algorithm for such exploration. We expect that the formalization presented in this paper will lead to new research in the area of ranking problems for E-com marketplaces.

1 Introduction

One of the most critical components of an e-commerce (e-com) marketplace is its search functionality. The goal of an e-commerce search engine is to show the buyers a set of relevant and desirable products and facilitate the purchasing transactions that generate the revenue for the platform. Additionally, the e-com search also need to facilitate the discovery of the new or less exposed items to the buyers. This is in-fact critical for some categories such as apparel where new items are added periodically. However, a search ranking algorithm uses the behavioral signals such as sales, clicks, cart adds as features in its learning to rank algorithm. Therefore, the search engine may favor certain items that are purchased more by customers than other items in order to maximize the revenue, but the more an engine favors certain items, the higher those items would be ranked in the search. This creates a conflict between the revenue and discovery metrics since some less-favored items might never have a chance of being exposed to the users. It is also easy to see maximizing discovery can compromise relevance of search results since those "unseen products" may not be relevant to a user's interest. We thus see that an e-com search engine must deal with a much more challenging optimization problem dealing with optimizing relevance and revenue as well as providing a discovery mechanism for the buyers. We address this problem in this paper and have made three contributions: Firstly, we suggest a formal framework for optimizing E-Com search and define multiple objectives to form a theoretical foundation for developing effective E-Com search algorithms. Secondly, we propose a simple and practical framework for conducting regulated discovery in e-com search. We then provide an exploration algorithm (eLTR) with a theoretical guarantee that can be easily integrated with traditional learning to rank algorithms. We also discuss how existing multi-armed bandit algorithms such as upper confidence bound (UCB) can also be used to address this problem in e-com search. Thirdly, we suggest a possible evaluation methodology based on simulation with E-Com search log data and show the effectiveness of our proposed eLTR algorithm using our evaluation methodology with synthetically generated data. We also compare different exploration strategies and show the effectiveness of eLTR algorithm.

2 Related work

There has been extensive research on learning to rank (LTR) algorithms particularly in the context of web search [11]. Most of the algorithms are designed to optimize a single metrics. Recently, Svore et al. [17] proposes a variant of LambdaMart [3] that can optimize multiple objectives particularly when two objectives are positively correlated. Authors conducted their experiments showing optimization of two different variants of normalized discounted cumulative gain (NDCG) [8] metrics that are based on judgments of human raters and based on click feedback respectively. In case of e-com search, aiming to maximize exploration can hurt the main business objectives and hence using this approach is not possible. The exploration algorithms are well researched in machine learning [16, 2, 7], particularly in the context of recommender systems [14, 15], news content optimization problems [10]. However, in e-com search we also need to ensure maximization of revenue and the exploration needs to be well regulated to minimize the expected loss. Vermorel et al. [18] in their paper compared the effectiveness of several multi-armed bandit (MAB) algorithms including heuristics such as ϵ-explore, soft-max etc., and also approaches based on upper confidence bound (UCB) [1] which has nice theoretical regret guarantee. The authors suggested often simple heuristics can provide very good practical performance for exploration. In this paper, we use a sub-modular function [12, 20] for exploration in order to have a nice theoretical guarantee for the exploration component. Our approach can be considered similar to the approaches used in learning adaptive sub-modular function [6]. However, we integrated this with a ranking function and propose a novel function and prove the monotonic sub-modularity of it.

3 Optimization of e-com search

We consider the problem of optimizing an E-Com search engine over a fixed period of time $\{1, \cdots, T\}$. We assume that the search engine receives N queries, denoted by $Q = (q_1, q_2, \cdots, q_N)$ during this time. Let $\mathcal{Z} = \{\zeta_1, \cdots, \zeta_M\}$ be the set of M items during the same time. Let's denote the all the relevant items (recall set) for a query q_i by $R_i \subseteq \mathcal{Z}$. Consequently, we have $\mathcal{Z} = \bigcup_{i=1}^{N} R_i$. Now, we define a ranking policy by $\pi : 2^{(Q \times \mathcal{Z})} \rightarrow \Re$, where the input is the set of query item tuples where the items are from the recall set for the query and the output of the policy function is a subset of K items. These items are shown to the users and then an user browses the items one after another in the order they are shown. The user may click an item, add it to the shopping cart, and can also purchase. If a purchasing transaction happens then either the revenue generated or a sale can be considered to be a reward for the π. If the reward is designed to be using revenue it then needs to be real valued. If the reward is based on a sale, it can be a binary variable. It is also possible to construct the reward using clicks or cart-adds or a combination of all or some of these. An e-com search intends to maximize all these measures. However, the policy functions space is exponential and we require to formulate an optimization problem for e-com search. We don't generally have the knowledge when a purchasing transaction can happen. Hence, we introduce a binary random variable $\lambda_{ij} \in \{0, 1\}$ to indicate whether a purchasing transaction will happen with $\lambda_{ij} = 1$ meaning a purchasing event. Naturally, $p(\lambda_{ij} = 1|\zeta_j, q_i) + p(\lambda_{ij} = 0|\zeta_j, q_i) = 1$ for an item ζ_j shown for query q_i. The expected RPV for this query is then given by

$$RPV(q_t) = \sum_{\zeta_j \in \pi(q_i)} price(\zeta_j) \times N(\lambda_{ij} = 1|\zeta_j, q_i).$$

The total revenue defined on all the query results for the fixed period of time T when using policy π is thus

$$g_{RPV}(\pi) = \sum_{i=1}^{N} RPV(q_i)$$

Similarly, we can also define the relevance objective function as

$$g_{REL}(\pi) = \sum_{i=1}^{N} \rho(\pi(q_i))$$

where ρ can be any relevance measure such as nDCG, which is generally defined based on how well the ranked list $\pi(q)$ matches the ideal ranking produced based on human annotations of relevance of each item to the query. The aggregation function does not have to be a sum (over all the queries); it can also be, e.g., the minimum of relevance measure over all the queries, which would allow us to encode the preference for avoiding any query with a very low relevance measure score.

$$g_{REL}(\pi) = min_{i \in [1,p]} \rho(\pi(q_i))$$

We can now define the notion of discoverability of an e-commerce engine by considering a minimum number of impressions of items in a fixed period of time. The notion of discoverability is important because the use of machine learning algorithms in search engines tends to bias a search engine toward favoring the viewed items by users due to the use of features that are computed based on user behavior such as clicks, rates of "add to cart", etc. Since a learning algorithm would rank items that have already attracted many clicks on the top, it might overfit to promote the items viewed by users. As a result, some items might never have an opportunity to be shown to a user (i.e., "discovered" by a user), thus also losing the opportunity to potentially gain clicks. Such "undiscovered" products would then have to stay in the inventory for a long time incurring extra cost and hurting satisfaction of the product providers. To formalize the notion of discoverability, we say that the LTR function f is β-discoverable if all items are shown at least β times. Now, we can further define a β-discoverability rate as the percentage of items that are impressed at least β times in a fixed period of time. Let us now define again a binary variable γ_i for every item ζ_i and then assume that $\gamma_i = 1$ if the item got shown in the search results for β times and $\gamma_i = 0$ in case the item is not shown in the search results more than β times. We can express this as follows:

$$g_{\beta-discoverability} = \frac{\sum_{i=1}^{i=M} \gamma_i}{M}$$

Given these formal definitions, our overall optimization problem for the e-com search is to find an optimal ranking policy π that can simultaneously maximize all three objectives, i.e.,

$$\textbf{Maximize} \quad g_{RPV}(\pi), g_{REL}(\pi), g_{\beta-dicoverability}$$

.

The above is a multi-objective problem and maximizing simultaneously all of the above objective may not be possible and it may also not be a desirable business goal from the platform side. The optimal tradeoff between the different objectives would inevitably application dependent.

The challenging aspect of this multi-objective problem is that the objectives such as discovery requires exploration that can also hurt the relevance and revenue.

4 Strategies for solving the optimization problem

Since there are multiple objectives to optimize, it is impossible to directly apply an existing Learning to Rank (LTR) methods to optimize all the objectives.

However, there are multiple ways to extend an LTR method to solve the problem as we will discuss below.

4.1 Direct extension of LTR

One classic strategy is to use a convex combination of multiple objectives to form one single objective function, which can then be used in a traditional LTR framework to find a ranking that would optimize the consolidated objective function. One advantage of this approach is that we can directly build on the existing LTR framework, though the new objective function would pose new challenges in designing effective and efficient optimization algorithms to actually compute optimal rankings. One disadvantage of this strategy is that we cannot easily control the tradeoff between different objectives (e.g., we sometimes may want to set a lower bound on one objective rather than to maximize it). Additionally, it does not have any exploration component and hence we can not ensure optimizing discovery with such algorithm.

4.2 Incremental Optimization

An alternative strategy is to take an existing LTR ranking function as a basis for a policy and seek to improve the ranking (e.g., by perturbation) so as to optimize multiple objectives as described above; such an incremental optimization strategy is more tractable as we will be searching for solutions to the optimization problem in the neighborhood. We can then construct such a perturbation by keeping a fixed number of x positions for exploration out of the K top results. Then, the rest of the $(K - x)$ items can be selected using a LTR function based on other criteria such as combination of revenue and relevance. This framework is so simple that it is very easy to realize in practice but it is possible to conduct exploration based on several strategies such that the regret in the form of loss of revenue and relevance can be minimized. In the next section of the paper, we discuss a few such strategies.

5 Exploration with LTR (eLTR)

Let us define the set from which the LTR function selects the items as $L_i \subset R_i$ for a given query q_i. We assume that all the items outside set L_i are not β-discoverable. Then, $L = \cup_{i=1}^{i=N} L_i$ is the set of all β-discoverable items. Hence, the set $E = R \backslash L$ can then be consisting of all the items that require exploration.

Now, we propose three strategies to incorporate discovery in an e-commerce search.

Random selection based exploration from the recall set (RSE): This is a baseline strategy for continuous exploration with a LTR algorithm. In this, for every query q_i, we randomly select x items from the set $E \cap R_i$. Then, we put these x items on top of the other $(k - x)$ items that are selected using LTR from the set R_i. The regret here will be linear with the number of

Upper confidence bound (UCB) based exploration from the recall set (UCBE): This is another simple strategy that uses a variant of UCB based algorithm for exploration instead of random sampling. Here, we maintain a MAB for each query. We consider each item in the set $E \cap R_i$ as an arm for the MAB corresponding to a query q_i. We maintain an UCB score for each of those items based on sales over impression for the query. If an item ζ_j is in the set $E \cap R_i$ and is shown b_j times in T iterations, and is sold a_j times in between, then the UCB score of the item ζ_j is $ucb_j = \frac{a_j}{b_j} + \sqrt{\frac{2 \log_2 T+1}{b_j}}$. Note, this is for a specific query. We then select x items based on top UCB scores.

Explore LTR (eLTR In this, we define a function that we call explore LTR (eLTR) to select the x items. The rest of the items for top K can be chosen using the traditional LTR. Then, we can either keep the x items on top or we can rerank all K items based on eLTR.

The main motivation for the eLTR is the observation that there is inherent overfitting in the regular ranking function used in an e-com search engine that hinders exploration, i.e., hinders improvement of β-discoverability and STR. The overfitting is mainly caused by a subset of features derived from user interaction data. Such features are very important as they help inferring a user's preferences, and the overfitting is actually desirable for many repeated queries and for items that have sustained interests t users (since they are "test cases" that have occurred in the training data), but it gives old items a biased advantage over the new items, limiting the increase of β-discoverability and STR. Thus the main idea behind e-LTR is thus to separate such features and introduce a parameter to restrict their influences on the ranking function, indirectly promoting STR. Formally, we note that in general, a ranking function can be written in the following form:

$$y = f(\mathbf{X}) = g(f_1\mathbf{X1}), f_2(\mathbf{X2}))$$

where $y \in \mathbb{R}$ denotes a ranking score and $\mathbf{X} \in \mathbb{R}^N$ is a N dimensional feature vector, $\mathbf{X1} \in \mathbb{R}^N 1$ and $\mathbf{X2} \in \mathbb{R}^N 2$ are two different groups of features such that $N1 + N2 = N, \mathbf{X1} \cup \mathbf{X2} = \mathbf{X}$. The two groups of features are meant to distinguish features that are unbiased (e.g., content matching features) from those that are inherently biased (e.g., clickthrough-based features). Here g is an aggregation function which is monotonic with respect to both arguments. It is easy to show that any linear model can be written as a monotonic aggregation function. It is not possible to use such representation for models such as additive trees. However, our previous techniques do not have such limitation since they are completely separated from the LTR. In this paper, we keep our discussion limited to linear models. We now define explore LTR (eLTR) function as follows:

$$y^e = f_e(\mathbf{X}) = g(f(\mathbf{X1}), \epsilon \times f(\mathbf{X2}))$$

where $y^e \in \mathbb{R}$ and $0 \leq \epsilon \leq 1$ is a variable in our algorithmic framework. Since, g is monotonic, $f_e(\mathbf{X}) <= f(X)$ when $\epsilon \leq 1$. Since feature set $X2$ is a biased feature set favoring old items, we can expect ranking based on f^e would be more in favor of new items in comparison with the original f, achieving the goal of emphasizing exploration of new items. Note that ϵ controls the amount of exploration: the smaller ϵ is, the more exploration (at the cost of exploitation). Since the maximum exploration is achieved when ϵ=0, in which case, ranking is entirely relying on f_1, the only loss in the original objective function is incurred by the removal of f_2. By controlling what features to be included in f_2, we can control the upper bound of the loss. In this sense, eLTR ensures a "safe" exploration strategy since f_1 is always active. Note, this function gradually can become very same as the LTR function when ϵ is close to 1. There can be various ways of constructing the ϵ. In this paper, we experimented with three different expressions for ϵ. These are as follows:

eLTR basic exploration (eLTRb): In this strategy, we keep $\epsilon = \frac{I}{T_{max}}$. Here, I is an iteration and T_{max} is a maximum number of iteration after which everything can be reset. This is a very simple strategy where the eLTR just increases the importances of the behavioral features gradually with every iteration.

eLTR ucb weighted exploration (eLTRu): In this strategy, we keep $\epsilon = \frac{ucb_j}{U_j}$. Here, U_j is a normalization factor and in our experiment it is chosen to be the maximum UCB score in the set $E \cap R_i$. This can be intuitively considered as the expected LTR score based on a sales estimation. It is motivated by adaptive sub-modular optimization in bandit setting [6] that has nice regret guarantee.

eLTR ucb weighted exploration and reranking (eLTRur): This strategy first selects the top x items using eLTRu and it selects the remaining $(k - x)$ items using the classic LTR and then it reranks the k items using eLTRu.

6 Theoretical analysis

In this section, we discuss the regret bounds of all the strategies. We express the regret in terms of total number of search session n in a fixed period of time T. Our first strategy RSE can be arbitrarily bad and can have a worst case regret proportional to $O(xn)$. However, it can have a fast discovery. The UCB is a better strategy compared to RSE. The regret of stochastic variant of UCB can be estimated as $O(\log(xn))$. The discovery in this algorithm will be not as good as the RSE and it can be worst if the MAB arms converge fast towards optimality. On the other hand, we can construct the eLTR function as monotonic sub-modular. Then, the regret for eLTR can be estimated as $O(1+1/e^{-\frac{|E|}{x}})$ times worst compared to the optimal. In our case, the optimal algorithm is LTR [13]. The eLTR algorithm is inspired from ϵ-greedy style MAB algorithm and hence can have better discovery compared to UCB. However, it is not clear if the regret is necessarily better than UCB based strategy. In section 8 we conduct a simulation to understand how these algorithms compare with each other. Here, we now show that eLTR can be indeed monotonic sub-modular.

6.1 Monotonic sub-modularity of eLTR

Let's call the ranking policy for selecting x items from the set E as

$$\pi^e : 2^{(Q \times \mathcal{E})} \rightarrow \Re$$

, where the cost function for our policy can be as follows:

$$c(E) = arg \max_{\zeta \in E} \sum_{i=1}^{i=x} y_i^e$$

We now show that this cost function is monotonic.

If we add a new item in set E, that will be added to the result of a query if the eLTR score for that query and that item is greater than the score of existing top x items. In that case, the cost of eLTR will increase. If the eLTR score for the query and the item is less than the existing top x items, the overall score from eLTR will be unchanged. Hence, the function is monotonically nondecreasing.

Now, we show that this function is sub-modular.

Let us assume that $A \subset B \subseteq E$. Let's also assume that there is an item $\zeta_g \notin (A \cup B)$. Consequently, we can have, $a = c(A \cup \{\zeta_g\}) - c(A)$ and $b = c(B \cup \{\zeta_g\}) - c(B)$.

There can then be three cases: case 1: $c(B) \geq c(A)$

In this case, there must be one or more high eLTR items in set B. Now, if we add the item ζ_g, it will either get added to the top x or not. If it is added to the top items in set B, that means it replaces at least the one item with the minimum eLTR score in top x items in set B. If there are no common items in the top x items for A and B, and since $c(B) \geq c(A)$, the new item has a higher eLTR value than any items in set A and will also replace an item in top x for A. Hence, $a = b$.

Now, if the item does not get added to top x items in B, that means the item does not have higher value compared to the top x items in B. Then, we have $b = 0$. Now, the item can be added in top items for A or not. If it is added in A then we will have $a > 0$ and if it is not added then we have $a = 0$.

case 2: $c(B) \leq c(A)$

This case will never happen since all the items in set A are also in set B and if there are top items in set A, all of those items will be in set B. Hence, unless there are items with higher eLTR compared to the top items in A, top items in B will never be different.

case 3: $c(B) = c(A)$

This is the simplest case. All top items are same and the new item will either get added in both or not since it need to replace one of the top items. Hence, $a = b$.

We have now shown that this cost function always have $a >= b$ and hence this function is sub-modular.

7 Evaluation Methodology

Due to the involvement of multiple objectives, the evaluation of E-Com search algorithms also presents new challenges. Here we discuss some ideas for evaluating the proposed e-LTR algorithm, which we hope will stimulate more work in this direction. The ideal approach for conducting such an evaluation would require simultaneously deploying all candidate methods to live user traffic, and computing various user engagement metrics such as click through rate,sales, revenue etc. However this strategy is difficult to implement in practice. Since user traffic received by each candidate method is different, we need to direct substantial amount of traffic to each method to make observations comparable and conclusions statistically significant. Deployment of a large number of experimental and likely sub-optimal ranking functions, especially when evaluating baselines, can result in significant business losses for e-Commerce search engines. Perhaps a good and feasible strategy is to design a simulation-based evaluation method using counterfactual techniques [9]. Here, we use historical search session data to replay the sessions for a fixed period of time. We then artificially make a set of items selected randomly as candidates for exploration where we do not have estimation of purchase probabilities. We keep these items in set E. We use the true purchase probabilities estimated from the data fro the items that have been shown sufficient number of time in our rank function but use zero values for the same probabilities for the items in set E.

On the surface, it appears that we may simply use the clicks or sales of the items to estimate the utility of each product. However, such a commonly used strategy would inherently favor already exposed items, and if an item has never been exposed, its utility would be zero, thus this strategy cannot be used for evaluating discoverability. To ensure discoverability for potentially *every* item in the collection, we can define the gold utility of a query product pair $u_{q,d}$ as a number randomly sampled between $[0, 1]$. Such a random sampling strategy would give every item a chance of being the underexposed target to be "discovered." Thus although the assigned utilities in this way may not reflect accurately real user preferences, the simulated utility can actually give more meaningful evaluation results than using click-throughs to simulate utility when comparing different exploration-exploitation methods where only the relative difference of these methods matters.

8 Experimental results

In this section, we first construct a synthetic historical dataset with queries, items and their prices. We also generate the true purchase probabilities and utility scores for the item and query pairs. Additionally, we use a specific rank function to simulate the behavior of a trained LTR model.

Then we conduct a simulation as described in section 7 with various exploration strategies. During the simulation we use the observed purchase probabilities estimated from the purchase feedback as the most important feature for the rank function but we use the true probabilities generated during the initial data generation phase to simulate the user behavior.

The main goal of this experimental study is to evaluate the behavior of the exploration strategies (a) with various different sets of number of queries and number of items, (b) with different values of β-discoverability at the beginning, (c) with different distributions of the utility scores representing different state of the inventory in an e-com company.

We evaluate our algorithms by running the simulation for T times. We compute RPV and β-discoverability at the end of T iterations. We also compute a purchase based mean reciprocal ranking [4] metric (MRR). This metric is computed by summing the reciprocal ranks of all the items that are purchased in various user visits for all queries. Moreover, we also discretize our gold utility score between 1 to 5 and generate a rating for each item. This also allows us to compute a mean NDCG score at k-th position for all the search sessions as a relevance metric.

We expect to see that the RPV and NDCG of the LTR function will be the best. however the β-discoverability values will be better in ranking policies that use an exploration strategy. The new ranking strategies will incur loss in RPV and NDCG and based on our theoretical analysis we expect the eLTR methods to have less loss compared to the RSE and UCB based approaches in those measures. We also expect to see a loss in MRR for all exploration methods. However, we mainly interested in observing how these algorithms perform in β-discoverability metric compared to LTR.

8.1 Synthetic data generation

We first generate a set of N queries and M items. We then assign the prices of the items by randomly drawing a number between a minimum and a maximum price from a multi-modal Gaussian distribution that can have up to 1 to 10 peaks for a query. We select the specific number of peaks for a query uniform randomly. We also assign a subset of the peak prices to a query to be considered as the set of it's preferred prices. This makes a situation where every query may have a few preferred price peak points where it may also have the sales or revenue peaks.

Now that we have the items and queries defined, we randomly generate an utility score, denoted by (u_{ij}) for every item ζ_j for a query q_i. In our set up, we use uniform random, Gaussian and a long tailed distribution for selecting the utilities. These three different distributions represent three scenarios for a typical e-com company's inventory. Additionally, we generate a purchase probability between 0.02 to 0.40 for every item for every query. We generate these probabilities such that they correlates with the utility score. We generate these numbers in a way so that these are correlated with the utility scores with a statistically significant (p-value less than 0.10) Pearson correlation coefficient [19]. We also intend to correlate the purchase probability with the preferred peak prices for a query. Hence, we give an additive boost between 0 to 0.1 to the purchase probability in proportion to the absolute difference of the price of the item from the closest preferred mean price for that query. By generating the purchase probabilities in this way, we ensure that the actual purchase probabilities are related to the preferred prices for the queries, and also it is related to the utility scores of the items for a given query. Now, we define a β-discoverability rate $\beta = b$ and selects $b \times M$ items randomly from the set of all items. In our simulation, we assume that the estimated (observed) purchase probability for all the items in set E at the beginning can be zero. The rest of the items purchase probability are assumed to be estimated correctly at the beginning. Now, we create a simple rank function that is a weighted linear function of the utility score (u), the observed purchase probability (p_o), and the normalized absolute difference between the product price and the closest preferred mean price ($\hat{m}_p$ for the query such that $l = 0.60p_o + 0.20u + 0.20\hat{m}_p$. Here l denotes the score of the ranker. This ranker simulates a trained LTR function in e-com search where usually the sales can be considered the most valuable behavioral signal.

We now construct an user model. Here, an user browses through the search results one after another from the top and can purchase an item based on that item's purchase probability for that query. Note, in order to keep the simulation simple, we consider an user only purchases one item in one visit and leaves the site after that. We also can apply a discount to the probability of purchase logarithmically for each lower rank by multiplying $\frac{1}{\log_2(r+1)}$, where r is the ranking position of the item. This is to create an effect of the position bias [5].

8.2 Description of the experimental study

We conduct four sets of experiments with this simulated data.

In the first set of experiments, we use a small set of queries and a small set of products to understand the nature of the algorithms. The utility scores for all the products are generated from an uniform random distribution.

The table 1 shows the RPV, NDCG@6,PMRR, and β-discoverability. We note that all the variants achieve high discoverability score with relatively small loss in RPV, NDCG and MRR. It is clear that eLTRur performs better than all other approaches. It in-fact performs even better than the LTR algorithm in RPV metric along with doing well in discovery.

In the second set of experiments, we use a larger number of queries and products and select a smaller starting value for β-discoverability. We also run this simulation longer. In table 2, we find the eLTR variants perform much better compared to the UCBE, and RSE. In-fact, this time eLTR variants also perform as good as the LTR also in NDCG metric.

In the third set of experiments we use a Gaussian distribution with mean 0.5 and the variance 0.1 for generating the utility scores, but everything else is same as the previous experiment. We again see in table 3 that eLTR variants perform well compared to UCBE and RSE and they also do better in terms of

Algorithms	RPV	NDCG	MRR	$\beta - d$
LTR	0.09	0.94	0.41	0.37
RSE	0.089	0.86	0.38	0.97
UCBE	0.09	0.87	0.39	0.96
eLTRb	0.09	0.88	0.39	0.97
eLTRu	0.09	0.88	0.39	0.97
eLTRur	0.092	0.88	0.40	0.98

Table 1: Simulation of eLTR framework, with $|Q| = 10, |\mathcal{Z}| = 100, |L| = 50, \beta - d = 20\%, \beta = 50, K = 6, x = 3, T = 10000$.

Algorithms	RPV	NDCG	MRR	$\beta - d$
LTR	0.12	0.90	0.42	0.12
RSE	0.09	0.73	0.27	0.30
UCBE	0.10	0.73	0.27 0.66	
eLTRb	0.11	0.91	0.32	0.68
eLTRu	0.11	0.92	0.32	0.68
eLTRur	0.11	0.92	0.32	0.68

Table 2: Simulation of eLTR framework, with $|Q| = 100, M = 5000, |L| = 200, \beta - d = 10\%, \beta = 50, K = 6, x = 3, T = 50000$.

NDCG compared to LTR. The table **??** shows the convergence plots for the six competing algorithms for RPV, MRR, and the discovery.

kept all the parameters same except the distribution of utility score. We generate the scores for all the products from a Gaussian distribution with mean 0.5 and the variance 0.1. The table 3 shows the tables with final metrics for all the algorithms. We observe that with a Gaussian distribution of utility scores the eLTR approaches have better MRR, and β-discoverability.

Algorithms	RPV	NDCG	MRR	$\beta - d$
LTR	0.10	0.92	0.44	0.10
RSE	0.08	0.86	0.28	0.29
UCBE	0.08	0.87	0.28	0.66
eLTRb	0.09	0.94	0.33	0.67
eLTRu	0.09	0.94	0.33	0.67
eLTRur	0.09	0.94	0.33	0.67

Table 3: Simulation of eLTR framework, with $|Q| = 100, |\mathcal{Z}| = 5000, |L| = 200, \beta - d = 10\%, \beta = 50, K = 6, x = 3, T = 50000$.

In the fourth set of experiment, we use a power law to generate the utility distribution. This means that only a small set of items here can be considered valuable in this scenario. The table 5 shows the final metrics for this case and

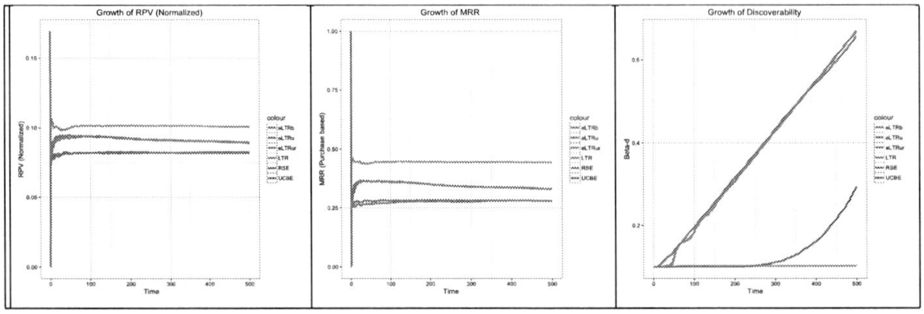

Table 4: Simulation of eLTR framework, with $|Q| = 100, |\mathcal{Z}| = 5000, |L| = 200, \beta - d = 10\%, \beta = 50, K = 6, x = 3, T = 50000$.

the figure 6 shows the convergence plots for RPV, NDCG and discoverability for the six different algorithms. We notice that even with this distribution of utility scores the eLTR variants have smaller loss in RPV, NDCG, and in MRR. Note that in this distribution, the discoverability can be considered to be naturally not so useful since a large number of items are not that valuable. We expect in such situation, a nice discoverability algorithm can help to eliminate items that do not get sold after sufficient exposure and enable the e-com company to optimize it's inventory. The table 6 shows the convergence plots of all the algorithms in this scenario.

Algorithms	RPV	NDCG	MRR	$\beta - d$
LTR	9.56	0.57	0.45	0.11
RSE	7.55	0.27	0.25	0.30
UCBE	7.55	0.27	0.26	0.66
eLTRb	8.2	0.33	0.31	0.67
eLTRu	8.3	0.33	0.31	0.67
eLTRur	8.4	0.33	0.32	0.67

Table 5: Simulation of eLTR framework, with $|Q| = 100, |\mathcal{Z}| = 5000, |L| = 200, \beta - d = 10\%, \beta = 50, K = 6, x = 3, T = 50000$.

9 Conclusions

This paper represents a first step toward formalizing the emerging new E-Com search problem as an optimization problem with multiple objectives including the revenue per-visit (RPV), and discoverability besides relevance. We formally define these objectives and discuss multiple strategies for solving such an optimization problem by extending existing learning to rank algorithms. We also proposed a novel exploratory Learning to Rank (eLTR) method that can be

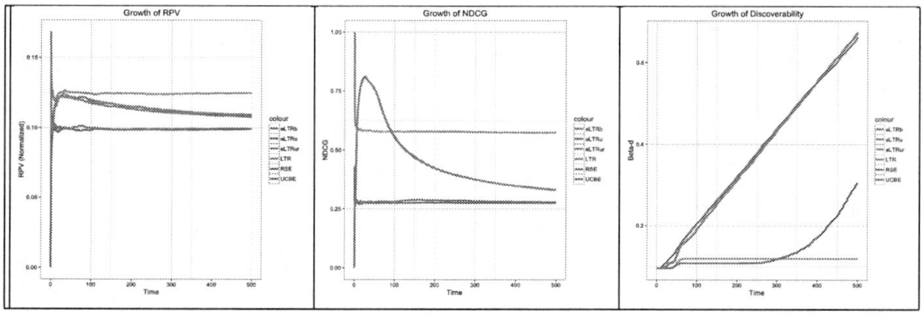

Table 6: Simulation of eLTR framework, with $|Q| = 100, |\mathcal{Z}| = 5000, |L| = 200, \beta - d = 10\%, \beta = 50, K = 6, x = 3, T = 50000$ and with Pareto distribution for the utility scores and the purchase probabilities.

integrated with the traditional LTR framework to explore new or less exposed items and discussed possible methods for evaluating eLTR. We show that selecting the items from a set of yet not discovered items using eLTR can be mapped to a monotonic sub-modular function and hence the greedy algorithm has nice approximation guarantees.We hope that our work will open up many new directions in research for optimizing e-com search. The obvious next step is to empirically validate the proposed eLTR strategy by using the proposed simulation strategy based on log data from an e-com search engine. The proposed theoretical framework also enables many interesting ways to further formalize the e-com search problem and develop new effective e-com search algorithms based on existing multi-armed bandit and sub-modular optimization theories. Finally, the proposed eLTR algorithm is just a small step toward solving the new problem of optimizing discoverability in e-com search; it is important to further develop more effective algorithms that can be applied with non-linear learning to rank algorithms.

References

1. Auer, P., Ortner, R.: Ucb revisited: Improved regret bounds for the stochastic multi-armed bandit problem. Periodica Mathematica Hungarica 61(1-2), 55–65 (2010)
2. Bubeck, S., Cesa-Bianchi, N.: Regret analysis of stochastic and nonstochastic multi-armed bandit problems. FOUNDATIONS AND TRENDS IN MACHINE LEARNING 5(1), 1–122 (2012)
3. Burges, C.J.: From ranknet to lambdarank to lambdamart: An overview. Learning 11(23-581), 81 (2010)
4. Craswell, N.: Mean reciprocal rank. In: Encyclopedia of Database Systems, pp. 1703–1703. Springer (2009)
5. Craswell, N., Zoeter, O., Taylor, M., Ramsey, B.: An experimental comparison of click position-bias models. In: Proceedings of the 2008 International Conference on Web Search and Data Mining. pp. 87–94. WSDM '08, ACM (2008)

6. Gabillon, V., Kveton, B., Wen, Z., Eriksson, B., Muthukrishnan, S.: Adaptive submodular maximization in bandit setting. In: Advances in Neural Information Processing Systems. pp. 2697–2705 (2013)
7. Gittins, J., Glazebrook, K., Weber, R.: Multi-armed bandit allocation indices. John Wiley & Sons (2011)
8. Järvelin, K., Kekäläinen, J.: Cumulated gain-based evaluation of ir techniques. ACM Transactions on Information Systems (TOIS) 20(4), 422–446 (2002)
9. Li, L., Chen, S., Kleban, J., Gupta, A.: Counterfactual estimation and optimization of click metrics in search engines: A case study. In: Proceedings of the 24th International Conference on World Wide Web. pp. 929–934. ACM (2015)
10. Li, L., Chu, W., Langford, J., Schapire, R.E.: A contextual-bandit approach to personalized news article recommendation. In: Proceedings of the 19th international conference on World wide web. pp. 661–670. ACM (2010)
11. Liu, T.Y.: Learning to rank for information retrieval. Foundations and Trends in Information Retrieval 3(3), 225–331 (2009)
12. Lovász, L.: Submodular functions and convexity. In: Mathematical Programming The State of the Art, pp. 235–257. Springer (1983)
13. Nemhauser, G.L., Wolsey, L.A., Fisher, M.L.: An analysis of approximations for maximizing submodular set functionsi. Mathematical Programming 14(1), 265–294 (1978)
14. Park, S.T., Chu, W.: Pairwise preference regression for cold-start recommendation. In: Proceedings of the third ACM conference on Recommender systems. pp. 21–28. ACM (2009)
15. Schein, A.I., Popescul, A., Ungar, L.H., Pennock, D.M.: Methods and metrics for cold-start recommendations. In: Proceedings of the 25th annual international ACM SIGIR conference on Research and development in information retrieval. pp. 253–260. ACM (2002)
16. Sutton, R.S., Barto, A.G.: Reinforcement learning: An introduction, vol. 1. MIT press Cambridge (1998)
17. Svore, K.M., Volkovs, M.N., Burges, C.J.: Learning to rank with multiple objective functions. In: Proceedings of the 20th international conference on World wide web. pp. 367–376. ACM (2011)
18. Vermorel, J., Mohri, M.: Multi-armed bandit algorithms and empirical evaluation. In: ECML. vol. 3720, pp. 437–448. Springer (2005)
19. Wilcox, R.R.: Introduction to robust estimation and hypothesis testing. Academic press (2011)
20. Yue, Y., Guestrin, C.: Linear submodular bandits and their application to diversified retrieval. In: Advances in Neural Information Processing Systems. pp. 2483–2491 (2011)

Prediction of Re-tweeting Activities in Social Networks Based on Event Popularity and User Connectivity

Sayan Unankard

Information Technology Division, Faculty of Science,
Maejo University, Thailand
sayan@mju.ac.th

Abstract. This paper proposes an approach to predict the volume of future re-tweets for a given original short message (tweet). In our research we adopt a probabilistic collaborative filtering prediction model called Matchbox in order to predict the number of re-tweets based on event popularity and user connectivity. We have evaluated our approach on a real-world dataset and we furthermore compare our results to two baselines. We use the datasets crawled by the WISE 2012 Challenge[1] from Sina Weibo[2], which is a popular Chinese microbloging site similar to Twitter. Our experiments show that the proposed approach can effectively predict the amount of future re-tweets for a given original short message.

Keywords: re-tweets, prediction, micro-blog, social networks

1 Introduction

The prediction of message propagation is one of the major challenges in understanding the behaviors of social networks. In this work, we study that challenge in the context of the Twitter social network. In particular, our goal is to predict the propagation behavior of any given short message (i.e., tweet) within a period of 30 days. This is captured by measuring and predicting the number of re-tweets.

To model the re-tweeting activities, we use the datasets crawled by the WISE 2012 Challenge from Sina Weibo, which is a popular Chinese microbloging site similar to Twitter. In Sina Weibo, retweet mechanish is different from Twitter. In Twitter, users can only re-tweet a tweet without modifying the original tweet. However, in Sina Weibo user can modify or add information from other users' in the re-tweeting path in their own re-tweet.

The dataset that to be used in this challenge contains two sets of files. Firstly, Followship network, it includes the following network of users based on user IDs. Secondly, Tweets, it includes basic information about tweets (time, user ID,

[1] http://www.wise2012.cs.ucy.ac.cy/challenge.html
[2] http://weibo.com

Table 1: Number of original messages re-tweeted in 30 days

number of	Original messages		Annotated with events	
re-tweets	#messages	%	#messages	%
< 10	42,551,891	94.749	882,191	2.073
10-99	2,171,214	4.835	65,809	3.031
100-499	173,803	0.387	5,464	3.144
500-999	10,283	0.023	400	3.890
1,000-4,999	2,838	0.006	158	5.567
5,000-9,999	26	0.00006	2	7.692
≥10,000	11	0.00002	1	9.091
Total	44,910,066	100.00	954,025	2.124

Table 2: Number of re-tweets in 10 levels within 30 days

level	number of re-tweets	%
1	107,025,967	56.056
2	49,401,724	25.874
3	16,934,845	8.869
4	8,045,285	4.213
5	4,196,992	2.198
6	2,315,732	1.212
7	1,294,638	0.678
8	746,494	0.390
9	428,158	0.224
10	240,606	0.126

messages ID), mentions (i.e., user IDs appearing in tweets), re-tweet paths, and whether containing links. User IDs and message IDs are anonymized. Content of tweets are removed, based on Sina Weibo's Terms of Services. Some tweets are annotated with events. For each event, the terms that are used to identify the event and a link to Wikipedia[3] page containing descriptions to the event are given. For the purpose of this challenge, 369 million messages and 68 million user profiles were extracted. The sizes of the followship dataset and the microblog dataset are 12.8 GB and 64.8 GB, respectively. It should be note that the dataset is not complete but it is sufficiently large to predict the re-tweeting behavior of users on Sina Weibo.

In preparation for the challenge, we further collected some statistical information for a better understanding of the available datasets. In particular, for the followship dataset (i.e., the who is following whom relationship), we found that the majority of users have less that 10 followers (approximately 91%) as shown in Figure 1. Additionally, for the microblog dataset (i.e., whose tweets are re-tweeted by whom), we ranked the distribution of the original tweets based on how many re-tweets they received within 30 days as shown in Table 1.

[3] http://wikipedia.org

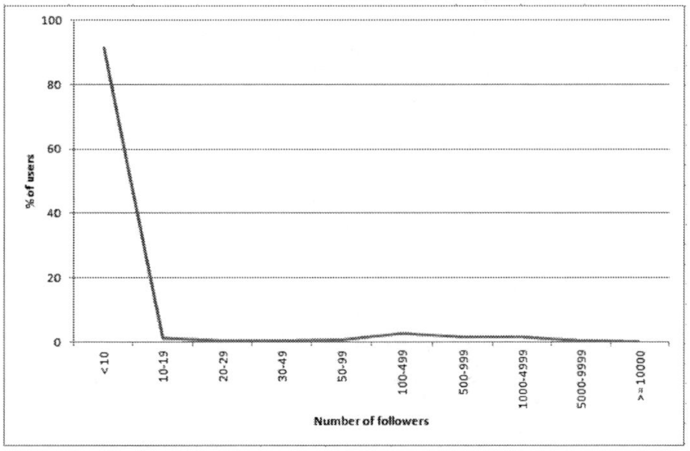

Fig. 1: User distribution based on numbers of followers

The table also shows the subsets of tweets that have been annotated with events. As the table shows, approximately 95% of the original tweets were re-tweeted less than 10 times, of which approximately 2% were annotated with events. In addition, most original tweets were re-tweeted in 3 levels within 30 days (approximately 91%) as shown in Table 2 and Figure 2.

In order to understand the re-tweet activity, we also studied the re-tweet activity by day of the week and time of the day. We selected original tweets associated with events which have the number of re-tweets more than 100 for our study (6,934 messages). In Figure 3, the graph shows the number of re-tweets per day of week. Based on a sample of tweets, Monday is the most popular day for re-tweet activity; followed by Tuesday and Friday. In Figure 4, the chart shows the number of re-tweets per hour of the day. During the day, the most re-tweet activity happens from 10 a.m. to 12 p.m.

The contributions of this paper are summarized as follows: 1) An extensive statistical studies on the re-tweeting activities of users' behaviors in the widely used social network are provided. 2) The number of re-tweets is measured to understand the users' participation for spreading information in social network. 3) An approach to automatically predict the number of re-tweets over micro-blogs is proposed.

This paper is organised as follows, Section 2 is about related work. The proposed approach is presented in Section 3. In Section 4, we present the experimental setup and results, the conclusions are given in Section 5.

2 Related work

Microblogging activities in social networks have been attracting growing attentions from researchers in Data Mining and Information Retrieval. One interesting

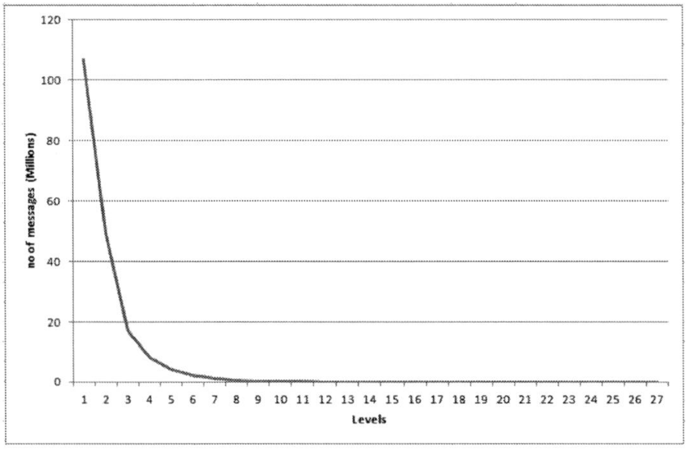

Fig. 2: Number of re-tweets in each level

problem is the study on the re-tweeting behaviours from an information diffusion perspective. Most works had focused on Twitter, a popular microblogging site. Insightful studies on re-tweeting behaviors can be seen from [1, 2, 4, 9].

In [1], Boyd et al. studied the various aspects of re-tweeting. They conducted interviews with Twitter users and investigated the reasons why they re-tweet. Letierce et al. in [4] surveyed how researchers used Twitter to spread scientific messages. However, neither of them attempted to predict on whether a given message is to be re-tweeted. Galuba et al. in [2] focused on the URL propagation via re-tweets. In [9], Suh et al. gathered content and contextual features from Twitter and identified factors that impact re-tweeting. They found that URLs and hashtags have strong relationships with re-tweetability and identified the number of followers and followees as important factors.

Zaman et al. in [12] adapted a probabilistic collaborative filtering model called Matchbox [8] to predict information spreading in Twitter based on features such as tweeter and re-tweeter information, and the tweet content. In [11], Yang et al. proposed a factor graph model based on users' re-tweeting history.

Recently, Petrovic et al. in [7] built a time-sensitive model based on the passive-aggressive algorithm (PA) to automatically predict re-tweets activities. Hong et al. in [3] trained a binary classifier to predict if a message will be re-tweeted or not and a multi-class classifier based on logistic regression to predict the volume of re-tweets for a given message. For the multi-class classification, they used four class labels (0: no re-tweet, 1: re-tweets less than 100, 2: re-tweets less than 10000, and 3: re-tweets more than 10000).

In [6], Peng et al. modelled the re-tweeting activities by using conditional random fields with three types of features, namely content influence, network influence and temporal decay factor. Naveed et al. in [5] argued that the tweet content is the key for re-tweeting prediction. They used logistic regression to

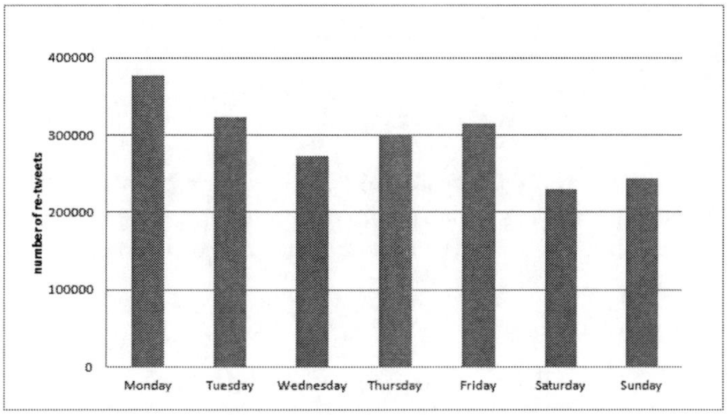

Fig. 3: Re-tweet activity by day of the week

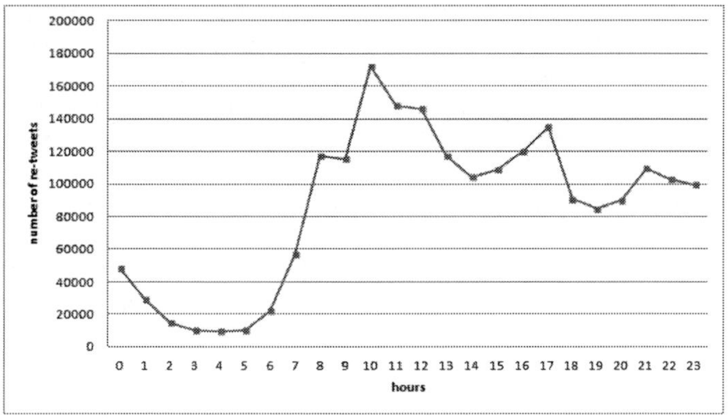

Fig. 4: Re-tweet activity by time of the day

compute re-tweet likelihood based on various interesting content features such as emotion positive/negative, exclamation/question mark, etc.

In our work, the tweet content has been removed from Sina Weibo microblog dataset pre-processed by WISE 2012 Challenge due to Sina Weibo's Term of Services.

3 Proposed Approach

3.1 Assumptions

Based on the given datasets, together with our statistical information presented in Section 1, we make the following assumptions:

- An event category is a group of similar events (manually grouped).

- The more popular the event category is, the more likely the tweet will be re-tweeted by a user.
- Similar events have similar re-tweet patterns.
- A user who has re-tweeted frequently in the past is likely to re-tweet in the future.
- Most users are only interested in tweets under certain event categories. Most followers are users who have similar interests.
- Users' interests and preferences are assumed to be stable.

3.2 Event Category

In WISE 2012 Challenge, the given original tweets are annotated with some social events together with their corresponding keyword lists. It is difficult to automatically group events into different categories and it is neither in our focus in this report because some events are simply labelled by personal names or by location names. Moreover, their relevant keyword lists are arbitrary and do not show clear contextual information between the keyword list and the event title. To solve this problem, we manually divide the WISE 2012 provided 46 events that have links to Wikipedia pages into 12 categories such as Natural Disaster, Celebrities, Product Release, Sports, and etc. The examples of event categories are shown in Table 5.

In order to predict the number of re-tweets, we adopt a probabilistic collaborative filtering prediction model called Matchbox which is a probabilistic model for generating personalized recommendations of items to users of a web service. Matchbox is used for the prediction of rating that users are likely to assign to items. It uses content information in the form of user and item metadata to learn correlations between them. Details of the Matchbox model can be found in [8]. This model can be applied to cope with our problem by the prediction of re-tweeting probability instead of the prediction of rating.

Matchbox is a factor graph for Bi-linear rating model. Each user and item are represented by a vector of features. Each feature is associated with a latent trait vector and the linear combination of the trait vectors for a particular user or item. An existing implementations of the Matchbox Recommender can be found at this link[4]. We adopt this model to predict whether followers of user will re-tweet the message posted by user who has posted an original tweet. For our approach, each tweet is regarded as an item while re-tweeter is considered as a user.

3.3 Tweet and Re-tweeter Features

According to datasets which have been pre-processed by WISE 2012 Challenge, we have Followship network and Tweets data without content. Although keyword lists are provided, they are arbitrary and do not show clear contextual

[4] https://docs.microsoft.com/en-us/azure/machine-learning/studio-module-reference/train-matchbox-recommender

Algorithm 1: *PredictRetweetviaMatchbox*

```
Input: mid:message id
Output: num_r:predicted number of re-tweets
tweets = GetPrevious100Messages(mid); //Get the latest 100 messages of the
  user before the predicted message (mid) has been posted.
users = GetRetweeters(tweets);
retweets = GetRetweetHistory(tweets);
tw_vectors = CreateTweetFeatures(tweets);
usr_vectors = CreateUserFeatures(users);
model = TrainModel(tw_vectors, usr_vectors, retweets);
foreach u ∈ usr_vectors do
    predict = model.predict(u, mid);
    if predict.getProbTrue() ≥ threshold then
        num_rt = num_rt + 1;
    end
end
return num_rt;
```

information between the keywords and the event. For our approach, each tweet is regarded as an item while re-tweeter is considered as a user to train the model.

Tweet features consist of tweet id, user id who posted the original tweet, number of followers, number of followees, day of the week, time of the day and event category. Re-tweeter features include user id who re-tweeted the tweet, number of followers and number of followees. Re-tweeters are extracted from all users who have re-tweeted in the past of each tweet. The binary feedback is 1 if the re-tweeter re-tweeted the tweet within 30 days and 0 otherwise. The output of the model will be the probability of a re-tweet of the tweet by the re-tweeter.

3.4 Training Data

In order to train the model, it is required the positive binary feedback and also negative feedback. The positive feedbacks are from all re-tweet action in the past of each tweet in the same event category. For a given tweet, the negative feedbacks are from all followers in the re-tweet network who did not re-tweet a given tweet. For each test event, we train the model by random select 1,000 original tweets in the same event category as items and extract re-tweeters from re-tweet history of each tweet.

3.5 Prediction

To predict the number of re-tweets, for given original tweet and set of users if user has the high probability of a re-tweet greater than threshold, the user is likely to re-tweet the original tweet. In order to find the most suitable value for threshold, we did the prediction on different threshold values. When threshold = 0.4 it render the best performance. The algorithm is shown as Algorithm 1.

4 Experiments and Evaluations

4.1 Baselines

The two baselines were compared with our results.

Baseline 1: Regression based on Popularity and Connectivity. It is a model to predict re-tweet activities based on event popularity and user connectivity by using a naïve approach. The intuition is that a tweet is more likely to be re-tweeted if it is about a popular event and its author is highly connected with others. The prediction will be the estimation of the probabilities of these two parameters in the space (connectivity of the user and category popularity). The formula for re-tweet prediction is shown as Eq. 1.

$$NumberOfRTs = 19.950(0.024C(uid) + 0.976P(uid, category)) \quad (1)$$

where function $C(uid)$ is to find how many re-tweets a uid (user ID) may have based on the number of followers she has, function $P(uid, category)$ is to predict how the event category popularity influences a tweet being re-tweeted. More details can be found in [10].

Baseline 2: Classification based on User Preferences. User preferences are used to train a classifier to predict the possible number of re-tweets in 30 days for a given original tweet. Given an original tweet, the authors need to compute how possible a user will re-tweet the original tweet in the category. The candidate users are extracted from re-tweet history in a form of "who-retweet-who". The authors use $P(r, u, c)$ to denote the interestingness of candidate re-tweet user r to original user u on category c. The function is defined as Eq. 2.

$$P(r, u, c) = \sum RT(r, u, c) / \sum T(u, c) \quad (2)$$

where $RT(r, u, c)$ returns the number of re-tweets by user r from user u on category c; $T(u, c)$ returns the total number of u's tweet on category c. More details of this algorithm can be found in [10].

4.2 Evaluations

For evaluation our approach, we predicted 33 test tweets and the ground truth of 33 tweets are provided by WISE 2012 Challenge[5]. For each tweet we compute the prediction error score (PE).

$$PE_i = \frac{|A_i - P_i|}{A_i} \quad (3)$$

where A_i is the actual value for tweet i and P_i is the predict value for tweet i. For each approach, the average of prediction error scores is computed.

$$Average_j = \frac{\sum_{t=1}^{N} PE_t}{N} \quad (4)$$

[5] http://content.wuala.com/contents/imc_ecnu/wise_challenge/A4_T2GTruth.zip?dl=1

Table 3: Average prediction error scores

Methods	Error Scores
Baseline 1 : Regression based on Popularity and Connectivity	0.700
Baseline 2 : Classification based on User Preferences	0.666
Our approach : Probabilistic collaborative filtering prediction model	**0.627**

where N is the number of test tweets. The small number is the better prediction result. Table 3 shows the performance of our approach againt baselines. Table 4 lists the predictions for the given 33 original tweets over 6 given events. In Table 3, our approach shows a better performance than others on the prediction number of re-tweets.

5 Conclusions

In this paper, we proposed an approach to automatically predict the number of re-tweets over micro-blogs. Our contributions can be summarized as: (1) We proposed a solution to estimate the volume of re-tweets for understanding the behaviors of social networks. (2) We adopt probabilistic collaborative filtering prediction model named Matchbox by the prediction of re-tweeting probability instead of the prediction of rating. (3) We provide an evaluation for the effective re-tweet prediction on a real-world dataset. Our experiments show that the proposed approach can effectively predict the number of re-tweet over the baselines. In future work, we will retrospectively study the assumptions that we have made on the given datasets and develop a hybrid approach to integrate the proposed methods.

References

1. D. Boyd, S. Golder, and G. Lotan. Tweet, tweet, retweet: Conversational aspects of retweeting on twitter. In *HICSS*, pages 1–10, 2010.
2. W. Galuba, K. Aberer, D. Chakraborty, Z. Despotovic, and W. Kellerer. Outtweeting the twitterers-predicting information cascades in microblogs. In *Proceedings of the 3rd conference on Online social networks*, pages 3–3, 2010.
3. L. Hong, O. Dan, and B. D. Davison. Predicting popular messages in twitter. In *WWW (Companion Volume)*, pages 57–58, 2011.
4. J. Letierce, A. Passant, S. Decker, and J. G. Breslin. Understanding how twitter is used to spread scientific messages. In *ACM WebSci Conference 2010*, pages 1–8, 2010.
5. N. Naveed, T. Gottron, J. Kunegis, and A. C. Alhadi. Bad news travel fast: A content-based analysis of interestingness on twitter. In *ACM WebSci Conference*, pages 1–7, June 2011.
6. H.-K. Peng, J. Zhu, D. Piao, R. Yan, and Y. Zhang. Retweet modeling using conditional random fields. In *ICDM Workshops*, pages 336–343, 2011.
7. S. Petrovic, M. Osborne, and V. Lavrenko. Rt to win! predicting message propagation in twitter. In *ICWSM*, 2011.

Table 4: The 33 predicted re-tweets of our approach and baselines

Mid	Ground truth	Baseline 1	Baseline 2	Our approach
Death of Steve Jobs				
8872263516485596	165	228	127	428
8872961090747701	3550	135	128	312
8872983825828431	154	184	137	128
8872990233170214	121	126	140	156
Fuzhou bombings				
27000599582694434 92	798	476	152	185
2700117991448817596	242	93	132	303
2700176673306864228	686	223	140	624
2701374467440601577	384	418	222	449
2701431322360449433	1271	10	148	488
Japan earthquake				
51000180083282169	576	68	157	138
51000180083492814	187	46	142	169
51000180091104384	188	46	172	42
55000180091534860	2119	43	147	463
55000180527027036	1068	5	134	40
58000180083553705	699	30	740	114
Li Na win French Open tennis				
2709258383303085289	620	3	260	281
2709864654666932643	13638	33	117	52
2709870697693881414	417	25	114	246
2709871713230486085	1383	53	132	232
2709893077170155796	163	33	130	403
Xiaomi release				
8896800636296312	1230	20	119	83
8896822338137478	114	95	257	101
8896858839607761	1681	23	136	555
8896889634186199	808	4	178	185
8896952812610010	249	12	129	154
Yao Jiaxin murder case				
2243526721410152330	700	232	160	141
2243578214587694822	129	142	142	159
510001856830842390	534	170	182	159
510001856834367317	121	39	298	152
510001904903643837	1001	946	143	128
510001908564754698	3474	9	616	106
5100019107401880	1126	609	170	187
550001906873838396	4900	31	184	164

Table 5: The 12 event categories in *WISE 2012* dataset

Category	Event
Natural Disaster	Earthquake of Yunnan Yingjiang
	Japan Earthquake
	Yushu earthquake
	Zhouqu landslide
Product Release	iPhone 4s release
	Windows Phone release
	Motorola was acquisitions by Google
	Xiaomi release
Sports	Yao Ming retirement
	Spain Series A League
	Li Na win French Open in tennis
Famous people	The death of Muammar Gaddafi
	The death of Steve Jobs
	Family violence of Li Yang
	Tang Jun educatioin qualification fake
	The death of Kim Jongil
	The death of Osama Bin Laden
Social problem	Anshun incident
	China Petro chemical Co. Ltd.
	Foxconn worker falls to death
	Guo Meimei
	Incident of self-burning at Yancheng, Jangsu
	Shanghai government's urban management officers attack migrant workers in 2011
	Yao Jiaxin murder case
	Yihuang self-immolation incident
	The death of Wang Yue
	Case of running fast car in Heibei University
Public Security	Bohai bay oil spill
	Foxconn bombing in Chengdu
	Fuzhou bombings
	Shanxi
Protests	Chaozhou riot
	Mass suicide at Nanchang Bridge
	Protests of Wukan
	Qianxi riot
	Zhili disobey tax official violent
Development Projects	Line 10 of Shanghai-Metro pileup
	Shenzhou-8 launch successfully
	Tiangong-1 launch successfully
Economy	House prices
	Individual income tax threshold rise up to 3500
Human right	Qian Yunhui
	Deng Yujiao incident
Accident	Gansu school bus crash
	Wenzhou train collision
Crime	Chongqing gang trials

8. D. H. Stern, R. Herbrich, and T. Graepel. Matchbox: large scale online bayesian recommendations. In *WWW*, pages 111–120, 2009.
9. B. Suh, L. Hong, P. Pirolli, and E. H. Chi. Want to be retweeted? large scale analytics on factors impacting retweet in twitter network. In *SocialCom/PASSAT*, pages 177–184, 2010.
10. S. Unankard, L. Chen, P. Li, S. Wang, Z. Huang, M. A. Sharaf, and X. Li. On the prediction of re-tweeting activities in social networks – a report on wise 2012 challenge. In *Web Information Systems Engineering - WISE 2012*, pages 744–754, Berlin, Heidelberg, 2012. Springer Berlin Heidelberg.
11. Z. Yang, J. Guo, K. Cai, J. Tang, J. Li, L. Zhang, and Z. Su. Understanding retweeting behaviors in social networks. In *CIKM*, pages 1633–1636, 2010.
12. T. R. Zaman, R. Herbrich, and D. H. Stern. Predicting information spreading in twitter. *Computational Social Science and the Wisdom of Crowds*, 55:1–4, 2010.

Ensemble of Heterogeneous Regressors Applied to Forecasting in Cosmetics Industry

Leandro dos Santos Coelho[1,2], Viviana Cocco Mariani[1,3], Frederico Gonzalez Colombo Arnoldi[4] and Donald Neumann[5]

[1] Department of Electrical Engineering, Federal University of Parana (UFPR)
[2] Industrial and Systems Engineering Graduate Program (PPGEPS)
[3] Mechanical Engineering Graduate Program (PPGEM),
Pontifical Catholic University of Parana (PUCPR)
[4] O Boticário, São José dos Pinhais, Curitiba, PR, Brazil
[5] Department of General and Applied Management, Federal University of Parana (UFPR)
leandro.coelho@pucpr.br

Abstract. Cosmetic products serve the beautifying purposes and cover a wide range of products. Despite the recent advances in production, planning and management processes in the cosmetic industry, few studies have explored machine learning (ML) methods to predict the derived demand from point-of-sales (sell-in) based on end consumer demand (sell-out). In terms of regression, ML can be useful to identify and discover patterns in complex datasets related to products and predict point-of-sales behavior affecting the sell-in demand. The contribution of this paper is the comparison of the predictive performance of ten regressors and its heterogeneous ensemble generating estimates of the sell-in demand using datasets from a Brazilian cosmetics company that operates in a franchising business model. The results show that ensemble learning method can be a convenient and accurate approach to predict monthly cosmetic sales up to 200 SKUs (Stock Keeping Units) with 15 steps ahead, reducing the Bullwhip Effect, improving stock and service levels along the supply chain.

Keywords: Ensemble learning, Forecasting, Regression, Cosmetics Industry, Supply chain management, Bullwhip effect.

1 Introduction

During the last years, the cosmetic industry has dramatically diversified its managerial and marketing orientation towards customer requirements due to the growth in response to the customer trends towards a healthier lifestyle and requirements for natural cosmetics [1]. In 2015 the industry generated $56.2 billion in the United States. Hair care is the largest segment with 86,000 locations. Skin care is a close second and growing fast, expected to have revenue of almost $11 billion by 2018. This growth is being driven in part by a generally increasing awareness of the importance of skin care, but also specifically due to an increase in the market for men [2]. Since the turn of the century the cosmetic markets of the BRIC countries (Brasil, Russia, India and China) have been growing fast. In 2011 all those countries generated 81% of the global cosmetics sales growth, according to *Euromonitor International's* data, more than half of which (54%) was attributed to BRIC [3]. According to Euromonitor, the Brazilian market for Beauty and Personal Care (BPC) products was about 102 billion of real in 2016 and should reach 120 billion of real in 2020. Although it is a health market, the compound annual growth rate (CAGR) is expected to decrease from 8.3% (2011-2016) to 4.8% (2016-2021) with a weak period in 2016 and 2017 with a CAGR of 2.6% [4]. This scenario motivates many companies to review internal processes in order to eliminate inefficiencies.

The Brazil BPC market has many different product categories, with hundreds and even thousands of products within each group. As consequence, a large company can have thousands of SKUs in its portfolio and complex demand plans along the whole supply chain, from consumer (independent, sell-out demand) to OME (derived, sell-in demand) are necessary to keep the global efficiency of system. Increase in the BPC complexity and the massive data production have caused an exponential growth in databases and repositories. In addition, forecasting is crucial for the cosmetic industry, but an effective sales forecasting model is challenging due to the sizeable amount of purchasing information obtained from diverse sources in a BPC industry. Machine learning (ML) and big data methods are emerging technologies actively being adopted across many knowledge fields. In last years, several ML applications for regression approaches have been studied and proposed using ensemble-based frameworks [5-7].

The main contribution of this paper is a validation of ten regressors (multilayer perceptron, Elman partially recurrent network, support vector regressor, extreme learning machine, Cubist, *k*-nearest neighbor, multivariable adaptive regressor splines, ordinary random forest, regularized random forest, and extreme gradient boosting) and the combination of the mentioned methods in the ensemble approaches for regression. The regressors were evaluated with a dataset including 200 SKUs from a Brazilian cosmetics company that operates in a franchising business model with thousands of stores. The remainder of the paper is organized as follows. In Section 2, we briefly introduce the regression case study of the Brazilian cosmetics company. In Sections 3, comments about the adopted ensemble form are mentioned. Section 4 presents a results analysis. Finally, this short paper is concluded in Section 5.

2 Brief Description of Case Study in Cosmetics Industry

This complexity of the BPC is leveraged by the fact that sales usually happen in two distinct stages, from industry to stores (sell-in) and from stores to end consumers (sell-out). In the long term, the sell-in volume is similar to the sell-out one. However, in the short-term they are significantly different as the sell-in demand is deeply affected by the behavior of the independent, fully autonomous buying agent at the point-of-sale. This phenomenon is well known in the supply chain literature as the Bullwhip Effect, caused by sub-optimal decision policies, time delays, uncertainties and speculative behavior of the buying agent [10]. In case these differences are not forecasted, over stocking or out-of-stocks can happen in both stages, leading to inefficiencies in the management of the company's financial resources. Different approaches were tested to identify which methodology would help companies to convert sell-out forecasts to sell-in volumes, i.e. predict the behavior of the autonomous buying agent. Sell-out and sell-in volumes were made equivalent in time by adding the lead-time of the delivering products, differences in volume were the subject of our study. A schematic of the case study related to a regression problem is illustrated in Fig. 1.

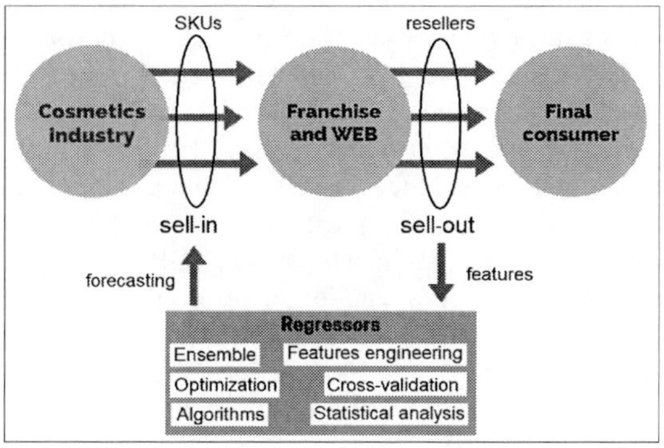

Fig. 1. Schematic linking the cosmetics industry and regressors.

3 Ensemble Learning

The process of ensemble learning for regression can be divided into three phases: the generation phase, in which a set of candidate models is induced, the pruning phase, to select of a subset of those models and the integration phase, in which the output of the models is combined to generate a prediction [4]. In this paper the proposed ensemble learning for regression is composed of simple and heterogeneous base models (base learners) linked with cross-validation procedure, including the following procedures:

Dataset setup: The dataset has 56 features for 200 SKUs as inputs and one output variable of the regressors. Among these features are holidays and marketing variables that affect the buying behavior of the downstream members of the chain. The time unit is the selling cycle of the company and forecasting horizon of the sell-in (output variable) was 15 steps ahead. More details about the contents of the dataset were not authorized by Brazilian cosmetics industry.

Features selection: The adopted design of ensemble learning of this research was based in the combination of three procedures: (i) correlation analysis of inputs to the output; (ii) ranking of the information gain obtained by a gradient boosting machine for regression called xgboost [8] in regression task; and (iii) features clustering linked with correlation analysis. General result of features selection was a decreasing of 43 initial to 36 to forecasting horizon with 15 steps ahead to 200 SKUs.

Model validation: Cross-validation (CV) is a resampling technique often used in ML for model selection and estimation of the prediction error in regression problems. In this paper, CV was equal to 10 folds repeated 100 times.

4 Results Analysis

Ten ML approaches were designed and tested alone in R Studio computational environment. In the tests phase, different combinations using a weighted sum of regressors outputs linked with a factorial experimental design [9] approach to the alone design was validated to obtain a best ensemble regressor in terms of generalization to prevent from having overfitting in a forecasting for 200 SKUs. The performance criterion adopted was the MAPE (Mean Absolute Percentage Error) to be minimized with 15 steps ahead of forecasting. The validated ten regressors were the following: multilayer perceptron (MLP), Elman partially recurrent network (EPRN), support vector regressor (SVR), extreme learning machine (ELM), Cubist, *k*-nearest neighbor (*k*NN), multivariable adaptive regressor splines (MARS), ordinary random forest (ORF), regularized random forest (RRF), and extreme gradient boosting (XGB). The best results with alone approaches were RRF, ORF and XGB, and for all tested approaches, in terms of MAPE performance (k=10 folds repeated 100 times) was the ensemble (BestEns) obtained by weighted sum of *k*NN, SVR, Cubist and XGB as illustrated in Table 1.

The SO, sale of franchisees to the final consumer, utilized as forecaster was more efficient than the regressors in SKUs. This result confirms the hypothesis that in many cases the behavior of the downstream agent is not rational could be identified over the sell-out demand. According to the supply chain literature, this might be due to uncertainties, sub-optimal decision policies and time delays for the agent to react to the consumer demand [10]. Even though this might appear to be a not very good result, for the company knowing which types of products are not subject to rational buying behavior helps to mitigate the amplification of the demand signal (bullwhip effect) upward in the chain. For another set of products, significant variables were identified, which drive buying behavior downstream on the chain. Business understanding of these variables helps preparing stocks assuring adequate service level.

Table 1. Mean quartile results of MAPE criterion. First best results in bold, second and third best results are underlined.

Regressors	Quartile (25%)	Quartile (50%)	Quartile (75%)
SO (Sell-Out)	0.130	0.273	<u>0.464</u>
MLP[1]	0.131	0.331	0.562
EPRN[1]	0.292	0.575	0.913
SVR[2]	0.231	0.440	0.654
ELM[3]	0.305	0.596	0.932
Cubist[4]	0.136	0.304	0.654
*k*NN[5]	0.153	0.315	0.573
MARS[6]	0.136	0.289	0.571
ORF[7]	<u>0.122</u>	*0.271*	0.510
RRF[7]	0.125	<u>0.263</u>	0.517
XGB[8]	*0.126*	0.278	*0.481*
BestEns	**0.104**	**0.239**	**0.430**

* Comprehensive R Archive Network (*https://cran.r-project.org/*)

5 Conclusion and Future Research

Ensemble methods has been proved be a promising alternative in many applications (see details in [5,6]). The combination of many regressors in an ensemble is a well-known method of increasing the quality of recognition and forecasting tasks. In this paper, the performance of ten ML approaches was applied alone and also in an ensemble form based in weighted sum. The solution obtained by this research was further extended for the whole product portfolio and implemented in a solution that combines R and SPSS and was fully deployed into the Integrated Sales and Operations process of the company. As a future research to do, the systematic way to improve the ensemble design based on bagging, boosting, and stacking approaches.

Acknowledgments

The authors would like to thank CNPq (Grants: 150501/2017-0-PDJ, 303906/2015-4-PQ, 303908/2015-7-PQ, 405101/2016-3-Univ, 404659/2016-0-Univ, 204910/2017-0-PDE and 204893/2017-8-PDE) for its financial support of this work.

References

1. Dimitrova, V., Kaneva, M., Gallucci, T. (2009), "Customer knowledge management in the natural cosmetics industry", Industrial Management & Data Systems, 109 (9), 1155-1165.
2. Beauty Industry Analysis 2018 - Cost & Trends, Available at: Beauty Industry Analysis 2015 - Cost & Trends, *https://www.franchisehelp.com/industry-reports/beauty-industry-analysis-2018-cost-trends/* (Accessed on: March 15, 2018).
3. A. Łopaciuk and M. Łoboda, Global beauty industry trends in the 21st century, Management, Knowledge, and Learning International Conference, 2013.
4. Euromonitor, Beauty and personal care in Brazil, May, 2017. *http://www.euromonitor.com/beauty-and-personal-care-in-brazil/report*
5. Moreira, J. M., Soares, C., Jorge, A. M., De Sousa, J. F.: Emsemble approaches for regression: a survey. ACM Computing Surveys, 45 (1), Article No. 10, 2012.
6. Ren, Y., Zhang, L., and Suganthan, P.N.: Ensemble classification and regression — recent developments, applications and future directions. IEEE Computational Intelligence Magazine, 11 (1), 41-53, 2016.
7. Ribeiro, G. T., Gritti, M. C., Ayala, H. V. H., Mariani, V. C., Coelho, L. S.: Short-term load forecasting using wavenet ensemble approaches. In: International Joint Conference on Neural Networks (IJCNN), pp. 727-734. IEEE, Vancouver, Canada (2016).
8. Chen, T., Guestrin, C.: XGBoost : Reliable large-scale tree boosting system. In: Proceedings of the 22nd ACM SIGKDD International Conference on Knowledge Discovery and Data Mining (KDD'16), San Francisco, CA, USA, pp. 785-794 (2016).
9. Onyaih, L. C.: Design and analysis of experiments: classical and regression approaches with SAS, Chapman and Hall/CRC, 2008.
10. Neumann, D.: Collaborative Systems: a systems theoretical approach to interorganizational collaborative relationships. Peter Lang Verlag. Frankfurt am Main, 2012.

Enhancing Outlier Detection by An Outlier Indicator

Xiaqiong Li[1], Xiaochun Wang[1], Xia Li Wang[2]

[1]School of Software Engineering, Xi'an Jiaotong University, Xi'an, 710049 CHINA
xiaqiongli@stu.xjtu.edu.cn
[1]School of Software Engineering, Xi'an Jiaotong University, Xi'an, 710049 CHINA
xiaocchunwang@mail.xjtu.edu.cn
[2] School of Information Engineering, Changan Univeristy, Xi'an, 710061 CHINA
xlwang@chd.edu.cn

Abstract Outlier detection is an important task in data mining and has high practical value in numerous applications such as astronomical observation, text detection, fraud detection and so on. At present, a large number of popular outlier detection algorithms are available, including distribution-based, distance-based, density-based, and clustering-based approaches and so on. However, traditional outlier detection algorithms face some challenges. For one example, most distance-based and density-based outlier detection methods are based on k-nearest neighbors and therefore, are very sensitive to the value of k. For another example, some methods can only detect global outliers, but fail to detect local outliers. Last but not the least, most outlier detection algorithms do not accurately distinguish between boundary points and outliers. To partially solve these problems, in this paper, we propose to augment some boundary indicators to classical outlier detection algorithms. Experiments performed on both synthetic and real data sets demonstrate the efficacy of enhanced outlier detection algorithms.

Keywords: outlier detection, distance-based outlier detection, density-based outlier detection, boundary detection, *k*-nearest neighbors.

1 Introduction

With the rapid development of information technology, a large amount of information has been produced from the real word. How to find import and useful information from these massive and multi-dimensional data has become an urgent problem. Therefore, data mining and database technologies come into being consequently.

In practice, data often come from different information individuals, departments, enterprises, and countries. These complex data sets may contain a small portion of data which differ significantly from other data objects in behavior or model. These data objects are called outliers. A general intuition of what constitutes an outlier was given by Hawkins in 1980. "Outlier is an observation that deviates so much from other observations as to arouse suspicion that it was generated by a different mechanism"[1].

In many fields, outliers are more important than normal data, as they imply some useful information.

At present, the study on outlier detection becomes very active. Many outlier detection algorithms have been proposed. Outlier detection methods can be divided into distribution-based methods, depth-based methods, distance-based methods, density-based methods and clustering-based etc. However, none of them have been proved to be completely applicable to all the situations. Each type of outlier detection algorithms has its advantages and disadvantages. In distribution-based methods, an object is considered as an outlier if it deviates too much from a standard distribution (e.g., normal, Poisson, etc.) [2]. However the underlying distribution is usually unknown and there are many practical applications which do not follow a standard distribution. As a result, distribution-based methods have a limited number of applications. Being an improvement, depth-based methods assign a depth value to each data object and map it to the corresponding layer in the two-dimensional space. Data objects in the shallow layers are more likely to be outliers than those in the deeper ones. Unfortunately, these methods suffer high computational complexity for data of more than three dimensions. Distance-based methods, also known as adjacency-based methods, believe that data objects are outliers if they are far away from the majority of data points and address more globally-oriented outliers in databases [3]. However, distance-based methods are often accompanied by the problem that the values of k have a great influence on the results. Density-based methods usually assign to each data object a measure of outlier degree as the classic LOF algorithm does and then regard those data objects which possess largest outlier degrees as outliers [4]. In comparison to distance-based methods, these methods address more locally-oriented outliers. Finally, clustering-based methods obtain outliers as a by-product and regard those data items that reside in the smallest clusters as outliers [5].

However, traditional outlier detection algorithms face some challenges. For one example, most distance-based and density-based outlier detection methods are based on k-nearest neighbors and therefore, are very sensitive to the value of k. For another example, some methods can only detect global outliers, but fail to detect local outliers. Last but not the least, in many existing outlier detection algorithms, the boundary points are mistakenly classified to be outliers. To partially solve these problems, in this paper, we propose to augment classical outlier detection algorithms with some boundary indicators so as to enhance traditional methods for outlier detection. When compared with some classical outlier detection algorithms on sample datasets, the enhanced method is more accurate with less sensitivity to k.

The rest of the paper is organized as follows. In Section 2, we review some existing work on classic outlier detection algorithms. We then present our proposed enhancer in Section 3. In Section 4, a performance evaluation is conducted and the results are analyzed. Finally, conclusions are made in Section 5.

2 Related work

If outliers exist in a data set, they will stay far away from other data points. Thinking about outliers in this way, Knorr and Ng proposed distance-based outlier detection method in 1998. Given a distance measure defined on a feature space, "an object O in a dataset T is a DB(p,D)-outlier if at least a fraction p of the objects in T lies greater than distance D from O", where the term DB(p,D)-outlier is a shorthand notation for a Distance-Based outlier (DB-outlier) detected using parameters p and D [3]. There are two classical algorithms based on this concept. "Given two integers, n and k, a Distance-Based outlier is the data item whose average distance to their k-nearest neighbors is among top n largest ones [6]" (referred to as "DB") and "Given two integers, n and k, a Distance-Based outlier is the data item whose distance to their k-th nearest neighbor is among top n largest ones [7]" (referred to as "DB-Max").

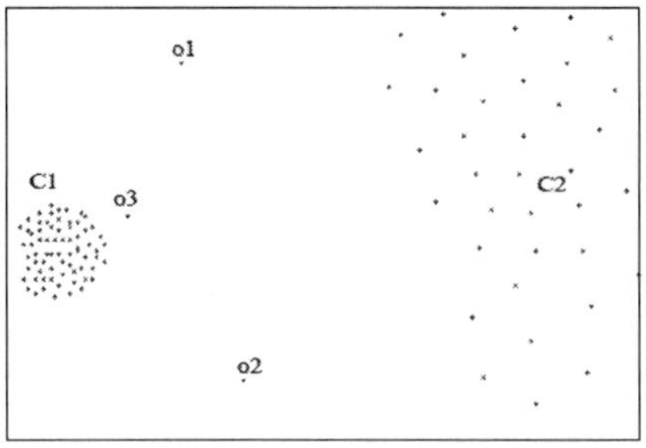

Figure. 1. A classic example of a local outlier.

The realization of distance-based outlier detection method is simple, but it is difficult to solve outlier detection problem in datasets with complex densities, as illustrated in Fig 1. To overcome this limitation, in 2000, Breunig et al. proposed the density-based outlier detection method by introducing an outlier factor for each data item, called Local Outlier Factor (LOF), which is a ratio between the local density of an object and the average of the local densities of its k nearest neighbors [4]. It represents the degree of separation of an object relative to its local area. The top n objects are returned as outliers because the higher value of a data object's LOF means the higher possibility of its being an outlier.

In 2006, Wen Jin et al. presented a new density-based outlier detection algorithm named INFLO to solve the problem when outliers exist in the location where the density distributions in the neighborhood are significantly different [8]. This method considers the union of a point's k-nearest neighbors and its reverse nearest neighbors to obtain a measure of outlierness. The reverse nearest neighborhood of a data point p is defined to consist of those of its k-nearest neighbors for which p is also among its k nearest neighbors.

In 2011, Huang et al. proposed a new approach for outlier detection, named RBDA [9]. RBDA method is based on a ranking measure that focuses on the question of whether a point is central from its nearest neighbors. The problem with RBDA is its high computation cost.

3 The proposed enhancer for outlier mining

3.1 A simple idea

Distance-based outlier detection methods are good at identifying global outliers. To identify the relatively small number of outliers, kNN for each data point is first computed, together with the corresponding distances between each data to their k nearest neighbors. The average of these distances or the k-th distance is used as an outlier score in distance based outlier detection method. However, there is no reason to assume that this must be the case for some outliers due to the existence of boundary data points. To face this challenge, an outlier indicator can be an aid. A problem with distance-based outlier detection algorithms is that these methods do not take the outlying degrees of a data point's k-nearest neighbors into consideration in the detection process. As a result, false positives can happen. For example, for the sample dataset shown in Fig. 2, though DB or DB-Max outlier scores can be calculated for each data point and four boundary data points of cluster C_2 can be mistakenly detected as DB or DB-MAX outliers, there are no outstanding outliers. To prevent the false positives from happening, there must be some ways to differentiate between boundary points and outliers existing in a dataset in the first place. To do so, as a first degree approximation, the distances of each data point and its *k*NN to their first nearest neighbor within a cluster can be assumed to follow a uniform distribution and the corresponding mean and standard deviation can thus be calculated. The ratio of the standard deviation over the mean can be used to judge to some degree whether outliers exist or not. For the sample dataset shown in Fig.2, if k is set to be 2 (i.e., 2NN), the distance of data point o_1 to its first nearest neighbor is the same as that of data point o_2 to its first nearest neighbor and that of data point o_3 to its first nearest neighbor. The corresponding ratio of the standard deviation over the mean is 0, indicating there are not outstanding global outliers.

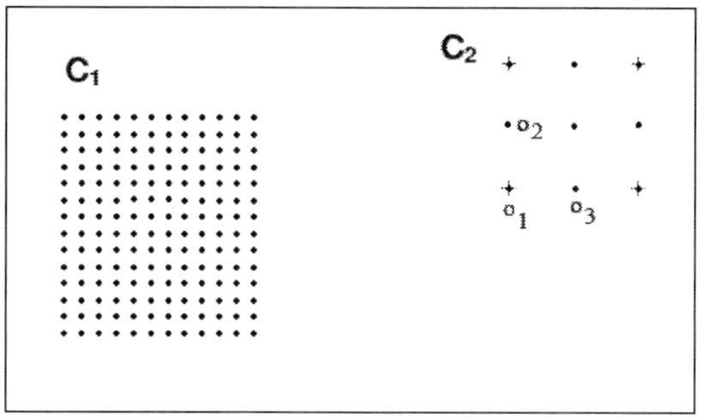

Figure. 2. An illustration of outlier indicator.

In the related work section, outlier definitions and some classical outlier mining algorithms are presented. These methods are able to identify some outliers, either global or local. However, for distance-based outlier detection methods, boundary points could be misclassified as outliers, while, for density-based outlier detection methods, global outliers may have low outlier scores and therefore be missed. Taking the dataset shown in Fig.3 as an example, data point A is farthest away from its six closest neighbors and therefore should be identified as a global outlier. However, for k=6, the LOF-based outlier detection method assigns a higher outlier score to data point B than to A and therefore, fails to identify A as the most significant global outlier. If global outlier detection is separated from local outlier detection, this will not happen.

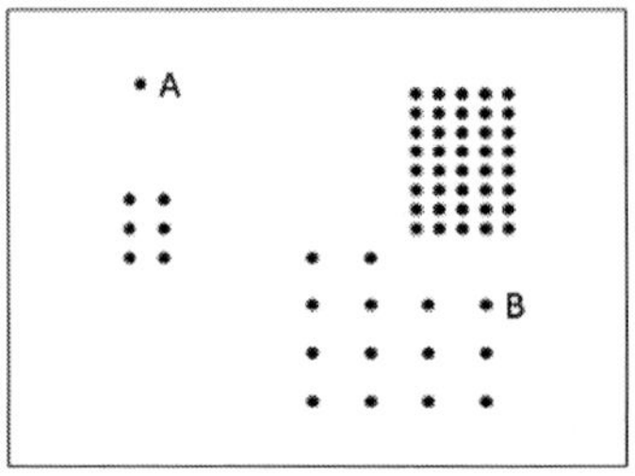

Figure. 3. An illustration of a difference between global outlier and local outlier definitions.

Based on these observations, we propose a new outlier detection algorithm, which enhances current state-of-the-art outlier mining methods by filtering out boundary points from outlier candidates, and formularize it in the following subsections.

3.2 Some definitions

In this paper, we propose an outlier indicator to separate boundary points from being mixed with outliers to some extent.

Definition 1 (*k*-Distance of an object *p*). For any positive integer *k*, the *k*-Distance of object *p*, denoted as *k*-Distance(*p*), is defined as the *distance*(*p*,*o*), or simply, *d*(*p*,*o*), between *p* and an object $o \epsilon D$ such that:

1) for at least *k* objects $o' \epsilon D \backslash \{p\}, d(p,o') <= d(p,o)$;
2) for at most *k*-1 objects $o' \epsilon D \backslash \{p\}, d(p,o') < d(p,o)$.

Definition 2 (*k*-Nearest Neighbors of an object *p*). For any positive integer *k*, given *k*-Distance(*p*), *k*-nearest neighbors of *p* contain the first *k* closest objects whose distance from *p* is not greater than *k*-Distance(*p*), denoted as $kNN_{k\text{-}Distance(p)}(p)$, for which, *kNN*(*p*) is used as shorthand.

For outlier detection, we are more interested in those data points whose distance to its first nearest neighbor is significantly larger than the average value of the distances of the point's kNN to their first nearest neighbor. To quantify the significance of a data point's positioning outside some cluster, the uniform distribution is used as a first degree approximation for the distances associated with a data point and its kNN's to their first nearest neighbors. To distinguish between boundary points and outliers, we therefore formulate an outlier indicator using the distances associated with the first nearest neighbor of the data point and its kNN as in the following to focus our attention on the small number of outstanding global and local outliers.

Definition 3 (Outlier indicator of an object p). Given *k* nearest neighbors of an object p, in the following, *dist*[*0*] denotes the distance of an object p to its nearest neighbor, and *dist*[*i*] denotes the distance of its i-th nearest neighbor to its corresponding nearest neighbor, the proposed outlier indicator of an object p, $SOM_{nn\text{-}dist}(p)$, is defined based on these distances in the following,

$$Mean_{nn-dist}(p) = \frac{1}{k+1}\sum_{i=0}^{k} dist[i] \tag{1}$$

$$Std_{nn-dist}(p) = \sqrt{\frac{1}{k+1}\sum_{i=0}^{k}(dist[i] - Mean_{nn-dist}(p))^2} \tag{2}$$

$$SOM_{nn-dist}(p) = \frac{Std_{nn-dist}(p)}{Mean_{nn-dist}(p)} \tag{3}$$

To manifest the effectiveness of the outlier indicator, for the test sample dataset shown in Fig. 4, we calculate the outlier indicators for all the data points and use the sum of their mean and standard deviation as a threshold to highlight the potential outliers. The results shown in Fig. 4 demonstrate that outliers O_1 and O_2, denoted by red color, are well identified because their indicator is much larger than the others.

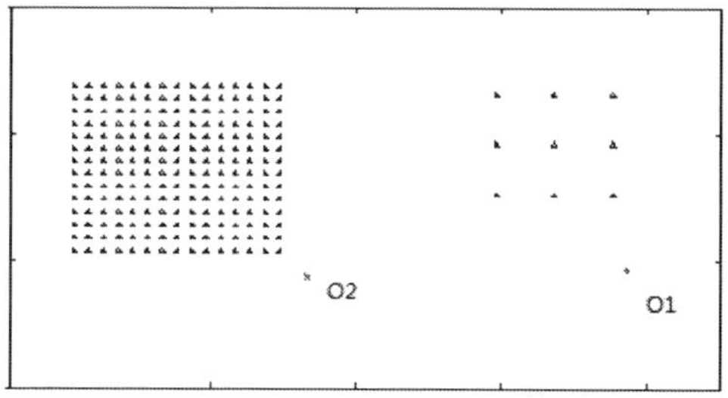

Figure. 4. An illustration of the effect of outlier indicator.

3.3 Our proposed outlier detection algorithm

To find global outliers, we follow the notion of kNN based distance outlier definition and calculate the distance-based outlier factors (i.e., DB-MAX) for all the data points, sort them in a non-increasing order, and searching for the largest factor values. If their corresponding outlier indicators are significantly larger than a threshold value, SOM, top n data points can be regarded as the global outliers. For local outliers, we follow the notion of kNN based density-based outlier definition and calculate the LOF outlier factors for all the data points, sort them in a non-increasing order, and searching for the largest factor values. We combine three proposed factors to create our kNN-based outlier detection algorithm. To improve the readability, our proposed outlier detection algorithm is presented in a pseudo code format in Table 1.

Table 1. A combined outlier detection algorithm

Input:	*S*: a set of *N* data objects;
	k: the number of nearest neighbors;
	SOM: threshold
	n: the required number of top outliers.
Output:	*Index*: the indices of top-*n* outliers
Begin:	
	Compute *k* nearest neighbors for each data point;
	Compute the global and local outlier scores, DB-MAX and LOF, and outlier indicators;
	Compute the *mean* and *std* of the outlier indicators, and the threshold value, SOM;
	Sort the outlier scores, DB-MAX and LOF, in a non-increasing order;
	While(*Index*.size<n)
	{
	if(DB-MAX.next>SOM) *Index*.push_back(DB-MAX.next.index);
	if(LOF.next>SOM) *Index*.push_back(LOF.next.index);
	}
	Return *Index*.
End	

To determine the threshold of indicators in a data set, let the outlier indicators of all points in dataset be computed, based on which the average of the indicators, mean, and the corresponding standard deviation, std, are calculated. The threshold of indicators, SOM, for finding potential outliers is defined as,

$$SOM = mean(\text{indicators}) + f \times std(\text{indicators}) \qquad (4)$$

To summarize, the numerical parameters the algorithm needs from the user include the data set, *S*, the loosely estimated number of outliers (i.e., the percentage of outlier candidates in the original data set), *n*, and the number of nearest neighbors, *k*.

4 Experiments and results

In this section, we compare the effectiveness of the proposed outlier detection method with several state-of-the-art outlier detection methods, including the DB method, the DB-max, the LOF, the INFLO and RBDA methods, on several different datasets. In the first set of experiments, two 2-dimensional synthetic data sets are used to show that our proposed outlier detection method augmented with outlier indicator can outperform classical outlier detection algorithms in classification accuracy. Further, it is important for an outlier detection method to work effectively on real-world data sets. Therefore, in the second set of experiments, a real high-dimensional data sets obtained from the UCI Machine Learning Repository [10] are used to check the effectiveness of this study and to illustrate the effectiveness of our method in real-world situation. All the data sets are briefly summarized in Table 2. We implement all the algorithms in java and perform all the experiments on a computer with AMD A6-4400M Processor 2.70GHz CPU and 4.00G RAM. The operating system running on this computer is Windows 7. In our evaluation, we focus on the outlier detection accuracy rate of these outlier detection algorithms on different data sets. The results show that, overall, our proposed outlier detection algorithm is superior over other state-of-the-art outlier detection algorithms.

Table 2. Description of all datasets

Data Name	Data Size	Dimension	#of outliers
syn_Data1	82	2	10
syn_Data2	473	2	6
LYMPHOGRAPHY	148	18	6

4.1 Performance of our algorithm on synthetic data

In this subsection, we use two synthetic datasets to show that the proposed outlier detection method performs better than traditional outlier detection methods. The two synthetic datasets, syn_Data1 and syn_Data2, are shown in the first plot of Fig.5 and Fig.6, respectively. For this set of experiments, the parameter *k*'s is set to be 3 for all the methods and the results for syn_Data1 and syn_Data2 are plotted in Fig.5 and Fig.6, respectively.

The first synthetic dataset, syn_Data1, consists of 82 instances, including six single outliers (i.e., A, B, C, D, E and F), and four clusters of different densities with 36, 8, 12 and 16 uniformly distributed instances. From the results depicted in Fig. 5, we can see that DB and DB-Max have the same ranks for A, D, E and F, but can not mine the two local outliers, that is, B and C. RBDA, INFLO, LOF and our outlier detection method detect all six outliers correctly. The plot at bottom left corner shows the corresponding $SOM_{nn\text{-}dist}$ values (which are actually 0 for boundary and inner points) thresholded by Equation (4), which correctly identifies the six outliers.

The second synthetic dataset, syn_Data2, consists of 473 instances, including six outliers and five clusters of different densities clusters. A particular challenging feature of this data set is that three denser clusters are buried into one sparse cluster on the upper right corner. From the results depicted in Fig. 6, we can see that this is a global outlier detection situation while the detection process is disturbed by the immediate connection of clusters with different densities. For detecting top 6 outliers, RBDA misses C but all other methods, that is, DB, DB-Max, LOF, INFLO and our method detect all six outliers correctly but with different rankings. The plot at bottom left corner shows the corresponding $SOM_{nn\text{-}dist}$ values thresholded by Equation (4), which correctly identifies the six outliers.

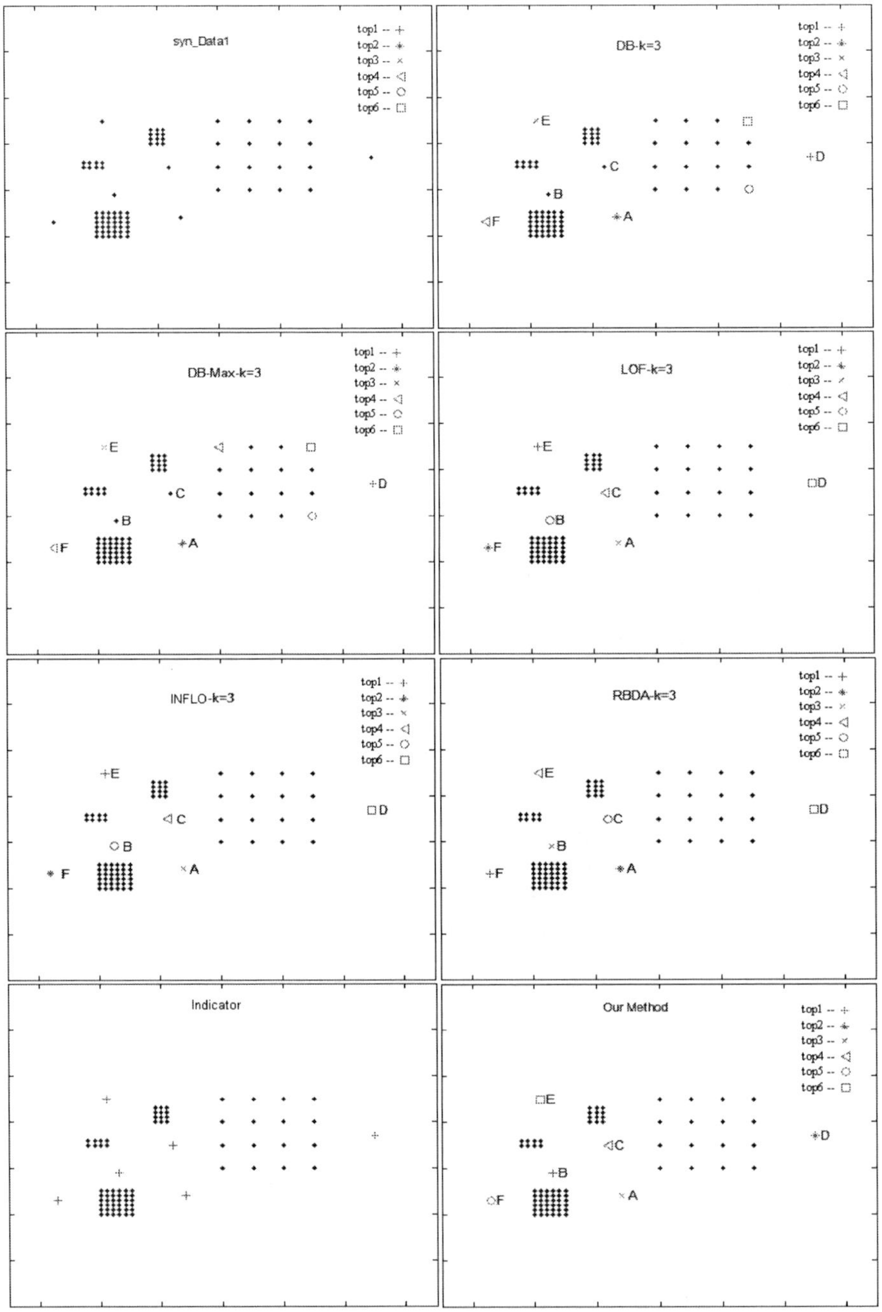

Figure 5. The outlier detecting results on syn_Data1 for *k*=3.

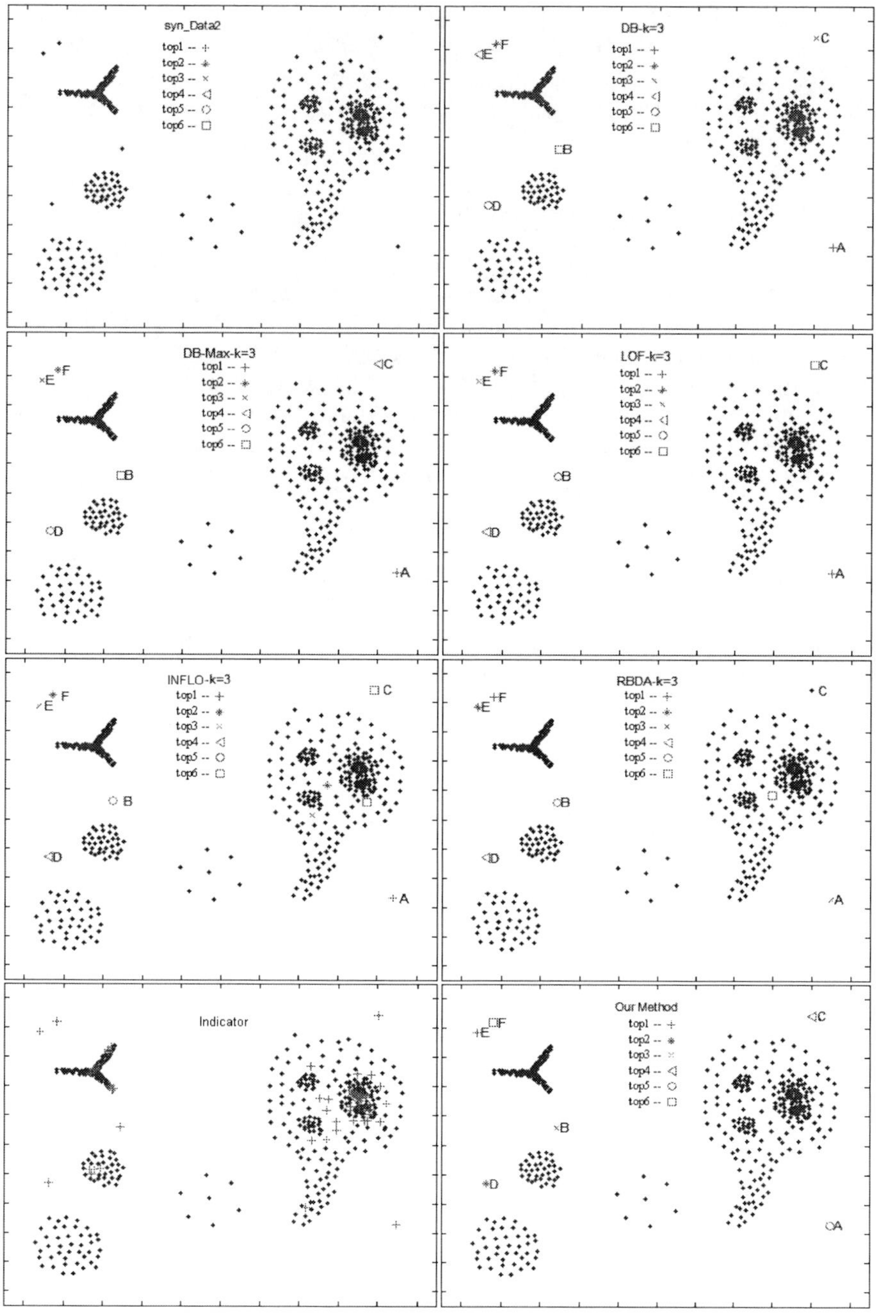

Figure 6. The outlier detecting results on syn_Data2 for *k*=3

To summarize, it can be observed from Fig.5 and Fig.6 that our method has no problems detecting all outliers and clearly offers the best ranking in three synthetic datasets while all other methods do not perform competently with detecting all the outliers one way or the other. The advantage of our outlier detection factors is very evident on these 2-dimensional data sets.

4.2 Performance of our algorithm on real data

It has been pointed out by Aggarwal and Yu that one way to test how well an outlier detection algorithm works is to run the method on the dataset and test the percentage of points which belongs to the rare classes [11]. In order to test how well our outlier indicator works on real dataset, we compare its ability in finding outliers with other methods in a real dataset, LYMPHOGRAPHY, which is downloaded from UCI [10]. This dataset has 148 instances with 18 attributes and contains a total of 4 classes. Classes 2 and 3 have 81 and 61 instances, respectively. The remaining two classes have totally 6 instances (2 and 4, respectively) and are regarded as outliers (i.e., rare classes) for they are small in size.

To quantitatively measure the performance of an outlier detection method, a popular metric, called recall, is used. Assuming that a dataset $D=D_o \cup D_n$ where D_o denotes the set of all outliers and D_n denotes the set of all normal data. Given any integer $m \geq 1$, if O_m denotes the set of outliers among objects in the top m positions returned by an outlier detection scheme, recall is defined as,

$$recall = \frac{|O_m|}{|D_o|} \tag{5}$$

In Equation (5), recall shows the percentage of detected outliers in all outliers.

Table 3 shows the experimental results of the proposed outlier detection method in comparison with five other methods, DB, DBMax, LOF, INFlO, RBDA respectively, for four values of k's (i.e., 7, 10, 20, 30) and six values of m's (6, 7, 8, 9, 10, 15). In the table, n denotes the correct number of outliers among returned m ones, and r denotes the corresponding recall. From the experimental results, it can be seen that the proposed method mines all the outliers correctly for all m's and all k's and thus performs the best. RBDA method and LOF method perform next since they mine outliers as well as our method for k=20 and k=30 but does not do well in cases for k=7 and k=10. Overall, with increasing k's, RBDA, LOF and INFLO methods work better and better while DB and DB-Max work worse and worse.

5 Conclusions

Traditional distance based and density based outlier detection algorithms can effectively detect two different kinds of outliers separately but not both at the same time.

Table 3 Experimental results for LYMPHOGRAPHY data

	DB		DB-Max		LOF		INFLO		RBDA		OUR	
m	n	r	n	r	n	r	n	r	n	r	n	r
k=7												
6	5	0.83	5	0.83	5	0.83	4	0.67	5	0.83	**6**	**1.00**
7	**6**	**1.00**	5	0.83	5	0.83	5	0.83	5	0.83	**6**	**1.00**
8	**6**	**1.00**	**6**	**1.00**	**6**	**1.00**	5	0.83	**6**	**1.00**	**6**	**1.00**
9	**6**	**1.00**	**6**	**1.00**	**6**	**1.00**	**6**	**1.00**	**6**	**1.00**	**6**	**1.00**
10	**6**	**1.00**	**6**	**1.00**	**6**	**1.00**	**6**	**1.00**	**6**	**1.00**	**6**	**1.00**
15	**6**	**1.00**	**6**	**1.00**	**6**	**1.00**	**6**	**1.00**	**6**	**1.00**	**6**	**1.00**
k=10												
6	5	0.83	5	0.83	5	0.83	4	0.67	5	0.83	**6**	**1.00**
7	**6**	**1.00**	5	0.83	5	0.83	5	0.83	**6**	**1.00**	**6**	**1.00**
8	**6**	**1.00**	5	0.83	**6**	**1.00**	5	0.83	**6**	**1.00**	**6**	**1.00**
9	**6**	**1.00**	**6**	**1.00**	**6**	**1.00**	**6**	**1.00**	**6**	**1.00**	**6**	**1.00**
10	**6**	**1.00**	**6**	**1.00**	**6**	**1.00**	**6**	**1.00**	**6**	**1.00**	**6**	**1.00**
15	**6**	**1.00**	**6**	**1.00**	**6**	**1.00**	**6**	**1.00**	**6**	**1.00**	**6**	**1.00**
k=20												
6	5	0.83	5	0.83	**6**	**1.00**	5	0.83	**6**	**1.00**	**6**	**1.00**
7	5	0.83	5	0.83	**6**	**1.00**	5	0.83	**6**	**1.00**	**6**	**1.00**
8	**6**	**1.00**	**6**	**1.00**	**6**	**1.00**	**6**	**1.00**	**6**	**1.00**	**6**	**1.00**
9	**6**	**1.00**	**6**	**1.00**	**6**	**1.00**	**6**	**1.00**	**6**	**1.00**	**6**	**1.00**
10	**6**	**1.00**	**6**	**1.00**	**6**	**1.00**	**6**	**1.00**	**6**	**1.00**	**6**	**1.00**
15	**6**	**1.00**	**6**	**1.00**	**6**	**1.00**	**6**	**1.00**	**6**	**1.00**	**6**	**1.00**
k=30												
6	5	0.83	5	0.83	**6**	**1.00**	5	0.83	**6**	**1.00**	**6**	**1.00**
7	5	0.83	5	0.83	**6**	**1.00**	**6**	**1.00**	**6**	**1.00**	**6**	**1.00**
8	5	0.83	5	0.83	**6**	**1.00**	**6**	**1.00**	**6**	**1.00**	**6**	**1.00**
9	**6**	**1.00**	5	0.83	**6**	**1.00**	**6**	**1.00**	**6**	**1.00**	**6**	**1.00**
10	**6**	**1.00**	**6**	**1.00**	**6**	**1.00**	**6**	**1.00**	**6**	**1.00**	**6**	**1.00**
15	**6**	**1.00**	**6**	**1.00**	**6**	**1.00**	**6**	**1.00**	**6**	**1.00**	**6**	**1.00**

Further, classical distance based outlier detection algorithms do not differentiate global outliers from boundary data points. To partially circumvent these problems, in this paper, we have proposed a novel outlier detection approach which can detect both global and local outliers in a separate and simultaneous way and, when augmented with an outlier indicator, can outperform traditional outlier detection approaches. To demonstrate the utility of our proposed outlier detection mechanism, a detailed comparison is performed with state-of-the-art distance-based and density-based outlier detection methods. Experimental results show that our algorithm is able to rank the best candidates for being an outlier with high recall.

Acknowledgment

The authors would like to thank the Chinese National Science Foundation for its valuable support of this work under award 61473220 and all the anonymous reviewers for their valuable comments.

References

1. Hawkins, D.M.: Identification of outliers, Monographs on Applied Probability and Statistics. Chapman and Hall, London (1980).
2. Barnett, V., Lewis, T.: Outliers in statistical data, vol. 3, Wiley New York, 1994.
3. Knorr, E.M., Ng, R.T.: Algorithms for mining distance-based outliers in large datasets. In: Proceedings of the 24th VLDB Conference, pp. 392-403, New York, USA (1998).
4. Breuning, M.M., Kriegel, H.P., Ng, R.T., Sander, J.: LOF: identifying density-based local outliers. In: Proceedings of the 2000 ACM SIGMOD international conference on Management of data, pp. 93-104 (2000).
5. Jiang, M.F., Tseng, S.S., Su, C.M.: Two-phase clustering process for outliers detection. Pattern Recognition Letters, vol. 22, pp. 691-700 (2001).
6. Angiulli, F., Pizzuti, C.: Fast outlier detection in high dimensional spaces. In: Proceedings of the Sixth European Conference on the Principles of Data Mining and Knowledge Discovery, pp. 15-26 (2002).
7. Ramaswamy, S., Rastogi, R., Shim, K.: Efficient algorithms for mining outliers from large data sets. In: Proceedings of the ACM SIGMOD Conference, pp. 427-438 (2000).
8. Jin, W., Tung, A.K.H., Han, J.: Ranking outliers using symmetric neighborhood relationship. Lecture Notes in Computer Science, vol. 3918, pp. 577-593 (2006).
9. Huang, H., Mehrotra, K., Mohan, C.K.: Rank-based outlier detection, Journal of Statistical Computation and Simulation. 83 (3) pp. 1–14 (2013).
10. UCI: The UCI KDD Archive, University of California, Irvine, CA. http://kdd.ics.uci.edu/.
11. Aggarwal, C., Yu, P.: Outlier detection for high-dimensional data. In: Proceedings of the 2001 ACM SIGMOD Conference (SIGMOD'01), pp.37–46, Santa Barbara, CA, USA, (2001).

A Method of Biomedical Knowledge Discovery by Literature Mining Based on SPO Predications: A Case Study of Induced Pluripotent Stem Cells

Zheng-Yin Hu[1], Rong-Qiang Zeng[1,2,⋆], Xiao-Chu Qin[3], Ling Wei[1], and Zhiqiang Zhang[1]

[1] Chengdu Library and Information Center of Chinese Academy of Sciences, Chengdu, Sichuan 610041, P. R. China
huzy@clas.ac.cn, zhangzq@clas.ac.cn, weiling@mail.las.ac.cn
[2] School of Mathematics, Southwest Jiaotong University, Chengdu, Sichuan 610031, P. R. China
zrq@swjtu.edu.cn
[3] Guangzhou Institutes of Biomedicine and Health, Chinese Academy of Sciences, Guangzhou, Guangdong 510530, P. R. China
qin_xiaochu@gibh.ac.cn

Abstract. A large amount of valuable knowledge is hidden in the vast biomedical literatures, publications, and online contents. In order to identify the previously unknown biomedical knowledge from these resources, we propose a new method of knowledge discovery based on SPO predications, which constructs a three-level SPO-semantic relation network in the considered area. We carry out the experiments in the area of induced pluripotent stem cells, and the experimental results indicate that our proposed method can significantly discover the potential biomedical knowledge in this area, and the performance analysis of this method sheds lights on the ways to further improvements.

Key words: biomedical knowledge discovery, SPO, induced pluripotent stem cells, semantic relation network, community detection.

1 Introduction

Knowledge Discovery in Text (KDT) is the process of identifying and extracting the new, useful, potential and understandable patterns from the literatures in a credible way. With the rapid growth of biomedical literatures, Knowledge Discovery in Biomedical Literature (KDiBL) has become an important research area [8].

Information extraction plays an important part in KDT, which automatically extracts the specific terms, the corresponding characteristics and the semantic relations among them from the texts as the basic knowledge unit of knowledge

⋆ Corresponding author.

discovery. Subject-Predication-Object (SPO) represents the semantic relationships among the knowledge units, which is widely used in the fields of knowledge organization, semantic network, knowledge discovery, and so on [3].

In this paper, we propose a new method of knowledge discovery based on SPO predications, which constructs a three-level SPO-based semantic relation network in the considered area. Then, we realize the community detection for the SPO-semantic relation network, so as to find the hidden valuable knowledge. The experimental results indicate that the proposed method can effectively discover the unknown biomedical knowledge. The performance analysis explains the behavior of our proposed method and sheds lights on the ways to further improvements.

The remaining part of this paper is organized as follows. In the next section, we briefly review the previous works related to the biomedical knowledge discovery. In Section 3, we investigate a new method of constructing three-level SPO-based semantic relation network to discover the potential unknown knowledge. Section 4 provides the experimental results and the performance analysis of the proposed method in the area of induced pluripotent stem cells. The conclusions are presented in the last section.

2 Literature Reviews

In this section, we present the literature reviews concentrating on the biomedical knowledge discovery.

In [1], with techniques from systems medicine, natural language processing, and graph theory, the authors created a molecular interaction network, which represents neural injury and is composed of relationships automatically extracted from the literature, in order to support the diagnosis of mild traumatic brain injury. Actually, they retrieved the citations related to neurological injury and extract the semantic predications that contain potential biomarkers. The experimental results on 99,437 relevant citations and 26,441 unique relations indicated a set of 17 potential biomarkers, which provides an opportunity to obtain more effective diagnosis than the current methods.

In [5], the authors investigated the use of deep learning methods, which have shown significant promise in identifying hidden patterns from large corpus of text in an unsupervised manner, in order to discover the hidden, interesting or previously unknown biomedical knowledge from free text resources. They used the text corpus from MRDEF file in the Unified Medical Language System (UMLS) dataset as training set to discover potential relationships. Taking a manual evaluation from a sample of the non-overlapping set, their proposed algorithm founded 32% of new relationships not originally represented in the UMLS, which provides provide a promising approach in discovering potential new biomedical knowledge from free text.

In [7], according to some semi-supervised learning methods named Positive-Unlabeled Learning (PU-Learning), the authors proposed a novel method to predict the disease candidate genes from human genome, which ia an important part of nowadays biomedical research. Since the diseases with the same phenotype have the similar biological characteristics and genes associated with these same diseases tend to share common functional properties, the proposed method detects the disease candidate genes through gene expression profiles by learning hidden Markov models. The experiments are carried out on a mixed part of 398 disease genes from three disease types and 12001 unlabeled genes, and the results indicate indicate a significant improvement in comparison with the other methods in literature.

In [9], the authors presented a set of knowledge discovery framework to identify the unknown knowledge from the biomedical literatures based on subject-predication-object predications. Actually, they extracted the SPO predications from the biomedical literature by using UMLS corpus and SemRep. Then, they constructed the corresponding semantic network diagrams with NetMiner [10], which is applied to the field of induced pluripotent stem cells. The experimental results showed that can effectively reveal the knowledge content from the biomedical literatures.

In [11], the authors proposed a novel Sequence-based Fusion Method (SFM) is proposed to identify disease genes from human genome, which is of great importance to improve diagnosis and treatment of disease. In this method, the amino acid sequence of the proteins has been carried out to present the genes into four different feature vectors, instead of using a noisy and incomplete prior-knowledge. Then, the intersection set of four negative sets generated by distance approach is used to select more likely negative data from candidate genes, and the decision tree has been applied as a fusion method to combine the results of four independent state-of the-art predictors based on support vector machine (SVM) algorithm for the final decision. The experimental results confirm the efficiency and validity of the proposed method.

In [12], the authors proposed a method based on degree centrality that measures connectedness in a graph, in order to automatically summarize the semantic predications representing assertions in MEDLINE citations in the large graph with more than 500 citations. The experiment was carried out on the four categories of clinical concepts related to treatment of disease, the results showed that their proposed method are very competitive, in comparison with the reference standard produced manually by two physicians.

In [13], the authors presented a hybrid model for the extraction of biomedical relations that combines Recurrent Neural Networks (RNNs) and Convolutional Neural Networks (CNNs), in order to extract high-quality biomedical relations from biomedical texts. In this model, RNNs and CNNs are employed to automatically learn the features from the sentence sequence and the dependency sequences to generate the shortest dependency path for the biomedical relation extraction. The experiments are carried out on five public (protein-protein interaction) PPI corpora and a (drug-drug interaction) DDI corpus, and the experimental results indicate the proposed model can effectively boost biomedical relation extraction performance.

3 Methodology

In our work, we propose a new method of knowledge discovery based on SPO predications, which constructs a three-level SPO-based semantic relation network in a certain area. First, we present an introduction to the SPO-based semantic relation network. Then, we construct a three-level graph, which is different from the graph generated by the NetMiner. Afterwards, we investigate the method of detecting the community in the three-level graph.

3.1 Network Construction

Generally, we construct the SPO-based semantic relation network, according to four basic principles proposed by M. Fiszman et al., which are relevancy, connectivity, novelty and saliency, more information about these principles can be found in [2].

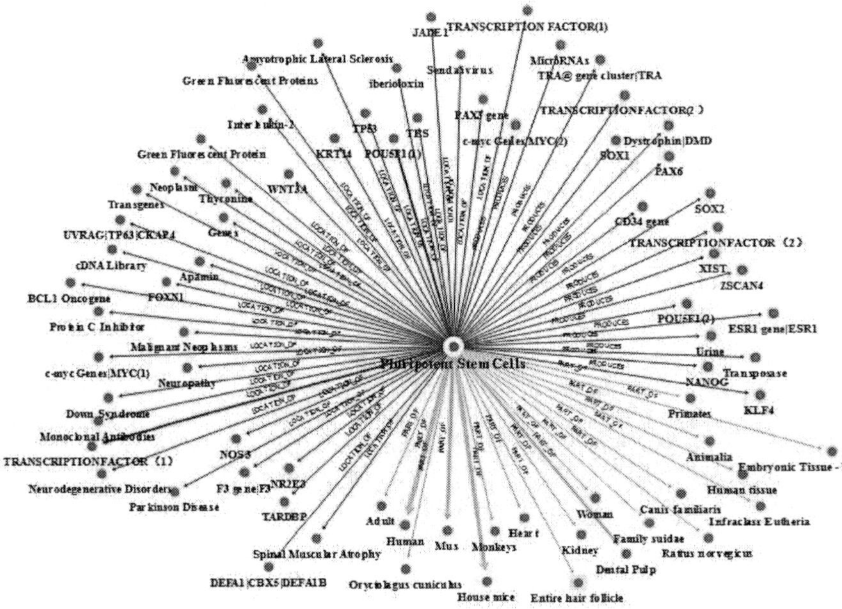

Fig. 1. An example of semantic network based on the subject of induced pluripotent stem cells [9].

Two examples of directed semantic networks of induced pluripotent stem cells are respectively illustrated in Fig. 1 and Fig. 2, which are both depicted by NetMiner. In these two figures, the node in the network represents the semantic concepts, and the corresponding color represents the type of semantic concept.

In addition, the edge represents the semantic relationship with the direction from the subject to the object, the color and the width of the line represent the semantic type and the frequency of semantic description respectively.

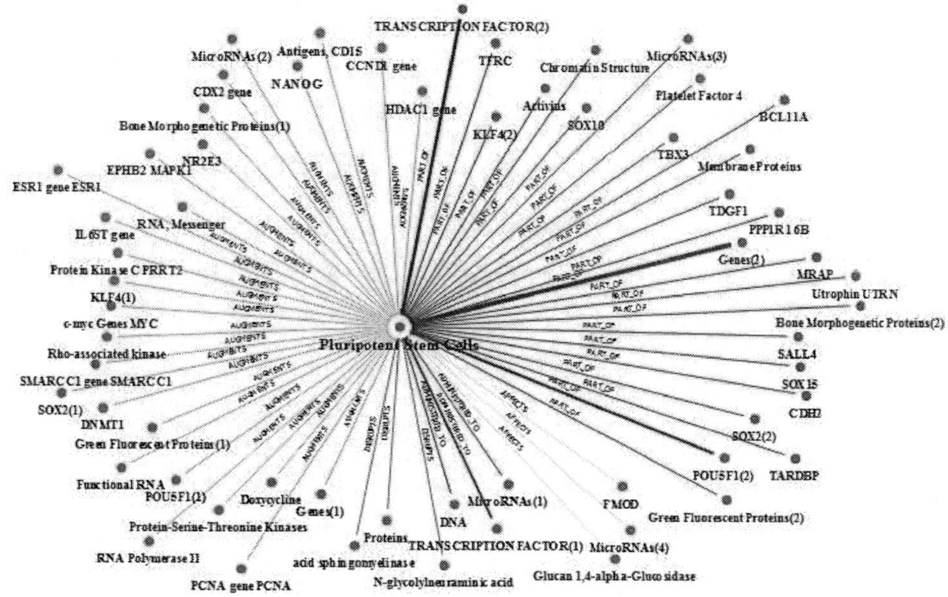

Fig. 2. An example of semantic network based on the object of induced pluripotent stem cells [9].

In Fig. 1, the Induced Pluripotent Stem Sells (IPSC) is the subject, the other nodes are the objects. Whereas, in Fig. 2, the Induced Pluripotent Stem Sells (IPSC) is the object, the other nodes are the subjects. Actually, these two figures present the semantic relation between the IPSC and the other nodes from two different angles.

However, we can only obtain the local semantic relation between one subject and the other objects (or between one object and the other subjects) in Both Fig. 1 and Fig. 2. In fact, it is very difficult to illustrate the global semantic relation between different subjects and different objects in one figure with NetMiner, which is the disadvantage of discovering the hidden biomedical knowledge. Then, it is essential that we construct the global semantic relation network for knowledge discovery.

An example of global SPO-based semantic relation network is illustrated in Fig. 3, which is composed of thousands of nodes and edges. In this figure, the grey node denotes the subject, the orange node denotes the object, and the green node

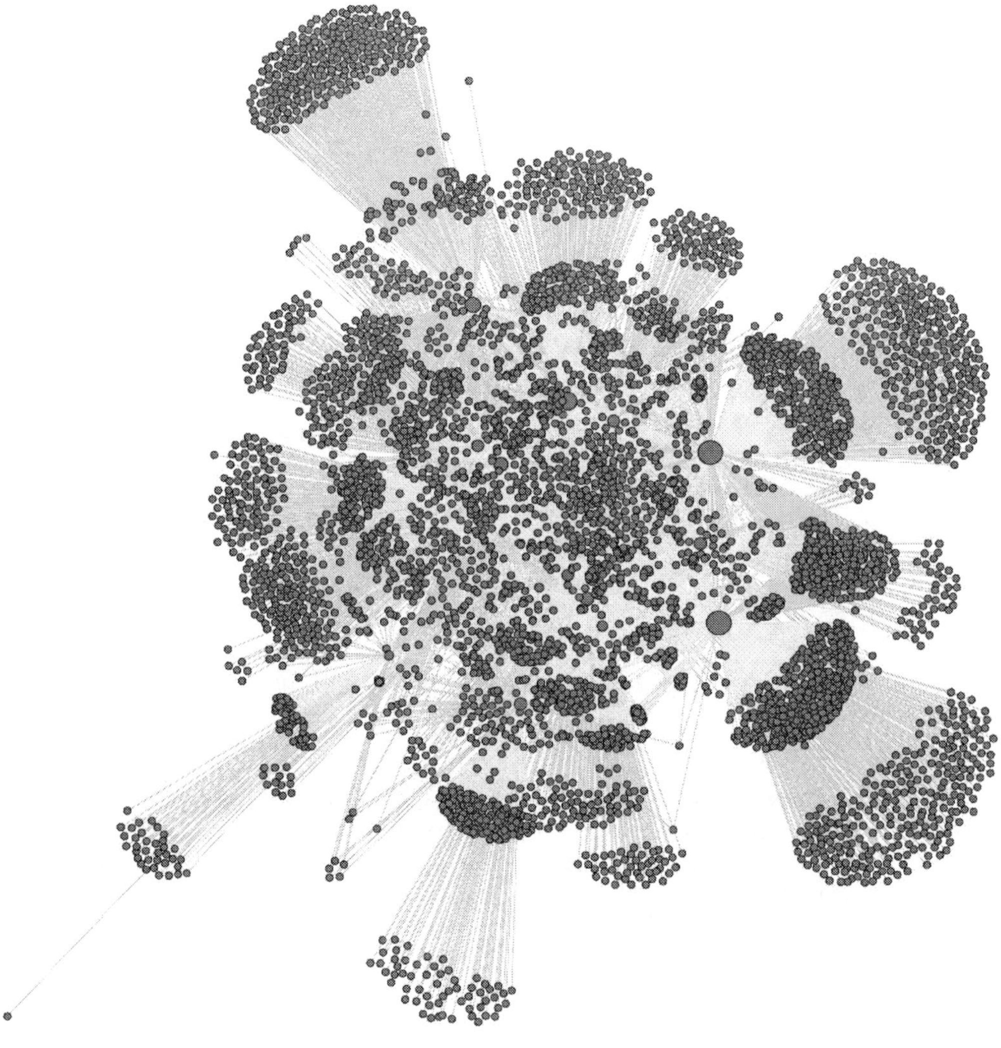

Fig. 3. An example of global SPO-based semantic relation network.

denotes the semantic relation. Actually, many nodes can be both the subjects and the objects, which makes the whole network very complicated. That's to say, it is very difficult for the experts to recognize the valuable biomedical knowledge from the network.

3.2 Community Detection

In order to clearly recognize the valuable biomedical knowledge from global SPO-based semantic relation network, it is essential to detect the community structure, which is the intrinsic properties of networks. In our work, we take the widely accepted modularity function proposed by Newman and Girvan, which is defined as follows [6]:

$$Q = \frac{1}{2m} \sum_{vw} [A_{vw} - \frac{k_v k_w}{2m}] \delta(C_v, C_w), \tag{1}$$

Suppose the vertices are divided into the communities such that vertex v belongs to community C denoted by C_v. In Formula 1, A is the adjacency matrix of graph G. $A_{vw} = 1$ if one node v is connected to another node w, otherwise $A_{vw} = 0$. The δ function $\delta(i, j)$ is equal to 1 if $i = j$ and 0 otherwise. The degree k_v of a vertex v is defined to be $k_v = \sum_v A_{wv}$, and the number of edges in the graph is $m = \sum_{wv} A_{wv}/2$.

In addition, the modularity function can be represented in a simple way, which is formulated below [6]:

$$Q = \sum_i (e_{ii} - a_i^2), \tag{2}$$

where i runs over all communities in graph, e_{ij} and a_i^2 are respectively defined as follows [6]:

$$e_{ij} = \frac{1}{2m} \sum_{vw} A_{vw} \delta(C_v, i) \delta(C_w, j), \tag{3}$$

which is the fraction of edges that join vertices in community i to vertices in community j, and

$$a_i = \frac{1}{2m} \sum_v k_v \delta(C_v, i), \tag{4}$$

which is the fraction of the ends of edges that are attached to vertices in community i.

Then, we employ the local search procedure to effectively detect the community structure, which is presented in the Algorithm 1 [4].

In this algorithm, we randomly divide the whole network into two communities, and each smaller community is further divided into two smaller communities. Let C_i and C_j be two communities, w be a vertex from C_i or C_j, we assume

Algorithm 1 Community Detection Algorithm

```
Input: network adjacency matrix A
Output: the best value of the modularity function
P = {x^1, ..., x^p} ← Random_Initialization (P)
repeat
    x^i ← Local_Search (x^i)
until a stop criterion is met
```

that $w \in C_i$ and the corresponding change by moving vertex w from C_i to C_j can be computed as follows [4]:

$$\Delta Q(w, C_i, C_j) = \frac{k_w^j - k_w^i}{m} + \frac{k_w(a_i - a_j)}{m} - \frac{k_w^2}{2m^2}, \tag{5}$$

where k_w^i and k_w^j are respectively the number of edges connecting vertex w and the other vertices in communities C_i and C_j. While, for any vertex v in community C_i, we can also obtain the updated ΔQ value $\Delta Q'(v, C_i, C_j)$ with the formula below [4]:

$$\Delta Q'(v, C_i, C_j) = \Delta Q(v, C_i, C_j) - (\frac{k_w^2}{m^2} - \frac{2A_{wv}}{m}). \tag{6}$$

With the incremental value of the modularity function in Formulas 5 and 6, the local search procedure can chooses the best move at each step until the modularity does not improve any more. Then, we obtain the communities of the considered network.

4 Case Study

Induced pluripotent stem cells technology is one of the most important emerging frontier technologies in the biomedical field, which can nurture new stem cells with similar differentiation potential as embryonic stem cells by reprogramming the mature cells [9]. Then, it is of great significance to realize the knowledge discovery in the SPO-based semantic network. In this section, we apply our proposed method in the area of IPSC and present the experimental results with performance analysis.

4.1 Data Information

In order to carry out the experiments, we obtain the data from the PubMed Database by inputting the key words "Regenerative Medicine" from 2000 to 2014. Then, we select the literatures retrieved by the Semantic Medline Database, the type of literature is "Journal Article". The exact data information is presented in Table 1

In this table, we have retrieved 10,687 papers and obtained 65,042 SPO-based semantic relations, which consists of 2055 subjects, 1821 objects and 45

Table 1. The information of SPO-based semantic relation network.

	SPO
Number of Subjects	2055
Number of Objects	1821
Number of Actions	45

actions. With these information, we can construct a three-level SPO-based semantic relation network.

4.2 Experimental Results

In this subsection, we present the experimental results in the area of IPSC, which are classified into different communities according to the corresponding actions. The global SPO-based semantic relation network of IPSC is illustrated in Fig. 4 below.

In this figure, the upper level and the lower level respectively represents the subjects and the objects, which are linked by the edges with different colors. The middle level represents the actions, in which the frequency is proportional to the size of the circle.

Furthermore, different communities are represented in different colors, which are composed of the subjects, the objects and the corresponding actions. For example, there is a community colored in green with the action "LOCATION_OF" in Fig. 4.

The computational results are summarized in Table 2. In this table, we do not present all the found communities in the network but to provide parts of three different communities, which are colored in green (located in the center of Fig. 4), in pink (located in the center of Fig. 4) and in red (located on the left of Fig. 4).

Moreover, the subjects and the objects of the community in pink are linked by the action "PART_OF", which is the highest frequency among all the actions. From Fig. 4, we can clearly recognize the different communities, which is very helpful to realize the biomedical knowledge discovery.

5 Conclusions

In this paper, we have investigated a new method of constructing the three-level SPO-based semantic relation network for biomedical knowledge discovery. To achieve this goal, we have carried out the experiments in the area of induced pluripotent stem cells. The experimental results indicate that our proposed method can significantly discover the potential unknown biomedical knowledge in the considered area.

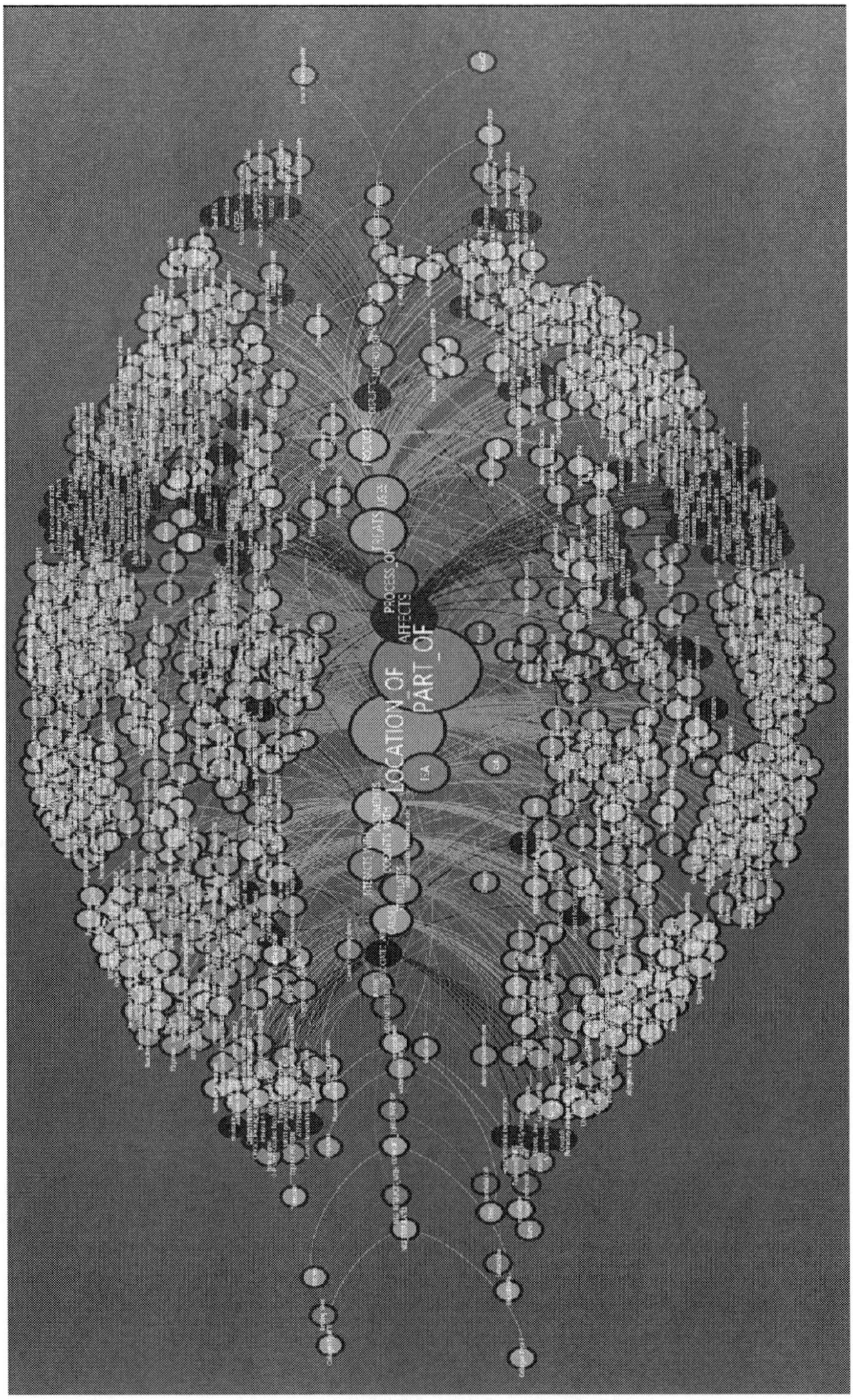

Fig. 4. The global SPO-based semantic relation network.

Table 2. The communities detected in global SPO-based semantic relation network.

Action	Subject	Object
LOCATION_OF	Embryo, Liver, Epidermis	Toxic effect, Purinoceptor
	Body tissue, Basement membrane	Injury wounds, Tissue Engineering
	Entire bony skeleton, Retina, ···	Cell Transformation, Neoplastic, ···
PART_OF	Mammary gland, Chorionic villi	Infraclass Eutheria, Equus caballus
	Bone Marrow Cells, Serum	Cementoblasts, Entire tendon
	Mesenchymal Stem Cells, ···	Rattus norvegicus, ···
ADMINISTERED_TO	Small Interfering, MicroRNAs	Cells, Patients, Mus
	RNA, Growth Factor, Adiponectin	human embryonic stem cell
	High Throughput Screening, ···	Urothelial Cell, ···

Acknowledgments. The work in this paper was supported by the key projects of the National Social Science Foundation of China "Theory and Applications Research of Subject-Informatics for Domain Knowledge Discovery" (Grant No: 17ATQ008), supported by the Informationization Special Project of Chinese Academy of Sciences "E-Science Application for Knowledge Discovery in Stem Cells" (Grant No: XXH13506-203), and supported by the Fundamental Research Funds for the Central Universities (Grant No. A0920502051722-53).

References

1. M. J. Cairelli, M. Fiszman, H. Zhang, and T. C. Rindflesch. Networks of neuroinjury semantic predications to identify biomarkers for mild traumatic brain injury. *Journal of Biomedical Semantics*, 6(25):1–14, 2015.
2. M. Fiszman, T. C. Rindflesch, and H. Kilicoglu. Abstraction summarization for managing the biomedical research literature. In *Proceedings of the HLT-NAACL Workshop on Computational Lexical Semantics*, pages 76–83, 2004.
3. A. Keselman, G. Rosemblat, and H. Kilicoglu. Adapting semantic natural language processing technology to address information overload in influenza epidemic management. *Journal of the American Society for Information Science & Technology*, 61(12):2531–2543, 1990.
4. Z. P. Lü and W. Q. Huang. Iterated tabu search for identifying community structure in complex networks. *Physical Review E*, 80:026130, 2009.
5. R. N. Nadeem, P. O. Chintan, and K. A. Sharib. Using deep learning towards biomedical knowledge discovery. *I. J. Mathematical Sciences and Computing*, 2:1–10, 2017.
6. M. E. J. Newman and M. Girvan. Finding and evaluating community structure in networks. *Physical Review E*, 69(2):026113, 2004.

7. O. Nikdelfaz and S. Jalili. Disease genes prediction by hmm based pu-learning using gene expression profiles. *Journal of Biomedical Informatics*, 81:102–111, 2018.
8. D. R. Swanson. Medical literature as a potential source of new knowledge. *Bulletin of the Medical Library Association*, 78(1):29–37, 1990.
9. L. Wei, Z. Y. Hu, H. S. Pang, X. C. Qin, H. M. Guo, and S. Fang. Study on knowledge discovery in biomedical literature based on spo predications: A case study of induced pluripotent stem cells. *Digital Library Forum*, 9:28–34, 2017.
10. T. E. Workman, M. Fiszman, J. F. Hurdle, and T. C. Rindflesch. Biomedical text summarization to support genetic database curation: using semantic medline to create a secondary database of genetic information. *Journal of Medical Library Association*, 98(4):273–281, 2010.
11. A. Yousef and N. M. Charkari. Sfm: A novel sequence-based fusion method for disease genes identification and prioritization. *Journal of Theoretical Biology*, 383:12–19, 2015.
12. H. Zhang, M. Fiszman, D. Shin, C. M. Miller, G. Rosemblat, and T. C. Rindflesch. Degree centrality for semantic abstraction summarization of therapeutic studies. *Journal of Biomedical Informatics*, 44:830–838, 2011.
13. Y. Zhang, H. Lin, Z. Yang, J. Wang, S. Zhang, Y. Sun, and L. Yang. A hybrid model based on neural networks for biomedical relation extraction. *Journal of Biomedical Informatics*, 81:83–92, 2018.

Online Evaluation of Classifier Accuracy, False Acceptance Rate and False Rejection Rate

Sabit Hassan[1], Shaden Shaar, Bhiksha Raj, and Saquib Razak

Carnegie Mellon University, Pittsburgh, PA, USA,
{sabith, sshaar}@andrew.cmu.edu ,bhiksha@cs.cmu.edu, srazak.cmu.edu

Abstract. Classifier evaluation is an important phase in machine learning systems which requires obtain true labels for data. Although in many scenarios, large scale data is easily available, obtaining true labels for the data can be expensive and difficult. Therefore, our goal is to select a subset of the data to obtain true labels for, such that they provide the best estimate of classifier accuracy. In this paper, we propose strategies based on stratified sampling to address this problem. In stratified sampling, the data is divided into several strata and samples are taken from the strata. However, allocation of samples among the strata is a challenging problem. Because optimal allocation can not be achieved, we propose an online allocation algorithm for approximating Optimal Allocation, which outperforms existing online algorithms and offline algorithms such as equal allocation or proportional allocation. Then, we extend our algorithm to evaluate False Acceptance Rate and False Rejection Rate of classifiers as well.

Keywords: Classifier Evaluation, Stratified Sampling, Optimal Allocation, False Acceptance Rate, False Rejection Rate

1 Introduction

Deploying a classifier without a proper estimate of its accuracy can be disastrous on many occasions. For example, if we use a low accuracy classifier for predicting diseases without knowing that the classifier is actually unreliable, it can lead to harmful decisions, making classifier evaluation an extremely important phase. The evaluation phase requires obtaining true labels which are then compared with the classifier output to compute accuracy of the classifier. However, obtaining true labels can be an expensive and difficult process. In our earlier example of predicting disease, to obtain true labels we would need to acquire diagnosis reports of patients which is an expensive process. Then, we would like to minimize the amount of true labels to be obtained while achieving a good estimate of classifier accuracy.

For binary classifiers, an important metric of evaluation is False Acceptance Rate (FAR) and False Rejection Rate (FRR). Consider the scenario described earlier. A classifier wrongly identifies a patient to *have* a disease but the patient *doesn't* have the disease. This is an instance of False Acceptance. If the classifier identifies the patient to *not have* a disease when the patient *does* have the disease, it is an instance of False Rejection. In many scenarios, evaluation of FAR and FRR is extremely important. In the example scenario of medical diagnosis, a False Rejection is much more harmful than a False Acceptance. Therefore, it's often essential to have a measure of FAR and FRR rather than the overall accuracy.

In this paper, we address the problem of classifier evaluation under limited resources for both of the scenarios described earlier. First, we propose a novel algorithm to estimate overall accuracy of the classifier. Then, we extend the algorithm to estimate FAR and FRR for the classifier.

The most general approach for evaluating accuracy under limited resources is Simple Random Sampling (SRS), where samples are chosen randomly from available data. However, SRS doesn't take into account distribution of data. In real world, we would expect distribution of data to provide us information about the accuracy. Consider the following example: if the data could be partitioned into two regions R_1 and R_2 such that a classifier is 100% accurate in R_1 and 0% accurate in R_2, it would be sufficient to sample 1 instance from R_1 and 1 instance from R_2 to achieve a perfect estimate of the classifier's accuracy. Of course, in real world, we cannot expect the data to be separable in such a perfect way. However, if we could partition the data in a way such that data with similar accuracy are in the same region, we would be able to achieve better estimate of the accuracy with same amount of labeling resources. By a better estimate, we mean the estimation will be consistent (low variance) and precise (low bias). This is the fundamental principle of Stratified Sampling [2], where the data is partitioned into different strata and samples are allocated from each stratum. As shown in existing research [1, 5] Stratified Sampling can result in significant reduction in error compared to simple random sampling for classifier evaluation.

A difficult challenge associated with Stratified Sampling is how to choose samples from each stratum. We would like to sample more instances from strata where classifier or human labeling is more inconsistent compared to strata where they are more consistent. In our earlier example, if a classifier has same output label for all instances in R_1, we can sample only 1 instance to estimate classifier's behavior in this region. If the classifier, on the other hand, behaves more randomly in R_2, we would need more samples to have a good guess of the classifier's behavior in R_2. Mathematically, we should allocate more samples in strata which have high variance and less samples in strata which have low variance. We can find an Optimal Allocation scheme only if variance of the data is known [1]. But to know the variance of the data, we would need to know accuracy of classifier, which is the very quantity we are trying to estimate. Existing allocation methods such as proportional allocation and equal allocation can be used with Stratified Sampling. However, these allocation methods are not optimal. Since Optimal Allocation cannot be achieved before the sampling process itself, the question we want to ask is how can we approach Optimal Allocation? We answer this question by proposing an online algorithm that use estimated variance to approximate Optimal Allocation. In our online algorithm, we first obtain an estimate of variance using classifier score, then iteratively allocate more samples and re-estimate the variance. As our results will show, these algorithms are more consistent compared to Equal Allocation, Proportional Allocation and state-of-the-art online allocation methods that approximate Optimal Allocation. Moreover, none of the existing methods [1, 5] evaluate FAR and FRR of classifiers. To address this issue, we extend our proposed online algorithm to evaluate FAR and FRR of classifiers. In this case, we show that our online algorithm performs significantly better than Simple Random Sampling (because there is no other existing methods of evaluating FAR and FRR simultaneously). As illustrated in the earlier example of medical diagnosis, we may want to be more confident about FRR compared to FAR in certain scenarios (or vice-versa). Our algorithm offers the flexibility of choosing more accurate estimate of either FAR or FRR.

In section 2, we discuss prior work regarding Stratified Sampling and approximation of Optimal Allocation in the context of accuracy evaluation. In section 3, we formulate the problem of evaluating accuracy, in section 4, we discuss mathematical formulation of Simple Random Sampling and Stratified Sampling. In section 5, we discuss existing allocation schemes, propose our online algorithm for approximation of Optimal Allocation and then extend the algorithm for evaluation of FAR and FRR. Our experiments in section 6 show that the newly proposed algorithm outperforms the existing algorithms.

2 Related Work

Classifier evaluation has received limited attention under the constraint of limited resource: when we can obtain true labels for only a subset of the entire dataset. Existing work in unsupervised evaluation of classifiers assume no labelled data are available but multiple classifiers are available for comparison [3, 10, 11, 9]. In our paper, our objective is to evaluate a *single* classifier, and although limited, we do have access to labels. Our objective is to utilize the limited number of true labels available so that we can achieve the best estimate of classifier accuracy.

In the context of classifier evaluation under limited resources, existing approaches are based on Stratified Sampling, which has been shown to perform significantly better than Simple Random Sampling [1, 5].

The *Optimal* Allocation method assigns samples to each stratum in proportion to the variance of the estimator of the classifier's accuracy in that stratum [5]. As discussed earlier, existing allocation methods such as Equal and Proportional allocation are not optimal. There is existing work that proposes allocation methods that approximate Optimal Allocation [1, 5]. To approximate optimal allocation, these methods initially allocate some samples to the various strata to estimate the variance, then iteratively allocate samples based on the estimated variance, and use the obtained labels to update both the estimate of the classification accuracy and the estimated variance in each stratum.

However, when available resources are small, not many samples can be allocated to obtain the initial bootstrap estimate of the variances. Since allocation in subsequent iterations depends on the estimated variance, this can result in significant error. To address this problem, we propose a new algorithm which achieves an initial estimate of the variance by utilizing classifier score. Moreover, existing methods [1, 5] do not address evaluation of FAR and FRR. We extended our proposed algorithm to evaluate FAR and FRR simultaneously with the same labeling instances.

3 Problem Formulation

3.1 Accuracy Evaluation

Let there be N instances in a dataset. Our objective is to estimate the accuracy of a classifier's predictions on the entire dataset. However, we have limited resource allowing us to sample only n instances for labelling, where n is much smaller than N. Let the true label for the ith instance be l_i. The label predicted by the classifier for the ith instance is $\hat{l}_i$. The true accuracy, A, of the classifier can be expressed as following:

$$A = \frac{\sum_{i=1}^{N} I(l_i = \hat{l}_i)}{N} \tag{1}$$

where $I()$ is an indicator function.

To compute the true accuracy A, we require the true labels l_i for each instance. Since we can obtain true labels for only n instances, we would like to choose a subset of n instances from the dataset so that comparing the true labels for those instances with the classifier labels will provide us a good estimate $\hat{A}$ of the true accuracy A. We would like our estimator of accuracy $\hat{A}$ to be consistent (low variance) and close (low bias) to the true accuracy A.

3.2 False Acceptance Rate (FAR) and False Rejection Rate (FRR)

False Acceptance is the event of classifier wrongly identifying a negative instance as positive. And False Rejection is the event of classifier wrongly identifying a positive instance as negative.

$$FAR = \frac{\sum_{i=1}^{N} I(l_i = 0 \wedge \hat{l}_i == 1)}{N} \tag{2}$$

$$FRR = \frac{\sum_{i=1}^{N} I(l_i = 1 \wedge \hat{l}_i == 0)}{N} \tag{3}$$

where $I()$ is an indicator function.

Since the equations for FAR and FRR are analogous to overall accuracy A, to avoid complications, we will use A in the section 4 and 5 to derive equations.

4 Estimation Methods

In this section, We formulate equations of estimated accuracy and variance for Simple Random Sampling and Stratified Sampling, which will be used later.

4.1 Simple Random Sampling

If we have resource to choose n samples then we can choose these instances randomly from the dataset; this method is Simple Random Sampling (SRS). The estimate of the accuracy is,

$$\hat{A}^r = \frac{\sum_{i=1}^{n} I(l_i = \hat{l}_i)}{n} \tag{4}$$

It is trivial that SRS does not have any bias, *i.e.* $E[\hat{A}^r] = A$

For SRS, if n instances are sampled, variance of the estimator, $\hat{A}^r$ is given by:

$$V(\hat{A}^r) = \frac{S^2}{n} \tag{5}$$

S^2 is the variance of the indicator variable $\mathcal{I}(l_i = \hat{l}_i)$ over N instances. S^2 is given by:

$$S^2 = \frac{\sum_{i=1}^{N}(I(l_i = \hat{l}_i) - A)}{N-1} \tag{6}$$

True accuracy A is not available prior to sampling. But [5] shows, if $\hat{A}^r$ is an unbiased estimator of A, the unbiased estimate of S^2 is given by:

$$\hat{S^2} = \frac{n}{n-1} A^r(1 - A^r) \tag{7}$$

Since SRS provides us with an unbiased estimator $\hat{A}^r$ [5], replacing S^2 by $\hat{S^2}$ in Eq. 3 gives us an unbiased estimate of the variance of $\hat{A}^r$ of SRS:

$$v(\hat{A}^r) = \frac{\hat{A}^r(1 - \hat{A}^r)}{n-1} \tag{8}$$

4.2 Stratified Sampling

In Stratified Sampling the data are partitioned into disjoint strata and samples are chosen from each stratum. The *weight* of a stratum is the proportion of all data instances that are in it. So, if our data is partitioned into K disjoint strata and there are N_k instances in the kth stratum, the weight of kth stratum, $W_k = \frac{N_k}{N}$. The overall accuracy is calculated by taking into account both the weight and the accuracy of each stratum. If we sample n_k instances randomly to estimate the accuracy in the kth stratum to be $\hat{A}_k^r$, the overall estimate of the accuracy $\hat{A}^s$ is:

$$\hat{A}^s = \sum_{k=1}^{K} W_k \hat{A}_k^r \tag{9}$$

The accuracy of each stratum is estimated by preforming SRS within the stratum. For the kth stratum, if we select n_k samples from N_k instances and obtain an unbiased estimate of accuracy A_k^r, similar to previous subsection, we get:

$$\hat{S_k^2} = \frac{n_k}{n_k - 1} A_k^r (1 - A_k^r) \tag{10}$$

The unbiased estimate of the variance of $\hat{A}^s$ is given by [5] Eq. 11:

$$v(\hat{A}^s) = \sum_{k=1}^{K} W_k^2 \frac{\hat{S_k^2}}{n_k} = \sum_{k=1}^{K} W_k^2 \frac{\hat{A}_k^r(\hat{A}_k^r - 1)}{n_k - 1} \tag{11}$$

To achieve a good estimate of the accuracy, we want to reduce the variance of the estimate so that it is consistent. To reduce the variance in the estimate of the accuracy, our goal is to find a good stratification and allocation method so that when n_k samples are allocated to the kth stratum, the quantity in Eq. 11 is minimized under the restriction that $\sum_{k=1}^{K} n_k = n$ where n is the number of samples we can obtain true labels for.

5 Allocation Methods

In this section, we first discuss formulation of offline allocation methods Equal Allocation and Proportional Allocation. We then discuss Optimal Allocation and current methods that approximate Optimal Allocation. We discuss the limitations of offline and existing approximation algorithms. Then, we propose a novel algorithm that estimates Optimal Allocation which addresses issues with existing algorithms.

5.1 Equal Allocation

In Equal Allocation, samples are allocated equally to all strata. If there are K strata, the number of samples allocated to the kth stratum is:

$$n_k = \frac{n}{K} \tag{12}$$

Equal Allocation does not take into account the size or the variance of accuracy within a stratum. This means, Equal Allocation may end up allocating many samples to a small stratum with really low variance, deviating from Optimal Allocation.

5.2 Proportional Allocation

In Proportional Allocation, samples are allocated according to the weight of each stratum. If there are K strata, with W_k being the weight of the kth stratum, the number of samples allocated to the kth stratum is:

$$n_k = n * \frac{W_k}{\sum W_k} \tag{13}$$

However, this means Proportional Allocation always allocates a high number of samples to larger strata. But if a large stratum is has very low variance, Proportional Allocation will over-allocate samples to it, deviating from Optimal Allocation.

5.3 Optimal Allocation

In Optimal Allocation, samples are allocated according to both the weights and the variance of the strata. If there are K strata, and the weight and variance of kth stratum are W_k and S_k^2 respectively, the number of samples allocated to the kth stratum is:

$$n_k = n * \frac{W_k S_k}{\sum W_k S_k} \tag{14}$$

5.4 Approximating Optimal Allocation

Prior to the sampling process, we do not know the variance within a stratum. To address this issue, current methods [1, 5] obtain estimate of the variance by pre-allocating samples to all strata (i.e. drawing samples from all strata for labelling), using these to re=estimate the variance within the strata, and reallocating samples to strata depending on the estimate. The algorithm used by [1, 5] is summarized in Estimated-OPT (EST-OPT). In all the algorithms presented in this section, P is a stratification of dataset, P_k is the subset of the dataset that belong to the k_{th} stratum, n is the available sampling resource, n_{ini} is the initial number of samples to be chosen from each stratum, and n_{step} is the number of samples to be allocated in each iteration.

The EST-OPT algorithm is prone to initialization bias. If the accuracy within a stratum is overestimated, its variance is underestimated, and as a result the stratum receives fewer samples than it requires. Since the subsequent allocations depend on the estimated variance, this results in significant bias. In the limit, if the accuracy of the classifier in a stratum is estimated to be 100%, the variance assigned to it is 0 and no further samples are drawn from the stratum.

To address this issue, we propose the algorithm Classifier-OPT(CLF-OPT). In CLF-OPT, we do not rely on variance estimated by small number of samples. Rather, we assume classifier score itself is a good estimation of accuracy and use it in eq.10 to obtain an estimate of variance.

Algorithm 1 Estimated-OPT

procedure VI-OPT(P, n, n_{ini}, n_{step})
  Randomly sample n_{ini} from each stratum
  Estimate A_k, S_k for each stratum
  $n_{rem} = n - K * n_{ini}$
  while $n_{rem} > 0$ **do**
    $n_{cur} = min(n_{rem}, n_{step})$
    Allocate n_{cur} among the strata using Eq. 10
    Update estimates of A_k, S_k
    $n_{rem} = n_{rem} - n_{cur}$
  end while
  Using Eq. 9 calculate overall estimate of A^s
  Return estimate of A^s
end procedure

Algorithm 2 Classifier-OPT

procedure CLF-OPT(P, n, n_{step})
  $n_{rem} = n$
  $total\_iters = n/n_{step}$
  $current\_iter = 0$
  train logistic regression proposed in Section 5
  for `i = 1, i<= N, i++` **do**
    $S_i = max($ classifier scores for each class $)$
  end for
  for `k = 1, k<= K, k++` **do**
    $L_k =$ average of S_i for $i \in P_k$ stratum
    $H_k^2 =$ substitute $A_k = L_k$ in $Eq.10$
  end for
  while $n_{rem} > 0$ **do**
    $n_{cur} = min(n_{rem}, n_{step})$
    $n_{var} = (current\_iter/total\_iters) * n_{cur}$
    $n_{fix} = n_{cur} - n_{var}$
    Allocate n_{var} using Eq. 14, with $S_k = H_k$
    $\hat{S_k} =$ Estimate S_k for every stratum k
    Allocate n_{var} using Eq. 14, with $S_k = \hat{S_k}$
    $\hat{A_k} =$ Estimate A_k for every stratum k
    $current\_iter++$
    $n_{rem} = n_{rem} - n_{cur}$
  end while
  Return $\hat{A_k}$
end procedure

We split our sampling resource n_{step} at each iteration into n_{fix} and n_{var}. We allocate n_{fix} according to classifier scores. We allocate n_{var} according to our estimate of variance. As the number of iterations increase, we become more confident of our estimate and in subsequent iterations, we lower n_{fix} and increase n_{var}.

5.5 Evaluation of FAR and FRR

To evaluate FAR and FRR, we modify CLF-OPT by taking weighted average of variance computed from the classifier scores of the two classes (we are interested in binary classifiers) for an initial estimate of variance. We evaluate FAR and FRR by taking new samples (same ones for both FAR and FRR), compute variance for each of them, then use their weighted average as re-estimated variance. Then, in subsequent iterations, we split our sampling resource n_{step} at each iteration into n_{fix} and n_{var}. Similar to CLF-OPT, we allocate n_{var} according to this estimated variance and allocate n_{fix} according to the initial estimate of variance obtained from classifier scores. As number of iterations increase, similar to CLF-OPT, we become more confident in our estimated variance. Therefore, we increase n_{var} and decrease n_{fix} as number of iterations increase. The weights of FAR and FRR can be adjusted depending on which one is more important to the user. For example, if we are interested in a more accurate evaluation of FRR, we can have higher weight for FRR and this will result in more accurate estimate of FRR. Although this will penalize estimate of FAR, this provides the user with flexibility to choose whether FAR and FRR are equally important or either of them is more important.

6 Experiments and Results

This section is split into two subsections. In Subsection 6.1, we compare allocation algorithms CLF-OPT with EST-OPT, Equal Allocation and Proportional Allocation described in Section 5. In Section 6.2, We use modification of CLF-OPT to evaluate FAR and FRR, We use two publicly available datasets for the experiments. The first one is the binary form of the *rcv1* [8] text classification dataset. This corpus has around 20,000 training instances and around 670,000 test instances. In 6.1 and 6.2, we train logistic regression classifiers on subsets of the training set to achieve different accuracy. For evaluation purposes, we choose our samples from the whole testing set. The other dataset we use is *News20 binary*, which is a binary form of the text classification UCI News 20 dataset [6]. This dataset contains around 20,000 total instances. In 6.1 and 6.2 we take subsets of this dataset to train linear-SVM classifiers and use the rest of the data as testing dataset. We pick our samples for evaluation from this testing dataset. All the classifiers are trained using scikit-learn [7]. For all the experiments in Fig. 3 and Fig. 4, we stratify the testing data by using K-Means on the classifier score.

6.1 Comparison of Allocation Methods

Although Proportional and Equal Allocation schemes are easy to implement, as discussed in Section 5, these schemes are not optimal. Since optimal allocation cannot be achieved, we compare performance of these schemes with the interactive algorithms that approximate optimal allocation.

In Fig. 1 and Fig. 2, we compare the Mean Absolute Error (MAE) between the true and estimated accuracies for Random Sampling, Equal Allocation and Proportional Allocation, state-of-art online algorithm (EST-OPT), and our proposed algorithm, CLF-OPT. We experiment by (a) varying the number of samples (b) and number of strata (b). Fig. 1 and Fig. 2 show results of the experiments on the *rcv1* and *News20 binary* datasets respectively.

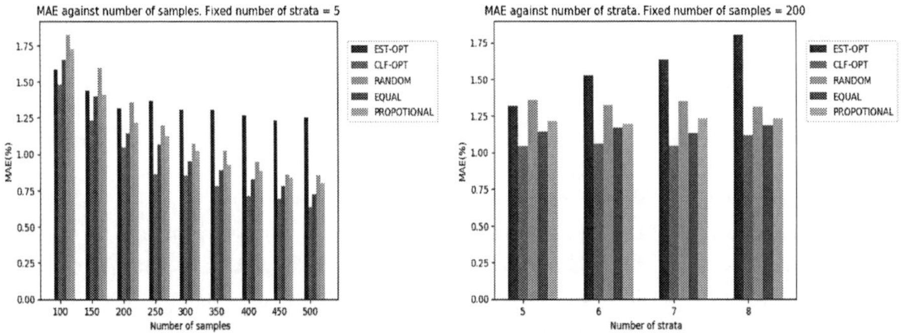

(a) rcv1, K = 5

(b) rcv1, n = 200

Fig. 1: Comparison of MAE for rcv1 Dataset

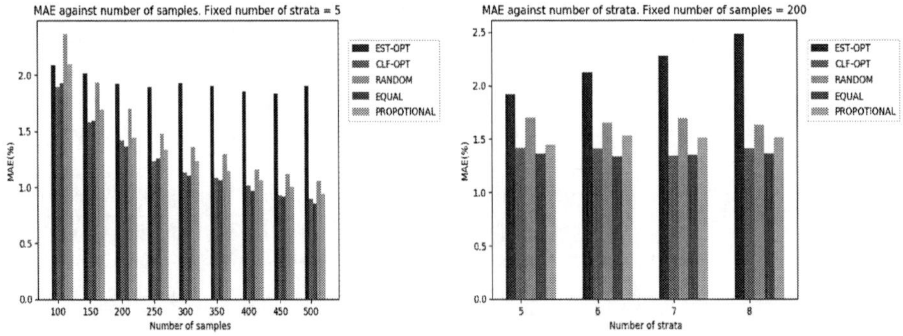

(a) news20, K = 5

(b) news20, n = 200

Fig. 2: Comparison of MAE for news20 Dataset

An important result from Fig. 1 and Fig. 2 is that performance of EST-OPT is worse than all other methods and performance does not improve even when the number of samples is increased. Although EST-OPT may perform well in certain scenarios as claimed in (Kumar and Raj, 2018), it performs poorly in the scenario present in Fig. 1 and Fig. 2. The fundamental issue with EST-OPT is that subsequent allocations depend heavily on initial estimate of the variance. As explained earlier, if the initial estimates are wrong, they do not get corrected in subsequent iterations, resulting in significant bias. Fig 3.a and Fig 4.a illustrate this issue when the number of samples allocated initially remains same (10 per strata) and the total number of samples increase but we see no decrease in error.

Performance of Equal and Proportional Allocation can depend heavily on the stratification. As discussed in Section 5, they can deviate from Optimal Allocation. In Fig. 1 and Fig. 2, we can see that CLF-OPT outperforms Equal and Proportional in all cases.

CLF-OPT address issues of Equal Allocation, Proportional Allocation and EST-OPT. In Fig. 1, CLF-OPT has MAE reduction of up to 23% and 19% compared to Proportional and Equal Allocation respectively.In Fig. 2, CLF-OPT performs similarly to Equal but has MAE reduction of up to 9% compared to Proportional. In all cases, CLF-OPT outperforms EST-OPT. Fig. 1(b) and Fig. 2(b) shows that the results are consistent even when number of strata is varied. This implies, CLF-OPT is the most consistent allocation scheme.

6.2 Evaluation of FAR and FRR

In Fig. 3, we use extension of CLF-OPT to evaluate FAR and FRR of classifiers. Since it was established by the experiments in Fig. 1 and Fig. 2 that CLF-OPT is the most consistent allocation scheme and results remain consistent even when number of strata is varied, in Fig. 3, we only compare CLF-OPT with Random Sampling for the two datasets.

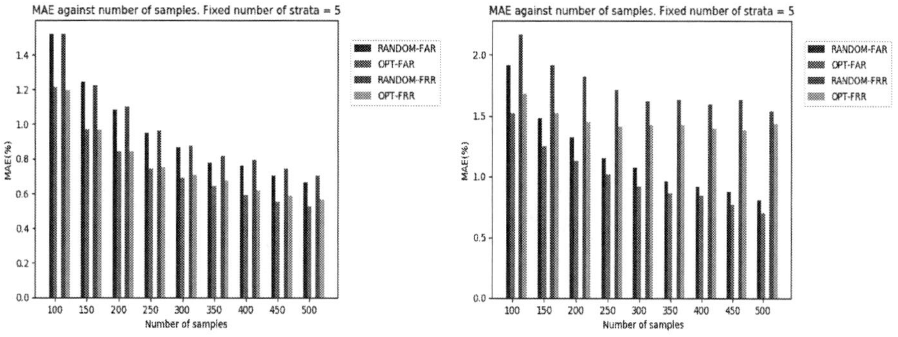

(a) rcv1, n = 200

(b) news20, K = 5

Fig. 3: Comparison of MAE for rcv1 Dataset

In both Fig. 3(a) and Fig. 3(b) we see that using our allocation scheme reduces MAE for both FAR and FRR simultaneously compared to Random Sampling. We can see that in both cases, there is up to 20% reduction in MAE.

7 Conclusion and Future Work

In this paper we proposed a new online algorithm that can approximate Optimal Allocation and outperform existing online methods by utilizing availability of classifier scores. We have shown that this allocation scheme also outperforms offline schemes such as Equal and Proportional Allocation. This algorithm can be adapted to evaluate FAR and FRR of classifiers simultaneously. Existing online algorithms do not address the issue of simultaneous evaluation of FAR and FRR. Adaption of our proposed algorithm has been shown to perform significantly better than Simple Random Sampling. In this paper, the algorithms are restricted to evaluation of a single classifier in every case. In the future, we hope to extend these algorithms for simultaneous evaluation of multiple classifiers.

References

1. P. N. Bennett and V. R. Carvalho. Online stratified sampling: evaluating classifiers at web-scale. In *Proceedings of the 19th ACM international conference on Information and knowledge management*, pages 15811584. ACM, 2010.
2. W. G. Cochran. Sampling techniques. John Wiley Sons, 2007.
3. P. Donmez, G. Lebanon, and K. Balasubramanian. Unsupervised supervised learning i: Estimating classification and regression errors without labels. The Journal of Machine Learning Research, 11:13231351, 2010.
4. J. F. Gemmeke, D. P. Ellis, D. Freedman, A. Jansen, W. Lawrence, R. C. Moore, M. Plakal, M. Ritter, Audio set: An ontology and human-labeled dataset for audio events, in IEEE ICASSP, 2017.
5. A. Kumar and B. Raj. Classifier Risk Estimation under Limited Labeling Resources. In *The 22nd Pacific-Asia Conference on Knowledge Discovery and Data Mining (PAKDD)*, 2018
6. S. S. Keerthi and D. DeCoste. A modified finite newton method for fast solution of large scale linear svms. In *Journal of Machine Learning Research*, pages 341361, 2005.
7. F. Pedregosa et al. Scikit-learn: Machine Learning in Python. In *Journal of Machine Learning Research*,12:2825-2830, 2011.
8. D. D. Lewis, Y. Yang, T. G. Rose, and F. Li. Rcv1: A new benchmark collection for text categorization research. *The Journal of Machine Learning Research*, 5:361397, 2004.
9. F. Parisi, F. Strino, B. Nadler, and Y. Kluger. Ranking and combining multiple predictors without labeled data. In *Proceedings of the National Academy of Sciences*, 111(4):12531258, 2014.
10. B. Raj, R. Singh and J. Baker. A paired test for recognizer selection with untranscribed data. In *IEEE International Conference on Acoustics, Speech and Signal Processing (ICASSP)*, pages 56765679, 2011.
11. E. A. Platanios, A. Blum, and T. Mitchell. Estimating accuracy from unlabeled data. 2014.

Announcement

World Congress DSA 2019
The Frontiers in Intelligent Data and Signal Analysis
New York USA, July 13 - 25, 2019

www.worldcongressdsa.com

Conferences

We are inviting you to our seventh World congress on the Frontiers of Signal and Image Analysis DSA 2019 to New York, USA.

This congress will feature three events:

- the 15th International Conference on Machine Learning and Data Mining MLDM,
- the 19th Industrial Conference on Data Mining ICDM,
- and the 14th International Conference on Mass Data Analysis of Signals and Images MDA.

Workshops and Tutorial will also take place.

Come to join us to the most exciting event on Intelligent Data and Signal Analysis.

Sincerely your,
Prof. Dr. Petra Perner

MLDM icdm mda

www.mldm.de www.data-mining-forum.de www.mda-signals.de